# Commercial motor transportation

# Commercial motor transportation

CHARLES A. TAFF, Ph.D.
Professor of Transportation
College of Business and Management
University of Maryland
College Park, Maryland

Sixth Edition

1980

CORNELL MARITIME PRESS, INC.
Centreville, Maryland

Library of Congress Cataloging in Publication Data

Taff, Charles Albert, 1916—
    Commercial motor transportation.

    Bibliography: p.
    Includes index.
    1. Transportation, Automotive—United States.
I. Title.
HE 5623.T3      1980      388.3'0973      80-12947
ISBN 0—87033—266-X

*Manufactured in the United States of America*
First edition, 1950. Sixth edition, 1980; second printing, 1981

# Preface

Of all the modern means of transport, motor transportation has proved to be the form most adaptable to today's multiplicity of needs. It is the dominant method of transport, and its impact is felt in almost every phase of our daily lives. We use automobiles and buses for almost 90 percent of our passenger transportation; and trucks transport practically all freight within urban areas, more than one-fifth of intercity traffic, and 75 percent of freight on a total cost basis. The mobility afforded by automotive transport and the modern highway system has given impetus to industrial growth and location and has broadened the social and economic opportunities of vast numbers of people. The technological advances that have occurred within a relatively short period of time give promise of continued improvement in this system of transport.

We have endured and, in large measure, adjusted to two fuel crises in 1973-74 and again in 1979. The 1980's are expected to be years when conservation efforts will be emphasized and the development of synthetic fuels will be pursued. Although uncertainties remain regarding petroleum supply and price and also regarding our commitment to an intensive synfuel development, our mobile society and a growing economy will require a continuing high utilization of trucks, buses, and automobiles to meet personal and business needs.

About three-fourths of our governmental infrastructure investment in transportation is in highways, but these expenditures are now receiving increasing scrutiny. The need for funding of alternative means of moving people, particularly in congested areas, and the demand for financial sharing of the Highway Trust Fund have injected new forces into the highway transportation field. The significance of the changes in direction in our planning in the 1980's is presented. The legislative changes in the Federal-Aid Highway Acts and the diversion of Trust Fund revenues to other transportation purposes are thoroughly discussed.

The emerging importance of consumer participation in transport planning, and the impact of environmental and sociological factors, such as noise, air pollution, congestion, relocation problems of displacement, and safety are treated in their relation to highway and urban transit development.

The trend in the last two decades in intercity highway transportation has been to insure that the users pay their fair share of the cost of facilities they use. We are now experiencing a reversal of this attitude in the urban transit field as there appears to be little expectation that the users will pay for either the facilities or the full operational costs. The implications of this change are assessed.

The managerial and economic aspects of motor transportation are discussed in order to provide an understanding of its role in our economic life. The significance of effective carrier management, including participative management, the functions of management, and management by objectives are examined. The growing importance of the computer in motor carrier decision making and as an operational aid is recognized, and the promise the computer holds for future shipper-carrier data exchange is treated. All phases of the broad field of trucking management and operations—economics, terminal operations, financing, equipment, rates, labor relations, claims, insurance, and other pertinent areas—are thoroughly explored. The problems that accompany carrier growth are presented in a manner designed to be of effective help in management decision making. The diverse types of motor carrier operations, including the growing competitive role of specialized carrier operations, are covered. The operations of independent truckers and owner-operators, their relationship to regulated motor carriers, their contributions to the trucking field, and their particular problems are discussed. The acquisition and merger activity of motor carrier management and its influence in changing the structure of the industry are assessed.

The speed, reliability, and flexibility of trucks have contributed to more effective distribution and closer inventory planning and control and provide the physical distribution manager with an array of trade-off alternatives. This has resulted in the increased use of all types of truck transportation—common, contract, exempt, and private carriage.

The continuing growth of private carriage is a shipper initiative that provides keen competition for the for-hire motor carrier. A separate chapter has been included to treat many of the facets of this field. Included among the topics are the pros and cons of private carriage, intercorporate hauling, leasing, equipment utilization, back-hauls, and others.

Since the passage of the Motor Carrier Act of 1935, and before that in state regulation, motor carriers have been subject to regulatory constraints. In the past several years, there have been proposals by the Administration, by Congress, and by others to modify or deregulate the motor carrier industry. Since 1977, the Interstate Commerce Commission has engaged in extensive rule making and policy statements that have significantly modified regulation. These matters are discussed in some detail. Continuing modification is expected.

The external constraints under which motor carrier management has operated for years have been further enlarged through recent legislation. The Environmental Protection Act, the Equal Employment Opportunity Act, the Occupational Safety and Health Act, and heightened concern for highway safety have their impact on management decisions and provide constant challenges to management.

The essential service provided by intercity passenger operations and the trends evident in the field are presented. The rapid growth of charter service and package freight as parts of intercity bus service are discussed. The competitive aspects of the government-provided rail passenger service of Amtrak and some of the implications are also covered.

Special treatment is accorded urban transit problems, including the continuing growth of city-owned or public authority transit systems. The developments that have been occurring in the urban mass transit field as a result of new funding from the Highway Trust Fund, as well as the funds provided by Urban Mass Transit Administration, are examined. The impact of fuel shortages and accelerating prices is covered as well as the role of automotive transportation in traffic congestion.

The Interstate Commerce Act was recently recodified with a five-digit numbering system and became effective in mid-1979. This edition has incorporated the new numbering system where reference is made to the Act.

This book is planned as a textbook for courses in motor transportation and carrier management; and as a reference for more general courses in transportation, physical distribution, logistics, and traffic management. It should also be of great value to people in the industry or those who are seeking understanding and knowledge of the field.

The author wishes to acknowledge with gratitude the important contribution made by his colleague, Dr. Garland Chow, Assistant Professor of Transportation, who reorganized and rewrote Chapter 7. The author is also indebted to many persons and organizations for their assistance in supplying information and for the suggestions of professors who have used earlier editions of this text. Appreciation is also expressed to his wife, Glatha M. Taff, for help in the preparation of the manuscript.

College Park, Maryland                    CHARLES A. TAFF

**TO**

**Jennifer, Robert, and Christopher**

# Table of contents

tive bill collection system. Bank clearings and electronic funds transfer.

Classification of motor carrier employees. Federal Labor legislation. Teamsters Union. Other unions. Independent truckers' organizations. Employers' groups. Settlement of grievances. Points covered in contracts. Questionable practices. Nonunion employees.

Terminal location in the urban area. Types of terminals based on ownership. Types of terminal design. Yard space. Freight terminal handling methods. Methods of freight checking. Receiving shipments. Weighing and marking. Stowing freight. Dispatching. Pickup and delivery operations. Two-way mobile radio. Terminal controls for management. Joint terminals.

CARGO CLAIMS: Known loss or damage. Concealed loss or damage. Damaged freight. Over and short freight. OVER-CHARGE CLAIMS: Tracing. INVESTIGATION AND DISPOSITION OF CLAIMS: Inspections after delivery. Salvage. Loss and damage claim register. REFUSED OR UNCLAIMED FREIGHT. RECOOPERING. CLAIM PREVENTION: Use of impact machines. Truck alarms. National classification rules. WEIGHING AND INSPECTION BUREAUS.

Types of insurance companies. Procedure of insuring companies. Bodily injury and property damage insurance. Cargo insurance. Workman's compensation. Personal lines group insurance. Additional coverages. Cost of insurance.

Development of motor classification. National Motor Freight Classification. Classification rules. New England area classification. Rail classifications. Factors influencing classification of articles. National Classification Board. National Classification Committee. National Motor Freight Traffic Association.

carriers of property. Dual status, private-public. MERGERS: Reasons for mergers. Types of mergers. Section 11343 (a). Section 11343 (d) (1).

What constitutes private carriage? Magnitude of private carriage. Managerial approaches to private trucking. Pro's and con's of private trucking. Operations.

Equipment and load factor. Advantages of intercity bus transportation. Service differentiation. Special services. Operating costs. Pricing and competition. The Greyhound Corporation. Trailways. Terminals. Federal regulation. Passenger-carrier exemptions to economic regulation. Federal and state assistance to intercity bus systems. Special or charter party service. State restrictions on intercity operations. State size and weight restrictions.

Urban growth and transit plans. Trends in equipment and its use. Economic factors. Public Ownership. Possible solutions to the transit problem. Role of the federal government. Private automobiles.

# chapter 1

# Motor transportation

Motor transportation is big business, for it is every man's individual mode of transport. It has become an integral part of our transportation system, indispensable to our way of life. Motor transportation is pervasive in our economy, for through automotive transportation the interchange of ideas and goods has been greatly accelerated, with inestimable benefits to society. It is so easy to learn to drive a motor vehicle, both automobiles and trucks, that motor transportation offers to most individuals and many companies a "do-it-yourself" method of transport. Beyond ownership, one may rent, lease, or even borrow a vehicle to perform a needed service. In addition, a wide range of services may be secured from companies whose business is that of motor transport.

Motor transport has virtually revolutionized production and distribution. Its scope is so broad that there is almost no phase of daily living that is not affected by some aspect of it. The social and economic effects upon the economy of the nation have been greater than those occasioned by any other single technological development. In the United States, there are 3,806,883 miles of roads and streets of which 84 percent is rural mileage and 16 percent municipal. There is currently one motor vehicle for every 1.5 persons, and annual highway travel represents the equivalent of about 9,577 miles per person in the United States. Highway travel now exceeds 1 trillion, 436 billion vehicle miles, and a conservative projection to 1985 shows vehicle miles in that year to be about 1.85 trillion and 2.61 trillion in the year 2000.

We are increasingly dependent upon automotive transportation—in traveling greater distances to and from work and for recreational purposes and in transporting commodities by truck. It enables people to enjoy a greater mobility in every phase of their activities. The Department of Labor reported in 1977 that since 1973 families have been spending a larger percentage of the family budget on transportation than on food. Transportation expenditures rank second only to those for shelter. Despite the necessity for fuel conservation, the reliance upon this flexible means of transport will remain strong. Generally, fuel costs have been a small share of the total cost of transportation service, and the effect fuel price changes have had on the traveler's choice of transport mode has been overshadowed by the service and travel differentials among modes. Due to the large cost and service differentials among the freight modes, the marginal changes in relative costs due to higher fuel prices are not expected to have much effect on modal choice for most freight. The degree will depend in some measure on the availability of fuel and the price of fuel. Thus, in the absence of foreign embargoes or domestic fuel allocation, there will be continuing use of and growth in highway transportation. However, our transportation system is almost totally dependent on petroleum energy and consumes about half of all energy used in our nation. As shown in Fig. 1-1, the use of the automobile accounts for 50 percent of that used in transportation and truck transportation accounts for almost one-fourth of the total. Almost three-fourths of all the petroleum energy used in the U.S. is consumed by highway users.

Motor vehicle registrations have had an annual compound growth rate of 4.16 percent during the period 1935-65. One hundred, fifty million motor vehicles were registered in 1978.[1] Passenger cars represented 76 percent of vehicles registered and accounted for slightly less than that amount of vehicle miles traveled. Trucks and truck combinations comprised about 21 percent but had higher average travel mileages—about 22.3 percent of vehicle miles. Motorcycles were 2 percent of all vehicles and buses one-third of 1 percent, with vehicle miles of about the same respective percentages.

Except for the restrictions on travel during World War II, motor vehicle travel has shown a very close relationship to Gross National Product. And during the past 20 years, it has increased at a slightly faster rate than has GNP. Improvement in the service industries has exceeded that in manufacturing, and service industries require more individual transportation which is provided by motor vehicles. The manufacture, servicing, and operation of motor vehicles, including the use of the highways, account for about 21 percent of our Gross National Product, of which slightly more than 9 percent is accounted for by passenger transportation, and about one-fifth of all employment.

Recent projections of transportation growth rates in revenues or expenditures show a continuing growth but at a slower rate than earlier years. For the period 1975-1990, a 2.5 percent annual growth rate has been forecast.[2]

The projected freight revenues from for-hire intercity carriers for 1979 are $84.2 billion and from for-hire local carriers $66.2 billion. By the year 2000 revenues are estimated at $140.1 billion and $108.3 billion respectively.[3]

The investment in highway transportation is tremendous. Approximately $546 billion has been spent for the construction and maintenance of highways, roads, and streets in the United States from 1921 to the present. In 1979, the revenues available for the highway infrastructure at all levels of government—federal, state, and county—were $30.5 billion, of which approximately half was for construction outlays. In addition, the net investment in the more than 118.5 million automobiles and the 31.5 million trucks is staggering, to which are added expenditures for fuel, maintenance, parts, and insurance.[4] The capital requirements for equipment and facilities for the trucking industry, both for-hire and private, have been projected to require expenditures of $213.6 billion from 1976 to 1985 and $454.6 billion from 1986 to the year 2000. This is at a medium growth rate and is based on 1975 dollars. These totals do not include expenditures for terminal facilities for private trucking companies.[5]

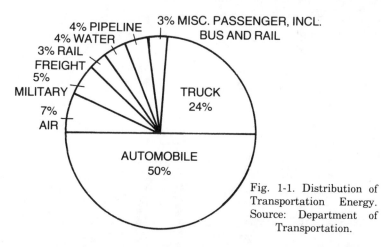

Fig. 1-1. Distribution of Transportation Energy. Source: Department of Transportation.

Automotive transportation is a significant factor in our defense planning. Statistically, there are enough private automobiles alone in the United States to evacuate at one time every man, woman, and child. Much of the success of our productive effort during wartime can be attributed to the availability and flexibility of motor vehicle transportation. Many manufacturers of tanks, planes, ships, and other essential equipment operate on the basis of long-distance production lines.

The Department of Defense has indicated the vital role of highways in defense planning by identifying 60,000 miles of Defense Strategic Highway Network. This network includes 18,000 miles of highway corridors in addition to the Interstate System.[6]

An estimate was made recently of the maximum capacity of just that portion of the trucking industry that operates between cities. This survey clearly indicates the defense potential of the industry. It was assumed that existing vehicles would be operating on two eight-hour shifts per day, six days a week, or about 300 days per year. An additional four hours were allowed per shift for unloading, servicing, and record keeping, and it was assumed that adequate personnel would be available to operate on two shifts a day. Since there would not always be capacity loads in both directions, and there would be operational details and dispatching problems, operating effectiveness of 75 percent was considered reasonable. Based on these assumptions, the total ton-mile capability of intercity carriers was computed to be about six times greater than the ton-miles actually being transported.[7] This estimated capacity under the assumed conditions emphasizes the role that intercity trucking could play in an emergency.

The decentralization of industry has continued and is receiving official encouragement in defense planning as a precaution against any

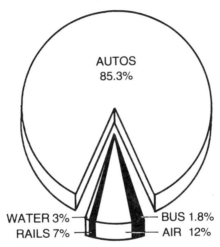

AUTOS
85.3%

WATER 3% ─┤     ├─ BUS 1.8%
RAILS 7% ─┤     ├─ AIR 12%

Fig. 1-2. Percent of total intercity passenger-miles by mode of transportation.

future emergency. It seems, therefore, that automotive transportation will be more essential in any future contingency than it has been in the past.

Automotive transportation has developed largely along two lines—freight and passenger. Each of these two types can be further subdivided into private and for-hire operations, the latter being conducted by common and contract carriers subject to federal regulation of business practices by the Interstate Commerce Commission and safety regulation by the Department of Transportation, and exempt carriers which are subject only to federal safety regulation.

At the present time, there are approximately 103,344 private carriers (that is, business firms that perform their own transportation or part of it), 42,033 exempt carriers (which operate on a for-hire basis), 16,874 for-hire carriers of property, and 1,176 for-hire passenger carriers subject to Interstate Commerce Commission regulation. Further discussion of the passenger aspects of motor transportation will be treated separately later.

Motor transportation is without question the dominant mode of transport today. Slightly more than 85 percent of all intercity passenger-miles is by automobile (Fig. 1-2); in the freight field in urban areas, all of the moves are by truck; and almost 25 percent of transport on a ton-mile basis in the intercity field is by truck. For-hire carriers are numerically the smallest group but they are essential to our productive and distributive process.

As significant as the contributions and the impact of automotive transportation are on our economy, however, there are some external diseconomies that it has developed. These externalities of air pollution, safety, noise, congestion, and impairment of aesthetic values are factors that affect the quality of our environment and hence the quality of our life. We will undoubtedly find more attention devoted in the future to solving some of these problems as we progress in our use of automotive transportation.

### Motor freight transportation

Thousands of communities are heavily dependent upon truck service for their everyday needs—their food, clothing, fuel, and movies. There is very little in their day-to-day living which does not come to them at least part of the way by truck. All communities, large or small, depend in some manner upon motortruck transportation for the satisfaction of their wants. Trucks transport practically all the milk, poultry, eggs, and livestock consumed in the United States, approximately 87 percent of all fresh fruits and vegetables, 85 percent of all the meat, and most of the short-haul grain. A strike or shutdown of the trucking industry or a portion of it, such as the independent truckers, is felt within a week's time. If it extends beyond that period, it can have significant effect upon the economy in terms of plant lay-offs and food shortages. In addition, there are 39,793 communities in the United States which depend completely upon truck service to supply them with their needs. This figure represents 65 percent of the communities in the United States. Many communities that formerly depended upon rail transportation are now relying upon truck transportation, since railroads are abandoning about 500 to 1,000 miles of lines each year.

Prior to World War I, there were approximately 250,000 trucks, most of which were engaged in local delivery service. At that time, the condition of the roads and the solid rubber tires on the vehicles, together with the frequency of mechanical failures, largely limited truck services to local operations. The development of pneumatic tires, as well as continuous highway improvements, did much to stimulate intercity carrying of freight; and the growth of the property-carrying phase of motor transportation has been spectacular.

By 1978, there were 30,500,000 motortrucks, not including more than 1 million government owned (excluding military vehicles) of all types operating upon the streets and highways of the nation. Truck registrations have almost doubled in the last decade. Trucks constitute 21 percent of the total number of vehicles and travel 22.3 percent of all vehicle miles. The

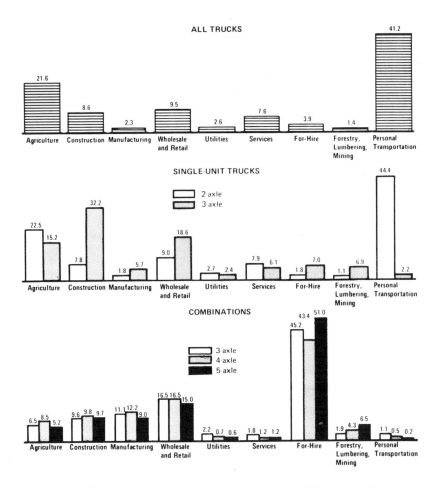

Fig. 1-3. Percent distribution of major uses for truck types: 1972. Source: Department of Commerce, *Truck Inventory and Use Survey*, October, 1973, p. XV.

majority of trucks in operation—about 96 percent—are privately operated by stores, dairies, farmers, industrial concerns, and individuals. The remaining 4 percent are for-hire trucks. Single-unit trucks comprise the largest share, 95.3 percent of all trucks in operation, most of which are 2-axle, the remainder 3-axle. About 4.7 percent are combinations (tractor-semitrailer), 0.7 percent are 3-axle, 1.4 are 4-axle, and 2.6 percent are 5 or more axles. [8]

The major uses of single-unit trucks and truck combinations are shown in Fig. 1-3. Personal transportation accounted for the major share of the 2-axle single-unit trucks, and the construction industry the 3-axle trucks. On the other hand, the dominant combination usage in 3-, 4-, and 5-axle units was in for-hire transportation.

Trucks are widely used by tradesmen as mobile workshops, by farmers for hauling, and by individuals for recreation purposes. Of the 28,366,901 private trucks, an estimated 3 million are farm trucks. In addition, many industrial firms perform a substantial amount or all of their own transportation in their own trucks, in both intercity and urban transportation. Some firms have very large private fleets, such as the Bell System, with more than 75,000 trucks.

Another measure of transportation service is the number of tons transported in intercity freight service. On this basis, truck transportation was found to be the leading mode with a total of 38.9 percent. Railroads handled 26.6 percent, and inland waterways, pipelines, and airlines 34.5 percent.[9]

The monetary measure is another method of measuring transportation service. This method reflects the market value which is paid for the service—that is, the operating revenues of the regulated for-hire carriers combined with the cost of operating private carriage. The for-hire property carriers which were subject to Interstate Commerce Commission regulation had operating revenues of more than $38 billion in 1979. The regulated motor carrier revenues exceeded rail freight revenue for the first time in 1963.

As shown in Fig. 1-4, an examination of the total freight revenues of the modes of transportation reveals that regulated motor carriers receive 32.6 percent of the total revenues, non-regulated motor carriers 38.2 percent, for a total of 70.8 percent of revenues. The rail carrier share was 20.6 percent, pipelines 2.8 percent, water carriers 4.1 percent, and air carriers 1.6 percent. There is a substantial difference among the modes of transport as to the carriers subject to regulation that has influence on the distribution shown in this figure. For example, 100 percent of railroads and 85 percent of pipelines are regulated, whereas but 44 percent of trucks and 7.5 percent of water carriers are subject to regulation.

The estimated revenues of motor carriers not subject to regulation by the Commission were $73 billion for local service and $43 billion for intercity service. Thus, the revenues from all motor carriers were estimated to be over $154 billion.

For intercity motor carrier service (excluding local service) both regulated and nonregulated, the value stated in terms of amounts paid for the service was about $81 billion, whereas the amount paid for all other domestic intercity freight service (rail, water, air, and pipeline) was about

$33 billion. On this basis, trucks accounted for 71.8 percent of the total monetary expenditures for transportation service.

Class I intercity motor common carriers received 11.1 cents per ton-mile in revenue in 1979.[10] The average revenue per ton-mile for motor carriers is five times that of the railroads.

The widespread use of motor transportation is also reflected in the growth of intercity ton-miles. It should be emphasized that the ton-mile is a physical measurement that does not take into account the quality

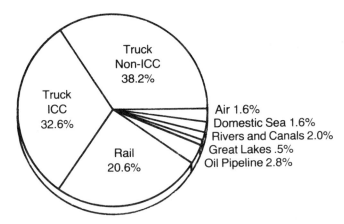

Fig. 1-4. Revenues of freight carriers (excluding indirect carriers: does not round to 100 percent). Source: based on statistics contained in *Transportation Facts and Trends*, Transportation Association of America, 1979, p. 18.

of transportation service or the costs of providing it. It is a widely used two-dimensional measure, namely tons and mileage, but it should be recognized that where there is substantial circuity, such as in inland water transportation, this will be reflected in ton-miles if it is compared with a more direct service such as rail or motor transportation. In 1946 the motor carrier share of total intercity ton-miles was 9 percent, amounting to 81 billion ton-miles, whereas the railroads were transporting 66 percent—602 billion ton-miles. By 1979, motor carriers had increased the ton-miles transported to 660 billion, which amounted to 25 percent of the total; and the rail share had declined to 35.8 percent, although ton-miles transported by rail increased to 915 billion (Fig. 1-5). During this period, total ton-miles transported by all modes increased from 903 billion to 2.5 trillion. Significantly then, with an expanding ton-mile market, the motor carrier share increased both absolutely and relatively while rail ton-miles increased, but the railroads' relative share of the market decreased.

As shown in Fig. 1-6, freight ton-miles are forecast to increase from 2.3 trillion ton-miles, based on a medium growth forecast, in 1975, to 3.5

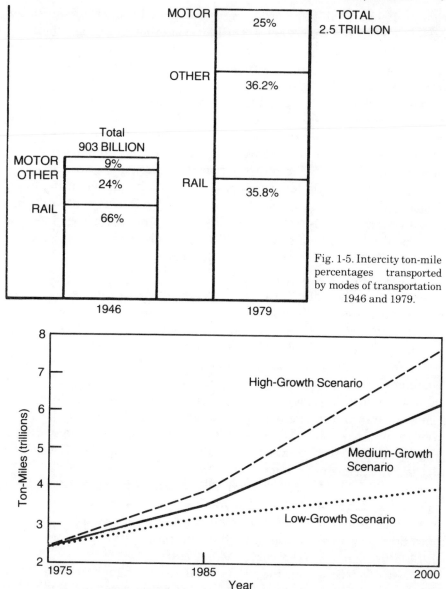

Fig. 1-5. Intercity ton-mile percentages transported by modes of transportation 1946 and 1979.

Fig. 1-6. Forecast of freight ton-miles to year 2000. Source: National Transportation Policy Study Commission, *National Transportation Policies*, Washington, D.C., 1979, p. 164.

trillion in 1985, and to 6.2 trillion in the year 2000. The high growth forecast is to 7.6 trillion ton-miles in the year 2000.[11]

Our economic growth is closely correlated to the increase in transportation of intercity freight. For the past several years, we have averaged about 10,000 ton-miles per person of intercity transportation, and this figure has been increasing. Using past linear relationships, it is estimated that by 1990 we will be transporting approximately 15,000 ton-miles per person, and in the year 2000, 1.3 trillion ton-miles. About one-fourth of this total will be transported by trucks. In 1985, it is estimated that private and for-hire intercity trucks will account for more than 832 billion ton-miles.[12]

The size of the trucking industry may be expressed in the number of people it employs. One estimate is that in 1979 there were 9,052,400 truck drivers and other employees in truck transportation in the United States.[13] This figure is derived by assuming that there are 0.8 drivers per nonfarm truck and includes drivers, helpers, mechanics, dock workers, and office staff. Excluded are employees of truck manufacturing firms, dealerships, truck stops, and body shops. The Department of Labor statistics show employment in establishments primarily engaged in local or long-distance trucking to be 1,253,000. This represents the average number of full-time and part-time employees.

### Advantages of truck transportation

Truck transportation provides a complete service on its own from shipper to consignee. It also can be used in combination with all other modes of transport. Thus, it is our most versatile mode of freight transportation. The diverse types of operations in truck transportation are reflected in the services that are available, whether urban or intercity, whether regional or transcontinental. Some carriers handle general commodities, whereas others handle only truckload lots. Some carriers specialize in transporting a single commodity or commodity group, such as steel, household goods, or perishables, flour, cement, and many others. Truck transport service may be available from companies of very large size to the one-man operation.

The trucking industry has been able to record its rapid advance because of its inherent ability to provide and render advantageous services in competition with other modes of transportation. Motortruck transportation has many advantages, but the primary benefits are speed, flexibility, economy, reliability, and convenience.

Speed of service from the platform of the consignor to the door of the consignee is one of the most important advantages possessed by the trucking industry. The shorter transit time by motor carrier has played a major role in increased patronage. This speed of service depends upon the transit time between terminals, the time spent in terminals, and pickup and delivery time. The ability to make expeditious deliveries would not be effective if only occasional service were offered. Frequency of schedule, therefore, is an important part of speed in service.

One of the paramount reasons why the trucking industry is able to provide comparatively fast transit time is its inherent flexibility. Operating with a unit of less capacity than the average freight car, the trucker does not have to wait too long to accumulate sufficient freight and usually is in a position to depart immediately after the vehicle is loaded. With the larger share of operations consisting of direct single-line service, the trucker is not delayed by the necessity of making connections. Freight can be collected at its source and delivered to its final destination with a minimum of rehandling. Trucks can be operated over the roads at night when traffic is relatively light. The fixed schedules of trains, on the other hand, often result in early closing hours of freight cars and late arrivals at intermediate points and at destination.

Monetary savings may be reflected in better transit time, such as faster turnover of stocks, reduced inventories, and broader market areas, which are receiving increased recognition of their trade-off values. Business firms are increasingly adopting the physical distribution or logistics approach, which embraces the interrelated costs of transportation, material handling, industrial packaging, warehousing, and inventory control.

Generally lower labor and packaging costs and the economy possible in truck transportation in loading and unloading shipments are other factors which are receiving greater attention. The truck driver and helper usually will load and unload truckload shipments, whereas, on rail carload movements, the expense of loading and unloading usually falls upon the shipper or the consignee.

Attached to the expense of rail carload shipments, also, but seldom present in truckload shipments, is the cost of delivery of the shipment to and from the railroad freight station when an industry does not have a rail siding. In addition, the truck driver is frequently more competent to load the vehicle than is shipping-room labor, which may represent intangible savings. Also, railroads do not offer pickup and delivery service on less-than-carload shipments at all of their stations, whereas this is the usual practice for all motor carrier service.

Motor carriers, as a whole, have dependable schedules of shipments and prompt collection and delivery. They have tended to improve and stabilize their standards of service through more efficient operations and to provide relatively careful handling of shipments en route, which is of vital importance to any shipper.

The flexibility of the truck enables the motor carrier to adapt its service to suit the convenience of a shipper if the occasion demands it. For example, a regular shipper can usually arrange to have a truck at his plant almost immediately and at almost any hour of the day or night whenever the tonnage to be shipped or the nature of the service warrants such special service. The same specialized service can be made available at destination as well. With a highway system exceeding 3.8 million miles as compared to a rail system of 204,000 miles, it is apparent that trucks have access to infinitely more origins and destinations than other modes of transportation are able to reach.

The designing of special equipment to meet the specific needs of particular kinds of shipments has become widespread in the trucking industry. For example, some trailers are designed to handle corrosive liquids or molten sulfur. Others are especially designed to haul edibles, and others inedibles. Certain trailers have built-in pneumatic conveying systems to facilitate rapid loading and unloading. The development of specialized equipment, although somewhat more costly than standard trailers, provides greater transport efficiency and tailors service to customers' needs.

Another advantage of the motor carrier is its ability to provide a more personalized service. Many trucking organizations are fairly small and are therefore capable of dealing promptly and directly with the shipper on his trucking problems. The fact that a shipment, in the majority of instances, is in the direct care of a single motor carrier from origin to destination also adds to the element of personal supervision.

Vast technological improvements, coupled with the many advantages inherent in this mode of transport, have broadened the scope of trucking operations. Many commodities which it was thought would not lend themselves to transportation by truck are being moved in increasing quantities. In addition, commodities that formerly were carried only relatively short distances by truck are being moved greater distances. The advantages of motor transportation are unparalleled by any other mode of transportation, and the increased reliance placed upon it by shippers is largely a reflection of its ability to meet any transportation requirement.

### QUESTIONS AND PROBLEMS

1. What are some examples of changes in the distribution pattern occasioned by motor transportation? Has this benefited the public? How?

2. Explain why the national-defense aspect of motor transportation is assuming increasing importance.

3. What is the status of the motor transportation industry as an employer? Why are there such wide variations in the estimates of the total number of persons employed in motor transportation?

4. Point out the significance to shippers, highway administrators, and the public of the fact that the total of trucks and buses at the present time is greater than the total of all vehicles in 1920.

5. During World War II, a group of experts in highway matters estimated the total number of vehicles that would be on the highways in 1965; yet that number was reached in the early 1950's. What factors accounted for this? What can we learn from this?

6. Carefully explain the difference between the tonnage carried by motor carriers and the total ton-miles transported by them.

7. What are the inherent advantages of motortruck transportation? Is there any evidence of a broadening of the scope of trucking operations in regard to commodities carried?

8. As a shipper of general commodities, what advantages possessed by motor transportation would largely influence you in your choice of transportation service? Comment.

9. What evidence is there to indicate that merchants can carry a smaller inventory because of the fact that they are able to replenish their stocks quickly through utilization of motor carriers? Can wholesalers likewise carry reduced inventories because of the speed of delivery by motor carriers? Discuss some of the aspects of inventory policy which may be attributed to utilization of motor carriers.

10. As an individual, how would you cope with some of the externalities of automotive transportation?

### FOOTNOTES TO CHAPTER 1

[1]Mr. C.F. Kettering, then vice president of research of General Motors, Inc., in 1934 predicted that there would be 42 million vehicles in 1960; and his low estimate for the same year, which his company thought more realistic, was 37 million. Actually, the 42-million estimate for 1960 was surpassed in 1948. His estimate was the highest of the prewar estimates. See *Need We Fail in Forecasting* by E.L. Kanwit, C.A. Steele, and T.R. Todd, presentation before the Highway Research Board, January, 1960.

[2]National Transportation Policy Study Commission, *National Transportation Policies*, Washington, D.C., 1979, p. 218.

[3]*Ibid.*, p. 210.

[4]*Ibid.*, p. 177.

[5]*Ibid.*, p. 302.

[6]*Ibid.*, p. 302.

[7]Bureau of Public Roads presentation at the National Academy of Sciences Transportation Research Study, August, 1960, Woods Hole, Mass. A ton-mile is a statistical unit measuring

weight and distance—1 ton transported 10 miles is 10 ton-miles. One passenger transported one mile is one passenger-mile.

[8]Bureau of Census, Department of Commerce, *Truck Inventory and Use Survey*, 1979.

[9]Transportation Association of America, *Transportation Facts and Trends*, 1979, and Supplements, p. 10.

[10]As classified by the Interstate Commerce Commission for accounting purposes through 1973, a Class I motor carrier was one that had gross revenue of $1 million or more per year; Class II, $300,000 to $1 million; and Class III, less than $300,000. Beginning in 1974, the classification is Class I, $3 million or more, Class II, $500,000 to $3 million; and Class III, less than $500,000. Beginning in 1979, the classification is Class I, $5 million or more, Class II, $1 million to $5 million, and Class III, less than $1 million.

[11]National Transportation Policy Study Commission, *op cit.*, p. 164.

[12]Department of Transportation, *1974 National Transportation Report, Summary*, Washington, D.C., December, 1974, p. II-19.

[13]American Trucking Associations, Inc., *Research Review*, April, 1979.

# chapter 2

# Highways

An elaborate system of improved highways has been developed in the United States over a period of years, with the majority of the improvements coming during the period since 1920. Many of the early roads were turnpikes of graded, graveled, or broken-stone surfacing which had been built by private companies expecting to profit through the imposition of tolls assessed for traveling upon the road. Prior to the advent of railroads, there was considerable activity, both governmental and private, dealing with the construction of this type of road. In 1830 there were about 27,000 miles of surfaced roads in the United States, most of which were turnpikes in the vicinity of the larger communities.

The impetus for highway improvement, however, did not occur until well after the invention of the first automobile. As ownership of automobiles became more widespread during the early part of the 20th century, increased attention was given to highway improvement.

Very limited funds were available for highway construction or improvement, and the control of highways was vested largely in cities, towns, villages, and other political subdivisions of the government. An awareness of the need for highway improvement manifested itself in a number of different ways, one of the most significant of which was the establishment in some states of state highway departments. During the years 1900-1920, some state highway departments were created to administer state grants-in-aid to local units for road improvement, although it appears that they exercised little power as to the nature of the road construction or the location of the roads.

The next step in the evolving pattern of state highway departments was their being given the responsibility for road construction with state funds, supplemented in some cases by local funds. Upon the completion of these roads, they were turned over to local government subdivisions for maintenance. It soon developed that local maintenance was not entirely satisfactory, which resulted in many instances of state highway departments assuming the responsibility for maintenance, as well as construction, involving state funds.

The granting of state aid to counties was inaugurated by New Jersey in 1891, and by 1900 six other states had enacted similar legislation. The main routes were those to which the state aid was applied. This practice was adopted by an increasing number of states, so that by 1917 all states were participating to some degree in highway aid.

The choice of routes which the state would aid was often made by drawing lines on a map which would connect the larger centers of population. These main roads were later classified as "primary roads" or a "primary system." Another type of highway—the road that performs a "feeder" service and is not of primary importance—is classified as a "secondary" highway.

During the past 50 years, our total road and street network increased a little more than one-third, from 2.7 million to 3.8 million miles (Fig. 2-1). From 1972 to 1990, an additional 8.8 percent miles of highways are expected to be constructed. All-weather surfaced mileage has increased from 12 percent of total mileage in 1914 to 80 percent of the total today. About 50 percent now has high-type bituminous or portland cement concrete pavement. Some of the other qualitative improvements include wider and additional lanes, reductions in steep grade and sharp curves, and smoother-riding surfaces.

At the present time, the mileage of existing roads and streets is as follows:[1]

|  | Miles | Percent |
|---|---|---|
| Primary state highways | 409,834 | 10.7 |
| Secondary state highways | 272,707 | 7.1 |
| County, town, and township roads | 2,249,446 | 59.0 |
| Municipal streets | 631,229 | 16.5 |
| State park, forest, toll, and other roads | 27,920 | 0.7 |
| National park, forest, reservation, and other federal roads | 215,747 | 5.6 |
| Total mileage | 3,806,883 | |

About 84 percent of our highway mileage is in rural areas and carries 50 percent of total vehicle miles of travel. Since 1920 about half of our motor vehicle miles have occurred in urban areas, but considerably less than half our federal and state highway investment during this time has been in urban highways. Vehicle miles is not a perfect indicator of highway investment needs, but until the past decade we have generally slighted urban highways, with the result that gross deficiencies have become widespread and in many areas critical.

It is estimated at the present time that about 6 acres of land are dedicated for highway purposes for each mile of highway. Therefore, about 1 percent of all of our land area is used for highway purposes. Obviously, the proportion of an urban area devoted to streets is much greater than this—usually about 25 to 30 percent. In the 1960's, increased concern about the amount of land being taken in constructing the interstate system in urban areas and the high costs of land acquisition led to reduction in the land acquired at interchange points. Interchanges, in some instances, have been made so tight that longer vehicle units are not able to negotiate them without modifications. This constitutes a constraint on current and future equipment technology.

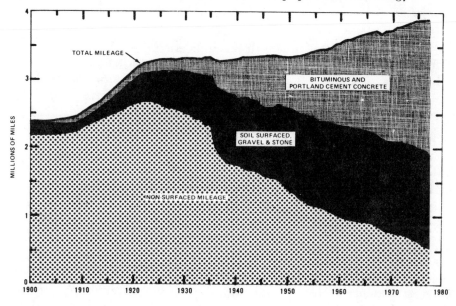

Fig. 2-1. Surface characteristics of the total road and street mileage in the United States. Source: Federal Highway Administration, Department of Transportation.

### Early roads

By modern standards, the type of road which was existent in 1900 was very inferior. Prior to 1900, the primary types of surfacing used were gravel and macadam. In 1900, of the 150,000 miles of surfaced rural roads, 72 percent were gravel, 24 percent were water-bound macadam, with 4 percent of miscellaneous materials. The increasing use of highways by automobiles caused the dust binder present in the gravel and macadam roads to be sucked out and blown away, with resulting rapid deterioration of the highways. Engineers devised tar and asphalt binders and, in general, began experiments with different types of road surfacing. The standards in highway surfacing were not high, and it was a common practice to surface a road without much alteration of base grade, curves, or width. The practice of following township or county lines, including the square corners, prevailed in certain sections of the country during the early stages of highway development.

### Early federal aid

The interest of the federal government in the development of improved highways in the United States was of very early origin. In 1806 aid by the federal government in the construction of the National Pike from Cumberland, Maryland, to Wheeling, West Virginia, later extended into Illinois (now U.S. Route 40), was indication of such interest.

In 1893 the Secretary of Agriculture established the Office of Road Inquiry, which became the Bureau of Public Roads in the Department of Agriculture in 1918. This agency was under various governmental departments through the years but was a part of the Department of Commerce from 1949 to 1967. In that year, it was transferred to the then new Department of Transportation. At the outset, this agency had no funds for actual construction of roads but was to investigate methods of road construction and distribute the information.

Shortly after the turn of the century, short strips of highway were constructed with local funds under the guidance of federal engineers in order to demonstrate desirable surfaced roads throughout the United States. From these demonstrations, valuable information was made available concerning the various types of road construction. More tangible evidence of the federal government's interest in road construction developed in 1912 when it authorized $500,000 to pay one-third of the cost of improving highways over which U.S. mail was carried. However, only 17 states raised the funds necessary to secure the federal assistance. In these 17 states, 425 miles of road were constructed with an expenditure of $1.8 million.

The federal-aid policy involving federal-state cooperation for highway construction became firmly established with the passage in 1916 of the Federal-Aid Road Act. This act authorized and appropriated $75 million over a period of five years for the improvement of any rural road used in mail delivery and specifically prohibited improvements in towns of more than 2,500 population. Federal participation was not to exceed 50 percent of the total cost of the roads constructed, provided the total cost did not exceed $10,000 per mile. The states had to match the federal contribution with funds under their control. The $10,000 limit per mile was later increased and then still later removed.

This act provided a formula for apportioning the federal funds among the states on the basis of three criteria, each to have equal weight: *(a)* the area of the state in relation to the total area of the United States; *(b)* the population of the state in relation to the total population of the United States; and *(c)* the mail road mileage of the state in relation to the total mail road mileage of the United States. A significant provision of the act was that this federal aid was to be available only to those states with state highway departments which could cooperate with the federal government. Those states lacking highway departments took steps toward the immediate formation of departments that would meet federal requirements. Under this act, the obligation of maintenance of highways was placed on the states or their political subdivisions. As other programs were developed, different apportionment formulas were established. There are a number of formulas that are now applicable which will be outlined in "Highway Financing."

Prior to the passage of the Federal-Aid Road Act, the principal executive officers of most of the existing state highway departments had joined in the formation of the American Association of State Highway Officials. This organization, which represented the views and desires of state governments on highway matters, was influential in shaping provisions of the act. This influence has been continuously and effectively exerted in all subsequent modifications of the federal highway program. The Federal-Aid Road Act became the pattern for later federal aid given in connection with airport construction.

The early federal-aid projects were randomly located, but it became apparent that the federal government's interest lay in an integrated highway system. This led to the passage of the Federal Highway Act of 1921, which required the state highway departments to designate a system of interstate and intercounty highways eligible to receive federal aid. Such aid was limited to 7 percent of the total mileage of rural roads in each state, and the highways so designated were divided into two classes—primary, or interstate, and secondary, or intercounty. In this manner, a federal-aid highway system came into being. Federal funds and matching state funds had to be spent on that system. The act also provided that the state was responsible for maintenance of highways constructed with the aid of federal funds. If a state failed to maintain these highways in proper fashion, the work could be carried out under direct federal supervision, the cost to be paid out of federal funds which otherwise would be available to the state for construction purposes. Certain roads which were considered to be of primary importance for national defense were also included in the federal-aid system.

The original formula governing apportionment of the federal authorizations remained unchanged in its application to the primary federal-aid system, except by the modification that no state shall receive less than one-half of 1 percent of the total authorized. However, the original requirement of at least equal matching with state funds of the federal contribution to the cost of roads built was modified by the Federal Highway Act, in respect to roads built in any state containing unappropriated public lands exceeding 5 percent of the total area of all lands in the state. It permitted payment of a federal share of the cost up to 50 percent plus a percentage equal to one-half of the percentage of unappropriated public lands in the state. This formula has resulted in the federal contribution in some western states amounting to 54 to 83 cents for each dollar expended.

The Federal Highway Act of 1921 appropriated $75 million for the fiscal year of 1922; but in 1923 the Congress provided for the authorization of federal funds, with specific appropriations to be made as needed. From 1921 through 1932, the federal funds authorized averaged about $100 million per year. When a state had completed and was maintaining 90 percent of its original federal-aid system of highways, the original limitation of 7 percent could be increased in 1 percent increments in accordance with a provision that was passed in 1932. Not charged against the 7 percent limitation are mileages in national forests, federal reservations, and urban areas. Currently, the federal-aid primary system ranges from 4 percent in North Dakota to 13 percent in Delaware. In some 22 states, it ranges from 7 to 10 percent. The federal-aid primary system has had a relatively slow growth from 169,000 miles in 1923 to 446,879 in 1973.

During the depression period of the 1930's, the federal-aid policy was liberalized because of the emergency, so that states did not have to match federal funds which were appropriated to provide employment. Furthermore, federal funds could be used for purposes of improvement of the federal-aid highway system through municipalities, as well as for construction of secondary roads.

The Federal-Aid Highway Act of 1944 authorized $500 million per year for the first three postwar years. This act continued the principles involved in the act of 1921 but also introduced the factor of making funds available for use in the federal-aid system in cities and urban communities of over 5,000 population. An important provision of this act was the establishment of a 40,000-mile interstate system of the more important highways in the United States so as to connect by direct routes the principal metropolitan areas. Specific provision was made for the designation of a separate federal-aid secondary system of principal secondary and feeder roads, including farm-to-market roads, rural free delivery mail, and public school bus routes.

The appropriations under the 1944 act were granted as follows: 45 percent to primary roads in the federal-aid system, which included urban extensions of these primary roads; 30 percent for expenditures on selected roads in the federal-aid secondary system; and 25 percent for federal-aid highways in urban areas which had populations of more than 5,000. This has since become known as the "ABC" or regular federal-aid program as distinguished from the interstate system. The percentage proportions have been retained in all subsequent authorizations.

The criteria used in the apportionment of federal-aid funds among the states for primary roads has continued to be area, population, and mileage. For secondary roads, the formula is the same except that rural population is substituted for general population.

The third division of federal-aid allocation to the states for urban areas is based on the ratio which the population in municipalities and other urban communities of 5,000 or more in each state bears to the total population in municipalities and other urban places, of 5,000 or more, in all the states as shown by the last federal census. Under the provisions of this act, the federal aid cannot in general exceed 50 percent of the total construction costs.

In 1948 and 1950, federal-aid legislation was enacted which continued, without any basic change, the principles of the act of 1944.

The federal-aid secondary system has grown much more rapidly than the primary system. It varies from 3 percent of all highway mileage in Wyoming to 35 percent in North Carolina. This system differs from the primary and interstate in that there is no legislative limit on system mileage; legislative criteria for route selection are broad and encompass almost any rural road; cooperation of state and local officials is required; and much of the federal review process is delegated to the states.

### Federal-aid legislation, 1950—60

For the first time in federal-aid legislation, specific funds were authorized in the Federal-Aid Highway Act of 1952 for the improvement of the national system of interstate highways. Before that, improvements were made with funds provided for the federal-aid primary highway system, of which it is a part, and for urban highway improvements. In order to accelerate the rate of improvement of the interstate highway system, the 1952 act authorized $25 million for exclusive use on the system for each of the fiscal years 1954 and 1955.

The loss of time to the highway improvement program caused by World War II and its aftermath has not been generally understood. The construction of federal-aid highway projects was stopped by Executive order late in 1941 and was in effect until October, 1945, when it was officially lifted. This stop order did not apply to state or local road construction, but other conditions imposed the slowing down of all operations and the abandonment of a major part of the authorized program.

The loss of engineering personnel from the highway departments, the disposal of contractors' organizations, the steel shortage, and other similar causes so severely restricted the program of construction that it was not until 1949 or 1950 that the program reached the level of the annual funds provided. Thus, nearly 10 years of construction and rehabilitation were lost when the major highways had suffered severe deterioration from war traffic and when new traffic was increasing at a rate greater than at any previous time. This was the major reason why there was an emergency highway condition existing after the war. The modernization of highways was disappointingly slow due largely to the insufficiency of financing.

After Presidential recommendations and extensive hearings, the Congress enacted the Federal-Aid Highway Act of 1956, authorizing the greatest long-range highway program ever undertaken as well as the greatest peacetime public works program. The act authorized an expenditure of over $24 billion for the interstate system for a 13-year period. This sum, together with about $2.6 billion to be contributed by the states, would provide an interstate system designed to meet the traffic anticipated in 1975. (It is now estimated that it will be completed in 1990 at a capital cost of $109 billion.) It increased the maximum mileage limitation of the interstate system to 41,000 miles and changed its title to the National System of Interstate and Defense Highways. The inclusion of toll roads in the interstate system was also authorized if they were suitably located and met the interstate standards, but their construction and improvement could not be paid for with federal funds.

The amounts authorized for the fiscal years 1957, 1958, and 1959 were to be apportioned as had been prescribed in the Federal-Aid Highway Act of 1954. For the remaining 10 years, the interstate system funds were to be apportioned according to a cost-of-completion formula—that is, in the ratio that the estimated cost of completing the system in each state bears to the total estimated cost of completing the entire system in order that the system could be completed throughout the country at the same time. The interstate system funds authorized by the act were to be expended on a 90 percent federal, 10 percent state matching basis. Under this act, the primary (other than the interstate), secondary, and urban federal-aid funds had to be matched on a 50-50 basis by the states.

Prior to this time, federal appropriations for highways were made from the general funds of the Treasury. Unlike some of the states that linked highway-user taxes to highway expenditures, the federal excise taxes had not been so earmarked. Certain federal excise taxes were increased under this act, and new excise taxes imposed. Varying percentages of these taxes were dedicated to highway expenditures and a Highway Trust Fund was created into which these revenues were to be paid.

This act contained a pay-as-you-go provision limiting the amounts to be expended to the balance in the Fund. The primary, secondary, and urban highways (the ABC system) have first call on the Trust Fund.

The act required that the standards governing the physical dimensions, control of access, and other design features of the interstate system had to be approved by the Secretary of Commerce (since 1967 the Secretary of Transportation) in cooperation with the state highway departments. The design standards were to be adequate to accommodate traffic in 1975. In order to insure control of access, the act provided that a state could not add points of access to or exit from a project on the interstate system without prior approval of the Secretary of Commerce. The latter, if requested by a state, could acquire rights-of-way for the interstate system where the state could not properly acquire and take possession of the needed land. Federal-aid funds apportioned to the states were available for acquiring rights-of-way on any of the federal-aid systems in anticipation of construction to start within five years.

A provision of the act froze the maximum weight and width limitation of highway vehicles by denying federal-aid funds to any state which permitted operation after July 1, 1956, over the interstate and defense highway system, of vehicles heavier or wider than those specified in the act, or those which on that date could be lawfully operated in the state, whichever was the greater. The amounts specified in the act were 18,000 pounds on a single-axle, 32,000 pounds on a tandem axle (2-axle); or an overall gross weight in excess of 73,280 pounds; or with a width in excess of 96 inches. About half of the states at that time permitted weights greater than the amounts specified in the act.

The Federal-Aid Highway Act of 1958 provided the regular biennial authorization for the ABC program by authorizing $900 million for fiscal 1960 and $925 million for fiscal 1961 in the usual proportions of 45 percent for the primary, 30 percent for the secondary, and 25 percent for the urban extensions. These funds were matched by the states on the traditional 50-50 basis.

The interstate system authorizations were $2.5 billion for each of the fiscal years 1960 and 1961. The act suspended the pay-as-you-go provision for a two-year period, allowing greater funds to be spent to combat the recession than otherwise would have been the case. (In 1959 Congress repealed the waiver of the pay-as-you-go provision by an amendment to the appropriation act for the Commerce Department.)

Control of outdoor advertising along the interstate system was another provision of this act. The Secretary of Commerce was required to develop national standards for regulating advertising within 660 feet of the right-of-way edge and visible from the interstate system. The states that entered into agreements with the Secretary of Commerce to carry out the national policy on a statewide basis were entitled to an increase of one-half of 1 percent in the federal share of interstate system project costs. By 1965 only 8 states had become eligible for such payments. It was clear by this time that the voluntary program had failed to control outdoor advertising.

The Federal-Aid Highway Act of 1959 made a number of changes in order to increase the amounts going into the Highway Trust Fund. It increased the federal motor fuel tax from 3 cents to 4 cents for the period October 1, 1959, to June 30, 1961. The 1-cent fuel tax increase was to be replaced as a source of additional revenue after that time by dedication to the Highway Trust Fund of one-half of the 10 percent excise tax on new automobiles and five-eighths of the 8 percent tax on motor vehicle parts and accessories to be effective from July 1, 1961, to June 30, 1964. None of the revenues from these two excise taxes had previously been dedicated to the Fund.

### Federal aid during the 1960's

During the 1960's, federal-aid legislation has been enacted which reflects greater consideration of social values. In 1962 federal relocation assistance was provided to the states for families and businesses displaced by highway construction. The same year, legislation provided that every urban area of 50,000 population or more must have a comprehensive, cooperative, continuing highway transportation planning process, including coordination of plans with other modes of transportation and with local land development, in order to receive federal aid.

Legislation in 1965 provided special funds for highway beautification and roadside junkyard and billboard control. The Highway Beautification Act provided for landscaping and roadside development on federal-aid highway systems; compensation to sign and property owners for the removal of billboards; and removing or screening of junkyards. By 1969, 14 states had signed agreements with the Department of Transportation to control outdoor advertising, and 20 states had signed agreements to control junkyards. It is estimated that 14,000 junkyards will be screened and 3,500 removed under this program.

In 1966 legislation required that full consideration be given in highway location to parks, wildlife and recreation areas, and historic sites. Legislation also authorized the use of airspace above or below highways for residential or commercial buildings or parking.

A national highway safety program was initiated in 1966 which authorized the establishment of safety standards for motor vehicles and authorized matching grants for this program. Also authorized was the issuance of federal standards covering a wide range of highway safety programs as goals which the states are expected to reach in the future. In the same year, Congress created the Department of Transportation, which began functioning in 1967 and moved toward the development of an integrated transportation system.

Federal matching funds were earmarked in 1968 legislation for traffic operation projects to increase capacity and safety (TOPICS) in urban areas. These projects are to be improvements that directly facilitate and control traffic flow, such as grade separation at intersections, widening of lanes, channelization of traffic, and loading and unloading ramps. By 1975, more than 4,600 projects had been authorized at an estimated cost of over $1 billion. Fringe parking demonstration projects were also authorized which could be financed with federal-aid urban highway matching funds if they were outside the central business district, were adjacent to federal-aid highways, and were located so as to be used with existing or planned public transportation facilities.

Another change enacted in 1968 strengthened relocation assistance. In addition to providing reasonable moving expenses and/or a dislocation allowance, this legislation permits payments up to $5,000 above the fair market value for homeowners whose properties are taken and up to $1,500 for tenants to rent suitable new quarters. The federal government paid all of displacement costs until July 1, 1970, by which time state laws were changed to enable the states to assist in the financing on a matching basis under the federal-aid highway program.

Another important development in 1968 related to future highway investment. A study was authorized to be completed by 1970 of a "functional" classification of highways made in cooperation with state highway departments and local governments. This study of highways by category of service and standards of quality could be used to establish future federal-aid highway priorities. In 1968, also, 1,500 miles were added to the interstate system, making a total of 42,500 miles, and the deadline for completion of the system was extended from 1972 to 1974 (later extended to 1977 and further extensions are probable). Another provision requires the Secretary of Transportation to make an affirmative finding that the inclusion of any additional toll road in the interstate system is in the public interest (about 6 percent of the system is toll facilities).

A somewhat different approach to highways was taken in the Appalachian Regional Development Act of 1965 and the Public Works and Development Acts of 1965 and 1967. The former act sought, by emphasizing better access through highways, to stimulate the economic and cultural growth of a deprived region embracing the Appalachian Mountains. It is not financed with regular federal-aid highway funds, but the Federal Highway Administration of the Department of Transportation and the state highway departments implement the development of highways programmed. Since regional development programs are based on broad considerations of public needs and benefits, the highway financing is from general rather than highway-user funds.

As part of the federal fiscal policy, highway expenditures have been accelerated at times to provide an antidepression or antirecession measure and, at other times, spending has been curtailed as an anti-inflationary measure. It is estimated that $1 billion of highway work during active construction provides on-site employment for 35,000 direct jobs and an equal number of indirect jobs. In 1966, highway funds were impounded by the President and, in subsequent years, succeeding presidents at times have impounded highway funds. There has been controversy between the Executive Branch and the Congress regarding actions of this kind. In 1974, $1.7 billion was impounded by the President.

### Federal aid in the 1970's

In the 1950's, there were four designated highway programs—the interstate, primary, secondary, and extensions of primary and secondary systems into the urban areas. In later years, the number of authorization categories grew until, by 1970, there were 15 separate programs funded from the Highway Trust Fund; and, in 1974, 34 program categories, 22 of which were funded by the Highway Trust Fund.

The major changes in the 1973 Federal-Aid Highway Act were the following: increased funding for the urban highway system and authorization for urban system funds to be used for mass transit; authorization for state and local governments in urbanized areas to substitute mass transit for interstate system routes; institution of new highway safety programs; and realignment of the federal-aid systems according to functional usage.

The Federal-Aid Highway Act of 1976 increased the program fund authorizations to 36 and extended the interstate program through 1990. Other important provisions included the establishment of the interstate 3-R program (resurfacing, restoration, and rehabilitation) which allocated money for interstate routes; continuation of the category of "high density urban" (which had been created in the 1973 act), as well as the annual authorizations for urban aid systems in general; continuation of existing safety programs at current or higher funding levels; establishment of a National Transportation Policy Study Commission of 19 members to develop national transportation systems to meet projected needs; and permission for the states to raise bus width limits from 96 inches to 102 inches for operation in the interstate system.

For the first time in 1978, the Surface Transportation Assistance Act of that year combined authorizations for highways, highway safety, and public transportation into one legislative act. Title I of the act was entitled the Federal-Aid Highway Act of 1978; highway safety was included under Title II; public mass transit under Title III; Title IV contained a "Buy America" provision that applied to the first three titles; and Title V extended the Highway Trust Fund.

For the first time, also, this legislation provided for a four-year authorization of funding which would allow for improved planning by state and local authorities. Funding provided by the act was as follows: a total $51.4 billion for the fiscal years 1979 through 1982, with $30.6 billion for highways, $7.2 billion for highway safety, and $13.6 billion for public transportation. The Highway Trust Fund was extended to 1984 without change in the tax rates. The 1990 date for completion of the interstate system continued unchanged, and authorization to allow federal funds to be used for both principal and interest on state highway bonds used to finance the interstate projects was included. Existing provisions that had permitted a state to transfer interstate mileage from one locality to another were eliminated and, after 1983, the authorization for substitution of new mass transit or highway projects for withdrawn interstate segments was eliminated. A new provision permitted states to use abandoned interstate right-of-way for other public uses without reimbursement of federal funds. The federal share of funding for all major non-interstate highway and safety construction programs was increased to a minimum of 75 percent.

The 3-R program was continued and received increased funding with 75 percent federal share, and the bridge program was expanded to include repair as well as replacement. The Secretary of Transportation was required to issue guidelines that would assure proper maintenance of interstate routes.

The funding levels for the primary, secondary, and urban systems of the federal-aid highway programs were increased from 70 to 75 percent, and a requirement was added that at least 20 percent of a state's apportionments for primary and secondary systems had to be used to resurface, restore, or rehabilitate those routes.

Numerous other programs were continued from previous highway acts, such as forest highways, public lands highways, economic growth centers, and control of outdoor advertising. The act also authorized the inclusion of bicycle paths and pedestrian walkways as elements of primary, secondary, or urban system projects. Car and van pooling programs were made eligible for funding from the federal-aid primary, secondary, and urban system funds.

The 1978 act also required a number of studies and reports, one of which was to study the desirability of uniform maximum truck weights, and the means to bring about such uniformity, to be based on recommendations by the Secretary of Transportation.

A special commission, the National Alcohol Fuels Commission, was created to study the potential of alcohol fuels as a part of energy development.

## National System of Interstate and Defense Highways

The National System of Interstate and Defense Highways constitutes 42,500 miles which will connect 90 percent of all cities having more than 50,000 in population. The routes comprising the interstate system have been selected by joint action of the state highway departments and the Bureau of Public Roads (now the Federal Highway Administration). An estimated 37,700 miles were designated in 1947. Additional routes around and through urban areas, totaling 2,300 miles, were specified in 1955. The latter routes were measured along principal existing highways, and no detailed engineering studies were made of these routes.

The act of 1956 increased the authorized length of the interstate system from 40,000 to 41,000 miles, but the additional 1,000-mile extension was not included in the original cost estimates for the program covered by the 1956 act. Later, the states, by more accurate measurement and selection of better locations for the routes already designated, found that there was a saving of 1,102 miles, and so a total of 38,898 miles of routes had actually been designated. In 1957, 2,102 miles (which represented the 1,102 miles in savings and the 1,000-mile extension) of interstate routes were designated.[2] In 1968 Congress appeared adamant in its views on adding to the interstate system, and the administration went along on a 1,500-mile increase in the system.

Essentially, the interstate system will be freeways because access will be controlled throughout the entire system and entry will be made only at selected locations. This is one of the most significant aspects of the interstate system. Grade crossings will be eliminated, and there will be no direct entrance for any commercial facilities.[3] The design and construction of this system was planned to provide highways which would adequately handle the traffic volumes of 20 years in the future.[4]

Most of the routes were planned to be four-lane, divided highways and with six to eight lanes in and near metropolitan areas. Federal legislation in 1966 required all sections to be a minimum of four lanes. The minimum design standards used on the interstate system provide for lane widths not less than 12 feet.

The median strip must generally be at least 36 feet wide, but in urban and mountainous areas, a minimum of 16 feet will be permitted. Under unusual conditions of terrain or right-of-way, it may be reduced

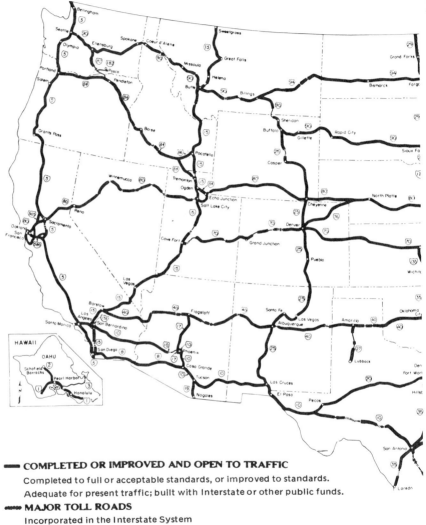

**COMPLETED OR IMPROVED AND OPEN TO TRAFFIC**
Completed to full or acceptable standards, or improved to standards.
Adequate for present traffic; built with Interstate or other public funds.

**MAJOR TOLL ROADS**
Incorporated in the Interstate System

**UNDER CONSTRUCTION**

**PRELIMINARY STATUS OR NOT YET IN PROGRESS**
Plan preparation and right-of-way acquisition completed or underway
on many portions of these sections

Fig. 2-2. The national system of interstate and defense highways.

Scale of map does not permit showing of status
in urban areas and for very short sections

U.S. DEPARTMENT OF TRANSPORTATION
FEDERAL HIGHWAY ADMINISTRATION

Source: Federal Highway Administration, Department of Transportation.

to not less than 4 feet. Shoulders 10 feet wide are to be provided, with 6 feet to be permitted in mountainous terrain.

The minimum right-of-way widths in rural areas range from 150 feet for a two-lane road to 330 feet for an eight-lane, divided highway with a frontage road on each side. A minimum clearance for bridges and underpasses of 16 feet is required.[5]

The design speeds established are 70, 60, and 50 miles an hour for flat, rolling, and mountainous terrain, respectively, where local conditions are favorable. The grades must be no steeper than 3 percent in flat country to 5 percent in mountainous country. The effect of these design standards is to provide for free-flowing traffic, as well as the safe movement of traffic. The primary consideration in the establishment of the minimum design standards was safety.

The interstate system consists of 33,189 miles of rural and 9,311 miles of urban highways. By 1980, 93 percent of the interstate system was open to traffic. There were 1,223 miles under basic construction, 1,395 miles with right-of-way in progress and 470 miles which were not yet in progress (Fig. 2-2).

The numbering system of the National System of Interstate and Defense Highways was devised by the American Association of State Highway Officials. Odd-numbered routes run north and south; even numbers east and west. The numbering begins at the west and south, and the numbers of the long, evenly spaced routes end with "0" or "5." In three-digit signs, a route through or around a city has an even first digit; a route into a city has an odd number as the first digit. Some of the principal highways have both U.S. and interstate markings. (Some of our main highways are marked by route markers with the initials "U.S." and a route number. This is done through joint action of the state highway departments in order to implement map making and simplify highway travel, and is without legal or administrative significance.)

The development of the transportation infrastructure represented by the 42,500-mile interstate system is one of the most significant transportation developments of the twentieth century. It has provided a linkage between major cities and regions that has enabled persons and property to be moved expeditiously, safely, and at a reasonable cost. The intercity portions of the interstate have enabled trucks to become a potent competitive force on both a service and cost basis. The beltways, or circumferential highways, around metropolitan areas have become a factor in shaping population patterns, industrial location and relocation, and recreational and cultural facilities. In some metropolitan areas, the suburban population densities adjacent to the beltways approach the densities of the inner city areas.

With some of the mileage on the interstate system more than 20 years old, it was apparent that improvements had to be made. One of the provisions of the Surface Transportation Assistance Act of 1978 required the Secretary of Transportation to issue guidelines to insure that interstate routes were being maintained to the level for which they were designed. Within one year from October 1, 1979, each state had to have a maintenance program that met the guidelines. If a state failed to do so, its interstate apportionment for that year would be reduced by 10 percent.

## Highway classification

The 1973 Federal-Aid Highway Act provided for the realignment of the federal-aid primary, secondary, and urban systems by the end of fiscal year 1976, based on the anticipated functional usage in 1980 or on a planned connected system. As directed by the provisions of this act, the federal-aid highway systems realignment issued a functional classification of highways. The functional classification is an analysis of services provided by each highway facility and the assignment of each facility to a system consistent with its principal function.

There are three basic highway classifications: principal arterial, minor arterial, and collector. These basic systems are further divided by area definitions—urbanized are those areas designated by the Bureau of Census as having a population of 50,000 or more; small urban are those having a population of 5,000 or more but less than 50,000; and rural includes all areas not falling in either of the above classifications. The principal arterial system is a network of routes that primarily serve state-wide and interstate travel. This system is divided into interstate, other freeways and expressways (in urban areas) and other principal arterials. The minor arterial system provides routes of access to principal arterial routes forming a network that links cities and larger towns to facilitate interstate and intercounty service. Collectors offer a balance between mobility and land access. This system is divided into larger collectors serving county seats and other traffic generators not directly served by arterial routes and minor collectors that link important traffic generators with smaller communities.

The Department of Transportation in 1977 made a calculation using the functional classification system as to estimated mileage traveled and expenditures by functional system by the year 1990. These figures were compared to actual 1975 figures for the same categories. As Fig. 2-3 shows, the division of rural and urban systems reflects significant changes in all three categories. The change to the new functional system of classification was estimated by the Department of Transportation to result in significant shifts in capital expenditures by 1990. The rural federal-aid highway system, which in 1975, had capital expenditures of 33 percent would decline to 19 percent by 1990. Capital expenditures for the same period on arterials would increase from 46 percent of the total to 62 percent. In urban

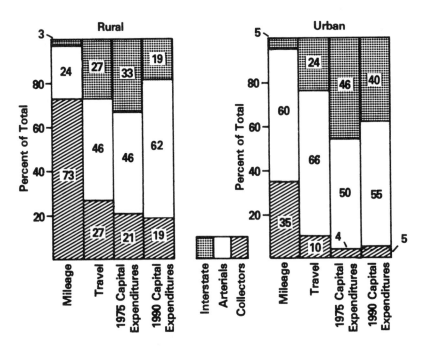

Fig. 2-3. Mileage, travel, and expenditures by functional system, 1975 and 1990. Source: Department of Transportation, *The Status of the Nation's Highways: Conditions and Performance*, 95th Cong., 1st sess. (Washington, D.C.: U.S. Government Printing Office, 1977), p. 178.

areas, the change was less marked. From 1975, capital expenditures on the interstate of 46 percent would decline to 40 percent by 1990, and arterials would increase from 50 percent to 55 percent in the same period. The figure shows the 1990 highway mileage and travel by interstate, arterials, and collectors.

Highways do wear out. Fluctuations in the conditions of service, standards of design and construction, and management policies affect the predicted average lives of highway pavements. Thus, one finds there is variation from state to state. When related to service of the highway, the variation is from 12 years for bituminous penetration to 25 years for portland cement concrete. A typical highway repair project can improve vehicle fuel efficiency by 10 percent according to the Federal Highway Administration. It has been found that the number of years a road surface on principal rural arterial highways remains in service before it is re-surfaced, reconstructed, or otherwise replaced ranges from five years for low-type surfaces, such as gravel,to 25 years for high-type surfaces, such as portland cement concrete or bituminous concrete.

The condition of highway pavement is classified on a scale that ranges from 5.0 (good) for new pavement to 0.0 (poor) for pavement in need of resurfacing or reconstruction. This scale is normally used as the present serviceability rating. Pavement rated below 2.5 is considered to be in immediate need of reconstruction. Between 2.5 and 3.0 is considered to be in fair condition, and 23 percent of the interstate system was so rated in 1979.

### Federal Highway Administration

The Federal Highway Administration was established in 1967 as a part of the new Department of Transportation. It is responsible for the total operation and environment of the highway system.

The Federal Highway Administration administers the Federal-Aid Highway Program of financial assistance to the states for highway con-struction. This program provides for construction of the 42,500-mile inter-state highway system and improvement of federal-aid primary and sec-ondary roads and their urban extensions. Emphasis is placed on improving the safety design of new highways, correcting high-hazard locations on existing roads, and improving the capacity and efficiency of urban street systems. It establishes technical standards for the various federal-aid systems and insures that these standards are met. These minimum design standards which guide in the construction of highways are subject to a number of variable factors, such as the daily volume of traffic, whether the terrain is flat or rolling (which affects design speed), the presence of curves, and many other factors. These standards for the same type of highway vary in different sections of the country as well as in the same general area, dependent upon the variable factors. [6]

The Bureau of Motor Carrier Safety has jurisdiction over the safety performance of all motor carriers engaged in interstate or foreign com-merce, including those whose operations are specifically exempt from economic regulation. It checks on driver qualifications and hours of service on the road, analyzes accident reports, and makes carrier and vehicle inspections.

## National Highway Traffic Safety Administration

Another operating agency of the Department of Transportation is the National Highway Traffic Safety Administration. It has the responsibility of establishing and requiring compliance with standards for newly-manufactured vehicles and identified components. It has issued 18 state program standards covering such matters as codes and laws, driver licensing and periodic motor vehicle inspection in an effort to assist the states through financial and technical assistance to implement state programs for drivers and motor vehicles. It is responsible for the development and administration of safety standards encompassing the identification and surveillance of accident locations, highway design, construction and maintenance. The states are expected to implement the federally established programs in accordance with the standards that are issued by the Secretary of Transportation.

The Surface Transportation Assistance Act of 1978 expanded the existing highway safety programs under the Federal Highway Administration and the National Highway Traffic Safety Administration. The authorizations were higher for the four years covered by the act and most of the increase was due to expanded funding for the bridge replacement and rehabilitation program. The following new safety activities were authorized: safety education; innovative safety grants; and enforcement of the 55-mile per hour speed limit.

The Highway Safety Grants Program under Section 402 is administered by both FHA and NHTSA and was designed to provide funding for implementation of the 18 highway safety standards and acceptance analysis programs and to conduct safety research covering highway travel and highway characteristics among other states. Each state's highway safety program must be administered by the governor through a state highway safety agency. A Section 403 program, that of safety research and development, provided funding for safety research. In this act, there is a hazard elimination program under which funding is provided for highway safety construction on non-interstate federal-aid highways to improve high hazard locations, eliminate roadside obstacles, and increase enforcement of traffic control devices including pavement marking.

### State and local highway management

Public highways in the United States are, in general, under the control of the states; and, because of this fact, different methods of management are employed. Because of the varying sizes of the states and the number of miles of highways within the states, the administrative organization necessary to manage properly the respective state highway systems differs likewise.

There are six types of state highway organizations. One of these is the single executive who has full responsibility and authority. The single executive and advisory commission is a second type. The full responsibility is vested in the single executive and the commission acts only in an advisory capacity at the request of the executive. Another type is the single executive and coordinate commission. In this kind of highway organization, the authority is divided either by law or by assignment between a single executive and a commission. The fourth type is the limited-control commission in which the authority of the commission is specifically restricted to policy determination or performance of limited administrative duties. The fifth type is the administrative commission which has complete responsibility and authority. The sixth type is a Department of Transportation. By 1975, more than 20 states had created such departments which encompassed highway administration, together with the other transportation responsibilities.

In the majority of the states, the state delegates some responsibility for county and local roads to those political subdivisions. However, counties have little or no responsibility for roads in the New England states, Delaware, North Carolina, West Virginia, and Virginia (except for two counties). Alabama has assumed responsibility for county roads in 10 counties and Maryland handles it on behalf of 6 counties.

The units below the state level which administer local roads include more than 2,500 counties, about 15,000 rural towns or townships, about 900 special districts and toll authorities, and about 16,000 incorporated and other urban places. The highway function is administered by approximately 34,000 governmental units, each having some degree of responsibility for the administration and support of highways.

An additional 500 counties, rural towns and townships, and special districts are responsible for paying principal and interest on debt incurred for highway purposes, but they have no other highway responsibilities.

Most states apportion highway funds to political subdivisions of the state. Population is a widely used factor for apportionment to urban areas. Some states combine other factors with population, such as vehicle registration, registration revenue, street and road mileage, and others. The states transfer to local governments about one-fourth of all state highway-use tax revenues as state aid for local roads and streets. The majority of states use a combination of factors in apportioning funds among counties, including area, population, vehicle registration, registration revenue, and local road mileage.

Procedures for the acquisition of right-of-way and the designation of highway systems by administrative bodies, as provided by existing laws, fall far short of what is needed. Highway administrators are compelled to act within the scope of legal authority as set forth in the statutes governing their administration. States have often constructed community bypasses only to find that failure to control access results in another bypass being constructed to bypass the bypass.

When land is acquired for limited-access highways, there is a great deal of speculation in land adjacent to the highways, particularly at the interchanges where motels, restaurants, apartments, and service facilities may be constructed. The price of this land skyrockets, which makes a considerable profit for land speculators. Since it is the location of the highway that enhances the value of this property and since highway construction costs are high, the state in acquiring land for rights-of-way should secure a large enough acreage at the proposed interchanges that it can be held for either leasing or future sale. This would recover some of the highway costs.

Many relationships between a state and its counties and cities, and between local units as well, are involved in the planning, improvement, and maintenance of the roads and streets throughout a state. Due to state and federal aid for highways, various intergovernmental relationships have gradually been established, and in recent years they have expanded. Such relationships range from joint participation in projects to the mere exercise of supervisory control. In many states, however, such development has been sporadic, expanding fragmentarily as specific problems and situations were encountered.

In view of the piecemeal growth of cooperative relationships, it is frequently found in the various states that existing legislative authority is inadequate, that responsibility and authority are not clearly defined and assigned, that policies and procedures are not uniformly executed, and that existing administrative machinery needs revamping.

The various requirements of cooperation among the several highway agencies in the state further intergovernmental relationships and encourage greater uniformity of standards and good engineering practices among counties and cities.

### Trends in highway use

There is a great variation in the use of our highway system. Some city streets carry as many as 200,000 vehicles daily, as do some rural highways; whereas on others, both urban and rural, the daily traffic is less than 50 vehicles. Certain freeways in urban areas during the rush hours from 7 to 9 a.m. operate at 50 percent above their designed capacity.

The possibility of highways designated for truck or bus service only may only be likely within the next two decades. A separate truck or bus highway would accommodate this type of traffic where the volumes are especially heavy and segregation of such traffic may be economically justified. The designation of exclusive or separate bus lanes in urban transit areas during the hours of peak traffic is being widely used and is effective in speeding traffic and handling large volumes. The possibility of this kind of lane on federal-aid highways in urban areas appears to offer even greater efficiency in the future.

Highways are constructed for the dual purpose of both private and commercial use, and design of major routes must be held to certain standards in the interest of national defense, a factor of vital significance. In addition, state highway engineers have stated frequently that they would construct highways to meet certain standards whether or not there were commercial vehicles operating on those highways, inasmuch as certain minimum standards must be met to take care of the weathering of a highway.

Of course, weight and volume of traffic are other factors which are considered. A commercial vehicle does occupy more road space than a passenger car. An average dual-tired commercial vehicle is said to have about the same effect as 2 passenger cars on multilane highways and 2.5 on two-lane highways in level terrain, and 4 passenger cars in rolling terrain. In mountainous areas this effect can be as great in relation to highway capacity as 6 passenger cars on a 3 percent grade 2,000 feet long or 20 passenger cars on a 6 percent grade of the same length.

A two-lane highway in level terrain and carrying traffic 30 percent of which is trucks, for example, will have the same congestion with about 69 percent of the number of vehicles which the same highway will carry if all vehicles are passenger cars.

Several programs have been undertaken by the Federal Highway Administration to reduce traffic congestion in urban areas. This has involved preferential treatment for transit buses (exclusive bus lanes), computerized traffic control systems, fringe parking facilities, and computerized bus pool and car pool programs.

### Social and environmental impact of highways

Increasing attention has been focused in recent years on the social impacts of highways, particularly in the urban areas. Greater participation by citizen groups have brought some needed changes in the planning for future highway construction. The social impacts include neighborhood disruption, overly rapid industrialization, destruction of historical facilities, and changes in land values that force unplanned changes upon society. In economic terms, these are referred to as externalities.

The concern with environmental factors, as reflected in legislation creating the Environmental Protection Agency, relates to air and water pollution, noise levels, and ecological impacts. Under this Act, certain regulations have been issued and proposed highway projects are required to consider these elements.

The Federal Highway Administration in a recent year processed more than 950 environmental impact statements on construction projects, more than any other governmental agency. One out of every eight dollars of highway improvements is spent on such environmental factors as landscaping, rerouting of roads to preserve wildlife, creation of such recreational amenities as roadside rest areas, ponds, and parks. Illustrative of the changes in highway planning is the attitude of the highway planner in disruptions necessitated by relocation. The Highway Administration may now provide up to $15,000 in payments over and above the fair market value of property for relocations due to a new highway right-of-way in order that the owner may secure comparable housing. Benefits are also provided to apartment dwellers who must move, as well as adjustments for commercial establishments.

### Effects of technological developments on highway needs

A recurring question regarding future use of highways and the need for future highway investment is that of the degree to which new or alternative modes of transportation may provide alternative means which might lessen future demands on highways. In the intercity field, significant technological improvements in aircraft have occurred, such as helicopters, vertical takeoff or short takeoff and landing aircraft, jets, and the supersonic transport. In addition, the Department of Transportation has spearheaded the Northeast Corridor High-Speed Train experiment operating from Washington to New York and Boston. Research is also being conducted on a number of concepts and techniques, such as tunneling, which could have future impact on highway needs. The research thus far applicable to the high-density travel area of the Northeast Corridor indicates that within that area only about 10 percent of all highway vehicle-miles of travel is intercity between the cities served, and only a portion of this might be diverted to high-speed mass transportation. Because of convenience, origins and destinations, party size, preference, and other reasons, heavy use will continue to be made of highways in the high-density areas. For travel within urban areas, research indicates that street and highway improvements will be required even though improved mass transportation is developed on a separate right-of-way, such as subways or rail lines. As in the case of intercity movements, trip requirements may be such that they can be made only by street or highway transportation.

### Benefits of improved highways

One of the primary benefits of improved highways is an improvement in safety. A federal government report indicated that where there was full control of access, there were 3.3 fatalities per 100 million vehicle-miles of travel on rural roads. Where only partial control of access existed on rural roads, fatalities per 100 million vehicle-miles almost doubled. On rural roads with no control of access, there were 8.7 fatalities per 100 million vehicle-miles.[7] It is estimated that completion of the interstate system will save 4,000 lives each year, since the fatality rate on this system is only one-half the national average.

Highway improvements bring additional benefits to highway users of reduction in travel time and saving in fuel. Travel time is saved whenever highway improvements reduce distance, permit higher speeds, or reduce the frequency of speed changes. Fuel savings are effected when highway improvements reduce travel distance, reduce the frequency of stop-and-go operations or slowdowns, or reduce traffic congestion. A study of the effect of traffic congestion upon fuel consumption of trucks showed that the number of times a truck had to change its speed in a mile of travel increases with the density of traffic on different types of highways.

Improved highways usually cause an increase in the value of land and property close to the highway. Conditions are often created which result in new or more intensified uses of nearby land. In urban areas, the conversion of land to industrial and commercial uses often causes very significant upward changes in land values. However, some uses, such as residential, may be bothered by highway proximity. Farmland values are also affected by highway improvements as they reduce travel time and increase the marketing radius for perishable commodities.

Improved highways have brought shopping centers and industrial parks closer, in terms of time, to areas of consumer and labor concentration. Moreover, there has been an increase in commuting radius which has broadened the availability of labor supply.

### Road tests

A number of road tests have been conducted from time to time to develop data concerning road design and durability of various surfaces under controlled conditions. The first important road test in this country was carried out in Illinois in the early 1920's and was known as the "Bates Test Road." The information it provided is still being used in road design.

In 1950-51, several northeastern and midwestern states sponsored a test in Maryland known as "Road Test 1—Md." This test was run on an existing concrete pavement and was supervised by the Highway Research Board. Among other things, it showed that the nature of the prepared subsoil had much to do with the durability of the concrete pavement.

A second test was run on two test loops, especially constructed of asphaltic concrete pavement, near Malad, Idaho, in 1952-54. This test was a cooperative effort of a group of western states and was supervised by the Highway Research Board. It was found that paving of shoulders greatly increased the load-supporting value of pavements; and thicker asphaltic surfacing greatly increased the load-supporting ability of pavements.

Test sections with 4-inch surfacing were far better than those with 2-inch surfacing and comparable pavement depth. The cracking and breaking of the pavement which occurred in the thin 6-inch and 10-inch pavement sections occurred primarily during the period when subsurface conditions were adverse because of moisture.

Although less than 14 percent of the test traffic was applied during two of these critical periods, 67 percent of the square feet of pavement cracked or was broken during this time. On the other hand, when conditions were favorable from July 24 to November 21, 1953, only 1.6 percent of the total pavement cracking or breaking occurred under 45 percent of the total load applications. The results of this test were of particular help to western states in connection with their size and weight limits.

The most comprehensive study was the AASHO road test sponsored by the American Association of State Highway Officials (now the American Association of State Highway and Transportation Officials) and administered by the Highway Research Board (now the Transportation Research Board) in cooperation with other organizations which provided grants or contributed services to the $27 million test. The test road was constructed between Ottawa and La Salle, Illinois. Basically, the test was a study of the behavior of concrete and bituminous road pavements of different thicknesses and layer composition and of bridges of varying design, subjected to repeated passages of trucks and truck combinations of known weights. There were 836 test sections in 10 test lanes representing almost 200 different combinations of various thicknesses of surfacing, base, and subbase material. Half of each test loop was surfaced with Portland cement concrete and half with asphaltic concrete. The test facility included 16 short-span highway bridges.

The controlled traffic was started in 1958 and continued on an 18 or 19 hour day, six to seven days a week until October, 1960. One million load applications were completed during that time. Over 7,000 measuring devices were installed to measure the effects of the traffic. There were 19 variables that affected the behavior of the test sections. During the winter of 1960-61, special tests were conducted on the bridge spans. Studies were also made during the spring of 1961 of the effect of certain types of military vehicles on the test pavements.

The research results of this test have had and will continue to have an influence upon highway design and construction and upon vehicle sizes and weights.

### Restrictions on interstate movement

An internal trade barrier is a restriction imposed by a state or municipality in the form of a law, regulation, ordinance, or administrative order which discriminates or unreasonably obstructs, whether intentionally or unintentionally, the free flow of legitimate interstate commerce. One of the continuing problems of interstate trucking is the lack of uniformity in the restrictions imposed by the various states. Some of the restrictions are those involving size and weight limitations; taxation, licensing, and registration requirements; and miscellaneous restrictions. Carriers point out that the varying state restrictions upon size and weight limits have an effect on the technology and productivity of the industry and the cost of transportation.

The states, on the other hand, declare that they must protect their highways and bridges from destructive loads or loads that are considered to be destructive; that they must conserve the resources of their states and build only those highways and bridges which meet the needs of their states; that they wish to promote safety and minimize nuisances in road use; that they want to equalize the tax burden between local and outside carriers; and that they seek to advance the interests of the states through the control of competition among the modes of transportation. There have been instances in which a state has granted special overweight permits for a limited period of time to a particular group of carriers, such as to agricultural haulers to transport a bumper crop to market.

During the last decade, considerable progress toward liberalization in state size and weight limitations has been achieved. The interstate barrier problem possesses such importance, due to its effect upon carriers, shippers, and the public, as to warrant a more thorough examination by public officials. The costs of these barriers are borne by one or all of the groups, depending upon economic circumstances.

## Size and weight restrictions

Varying state size and weight restrictions have continued to cause industry operational problems. Substantial uniformity has been achieved in width limitations, 96 inches being almost standard, except in Connecticut, Hawaii, Maine and Rhode Island which are higher. Height varies from 12 feet 6 inches to 14 feet—with 13 feet 6 inches being the most common. In many states, maximum gross weight depends on a formula or a table in which the deciding factor is the length from the center of the first axle to the center of the last axle, that is, the overall wheel base of the vehicle or combination of vehicles.

The laws of most states do not differentiate between front and rear axles in limiting maximum axle loads. It is, however, impractical to load the front axle beyond a certain point which has been assumed to be 10,000 pounds. For example, if the law allows only 18,000 pounds per axle, the practical gross load on a two-axle truck-tractor and single-axle semitrailer would be 10,000 pounds on the front axle, 18,000 pounds on the rear truck-tractor axle, and 18,000 pounds on the semitrailer axle, or a total of 46,000 pounds.

The combination tractor-semitrailer is permitted throughout the country, but until 1962 only 11 western states permitted "double bottoms," which can be a truck-full trailer or a tractor-semitrailer-full trailer. By 1975, 29 states allowed the use of "double bottoms." Similar combinations of overall length from 98 to 110 feet are legal on toll roads in New York, Massachusetts, Ohio, Indiana, Kansas, and Florida. "Triple bottoms" are permitted in Oregon, Idaho, Nevada, Arizona, and Utah.

It is known that size and weight limitations influence the choice of operating equipment today, as in the past. The most efficient type of equipment may not always be employed because of state restrictions, and this influences the determination of rates charged the public for the carrying of commodities. An illustrative problem is that which confronts a large motor carrier on its interstate traffic moving through Pennsylvania, the latter not permitting "double bottoms." In order to operate the "double bottoms" from Ohio into New York through Pennsylvania, the carrier has to break the double into singles on the route between the Ohio line and the New York line. On traffic into and out of Pennsylvania the company must operate with varying types of equipment other than the two 27-foot doubles within a 65-foot limit—in excess of 19 million miles per year. If the present total linear footage of trailer space was converted back into linear footage of 65-foot doubles, this company estimated a yearly savings through the use of the "double bottoms" in Pennsylvania of 5,748,800 miles or 1,402,146 gallons of diesel fuel annually.

For many years, the American Association of State Highway and Transportation Officials (AASHTO) has attempted to find a satisfactory basis for uniform regulation of sizes and weights of motor vehicles. This association has at intervals offered recommendations concerning limits suitable for adoption. The current recommendations are:

Height ................................................................................. 13 feet 6 inches
Width (102 inches recommended for future adoption) .......... 96 inches
Length:
    Single truck ...................................................................... 40 feet
    Single bus (2 or 3 axles) ..................................................... 40 feet
    Single semitrailer or trailer ................................................. 40 feet
    Truck-tractor with semitrailer ............................................. 55 feet
    Other combinations (not more than 2 units) ..................... 65 feet
Axle load ......................................................................... 20,000 pounds
Tandem axle load ....................................................... 32,000 pounds

Bridge formula:

$$W = 500 \left( \frac{LN}{N-1} + 12N + 32 \right)$$

where $W$ = maximum weight in pounds carried on any group of two or more axles, including any and all weight tolerances.

$L$ = distance in feet between the extremes of any group of two or more consecutive axles.

$W$ = number of axles in the group under consideration.

Some states, undoubtedly, will continue to have more liberal standards than the AASHTO standards.

The weight of vehicles affects the condition and life of the pavement by the amount of stress placed upon it. Heavier axle weights require greater pavement thickness and stronger bridges. The gross weight of short-wheelbase combination vehicles can also be a critical factor in bridge stress. Lengthening vehicles and adding more axles allow higher gross weights without a corresponding increase in highway stress. Unless minimum performance requirements are established, however, weight can affect highway capacity, since slow-moving vehicles can adversely affect the speed of others.

Vehicle size also has an effect upon highways. Greater length and height require increased dimensions of highway geometric patterns and clearances. Greater width requires wider pavements and bridges. Thus, vehicle size affects highway capacity.

In considering size and weight standards, the safety factor must be paramount. The principal determinent factor of a motor carrier's safety record is the quality of its operation rather than the weight or configuration of its vehicles.

An extensive study of maximum sizes and weights of vehicles operated on the federal-aid systems, including data based on the AASHTO road test, contained a number of recommendations.[8] Due to the need for analyzing additional information, it was recommended that the then

Fig. 2-4. An 11-axle tractor, semi-trailer, legal in Michigan for intrastate operations.

existing basic weights and widths on the interstate system, applied first in 1956, be continued through June 30, 1967. (Actually, the present federal limitations on vehicle dimensions and weights enacted in 1956 were based on a 10-year-old recommendation.) However, additional limits on sizes of vehicles using the interstate system were recommended. These included 40-foot maximum lengths on single-unit trucks, buses, semitrailers, and trailers; 55-feet maximum overall length of truck-tractor and semitrailer; and 65 feet on all other combinations;

and 13 feet 6 inches maximum overall height. Performance standards were also recommended relating to engine horsepower, braking, and connecting combinations.

After July 1, 1967, it was recommended that the standards for vehicles using the interstate system be increased to 102-inch vehicle width, 20,000-pound single-axle maximum and 34,000-pound tandem axle; and a more liberal maximum gross weight using the bridge formula $W = 500 \ (LN/N - 1 + 12N + 36)$.

There is no present federal limitation in sizes or weights for vehicles using the federal-aid primary, secondary, and urban systems as these standards are set by states and cities. The latter have shown more flexibility in adjusting standards over the years than has been the experience so far with the federal government in its standards on the interstate.

The Federal Highway Administration completed a comprehensive sizes and weights report of several volumes in 1968. It was not released, however, until 1974. The report recommended the following dimensions and weights to be desirable:[9]

1. Vehicle height of 13.5 feet.
2. Vehicle width of 102 inches.
3. Maximum lengths on all highways of 40 feet for single-unit trucks and trailers, 55 feet for tractors and semitrailers, and 65 feet for any other combination of vehicles.
4. Axle weight limits of 22,000 and 38,000 pounds for single and tandem axles respectively.
5. Gross weight limit of at least 120,000 pounds, or better yet, no gross weight limit at all with control of axle weight and spacing.

An assessment of this report, issued in 1974 by the Federal Highway Administration, concluded that the technical input data to the 1968 study were adequate but that benefit cost analyses support the economic justification of increasing the single and tandem axle weight limits to 26,000 and 44,000 pounds respectively on the federal-aid systems. Gross loads could either be increased to 120 kips (1 kip = 1,000 pounds) or no gross load specified; instead use axle weight and spacing as the control.[10]

The anticipated increase in construction and maintenance costs for the federal-aid highway systems which would result from the increase in axle weight limits would be $297 million. The estimated annual reduction in truck operating costs would be $3.61 billion or more than 12 times the cost—a benefit cost ratio of 12 to 1. The productivity increase for trucking that would be possible under such an increase in weight limits should be sufficiently desirable to the trucking industry that it would support an increase in truck taxes to offset the increased cost in construction and maintenance.

When the Federal-Aid Highway Act of 1956, which created the interstate system, was passed it imposed limits on the interstate system of 18,000 pounds on a single axle, 32,000 pounds on tandem axles, 73,280 pounds gross weight, and 96 inches in width. Under a grandfather clause, states were permitted to retain higher 1956 limits. In 1975, 22 states had maximum single-axle weights in excess of 18,000 pounds, 24 states permitted tandem axle weights in excess of 32,000 pounds, and off the interstate system 11 states permitted greater widths or weights.

Numerous bills have been introduced in Congress through the years to modify the restrictions but none were successful. The fuel crisis in late 1973 and the reduction to 55 miles an hour passed by the Congress (and made permanent in 1974) made it apparent that there would be a serious loss in transportation productivity. During the energy crisis, seven states eased their weight restrictions at that time in order to improve fuel conservation for truck users. In states where the speed limit had previously been 65 miles an hour, average truck speeds under the new speed limit resulted in an average increase of 10 to 15 percent in freeway travel times. On limited-access roads, the increase was not as great. However, this loss of productivity amounted to a reduction in total trucking capacity of about 8 percent over all highways.

Both shippers and carriers were concerned about this situation because it resulted in higher transportation costs. One means of offsetting the reduction in speed was to raise the weight limits on the federal-aid interstate system through legislation. This was done through Congressional legislation, signed by the President in early 1975, in which the federal limits on truck axle and gross weights on the interstate highway system were increased as follows: single axle from 18,000 to 20,000 pounds; tandem axle from 32,000 to 34,000 pounds, and gross vehicle weight from 73,280 to 80,000 pounds. The law is permissive and so does not go into effect without action by the states except in those states which already have laws that tie their limits to the federal law. By 1979, 12 states had not increased their limits. In response to the 1979 fuel crisis and the President's plea to the states for an increase in state limits to the federal weight limits, six of these states and the District of Columbia increased their weight limits to the federal limits, most of them on a temporary basis. The President also drafted legislation that would permit him to set uniform nationwide truck length and weight limits in the event of a national emergency.

A quantum jump in long-haul truck productivity could be secured by permitting the use of two 40-foot twin trailers powered by a 500- to 600-horsepower tractor on designated interstate highways as is currently permitted on certain toll roads. This, in combination with uniform single axle and tandem axle weights, could save as much as $2 billion annually.

It is very difficult to insure complete compliance with weight limitations. Although truckers generally strive to stay within the weight limits, the rewards of overloading are a built-in incentive. For example, a 10,000 pound overload may result in an additional $200 revenue and the equipment has the capacity to carry this load.[11]

The Surface Transportation Assistance Act of 1978 required states to certify by January 1 of each year that they are enforcing all state laws governing vehicle size and weights on federal-aid routes. If a state failed to certify or the Secretary determined a state was not enforcing size and weight laws, its apportionment for interstate, primary, secondary, and urban system projects would be reduced by 10 percent. The Secretary and the states must annually inventory state regulations, penalties, and special permit procedures dealing with vehicle weights. The act permitted the use of federal-aid highway funds for equipment used in enforcement, such as fixed or portable weighing scales. The Secretary of Transportation was required to study the need for enforcements in maximum truck sizes and weights and report to Congress in 1981.

### Taxes, licensing, registration, and other fees

Commercial vehicles are subject to numerous taxes and fees. Usually, interstate vehicles must pay a registration fee the same as intrastate vehicles. In some instances, an interstate vehicle is not required to pay the registration fee; therefore, other taxes are imposed. In addition, the commercial carriers may be subject to other taxes such as gross receipts and mileage taxes, certificate fees, plate fees, and the like. The problems created by the diverse action of states in matters of taxation may be more difficult to solve than the state size and weight limitations.

Theoretically, states are justified in establishing systems of taxation which will secure revenues in proportion to the use made of their highways. Actually, the cumulative effect of taxes levied by a number of states upon an interstate carrier may create a restrictive burden.

The restrictions that arise from the taxation of motor fuels prove to be burdensome upon commercial motor carriers, that is, the imposition by one state of a tax on fuel for which such a tax has already been paid in another state. This practice developed because the states that levied higher motor fuel tax rates than neighboring states found that unless there was legislation enacted specifying the amount of motor fuel that could be brought into the state without payment of the state motor fuel tax, the carriers would load their gas tanks in a neighboring state and try to go through the higher motor fuel tax state without purchasing gasoline. The majority of states had enacted legislation of this kind by 1942; and it was not uncommon for the state laws to stipulate the limit that could be brought in, such as 10, 15 or 20 gallons. The so-called "bridge states" imposed regulations of this type in order to secure from interstate commercial users of their highways some compensation in gasoline tax for the use of those highways. It is possible for a trucker to fill his gas tank in Pennsylvania and go across a bridge state, such as Maryland, without purchasing any gasoline; yet he makes use of the highways.

The special taxes and fees which are imposed by states upon motor carriers may be classified as (a) regulatory charges, and (b) measures of highway use. Under regulatory charges are certificates or permit fees, identification plate fees, and franchise taxes, except where these are graduated according to weight, capacity, or earnings. Under the measure of highway-use classification are gross earnings taxes, mileage taxes, and weight and capacity taxes. These can constitute a barrier for interstate commerce where there is a pyramiding of these charges through operation in various states. Other fees are more in the form of nuisances than barriers, such as weighing charges and inspection fees.

One of the largest motor carriers of general commodities in a recent year spent $2,975,000 on licensing line-haul and city fleets. This carrier's line-haul equipment consisted of 6,821 trailers and 1,955 tractors, and 659 converter dollies. Its city fleet operation consisted of 4,411 tractors, trailers, and trucks. This carrier applies for 81 licenses and permits per tractor and nine per trailer.

## Reciprocity

In its broadest form, reciprocity means that a state permits vehicles from other states to operate in and through the first state providing a similar privilege is given to vehicles domiciled in the first state and operating in and through other states. Reciprocity was originally secured by agreements between states regarding passenger cars. The relative ease of accomplishing reciprocity for passenger vehicles did not continue with regard to trucks because more complex factors were involved. Reciprocal agreements would do much to alleviate some of the restrictions which presently exist.

Reciprocity is a privilege and not a right. Therefore, it may be granted or removed unilaterally. Full reciprocity on all matters between any two states is the rare exception for the trucking industry, but there have been many agreements entered into which have facilitated the free flow of commerce between the states. Historically, reciprocity has dealt with two structures of taxes, namely the registration fee or license fee and motor fuel taxes. Some of the agreements between states have been informal, whereas others have been formal and have provided for reciprocity on license fees or on motor fuel taxes or both.

Reciprocity has taken on a regional pattern in recent years. Over half the states are members of some type of regional agreement. The laws of 43 states currently provide that written reciprocal agreements with other states are permissible. The fact that through these agreements carriers and administrators have been able to work cooperatively is encouraging.

There are four methods of reciprocity for commercial vehicles: bilateral agreements, multistate agreements, proration agreements, and International Registration Plan. Sixteen states are operating under the Multistate Reciprocal Agreement. The original 10 states were southern states that were later joined by four midwestern and one eastern state. This agreement operates on the theory of the basing point, and carriers license equipment in the state where the equipment is controlled, leaves, and returns. The basing point theory distributes the registration fees according to the operation of the vehicles. There are no reports or other administrative details. This agreement grants full reciprocity between the states that are parties to the agreement on registration and weight taxes, but there are provisions which do not permit reciprocity on certain for-hire carrier regulatory fees. The agreement does not exempt carriers from the application of requirements concerning fuel purchase laws that some of the states have restricting the amount of gasoline that may be brought into the state without paying state fuel taxes.

Eighteen states operate under the Uniform Proration Agreement. This agreement is a combination of reciprocity and apportionment of fees. The proration applies only to fleets of three vehicles or more, and registration fees are apportioned to the various states according to the miles traveled in each state. This enables a carrier to license its vehicles within one state, but the fee paid is prorated among the member states, based on each state's schedule of fees and in proportion to the mileage operated by the carrier within each state. This type of agreement requires some administrative details in making reports and maintaining certain records not required under the basing point theory.

The International Registration Plan, developed by the American Association of Motor Vehicle Administrators, is presently in effect in twenty-three states, and a large number of others are considering it. A single home registration plate is used and a cab card carries the additional states where the truck may operate. At the beginning of each year, the registration fee is divided on the basis of anticipated mileage within each state; and at the end of the year a final accounting based on actual miles is made. There is a possibility of combining the cab card and fuel reporting permits so that one settlement can be made at the same time.

There are several possible ways to improve the situation of multiple permit and licensing fees, of which increased reciprocity is one. Another possibility would be for the federal government to require the establishment of uniform registration, tax, and permit laws as a condition for the receipt of federal-aid funds; or the creation of a federal permit that would supersede state registration, taxes and permits, with the revenue derived from the permit to be distributed to the states. The establishment of an interim plan by the federal government that would provide federal funds for the establishment of uniform reciprocity and proration agreements and the administrative framework could be a starting point.

The registration permit and licensing fees imposed by states are relatively more burdensome to the owner-operator (independent trucker) than to the fleet operator.

## QUESTIONS AND PROBLEMS

1. Trace the early federal highway activity in the period prior to the passage of the Federal-Aid Road Act of 1916. What prompted this

federal interest? Explain why in your judgment the federal interest continues.

2. Truck productivity can be enhanced by increasing the permissible sizes and weights. Carefully explain the ramifications of this to consumers, state highway and/or transportation departments, and motor carrier management.

3. What are the significant changes in the federal-aid highway programs of the 1970's as compared with the 1950's?

4. Explain the functions of (a) the National Traffic Safety Administration, and (b) the Bureau of Motor Carrier Safety. Why are there two organizations?

5. It is estimated that $1 billion of highway construction work provides 35,000 direct jobs and an equal number of indirect jobs. Should highway improvements be accelerated in recession periods as a stimulus to the economy? Why or why not?

6. Compare the formulas used for apportioning federal funds among the states. Why are there so many?

7. What are the systems of federal-aid highways? Why are they important?

8. The advisability of broadening federal participation in highway aid, particularly as applied to secondary roads, has been questioned as being a matter for state and local authorities. What is your opinion? Why?

9. What accounts for the different methods of highway management employed in the various states? What are the advantages and disadvantages of about 34,000 governmental units each with some degree of responsibility for highway administration?

10. "A relatively small percentage of the highways in the nation carry the greatest amount of the traffic." What are the implications of this statement as far as motor transportation is concerned?

11. "Highways are constructed for the dual purpose of both private and commercial use." What are the advantages of this to the public?

12. "The control of access and the regulation of land use adjacent to highways as provided now by most states are wholly inadequate." Cite some examples of the economic effects which are the result of these factors.

13. Classify the benefits of improved highways according to user benefits and nonuser benefits.

14. How do you account for the concern for social values regarding our recent highway programs?

15. The establishment of trade barriers between the states is often referred to as an effort to Balkanize the United States. Do you agree? Explain the effect of such Balkanization (*a*) upon the motor carrier; (*b*) upon the shipper; and (*c*) upon the consumer.

## FOOTNOTES TO CHAPTER 2

[1] *Highway Statistics, 1973* (Washington, D.C.: U.S. Government Printing Office, 1974), p. 210.

[2] The states suggested the inclusion of some 14,000 additional miles. In subsequent years, some individuals have proposed a doubling of the system mileage.

[3] Grade crossings may be permitted in sparsely settled rural areas, principally in the West. The toll roads which are designated as a part of the system have commercial facilities with direct access to the highways.

[4] Highway officials design highways to meet the traffic load of the 30th highest hourly traffic volume of the year for which the highway is being built. This is often referred to as the "30th-hour factor."

[5] Until 1960, the minimum clearance had been 14 feet.

[6] Some of the other federal agencies administer highway programs, such as the Forest Service of the Department of Agriculture and the National Park Service in the Bureau of Indian Affairs in the Department of Interior. The Department of Defense and the Bureau of Land Management of the Department of Interior finance construction of roads leading to military installations in timber areas. In all of these programs, there is a close working relationship with the Federal Highway Administration, and in some instances, the latter administers the construction programs.

[7] In 1960, Congress established a Driver Register that has been placed in the Bureau of Public Roads of the Department of Commerce (now in the Department of Transportation). The Register serves as a clearinghouse for states to identify those drivers whose licenses have been revoked because of driving while intoxicated or conviction of a traffic violation resulting in loss of life. There are about 1 million license revocations annually, one-fourth of which are due to these two causes. Currently, about 120 million drivers' licenses are in effect.

[8] Committee on Public Works, *Maximum Desirable Dimensions and Weights of Vehicles Operated on the Federal-Aid Systems* (88th Cong., 2d sess. [Washington, D.C.: U.S. Government Printing Office, 1964]), p. 2.

[9] Department of Transportation, Federal Highway Administration, *Summary and Assessment of Sizes and Weights Report,* Washington, D.C., August, 1972, Introduction.

[10] *Ibid.*, p. 4.

[11] The Supreme Court in 1958 ruled that motor carriers may not deduct as business expenses fines imposed on them or their drivers for violations of state maximum weight laws, whether or not the violations were intentional.

# chapter 3

# Highway financing

A basic problem in highway construction has been financing. Engineers can build highways to any required specifications, but inadequate finances have seriously limited adequate construction for modern highways. The expenditures necessary to eliminate the deficiencies in our highway system are tremendous. It is expected that about $900 billion may be spent on highways in the next two decades. Currently, about 44 percent of highway expenditures are spent on highway improvements, an additional 28 percent for maintenance, and 28 percent for administration, safety, research, highway police, and interest on highway debt. To raise the required funds and to assign the costs fairly among the different levels of government and the various users of the facilities are tasks which are receiving a great deal of attention.

It is a curious fact that of the total expended on highways and vehicles by the public (including items such as cost, insurance, and maintenance), about 90 percent is spent on vehicles and only about 10 percent for the provision of highways. The cost of automatic transmission on a new $6,000 automobile is about $500. If the cost of the automatic transmission efficiency loss of about 12 percent is considered, a customer pays substantially just to keep from shifting gears. In 1979, more than 90 percent of cars produced in this country had automatic transmissions and 81 percent were air-conditioned. Perhaps the willingness of the individual to share in the expenses of providing an adequate highway system has been underestimated.

Several methods that have been used in financing highways are analyzed in this chapter. A part of the problem of highway financing involves the allocation of cost to different classes of vehicles on an equitable basis, which factor is also analyzed.

### Highway finances, taxes, and revenues

During the development of highways in the period prior to 1920, property taxes constituted an important source of revenue for state highway purposes. Although today such taxes are not so important as a source of highway income for the states, they are still a fundamental source of tax revenue for counties and municipalities for use in highway improvement and maintenance. However, highway-user taxes have emerged as a major source of revenue. These are taxes levied on the owners and operators of motor vehicles because of use of the public highways. There are three categories—motor vehicle revenues, fuel taxes, and motor carrier or special taxes. Some of the revenue from highway-user taxes is refunded to users because of nonhighway uses of motor fuel, such as agriculture, aviation, and marine purposes. Some states exempt or refund the tax for federal or other public use for transit bus operations and, in one state, for fuel consumed on toll roads. New York led the way in the establishment of a registration fee in 1901 and was followed in this practice by other states. By 1915 all states had registration requirements of some kind, and this was the first of the highway-user charges to be imposed. During World War I, the practice of registration fees which varied with the weight and capacity of the vehicle was introduced and soon became widely adopted.

A number of bases have been employed in the application of a registration fee, particularly for private motor vehicles, such as weight, price, horsepower, flat rate, number of times registered, and combinations of these. For truck-tractors, 41 states base registration fees on gross vehicle weight, one state uses load capacity, one state uses chassis weight, and 7 states and the District of Columbia use net or unladen weight figures. Some states register a tractor-semitrailer combination as a single unit, whereas others register the tractor and semitrailer separately.

Registration taxes, fees, operators' licenses, and title fees were the primary sources of income received by the states from motor vehicle owners until 1929. The inauguration in Oregon in 1919 of a tax of 1 cent per gallon on the sale of motor fuel, the revenue derived therefrom to be used for maintenance of state highways, soon led to the adoption of this second highway-user charge in other states.

Since 1929 the gasoline tax has produced the greatest amount of revenue and has been the primary source of highway revenues. Variations among states as to the amount of tax imposed on gasoline ranged in 1979 from 6 cents per gallon to 11 cents per gallon. Currently, a majority of the states charge 8.3 cents or more per gallon. In addition to the state gasoline tax, there is also a federal excise tax of 4 cents per gallon on gasoline. States have imposed taxes on both motor fuel and special fuels. The motor fuel tax usually applies to gasoline, whereas special fuels include diesel fuel and liquefied petroleum gas. Of the latter type, diesel is the most widely used, but the use of LPG, particularly butane, is increasing as a power source. Currently, 10 states have imposed higher tax rates on diesel fuel than on gasoline due to the greater mileage secured by diesel-powered vehicles. The average nationwide miles per gallon for passenger automobiles is 14, for single-unit trucks a little more than 10 miles, and for combinations and buses about 4.6 miles. For a passenger car, the total of state and federal gasoline taxes averages about 0.8 cents per mile.

It was found that the taxes on motor vehicles as well as those on tires and rubber are desirable taxes, since they increase with the size of vehicle as well as use. The federal manufacturers' excise taxes, based on manufacturer's price, are not as well designed for user taxes inasmuch as the variation of price with either axle load or gross load is not clearly defined. The use tax of $3.50 per 1,000 pounds of gross weight levied on vehicles weighing more than 26,000 pounds would seem to be a more satisfactory basis for the user tax than the manufacturers' excise tax.

The demand for gasoline is relatively inelastic as was shown in 1973-74 when the fuel shortage resulted in a 40 percent rise in gasoline prices. Another 40 percent occurred during the 1979 fuel crisis. Initially, consumption dropped due to the unavailability of fuel in some areas but returned to the pre-crisis level as more fuel was available. This would mean that increases in its price result in a relatively small change in consumption. Nevertheless, recommendations to legislatures to increase this tax are met by formidable opposition, particularly from the petroleum industry at legislative hearings.

It is suggested that the traditional opposition of the petroleum industry to the principle of increasing the gasoline tax might be reexamined in view of the critical need for financing highways and the fact that the petroleum industry is a substantial beneficiary of improved highways. The gasoline tax is often referred to as a "pay-as-you-go" method of highway financing; actually it is a "pay-before-you-go" system, since the tax is paid before the user uses the highways.

Escalating construction and maintenance costs will necessitate significant fuel tax increases in the 1970's if the highway system is to be maintained at its present service level. Unless the federal highway revenues are doubled, the highway system will continue to deteriorate nearly 50 percent faster than it is being rebuilt and reconstructed.

The registration fee does not measure highway use to the degree that is true of the gasoline tax. On the other hand, some states have felt that the gasoline tax does not provide a complete measure of highway use, for it is alleged that as the size of the vehicle increases it does not use proportionately more gasoline. Therefore, the states have turned to a third group of taxes on the for-hire carriers of persons and property, which are called "special highway-user taxes." In some states, these taxes have also been applied to private carriers. These have proved to be an increasingly important source of highway revenue. They have taken the forms of mileage tax, gross receipts tax, ton-miles tax, excise tax, and highway-use compensation tax, and are sometimes called third-structure taxes. Currently, 17 states have some form of mileage tax.

Total highway-user taxes are of such proportions that it is not unusual for a for-hire motor carrier which operates a truck regularly to pay in a single year taxes which approach or exceed one-third the market value of the vehicle.

The participation of the federal government in the early encouragement of road construction and the tangible evidence of such encouragement in the appropriation of federal funds have made an important contribution in the development of our highway systems. The American Association of State Highway Officials (now AASHTO) recommended in 1953 that federal contributions be increased from 50 to 75 percent of the expenditures on the primary system of interstate highways. At that time there was considerable resentment on the part of some states because the revenue from the federal excise taxes their users paid greatly exceeded the amount the federal government returned to the states in federal aid for highways. (At that time, none of the federal excise tax on gasoline was earmarked.) Therefore, a number of the states wanted the federal excise tax eliminated entirely; and the states could then impose additional taxes to raise the necessary revenue. This was not done, however. Somewhat later, the Highway Act of 1956 was enacted, which substantially increased the federal contribution.

Highway financing during the past half century has shifted from lower to higher levels of government. Local governments in 1915 provided 90 percent of highway funds. By 1965 federal and state governments provided over 80 percent of the financing. Federal aid for highways had grown during that period from $5 million to $4.8 billion. In 1978, federal and state disbursements accounted for 66 percent of the total $15.7 billion of capital outlays and 75 percent of the $35.0 billion total highway expenditures.

Another marked change has been the type of revenue used. In earlier years, property and other general fund taxes were the primary sources of revenue, accounting for as much as 90 percent of all funds. Highway-user taxes collected by federal and state governments provided about 80 percent of all highway funds by 1965, with property taxes and bonds collected locally accounting for the remainder. With the increase in state highway revenues and greater amounts being transferred to local government as grants-in-aid, the local units have been able to maintain local support for highways at about the same dollar revenue as previously. At the present time, states, with federal-aid assistance, spend almost half as much on capital improvements on county and township roads as these governmental units spend directly. In addition, the states, with federal-aid assistance, spend about three times as much on improvements in municipalities as the municipalities themselves.

The increase of highway construction costs in recent years has been very dramatic. The composite construction price index for highway construction in 1979 was 277 percent of 1967 base-year costs.

A greater portion of total federal and state highway revenue is being contributed by users. This has increased from 62 percent in 1945 to 71 percent in 1967. Currently, 86 percent of the funds contributed by the federal government for highway purposes are derived from highway-user taxes, primarily fuel taxes. Since the primary beneficiaries of improved highways are the users, this is a sound policy. It is exceedingly difficult to determine, on any but an arbitrary basis, what portion of highway revenue should be contributed by nonusers, yet this is a very important matter. With highway expenditures at record levels, it will vitally affect highway financing and taxation.

### Apportionment formulas

At the present time, there are 13 funds that are used to apportion the authorized sums according to established formulas for certain classes of federal-aid highways. These formulas are specified by statute and vary as to weight assigned to the various factors, as shown in Table 3-1.

Not all authorizations, however, are coupled with legislative apportionment formulas. Several funds have not been given a specific distribution procedure by Congress, such as bridge replacement, the basis for distribution of which is that of relative need. Another such fund is the special urban high density fund for which the basis for distribution is that of project by project.

## Matching ratios

Our early federal-aid program provided a 50 percent payment by the federal government and the remainder by the states for federal-aid highways. A sharp break with this program occurred in 1956 when legislation creating the interstate system was enacted. The federal share was raised to 90 percent and the state share lowered to 10 percent. Over the years, modifications of this early ratio occurred and currently the federal share varies by program. The federal share is 100 percent for certain demonstration projects and emergency relief, 90 percent—10 percent on the interstate, and 70 percent—30 percent on other major programs. States with large amounts of land under federal control receive an increase in the federal share.

### Determining future needs

Determining highway "needs" has become the established pattern in formulating some of our recent federal-aid highway programs. The projection of expected use of the highway system is made in terms of traffic volumes, which involve quantifiable physical improvements and estimated costs. In such a manner, future federal and state highway "needs" have been estimated to total about $900 billion to 2000 (based on 1975 constant dollars).

The Department of Transportation has incorporated the former *Highway Needs Study* as a part of total transportation needs. The first such report, the *National Transportation Report* was issued in 1972 and biennially since that time. This report encompasses both public and private sector transportation plans and integrates the needs of the respective components of the total system. The NTS secured from the governors of all of the states a wide array of data including an inventory of the physical state of the transportation system in the state, the amount of transportation activity which the system carries, the quality of performance, the cost of operating and maintaining various components of the system, and the side effects of the components, such as pollution and noise.

The long-range plans in the 1974 report were projected for the years 1980 and 1990 and dealt with public expenditure needs. Viewpoints and positions of transportation policy makers with regard to key issues and information regarding the private sector were obtained. In the 1974 report, the results of a survey of the current performance of various transportation modes as viewed by shippers was incorporated.

TABLE 3-1

Apportionment Formulas

Formulas for apportioning authorized sums for certain classes of Federal-aid highways are specified by statute. These are shown below.

| Fund | Factors | Weight | Statute* | Minimum Apportionment |
|---|---|---|---|---|
| Primary System | Area<br>Rural Population<br>Rural Delivery Route Mileage and Inter-city Mail Route Mileage<br>Urban*** Population | 2/9<br>2/9<br>2/9<br><br>1/3 | 104(b)(1) | 1/2 percent (except for D.C.) |
| Secondary System | Area<br>Rural Population<br>Rural Delivery Route Mileage and Intercity Mail Route Mileage | 1/3<br>1/3<br>1/3 | 104(b)(2) | 1/2 percent (except for D.C.) |
| Interstate System (for completion only) | Relative Federal Share of Cost to Complete the System** | 1 | 104(b)(5)(A) | 1/2 percent (including Alaska) as specified in Sec. 104(b)(1) of the 1978 STAA |
| Interstate Resurfacing, Restoration, and Rehabilitation | Interstate System Lane Miles in Use for More than 5 Years<br>Vehicle Miles Traveled on IS Interstate System Lanes in Use for More than 5 Years | 3/4<br><br><br>1/4 | 104(b)(5)(B) | -------------- |
| Urban System | Urban*** Population | 1 | 104(b)(6) | 1/2 percent |

62

| Program | Apportionment Factors | Weight | Section | Percent Limitation |
|---|---|---|---|---|
| Urban Transportation Planning | Urbanized**** Population | 1 | 104(f)(2) | 1/2 percent |
| National Scenic & Recreational Highway (Great River Road) | Relative Needs | 1 | 148(d) | ———— |
| Hazard Elimination | Total Population<br>Public Road Mileage | 3/4<br>1/4 | 152(e) | 1/2 percent***** |
| Forest Highways | Area of Forests<br>Value of Forests | 1/2<br>1/2 | 202(a) | ———— |
| Safer Off-System Roads | Area<br>Rural Population Off-System Road Mileage<br>Urban Population | 2/9<br>2/9<br>1/3 | 219(b) | ———— |
| Highway Safety Programs | Total Population<br>Public Road Mileage | 3/4<br>1/4 | 402(c) | 1/2 percent***** |
| Rail-Highway Crossing | Area<br>Rural Population<br>Rural Delivery Route Mileage and Intercity Mail Route Mileage<br>Urban Population<br>Number of Rail-Highway Crossings | 1/12<br>1/12<br>1/12<br>1/4<br>1/2 | Sec. 203(d) of the 1973 Highway Act | ———— |
| Bridge Replacement & Rehabilitation | Relative Needs | 1 | 144(e) | 1/4 percent (8 percent maximum) |

* Denotes appropriate section in Title 23, U.S.C., unless otherwise indicated.
** Apportionment factors are contained in the periodic reports, "A Revised Estimate of the Cost of Completing the National System of Interstate and Defense Highways," submitted to Congress as required in 23 U.S.C. 104(b)(5)(A).
*** Places of 5,000 or more persons.
**** Usually places of 50,000 or more persons—definition contained in 23 U.S.C. 101(a).
***** Except that the Virgin Islands, Guam, and American Samoa each get only one-third percent.

Source: Federal Highway Administration.

For a number of years, capital expenditures for highways have represented about 1.2 percent of our Gross National Product. In the 1974 report, the survey results of the states indicated that these expenditures would be about 1.5 percent for the period 1972-90.[1] However, based on the past trend analysis of federal, state, and local funds for highways, only an amount equal to 1.0 percent of GNP would be available for capital improvements, i.e., $286 billion.

Whereas earlier needs studies had been based on the estimated costs of improving all highways so that by 1990 all highways would meet certain uniform and physical standards, a 1977 report, *The Status of the Nation's Highways: Conditions and Performance*, recognized the inability to finance the earlier approach of maximum standards. This report adopted instead the concept of *performance* in which estimates of dollar needs were based on the cost of maintaining or improving 1975 levels of performance. Performance was introduced as a standard of measurement and was defined as the composite of the operating conditions and service that were to be determined by physical conditions and travel on all highway systems. Under performance-related investment, funds would be concentrated in areas of highest priority.

A need for new federal programs was expressed by 87 percent of the states, while 60 percent felt there were existing federal transportation programs or program requirements which were considered to be either of marginal value or which could be modified or eliminated. A number of suggested modifications were aimed at loosening program requirements to provide more flexibility and intermodal programs.

Better estimates of future demand for various modes of transportation are particularly needed when there are public facilities provided, such as in the case of air, motor, and water transportation. One of the analytical methods which should be used more extensively is that of *demand forecasting*. This, though, needs to be tied closely to the objective of such forecasts, and investment planning is one of the linkages in such a relationship. Demand forecasting can provide a foundation for needs, alternatives, priorities, and goal setting.

Although the state of the arts in demand forecasting is relatively new, the magnitude and complexity of future needs is so great that concerted effort should be directed toward the best means of accurately measuring future demand. In the use of analytical forecasts, care must be taken to insure that the imprecise nature of behavioral aspects of demand, which are not easily quantified, receive adequate recognition.

**Highway Trust Fund**

The trust fund concept has been widely used by the federal government as there are more than 800 of them, 15 of which are major funds. The Social Security trust fund is probably the best known. Most federal trust funds are financed through special "earmarked" taxes. However, many also receive substantial contributions from general tax dollars. The Federal-Aid Highway Act of 1956 created a Highway Trust Fund to provide the necessary federal financing of highways. At the time the Act was written, with its pay-as-you-go provision, a close balance of revenues and expenditures was planned, but not on a year-to-year basis. It was expected that an early surplus would arise in the Highway Trust Fund, followed by a period of deficit, and then a period of surpluses that would compensate for the deficit years. To cover the deficits, advances from the Treasury were planned, to be repaid from later surpluses. However, the inclusion of the pay-as-you-go clause, known as the Byrd amendment, required year-by-year balancing. The Highway Trust Fund is based on user taxes and, until 1973, did not receive contributions from the general tax dollars. In 1973, contributions of $3.8 billion from general funds were authorized, basically for mass transportation capital grants.

The law increased most automotive taxes and earmarked for the Trust Fund all those on gasoline, diesel and special fuel, tires, and tubes; motor vehicle use tax; and half of the tax on new trucks, buses, and trailers. At the time this act was passed, the Bureau of Public Roads estimated the amount of excise taxes that would be paid annually by vehicles of different sizes. The medium-weight automobile would pay federal automotive excise taxes of $52, of which $25 would go into the Trust Fund and $27 into the General Treasury. A two-axle, six-tire stake truck having a gross vehicle weight of 12,500 pounds would contribute $53 to the Trust Fund and $23 to the General Treasury. A three-axle tractor-semitrailer, gasoline powered, with a gross weight of 40,000 pounds would pay $465 annually of which $362 would go to the Trust Fund and $103 to the Treasury. A four-axle, diesel-powered, tractor-semitrailer would pay a total of $668 annually of which $488 would go to the Trust Fund and $180 to the Treasury. When state road-user tax payments are added to these figures, they are substantially higher. Except for the tax on lubricating oil, no similar taxes are levied on other forms of transportation.

In order to cover anticipated deficits in the Highway Trust Fund, the Federal-Aid Highway Act of 1959 provided additional revenue through further temporary dedication of certain excise taxes and a temporary 1-cent increase in gasoline taxes. Two additional tax increases were required—the first in 1961 and the other in January, 1966—in order to pay for an increase in costs for completing the interstate system. The excise and gasoline taxes were still in effect in 1979.

In 1977, the Federal Highway Administration forecast estimated revenues in 1975 dollars for 1976 through 1990 at three levels: low, moderate, and high. The agency used different assumptions to arrive at the three levels. The average annual dollars for the 15-year period are as follows:

| High | Moderate | Low |
|------|----------|-----|
| $47.5 billion | $42.9 billion | $36.0 billion |

Since the creation of the Trust Fund, some changes have been made in the amount of funds dedicated to it. At the present time, the Trust Fund receives the total revenues from the federal 4-cents-per-gallon tax on gasoline, diesel, and special fuels used in motor vehicles (except buses); the 10-cents-per-pound tax on tires and inner tubes (except buses) used on highways and 5-cents-per-pound on others; the 5-cents-per-pound tax on tread rubber (except buses); the 10 percent tax on the manufacturers' wholesale price on truck parts and accessories; 6 cents per gallon on lubricating oil used for highway purposes (except that used in buses); and $3 per 1,000 pounds annually on the total gross weight of vehicles rated at more than 26,000 pounds gross weight.

The Trust Fund was scheduled to go out of existence in 1972 but has been extended to 1984. The total received by the Trust Fund from those federal taxes so earmarked averages about $8 billion annually. Of this amount, the federal gasoline tax amounts to three-fourths of the revenue (1 cent per gallon generates over $1 billion annually, plus an additional amount from diesel fuel).

The total cost of completing the interstate system (at that time 41,000 miles) was estimated in 1961 to be $41 billion, of which $37 billion would be federal funds and $4 billion state money. This was considerably more than the original cost estimate. The estimate was further revised upward in 1965 and again in 1968 to a total in the latter year of $56.5 billion. By 1979, $70.5 billion had been expended on the interstate system, and the current estimate of the total cost of the interstate system is $109 billion.

Several billion dollars additional will have to be spent to upgrade certain existing parts of the interstate. Inflation during the last decade has been a major factor in the rising costs.

About 11 percent of the interstate mileage is located in urban areas but accounts for about half of the cost of the interstate system. The urban areas, however, generate approximately half of the Trust Fund revenues, so the amount spent in these areas is about equal to that generated.

From 1917 to 1955, when there was no linkage of federal automotive excise taxes to highway financing, only $8,135,000,000 of the $23,887,773,000 collected was expended for highway purposes.[2]

The excise taxes that go into the Highway Trust Fund are paid to the Internal Revenue Service by the producer of the taxed product and then they are collected from the consumer; except for taxes on diesel and special fuels which are paid by the retailer, and the heavy vehicle tax that is paid by the consumer. A tabulation showing taxes paid into the Highway Trust Fund is thus only an estimate of what is ultimately paid by consumers in that state and does not show exactly where travel has occurred. Because of the home office locations of major producers of taxable products, over half of the federal gasoline tax revenues are received from but three states—New York, Pennsylvania, and Texas.

The Highway Trust Fund has performed so successfully as a means of financing that increasing efforts have been made at different times to "break" the Trust Fund and use a portion of the funds for pressing nonhighway transportation purposes. The 1970 Highway Act broadened the uses of the Trust Fund for exclusive bus ways, passenger loading facilities, bus shelters, and fringe parking facilities to serve any type of public mass transportation. A number of other areas were included, such as financing safety. In the Federal-Aid Highway Act of 1973 (covering three years instead of the usual two) the Congress provided that where a state used a portion of its total highway funds apportionment for a transit project in lieu of a highway project, limited withdrawals could be made in specified amounts from the Trust Fund, but not during the fiscal year 1974. In fiscal 1975, $200 million could be spent for the purchase of buses out of the Trust Fund by a state, and in fiscal 1976, all the funds would come from the Highway Trust Fund. The total federal share of a substituted mass transit project is 80 percent. This provision of the Act is a trading of Trust Fund money for general funds.

As pointed out earlier, certain excise taxes levied on highway users were dedicated to the Highway Trust Fund whereas only certain percentages of other excise taxes on highway users were so dedicated. The result has been that from 1957 through 1979, the users of highways paid $122 billion in excise taxes.

The Surface Transportation Assistance Act of 1978 authorized funds for a four-year period with $30.6 billion for highways, of which $27.6 billion was to be provided from the Highway Trust Fund. There was no change in excise tax rates. However, the Energy Tax Act of 1978 exempted gasoline mixed with at least 10 percent alcohol from the 4-cents-per-gallon federal tax and repealed the 10 percent excise tax on buses, as well as removing a variety of other federal excise taxes on parts, tires, fuel, and lubricating oil used by buses. By 1979, 16 states had reduced or eliminated state taxes on gasohol.

The Byrd amendment (pay-as-you-go) was changed to require that all apportionments to the states from the Trust Fund, not just the interstate, would be reduced by an equal percentage to prevent a shortfall if Trust Fund revenues were inadequate to finance projected expenditures.

A Trust Fund for Airport and Airways, based on user taxes, was established in the early 1970's. We may ultimately see the creation of a single Transportation Trust Fund to take the place of the separate funds. Transportation investment might then be geared to total needs.

### State user taxes

State highway-user tax revenues amounted to $16.4 billion in 1979. These consisted of fuel tax, registration fees, and motor carrier fees. In addition, the states received approximately $3.8 billion from proceeds of highway construction bonds and $1.5 billion from tolls. Of course, federal-aid funds derived from federal highway-user taxes were in addition to this and amounted to $9.1 billion in revenues.

Currently 48 states provide for the sharing of state-collected highway funds, primarily from user tax revenues, with local governments for road and street purposes. In addition, 43 states provide aid from road-user taxes to municipalities. Counties in four states and municipalities in four states levy local motor fuel taxes. Vehicle fees are levied in many local communities.

An estimate of the 1973 state road-user and property taxes paid on selected motor vehicles indicates a considerable variation among the states in their tax structures.[3] This is illustrated in Fig. 3-1A. The

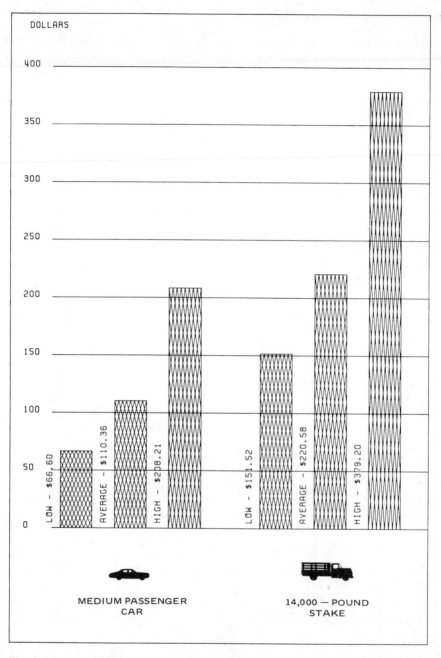

Fig. 3-1A. Annual rates of low, high, and average road-user and personal property taxes on selected vehicles in private operation. Source: Federal Highway Administration, Department of Transportation, *Road-User and Property Taxes on Selected Motor Vehicles*, 1973 (Washington, D.C.: U.S. Government Printing Office, 1973), p. 9.

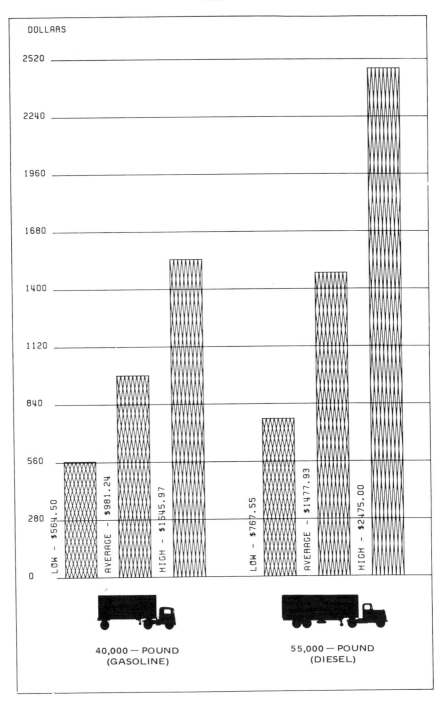

Fig. 3-1B. Annual rates of low, high, and average road-user and personal property taxes on selected vehicles in private use.

annual rate of road-user and personal property taxes for the medium-sized passenger car in the state with the lowest taxes is $66.60, and with the highest $208.21; the average is $110.36. For the stake truck having 14,000-pound gross weight, the low is $151.52, the high $379.20, and the average is $220.58.

State user taxes for two combination units in private operation are also shown in Fig. 3-1B. For the 40,000-pound gross weight gasoline combination, the range is from $564.50 to $1,545.97, with an average of $981.24. The larger diesel unit would pay in the lowest state $767.55, whereas in the highest state it would pay $2,475. The average payment is $1,477.93.

The state tax structure continues to reflect the tendency to impose greater taxes on for-hire carriers than on private carriers. Generally, farm trucks are treated the most favorably taxwise. For example, in Kentucky farm trucks of 24,000 pounds or less may be registered for $12.50 a year but the same-sized vehicle used in that state in private use, other than farming, would be charged $161. In five states, a 14,000-pound stake truck, if classified as a farm truck, is allowed a reduction of more than 75 percent of the normal registration fee; and in 12 states a reduction of 50 to 75 percent.

Of total state highway-user taxes, trucks currently pay 42.7 percent of registration fees, 32.3 percent of motor fuel taxes, 97 percent of motor carrier taxes, and 32 percent of miscellaneous fees.

### Bond issues as means of financing

Extensive use of borrowing for highway construction purposes has been practiced by counties, municipalities, and states. There has been considerable variation from state to state in the amount of borrowing for highway purposes.

Some state highway departments have felt that the construction and improvement of highways had to be advanced by means of borrowed funds, inasmuch as construction of highways from operating revenues alone would have been very slow. In some instances, states have had sufficient funds from operating revenues to surface only one lane of a main route, and several years have elapsed before the surfacing of the other lane could be accomplished. Vestiges of this practice still exist. With borrowed funds, however, the double lane could have been constructed; and it is less expensive to do the complete surfacing of a road at one time.

The type of bond most widely used by the states for securing funds for highway purposes has been the general-obligation type, which is backed by the credit of the respective states. It is customary to cover the payment of the debt so incurred by the revenue secured from highway-user taxes. The limited-obligation type of bond has been issued by some states; this type does not pledge the general credit of the state but is limited rather to the funds derived from highway-user revenues. A third type is the revenue bond, which is used to finance the construction of a specific facility. The revenue to retire such bonds is dependent entirely, except for insurance, upon that facility. Toll bridges are usually financed in this manner.

In some states, the counties were encouraged to issue bonds and turn the proceeds over to the state, with the understanding that the state would provide funds for the payment of principal or principal and interest on the bonds. The state used the credit of the local governments to borrow for state highways. This resulted in reimbursement obligations. Although this is not evidenced by state bonds, it forms a fourth type of obligation for highways.

There are two general types of provision for the retirement of bonds: the term-issue or sinking-fund method and the serial method. Under the term-issue plan the entire amount borrowed falls due at a certain date fixed when the debt is assumed. A sinking or amortization fund is provided to which annual payments of a fixed amount are made. The plan is so devised that the sum of these payments, plus whatever income is obtained from investing them, will be sufficient when the debt falls due to pay the entire amount.

In recent years, the serial method of retirement has become more popular. Under this plan a predetermined amount of the principal is scheduled to be paid each year, beginning at a certain time after the bonds are sold—usually not less than one year nor more than three. This plan of retirement does not require a sinking fund. The annual principal payments are usually made directly from current income, upon which they customarily have a prior claim.

At the present time, 39 states may incur debt for general or highway purposes, although all but 12 of that number are subject to constitutional limitation of the amount borrowed. Six states authorize borrowing and have no constitutional debt limit. Nine states may borrow only for reasons such as "casual indebtedness" or "failure in revenue." Constitutional limitations on indebtedness in those states which may borrow take several forms, such as limiting it to a specified percentage of the assessed value of property (for example, 1 percent) of the state.

Borrowing for state highways was used extensively during the large road-building program of the 1920's. Since World War II, bond issue proceeds for highways increased from 3.2 percent of total funds available in 1945 to a high of 18.1 percent in 1952. Currently, the figure is about 10 percent or over $2 billion.

### Diversion of state highway-user revenue

It should not be assumed that the total revenues secured from highway-user taxes are expended entirely for highway purposes. Highway-user revenue has been used in some states for such nonhighway purposes as mosquito control, state parks, welfare funds, probation and parole commissions, and the like. At the present time, 28 states prohibit the diversion of fuel tax receipts to nonhighway purposes. Fifteen states permit diversion for nonhighway purposes and eight permit diversion to the state general fund. Thirty-three states "earmark" portions of the tax for one or more specific nonhighway transportation purposes.

In recent years, increasing pressures have been placed upon state legislatures to divert road-user tax receipts to the general revenue fund or to use it for a special purpose, such as aid to education or mass transit. Some states divert as much as 50 percent, whereas others divert as little as one-tenth of 1 percent. Where the diversion is large, there have sometimes been offsetting appropriations for highways out of a state's general funds. The amount of revenues diverted by all states not prohibiting diversion has been running about $ 1.3 billion.[4]

The proponents of antidiversion laws feel that if a gasoline tax is imposed for the express purpose of using the funds to improve highways, it is logical that the receipts from gasoline tax imposts should be required to be expended only for highway purposes. Some of the first state gasoline taxes enacted contained this provision, but other states, in enacting the gasoline tax legislation, did not so provide, although many people assume that the funds are spent only for highway purposes. The opponents of the antidiversion law feel that such a law places a legislature in a straitjacket, since it handicaps the state in applying the revenue of the state to the needs of the state.

About half of all state tax collections are now earmarked for specific purposes. Opponents of this practice maintain that, carried to the logical conclusion, a state tax on alcohol presumably would be used for rehabilitation of alcoholics, and a state inheritance tax for the beautification of cemeteries.

### Toll roads

The term *toll road* is usually understood to mean any road for which a service charge is collected each time it is used in addition to any general taxes or fees which may be paid by all highway users. In the early part of the 19th century, a number of improved roads were developed on which tolls were charged. Some of these roads were privately owned and operated, whereas others were owned and operated by a state or its political subdivisions. The federal government participated, in a limited manner, in the construction of some turnpikes. The advent and early growth of the railroads were largely responsible for the decline and lack of further development of this type of highway facility.

During the present century, in which tremendous strides have been made in automotive transportation, highway development has been characterized by the construction of so-called "free" roads. Although the Pennsylvania Turnpike, on which tolls are imposed, was opened in 1940, not until after 1946 was there considerable activity regarding the contruction of toll roads.

There were several reasons for the growing interest in toll-road construction. One of these was that the supply of highways was limited in relation to the greatly accelerated traffic demand. Highway capabilities did not keep pace with the demands imposed upon them by the substantial increase in vehicles that has occurred in the past 20 years.

Another factor which has accounted for toll-road activity was the virtual moratorium on highway construction necessitated by World War II. Inadequate maintenance during this period due to shortages of labor and materials also accelerated obsolescence of highways. The higher costs of construction which followed the end of hostilities and the backlog of improvements which were necessary combined to make a total which was staggering to many states. The purchasing power of the dollar had shrunk, and many states were unable to finance necessary highway construction. Many believed that the cost of construction would drop during an anticipated deflationary period, so badly needed highway construction was often postponed. The combination of postponed highway improvements and higher construction costs accentuated the interest in toll roads.

With inadequate funds for a pay-as-you-go highway program states might normally turn to bond issues. In some states, however, there was a constitutional limitation on the amount of bonded indebtedness of the states, which also was a contributing factor to increased toll-road activity. In a state in which the amount of bonds already issued was close to the constitutional limit, the state had to consider some other means of financing needed highways. The establishment of a Turnpike Authority by a state created a means by which bonds could be issued without regard to constitutional limitations, the security for which was the revenue derived from tolls.

Many states, also, had a limitation on the funds which were available for improving the main arteries due to state statutory requirements which specified that certain percentages of registration fees and gasoline taxes had to be returned to political subdivisions of the state, that is, counties, townships, and local governments. In some instances, the amount returned to the local government was as much as 50 percent. It should not be inferred that the local highway needs did not require this but rather that the state was left with an insufficient amount to bring about all of the required improvements in the heavily traveled highways.

In some of the heavily populated states which are relatively small geographically and are often referred to as "bridge" or "corridor" states, the toll road has had considerable appeal as a means of constructing a modern and adequate facility and getting the out-of-state user to help pay for it. On the New Jersey Turnpike, the out-of-state vehicles range from 60 to 75 percent of the total traffic, which was an important factor in its construction.

The cost of limited-access highways is appreciable. In many states, the legislators questioned the feasibility of these undertakings when such facilities could be provided by means of a toll road. In those states also in which the rural interest in the legislature was particularly strong, the disadvantages of limited-access highways to rural residents, with the points of ingress and egress widely spaced, led to suggestions that such limited-access projects be made toll roads.

Since 1916 the federal government has discouraged the building of toll roads and has encouraged the construction of free roads. The manner in which the toll roads have been discouraged is that no money appropriated under the federal-aid highway programs can be spent on toll-road projects. The Federal-Aid Highway Act of 1916 specifies that "all highways constructed or reconstructed under the provisions of this act shall be free from tolls of all kinds." This provision has been carried forward in subsequent acts. The Bureau of Public Roads made a study in 1938 at the request of Congress concerning the feasibility of constructing six superhighways, three east and west and three north and south. The conclusion of this report, issued in 1939, was that only a small mileage of roads could secure sufficient traffic to be self-supporting if they were improved and operated as *toll* highways.

A report to Congress in 1955 by the Secretary of Commerce recommended the continuation of the law forbidding the collection of tolls on highways constructed with federal-aid funds. This report did recommend that the law should be modified to permit inclusion of toll roads as a part of the interstate system when they meet the standards for that system and when there are reasonably satisfactory alternate free roads on the federal-aid primary or secondary systems which permit traffic to bypass the toll road.

The act of 1956 included this provision and stated also that federal-aid funds may be used on toll-road approaches if the toll road is to become free when the bonds are retired. Federal-aid funds may also be used for the construction of toll tunnels under certain conditions.

Congress sought to determine, in 1956, whether states should be reimbursed for toll facilities on the interstate system, as well as for free sections constructed without federal funds or with federal funds at less than the 90:10 matching ratio. Congress so far has not decided on a policy of reimbursement, although numerous hearings have been held on the subject.

By 1980 there were 4,746 miles of toll roads, bridges, and tunnels in operation in the United States, of which 2,264 miles were on the interstate system. Of the major toll roads, only two—the Calumet Skyway in the Chicago area and the Chesapeake Bay Bridge and Tunnel—have failed to cover their bond interest requirements. The other toll roads have been able to cover their interest requirements, and some have redeemed bonds as much as 20 years prior to the scheduled redemption date.

The passage of the Highway Act of 1956 providing for federal aid in the amount of 90 percent on the interstate system resulted in the virtual abandonment of quite a number of toll-road plans. By 1960 a number of states were once again considering toll-road construction, and some toll roads were built within the next few years. Some of the reasons for the revival of interest in toll-road construction were that the construction of the interstate system had not progressed as rapidly as had been anticipated and states were hard pressed to provide the 10 percent matching funds; the public had become more accustomed to paying toll charges; out-of-state users would help pay for the highways through tolls; and bond prices had become more favorable for financing. A person is now able to make the trip from New York to Chicago on toll roads without encountering a single stoplight.

There are four types of toll projects based upon the method of providing the funds. The first is one in which the construction cost is provided from public funds. On completion the service charge is fixed for the use of each section, which is determined to be a fair charge for the service rendered. Another method is for construction funds to be provided by the sale of revenue bonds, with the interest and amortization of the bonds guaranteed by the state. The interest rate is considerably lower on this type.

The third method is for construction funds to be provided by the sale of revenue bonds, which are wholly dependent upon the earnings of the project for amortization and interest. These projects are administered by a commission created by the state, but the state does not guarantee the payment of either bonds or interest. This is often termed the "conventional method" of toll-road financing, since there is more of this method of toll financing than any other kind.

The last method is for a state by legislative action to grant authority to private interests to build a toll-road project. The construction funds are provided by the sale of revenue bonds, and the revenue from tolls is expected to cover the amortization and the interest accruals of the bonds. Practically all states either have toll facilities or enabling legislation which permit their construction.

Toll roads are usually financed by the issuance of revenue bonds which pledge the tolls, and the rate of interest is usually higher than general-obligation bonds which the state might issue to build free roads. Since revenue bond issues can carry "call" privileges for redemption or refinancing which can be exercised after issuance, it may develop that refinancing could be undertaken at rates which would compare favorably with general-obligation bonds. For the New York State Throughway and the Garden State Parkway in New Jersey, which, in 1954, were constructed as toll facilities, the bonds were guaranteed as to principal and interest in each instance by the parent state. Both these projects are expected to be self-liquidating. The pledge of the general credit and taxing powers of these states, if needed, effected material savings in financing costs.

Since tolls must be collected, such a collection charge is often regarded as being an added cost of this type of facility. The collection costs vary on the toll-road turnpikes now in operation and range from 3 to 10 percent.

The operation of toll roads is the responsibility of an independent commission or authority created for this specific purpose. The only compensation the members of such authorities receive is their expenses. As a rule, the commissioner of the state highway department is an ex officio member.

Trucks and buses provide a substantial portion of all revenue from toll roads. On the major toll roads, the heavier vehicles account, on the average, for 27 percent of the total revenue and constitute but 8 percent of the total vehicles. This ranges from a high of 53 percent of total revenue on the Pennsylvania Turnpike to a low of 2 percent on New Jersey's Garden State Parkway. Even so, the number of trucks using toll roads, in some instances, has not come up to advance estimates made by engineers. As a result, some toll roads have modified the charges for trucks in order to encourage greater use of toll facilities. A number have established volume discounts on monthly billings for trucks and buses. Some are graduated scales with a discount of 10 percent given on $200 to $400 per month and ranging up to 50 percent discount for more than $1,000.

One of the toll roads has also instituted reduced toll rates for all users during the period of lightest traffic—from 10 p.m. to 6 a.m. The reductions range from 20 to 40 percent, depending upon the type of vehicle and the distance traveled.

Most toll roads charge on a per-mile basis, but others collect flat fees for passage at fixed points or "barriers." For example, the Connecticut Turnpike extends 127 miles across the state, but 106 of these miles can be traveled without payment of toll by the use of exit and entrance points ahead and beyond the toll stations. Those toll barriers thus physically control a total of only 21 miles. Local Connecticut drivers, familiar with the route, are more likely to take advantage of this situation than long-trip drivers.

The current rate of tolls charged for a passenger automobile ranges from 1.5 cents to 4.5 cents per mile, which is equivalent to a tax of 21 to 67.5 cents per gallon. In other words, if an automobile averages 15 miles per gallon on the New Jersey Turnpike where the toll charge is 1.9 cents per mile, this means that the motorist is willing to pay in addition to the gasoline tax he has already paid the equivalent of an additional 28.5 cents per gallon to go 15 miles. The average federal and state tax on gasoline is 10.6 cents per gallon. The toll charges added to this are a form of double taxation, but this could be solved by having the state grant to the Turnpike Authority a fair amount for the gasoline tax earned by operating over the toll road.

On toll roads much less gasoline is sold than is consumed. On four representative turnpikes, a study of gasoline consumption indicated that only about one-third of the amount consumed is purchased on the toll roads. One of the reasons for this is that the average length of trip is short. Even on the 327-mile Pennsylvania Turnpike, the average trip is only 103 miles.

One of the factors of considerable importance in toll-road operation is that they should be self-liquidating projects. The laws in some states creating the Turnpike Authority stipulate that on the retirement of the bonds, the toll road will be operated free of tolls. In other instances, the statute provides that after the retirement of the bonds for the toll road, the tolls may continue to be charged and the revenues which are derived can be used to finance other toll roads. Most of the toll roads have been built since 1948, and only a few have been freed. When the revenue bonds are retired, toll roads should become free roads. If they are not conceived as self-liquidating projects and the general tax revenues or the credit of the states is pledged, the determination of where the toll facility should be built may be based upon political considerations rather than upon economic tests.

The original investment in all toll roads was slightly more than $7 billion but current replacement cost is estimated to be over $24 billion. There are periodic proposals for the federal purchase of the toll roads that are now a part of the interstate system. However, these proposals involve not only substantial funds needed for purchase but also that the states assume the escalating cost of maintenance. Completing the interstate system has higher priority. In addition, toll revenues are not only applied to debt service, collection, operating, and administrative expenses but also, in some cases, to other public services, which further complicates the problem.[5]

A provision of the Surface Transportation Assistance Act of 1978 required the determination of the amount of bonded indebtedness for each state as of January 1, 1979, for toll roads incorporated in the interstate system, with recommendations by the Secretary of Transportation on alternative methods for making such toll roads free. This act also provided that if requested by a state, the Department of Transportation could advance from that state's apportionment 100 percent of the cost of constructing a publicly-owned toll bridge, tunnel, or approach which completes an essential gap in the interstate system. The amount of the advance in excess of the normal federal share must be repaid with interest within three years of its being opened to traffic. All tolls must be applied to operating and maintaining the facility and repaying the local share of the debt. After full repayment, the facility must be toll free.

Congress has a continuing interest in having all portions of the interstate system free of tolls by the time the system is completely constructed. However, no program has been established to effectuate this plan. One method might be to use the Trust Fund to set up an escrow account amounting to the expected revenues derived from the travel increases, which fund would be made available at the end of the interstate construction program to pay off the revenue bonds on toll highways outstanding at that time. Another proposal is to extend the life of the Highway Trust Fund beyond its expiration date and use such revenues to establish the escrow account for meeting the annual future debt retirement of the outstanding bonds.

### Allocating highway tax responsibility

The argument over the question of public aid is basically one of equity of treatment by the federal government of the various modes of transportation. In recent years, this problem has become more critical because of the increasing competitive relationships which have developed among the several forms of transportation. The most impartial observers in the field of transportation feel that the users of transportation facilities should pay their fair share of the cost and maintenance of those facilities, with the exception that national-defense requirements might justifiably modify this desired objective to some extent. This appears to be a fair approach to the issue.

With the foregoing approach in mind, let us examine some of the salient facts concerning the highway users' contribution to the construction and maintenance of the facilities they use. This will give us a basis for a better understanding as to whether highway users are receiving any public aid.

As has been pointed out earlier, the highways, with but minor exceptions, are owned and maintained by the states and their various political subdivisions. It is further recognized that, through various taxes and assessments, the users of the highway facilities make definite revenue contributions for construction and maintenance. Since there are different types of highways (such as primary and secondary highways, local roads, and city streets) and facilities, as well as different classes of users (such as private automobiles, commercial freight, and commercial passenger users), we must seek to ascertain whether the users of the highways as a whole, as well as the various classes of users in particular, pay their fair share for the use of these facilities.

A number of studies have assigned specific percentages for highway costs to motor vehicle users as the amount for which they should be held responsible for road and street costs. There are sharp differences of opinion among the various investigators as to the percentage of responsibility which should be assigned to motor vehicle users. Since there are benefits to nonhighway users, such as property owners, there is the question of what percentage of the total cost of the highways should be borne by motor vehicle users. The same basic figures could be used in computation by these various investigators and quite different results obtained because of the differentiation in percentages of responsibility which each had assigned for highway use to motor vehicle users. It appears likely that some of these investigations may have been prompted by special groups with axes to grind.

Section 210 of the Highway Revenue Act of 1956 required the Secretary of Commerce to study and report to Congress information on the basis of which it could determine the federal taxes which should be imposed, and the amount of such taxes, in order to assure an equitable distribution of the tax burden among the various classes of persons using the federal-aid highways or otherwise deriving benefits from such highways.[6] The study, known as the *Highway Cost Allocation Study,* was made by the Bureau of Public Roads. It does not contain any recommendations regarding federal fiscal policy relating to highways but contains findings of highway cost responsibility on which Congress can act if it so desires.

In attempting to allocate highway costs between users and nonusers, a number of concepts have been developed and used in various studies. The two that are used in the study are explained. The *relative-use* method is one in which the cost allocation is based on the extent to which different highways of different classes render different kinds of service.

The primary classes of service are service to the through-traffic stream, providing access to land, and providing neighborhood access or facilitation of community activity.[7] This method was used in a number of the studies.

The *earnings-credit* method is one in which it is assumed that each road and street system should receive an allocation of road-user tax revenue at a rate—per vehicle-mile of travel on it—adequate to support the top systems of arterial and primary highways, rural and urban; and that each road and street system should receive an allocation of nonuser tax revenues at a rate—per mile of road on it—adequate to support the lowest systems of access roads and streets. Each system is credited with its estimated earnings of user-tax revenues.

The Bureau of Public Roads (now the Federal Highway Administration) computed cost responsibility, using both of these methods. It then took the mean of the two studies and concluded the following nonuser cost responsibility:

Interstate system............................................................................. 5.37
Other federal-aid primary ............................................................... 7.41
Federal-aid secondary....................................................................... 28.44

The net result is the assignment of about 8 percent of the tax burden to revenue sources other than taxes on motor vehicle users. The Bureau stated, however, that definitive answers to cost allocation between users and nonusers cannot be reached solely through analysis. It feels these answers are ultimately matters of policy. Congress and the Executive Department will decide what percentage will be assigned to nonusers. That portion of highway costs would then come from the general revenue funds.

### Theories of highway cost allocation

Some of the theories which have been proposed for the solution of the problem of graduating motor vehicle taxes in an equitable manner among vehicles of different sizes will be discussed. Each of the theories has certain shortcomings.

In order to accomplish equity in highway taxation, the theories of the manner in which the tax support should be allocated are based on one or a combination of two basic concepts: (1) the theory that tax support should be allocated among the beneficiary groups in proportion to the highway costs occasioned by each; and (2) that tax support should be allocated in proportion to benefits received, which is often termed "value of service."

The *incremental theory* uses what is termed the "costs-occasioned" concept. A theory based on benefits received is the *gross-ton-mile theory.*

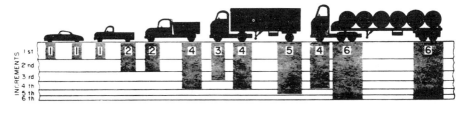

Total pavement broken into increments.
Shading under each axle group identifies the number of
pavement increments for which they must share the cost.

Fig. 3-2. Incremental concept of highway cost allocation.

In making an *incremental study,* there must be a scientific determination of what type of road would be necessary if there were no large and heavy vehicles using it and the highway was built only to withstand the elements and carry light passenger car traffic. Such a highway would be referred to as a "basic road." Once the cost of the basic road has been determined, the cost of such a road is assigned equally among all motor vehicles (passenger cars, trucks, and buses) on the basis of vehicle-miles operated. The difference in the cost of the basic road and the cost of the roads which are actually built to accommodate all traffic is assigned in its entirety to the heavy vehicles—that is, the additional or incremental costs which are incurred to accommodate these vehicles are assigned entirely to these vehicles. A factor to be considered is that not all types of roads are used to the same extent by vehicles of varying sizes and weights. The incremental concept as it applies to the structural design of highway pavement is illustrated in Fig. 3-2.

The six cost increments for the pavement structure are shown as though there are six component parts of a pavement structure.

Actually, each cost increment includes its proportionate share of the cost of the pavement's structural courses, surface, base, and subbase. Since the first increment is required by even the lightest axle loads and is an integral part of the total pavement thickness required by heavier axle loads, its cost is attributed to a single cost per mile among all axles. Similarly, the second increment is divided among all axles except those that require only the first increment. Each axle is assigned its share of the cost of each of the increments that make up the total pavement it requires in its travel.

The use of the incremental theory requires a complex analytical procedure. It also entails many technical problems. Basic assumptions must be made, and these must be reasonable and fairly and realistically made if the results are not to be distorted. For example, an incremental analysis conducted in California which did not go into great detail assumed that from the standpoint of highway thickness, a highway capable of carrying 8,000-pound axle loads would be adequate; yet the Bureau of Public Roads indicates that a highway capable of withstanding the elements is adequate to carry axle loads of 11,200 pounds.

Some parkways, like the Merritt Parkway in Connecticut and the Outer Drive in Chicago, are designed exclusively for passenger cars, and trucks are prohibited from using them; yet these highways are built 9 inches at the edge and 7 inches in the center.

It can be seen, then, that the basic assumptions in an incremental study are of great significance. Even though in theory the incremental approach to highway cost allocation possesses merit, the basic assumptions must be reasonable if the results of a study of this kind are to have validity.

The *gross-ton-mile theory* is one which assumes that the motor vehicle tax responsibility for vehicles of every type and size should be measured by multiplying the weight of the vehicle, usually the average operating gross weight, by the miles traveled and distributing the total tax responsibility among all vehicles or all weight groups of vehicles in proportion to this product. The product, weight times distance, is supposed to represent a measure of value of use or value of service which has been rendered to the highway user by the highway facility used.

It has been pointed out that there is no affirmative proof which can be offered that the product, weight times distance, is a measure of value of service. Is the service rendered by a truck filled with sand or one loaded with jet engine parts for an airplane of more or less value than the service rendered by a public-utility truck?

A passenger car weighing 3,500 pounds which travels 10 miles and a truck weighing 35,000 pounds which travels 1 mile will have identical gross ton-miles. However, these two operations are quite different, and different monetary considerations are involved. For various types and sizes of vehicles, the value received from the use of the highways is not proportional to their weight because value of service must be measured in fiscal not in physical terms.[8]

Generally, the use of the gross-ton-mile method would impose heavier tax burdens on vehicles in the higher weight groups than other methods. There are numerous shortcomings of the gross-ton-mile theory, and it has been authoritatively stated: "There can be no pretense that the gross-ton-mile analysis produces an accurate appraisal of the costs occasioned by vehicles of different sizes and weight."[9]

Gross weight and ton-miles are not necessarily related to highway costs. In highway construction, engineers consider the weight placed upon individual axles and not vehicle gross weight. What this means in terms of gross weight and axle loads is exemplified in the comparison of two trucks, one with two axles and a gross weight of 26,000 pounds and one with five axles with a gross weight of 86,000 pounds. The smaller truck having one 20,000-pound axle load requires the same standard of highway construction as the larger vehicle which has four such axles. The vehicles have vastly different gross weights, but the axle weights are identical. If the rear axle of the smaller truck were to carry 25,000 pounds, it would actually require a better and more costly highway than the larger truck, although its gross weight would still be only 31,000 pounds.[10]

The incremental theory and the gross-ton-mile theory have received by far the most attention. Two early governmental studies were made using these methods—the Federal Coordinator of Transportation or the Eastman report, and the Board of Investigation and Research. Both groups concluded that over the years motor vehicle users as a whole had paid their fair share for the use of the facilities.

Using the gross-ton-mile method, the Board of Investigation and Research allocated the motor vehicle users' percentage of responsibility which it had assigned and arrived at the conclusion that a number of commercial users, as well as private-user groups, were not paying their share of highway costs; but motor vehicle users, as a whole, were paying their fair share.

The Eastman report made use of a system of allocation of highway costs among highway users on the basis of the incremental theory. The Eastman report listed 27 different types of motor vehicles and showed that 22 of them had more than paid their fair share of highway costs. One of the classes found to have not quite paid its share was the school bus. Three other classes were privately operated trucks, which were found to have made underpayments—that is, they were not paying their fair share of highway costs. Only one class of for-hire trucks in the Eastman report was found to have underpaid, and that was the 5-ton single truck. These figures were for the year 1932. Using 1937 figures, but with less exact detail, the Eastman report found that the preponderance of the classes of motor vehicle users were more than paying their fair share.

Since the end of World War II, several states have undertaken comprehensive studies of highway needs for their respective states.[11] As one phase of the studies, some states have attempted to ascertain whether the various classes of highway users were paying their fair share of highway costs.

The trucking industry has felt that of the theories described, the incremental theory provides the soundest method to be used in allocating motor vehicle tax responsibility, providing that the data used as the basis are adequate and that assumptions are fairly made. The trucking industry has developed a method which has become known as the *cost-function method.* Under this system of highway cost allocation, the many individual and different items of cost are divided into three categories, with a different yardstick being used in assigning cost responsibility in each category.[12]

The Bureau of Public Roads, however, in its use of this theory in the *Highway Cost Allocation Study* altered the assignment of costs to the various categories from those used in the earlier trucking industry studies. As used by the Bureau, the first category is that of vehicle-function costs which are not affected by either miles traveled or variations in sizes and weights of vehicles. These costs are generally independent of fluctuations or variations in traffic, examples of which are cost for beautification and landscaping. These costs are assigned to the different groups of vehicles on the basis of the number of vehicles in each group.

The second category is referred to as traffic-function costs. These are essentially the highway costs and costs of maintaining and regulating traffic for a basic highway adequate for passenger cars and pickup trucks. The costs in this category are assigned to the different groups of vehicles on the basis of mileage traveled.

The third category, weight-function costs, includes the costs affected both by miles traveled and variations in sizes and weights. Weight-function costs are allocated on the basis of gross ton-miles. All costs affected by vehicle size or weight are shared by all vehicles at the same rate per ton-mile. A weakness of this method is that the distribution of the weight-function cost through the use of ton-miles does not assign solely to the heavy vehicles the cost of design features which are required only by these vehicles. The cost-function method was devised with the objective of making it possible to approximate the result of the incremental method while reducing the volume of data and analysis required for that method.

The theory of *differential benefits* is one in which an attempt is made to determine the benefits which are derived by vehicles of different types and sizes from the use of the highways by the various users of the highways and to allocate highway costs accordingly to these beneficiaries.

One of the methods used in this theory is to divide the benefits into the following categories: (1) reduction in operating costs; (2) reduction in time costs; (3) reduction in accident costs; and (4) reduction in strain and discomforts of driving in congested traffic. One or more of these benefits is achieved through each of the various categories of highway improvements: (*a*) reduction in distance between termini; (*b*) improvement in roadway surface; (*c*) reduction in rise and fall and improvement in gradients; (*d*) improvement in alinement and other geometrics; and (*e*) elimination of impediments to free traffic flow. The major problem in the allocation of highway costs according to user benefits is the computation of benefits differentiated according to weights and dimensions of vehicles.

### Allocation of costs to different classes of vehicles

The four theories just described were used by the Bureau of Public Roads in making the *Highway Cost Allocation Study*. The findings based on the ton-mile, differential benefits, and cost-function theories were completed by the Bureau and submitted to Congress in January, 1961, as the incremental study was not complete at that time. These findings were expressed in terms of ranges of the high and low values for any given category and were illustrated by the tax payments required by 14 different vehicles. The inference was that the most equitable figure was within the range given in each instance. The assignment of cost responsibility to the various vehicles was computed solely on the basis of the federal-aid portion of highway costs and did not include state highway costs.

The divergence between the range of required payment based on study findings and actual payment was slight in the lighter-weight vehicles but became very pronounced in the heavier vehicle combinations.

For example, the tractor-semitrailer, diesel, 62,000 gross vehicle weight, was underpaying from $424.68 to $2,773.88. According to the findings, pronounced underpayments became apparent in vehicle combinations. The four-axle vehicles, one gasoline-powered and the other diesel-powered, have the same requirements, $870.60 and $2,003.40, but their contributions differ because of the greater efficiency of the diesel-powered vehicle in the consumption of motor fuel. The gasoline-powered pays $724.08 while the diesel-powered pays $613.05.

The study made a comparison of the assignment of cost responsibility by the cost-function, differential-benefit, and ton-mile methods. The gross-ton-mile study gave the lowest values for the passenger car and for the pickup truck, since this method allocates all highway costs in proportion to the weight of the vehicle. Other methods took into account the fact that many elements of highway cost were affected little by weight of vehicle. The differential-benefit study gave the highest values to the passenger car and the pickup truck because of the inclusion of estimated benefits of reduction in travel time of private automobiles and reduction in strain and discomfort of driving. The use of these two items was a reflection of the demand of automobile users for modern highways.

For all vehicles heavier than the passenger automobile and the pickup truck, the cost responsibility given by the ton-mile study was the highest, and that given by the differential-benefit study, the lowest; that given by the cost-function study fell in between.

The divergence between the differential-benefit and the ton-mile values was very substantial for all heavier vehicles. The gross-ton-mile values were more than double in almost every instance and were almost triple those of the differential benefit in the five-axle combinations. Generally, the differential-benefit method allocates higher payments to the lighter vehicles, and lower payments to the heavier vehicles.

The results of these three allocation studies showed that the heavier trucks and combinations should be paying considerably more in comparison to the payments of the lighter vehicle groups than they were at that time.

## Incremental cost allocation[13]

The final report of the *Highway Cost Allocation Study* utilized one primary method—the incremental. The AASHTO road test results were used in connection with the incremental study and were found, in the judgment of the researchers, to be the most valid. The differential-benefit study was considered to be experimental in nature. By introducing the benefits of time savings and reductions in the strain and discomfort of nonuniform driving, the study relied on the demand aspect as a measure of the willingness to pay taxes. This particular study was used to supplement the incremental study. The cost-allocation values of the two methods were not averaged.

In comparing the results of the preliminary and final study, it was found that there was very little difference in the allocations that were made. Table 3-2 gives the variations in the two studies for six typical vehicles.

TABLE 3-2

Comparison of Preliminary and Final Allocations by the Incremental Method, for Six Typical Vehicles

| Vehicle | Registered Gross Weight (Pounds) | Assumed Annual Travel (Miles) | Preliminary Incre- mental* | Final Incre- mental† |
|---|---|---|---|---|
| Passenger car............................ | 4,413 | 9,600 | $   30 | $   31 |
| Pickup truck............................. | 5,000 | 9,000 | 24 | 25 |
| Stake truck.............................. | 15,000 | 12,000 | 55 | 59 |
| 3-axle tractor-semitrailer combination (2–S1)... | 40,000 | 40,000 | 571 | 584 |
| 4-axle tractor-semitrailer combination (2–S2)... | 55,000 | 60,000 | 1,085 | 1,077 |
| 5-axle tractor-semitrailer combination (3–S2)... | 72,000 | 70,000 | 1,769 | 1,623 |

* As shown in Figure 5 of the Federal Highway Administrator's statement of the House Ways and Means Committee hearings on the President's proposals for financing the Federal-aid highway program, March 1961 (3).
† Findings of the incremental allocation employing the final results of the AASHO road test.
Source: House Ways and Means Committee, *Supplementary Report of the Highway Cost Allocation Study* (89th Cong., 1st sess. [Washington, D.C.: U.S. Government Printing Office, 1965]), p. 3.

Figure 3-3 shows the allocated cost responsibility for certain vehicles and their estimated payment of Highway Trust Fund taxes. This indicates that under the incremental method automobiles do not quite pay their share, but it should be noted that this is due to the fact that the manufacturers' excise tax paid on new automobiles goes into the general revenue fund and not the Trust Fund. If these payments were made into the Trust Fund, automobiles would be paying their share. The fact that they travel so much of their mileage on federal-aid systems and that they travel greater mileages than the smaller of the single-unit trucks accounts for the costs attributed to them.

It was found that inequities still exist in the tax contributions of the different classes of users. Figure 3-3 shows that the heavier vehicles are not paying their fair share, as that share is computed under the incremental theory. All classes of single-unit trucks are overpaying the amount of cost responsibility assigned to them. This is due to the fact that generally such vehicles travel a relatively small mileage on the federal-aid systems. They account for about 13 percent of the vehicle-

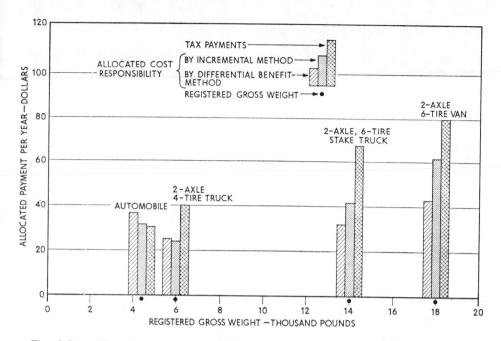

Fig. 3-3A. Allocated cost responsibility, per year of selected single-unit motor vehicles and comparison with estimated payment of Highway Trust Fund taxes.

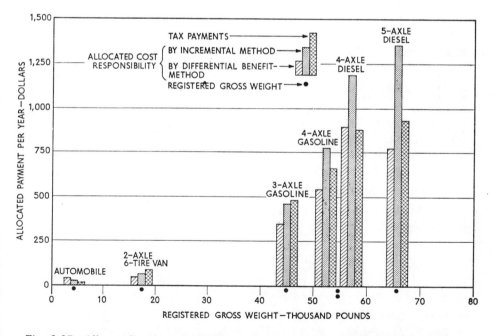

Fig. 3-3B. Allocated cost responsibility, per year, of selected single-unit and combination motor vehicles and comparison with estimated payment of Highway Trust Fund taxes. (Note: Different scale is used in these two figures.)

miles and were estimated in 1964 to pay approximately 20 percent of the Highway Trust Fund taxes. Under the incremental theory, this vehicle class should pay 12 percent of Trust Fund taxes. In the heavier weight groups of vehicles, those that use diesel fuel were found to be underpaying their assigned cost responsibility under the incremental method. In contrast to single trucks, tractor-semitrailer combinations have 80 to 90 percent of their travel on federal-aid systems. These combination vehicles accounted for 4.2 percent of all vehicle-miles, and 5.8 percent of the vehicle-miles on federal-aid highway systems. Their payments to the Trust Fund, in 1964, were estimated to be 15.7 percent of the total whereas, under the incremental theory, they should pay 18.8 percent. All combinations, including those with full trailers, accounted for 4.7 percent of total vehicle-miles and 6.3 percent on the federal-aid highway system. Their payments to the Trust Fund amounted to 17.7 percent of the total, but their responsibility was estimated to be 21.3 percent.[14]

The findings indicated that it would be desirable to have vehicles which impose axle and gross loads of the same magnitude on the highways pay the same or about the same amounts in user taxes. It noted, however, that diesel vehicles had better mileage than gasoline vehicles, so that the former had an advantage. If diesel vehicles were on a parity in terms of fuel tax with gasoline vehicles, they would pay a fuel tax in the range of 5 cents to 5.8 cents per gallon on diesel fuel, depending on the gross operating weight, where the gasoline tax is 4.0 cents per gallon.

A subsequent report was issued in 1970 updating the findings contained in the supplementary report of the Highway Cost Allocation Study in 1965.[15] This study provided a more complete analysis of highway-user cost responsibility. The study showed that of the total Trust Fund allocations and tax payments in 1969 automobiles were paying 94 percent of their appropriate share of the cost and combinations 76 percent. Two-axle, 4-tire trucks were paying 66 percent more than their share. The payment deficiency of some of the larger combinations was found to be due in part to the advantage in miles per gallon of diesel-powered units as compared with those using gasoline engines. Greater equity of federal highway user taxation could be secured by an adjustment of the diesel fuel tax, together with a revision of the annual use tax to a more realistic weight gradation schedule.[16]

For at least the next decade it appears that the problem of adequate user charges on inland waterways, airways, and highways will be a public policy issue of some magnitude. Currently, there are no user charges on inland waterway users and only in 1970 were airway user charges instituted whereas significant user charges have been levied against motor carriers for many years. The controversy will likely be heightened by efforts of the federal government to resolve the northeast and middle west railroad crises with federal proposals that, among other things, all classes of users pay their fair share of the cost and maintenance of waterways, airways, and highways. The motor carrier contribution, through truck user charges, is significant, as federal studies have shown, yet the competitive relationship with railroads is still sufficiently strong to cause administrative and legislative actions to be instituted. Moreover, if further productivity gains in truck transportation are geared to increased size and/or weights the adequacy of user charges will likely escalate.

The Surface Transportation Act of 1978 directed the Secretary of Transportation, assisted by the Congressional Budget Office, to conduct a cost allocation study to determine whether different types of vehicles are paying their fair share of the costs of federal-aid highways. This study is to be completed in 1982.

## QUESTIONS AND PROBLEMS

1. Trace the development of highway-user taxes, and indicate which tax constitutes the largest source of revenue today.

2. How do you explain the large number of apportionment formulas used to apportion sums for federal-aid highways? Are there better methods?

3. What is the National Transportation Report? Will future highway needs be subordinated in the National Transportation Report approach? Discuss both advantages and disadvantages.

4. To effect fuel conservation, there have been federal executive department suggestions that the gasoline tax be increased by amounts of as much as 10 cents to 40 cents. Considering the demand elasticity or inelasticity of gasoline, would you recommend such increases? Why or why not?

5. A number of Presidents have impounded or released federal highway funds to cool down inflation or stimulate economic activity. Discuss the pros and cons of such action.

6. What is meant by the statement that the gasoline tax is a pay-before-you-go system of financing?

7. What is the linkage theory concerning the federal excise tax on gasoline? Discuss its advantages and disadvantages.

8. To what extent has the use of bonds been a source of highway financing? What are the different types used?

9. What traffic volume, as one factor, is considered necessary to justify the construction of a toll road?

10. Why do toll roads "afford more relief in total dollars than in total percentage of highways?"

11. Trucks constitute about 17 percent of all motor vehicles but pay 37 percent of all highway taxes paid by all motor vehicles. Comment.

12. Should we abolish the Trust Fund? Why or why not?

13. Explain the incremental theory of highway cost allocation used in the Eastman report. What merit does it possess?

14. What is the gross-ton-mile method of allocation used in the Board of Investigation and Research report? Why is this method used in some of the state studies?

15. For the complex problem of financing highways, what program would you suggest as a state legislator? As a taxpayer?

16, Carefully explain the cost-function method of cost allocation.

17. What methods were used to allocate cost responsibility between users and nonusers in the *Highway Cost Allocation Study?* Critically analyze the finding.

### FOOTNOTES TO CHAPTER 3

[1] Department of Transportation, *1974 National Transportation Report Summary*, Washington, D.C., December, 1974, p. III-13.

[2] The federal automotive excise taxes were first levied during World War I on automobiles, trucks, and buses, and were repealed after the termination of the war emergency. The excise taxes on gasoline, lubricating oil, motor vehicles, parts and accessories, and tires and tubes were imposed on 1932. Diesel fuel used on the highways was added in 1951, and the tax on tread rubber and the use tax on vehicles of more than 26,000 pounds gross weight were levied in 1956.

[3] Department of Transportation, Federal Highway Administration, *Road-User and Property Taxes on Selected Motor Vehicles, 1973* (Washington, D.C.: U.S. Government Printing Office, 1973).

[4] See annual issues of *Highway Statistics*, Federal Highway Administration.

[5] Department of Transportation, *Feasibility of Toll Removal from the Interstate Highway System*, 1974, p. 92.

[6] House Committee on Ways and Means, *Final Report of the Highway Cost Allocation Study* (87th Cong., 1st sess. [Washington, D.C.: U.S. Government Printing Office, 1961]), p. 1.

[7] A variation of this is a predominant-use method in which tax support is allocated in accordance with the predominant service which a given road or street system renders. For example, general-use highways would be supported entirely by vehicle users, whereas community service roads would be supported by local revenues.

[8] Senate Committee on Interstate and Foreign Commerce, *Study of Domestic Land and Water Transportation* (81st Cong., 2d sess. [Washington, D.C.: U.S. Government Printing Office, 1950]), p. 1051.

[9] *Ibid.*, p. 1029.

[10] *The Basic Problems of Distributing the Highway Tax Burden among the Various Highway Beneficiaries,* prepared by Research Director, American Trucking Associations, 1954.

[11] California, Washington, Oregon, Illinois, New York, Kansas, Nebraska, North Dakota, Michigan, Kentucky, Montana, Louisiana, Minnesota, Ohio, and others.

[12] Virginia Highway Users Association, *Testing the Equity of Virginia's Motor Vehicle Tax Structure* (June, 1953), pp. 36-66.

[13] The Bureau of Public Roads in March, 1961, submitted to Congress a preliminary allocation of highway cost responsibility by the incremental method. Although no assurance was given that the cost allocation to the various vehicle groups would not change when the final incremental report of the road test was received, the Bureau noted that the AASHTO road test findings would affect the allocation of little more than one-fourth of the total 1964 expenditures since nearly three-fourths of the expenditures are for right-of-way, grading, structures, utility adjustment, roadside development, traffic and pedestrian services, and administration. The Bureau concluded, therefore, that there was good reason to believe that the final results of the AASHTO road test would be very little different from those of the preliminary solution. The preliminary study was based on a pavement thickness of 4 inches for the 3,000-pound axle load. This, it might be pointed out, is about the same thickness as many sidewalks. The study made use of an equation to compute incremental bituminous pavement designs.

[14] House Ways and Means Committee, *Supplementary Report of the Highway Cost Allocation Study* (89th Cong., 1st sess. [Washington, D.C.: U.S. Government Printing Office, 1965]), p. 3.

[15] Department of Transportation, Federal Highway Administration, *Allocation of Highway Cost Responsibility and Tax Payments, 1969,* Washington, D.C., 1970.

[16] *Ibid.*, p. 88.

# chapter 4

# Equipment

Our first trucks were converted automobile carriages with heavier axles and springs and strengthened frames. These appeared around 1900; and, for a period of about 25 years, the preponderance of trucks were 1 ton or smaller and were largely modifications of passenger cars. The differentiation between heavy-duty and light-duty trucks in those early days was marked. The latter were largely standardized and were produced at low cost. The heavy-duty trucks were largely produced to specialized requirements; and, as might be expected, the volume produced was low. About 1929 the passenger car manufacturers began specialization in light-duty trucks to meet each specific set of operating requirements. The rating of the small trucks was increased from 1 ton to 1½ tons, which caused a greater change from passenger car design. Today there is almost no such thing as a standard truck, even in the 1½-ton field. Chassis requirements may be standard, but the variety of options is so great that the operator can purchase a truck in the 1½-ton field, as well as in the heavier truck sizes, almost to specifications.

The manufacture of truck bodies is a separate industry in itself. With the exception of the production of a few simple body types, largely of the delivery type, truck manufacturers have not found it possible to standardize trucks for any type of operation. There are special designs which increase in number each year. Manufacturers of trucks have designed and manufactured trucks in a manner that has given them extreme flexibility from unit to unit, and that has enabled them to develop better trucks to meet the increasing demand for specialized vehicles resulting from the evolution of motor transportation.

In the early beginnings of the trucking industry, most of the commercial vehicles were built by manufacturers not associated with the passenger car industry. Passenger car manufacturers entering the light-truck field reduced the proportion of units handled by the independent manufacturers; nevertheless, the total number of trucks built by the independent companies has steadily increased. The manufacturers who are independent of the passenger car industry can be divided into two groups: (a) those who produce all types of trucks and truck-tractors for almost any purpose,[1] and (b) those who produce only a few limited and specialized types.

The necessity for individual engineering of one type or another, whether major or minor in nature, characterizes the construction of practically all units except the light-truck units. The truck manufacturer, then, in order to meet specific transportation problems, must have a large number of variations of his truck design. The producer of trucks has a variety of optional clutches, transmissions, and the like which are produced by independent "parts" manufacturers, so that it is possible for him to offer many variations without having to tool up for each completely new unit. Some truck manufacturers provide their salesmen with questionnaires on which are listed all of the factors relating to the specific hauling operations of each potential customer. The truck manufacturer, using each questionnaire as a guide, will select the correct units which will best serve the needs of the individual operator.

A large truck manufacturer may offer about 400 different models which include several thousand variations in bodies and special equipment. The various models which are offered by one truck manufacturer may be made up to include any one of 50 different engines of from 20 to 1,500 horsepower. For heavy-duty truck-tractors, 250 horsepower was the standard unit for a number of years but, by 1975, 350 horsepower had become much more common. However, with the 55 mile speed limit and the need for fuel economy, the likelihood is that there will be a return to 250 to 300 horsepower. Because of the speed limit and fuel conservation, a number of road speed governors that would limit vehicle maximum speed are being seriously considered by operators. In hilly or mountainous terrain, it is not uncommon to have 400 horsepower tractors in order to maintain reasonable speed going up grades.

Trucks may have as many as 16 forward and 4 reverse speeds. There is a wide range of differences in brakes, springs, frames, axles, and the like. For example, there are 1,000 different sizes and types of brake linings. "New models" among heavier trucks generally appear about every three to five years. Some of the manufacturers of specialized equipment redesign about once every 10 years. A number of federal safety and environmental standards have been formulated that are applicable to trucks. Some standards also apply to trailers. The most controversial requirement is the so-called "121" braking standard which has been strongly protested by the trucking industry for a number of years. The cost of installing such a system has been estimated to be $180 to $500 per axle.

Figure 4-1 shows the sale of trucks by gross vehicle weights from 1971 through 1978. Over the period covered, there has been an increase in the percentage of trucks with gross vehicle weights of less than 10,000 pounds, as well as those over 26,000. The units in the 10,000 to

26,000-pound group are becoming standard for local delivery and local cartage work. An increasing number are also being used in twin trailer combinations in over-the-road operation. The market share of heavy-duty trucks is divided as follows: International Harvester, 21 percent; Ford, 18 percent; General Motors, 16 percent; Mack, 15 percent; White, 13 percent; and others, such as Kenworth and Peterbilt, 15 percent.

Illustrative 2-axle and 3-axle truck-tractors are shown in Fig. 4-2, some with cab-over-engine. Truck-tractors powered by diesel fuel are predominantly used in intercity operations. Diesel mileage is better

| YEAR | 6,000 & Less | 6,001- 10,000 | 10,001- 14,000 | 14,001- 16,000 | 16,001- 19,500 | 19,501- 26,000 | 26,001- 33,000 | Over 33,000 | TOTAL |
|------|------|------|------|------|------|------|------|------|------|
| 1978* | 1,334,392 | 2,139,644 | 73,119 | 5,792 | 2,699 | 155,616 | 41,032 | 161,608 | 3,913,902* |
| 1977* | 1,305,788 | 1,802,692 | 36,478 | 3,237 | 4,847 | 163,370 | 28,491 | 140,643 | 3,485,546* |
| 1976* | 1,318,492 | 1,400,947 | 43,399 | 178 | 8,780 | 152,759 | 22,282 | 97,286 | 3,044,123* |
| 1975* | 1,101,242 | 951,710 | 23,054 | 1,253 | 9,073 | 158,584 | 22,993 | 83,148 | 2,351,057* |
| 1974* | 1,466,586 | 696,248 | 21,038 | 2,693 | 14,455 | 207,001 | 31,036 | 147,533 | 2,586,590* |
| 1973* | 1,754,254 | 758,236 | 49,771 | 3,118 | 15,709 | 235,569 | 37,030 | 154,571 | 3,008,258* |
| 1972* | 1,497,630 | 598,813 | 54,695 | 10,819 | 28,6C8 | 181,771 | 35,357 | 126,225 | 2,533,918* |
| 1971 | 1,184,741 | 487,633 | 6,173 | 14,643 | 46,094 | 139,587 | 33,749 | 98,664 | 2,011,284 |

*Includes imports by U.S. manufacturers—approximately 133,292 in 1977 and 140,736 in 1978, but excludes other imports.
Source: Motor Vehicle Manufacturers Association of the U.S., Inc., 1979, p. 23.

Fig. 4-1. New truck sales by gross vehicle weight, 1971-78.

than gas mileage. A greater number of trucks in local pickup and delivery service are also diesel powered. This trend was accelerated by the fuel shortages of 1973-74 and 1979. At the typical truck stop, 90 percent of the fuel sold is diesel. Diesels, for equal horsepower, weigh more than gasoline trucks, and their initial cost is about $2,000 to $3,000 higher.

Liquefied petroleum gas-powered engines have recently been intro-duced in intercity trucking. Propane gas and butane gas, so-called "bot-tled gas," are used. The cost of LPG as a fuel averages about 5 cents per gallon less than gasoline. Reduction in maintenance and operating costs and the elimination of exhaust odor are other advantages. As was true in the early stages of diesel-powered units, LPG is available at a limited number of points, and it has not expanded rapidly due in part to the continued improvements in diesel engines, which have made the latter more economical.

Currently, there is considerable experimentation with gas turbine engines for trucks. A substantial reduction in weight of the power unit is possible with such an engine, since it weighs only 330 pounds. Thus far, fuel consumption is very high. It is expected that it will have very low maintenance requirements and that many different types of fuels may be used, including kerosene. Such a unit is also air-cooled.

Federal Highway Administration research has concluded that truck fuel consumption per mile increases in direct proportion to speed. Utilizing two carriers that cooperated in the study, six vehicles pulling a sealed payload of 27,700 pounds at 50, 55, and 60 miles per hour on an interstate highway with terrain ranging from mountainous to rolling to virtually flat, the fuel economy results were conclusive. They showed that as speed is lowered, the consumption rate improves. It was also found that wind speed has an effect on fuel use. Where the wind was very strong and the test truck was traveling at 50 miles an hour, the average was 4 miles per gallon into the wind and 9.3 miles per gallon with a following wind.

One of the most significant developments in the postwar period was the trend toward automatic transmission. This was first started with

Fig. 4-2. Two-axle and three-axle truck tractors.

light-duty models. In the following years, it was used on medium-duty models, and it is now widely found on the heavy-duty trucks. Heavy-duty tractors with automatic transmissions first appeared in 1954. The savings of time through faster automatic shifting and decrease in driver fatigue are significant advantages of the automatic transmission.

The substitution of rubberized bellows containing compressed air for conventional metal leaf springs is being used in some trucks and tractors. This lowers the weight and reduces maintenance as well as making a more comfortable ride. Individual front wheel suspension is also used.

Another important development in tractors has been the growing use of cab-over-engine tractors to improve load distribution and permit use of longer trailers.

The cab-over-engine possesses particular advantage in those states in which the state law permits a specified maximum overall length with no restrictions on the length of the vehicles in the combination. When a 65-foot overall length is permitted, many operators desire a 45-foot semitrailer or twin trailers.

Also, some operators turn to the cab-over-engine chassis in order to place more of the weight of the payload on the front axle. The cab-over-engine can carry on the front axle as much as 10 percent more of the load imposed on the kingpin than can conventional models.

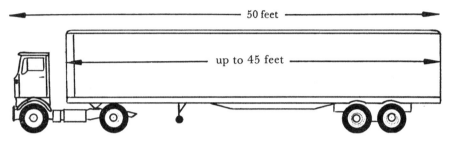

Fig. 4-3. A shortened cab measuring only 48 inches from bumper to back of cab.

As the pressure for increased size of trailers has developed, truck-tractor manufacturers have shortened the cab drastically. Some current models measure only 48 inches from the bumper to the back of the cab. Where state laws permit, it is possible to have a semitrailer 45 feet in length within an overall length limit for the combination of 50 feet, as shown in Fig. 4-3. Even with the addition of sleeper space, a 42-foot trailer can be used. Some of the truck-tractor cabs are being constructed of fiberglass and are about 1,200 pounds lighter than the standard metal cabs, allowing for additional payload. Further weight reduction will be sought through the use of new materials such as graphite fiber plastics. Greater use of electronics is anticipated in energy speed control, emission control, and instrumentation.

The greater steering effort needed as front axle loads are increased to the maximum has met with driver resistance. However, the use of power steering and the placement of more of the chassis overhanging the front axle permit the increase of the payload from 500 to 1,000 pounds.

A cab-forward-of-engine tractor which has two front axles, both of which steer, is in use in the West. The engine is mounted horizontally about midway beneath the frame.

A recent development has been a cab-under, which is a 49-inch high tractor that carries one trailer on its back and pulls another. This maximizes capacity within the 55-feet length.

TABLE 4-1

Truck Vehicle Distribution

| Trucks & Combinations | Private | | For-Hire | | Total | |
|---|---|---|---|---|---|---|
| | Number | Per-cent of Total | Number | Per-cent of Total | Number | Per-cent of Total |
| Single Unit Trucks— | | | | | | |
| 2 axles | 25,788,905 | 94.9 | 435,041 | 39.4 | 26,223,946 | 92.7 |
| 3 axles | 720,709 | 2.5 | 50,792 | 4.6 | 771,501 | 2.6 |
| All Single Unit Trucks | 26,509,614 | 97.4 | 485,833 | 44.0 | 26,995,447 | 95.3 |
| Combinations— | | | | | | |
| 3 axles | 106,963 | 0.4 | 80,604 | 7.3 | 187,567 | 0.7 |
| 4 axles | 217,917 | 0.8 | 167,833 | 15.2 | 385,750 | 1.4 |
| 5 or more axles | 373,293 | 1.4 | 369,896 | 33.5 | 743,189 | 2.6 |
| All Combinations | 698,173 | 2.6 | 618,333 | 56.0 | 1,316,506 | 4.7 |
| Total | 27,207,787 | 100.0 | 1,104,166 | 100.0 | 28,311,953 | 100.0 |

Of the 27,207,787 private trucks, approximately 3,000,000 are farm trucks.
Source: American Trucking Associations, *Trends*, 1977-78, p. 37.

Although fast schedules are quite important in motor transportation, high speed is expensive because road horsepower requirements increase approximately as the cube of vehicle velocity. As a result, the average speeds are limited to about 50 miles per hour.

There has been considerable cooperation between carriers and manufacturers of trucks and trailers in an effort to secure sufficient standardization to permit an interchange of tractor and trailer units. Some of the standardization sought is elimination of differences in location of operating instruments, reduction in the number of variations in fifth wheels, uniform electrical connections, distance from front of trailer to center line of kingpin set at 36 inches, as well as a number of others.

Approximately 95.3 percent of all registered trucks are single-unit trucks—essentially two-axle trucks. The remaining 4.7 percent consist of tractor-semitrailers and truck-trailers as shown in Table 4-1.

### Factors in equipment selection and fuel efficiency

Many factors in equipment selection must be considered.[2] Since equipment represents a sizable portion of a carrier's total investment, particular care should be given to its proper selection.

A basic starting point is to make a detailed study of the carrier operation. Different equipment will be used for an over-the-road operation than will be used for local. Equipment requirements will vary also for a short-haul carrier and for pickup and delivery operations for the over-the-road carrier. Road conditions should be considered also, the terrain, and the maximum grades, as well as other physical factors affecting the operation, such as temperature. Size and nature of the load are also factors to be considered. Fuel surcharges and price increases since 1973 have also emphasized the need to consider fuel efficient options in equipment.

The specifications of the component parts—such as axles—should be studied in regard to relative capacities of the components in order that undersized units may not be selected. Selection of engine size should take into account various operational factors, and the transmission should be selected in relation to the road speeds and the terrain. A thorough examination must be made of tire sizes in regard to their cost and their effect on other components, such as the engine and transmission.

It should be ascertained if special tools will need to be purchased in order to insure a maximum reduction in maintenance time. One of the important design features of a vehicle is accessibility for inspections and necessary servicing and repairing. The time required for performing various operations on the vehicle should be determined so that relative costs can take into account such design features. Many manufacturers will supply information concerning the time required for servicing that can be used as a standard in making a comparative study of inspection and repair costs on a number of vehicles.

As fuel became more expensive, operators of trucks and tractor-trailer combinations sought new vehicle options that would help in fuel conservation. One or more of the options that have been developed can result in fuel savings. Such options as variable fan drives which permit the fan to idle when it is not needed to cool the engine, aerodynamic devices that reduce air drag and may be mounted on the front of either the tractor or the trailer as shown in Figure 4-4 (due to differing frontal profiles, air deflectors are practicable only for vans), smooth-sided trailers that reduce wind resistance rather than exterior post trailers, radial tires that reduce rolling resistance, fuel efficient diesel engines, and especially low engine speed (RPM) and high torque are some of the technological devices. Some operators secure better results from some options than other operators do but all offer some fuel savings.

### Truck trailers

Hooking or hitching a two-wheel wagon to an automobile and thus increasing the carrying capacity available to the owner of a small car or truck was the first example of the use of trailers. In the early days, trucks or cars and trailers were hitched together with a loose-hanging clevis made of a piece of metal. The result was that this type of knuckle-steer trailer would weave over the highway. By 1920 many organizations in the lumber and building supply business were using truck trailers. It was at about this time that the problem of attaching the trailer was solved by the development of an automatic fifth-wheel steer and a more satisfactory coupling hook. The fifth wheel is a disk behind the cab of the tractor. The forward end of the semitrailer rests on this disk. By shifting the fifth wheel closer to the cab or closer to the rear axle of the tractor, axle loads can be changed. The fifth wheel makes it easy to couple and uncouple the trailer unit (Fig. 4-5).

Fig. 4-4. Aerodynamic devices can reduce air drag and save fuel.

For straight trucks, the average design provides for about 90 percent of the payload on the rear tires, and 10 percent on the front tires. In contrast to this, the payload in trailers can be distributed equally between the rear tires and the fifth wheel which transfers its load to the truck-tractor. The rear axle of the semitrailer carries about 43 percent of the load, the rear axle of the truck-tractor carries about 43 percent, and the remaining 14 percent is on the front axle of the truck-tractor. Certain designs of truck-tractors and semitrailers may alter these percentages.

The advantages of truck trailers are as follows (a) a relatively large load can be hauled by a small power unit; (b) it is not necessary to unload the vehicle to release the power unit for other work; and (c) a truck trailer is more easily turned and maneuvered in traffic than a single-wheelbase truck of equal capacity.

The tailoring of trailers to suit the requirements of individual operators is as pronounced as in the manufacturing of trucks. Trailers are designed, as well, to meet various state laws as to size and weight requirements. These factors have combined to make it impossible to produce standard commercial units in any quantity, although the materials used in construction may be standardized. All trailer manufacturers, however, produce so-called standard models. One large company, for example, produces 6,000 standard models.

About 100 firms are engaged in truck-trailer manufacturing and are located all over the United States. The largest company, Fruehauf Trailer Company, produces about 45 percent of all the truck trailers built, and Trailmobile over 20 percent. The five largest trailer manufacturers produce an estimated 85 percent of the total volume. It is reported that 79 percent of orders for Fruehauf trailers call for only one or two vehicles.

Many truck-trailer manufacturers concentrate their sales efforts in a regional area. Some concentrate on fleet sales, whereas others divide their efforts between fleets and individual operators. One truck-trailer

Fig. 4-5. Fifth-wheel coupler on truck-tractor. Courtesy: General Motors Corporation, Inc.

manufacturer has no sales outlets and sells only f.o.b. plant, whereas the larger companies have branch operations. Others have dealer distributors. Fruehauf has 80 branches, 10 distributors, and 76 dealers in the United States.

Truck-trailer production has wide variations from year to year. In 1955, 73,700 units were produced, but in 1958, a recession year, only 51,800 were built. By 1964 production was a great deal higher—89,300—and, in 1978 it was 2,764,090.

The production of truck-trailer vans, both closed and open top, constitutes the largest single category of total trailer production. The number of vans produced in relation to total production was about 67 percent in 1978. A greater number of specialized types of trailers are being produced. About 4 percent of trailer production in 1978 was of tank trucks. Platform-type trailers constituted 11 percent. Low-bed trailers, dump trailers, pole trailers, as well as a number of miscellaneous types of specialized trailers, are also produced. Figure 4-6 shows van, tank, bulk commodity, platform, and low-bed trailers.

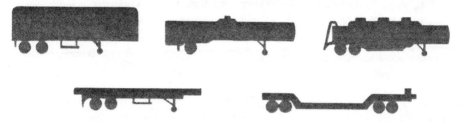

Fig. 4-6.  Typical van, tank, bulk commodity, platform, and low-bed trailers.

The average trailer carries about 300,000 ton-miles of freight per year in intercity service. This compares to 356,000 ton-miles transported by the average rail boxcar, which has a greater capacity but its capacity is not as well utilized.

Specialized equipment, such as a truckaway trailer, has also been designed to permit a return haul of freight. This is accomplished by providing side uprights and hinged sections, so that the tracks on which the cars are ordinarily placed are folded out of the way. A semitrailer and trailer designed to haul bulk cement one way and fuel oil on the return has been developed. Another such unit has a belly tank having a capacity of 7,300 gallons. The top of the tank forms the floor of a dry-freight trailer that can be used as a flatbed trailer for the hauling of a commodity, such as lumber. Low side-boards may be added to form an open-top trailer.

The transportation of products requiring specialized equipment has necessitated research into the most satisfactory designs and materials to be used. A greater volume of refrigerated commodities is moving by motor vehicle, for example. Both mechanical refrigeration units and crushed ice are used in insulated vans, depending on the commodity transported. The manner in which heat is transferred has caused changes in the interior design of refrigerated trailers, since it has been found that on an average hot summer day, steel channels to hold up meat rails conduct more heat into the trailer than refrigeration will take out.

Some trailer manufacturers have developed compartmentized van trailers, particularly for hauling commodities requiring refrigeration. It is possible to have one area capable of subzero temperatures for frozen foods, and the other part of the unit provide temperature at a different level. Drop-floor or depressed center van trailers are used in some types of service such as the transportation of household goods or livestock. Such trailers are sometimes referred to as "possum bellies." Livestock trailers have been developed with greatly increased capacity. They have three levels that can be converted into a dry freight, straight-floor trailer on the return load, thus minimizing empty return hauls as in Figure 4-7.

For some years attempts have been made to design trailers that can be used for both highway and rail movements by designing the truck trailer with a single set of retractable, steel-flanged wheels for rail use in addition to retractable, standard rubber tires for use on highways. About 3,000 to 4,000 pounds of weight are added to the trailer.

Fig. 4-7. Convertible tri-level aluminum trailer for use in transporting livestock one-way and dry freight the other. Courtesy: Wilson Trailer Co.

The service life of trailers is usually considerably greater than that of power units, although there are wide variations depending upon the type of equipment. The power unit may have a relatively short service life of 5 years and trailers approximately 10 years. The average number of semitrailers to tractors for Class I intercity motor carriers is 217 to 100. This is due to the fact that the semitrailer can be "dropped" at destination and remain at the dock until unloaded. In the meantime, the tractor can pick up another semitrailer and pull it to its destination.

The shiftable tandem axle is one of the most important developments in semitrailers. When different tractors are being used with a semitrailer, the shifting of rear axles to compensate for the load position can secure proper load distribution. Thus, axles can be shifted to comply with the different state requirements through which the unit operates, and a carrier can standardize on a trailer of one size for its over-the-road operations. Another advantage of the shiftable tandem is that removal of the entire sliding suspension can be made by disconnecting the airlines, removing the pins, and hoisting the body. This allows for the replacing of a unit with an overhauled one in a matter of 30 minutes.

TABLE 4-2

TRENDS IN VAN TRAILER LENGTHS

(all values are percentages, %)

| LENGTH IN FEET | 1946 | 1948 | 1953 | 1956 | 1958 | 1960 | 1962 | 1964 | 1966 | 1968 | 1970 | 1972 | 1974 | 1976 | 1978 |
|---|---|---|---|---|---|---|---|---|---|---|---|---|---|---|---|
| 45' or over | -- | -- | -- | -- | -- | -- | -- | -- | -- | 6.1 | 13.3 | 31.7 | 41.8 | 37.0 | 52.08 |
| 42'6" to 45' | -- | -- | -- | -- | -- | -- | -- | .8 | 2.3 | .9 | 2.0 | 3.1 | 5.3 | 18.5 | 7.23 |
| 40' to 42'6" | -- | -- | -- | -- | 3.0 | .1 | 3.2 | 1.1 | 2.3 | 64.6 | 70.8 | 50.2 | 41.4 | 28.2 | 32.68 |
| *38' to 40' | -- | -- | -- | -- | 10.0 | 60.0 | 81.8 | 82.4 | 73.0 | 1.7 | 1.3 | .6 | 2.6 | .8 | .21 |
| 36' to 38' | -- | -- | 2.4 | 6.7 | 8.5 | 6.5 | 2.4 | 1.2 | 1.6 | .4 | .3 | .1 | .1 | .4 | .10 |
| 34' to 36' | -- | -- | 18.9 | 68.6 | 64.0 | 16.6 | 7.4 | 3.3 | 1.8 | 1.2 | .8 | .8 | .3 | .6 | .25 |
| 32' to 34' | 4.3 | 16.6 | 58.7 | 14.8 | 5.5 | 2.8 | .9 | .7 | .3 | .7 | .1 | .4 |  | 1.3 | .07 |
| 30' to 32' | 4.1 | 23.9 | 10.4 | 2.0 | 3.0 | 2.0 | .6 | 1.2 | .8 | .4 | .9 | 1.0 | .9 | 1.2 | .08 |
| 28' to 30' | 17.9 | 27.5 | 3.2 | .9 | 2.0 | 2.5 | .6 | 1.7 | .5 | 2.8 | 1.0 | 1.4 | .6 | .3 | .01 |
| 26' to 28' | 23.5 | 18.8 | 1.1 | .6 | 1.0 | 6.4 | 1.3 | 4.4 | 15.4 | 19.8 | 7.6 | 10.4 | 5.9 | 8.6 | .25 |
| 24' to 26' | 24.3 | 6.5 | 1.8 | 1.0 | .5 | 1.0 | .9 | 2.9 | 1.3 | 1.5 | 1.2 | .6 | .6 | 2.4 | 4.18 |
| 22' to 24' | 21.4 | 5.3 | 1.6 | 1.6 | 2.5 | .5 | .2 | .2 | .6 | .2 | .1 | -- | .1 | .4 | .91 |
| Under 22' | 4.5 | 1.4 | 1.9 | 3.8 | -- | 1.6 | .7 | .1 | -- | .1 | -- | -- | -- | .3 | -- |

* - Through 1966 this figure included 40' units.

Source: Truck-Trailer Manufacturers Association, Inc., 1979.

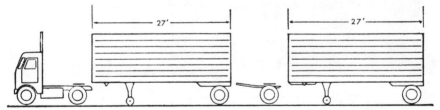

Fig. 4-8. A trailer-converter dolly used to convert a semitrailer into a full trailer.

Truck operators have demanded more payload space or more "cube." This growing demand must be reconciled by trailer manufacturers with state limits on sizes of units. The trend toward larger trailers over a period of years is shown in Table 4-2. The largest percentage of vans produced in 1946 was in the 24-26 foot length, which was 24.3 percent. As recently as 1956, no units were over 38 feet in length; yet by 1964, 82 percent were of this length or longer. In 1974 about 42 percent were 45 feet or over. In that year, 88 percent of all van trailers were 40 feet or longer. Use of 27-foot doubles in 65-foot combinations of tractor-semitrailer and full or semitrailer is widespread. The 26-28 foot trailer constituted 5.3 percent of production in 1979. The second semitrailer in doubles may be converted into a full trailer by using a trailer-converter dolly as shown in Fig. 4-8. A dolly may also be used to convert a two-axle tractor into a three-axle tractor.

An experiment was undertaken over the New York Thruway and Massachusetts Turnpike, both of which are toll roads, in which "double-bottom" (tandem trailers) combinations with an overall length of 98 feet and gross loads up to 120,000 pounds were permitted. Speed limits were established with a minimum of 20 miles an hour and a maximum of 50 miles an hour. This proved to be successful and is no longer considered experimental. It has since been extended to other toll roads, including the Ohio Turnpike and the Indiana Turnpike. On the Kansas Turnpike, special authorization has been given to permit double-bottom equipment with two 40-foot semi-trailers, making the unit 105 feet in length and having a gross weight capacity of 130,000 pounds. A substantial increase in long-haul trucking productivity could be gained by permitting the same type of equipment to be operated on designated interstate highways.

Fig. 4-9. Combination unit of twin trailers, 28 feet in length, with rounded nose, and sloping from front to rear for more cube. Courtesy: Consolidated Freightways, Inc.

Although the 27-foot twin trailers are being widely utilized, there were 1,674,000 40-foot commercial trailers in use in 1979. This compares to 380,000 27-foot trailers, or a ratio of 5 to 1. Some of the newer twin trailers are 28 feet in length with a rounded nose. They are sloped from front to rear for more cube and are called "wedge trailers." As shown in Fig. 4-9, such a combination provides 3,750 to 3,800 cubic feet.

It is estimated that to use 40- or 45-foot trailers in double-bottoms, the additional cost for a towing device and strengthening of the frame would cost $250 to $300 for new trailers and $350 to $400 for existing equipment.

The use of a "trailing trailer," which is about 15 feet in length, behind a regular semitrailer for line service has been developed. The trailing trailer is equipped with a fifth-wheel attachment making it possible to use it for a city pickup and delivery with standard tractors. The shipments can be picked up in this unit, make the over-the-road trip in it, and then be delivered at destination directly from the unit, eliminating extra platform handling at origin and destination. The same principle has been used with trucks built like boxes and coupled together so that they may be operated as one unit in over-the-road service, and as two units in pickup and delivery at origin and destination.

Additional cubic capacity in new semitrailers has been accomplished by lengthening the semitrailer through the use of cab-over-engine tractors which require less tractor length, reduced clearance of trailers over the tires, smaller-diameter wheels and tires, lower fifth wheels and fifth-wheel mountings, thinner wall sections, and flatter and thinner roof construction, as well as in a number of other ways.

There is increasing use of doubles or twin trailers because of the greater cubic capacity. The 40-foot semitrailer has to carry freight with a density of about 17.5 pounds before it "cubes out." The general commodities transported today, however, have an average of about 12.5 pounds per cubic foot. Two 27-foot doubles can secure full weight and full visible load at a density of just over 12 pounds per cubic foot. A combination of this type has a cubic capacity of approximately 33 percent more than one 40-foot semitrailer.

As early as 1966, a number of western states began permitting triple trailers on their highways, initially on a test basis and only on designated highways. The operational and safety experience in these states has been excellent, and the states have established guidelines for their operation. Fuel economy is significant in this type of operation. Five western states have legalized it, and four others are testing its operation. Figure 4-10 is illustrative of this type of equipment used in this operation.

Instead of conventional steel springs, an air suspension has been used on some of the newer trailers. Under this method of construction, the load actually rides on an air cushion. As a trailer is loaded, air is automatically pumped to expand the air cushions. When unloaded, the air is released. This makes it possible to maintain a constant height of the trailer. With conventional springs, a trailer must be designed to meet the legal height when empty, and when loaded, sometimes the height is as much as 3 inches lower than allowed.

In order to increase the payload, there has been greater use of lighter metals in trailer construction, and manufacturers make almost three times as many aluminum as steel vans. With lightweight construction material, manufacturers are producing trailers that can carry six times their weight in payloads.

Plastics have had limited use so far. In some of the new trailers, skylight panels of plastic are being placed in the forward part of the roof of the trailer which gives added light for loading and unloading. Some plastic sides have been constructed for trailers, and a few tank trailers have been constructed of reinforced plastic. It appears that plastic will be used when its use is economically sound, but so far it has had limited application.

Fig. 4-10. Triple-trailer equipment that is legal in certain western states. Courtesy: Garrett Freightlines, Inc.

### Containers

Shipping containers are used primarily for shipping packaged goods and bulk materials in order to minimize damage and loss in transit. They are also extensively used for small articles to avoid individual rehandling. Containers are becoming increasingly popular. They vary in size from a few cubic feet of capacity to 2,200 cubic feet and more. They may be as much as 40 feet in length. Standards for freight container size have been established by the U.S.A. Standards Institute in lengths of 5, 6-2/3, 10, 20, 30, and 40 feet, with height and width dimensions of 8 by 8 feet. It is hoped that the standards will be adopted by all types of carriers in order to facilitate interchange between carriers.

The air carriers have made use of 10 x 8 x 8 and 20 x 8 x 8 containers in the larger 747's. Alphabetical designations are used by the airlines to identify their containers. Type A containers range from 375 to 500 cubic feet and are carrier owned. Types B, B-2, and D are shipper-owned containers and vary up to 197 cubic feet. Type B is the largest with 197 cubic feet, and the others are smaller. The 747's that are designed only for carrying freight have a capacity of about 171,000 pounds. This is far in excess of that permitted by size and weight limitations on trucks.

A container in the trucking field usually refers to a demountable van container with a length of 10 feet or more, which is designed to serve as a van component of a truck or trailer body but is detachable from the chassis or other running gear for interchange between modes of transportation. Forklifts or cranes are used to place them on flatbed bodies or trailers. Approximately 5 percent of total van production is container production.

Fig. 4-11. A typical 5-axle tractor-semitrailer combination unit. Courtesy: Spector Motor Freight System, Inc.

### Vehicle combinations

A wide variety of vehicle combinations are in use today. The adaptability and capacity of combination units have proved their value in intercity transportation. In 1936 single-unit trucks transported 57 percent of ton-mileage while combinations transported 43 percent. For more than 20 years, though, combinations have transported over twice that carried by single-unit trucks—70 percent for combinations and 30 percent for single-unit trucks. A typical 5-axle combination unit is shown in Fig. 4-11.

Throughout the motor-carrier industry, terms are applied to equipment which are only applicable in a particular area. In referring to a piece of equipment, the expression used in one area may have a completely different connotation in another area. These terms become firmly entrenched through usage and are widely found in labor contracts. For instance, a labor agreement in one area may make reference to a piece of equipment called a "jeep." The same term in a labor contract in an area just 500 miles distant may refer to an entirely different piece of equipment. What is referred to as a "double-bottom" in Ohio is known as a "train" in another area. A trailer less than 20 feet in length may be called a "pup," and one more than 20 feet long may be called a "dog."

### QUESTIONS AND PROBLEMS

1. Trace the early development of the motortruck. Is there any specialization in the production of trucks?
2. Enumerate the advantages of truck trailers.
3. What does the fact that there is a truck-trailer manufacturer which produces 6,000 "standard" models mean (a) to the motor carrier, and (b) to the truck-trailer manufacturer?
4. What are some of the current trends in power units used in trucks?
5. Discuss the effects of the shiftable tandem axle and the larger cube trailer upon (a) motor carriers, (b) shippers.
6. What points should be considered in selecting equipment? How could this be done more scientifically?
7. Analyze the technological advance in truck and trailer equipment during the past 25 years. Who has benefited most from the advance?
8. Should equipment utilization during peacetime influence material allocation for equipment during war?
9. Twin or triple trailers have been increasingly used where permitted by size and weight laws. How can you analyze their prospective productivity?
10. Have containers been widely used in truck transportation by general commodity carriers? Why not?

### FOOTNOTES TO CHAPTER 4

[1] A motortruck carries its load on its own wheels whereas a truck-tractor is designed primarily for drawing truck-trailers and constructed to carry part of the weight and load of a semitrailer. A semitrailer is a truck trailer equipped with one or more axles and constructed so that a substantial part of its weight and load is carried by a truck-tractor. An extensive standard nomenclature has been developed by the Society of Automotive Engineers and can be found in the *SAE 1949 Handbook* (New York: Society of Automotive Engineers, Inc.), pp. 868-71.

[2] The Society of Automotive Engineers publishes *Truck Ability Prediction Procedure*, which is a report providing a practical method for the prediction of truck performance and is helpful in truck selection.

# chapter 5

# Types of operations

Motor carriers of property can be classified according to a number of different bases. Many of these classifications will be listed and described in order to familiarize the reader with a number of the operations in the motor carrier industry. The Interstate Commerce Commission, acting under Section 204 (c) (now 11102) of the Motor Carrier Act, adopted the following classification in 1937 after a national investigation: [1]

*Classification of Motor Carriers of Property*

I. By type of carrier:
  1. Common carriers of property
  2. Contract carriers of property
  3. Private carriers of property
  4. Brokers of property transportation
  5. Exempt carriers

II. By type of service in which engaged:
  A. *Regular route, scheduled service.* A regular route scheduled service carrier is any person which undertakes to transport property or any class or classes of property in interstate or foreign commerce by motor vehicle for compensation between fixed termini and over a regular route or routes upon established or fixed schedules.
  B. *Regular route, nonscheduled service.* A regular route nonscheduled service carrier is any person which undertakes to transport property or any class or classes of property in interstate or foreign commerce by motor vehicle for compensation between fixed termini and over a regular route or routes at intermittent intervals and not upon an established or fixed schedule.
  C. *Irregular route, radial service.* An irregular route radial service carrier is any person which undertakes to transport property or any class or classes of property in interstate or foreign commerce by motor vehicle for compensation over irregular routes from a fixed base point or points to points or places located within such radial area as shall have been fixed and authorized by the Interstate Commerce Commission in a certificate of pub-

lic convenience and necessity or permit, or from any point located within such radial area to such carrier's fixed base point or points.

  D. *Irregular route, nonradial service.* An irregular route nonradial service carrier is any person which undertakes to transport property or any class or classes of property in interstate or foreign commerce by motor vehicle for compensation over irregular routes between points or communities located within such general territory as shall have been defined geographically and authorized in a certificate of public convenience and necessity or permit, and any other points or communities located within the same general territory without respect to a hub community or a fixed base point of operation.

  E. *Local cartage service.* A local cartage carrier is any person which undertakes to transport property or any class or classes of property by motor vehicle for compensation when such transportation is performed in interstate or foreign commerce wholly within a municipality or between contiguous municipalities or within a zone adjacent to and commercially a part of any such municipality or municipalities.

III.  By type of commodities transported:
1. Carriers of general freight
2. Carriers of household goods
3. Carriers of heavy machinery
4. Carriers of liquid petroleum products
5. Carriers of refrigerated liquid products
6. Carriers of refrigerated solid products
7. Carriers engaged in dump trucking
8. Carriers of agricultural commodities
9. Carriers of motor vehicles
10. Carriers engaged in armored truck service
11. Carriers of building materials
12. Carriers of films and associated commodities
13. Carriers of forest products
14. Carriers of mine ore, not including coal
15. Carriers engaged in retail store delivery service
16. Carriers of explosives or dangerous articles
17. Carriers of specific commodities, not subgrouped

This classification enables the Interstate Commerce Commission to have a system of identification for any motor carrier. For example, a motor carrier transporting household goods over irregular routes in radial service, which is a common carrier, is classified as a Common Carrier, Class C-2. A motor common carrier transporting new automobiles over irregular routes in radial service is classified as a Common Carrier, Class C-9.

The regulation of interstate for-hire trucking was placed under the jurisdiction of the Interstate Commerce Commission in 1935 with the passage of the Motor Carrier Act. Under this act, all interstate motor carriers are subject to safety regulations, and a number are subject to economic regulation as well.[2] The various states regulate intrastate highway transportation.

### Classification by gross revenue

The Interstate Commerce Commission also classifies for statistical purposes the motor carriers which are subject to its jurisdiction on the basis of gross revenue. Through 1973, a Class I motor carrier was one that had gross revenue of over $1 million per year; a Class II carrier, $300,000 to $1 million per year; and a Class III motor carrier, less than $300,000. Beginning in 1974, the classification was changed to Class I carriers, $3 million and over; Class II, $500 thousand to $3 million; and Class III, less than $500 thousand. Again in 1979, the classification was changed to Class I, $5 million and over; Class II, $1 million to less than $5 million; and Class III, less than $1 million.

There are a relatively small number of Class I carriers. In 1979, they constituted just 6 percent of all motor carriers, yet accounted for 78 percent of the revenue. Class II carriers constituted 17 percent and accounted for 14 percent of the revenue; and Class III carriers, 77 percent of the total and 8 percent of the revenue.

### For-hire and private carriers

A workable classification used for differentiating between the various kinds of motor carriers is that of for-hire carriers and private carriers. The for-hire carriers are those carriers which engage in transportation for compensation of one or more classes of freight that is the property of others. The for-hire group embraces the common, the contract, and certain exempt carriers. A brief explanation of each of these groups of carriers follows.

### Common carriers

The motor vehicle common carrier is defined by statute as any person which holds itself out to the general public to engage in the transportation of property by motor vehicle over regular or irregular routes in interstate or foreign commerce. A common carrier is granted a certificate of public convenience and necessity by the Interstate Commerce Commission which constitutes its operating authority. Common carriers may be subdivided into two broad groupings based on the commodities transported: (1) the carriers of general commodities with the usual exceptions—dangerous explosives, commodities of unusual value, household goods, commodities in bulk, and those requiring special equipment. This gives rise to the second category (2) specialized common carriers, which transport a generic commodity group such as petroleum and chemicals, household goods, automobiles, heavy haulers, etc. As common carriers, both categories hold themselves out generally to serve the public.

Common carriers of general commodities usually operate over regular routes between fixed termini. This group is comprised of localized carriers, small regional carriers, large regional carriers, and large transcontinental carriers. Currently, there are fourteen motor carriers of general commodities that, through mergers and acquisitions, are now able to provide single-line transcontinental service. Two of these, Consolidated Freightways and McLean Trucking Co., have route miles of 87,000 and 84,000 respectively. Specialized divisions have been created in some general commodity carriers, and these divisions handle a limited number of commodities including frozen foods, building materials, and steel, in truckload lots. These operations are typically conducted by owner-operators (independent truckers) for the regulated general commodity carrier.

Specialized motor common carriers generally operate over broad geographical areas via irregular routes and handle truckload lots. Examples include transporters of paper products, tank trucks for liquid and dry flowables, and household goods carriers. Others have specialized equipment to transport items of unusual size or weight. Another type of specialized carrier is that of United Parcel Service that limits its service to packages which do not exceed 50 pounds and serves the continental United States.

The revenue per ton-mile received by carriers of general commodities was 14.2 cents and that received by other than carriers of general commodities was 7.1 cents.

Currently there are 16,874 motor common carriers of property certificated by the Interstate Commerce Commission. The for-hire common carriers constitute the predominant segment of interstate property-carrying for-hire motor carriers which are subject to economic regulation by the Interstate Commerce Commission. The material in this text emphasizes and deals later in more detail with the many aspects of the common-carrier operations of general commodities.

The operations of general commodity carriers typically involve a distributive type of operation or a key-point operation. The distributive operation is the type in which the motor carrier performs a distribution service in many small towns and communities. This operation is inherently more expensive to conduct because the charges per unit are higher. Such carriers have a network of routes serving local areas where the carrier is engaged in assembly and distribution service. The operator may be unable to secure as much outgoing traffic from a small community as it carries in, and unit charges are higher. Key-point operation is between key points, such as two cities, in which a truckload is dispatched from one key point and continues all the way through to the other key point. This type of operation is one that secures heavy and balanced loads. Moving traffic only between these key points holds costs at a minimum. Common carriers operate over regular and irregular routes as specified in their certificate. They issue a bill of lading or receipt for goods which is uniform for all shippers served.

### Contract carriers

The contract carrier, as redefined by Congress in August, 1957, is a for-hire carrier that engages in transportation for compensation under continuing contracts with a person or a limited number of persons either (a) for the furnishing of transportation services through the assignment of motor vehicles for a continuing period of time to the exclusive use of each person served; or (b) for the furnishing of transportation services designed to meet the distinct need of each individual customer. The operating authority of the contract carrier in interstate operations is contained in a permit issued by the Interstate Commerce Commission.

The contract carrier makes an individual contract with one or more shippers. It is essentially an independent contractor whose undertaking of transportation service is defined and limited by an individual contract which calls for a service specialized to meet the peculiar needs of a particular shipper or a limited number of shippers. (Fig. 5-1.) A contract carrier then will pick and choose among shippers those whom it will serve, and this may be done by choosing any particular segment of traffic desired, provided it is within the scope of its operating rights. It may legally refuse to handle any other class of traffic. Currently 3,165 permits are issued to an estimated 2,800 contract carriers that are subject to regulation by the Interstate Commerce Commission. There are 127 Class I and 243 Class II contract carriers.

Under the new definition, there are two types of contract carrier. The first of these is the carrier which assigns a fleet of vehicles to a single shipper for its exclusive use. This is what has been termed "dedication of vehicle to the shipper." An example of this type of contract carrier is one that operates a fleet of vehicles for the exclusive use of a chain-store firm in distributing from warehouse to retail outlets. The Commission has ruled that

Fig. 5-1. Five-axle refrigerated unit used in transportation of meat by contract carrier. Courtesy: Monfort of Colorado.

such assigned vehicles may be used for other shippers providing such use does not result in any less availability of equipment to the original contracting shipper than a return movement would have. In a later case, the Commission ruled that a carrier may utilize empty space remaining in a trailer that is designated to one shipper for the freight of another shipper under the same conditions as in the previous case. The second type of contract carrier is one that uses the same equipment to serve more than one customer in a manner which meets the distinct need of each.

Even before the redefinition of contract carriers, they had not shown the growth that has characterized other segments of the trucking industry. In 1939 they accounted for 24 percent of intercity ton-miles transported by regulated motor carriers, but this had dropped to 4.5 percent by 1977, with revenue dropping from 16 percent to 4.8 percent of the total.

Certain differences in operations are reflected in operating costs between contract carriers and common carriers. Contract carriers usually have no terminal facilities for platform handling of freight because they

| Warehouse_____Date Delivered_____Date Loaded_____ |
| Consigned To_____Truck - Class_____No._____ |
| Location_____R. T. Mileage_____ |
| How Shipped_____Scale Weight_____ |
| Trip Time_____ |
| N. S._____    N. S._____Mty Man Hrs._____ |
| Seals - S. S._____End Door - S. S. _____Car Number_____ |
| Pieces Billed_____Date Started_____Refused_____ |
| Pieces Not Del'd._____    Short_____ |
| Pieces Delivered_____Date Finished_____Over_____ |

| KEY NO. | NUMBER OF PIECES | | | | | TOTAL WEIGHT | C'RGE RATE | CARTAGE AMOUNT |
|---------|------|------|--------|------|-------|------|------|------|
| | GROC. | PROD. | BAKERY | MEAT | TOTAL | | | |
| | | | | | | | | |
| | | | | | | | | |
| | | | | | | | | |
| | | | | | | | | |
| | | | | | | | | |
| | | | | | | | | |
| | | | | | | | | |
| | | | | | | | | |
| | | | | | | | | |
| | | | | | | | | |
| | | | | | | | | |
| | | | | | | | | |
| TOTAL | | | | | | | XXXXX | |

_____
Truckman

_____
Driver's Signature

We hereby certify that the above described meat or meat food products which are offered for shipment in interstate or foreign commerce, have been U.S. inspected and passed by Department of Agriculture, are so marked, and at this date are sound, healthful, wholesome and fit for human food.

THE GREAT ATLANTIC & PACIFIC TEA CO.

"This is to certify that the above named articles are properly described, and are packed and marked and are in proper condition for transportation according to the regulations prescribed by the Interstate Commerce Commission and the Commandant of the Coast Guard".

THE GREAT ATLANTIC & PACIFIC TEA CO.

Fig. 5-2. Form used in lieu of a bill of lading by a dedication of the vehicle to the shipper type of contract carrier.

make a contract only for volume freight—which means, in effect, truckload lots. They go to the shippers' plants, load the freight, and take it directly to the consignees; therefore, they have no need for terminal facilities for freight handling. Contract carriage also tends to be more limited in territorial scope than common-carrier service.

The documents used may also be different. Figure 5-2 is a form used in lieu of a bill of lading in a dedication of the vehicle to the shipper type of contract carriage.

The revenue per ton-mile received by intercity Class I common and contract carriers is shown in Table 5-1. The average revenue per ton-mile of contract carriers was below that of common carriers but from 1965 to 1970, revenue per ton-mile of Class I contract carriers exceeded that of Class I common carriers. Since 1970, Class I common

TABLE 5-1

Revenue per Ton-Mile—Class I Intercity Common and
Contract Carriers of Property

| Year | Common | Contract |
|------|--------|----------|
| 1965 | 6.457 | 7.663 |
| 1966 | 6.337 | 7.305 |
| 1967 | 6.645 | 7.355 |
| 1968 | 6.927 | 7.233 |
| 1969 | 7.081 | 7.354 |
| 1970 | 7.458 | 6.855 |
| 1971 | 7.853 | 7.200 |
| 1972 | 7.997 | 7.022 |
| 1973 | 8.341 | 6.683 |
| 1974 | 8.731 | 7.759 |
| 1975 | 9.200 | 7.800 |
| 1976 | 9.970 | 8.200 |

Excludes household goods carriers.
Source: Bureau of Economics, Interstate Commerce
Commission, *Transport Economics,* Vol. 5, No. 1,
1978, p. 2.

carrier revenue (both general commodity and specialized carriers) is again higher than that of contract carriers. On the other hand, revenue per ton-mile for Class II contract carriers has averaged about 1 cent less than that of Class II common carriers during the past decade.

The contractual terms will have a definite influence on the rate schedule which the contract carrier will charge. A contract may be drawn in which the carrier is relieved of all liability regarding the shipment, in which case the shipper would expect to find this reflected in lower rates. On the other hand, the contract can be drawn requiring the contract carrier to assume full common-carrier liability for the shipments which, likewise, will be reflected in the rates.

The liability of a contract carrier, unlike common carriers, is entirely dependent upon its contractual arrangements with the shipper. The contract carrier may contract under any terms except for total exemption from liability because of its negligence. This right to contract freely is not affected by the Interstate Commerce Act. Thus, dependent upon the contractual arrangements, a contract carrier may be liable for goods in transit merely as a bailee for hire, or, on the other hand, it may be liable to the same extent as a common carrier. As a bailee for hire, it owes the duty only to exercise reasonable care in handling the freight. The carrier would not be liable, therefore, for accidents which were not its fault, but it would be liable if it failed to exercise reasonable care to protect the goods. Actually, the majority of transportation contracts provide for full liability on the part of the carrier. The Commission does not require contracts of contract carriers to include provisions concerning the carrier's liability. It considered this general subject in *Ex parte No. MC–12* and felt that it had no jurisdiction over this aspect of the contract.

If an intrastate movement is involved and there is a question about the liability of the carrier, the state law would apply. Moreover since there is no overriding federal statute governing the liabilities of contract carriers, state laws would apply to both interstate and intrastate movements. In any particular case, the laws of the state having jurisdiction over the matter would have to be consulted.

Characteristics of a contract are: (1) it is bilateral in nature; (2) the shipper should agree to furnish the commodities to be transported by specifying the amount of tonnage to the point, points, or areas named; (3) it provides for a series of shipments within a given period of time; (4) it includes the rates and charges and the method by which the actual amount payable to the carrier can be determined; (5) it contains an agreement by the shipper to pay the specified compensation; and (6) it provides for transportation by the carrier for a particular shipper under the rules, conditions, or provisions which are set forth in the contract. The Commission requires that the contracts must be in writing and copies shall be preserved by carriers as long as they are in force and for one year thereafter. However, one group of contract carriers, those carrying bullion, currency, jewels, and other precious or very valuable articles, does not have to execute contracts. These contract carriers which offer armored-car service do not have to file schedules of their actual rates and charges.

In general, the contract for transportation is between the carrier and the one who pays the transportation charges. This is considered to be evidence that the person who pays is the one who controls the transportation. In a 1972 ruling[3] the Commission expanded this description of the "contract shipper" to make it clear that the person with whom the carrier has a contract is not necessarily the one who always pays the freight bill.

The shipper who makes the contract with the carrier cannot offer to others the privilege of shipping commodities under the contract which he holds, although there has been no formal ruling on this matter. When a parent corporation has a contract with a contract carrier and a subsidiary company wishes to ship commodities with the same contract carrier, separate contractual arrangements should be made by the subsidiary. The contract carrier may add or substitute contracts within the scope of its permit.

### Exempt carriers

The third group of for-hire carriers of property is the exempt-carrier group. These carriers are engaged in moving certain commodities for compensation interstate; but, under the provisions of the Interstate Commerce Act, they are specifically exempt from economic regulation by the Interstate Commerce Commission. These are property carriers using motor vehicles controlled and operated by farmers engaged in the transportation of agricultural commodities or farm supplies; vehicles controlled and operated by cooperative associations, as defined in the Agricultural Marketing Act; vehicles used in carrying livestock, fish, or agricultural commodities; vehicles used exclusively in the distribution of newspapers; vehicles used in the transportation of property incidental to transportation by aircraft; vehicles used in transportation of property wholly within a municipality or zone adjacent to or commercially a part of such a municipality; and vehicles used in casual, occasional, or reciprocal transportation of property in interstate or foreign commerce by a person not engaged in transportation by motor carriers as a regular business.

It is estimated that there were 42,033 exempt carriers operating interstate in 1979, which is about three times more than there were common and contract interstate carriers of property regulated by the Interstate Commerce Commission. Most of these exempt carriers are engaged in carrying agricultural commodities, livestock, and fish. Exempt interstate motor carriers are in their operations common or contract motor carriers but are excluded from economic regulation by the Interstate Commerce Act. Therefore, they do not have to secure operating authority in the form of certificates or permits from the Interstate Commerce Commission. They are subject only to safety regulations of the Department of Transportation.

The most important exemption in intercity transportation is the one covering agricultural commodities (not including manufactured products thereof), livestock, and fish. This exemption was redefined by the Transportation Act of 1958 and provides that the exemption applies to property consisting of ordinary livestock and fish (including shellfish), or agricultural (including horticultural) commodities (not including manufactured products thereof). Exempt and nonexempt commodities, as determined by the Commission, are now listed in an Administrative Ruling.[4] The amendment further provided that the agricultural exemption does not include frozen fruits, berries, and vegetables, cocoa beans, coffee beans, tea, bananas, or hemp and wool imported from any foreign country, wool tops and noils, or wool waste (carded, spun, woven or knitted) but does include cooked or uncooked (including breaded) fish or shellfish when frozen or fresh (but not including fish and shellfish which have been treated by preserving such as canned, smoked, pickled, spiced, corned, or kippered products).

Much of the transportation of agricultural commodities is over long distances. Apples from the state of Washington move by truck distances of more than two thousand miles. Lettuce is transported from California and Mexico to the East Coast, and snap green beans from Florida to Minnesota. There is also substantial long distance movement of shell eggs from the North Central region to other areas of the country.

The volume of traffic which moves in exempt transportation has grown considerably, but there are no overall figures showing the total volume. Eighty-seven percent of all fresh fruits and vegetables are moved by truck. This is expected to exceed 90 percent in the early 1980's. The majority of this traffic is transported by exempt carriers.

Many of these exempt haulers are owner-operators who own one unit. In other instances, several units may be owned by one individual, or as many as 200, and operated in this type of service. (Fig. 5-3.)

The arrangements for truck movement of exempt agricultural commodities are usually made by brokers. These brokers, some 1,000 in number, are not subject to regulation by the Interstate Commerce Commission as are brokers of general commodities. The truck operator contacts or calls the broker's office notifying him that he is available for transporting exempt commodities to some particular point. The broker then makes the arrangements with the shipper, some of which may require delivery within a specified number of hours; and such matters as late arrival, damaged goods, and similar details are handled by the broker with the agricultural hauler.

Many "truck stops" catering to truckers post on their bulletin boards notices of loads of exempt commodities which are available. Some grain companies are particularly active in arranging return loads of grain for exempt carriers. Typical arrangements are those in which the driver is given a 20 percent advance, and the balance is wired or mailed upon delivery of the grain.

Some exempt haulers follow a regular pattern of operation—that is, they operate from one general area to another area. Others, however, are more migratory in nature. For example, an exempt hauler of agricultural commodities in Michigan carried a load of fresh onions to

Fig. 5-3. Five-axle unit used by largest truck transporter of grain. Courtesy: Shupe Brothers.

Florida. Upon finding there was not an immediate return load of citrus products to Michigan, he carried a load to Washington, D.C., since he wanted to do some sightseeing in Washington. He then leased his unit to a certificated carrier and carried a load of nonexempt commodities back to Florida, and then carried exempt commodities back to Michigan.

It is difficult to secure precise data on the rates exempt carriers charge. In the perishable field, the author's research leads to the conclusion that early in the season for an item, such as citrus fruit, when there are a large number of trucks available, the rate tends to decline from perhaps $1.25 per 100 pounds to 85 cents. But as the full crop starts coming in and the truckers are busy, the rates go back to $1.25 and may go higher if a shortage of equipment develops.

A stabilizing rate factor is existent in different types of exempt transportation through the truck brokers as well as published rates. For example, suggested truck rates per 100 pounds or per carton from Florida points to all major metropolitan areas on all perishables are published and distributed by truck brokers. The suggested rates differentiate by commodity but all are geared to truckload lots. The rate pattern shows great similarity to regulated truck rates. Suggested rules covering count and weight, unloading charges, diversion, charges for extra stops as well as other matters are published. For example, the suggested watermelon truck rates per 100 pounds are established by zone (Fig. 5-4) and suggested rates are established to major points in the United States.

In many of the perishable markets, there are unloading fees which the exempt trucker must pay. Rail shipments that come into the same area are not charged the fees. Such fees may be assessed even though there is no help in unloading.

Some exempt truckers of perishables in 1979 felt that a minimum of 90 cents per truck-mile should be charged. On the other hand, there are some successful truckers of these commodities operating at 75 cents per truck-mile.

The turnover rate of exempt truckers is not known precisely and would certainly vary with the product transported. Livestock haulers have a lower turnover rate than the long distance perishable transporters. Based on the author's research, the latter ranges from 10 to 15 percent a year, conservatively speaking.

Approximately 99 percent of the cattle and calves, 100 percent of the hogs, and 98 percent of the sheep and lambs move from ranges, farms, and feed lots to markets and slaughtering points by trucks in exempt transportation.[5]

Livestock hauling tends to have a somewhat lower average haul than that of agricultural commodities. In livestock hauling, a conventional bill of lading is not used by most carriers. At the time that the shipment is picked up at the farm, no receipt is given to the farmer. The livestock yards, however, provide a form which is a truck consignment. One of these tickets is filled out for each shipper. This will contain information as to the livestock picked up by the trucker and delivered by him, as well as the rate per 100 pounds and other information.[6]

Livestock haulers are domiciled in the community in which they operate and hold themselves out as common carriers. The rates which they charge one farmer in a community will be the same as they charge another for the same minimum so, although they are free to establish rates which vary, their rates tend to be fixed rates for the same general weights.

Livestock haulers serving a particular livestock market may secure authority to transport certain specified nonexempt commodities for the return haul. The tendency, however, even if they possess such rights, is

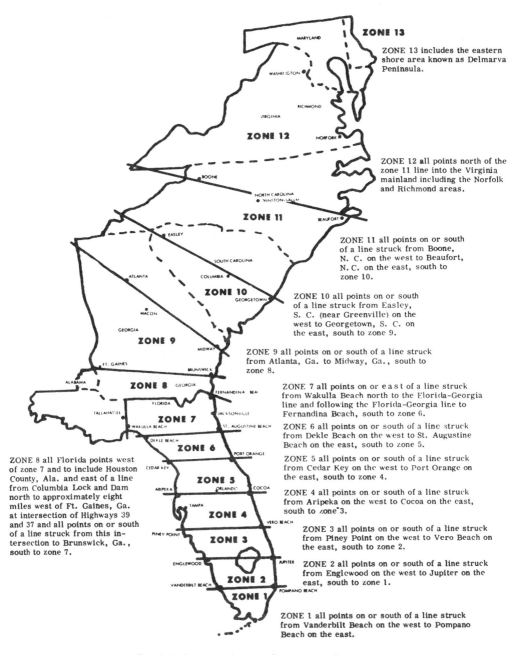

ZONE 13

ZONE 13 includes the eastern shore area known as Delmarva Peninsula.

ZONE 12 all points north of the zone 11 line into the Virginia mainland including the Norfolk and Richmond areas.

ZONE 11 all points on or south of a line struck from Boone, N. C. on the west to Beaufort, N. C. on the east, south to zone 10.

ZONE 10 all points on or south of a line struck from Easley, S. C. (near Greenville) on the west to Georgetown, S. C. on the east, south to zone 9.

ZONE 9 all points on or south of a line struck from Atlanta, Ga. to Midway, Ga., south to zone 8.

ZONE 7 all points on or e a s t of a line struck from Wakulla Beach north to the Florida-Georgia line and following the Florida-Georgia line to Fernandina Beach, south to zone 6.

ZONE 6 all points on or south of a line struck from Dekle Beach on the west to St. Augustine Beach on the east, south to zone 5.

ZONE 8 all Florida points west of zone 7 and to include Houston County, Ala. and east of a line from Columbia Lock and Dam north to approximately eight miles west of Ft. Gaines, Ga. at intersection of Highways 39 and 37 and all points on or south of a line struck from this intersection to Brunswick, Ga., south to zone 7.

ZONE 5 all points on or south of a line struck from Cedar Key on the west to Port Orange on the east, south to zone 4.

ZONE 4 all points on or south of a line struck from Aripeka on the west to Cocoa on the east, south to zone 3.

ZONE 3 all points on or south of a line struck from Piney Point on the west to Vero Beach on the east, south to zone 2.

ZONE 2 all points on or south of a line struck from Englewood on the west to Jupiter on the east, south to zone 1.

ZONE 1 all points on or south of a line struck from Vanderbilt Beach on the west to Pompano Beach on the east.

Fig. 5-4. Suggested zones for watermelon rates.

124

to lease their unit on the return from the livestock market to a certificated general commodity hauler, since the livestock hauler does not have a sales force nor the time to solicit business for the return haul. If the livestock hauler has a particularly heavy demand for his service, he may not even lease his truck for the return haul because this ties up his equipment longer, since he has to go to the terminal to load the freight. Therefore, he may make the return trip empty.

Many exempt carriers maintain no terminals, whereas others, such as livestock haulers, may have a concentration yard which serves as their terminal. When there are but two or three head of livestock to be shipped by one farmer, the stock may be picked up in a small truck and transported to the livestock hauler's loading area, where the stock may be loaded with others in an over-the-road vehicle.

It should not be assumed that all agricultural commodities are transported by exempt carriers. As a result of two court cases,[7] the Interstate Commerce Commission permits carriers of so-called "nonexempt" items—that is, carriers to which operating authority has been granted—to use their vehicles for transporting agricultural commodities, providing the exempt commodities are not moved in the same vehicle at the same time with a nonexempt commodity. Thus, when a regulated carrier finds it to its advantage to move an exempt commodity, perhaps on a return haul, it may do so. A certain amount of this traffic is moved by regulated carriers to reduce empty miles but so far it is less than 10 percent of revenue of Class I carriers.

The agricultural cooperative exemption has been broadened so that such an organization may transport both exempt and nonexempt commodities (PL-90-433). In addition to agricultural commodities, farm supplies may be transported for its members without limitation, and other products on a for-hire basis for nonmembers up to 15 percent of its total transportation as measured by tonnage.

**Independent truckers**

For many years, there have been owner-operators in the trucking industry who own their own tractor semitrailer unit and transport exempt commodities, as just explained, or who transport for regulated carriers under a contract or lease arrangement. These individual entrepreneurs who transport for regulated carriers may perform such service for a specialized division of a general commodity carrier, such as a steel division or a refrigerated food division. In other cases, the owner-operators render service to carriers which are themselves specialized common carriers of a commodity or a commodity group, such as paper products, building materials or household goods. (See Fig. 5-5 for carriers seeking owner-operators.) The intercity movement of the latter is performed almost entirely by owner-operators.

The exact number of independent truckers is not known but the estimates are from 200,000 to 250,000, 73,000 of which are under long-term lease to regulated carriers. About 30 organizations represent them such as the Fraternal Association of Specialty Haulers that claims to represent 25,000 owner-operators transporting iron and steel products. These organizations are loosely affiliated with the National Independent Truckers Unit Council.

The public's attention was focused on the independent truckers as a result of the fuel crisis in 1973-74 and again in 1977 and 1979. Some key highways were blockaded by the independent truckers, and a nationwide closedown was undertaken to protest skimming, higher fuel prices, in-

Fig. 5-5. Carrier advertisements seeking owner-operators.

ability to get fuel, energy-saving lower speed limits of 55 miles per hour, and lack of uniformity in truck size and weight. In the first six months of 1979, diesel fuel prices rose 40 percent and, in many areas, diesel prices exceeded gasoline prices. Fuel surcharge pass throughs granted by the Interstate Commerce Commission helped alleviate the situation.

The independent truckers who transport for exempt carriers receive varying amounts but 90 percent of the transport charge is a typical amount. The trucker has to pay his operating expenses from this percentage. In addition, he may also have to pay a market entry fee. These fees are applied at state farmers' markets and are used for sanitation, security, and upkeep. For agricultural transporters, there are often unloading charges at the receiver's dock, as well, that must be paid by the trucker from his percentage. Truckers are paid upon delivery of their load assuming they secure a clear receipt of delivery.

Typically, the grower or shipper will deal with five or six brokers and divide business among them. The broker who has arranged for the shipment between the shipper and the independent trucker usually charges a fee of from 8 to 10 percent of the total freight bill. He collects this amount from the shipper or receiver as a part of the overall freight bill. The broker deducts his fee prior to reimbursing the trucker for his agreed share of the total. Such fees vary in different regions and are higher in the northwest where 12 percent is the fee if an advance to the trucker is required. Some of the brokers of exempt commodities are also for-hire carriers.

The truck broker may deal with a produce broker (merchandise or buying broker) who, in turn, deals with the shipper or grower. In such cases, the produce broker also receives a commission, generally 5 percent, on the produce transported.

Independent truckers who are operating on a long-term basis with a specialized division of a regulated motor carrier have their revenues as a part of the collective bargaining agreement of the labor contract. The percentage from gross revenues per truckload is as follows: 13 percent for the trailer, 33 percent for the tractor, 29 percent for the driver, and 6 percent for fringes such as insurance. The independent trucker, in all cases, has to pay all his own operating expenses, such as fuel, etc. To continue in this type of relationship, an owner-operator must gross at least $71,000 minimum in order to secure $20,000 for driving. This would mean he is driving 90,000 miles a year and averaging $.79 a mile.

Some companies have a variable mileage pay scale. One company pays $1.50 for distances of up to 100 miles, $.65 for 250 to 700 miles, and $.59 for distances of over 2,000 miles. All empty miles are paid at the rate of $.50 a mile by this carrier.

Independent truckers make use of truck stops along their routes, particularly on the interstate system. These stops provide not only fuel but also many have barber shops, convenience stores, motels, restaurants, and weighing scales. Some can accommodate more than 100 trucks at any given time. The stop is also often a source of information regarding return loads as truck brokers are often located here.

### Private carriage

Private motor carriers are the second group of carriers in this general classification of for-hire and private carriers. A private carrier is a shipper (a manufacturer or merchant) who provides his own transportation service in whole or in part. His primary business is other than transportation.

The Transportation Act of 1958 further delineated private carriage by amending the Interstate Commerce Act to provide that no person engaged in any business enterprise other than transportation shall transport property by motor vehicle in interstate or foreign commerce for business purposes unless such transportation is within the scope and in furtherance of that person's primary business enterprise, other than transportation. The mere ownership of the commodity transported does not make the transporter a private carrier.

The transportation must be incidental to, and in furtherance of, some established non-carrier business. Private carriers require no operating authority from the Commission, since they are not subject to economic regulation but only to safety regulation by the Department of Transportation. In 1978, the Commission reversed a long-standing policy and now permits private carriers to operate also as for-hire carriers on return hauls.

There were 103,344 private carriers in 1979. The number of private trucks used in intercity operation has continued to increase at a relatively rapid rate. Of the total, the largest number is operated by manufacturers and distributors of food—23 percent; metal fabricators are next with 14 percent; and 9 percent is operated by petroleum companies. The remainder is distributed throughout industry.

There are a number of reasons that prompt business organizations to conduct all or a part of their own trucking operations rather than to rely on for-hire carriers. The use of its own equipment (a) assures general improvement in service; (b) assures absence of congestion at loading docks; (c) assures the safe arrival of goods not mixed with goods of other shippers and not exposed to extra or inexperienced handling; (d) assures on-time deliveries of finished goods at customers' doors and of raw materials and supplies at their plants; (e) makes possible the avoidance of expensive packaging; (f) provides advertising through the use of the company's own trucks which are, in effect, "rolling billboards"; (g) makes possible the charging for the service of an amount equal to or exceeding the rate of common or contract carriers, thus making private carriage a self-supporting enterprise; and (h) provides flexibility through the freedom to operate wherever desired.

Some of the disadvantages of private carriage are the cost of equipment, the cost of maintenance and difficulty in securing personnel capable of maintaining equipment properly (this may be handled by truck rental or truck leasing), the economic loss occasioned by operating the vehicle empty on return movements, and the burden on management of supervising a motor carrier operation which is different from the normal business of the company.

Because of their strong competitive position in relation to for-hire carriers, private carriers will be discussed further in Chapter 19.

### Diversity of motor carrier operations

As this chapter points out, the trucking industry is a very diversified, hetergeneous group. The different types of operations that have emerged from this diversity have special rate and service capabilities that fill the needs of a wide range of shippers, including the shipper as a carrier. Current ton-miles transported by each type of carrier have been estimated to be divided as follows: regular route common carriers of general freight, 20 percent; irregular route special commodity carriers, 22 percent; contract carriers, 6 percent; intrastate and local carriers, 10 percent; exempt agricultural carriers, 11 percent; and private carriers, 31 percent.[8]

## Property brokers

Property brokerage is a type of operation that is not a carrier operation. Property brokers which handle exempt commodities, as explained earlier, are not subject to Federal regulation (however, Florida and Texas require licenses) but property brokers that arrange for transportation of regulated commodities are subject to regulation by the Interstate Commerce Commission. These brokers were a part of the trucking industry before the passage of the Motor Carrier Act in 1935. Most motor carriers of freight in those days were small operators with a limited amount of equipment and without a need for or the means to support an organization that would include salaried salesmen. Many of the carriers offered specialized services—for example, household goods carriers operating in irregular route service over a large area. Others operated out of their home base and did not feel that they could maintain even part-time salesmen at all of the points that they served; yet, in order to have efficiency of operation, they sought some way of securing loads between and from these points away from their home base.

From these needs developed agencies, independent of both the shippers and the carriers, which were devoted to the solicitation of traffic to be moved by carriers selected by them and from whom they received a fee for their services. These became known as "motor transportation agents" or "brokers." Some states enacted laws regulating the business of these motor transportation agents which were not themselves engaged in transportation but which would make the necessary arrangements for or the selling of transportation. Some of the operations of the brokers in these earlier phases of the development of the motor carrier industry were beneficial, but there were other instances of irresponsible persons resorting to exploitation of the carriers through excessive charges and certain other questionable practices. The Motor Carrier Act of 1935 set forth regulation of brokers in Section 203 (a) (18) now 10924 and Section 221 now 11144.

As defined by the Commission, a "broker means any person not included in the term 'motor carrier' and not a bona fide employee or agent of any such a carrier, who, as principal or agent, sells or offers for sale transportation subject to Part II of the Interstate Commerce Act, or negotiates for, or holds himself out by advertisement, solicitation, or otherwise, as one who sells, provides, furnishes, contracts, or arranges for such transportation."[9] The operating authority issued by the Commission to brokers is a license.

This definition is particularly important to household goods carriers because many of them have authority to perform a part of the transportation haul, but they may turn over the shipment at the origin point to a carrier which will take it all the way to destination. The proviso does not require such carriers to secure licenses as brokers. Motor common carriers which surrender to others for compensation shipments the line hauls of which they are not authorized to perform in whole or in part are brokers.

The act provided that the Commission could establish reasonable requirements with respect to licensing of brokers, their financial responsibilities, accounts, records, reports, operations, and practices which became effective in 1952. Currently, 70 licenses have been issued to property brokers, most of which have been issued to brokers of household goods.

There are two classes of so-called "nonbrokerage" services: (1) those which are supplied to shippers, such as warehousing, sorting, storage, preparation of shipments for moving, packing, crating, stenciling, checking freight bills, and handling claims with carriers; and (2) those supplied to carriers, such as arranging for, or the leasing of, vehicles by or for carriers; maintenance of dock or terminal facilities; performing pickup and delivery service; preparing, arranging, and collecting freight bills; and processing claims.

The Interstate Commerce Commission has prescribed rules and regulations governing the practices of brokers of transportation of property. A broker may not advertise in any manner to offer his service as a broker without showing in such advertisement his status as a broker in type as large as any other used in the same advertisement.

Brokers may not issue any bill of lading or freight bill in any name except that of a carrier, nor may a broker issue an order for service which does not clearly show the name and address of the broker and the fact that the order is executed as a broker of transportation.

A broker may not charge or receive compensation from a motor carrier for brokerage service performed in connection with any shipment which he owns, or in which he has a material interest, or the routing of which he controls by reason of any affiliation with, or nonbrokerage relationship to, the shipper, consignor, or consignee. Under this ruling, a shipper is not prohibited from hiring a broker to route all his traffic, but when such a nonbrokerage service is rendered for a shipper, the compensation for it may not be collected by the broker from the carrier.

### Agents as distinguished from freight brokers

There have been a number of occasions when the Commission has had to distinguish between a bona fide agent and a broker, as those terms are used in the act.[10] In one case, it was pointed out that "every broker is in a sense an agent, but not every agent is a broker. The chief distinguishing feature is that a broker generally acts in a certain sense as an agent for both parties to a particular transaction. Strict agency implies exclusiveness, whereas brokerage involves a holding out generally."[11]

A "bona fide agent," as distinguished from a broker, according to the Commission, is a person who is part of the normal organization of a motor carrier and performs his duties under the direction of the carrier, pursuant to a preexisting agreement with the carrier, providing for a continuing relationship between them and precluding the exercise of discretion on the part of the agent in allocating traffic as between the principal and others.

### Commission agents

Large motor common carriers have adopted the practice of using the pickup and delivery and platform services of local cartage companies in communities too small to warrant the establishment of a company-operated terminal. In many instances, the traffic is dropped off at the agency station by the over-the-road unit at hours of the day when the consignee's dock or plant is not open. These agents, called "commission agents," are paid for the work they render, such as collection and delivery, platform handling, and billing and collecting, on the basis of a certain compensation per 100 pounds, with the commission per 100 pounds varying with the weight of the shipment; that is, the fee for a 300-pound shipment may be 10 cents per 100 pounds, but for a shipment of over 5,000 pounds, the fee may be 4 cents per 100 pounds.

### Freight forwarders

The surface freight forwarder holds itself out to the public to provide a through transportation service from point of receipt of shipment to the final destination in its own name and under its own responsibility. Freight forwarders are common carriers which have other regulated motor, rail, and water common carriers physically move their shipments for them. Therefore, freight forwarders are extensive purchasers of transportation. The over-the-road[12] movement is made in equipment not owned by the forwarder, except under one of the piggyback arrangements described later, in which the forwarder does own the equipment. The function of the freight forwarder is to combine numerous small shipments of individual consignors into consolidated consignments which move in carloads or truckloads, but its tariffs list through less-than-carload or less-truckload rates from origin to destination. The forwarder bears the cost of the transportation it employs, as well as the cost of solicitation, billing, platform handling, loading and unloading, and the investigation and payment of claims performed by it. Freight forwarders have, over a period of years, extensively used the services of motor common carriers. In addition, a number (11) of major motor carriers have secured freight forwarder operating authority and operate these companies as subsidiaries.

There are a number of ways in which freight forwarders utilize motor common carriers, but these can be grouped into essentially three classes: (a) the movement of individual shipments from the consignor to the forwarder's terminal (concentration point) and delivery from the forwarder's terminal (break-bulk point) to the consignee both before and after the transportation of such shipments as part of a consolidated consignment; (b) the movement of an aggregation of individual shipments in so-called truckloads between terminals preceding or following the carriage of consolidated consignments in carload by rail; (c) the movement of an aggregation of individual shipments in so-called truckloads between terminals.

It has been estimated that the motor common carriers of general commodities receive on the average between 1 and 2 percent of their revenues from freight forwarders' traffic. An estimated 3,000 motor common carriers have agreements with one or more freight forwarders, and a few motor common carriers transport exclusively for the forwarders. The latter carriers are often referred to as "captive carriers," since their entire service can be rendered only on behalf of freight forwarders in accordance with their operating authority.

The basis of compensation has been developed by trial and error over a long period of time and follows no uniform pattern. Contracts between the freight forwarder and the motor common carrier have been negotiated in terms of traffic requirements of the particular service to be rendered, and seldom have these requirements been the same between any two points. Some of the agreements are oral, and others are memoranda or letters confirming agreements made orally. Motor carriers have agreed to a lower basis of compensation where the freight forwarder traffic moved in the direction in which the trucks would ordinarily be returning empty or with light loads. Some of the factors that have been considered in individual negotiations are labor costs, amount of light and bulky traffic, volume of movement, traffic flow, and competition among forwarders.

Section 10766 (b) was amended in 1950 to prohibit the publication and maintenance of joint rates between freight forwarders and motor common carriers after September 19, 1951, and to permit motor common carriers to perform certain transportation services for freight forwarders under contracts to be filed with the Commission.[13] One freight forwarder has more than 4,000 contracts on file.

On shipments moving from origins to concentration points and from break-bulk points to ultimate destinations, less than published rates may be contracted for, regardless of distance or size of shipment.

On movements from a concentration point to a break-bulk point under the contracts, payment for less-truckload lots may be at less than the published rates over any distance figure. However, payment for truckload lots may be at less than the published rates only when the distance is less than 450 miles.

Another type of rates are assembly and distribution rates published under Section 10725 (b). These are published rates in tariff form which are on file with the Interstate Commerce Commission and are not the result of negotiation. They are lower than those applicable at the same time between the same points on nonforwarder traffic. This results in a rate of payment to the motor carriers for the handling of freight forwarder traffic which is generally below the level of the motor carriers' public local tariff rates.

Generally, regulatory bodies have not permitted a carrier in one mode of transportation to acquire a carrier in another mode of transportation except on a very limited basis and under restrictive conditions. The Civil Aeronautics Board in 1974 granted approval for two motor carriers to acquire control of cargo-only, air taxi operators. The latter are noncertificated carriers which operate smaller aircraft. The Board granted an exemption to these motor carriers to acquire the air taxi operators.

### Combination, intermodal, or bi-modal service

There are several types of service that use the facilities of two or more modes of transport in a single move. Service may be provided by a combination of rail and motor, rail/motor and water, or motor and air. The intermodal service of rail and motor is the one that is more frequently used.

Railroads have developed an increasing amount of service in which a trailer or container is loaded at origin and is then physically transported by the rail carrier on a flatcar to its destination; there a truck-tractor moves it to the area where it is unloaded. Six types of trailer-on-flatcar ("piggyback") service have developed. One type, Plan I, is the transportation of trailers or containers owned by motor common carriers. The motor carrier solicits the freight, ships it on motor carrier bills of lading, and bills the freight at truck rates. The motor carrier pays the railroad either a division of the revenue or a flat charge per trailer or container. Plan II is transportation provided by the railroads in their own trailers or containers. The railroad solicits business under rail-truck competitive rates. Plan II½ is a combination of Plans II and III whereby the shipper furnishes the trailer or container but the railroad performs the terminal service. A fourth type, Plan III, is that in which the shipper or forwarder provides his own trailers or containers, which he delivers to the railhead. The railroad transports them to destination. Railroad bills of lading are used, and rail rates are based on the commodity and quantity moved or on a flat amount per trailer or container. Plan IV is the rail movement of shipper or forwarder trailers or containers on shipper flatcars. The shipper takes trailers or containers to and from the railroads and loads and unloads the flatcar. Rates are based on a flat charge per car, whether the units are loaded or empty. Under Plan V, joint rail-motor rates are established. This has the effect of extending the territory of each carrier to that served by the other. Either may solicit traffic for the through movement. The motor carrier portion of the haul is over the highway in the area which it is authorized to serve, while the rail portion of the haul is in TOFC or COFC service over the railroad. More than 60 railroads participate in one or more of the plans.

Increased use is being made of containers on flatcars or flatbed trailers which are cargo-type body equipment without running gear. Containers may be transferred among rail, motor, water, and air carriers.

Trailer-on-flatcar and container-on-flatcar have developed from 3.0 percent of the revenue freight carloadings in 1964 to 7.8 percent in 1978. Of the six TOFC-COFC plans, Plan II in which the railroad provides its own door-to-door service has declined relatively in an expanding TOFC market. On the other hand, Plan II½ in which the railroad furnishes the trailer or container, and the shipper performs the service to and from the rail terminal is where significant growth has occurred. More than 50 percent of all TOFC-COFC traffic moves under this plan. In Plans III and IV, where the trailers or containers are owned or leased by freight forwarders or shippers, there has been modest growth.

There is some evidence that the railroad TOFC-COFC terminal operations are a deterrent to their providing the most effective service for these shippers. Although this traffic, from a revenue point of view, appears attractive, the service that is provided has not been good enough to attract the volume of traffic that many people had forecast.

Trailer-on-ship, or "fishyback," has developed somewhat more slowly. One type of operation is that in which the trailers are rolled on and rolled off the ship. Another type uses a demountable container moved on a flatbed trailer or flatcar to shipside where the container is lifted on the ship and at destination is lifted off. The trend is toward the latter operation because the undercarriage of a trailer is space consuming on a ship.

Several ships have been converted to container handling, and containers designed to stack six high are in use. Some container ships are in coastwise service, whereas others are in service to foreign countries. A greater volume of household goods is moving in containers from interior points by highway and then by water to overseas destinations. Several motor carriers have secured operating authorities to transport containers from and to certain U.S. ports. The volume of this traffic is expected to grow.

Attention is also being given to bi-modal service which utilizes a highway trailer that is equipped with both steel wheels and rubber wheels that are retractable and can be operated on both rail and highway. A unit such as this eliminates the need for rail flatcars that are used in TOFC operations. Currently, however, these units are designed to operate only in complete trains since they cannot be coupled to conventional rail cars. Special truck tractors, rather than switching locomotives, are used to make up or break the trains.

Some intercity motor carriers have developed a truck-air service, which is a combination service with air carriers. Service is provided from a point on the motor carrier's route not served by the airline. Some shipments are made in shipping containers sealed at origin point and moved by truck and air to ultimate destination.

### QUESTIONS AND PROBLEMS

1. Differentiate between (a) irregular route, radial service, and (b) irregular route, nonradial service.

2. List the motor carriers of property on the basis of (a) type of carrier, and (b) type of commodities.

3. What type of operation would a common carrier, Class C-2, be? Common carrier, Class C-9?

4. What are independent truckers? How would you determine if they have grown in number and importance in the past decade?

5. Do you feel it wise for motor carriers to acquire freight forwarders? Why or why not?

6. Define (a) distributive operations, and (b) key-point operations of a common carrier of general commodities.

7. What are the types of contract carriers? How do contract carrier operating costs compare with those of common carriers? Why?

8. What is the statutory difference between a common and a contract motor carrier?

9. "It is estimated that there were about three times more exempt carriers operating interstate . . . than there were common and contract interstate carriers of property." Comment.

10. Enumerate the reasons that prompt business firms to operate their own fleets of private trucks and not to rely on for-hire carriers. What is the trend?

11. Distinguish between household goods brokers and freight brokers.

12. How can an agent be distinguished from a freight broker?·

13. Describe the different ways in which freight forwarders utilize motor common carriers.

14. Will the growth of containerization have much effect upon for-hire motor carriers?

### FOOTNOTES TO CHAPTER 5

[1] This section of the Motor Carrier Act of 1935 provided that the Interstate Commerce Commission could establish classification of brokers and carriers as the special nature of the service performed required; this was accomplished in 2 MCC 703 (1937). The Motor Carrier Act was later incorporated into Part II of the Interstate Commerce Act.

[2] Interstate Commerce Commission economic regulation and state regulation of motor carriers are discussed in a later chapter.

[3] Administrative Ruling No. 76, 117 MCC 433, 1972.

[4] Administrative Ruling No. 119, October, 1974.

[5] Motor Vehicle Manufacturers Association, *Motor Truck Facts* (Detroit, 1974), p. 36.

[6] No standard document is used as a receipt when exempt shipments are made. The International Apple Association, Inc., had one of its committees prepare a Uniform Exempt Commodity Bill of Lading which was suggested for use by exempt carriers but it has had limited acceptance.

[7] *ICC* v. *Dunn*, 166 F. 2d. 116 (1948); *ICC* v. *Service Trucking Co., Inc.*, 186 F. 2d 400 (1951).

[8] Paul O. Roberts, "Some Aspects of Regulatory Reform in the Trucking Industry," paper presented at Workshop on Motor Carrier Economic Regulation, Washington, D.C., April 7, 1977.

[9] Section 203 (a) (18).

[10] *Cain Broker Application*, 2 MCC 633 (1937); and *Copes Broker Application*, 27 MCC 161 (1940).

[11] *Copes Broker Application*, 27 MCC 161 (1940).

[12] The term *over the road* is used interchangeably with *line haul* and means the same type of movement, that is, intercity movement of freight using heavy equipment.

[13] Public Law 881, 81st Cong., 2d sess., December 20, 1950.

# chapter 6

# Local and specialized carriers

## LOCAL CARRIERS

Urban (local) freight movements have elicited little research, planning, or public interest. This facet of transport does not possess the glamour or political appeal of urban passenger transportation; yet the cost of urban freight is reflected in the myriad of goods we consume and use. Such costs have increased disproportionately to intercity truck costs. Our research in this area has been thin and limited, and public sector efforts directed toward understanding the problems and formulating systematic solutions for more efficient movement of freight within the urban area have been minimal.[1]

Local cartage operations are the beginning and the end of every motor carrier operation in pickup and delivery service, and they represent extensive local operations in motor transportation. The Interstate Commerce Commission's definition of local cartage service, as given earlier, is that a local cartage carrier is any person which undertakes to transport property or any class or classes of property by motor vehicle for compensation, when such transportation is performed in interstate or foreign commerce wholly within a municipality, or between contiguous municipalities, or within a zone adjacent to, and commercially a part of, any such municipality or municipalities. The majority of local cartage operations fall within the category of exempt carriers, under the exemption as defined in the Interstate Commerce Act for vehicles used in transportation of property wholly within a municipality or zone adjacent to or commercially a part of such a municipality.

For the purpose of accounting and the compilation of statistical data, the Commission defines the area of local cartage service as transportation performed within a city or town, including the suburban area contiguous thereto. It classifies those carriers that derive 50 percent or more of their operating revenues from local service as local carriers.

Local cartage operators would like to have included in local cartage service the area that could be reached and served by them by going out from and back to the local carrier's domicile in the course of a normal working day. This distance would vary, depending upon the type of truck used in the local cartage operation—a lighter vehicle increasing the distance covered and a heavier vehicle decreasing the distance. Another way of defining the area included in local cartage service is that which is contained in some of the labor agreements between local cartage carriers and labor unions; that is, the contract may define local cartage as service to any of the points within 40 miles of the city hall or the carrier's garage.

Virtually all of local urban freight needs are met today by use of trucks. Some operate primarily in downtown areas and others transport goods into the suburban areas. Some local truckers serving urban and suburban areas have inbound shipments only whereas others are both collectors and distributors. One study analyzing the urban freight aspects has made a mathematical analysis of the relationship of local for-hire trucking needs, the standard of living as expressed in effective buying income, and metropolitan area populations.[2] The findings indicated that by utilizing mean value substitution, one local service for-hire truck is required for every 300 urban dwellers or for every $1.2 million in effective buying income.[3]

An increasing number of local operations are more aptly described as short haul in nature.[4] One factor that has been instrumental in this development has been the loss of transfer hauling between stores and rail depots because of the door-to-door service rendered by over-the-road motor carriers. The location of many new plants in suburban areas and the shift of population to the suburbs with the resultant change in market areas are other factors causing an alteration in the operations of local cartage carriers.

Special package delivery and courier services are available in larger urban areas, and increasing use is made of taxicabs for intercity deliveries. Although important in meeting customer needs, the volume is small.

Local operations were the antecedents of for-hire motor transportation. Local operators started by using teams and wagons to deliver local merchandise, to haul coal, and the like. It was from this early beginning in wagons and carts that the term *local cartage* developed. Some of these companies have been operating for more than a century. These organizations vary greatly in size, from one-truck operators in small towns to organizations operating in metropolitan areas which offer many different types of local cartage service and use 100 or more trucks. Each one operates in a different manner and handles different commodities, although many of them are common carriers. Far more vehicles are used in local operations than in intercity operations, both in private and in for-hire carriage. In private operations, there are almost nine times as many vehicles in local transportation as in intercity, and in for-hire transportation, almost twice as many.

### Commercial zones

Most local cartage carriers are not economically regulated by the Interstate Commerce Commission, since their operations are within so-called commercial zones. Even though the operations may be interstate in nature within the zone, they are exempt from Commission economic regulation. For example, a local cartage carrier operating in St. Louis, Missouri, may have operations that cross the river to East St. Louis, Illinois. Such operations are interstate in nature; but, inasmuch as the carrier is operating in a commercial zone of a municipality of contiguous municipalities designated by the Commission, it is exempt from economic regulation as an interstate motor carrier. Such interstate local cartage intrazonal operations are subject, however, to Department of Transportation safety regulation as to qualifications and maximum hours of service of employees. If a vehicle is transporting dangerous articles, such as flammables, in quantities that require the vehicle to be placarded, all safety regulations apply.

The limits of the commercial zones are determined by the Commission, and carriers operating wholly within a commercial zone are exempt from economic regulation by the Commission. This exemption does not apply, on the other hand, if the transportation is under a common control, management, or arrangement for a continuous carriage or shipment to or from a point without such municipality. This would mean that if the pickup and delivery at either end of an interstate over-the-road carriage is performed under common control, management, or arrangement for continuous carriage, the carrier would be subject to regulation even though it was operating in a commercial zone. In this manner, some local cartage operators do come under the economic regulation of the Interstate Commerce Commission.

The first commercial zones were established in 1937 by the Commission. Through conferences and field surveys and development of certain other facts, the Commission initially established the commercial zones for a number of the larger cities. Subsequently, 38 commercial zones were specifically prescribed.

In addition, the Commission using a population-mileage formula defined commercial zones for all cities for which such zones had not been previously established. Commercial zones applied only to incorporated cities and, as they grew and industrial and commercial activity expanded, busi-

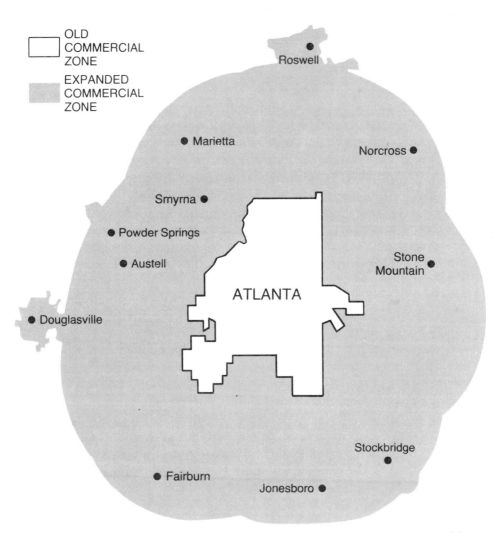

Fig. 6-1. The expansion of the commercial zone of Atlanta as a result of the application of the new population-mileage formula.

ness interests in many instances sought to have the zones expanded. Some individual modifications resulted from litigation that sometimes extended over a decade. The Commission in 1977 increased the population-mileage formula to embrace broad territorial areas. All specifically designated zones were replaced with zones based on this formula. This action was opposed by local and short-haul carriers but supported by long-haul carriers and some shippers. The formula was upheld by the courts in 1978 and is as follows:[5]

1. The municipality itself, hereinafter called the base municipality.
2. All municipalities within the United States which are contiguous to the base municipality.
3. All other municipalities within the United States and all unincorporated areas within the United States which are adjacent to the base municipality, as follows:
    *a)* When the base municipality has a population less than 2,500, all unincorporated areas within 3 miles of its corporate limits and all of any other municipality any part of which is within 3 miles of the corporate limits of the base municipality.
    *b)* When the base municipality has a population of 2,500 but less than 25,000, all unincorporated areas within 4 miles of its corporate limits and all of any other municipality any part of which is within 4 miles of the corporate limits of the base municipality.
    *c)* When the base municipality has a population of 25,000 but less than 100,000, all unincorporated areas within 6 miles of its corporate limits and all of any other municipality any part of which is within 6 miles of the corporate limits of the base municipality.
    *d)* When the base municipality has a population of 100,000 but less than 200,000, all unincorporated areas within 8 miles of its corporate limits and all of any other municipality any part of which is within 8 miles of the corporate limits of the base municipality.
    *e)* When the base municipality has a population of 200,000 but less than 500,000, all unincorporated areas within 10 miles of its corporate limits and all of any other municipality any part of which is within 10 miles of the corporate limits of the base municipality.
    *f)* When the base municipality has a population of 500,000 but less than 1,000,000, all unincorporated areas within 15 miles of its corporate limits and all of any other municipality any part of which is within 15 miles of the corporate limits of the base municipality.
    *g)* When the base municipality has a population of 1,000,000 or more, all unincorporated areas within 20 miles of its corporate limits and all of any other municipality any part of which is within 20 miles of the corporate limits of the base municipality.
4. All municipalities wholly surrounded, or so wholly surrounded except for a water boundary, by the base municipality, by any United States municipality contiguous thereto, or by any United States municipality adjacent thereto which is included in the commercial zone of such base municipality under the provisions of (3) of this finding.

In determining distances, airline mileage (statute miles rather than nautical miles)[6] must be used; and the population for any municipality shall be that shown in the last decennial census.

Figure 6-1 shows the substantial expansion in the Atlanta commercial zone as a result of the application of the new formula. If one analyzes the effects of the rules, one can observe instances, such as Baltimore and Washington, D.C., in which the zones are co-extensive. Operations between the two cities, therefore, are free from economic regulation even though the transportation is interstate in nature.

The fact that a local carrier is under common control, management, or arrangement with a line haul carrier which serves the same city is not, in itself, sufficient to nullify the exemption of Section 10526 (b)(1)(A) when there are not joint services or interchange of traffic. However, the common arrangement which would nullify the exemption is one involving arrangement for continuous carriage or shipment between a local carrier and another carrier, either motor, rail, water, air, forwarder, or express. The arrangement may be either oral or written, or in the form of a contract or an agreement. It must be between the local carrier and another carrier for through shipment to or from a point outside the zone to void the exemption.[7]

An arrangement between a local cartage carrier and a shipper or consignee does not nullify the exemption. The local cartage company, under these circumstances, would establish its own rates and make its own contracts, as well as take its instructions from the shipper or consignee; and it may transport within a zone to or from the docks of line haul carriers under the commercial zone exemption.[8]

Most local transportation which does not fall within the commercial zone exemption is exempt under the pickup and delivery exemption contained in Section 10523 (A,B,C). Service under this exemption must be limited to areas in which the motor vehicle transportation consists of genuine transfer, collection, or delivery service as distinguished from line haul service.

Some local transportation does require authority, examples of which are transportation performed for a carrier to or from a point beyond its terminal area or that performed for a carrier not subject to the act, such as a water carrier not subject to subchapter III.

The Commission has held that no common arrangement exists when the pickup and delivery carrier receives compensation from the line haul carrier but is employed by the shipper or consignee, such compensation being the line haul carrier's published collection and delivery allowance.[9] (There are also zones around airports in which the transportation by local carriers of shipments having a prior or subsequent movement by air is exempt from economic regulation. This is called the incidental-to-air exemption and involves the pickup, delivery, or transfer of shipments. The extent of such a zone was 25 miles but was increased, in 1979, to 35 miles from the boundaries of the airport, as well as 35 miles from the corporate municipality any part of whose commercial zone falls within 35 miles of that airport.)

### Terminal areas

Local transportation which is performed under common control, management, or arrangement is exempt from economic regulation under Section 10523. This section excludes those operations which are already subject to the provisions of subchapter I of the act—that is, those motor common carriers which are performing collection, delivery, or transfer services which are a part of rail and rail express services. Under Section 10523 (A,B,C) all transportation by motor vehicle in the performance within terminal areas of collection, delivery, or transfer services by railroads subject to subchapter I, by water carriers subject to subchapter III, or by freight forwarders subject to subchapter IV of the act, or for such carriers or for express companies subject to subchapter I, or for motor carriers subject to subchapter II, is exempt from economic regulation except as a part of the line haul or intercommunity services to which such collection, delivery, or transfer service is incidental.

An exempt freight forwarder that is exempt from economic regulation under subchapter IV of the act does require authority to perform its own pickup and delivery service.[10]

The terminal area of a motor carrier within the meaning of Section 10523 (A,B,C) at any municipality the carrier is authorized to serve consists of and includes all points or places which are within the commercial zone of that municipality and not beyond the limits of the operating authority of the carrier. Thus, the terminal area of a line haul motor carrier at any point which it serves is that area within which it performs or has performed for it bona fide collection, delivery, and transfer service. The phrase "collection, delivery, and transfer service" means intracity or intraterminal transportation performed in the picking up, gathering together, or assembling at origin or in the distribution at destination of less-truckload or less-carload shipments prior or subsequent to an intercity or intercommunity line haul movement and as an incident to such line haul movement.[11] The terminal area of regulated freight forwarders is considered by the Commission to be the same as that of regulated motor carriers.

Pickup, delivery, and transfer of loaded trailers moving in trailer-on-flatcar service is within the exemption when confined to the rail carrier's terminal area.[12]

The terminal area under Section 10523 (A,B,C) of any motor carrier at an unincorporated community has been prescribed by a population-mileage formula by the Commission. Using the post office of the community as the central point, the following distances were prescribed: (1) all points in the United States located within the limits of the operating authority of the motor carrier and within 2½ miles of the post office if the community has a population of less than 2,500, within 4 miles if it has a population of 2,500 but less than 25,000, and within 5½ miles if it has a population of 25,000 or more; (2) all points in any municipality, any part of which is within the limits described in (1); and (3) any municipality wholly surrounded or so surrounded except for a water boundary included in (2).[13]

### Implied authority

The Commission has held that terminal areas may not at any point extend beyond the particular carrier's operating authority, including implied authority. Although a terminal point which is authorized to be served may be a city, it is implied that the grant of authority is to serve the immediate community rather than merely the city. In other words, the authority which is implied is that of serving the community and surrounding industry rather than just the city itself.

Although there has been no formal cancellation of Administrative Rules No. 84 through 87,[14] which deal with commercial zones and terminal areas, Rule No. 84 complements the interpretation which the Commission made in the *Commercial Zone* case in that it permits service on both sides of all intermediate point portions of routes within one mile. Rules No. 85, 86, and 87 would appear to be superseded by the liberal interpretation as to implied authority in *Ex parte MC-37*.[15]

Carriers have the same obligation to serve points under implied authority as they have to serve points specifically described in their certificates and permits. This duty is to serve to the extent of the carrier's ability. If it does not want to render service under the implied authority, it can file with the Commission a request to modify its certificate or permit. [16]

## State regulation

Although local cartage is exempt in general from economic regulation by the Interstate Commerce Commission, Oregon, Washington, and Pennsylvania regulate intrastate local cartage operations. In Pennsylvania, common and contract carriers are under the jurisdiction of the Pennsylvania Public Utility Commission. The legislation in this state does not distinguish between local cartage operations and other types of for-hire carriers but includes all types of for-hire carriers under its jurisdiction. In instances where there has been some state or local regulation, it is possible to obtain specific information as to the nature of charges and rules and regulations governing the local cartage carriers in that particular state, and thus to gain a better understanding of this phase of the motor carrier industry.

## Services performed by local cartage carriers

Local cartage carriers offer a wide variety of services. Some of these services are as follows: (a) packaged delivery; (b) heavy hauling; (c) pool-car and pool-truck distribution; (d) machinery moving; (e) mobile crane service; (f) packing and crating; (g) merchandise storage; (h) pickup and delivery service for railroads, truck lines, and forwarding companies; (i) furnishing dump trucks; (j) local household goods moving; (k) leased truck service; (l) general hauling; (m) trash collection; (n) baggage service; (o) refrigerated truck service; (p) tank-truck service; and (q) armored-car service.

In some urban areas, local cartage companies furnish the truck, and travel under contract arrangements to what is termed a "steady house." Such accounts may be organizations like Sears or large department stores. This service usually involves packaged deliveries, although it may be more.

Typical local cartage operations in connection with interstate commerce may be generally divided into three classes as follows:

a) Full carload handling, which covers the loading and unloading of property at terminals, rail sidings, or team tracks and transportation to or from shippers or receivers.

b) Pool-car or pool-truck handling and distribution, which covers the assembling or loading of full or partial carloads or truckloads, or the unloading, tagging, marking, routing, sorting, or other such service as a part of the handling of such truckloads or carloads, and the transportation of such property to consignees.

c) Collection and delivery service of less-truckload or less-carload freight within cities and their commercial areas for line haul motor, rail, or forwarding companies.

The equivalent of (a) and (b) is also performed from warehouses, warehouse platforms, or similar facilities, and may or may not involve interstate commerce as such.

Services performed under (a) contemplate, as a general rule, merely the trucking between the car and shippers' premises. No sorting, checking of kinds, colors, or the like is usually required. Services under (c) are a continuation, under original bills of lading, of a movement between terminals and consignees or consignors. Billing is often greatly simplified, based on agreed contract rates under which the local carrier acts as independent contractor for the line haul carrier or forwarder.

Services under (b), however, present an entirely different situation. Shipment in such a pool car or pool truck must be sorted and carefully checked, since all packages may be almost identical in size, shape, or color, but containing an assortment of articles, different colors, quality, and brands. This sorting and checking is a job requiring care, skill, and time. Cartons or containers may not be marked, and the shipper's directions as to segregation and distribution must be carefully followed. Routing of shipments consigned beyond is also an important service. Along with the transportation comes such items as taking proper receipts, making redeliveries, collecing c.o.d.'s, accounting to the shipper for all such items, and, in some instances, storage.

Pool-car distribution is an important function of the cartage industry. It is a departure from the ordinary receiving, transporting, and delivery of carload traffic, of doing or performing many special services for the shipper between the acceptance of the carload of traffic and the ultimate delivery and accounting to shipper, such as providing dock and storage space, since all shipments in the load cannot be delivered immediately, providing sorting, checking, marking, routing, preparing bills and receipts, and then the transporting, handling of c.o.d.'s, and finally accounting to the shipper. The cartage operator is able to consolidate handling with other services and is therefore in a position to give the shipper a complete and economical service throughout an entire metropolitan area. The amount of service to be rendered is generally defined by contract with the shipper.

It is an economical operation for both shippers and receivers to utilize pool-car distribution service in connection with consolidated distribution by a single local cartage operator. The payer of the freight gets the benefit of the carload or volume rate for the line haul movement and the benefit of specialized handling as a consolidated lot by the cartageman at the destination. This type of service and distribution is an economical one for shippers and carriers because it provides the advantages and benefits of line haul movement in volume and of specialized distribution by a single local operator at destination. Frequently such operators are making other deliveries to the same consignees or areas at the same time.

Pool-truck distribution performed by many local cartage operators is somewhat similar to pool-car distribution. One of the principal exceptions is that the cartage operator is often required to provide special facilities for handling such pool truckloads or lots.

The charges made by pool-car and pool-truck distributors are usually tailor-made to fit a particular movement. The factors taken into consideration include the type of freight volume involved, weight per shipment and per stop, number of stops, amount of handling needed, the number of separate and distinct services covered, available facilities of consignees, distance traveled in making deliveries, and similar factors. Scarcely any two operations are alike as to service required or cost of handling. Some large manufacturing firms are making extensive use of pool-car and pool-truck services.

Local cartage carriers also perform pool-car and pool-truck distribution out of warehouses and storage facilities which they operate. These warehousemen and cartage operators have regular established charges for handling, sorting and tagging, making bills of lading, routing, and other accessorial services in connection with pool-car or pool-truck handling and distribution.

Another of the services which may be offered by local cartage carriers is that of armored-car service. Armored-car carriers generally operate as contract carriers and perform a variety of services. Their basic service is the collection of customer's receipts for subsequent bank deposit, but there are other services, such as distribution of payrolls to workers, mint and bank work, department and chainstore services, service for currency exchanges, and service to brokerage offices. Approximately two thirds of the nation's armored-car fleet is operated by Brink's Express, Inc.

### Contracts and rates

The local cartage carrier may have a majority of its volume of business coming from but two or three customers with which it will have contracts covering terms and conditions of service. These contracts may be formal documents of great length, or they may be informal agreements confirmed by letter. A formal contract covers one year or a number of years and usually contains an escape clause whereby either party may cancel the contract after proper notice. Even in a long-term contract, it is possible to make it flexible enough to be suitable to both parties. As an example, the contract may be drawn so that it allows for an adjustment of rates should the profit to the local carrier in the contractual carriage fall below a designated minimum or rise above a designated maximum.

Local cartage rates are tailor-made. Some of the factors which will affect costs are: (1) the facilities at shipping and receiving points; (2) traffic congestion; (3) point of delivery whether on the dock or inside the building; and (4) special handling. In pricing a cartage job, the time required and the cost of the labor and equipment for the time required are most important.

## HOUSEHOLD GOODS CARRIERS

The household goods carriers constitute one of the largest of the specialized motor carrier groups subject to Commission regulation. This group of carriers has developed responsive to the needs of the public which it serves. Prior to the advent of the motor van, the transporting of the contents of a household to a new location was performed by rail. This involved cartage of household effects to a warehouse, packing and crating, transportation by the rail carrier, carting to the residence, and unpacking there. The development of household goods motor carriers made possible transportation from a household to the new location without the extensive crating and packing, rehandling, and longer time in transit.

The moving van has virtually revolutionized the transportation of household goods. It is estimated that over 90 percent of household goods are now being moved by motor van. This is an example of the tremendous inroads made by specialized motor transportation on the traffic previously transported by rail.

Many of the early household goods carriers had performed packing, crating, and local cartage service for railroads. With the improvement in highways and motor carrier equipment, some of these carriers started rendering service within a limited radius. The success of these carriers led to a broadening of operations, so that at the time of the passage of the Motor Carrier Act in 1935 there was a well-established pattern of household goods carrier operations. Currently, there are 2,850 such carriers.

Practically all intercity transportation of household goods is by owner-operators. These individuals own their equipment which is painted in the colors of the company for which they work. Typically, these truckers will remain in the employ of the same company for a long period of time.

The extent to which the civilian population of the United States moves each year is not generally realized. Figures compiled by the U.S. Bureau of the Census from a sample survey shows that approximately 20 percent of the civilian population moves each year. Further, the majority of the persons moving stay within the same community or nearby areas, but about 15 million move within the same state and 17 million move across state lines. Only 2 percent of the adult population have always lived in their present homes. This is some indication of the potential market of the household goods carriers.

The busiest months for household goods movers are from June to September, during which time between 40 and 45 percent of the total year's volume of business is moved. The largest single shipper of household goods is the Department of Defense, which is occasioned by the rotation of personnel. Currently, this is the largest single expenditure by the Department of Defense for a commodity group. It spends more than $700 million a year in moving household goods for military personnel.

### Radial and nonradial operations

The household goods carriers which transport interstate by motor are classified by the Interstate Commerce Commission as irregular-route common carriers of household goods. [17] The nature of household goods operations lends itself to irregular-route operations, inasmuch as the origin and destination may differ for each and every shipment. The authority to operate over irregular routes enables the carrier to take the shortest practicable route.

The certificate which is granted may cover operating authority which is radial or nonradial. When the operating authority granted is radial, it authorizes operations only from or to a specified base, which may be a city, county, a part of a state, or an entire state or area to specified points or places. An example of this type of certificate is one which reads: "Between points and places in Marshall County, W.Va., on the one hand, and, on the other, points and places in Md., Ky., Ohio, Pa., Va., and the D.C."

Nonradial operating authority permits the carrier to operate to, from, or between any points within a prescribed area, which may be only two states or may embrace all of the states. In recent years, there have been mergers of companies resulting in the new company having nationwide authority. In 1979, there were 27 carriers what could serve all points in the United States in nonradial service. Examples are Aero Mayflower Transit Company, Allied Van Lines, Bekins Van Lines, Greyhound Van Lines, John F. Ivory Co., and Wheaton Van Lines.

The radial-type carrier may possess a more limited area of operation. On the other hand, in many instances such a carrier serves as the local agent for household goods carriers possessing broader operating authority, such as the nationwide moving companies.

The largest household goods carrier based on gross revenues, Allied Van Lines, owns no vehicular equipment, and the drivers, helpers, and mechanics engaged in its operations are hired and paid for by its agents. Under hauling-agency contracts, the carriers from which it has purchased operating rights have become its hauling agents. It also has a number of booking agents. The agents of the company own the stock and receive a share of profits based on the revenue the agent generates.

The corporate organizations of other nationwide movers are along conventional lines, although there is considerable variation in the manner in which they secure their equipment. Some of them are family companies, such as, Stevens Van Lines. North American Van Lines is owned by a conglomerate, Pepsico. United Van Lines is one in which the agents are the stockholders. In Atlas Van Lines, the agents are also the stockholders but the certificate is held by a trustee. One of the large carriers, Bekins Van Lines, is a holding company for several of the operating companies under it.

The Big Four of the moving industry—Allied, North American, Aero Mayflower, and United—received approximately one-half of the total revenue of Class I and II interstate moving companies in 1979. North America has the 9th largest gross revenues of all motor carriers in the United States.

Another segment of the interstate household goods carries consists of the local moving and storage company which has a certificate covering a limited territory, but its operation is conducted independently of all other carriers in handling shipments within its authorized territory.

### Cooperative arrangements

Another group of carriers, the majority of which have limited operating authority, has combined its service through cooperative arrangements. In this manner, the group handles shipments to and from most sections of the country through interline or interchange arrangements. There are several of these groups of carriers which have made these cooperative arrangements. As a rule, their services are complementary rather than competitive. In some instances, however, the authority which one carrier possesses overlaps that of another in the same group. In one of the groups, there are about 48 carriers which have an arrangement whereby they interchange or interline shipments among themselves. A carrier which is a member of one of these groups will turn over a shipment to another, with the originating carrier assuming carrier responsibility to the owner of the goods. These cooperative arrangements are similar to the return-load bureaus which were existent during the 1920's.

### Agents

The larger carriers make extensive use of agents which they appoint in local communities to represent them. These agents, or agencies, operate under bona fide agency agreements which establish their duties and responsibilities in their respective territories. Some agency agreements provide for exclusive franchised territory, but this is not usual. While the bona fide agency agreements used by various large carriers may vary in detail to fit the particular needs of a carrier's operations, they are much alike in the minimum requirements. Some of the typical responsibilities of the local agent include the solicitation and procurement of business, arranging for helper labor to load and unload, aid in the adjustment of claims, assistance in the dispatch of vehicles, assistance in the collection of charges, the furnishing of accessorial services as required, compliance with the principal's tariffs, the use of only approved advertising, serving as a depository of records, refraining from selling on its own behalf any services for the transportation of household goods beyond the territorial limits of the agent's operating authority, the exclusive selling of the principal's service to all points within the United States beyond the limits of the agent's authority, and the carrying of necessary insurance. These agents are called "prime agents."

Some nationwide carriers require local agents to ship a stipulated percentage annually over the principal's operating rights before the agent may use its own rights. Although the operating rights of an agent cover a much smaller territory, it frequently occurs that shipments could be transported by the agent as a carrier using its own rights rather than as an agent. Other nationwide companies permit their agents to use the agent's own rights whenever the agent is able to do so without requiring any specified percentage of the business.

"Military agents," who solicit shipments only from the Department of Defense, are frequently used by the carriers.

When a bona fide agency arrangement exists, the carrier is obligated by and responsible for the acts of its agents within the provisions of the agency agreement and the scope of the carrier's authority.

The policy of the larger carriers on agency organizations varies. Some carriers appoint only local companies which have household-goods warehouse facilities. Those agents which operate storage warehouses but are not engaged in motor carrier operations are often termed "non-booking agents." "Hauling agents" are those which provide vehicles and perform the transportation service for the principal. They receive from 63 percent to 79 percent of the line haul revenue for this service, less for military shipments. Others appoint "booking agents" which have neither warehouses nor vehicles. For the services involved in booking, they are paid a percentage of the line haul charge. This varies from 16 to 25 percent. Thus, there are several common types of agents, *hauling,* *nonbooking,* and *booking,* as well as combinations of these. The number of agents will vary depending upon the type used. One nationwide moving company has over 1,400 agents. One of the advantages of numerous agents is that it enables a carrier with extensive operating authority to reduce the ratio of empty miles to loaded miles. The largest household goods carrier based on gross revenue has an empty mileage ratio of only 13 percent.

There are some household goods brokers who act as intermediaries between a shipper of household goods and the carrier. These brokers are licensed by the Interstate Commerce Commission. Their function is primarily that of selling and their commission comes from the purchaser of transportation.

The majority of the local moving and storage companies which formerly handled their own long-distance moving now act as agents for one of the larger household goods carriers.

### Pooling agreements

A number of the large household goods carriers have pooling plans under which traffic, service, and earnings are pooled.[18]  Pooling is permitted only if the Commission approves. It must find that the arrangement will be in the interest of better service to the public, will result in economy of operations, and will not unduly restrain competition. The terms and conditions of the arrangement must be just and reasonable, and the arrangement must be assented to by all the carriers involved. The Commission instituted a rule-making procedure in 1960 regarding the extent, arrangements, and possible regulations to be issued on pooling arrangements.[19] In 1965 it dropped the investigation and recommended that legislation be enacted by Congress to exempt household goods carriers who wanted to pool from the Commission requirements. However, Congress has taken no action.

A pooling agreement is a means whereby the principal—such as a nationwide household goods moving company—and its agents, with limited operating authorities competitive with those of the principal, enter into an agreement that minimizes competition. Such a plan stipulates the conditions under which the booking and surrender of shipments to the principal are handled, as well as other matters. In a typical agreement, four types of situations are covered: (1) If the shipper requests service by the principal, the traffic is booked with the principal regardless of whether or not the movement could be made under the agent's operating authority; (2) if the shipment is within the agent's scope of authority but it finds it more economical to have the principal make the movement, it may book the traffic to the latter; (3) if the agent books traffic for transportation on its own rights but later finds the movement can be made more rapidly and economically by the principal, it may surrender such traffic at its discretion; and (4) all shipments booked by the agent calling for service outside its operating authority are surrendered to the principal.

### Booking

The practice of booking is widespread in the household goods field and is usually done by agents. It is estimated that 75 percent of the certificated household goods carriers engage in the practice of turning over shipments to others for compensation.

Household goods carriers have felt that when the booking carrier issues the bill of lading in its own name and is responsible to the shipper, the commission which it is paid by the hauling carrier is not in reality a commission but a division of the revenue, since the performance of any service by the booking carrier constitutes participation in the transportation. The Commission, however, has rejected this concept. The Commission has felt that the mere booking of a shipment or even the performance of some accessorial or terminal service in connection with it does not constitute participation in the performance of transportation, so that the booking carrier cannot be classified as a participant in an interline movement and that compensation paid such carrier is not an interline settlement or division. [20]

Household goods carriers have referred to the practice of the booking carrier turning over shipments to the hauling carrier as "joint carriage." In effect, the booking carrier performs the terminal portion of the joint carriage, and the hauling carrier all of the physical transporting of the shipment. Interlining is not common in the household goods field as it is among the general commodity carriers.

Fig. 6-2. A typical moving van used in over-the-road operations. Courtesy: Andrews Van Lines.

### Operations

Household goods average approximately 7 pounds per cubic foot. The nature of the goods shipped, plus the pads in which they are wrapped, account for the large occupancy of space in relation to weight. It is possible to put the contents of more than one average home in the semitrailer used by the household goods carriers in interstate moves, but this will depend upon the amount of household goods in each shipment. The furnishings of as many as three average six-room houses may be placed in the larger vans. Figure 6-2 shows a typical moving van used in over-the-road operations.

In recent years, separate companies that specialize in packing and crating for household goods carriers have developed. Their charges are typically 70 to 80 percent of the carrier's packing tariff charge to the shipper. They assume liability for all damage claims.

Long-distance moving companies seek to consolidate shipments. Some shipments are taken from the home and held at the carrier's warehouse for consolidation with other shipments going to the same general area.

## Warehousing

An adjunct of many household goods carriers is a responsible warehouse service. The agents of some companies are warehousemen and furnish this service for the carrier. Others, however, are warehousemen-carriers. A third group are warehousemen who will provide household goods storage for any household goods carriers.

There are several different types of storage that are referred to in the industry, some of which are found in carrier tariffs. Storage-in-transit is the holding of a shipment in the warehouse of the carrier or its agent for storage pending further transportation. Generally, storage-in-transit is limited to 60 days by tariff provision, although it may be as high as 180 days. During the storage-in-transit period, the carrier is responsible for the shipment, and its tariff rates apply. At the end of this period and in the absence of final delivery instructions, the shipment is placed in permanent storage, at which time the carrier's liability ceases.

Permanent or regular storage is more complete, since goods are usually wrapped, treated for moth and vermin protection, and placed in a permanent or a regular location from a short period of time to possibly several years. In most states, the rates for this service are not under regulation but are determined by the warehouseman in possession. When permanent or regular storage is involved, there are "handling-in" and "handling-out" charges, which are usually applied by warehousemen in connection with this type of storage. These charges cover taking the goods from the unloading dock, proper preparation, and placing goods away in permanent location; and removing goods from permanent location, unwrapping, and delivery back to the loading dock.

The liability of the warehouseman is determined by the Uniform Warehouse Receipts Act and only extends to damage due to his negligence. This liability is less than that of common carrier liability. A limit of liability per piece or package is contained in the contract terms and conditions of the warehouse receipt.

## Regulation

The Interstate Commerce Act sets forth certain economic requirements with which carriers must comply, which are discussed in later chapters. In addition to this, the Interstate Commerce Commission has prescribed rules and regulations for particular segments of the motor carrier industry. In the case of household goods carriers, the Commission has prescribed rules and regulations to govern the practices of all motor common carriers engaged in the transportation of household goods in interstate or foreign commerce. The rules that are currently effective provide a framework within which operations can be conducted in a manner beneficial to both shipper and carrier. They cover such subjects as: the definition of "household goods"; the establishment of rates in amounts per 100 pounds; the manner of determining loaded weight, tare weight, and constructive weight;[21] accessorial or terminal services and charges; prohibition of discounts; restrictions on carriers serving as agents for other carriers; prohibition against carrier acting as agent for insurance company for compensation; prohibition against carrier issuance of receipt or bill of lading for transportation prior to receiving household goods; restriction of carrier liability; rules regarding estimates of charges made by carriers; prohibition of absorption of dock charges of warehouseman; prescription of printed information about service and rate aspects that must be furnished to shipper by carrier; and a rule stating that the carrier must advise the shipper as to minimum weight provisions prior to acceptance of shipments.[22]

The rule which defines the term "household goods" and thus indicates the goods that can be transported by the household goods carriers was prescribed by the Commission in 1939.[23] This early definition was reaffirmed by the Commission in 1951.[24] Part 1 of this rule relates to a change in the domicile of a householder and does not permit ordinary retail deliveries of new furniture. Part 2 relates to a change in the location of a store, office, museum, institution, hospital, or other establishment. Part 3 relates to the transportation of articles that are of an unusual nature or value and require the specialized handling and equipment of household goods carriers. The fact that commodities are uncrated does not make them of unusual value or nature. Part 3 does not necessarily relate, as do Parts 1 and 2, to removals of property due to a change in the location of a householder or an establishment.

Under the 1st Proviso (Part 1), there are three types of shippers—individual c.o.d. shippers, national account shippers, and military shippers. National account moves are personnel transfers for corporations. Approximately 45 percent of carrier shipments are c.o.d., 39 percent national account, and 16 percent Department of Defense.

There continue to be innumerable complaints from shippers of household goods. The common complaints are low estimates, excessive charges based on incorrect weights, failure to abide by pickup and delivery dates, and failure to adjust loss and damage claims. Unfortunately, some of these practices exist because a carrier takes advantage of the inexperience of shippers.

On different occasions, the Commission staff has conducted studies of household goods shipments and the complaints filed in connection with them and has found little, if any, improvement.

A number of orders have been issued and, in 1970, movers were required to make full disclosures to customers. The estimates of charges had to be clearly identified as estimates, the customer had to be given a span of days in which pickup and delivery would be performed, and the movers had to explain fully about liability limits and the filing of claims. [25]

Subsequently, the carriers were required by the Commission to submit a performance report on each of their agents. Further action required movers to file annual reports to the Commission containing data on pickup and deliveries, estimates (which cannot err more than 10 percent), and on the speed with which they settle claims. They must provide potential customers with an ICC document that gives information on loss and damage claims. They must also provide the customer with a document entitled "Summary of Information for Shippers of Household Goods." [26]

The Commission in *Ex Parte No. MC-19, sub 23*, issued rules providing that at the carrier's option a written estimate based on constructive weight may be given to a shipper. The shipper is then obligated to pay only the lower price determined using the actual or constructive weight of the shipment. This written estimate is binding for 60 days unless the shipper adds items to or removes items from the shipments; requests additional services or cancels previously requested services; a pending rate change becomes effective; or charges different from those originally quoted apply to the shipment.

Because of repeated violations of the Commission's regulations, the Commission has proposed to suspend some of the major carriers' authority to haul 2d and 3d proviso goods (goods covered under Part 2 and Part 3) for a period of several months but this has not been adopted.

Physical distribution or traffic managers, as professional purchasers of transportation, are much better able to secure the quality of service they desire than are individual householders who move infrequently.

With the development of large all-weather containers, some of which are large enough to hold the entire household effects of a home, motor carriers of household goods have started service to foreign countries using the containers. Such carriers often establish a separate freight-forwarding company to perform this service. Since freight forwarders of used household goods are exempt from economic regulation, a motor carrier which has household goods operating authority could also be a freight forwarder of used household goods. There has also been expanding use of containers for door-to-door domestic service. In early 1974, the Commission rejected a petition by the household goods carriers to extend the rules and regulations applying to the household goods carriers to freight forwarders of household goods.[27]

A number of freight forwarders have established service that is competitive with motor household goods carriers. They use motor carriers of general commodities to transport household goods for them. They also use motor carriers of household goods, particularly for military shipments.

Some household goods carriers have flatbed trailers on which they move containers. Household goods shipments having a prior or subsequent movement overseas are containerized and are handled by railroads, general commodity motor carriers, contract motor carriers, airlines, and household goods carriers.

In a case involving forwarders, the Commission held among other things that motor carriers that perform pickup and delivery service for forwarders of household goods operating under the exemption in Section 10562 (2)(D) of the Interstate Commerce Act are not themselves exempt from regulation. Prior to this ruling, such carriers had felt that their operations were not subject to regulation. The Commission termed these carriers (about 300) "color-of-right" operators and established guidelines for their applications for operating authority to transport household goods.[28] In 1969 the ICC granted authority to 53 firms to haul used household goods over irregular routes between the various points "restricted to the transportation of traffic having a prior or subsequent movement in containers, beyond the points authorized and further restricted to the performance of pickup and delivery service in connection with packing, crating, and containerization or unpacking, uncrating, and decontainerization of such traffic."

Household goods carriers have been permitted to transport valuable show cars and related display exhibits and automobile transporters may also transport such displays and exhibits. Household goods movers, however, cannot handle show cars by using double-deck automobile transports nor trilevel transports which are not the specialized equipment usually employed in moving household goods. This is an instance in which the shipper may use either of these specialized carriers.[29]

Numerous household goods carriers have pointed to the service rendered by household goods carriers as being different from that of general freight haulers. This difference is said to be due to the special equipment, the use of especially trained personnel, and the fact that movers remove the shipment from the place where the article is originally located, take it to destination, and place the article in the exact location at destination desired by the shipper. It should be pointed out, however, that there are numerous segments of the motor common-carrier industry which operate in a distinct or unique manner different from general commodity haulers, but all of them, without exception, are rendering a common-carrier transportation service, representing a general holding out to the public.

### Rates

Although household goods carriers originally published tariffs based on the cubic feet displacement of the goods carried, the dissatisfaction occasioned by such rates due to discriminatory practices resulted in the Commission's prescription of a rule that all rates must be published on a weight basis. The line haul rates, which are published in cents per 100 pounds, are graded in accordance with distance, that is, rates are published by weight brackets and mileage blocks. For example, the rate per 100 pounds would be higher for a light shipment than the rate named for the same distance as applicable on a heavy shipment.

In addition to the line haul charge, there are rates and charges for additional services (accessorial). Some of these are the result of requests which the shipper will make to perform a particular service, such as packing, unpacking, waiting time, storage in transit, and appliance servicing.

The shipper can secure exclusive use of the vehicle, but the charges are generally more for this service. Expedited service is also available upon request of the shipper so that delivery will be made on a definite date or within a specified period of time. The usual requirement is that the shipment must weigh 5,000 pounds, and the charges for this service are greater than when shipments are hauled at the carrier's convenience. Most tariffs also provide that shipments weighing less than 500 pounds are subject to a minimum charge of 500 pounds.

For moves wholly within urban areas, the charges are usually computed on an hourly basis, for the van and for each man, or on a per-job basis. These carriers do not always hold themselves out as common carriers. There are many thousand local household goods carriers—900 in New York City alone.

The Commission has authorized the use of rates that are based on the size and number of containers utilized. This is termed "constructive weight." The shipper is charged on a seven-pound-per-cubic-foot weight basis regardless of the actual weight of the shipment that is transported in the container.

Whereas the average revenue per ton-mile for general commodity carriers is 14.2 cents, that of household goods carriers is estimated to be about 35.0 cents. The average revenue per ton-mile for household goods carriers varies widely depending on the length of haul.

The Interstate Commerce Commission issued a *released rate* order which permitted the limitation of liability of the household goods carriers. [30] This order also authorized the payment of an additional amount if the shipper declared the value of the shipment to be higher than the prescribed maximum. The rate of 60 cents per pound per article, as provided in the tariffs, is considered to be the base rate, and the carrier's responsibility is limited to that amount in the case of lost or damaged articles. If the shipper wishes to be paid full value for lost or damaged items, he must declare a lump sum value for the entire shipment and pay an extra charge depending upon the value he declares. Under one option, the shipper does not declare a value or sign the valuation statement in the bill of lading in which case the mover's maximum liability is set at $1.25 times the weight of the shipment in pounds. Thus, if the shipment weighs 4,000 pounds, the lump sum valuation would be $1.25 times 4,000 pounds or $5,000. The second option for the shipper is to enter on the bill of lading a lump sum value which he considers adequate to cover his shipment. It cannot be less than $1.25 times the weight of the shipment but it can be more, whatever the shipper establishes as the value of his shipment. In either of the foregoing options, the shipper is charged 50 cents per $100 valuation for this higher protection. Released rates are applicable not only to the transportation of household goods but also to charges for accessorial services in connection therewith.

About 50 percent of household goods shippers release their goods at a value not to exceed 60 cents per pound per article. The effect of such limitation is that many persons take out transit insurance to provide additional coverage but the mover cannot sell this insurance. Currently, the average value of household goods is $2.20 per pound.

There are two major household goods rate bureaus—the Household Goods Carriers' Bureau and Movers' and Warehousemen's Association of America. Rates are identical, but some accesorial charges are different.

Substantial deregulation of household goods carriers, particularly with regard to rates, was being considered by Congress in 1980.

## TANK TRUCKS

Tank trucks[31] constitute a specialized type of operation using specialized equipment which is designed for handling a variety of commodities in bulk, both liquid and dry. The range of these commodities is very extensive, there being more than 700, the majority of which are petroleum and chemical products. Figure 6-3 is a typical tank truck used in transportation of petroleum products. There are many others, such as glue, molasses, milk, citrus juices, fingernail polish, penicillin, liquid latex, ink, plastic, and numerous others in liquid form. The transportation of liquid chocolate illustrates the adaptability of tank-truck operations to industry needs. Chocolate refineries used to harden liquid chocolate into large cakes which were cut into 10-pound slabs, placed in paper bags, and then sacked in burlap for shipment. The shipper and

Fig. 6-3. A typical tank truck used in transportation of liquids. Courtesy: O'Boyle Tank Lines.

receiver warehoused it in temperature-controlled rooms, and remelted it as needed. Tank trucks now transport chocolate in liquid form at 115°, and it is unloaded into the tanks of candy makers, thereby eliminating many intermediate steps, with a saving in time and money for shippers and consignees. Eggs, minus shells, are now being shipped in tank-truck quantities to bakers. A shipment of 442,000 eggs can be transported in one tank truck as compared to a trailer load of shell eggs of 300,000.

Plastic pellets are also being moved by tank trucks. The pellets are used by film converters and extruders to produce plastic products, such as wrappings, linings, milk cartons, and toys. Dry bulk tank vehicles are also used in the carrying of such commodities as carbon black, and a growing number of edibles, such as sugar and flour.

### Development of tank-truck operations

The early development of the tank-truck industry was largely in the transportation of petroleum products. During World War II, all rail tank cars, about 18,000, were withdrawn for hauls of less than 200 miles and were placed in long-distance movement to replace ocean tankers. Tank trucks were substituted for tank cars in this operation, which resulted in a tremendous growth in the tank-truck industry.

The experience of shippers in World War II in using tank trucks demonstrated that in the short-haul movement (1) tank trucks had faster turnaround time; (2) they required less expensive plant installations and receipts for loading use; (3) delivery could be made directly to service stations and large consumers, bypassing bulk plants; and (4) they provided greater flexibility, since it was no longer necessary to plan movements in keeping with train schedules.[32] During the war, it was found that on the average haul of less than 200 miles the turnaround time for a tank truck was between 11 and 13 hours as compared with an average of from 8 to 10 days for tank cars on similar hauls.

The expansion of the petroleum industry in the chemical field, and the expansion of production in the chemical industry in the postwar years, led to a greater diversification in tank-truck hauling than previously had been the case. Petroleum products are easy to haul, and the ideal arrangement is to have a volume sufficient to warrant putting specific units in a particular service, since this avoids a mixing of products and possible contamination. However, petroleum products usually constitute a one-way haul. In chemical transportation, there is greater possibility of a return haul because the same pound or gallon of chemical is generally hauled three or four times before it is ultimately consumed. Another advantage is that the commodity is heavier.

The extent of private carriage in the tank-truck field has always provided strong competition to the for-hire portion. Petroleum hauling has lent itself to the operation of company-owned trucks, and the oil industry has owned or controlled its own transportation facilities in other modes of transportation. Petroleum companies have felt that deliveries from bulk stations to their service stations should be made only in trucks which bear the company name, since an unidentifiable tank truck unloading at a service station might give the patrons the impression that a different brand of gasoline was being unloaded.

Because for-hire carriers serve more than one shipper, they have an inherent flexibility that private carriage does not possess. For-hire carriers have succeeded when they have provided a better service for the shipper than he can provide for himself and at a rate which does not encourage private operation.

The largest tank-truck carrier, Chemical Leaman Tank Lines, had gross revenues in 1978 of $ 163 million and was the 23rd largest carrier in revenue among all motor carriers. In the same year, there were 20 tank truck carriers that grossed $ 20 million or more and a total of 218 that grossed $1 million or more.

### Equipment

The equipment used in tank-truck operations varies widely, since commodities may be moved at temperatures which range from $-300^o$ to over $600^o$ above zero, and varying from no pressure to 2,500 pounds per square inch. There is no standard type. Furthermore, there is practically no interchange of equipment between carriers. Tank trucks must be constructed to specifications which are issued by the Department of Transportation. These specifications were prepared in cooperation with carriers and petroleum and chemical companies. They cover such matters as material, thickness, strength, baffling, valve design, test procedures, and marking.

Tank trucks are used to transport a wide range of products as discussed earlier. Some equipment is general purpose, and other equipment is designed for a particular use, such as transportation of corrosive products. Some are convertible between liquid and dry bulk service. Dry bulk tanks may be designed to be unloaded pneumatically through closed dump air slide hopper and screw conveyor. These product transfer systems are an integral part of the tank truck. Savings through distribution in bulk over shipments in bags have been reported to be as much as 25 percent.

There are many types of equipment, such as single, double, triple, or more compartments, insulated and uninsulated, lined and unlined, single-shelled and double-shelled with special valves and discharge equipment. Most petroleum tanks are unloaded from the bottom, as are many other tanks. On the other hand, the products carried in most acid tanks are forced out of the top by air pressure. Tank trucks used in transporting bulk solids, such as granulated sugar or flour, are often equipped for gravity (Fig. 6-4) or mechanical discharge or designed with pneumatic equipment. A load of 44,000 pounds of bulk flour can be discharged from a tank truck by pneumatic means to a height of 125 feet in less than one hour.

A nonrigid tank consisting of a two-ply rubberized container was introduced by some of the rubber companies, but it is not used to any extent. The tank when full assumes the shape of an elongated pillow and can be placed in a van or a flatbed trailer. When empty, it can be readily rolled up so the remaining cargo space can be used for dry cargo on the return trip. The capacity of this type of tank is about 4,400 gallons.

There was controversy between the general commodity carriers and the tank-truck carriers about the use of the rubberized container. In Docket No. MC-8902 (Sub No. 12) *The Western Express Company Extension-Sealdtanks* (March 29, 1961), the entire Commission ruled that whenever a rubber bag, or other type of so-called collapsible or stackable container, is filled after it has been placed on the vehicle

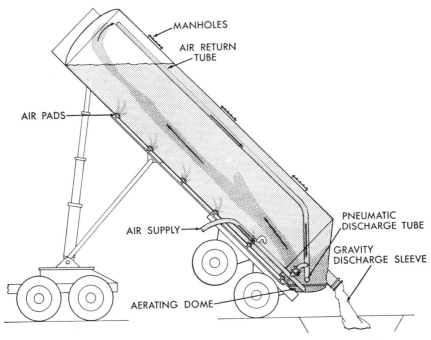

Fig. 6-4. Tank trucks equipped with gravity or pneumatic discharge. Courtesy: The Heil Company.

and/or emptied before it is removed, it is a tank-truck operation and precluded from transportation by general commodity carriers whose authority contains restrictions against the transportation of commodities in bulk or those requiring special equipment. General commodity carriers do, however, have authority to transport commodities in these containers, whether supplied by the carrier or shipper, when they are tendered to the carrier in dismounted containers and are loaded and unloaded with the product in them. These tanks have a capacity of 1,500 to 4,700 gallons.

Like general commodity carriers, the capacity of tank trucks has increased with state modifications in size and weight laws. Over half of all tank trailers are now being constructed of aluminum. A few plastic tanks have been constructed for transportation of chemicals.

The tank truck used in local delivery is an entirely different unit from over-the-road equipment. It is operated by another type of tank-truck business. The equipment used is smaller than over-the-road, consisting primarily of a straight truck with a special individual tank mounted on it, or a small tank semitrailer with multiple compartments. The operation of these local delivery tank trucks is almost exclusively that of a private carrier. They are owned and operated by major oil and refinery companies' wholesale and retail facilities, and the independent oil jobber, oil distributor, or retailer operating his own business.

These units are used for delivering petroleum products in relatively small quantities to industrial consumers, homes, and farms. They deliver gasoline and petroleum products to filling stations and fuel oil to homes.

### Operations

Many for-hire operators feel that the best type of operation is one in which they can have 24-hour-a-day loading and unloading. Some shippers have provided keys to permit the for-hire tank-truck operator to unload at night after closing hours. Such so-called "key-stop" operations have advantages to the shipper. For the carrier, it means operations closer to a 24-hour day. The nighttime operations avoid heavy traffic and congested streets.

There are some places where the tank-truck drivers perform the loading and unloading of the unit and serve the customer on a "keep-full" basis. The tank-truck operator watches the customer's storage tanks, and when there is room for additional loads they are automatically added. The majority of petroleum products move on standing orders which may be given to a carrier a week or a month at a time. In chemical transportation there are many specialized individual loads which require not only special handling but special equipment. Therefore, these shipments do not move on standing orders.

One of the services provided by many for-hire tank-truck carriers is what is termed "drumming" service. In this service, the contents of the tank truck are emptied into smaller containers of almost any size, even 1-gallon cans. There have been instances when 5,000 1-gallon cans were filled from a tank truck.

The terminals of for-hire tank-truck carriers are largely for administration, maintenance, fueling, interior tank cleaning, and driver training. Generally, tank-truck operations are of an irregular route type, many with one-way hauls (estimated 54 percent are loaded miles). Where feasible, a higher equipment utilization factor is attempted through a triangulated traffic development. This generally involves a loaded haul from A to B, from B to C empty, but from C back to A loaded. Varying products may be involved in such transportation.

With few exceptions, tank trucks operate in truckload shipments. Their rate structure is somewhat simpler than that of general commodity carriers. Bulk commodities are not fragile, and rates are typically based on the value of the shipment, volume of traffic, the cost of the equipment necessary to handle the shipment, safety hazards, and the problems involved in loading and unloading. Since bulk commodities are raw materials used in manufacturing, construction, and/or agricultural, the demand may be seasonal and therefore the movement may be seasonal.

Some bulk tariffs provide a return load rule in which a rate incentive is offered through a reduction of 50 percent of the regular one-way rate applicable on the return load, subject to the addition of a flat mileage charge for all empty mileage necessary for the connection.

Continuous movement service may be provided in some tariffs. A continuous movement would cover a shipment consisting of one or more separate loads in the same unit tendered consecutively by a consignor and covered by one bill of lading. The route of continuous movement of a unit begins at the originating carrier's terminal, then to the initial point of origin, then to subsequent origins and destinations, and return to originating terminal. Four or more legs in the continuous movement service are permitted.

There are service benefits as a result of equipment commitment by the carrier to the shipper but the primary incentive to the shipper is reduced cost. The rates are for various mileage brackets. The initial 350-mile movement is at $.96 and then drops to $.81 at 600 miles and over.

In hauling gasoline, motor carriers transport it from water and pipeline terminals into consuming areas, and thus their operations are usually confined to a radius of 200 miles. In the western states, however, there are hauls for distances as great as 600 miles one way. In tank-truck movements of chemicals, the average length of haul is greater than that of petroleum products.

It is particularly important in transportation of chemicals to see that the tank truck is properly cleaned and suited for the product to be hauled. At terminals of tank-truck operators, elaborate cleaning systems have been installed which make use of high-pressure steam, air cleaning, and chemicals to clean the tank. It is not unusual to put a man inside the tank to wipe it down. A claim of $5,000 was paid when a load of marashino cherries was spoiled because of failure to remove the residue of a cargo of printer's ink which had been transported in the tank truck earlier. An asphalt tank truck with as little as one quart of water in the bottom will erupt violently when loaded with hot asphalt.

## AUTOMOBILE HAULERS

Whether the carrier is a common or contract carrier depends, in part, upon the desires of shippers. Some automobile manufacturers use contract carriers, and others prefer the service to be offered by a common carrier. Because of the nature and characteristics of the transportation service rendered by automobile haulers, their operating authority embraces areas rather than specific points. Although 90 percent of the new automobiles were transported by carriers of motor vehicles in 1959, their share of the traffic has dropped to about 50 percent. The total market has been expanding, however, both in tons and in revenue. The railroads developed new equipment in the form of rack cars and lowered rates, thus regaining traffic that had earlier been lost to the motor carriers.

Two different types of transporting are used—the driveaway and the truckaway. If the vehicles which are being transported are moved by motive power which is furnished by one or more of the vehicles, the service is driveaway. If the motive power is not furnished by one or more of the vehicles being moved, it is truckaway service. Some companies engage in only driveaway service; others in only truckaway; while still others render service using both methods.

Most new automobiles are transported by the truckaway method. The equipment used in this service is especially designed for this purpose and varies with different carriers. A unit can haul six·or seven ordinary passenger cars.

A number of combinations may be used in driveaway service. There is single delivery, which means one car is driven under its own power; tow-bar delivery, which is one vehicle driven under its own power and the other towed; saddle-mount delivery, which is one vehicle driven under its own power and another vehicle partially mounted on the first; double saddle-mount delivery; and three-way combination delivery in which one vehicle is driven, one vehicle is completely mounted on the first, and another is towed. The term *caravanning*, used in driveaway operations, means the transportation of automobiles under their own power or the towing of one by another operated under its own power.

The driveaway method is used primarily in moving new trucks and buses, although there are instances in which the tow-bar method is used for new passenger automobiles. Figure 6-5 shows different types of driveaway deliveries.

In both truckaway and driveaway operations, the terminals operated by automobile haulers have greater land area than terminals of general

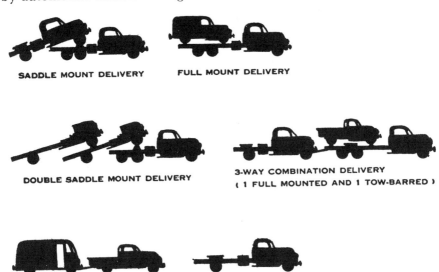

SADDLE MOUNT DELIVERY      FULL MOUNT DELIVERY

DOUBLE SADDLE MOUNT DELIVERY

3-WAY COMBINATION DELIVERY
( 1 FULL MOUNTED AND 1 TOW-BARRED )

TOW-BAR COMBINATION      SINGLE DELIVERY

Fig. 6-5. Different types of driveaway delivery.

commodity haulers. This is particularly the case at the origin terminal because the vehicles are brought there from plants or assembly lines and stored prior to shipment.

There are a number of what are termed *car-releasing companies* whose role is similar to that of an agent between the automobile manu-facturers and the automobile transporters. Their principal function is to eliminate congestion at the end of the factory production line by having men at the various plants who sign and receive the bills of lading for the new automobiles. When these receipts are signed and the cars released, company crews will take the cars either to their own lot or to lots maintained by some of the carriers. Each carrier is notified of the cars that have been received for its account. Some of these companies also deliver cars to the dealers in the city in which they operate.

**Nature of operating authority**

In the certificates and permits which are issued to motor carriers of automobiles, the terms "initial movements" or "secondary movements" may be found. Initial movement is considered to be the transportation of new motor vehicles from the place of manufacture or assembly to destination, or to a point of interchange with other common carriers. Secondary movement is the transportation of motor vehicles, whether new, used, damaged, or repossessed, between points authorized to be served by the carrier other than the point of manufacture or assembly.[33]

When there is a movement of motor vehicles from the factory to an adjoining parking lot by the manufacturer, the Commission has ruled that this constitutes intraplant movement and does not constitute an initial movement. The later movement from the parking lot by for-hire carriers would be the initial movement.[34]

In a situation similar to this when a for-hire carrier transported from the factory to the terminal of another carrier in the same city, this was held to be pickup and delivery service for the second carrier. Therefore, the second carrier's haul would be an initial movement. [35]

A common carrier which has operating authority to transport automobiles in initial movements was permitted by the Commission to purchase or lease a common carrier possessing authority for secondary movements. These authorities could be combined at any point common to both where interchange was possible when the rights were separately owned.[36] However, it has been held that where the combination of initial and secondary authorities will result in a completely new service, there would not be an approval unless there is a definite need for the service, there will be public benefits, and existing carriers will not be seriously affected by the new service.[37]

An individual who acted under a contract as a transport manager for a car manufacturer in transporting new cars was held to be a contract carrier. The drivers secured by the transport manager were obtained through advertisement. The drivers paid their sleeping accommodations, insurance on the car, and a deposit to cover any damage to the car. A part of the deposit was refunded if the car reached the destination without damage. The transport manager paid the car expenses.[38]

## HEAVY HAULERS

Another group of specialized carriers are heavy haulers. These carriers provide a variety of services in transporting commodities which because of size, shape, form, or weight require use of special carrier equipment (Fig. 6-6) or special carrier handling. They engage in rigging and erection, motor crane service, and steel erection. Some heavy haulers have confined their operation to urban areas, but many of them engage in interstate commerce; in that case they must have operating

Fig. 6-6. Low-bed trailers with the load-carrying surface close to the road.

Fig. 6-7. Oversize load with weight distributed over many tires and axles, moved by heavy hauler. Courtesy: Hoffman Companies.

authority from the Interstate Commerce Commission. This authority is usually in the nature of irregular route and involves a territorial grant of states.

The equipment used by heavy haulers is of special design to facilitate the movement of the items transported by such carriers. The gooseneck or lowboy is a common type of such equipment. There are also high flats with heavily reinforced underframe construction to support loads of 80,000 pounds or more; low-bed trailers with the load-carrying surface close to the road to transport high loads, such as shovels, cranes, and transformers (Figure 6-6); winch-equipped trailers, pole trailers, and those of odd and unusual design. Many missiles are transported on custom-built trailers, sometimes referred to as "special trailers."

Many of the loads of these carriers exceed the state weight and length limits, and it is necessary for the carrier to secure a special permit from the state to transport the load. Shipments weighing as much as 200 tons and including nuclear reactors, pressure vessels, and generators have been moved. Such loads require proper distribution in order to avoid damage to the highway (Fig. 6-7).

### Other specialized commodity carriers

There are many other specialized carriers that provide motor carrier service in specialized equipment and/or that are specialized as the commodities transported. These include film carriers, building materials carriers, carriers of forest products, carriers of mine ore, carriers of explosives or dangerous articles, armored truck service, and others.

There are about 200 regulated interstate carriers which limit shipments by size, weight, and number accepted per day to or from a shipper. These specialized carriers are package or small parcel carriers, which concentrate their service to parcel business only, with weight limits such as 50, 75, or 100 pounds as well as the other limitations.

The transportation of mobile or modular homes is another highly specialized type of carrier. Currently about 20 percent of all new housing units are of this type, and they are transported via highways for all or a portion of their movement from factory to building site. The use of escort vehicles is usually required in their movement. Most of the units are oversize and, in some instances, overweight, and state permits must be secured prior to their movement over the highways. Shipping costs, travel delays to the public, and safety hazards are greater on two-lane highways than on four-lane. Three carriers account for 85 percent of for-hire revenues in this field.

## QUESTIONS AND PROBLEMS

1. What factors would account for the emergence of so many specialized carriers in truck transportation?

2. Compare the various definitions of local cartage. What reasons are there for these different definitions?

3. What are commercial zones? Of what importance are commercial zones from a regulatory standpoint?

4. How has the Interstate Commerce Commission defined the boundaries of commercial zones? Of what importance are these zones to local cartage operators?

5. An over-all picture of local cartage is difficult to secure. Why?

6. Compile a list of the differences between local and over-the-road motor carriage.

7. Why have urban goods movements been neglected by researchers?

8. How would you differentiate between a commercial zone and a terminal area?

9. Describe the different types of agents. If you operated a nation-wide moving company, what type would you use? Why?

10. What is booking? What is included in the preliminary arrangements involved in booking?

11. Of what importance to shippers are released rates? Why are they used in the household goods field?

12. There is a greater possibility of a return haul in chemical transportation than in petroleum products. Why? What does this mean to the shipper? Carrier?

13. What is the difference between initial movements and secondary movements in the transporting of motor vehicles?

### FOOTNOTES TO CHAPTER 6

[1] See Highway Research Board, *Urban Commodity Flow*, Washington, D.C., 1970; Department of Transportation, *Urban Goods Movement Projects and Data Sources*, Washington, D.C., 1973; Transportation Research Board, *Urban Goods Movement*, 1974; Federal Highway Administration, *Goods Transportation in Urban Areas*, 1974.

[2] Richard A. Staley, *Trucks and Our Changing Cities* (Local and Short-Haul Carriers National Conference, Washington, D.C., 1973).

[3] *Ibid.*, iii.

[4] *Ibid.* This study defines short haul as a haul of up to 200 miles one way and local hauls as

exclusively urban and indicates that local and short haul for-hire trucks represent 70 percent of all for-hire trucks.

[5]*Commercial Zones and Terminal Areas,* 46 MCC 665 (1946).

[6]*Hall's Motor Transit Co.* v. *Buck Express, Inc.,* 82 MCC 139 (1960).

[7]*Bigley Bros., Inc., Contract Carrier Application,* 4 MCC 711 (1938).

[8]*Consolidated Freight Lines, Inc., Common Carrier Application,* 11 MCC 131 (1939).

[9]*Jeardoe Common Carrier Application,* 21 MCC 233 (1939).

[10]*Sky Freight Delivery Service, Inc., Common Carrier Application,* 47 MCC 233 (1947).

[11]*Commercial Zones and Terminal Areas,* 48 MCC 418 (1948).

[12]*Movement of Highway Trailers by Rail,* 293 ICC 93 (1954). Commercial Zones and Terminal Areas, 54 MCC 21 (1952).

[13]*Commercial Zones and Terminal Areas,* 54 MCC 21 (1952).

[14]The Bureau of Motor Carriers has issued 127 Administrative Rules which are considered authoritative in the absence of Commission rulings. In a number of cases, Commission rulings have superseded the Bureau's Administrative Rules.

[15]*Commercial Zones and Terminal Areas,* 54 MCC 21 (1952).

[16]*Commercial Zones and Terminal Areas,* 54 MCC 21 (1952).

[17]The author has found one contract carrier with "grandfather" rights to move household goods for employees of the cheese company whose products the contract carrier hauls. *Docket 31466. LCL Transit Co.*

[18]*North American Van Lines, Inc.—Investigation of Control,* 60 MCC 758 (1955). See also *Geitz Storage and Moving Co., Inc.—Investigation of Control,* 65 MCC 257 (1955); *United Van Lines, Inc.—Pooling,* 70 MCC 587 (1957); and *Atlas Van Lines, Inc.—Control and Merger—Atlas Van Service, Inc.,* 70 MCC 629 (1958) and 75 MCC 175 (1958).

[19]Ex Parte MC-51, *Pooling Motor Common Carriers of Household Goods,* 1960.

[20]*Ibid.,* 277, 293.

[21]If no adequate scale is available, a constructive weight based upon 7 pounds per cubic foot may be used to determine the weight.

[22]*Practices of Motor Common Carriers of Household Goods,* 17 MCC 467 (1939); 47 MCC 119 (1947); 48 MCC 59 (1948); 51 MCC 247 (1950); 53 MCC 117 (1951); and 71 MCC 113 (1957) (1967), MC-19 (1970).

[23]*Practices of Motor Common Carriers of Household Goods,* 17 MCC 467 (1939).

[24]*Practices of Motor Common Carriers of Household Goods,* 53 MCC 177 (1951).

[25]*Practices of Motor Common Carriers of Household Goods (Consumer Protection),* Ex Parte MC-19 (1970).

[26]119 MCC 585 (1974).

[27]344 ICC 862 (1972).

[28]*Kingpak, Inc., Investigation of Operations,* 103 MCC 318 (1967).

[29]*Automobile Shippers, Inc.—Extension—Show Cars and Displays,* 67 MCC 201 (1956).

[30]*ICC Released Rates Order MC-No. 2A,* January 29, 1948.

[31]This term also refers to semitrailers or trailers.

[32]Petroleum Administration for Defense, *Transportation of Oil* (Washington, D.C.: U.S. Government Printing Office, 1951), p. 12.

[33]Administrative Rule No. 75, July 15, 1938.

[34]*Payne Common Carrier Application,* 46 MCC 726 (1947).

[35]*George F. Burnett Co.,* 42 MCC 804 (1943) (not printed).

[36]*Clark—Lease—Ronken,* 36 MCC 195 (1940).

[37]*Fleet Carrier Corp.—Lease—George F. Burnett Co., Inc.,* 50 MCC 489 (1948).

[38]*Lord Contract Carrier Application,* 34 MCC 549 (1942).

[39]*George F. Burnett Co.,* 42 MCC 804 (1943) (not printed).

[40]*Clark—Lease—Ronken,* 36 MCC 195 (1940).

[41]*Fleet Carrier Corp.—Lease—George F. Burnett Co., Inc.,* 50 MCC 489 (1948).

[42]*Lord Contract Carrier Application,* 34 MCC 549 (1942).

# chapter 7

# Economics of commercial motor transportation

Commercial motor transportation is composed of many types of motor carriers offering a variety of services. The principal legal classifications were described in Chapters 5 and 6. The motor carrier freight market, competitively speaking, is also fairly well-structured according to shipment size. Motor carriers typically confine their service offerings to one of three weight categories: truckload, less-truckload, or parcels.[1]

Motor carriers of truckload freight provide door-to-door service for full trailerload freight that requires little, if any, terminal handling, and irregular route common carriers, contract, private, and exempt carriers typically concentrate on providing this type of service. Motor carriers of other than general freight are often irregular route carriers. Motor carriers of less-truckload freight provide service for both full trailerload freight and smaller less-truckload shipments that require terminal handling. Less-truckload shipments dominate in terms of revenue and number of shipments for these carriers. The principal supplier of less-truckload service is the general freight, regular route common carrier. Motor carriers of small parcels are a special category of the less-truckload carrier. Specialized carriers of small parcels have developed to take advantage of the size and uniformity of such shipments.

## Carrier Size and Economies of Scale

The 100 largest motor carriers based on gross revenue (those above $50 million) accounted for slightly more than half the revenue of all the Class I and II motor carriers in 1978.[2] The largest, United Parcel Service, grossed nearly $2.7 billion and was a small parcel operator, transporting parcels of under 50 pounds.[3] The next was Roadway Express with $918,054,000, Consolidated Freightways $758,443,000, and Yellow Freight System $678,265,000. Of the top ten in that year, eight were general commodity carriers, one was a household goods carrier, and one a small parcel carrier. These ten companies accounted for almost 25 percent of Class I and II motor carrier revenue.

In 1960 there were two regular-route general commodity carriers operating from coast to coast, but through acquisition, there are now 14. This is a substantial change in a relatively short period of time. Several motor carriers have authorized regular-route mileage greater than the mileage of any railroad.

The average number of units operated by Class I carriers in 1977 was 352 power units and 479 owned trailers.[4] The average revenue per power unit for these carriers was $79,410.[5]

Despite the fact there are some very large carriers, the motor carrier industry is still made up predominantly of smaller carriers. In 1978, of the 16,874 motor carriers regulated by the Commission, 12,900 were Class III carriers.[6] The Small Business Administration, a government agency established to assist small business, has classified 98 percent of the trucking industry as "small business" under its loan program. A "small business" for the trucking industry is defined for the purpose of business loans or government procurement as a trucking firm with annual receipts of $3 million or less. Many carriers have no desire to expand their operations by acquiring additional operating rights. They prefer the smaller size business in which they know all their customers and which can be managed effectively.

There are quite a number of carriers whose objective is to become very large carriers, presumably because of scale economies. Thus far, there does not appear to be an "ideal" size as far as economy and efficiency are concerned. This is due, in part, to the different types of services provided by motor carriers. The principal asset of truckload carriers providing door-to-door service is the line-haul vehicle. These units are relatively small. Truckload operations may be started with a very small investment and capacity adjusted in direct response to demand. Thus, the most common basis of scale economies, cost and asset indivisibility, is lacking for the truckload carriers. In contrast, less-truckload and the major parcel carriers operate integrated networks consisting of various types of vehicles and terminal facilities. Pickup and delivery vehicles, line-haul vehicles, local terminals, relay stations and breakbulk facilities are analogous to different machines in a manufacturing plant; and in order to utilize the most efficient combination of these parts, substantial size may be required.

A number of general freight, less-truckload carriers are actively expanding their geographic coverage and size in the belief that such an expansion strategy will result in the highest quality service produced at extremely efficient per-unit operating costs. The carrier with broad geographic coverage can pick up (or deliver) more shipments per stop and thus utilize pickup and delivery resources more efficiently. Broad coverage enhances the ability of the carrier to consolidate trailerloads quickly and reliably, improving the transit time and reliability of overall carrier service. Economies of service and marketing advantages are believed to improve with carrier size. With less coverage, the same carrier would have to move underloaded vehicles or increase its breakbulk (reship) activity in order to provide comparable service in terms of transit time.

Differences in truckload and less-truckload techniques explain why efficient less-truckload firms tend to be larger than efficient truckload firms, but at some size the economies of scale are offset by diseconomies of scale such as the increased cost of coordinating and managing larger enterprises. Just how large the most efficient less-truckload or truckload carrier should be is a matter of considerable dispute between economists.[7] Regardless of this, there are many acquisitions through merger which are motivated by reduced cost of operation, which would indicate advantage of large size.

### Size of shipments and motor carrier costs

In the motor carrier field, the average weight per shipment varies widely. Truckloads are defined by the Commission for statistical purposes as shipments weighing over 10,000 pounds. Usually, there is a further breakdown in the category of what is often called small shipments. Some analysts make the break at 1,000 pounds or less, others at 300 pounds or less. Shipments which weigh less than 50 pounds are typically classified as small parcels. It is in this category that the average weight per shipment of air carriers and air express, buses, parcel post and air parcel post, and motor carriers specializing in small parcels falls. General commodity motor carriers in the Middle Atlantic Territory, which embraces the area from Virginia north to New York City, had average shipments of 2,065 pounds. It was found in a continuing study of traffic conducted by the rate conference that about 75 percent of the total shipments moved were under 1,000 pounds.[8] These shipments represented 9.2 percent of the total tonnage carried and accounted for 27.1 percent of the revenue. However, truckloads in this region constituted 64.1 percent of total tonnage and 34.4 percent of the revenue.

It is estimated that general commodity Class I and II carriers transport 84 percent of all intercity tonnage under 10,000 pounds, and recently earned 56 percent of the revenue paid for small shipments.[9] If shipments of less than 50 pounds are excluded, this would rise to more than 90 percent. This factor has an economic impact on motor carrier operations because small shipments are more costly to handle. There are certain activities involved in any size shipment but on a weight basis the costs are proportionately greater for small shipments. These costs are termed "transaction costs," and general commodity carriers are essentially in a transaction business.

Fig. 7-1 indicates the present operational ranges for the movement of different size shipments by different types of motor carriers and other modes, as well as the manner in which they are manifested in the rates charged.

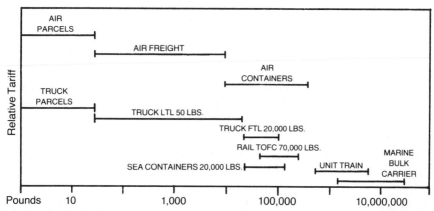

Fig. 7-1. Typical of effects of shipment size on transport tariff rates. Source: Department of Transportation, *National Transportation Trends and Choices* (Washington, D.C., 1977), p. 55.

All the major motor carrier rate bureaus for a number of years have conducted traffic studies. Based as they are on a sample of freight involving all sizes of shipments and different types of rates, the studies have been extensively used in general rate increase proposals as well as in the restructuring of motor carrier class rates. Such studies enable carriers and regulatory bodies to ascertain relationships of revenues and expenses, the potential impacts of a major change in freight rates, and reveal the trends in the patterns of traffic. These studies dealing with cost and revenue aspects have been of substantial benefit to carrier management.

In a careful costing of various weight brackets, it will be found there are some losses in the very small shipment category. This is offset by a very substantial margin on shipments from 2,000 to 25,000 pounds. The problem of *cross subsidization* is common and not easy to solve. Based purely on costs, certain segments of traffic are being subsidized by other segments.

In an effort to reduce rates on traffic that subsidizes traffic in the lower weight categories and thereby create a more cost-oriented rate structure, the Rocky Mountain Tariff Bureau in late 1974 made a submission to the Commission to justify a proposed restructuring of class rates and minimum charges between California and the Rocky Mountain states. Its proposal was to reduce rates for shipments of 2,000 pounds and less by 3 percent, 5,000 pounds 8 percent, 10,000 pounds 12 percent, and truckloads 3 percent. At the same time, the carriers proposed through the Tariff Bureau to increase the minimum charges 6 percent, the 0-499 pound shipments 6 percent, and 500 pound shipments 5 percent.

### Average length of haul and motor carrier costs

The average haul per ton of freight indicates that motor transportation is generally short haul. The average length of haul for all motor carrier traffic is estimated to be 300 miles. In contrast, the average haul for water, rail, and air freight traffic exceeds 370, 540, and 1,000 miles respectively.[10] Larger Class I motor carriers have longer hauls (331 miles) and smaller Class II carriers have shorter hauls (167 miles). Likewise, general freight carriers have longer hauls (430 miles) than specialized carriers (226 miles).[11] The average haul will vary widely within each carrier group. About 75 percent of the Class I general freight carriers have an average length of haul of 300 miles or less, 23 percent have an average between 300 and 800 miles, and 2 percent have an average exceeding 800 miles.[12] A carrier possessing broad operating authority can transport commodities great distances. However, there is a trend in the general commodity sector for carriers to develop their long-haul traffic and adjust their operations accordingly. Since 1962, the average length of haul for all Class I carriers has risen 25 percent.

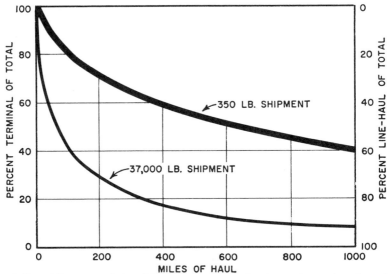

Fig. 7-2. Effect of distance and size of shipment on terminal and over-the-road portions of cost. Source: Interstate Commerce Commision, Bureau of Accounts, *Cost of Transporting Freight by Class I and Class II Motor Common Carriers of General Commodities, Middlewest Territory, 1959* (Washington, D.C., 1960), cover. See also, *Cost of Transporting Freight by Class I and Class II Motor Common Carriers of General Commodities, 1973* (November, 1974), p. 180.

Nearly all of the costs associated with loading vehicles for line-haul movement are insensitive to the length of the vehicle trip, and some line-haul costs increase less than proportionately with line-haul distance. The former is particularly true for terminal expenses which become a smaller portion of total cost as distance increases, as illustrated in Fig. 7-2.

The result is a sharp decline in the cost per ton-mile for less-truckload shipments as distance increases, as shown in Fig. 7-3. The decline is less significant for truckload shipments since terminal costs are less important for such movements.

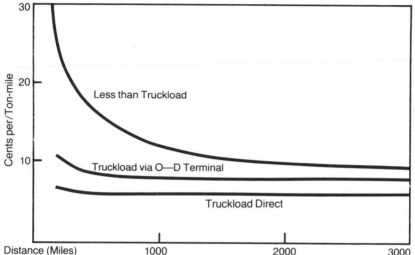

Fig. 7-3. Comparison of Trucking Costs. Source: Department of Transportation, *National Transportation Trends and Choices* (Washington, D.C., 1977), p. 165.

### Interline versus single-line traffic and motor carrier costs

The majority of general commodity hauls are characterized by a single-line haul; that is, the shipments are carried from origin to destination by a single motor carrier. This is true generally throughout the United States, although there are still substantial interline hauls. Interline traffic is that traffic which is exchanged between carriers. The single-line traffic for the Middle Atlantic area comprises 73.4 percent of the shipments, 82.7 percent of the weight, and 74.0 percent of the revenue for all traffic. Although single-line traffic is predominant in all weight groups, there is some interline traffic in each. On the other hand, 51 percent of the movements of transcontinental carriers involve joint-line service. (Transcontinental general commodity carriers are those that operate between points in the Rocky Mountain region or the Pacific region and points on and east of the Mississippi River.) Truckload specialists interline shipments the least. Over 95 percent of the tonnage of specialized carriers is originated and terminated by the same carrier.

Interlining of freight is necessary in instances where a carrier originating freight does not have the operating authority to deliver the freight. Interlining adds to the total cost of movement in the form of additional platform costs at the point of interchange, cost of freight transfer between carrier terminals and additional billing costs. The additional handling also increases transit time. Variable costs for two line movements were found to be 7.5 to 57.2 percent higher than comparable single-line movements.[13] The cost disadvantage increases as the shipment is smaller in weight and moves shorter distances. Many carriers have sought additional operating authority, frequently through merger, to reduce costs due to interlining as well as transit time.

There are also instances where interlining freight to another carrier is desirable even though the authority to complete a single-line movement exists. This case is discussed under pooling.

### Other factors impacting motor carrier costs

Figure 7-4 shows the gross operating costs for trailer combinations, showing vehicle mile costs and payload ton-mile costs in relation to loaded gross weights. The vehicle mile costs are charted with a payload in one direction, with a payload in both directions, and the payload with average loading. It will be noted that the upper curve has cost values which are twice that of the lower curve, since the upper curve represents the payload carried in only one direction. The vehicle mile costs for different degrees of loadings lie between these two extremes. This emphasizes the need for balanced loads by carriers.[14]

Using these data, it was suggested that substantial savings could be effectuated by heavier gross weights of trailer combinations; and such units would also reduce the number of vehicles in the traffic system.

The empty weight of a tractor-semitrailer used in transporting general commodities amounts to 20,000 pounds.[15] Refrigerator trailers that move perishables are approximately 4,000 pounds heavier. When full trailers are added to the combination, the weight increases according to the added length of the empty combination. Where a bridge formula provides a gross weight of 73,280 pounds, an increase to 80,000 pounds allows seven trucks to carry the payload of eight if one assumes a high density commodity.[16] A 20 percent increase in gross weight to 88,000 pounds enables four trucks to be the work of five assuming a high density commodity. In addition, more "cubage" in larger trailers or twin trailers can also afford fuel savings due to their larger capacity. A large transcontinental carrier of general commodities has estimated that its inability to operate twin trailers in two states, Iowa and Pennsylvania, causes it to use an additional two million gallons of diesel fuel annually.

The average density of general freight shipments is about 12½ pounds per cubic foot as packaged for transportation. It is estimated that this low density results in the closing out by volume of about one-half of all trailers by general commodity carriers;[17] that is, the semitrailer is loaded to full capacity before the maximum gross weight allowed is obtained. Twin trailer combinations provide up to 56 linear feet of cargo-carrying space within a 65-foot overall combination length, compared to the 40 to 45 feet available with a conventional tractor-semitrailer. Since the twin trailer is no higher, no wider, and designed to carry no more weight than present combinations, it has been suggested as a method for increasing motor carrier productivity. A cost reduction of about 4 percent has been estimated.

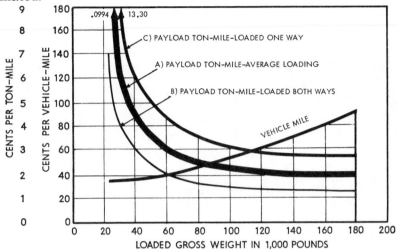

Fig. 7-4. Gross operating costs for all trailer combinations, showing vehicle-mile costs and payload ton-mile costs in relation to loaded gross weights. Source: Hoy Stevens, "Line Haul Trucking Costs Upgraded, 1964," *Highway Research Record*, 1966, p.19.

### Elements of Intramodal and Intermodal Competition

The intercity freight universe may be divided into three categories based on commodity classification and value. On the basis of ton-miles, bulk freight accounted for 29 percent of traffic, breakbulk 31 percent, and liquid 40 percent. All the liquid commodities are low value (value per ton under $200) and most of the bulk commodities are also low value. Break-bulk is basically medium value ($200 to $1,000 per ton) although some breakbulk is high value (over $1,000 per ton).

The quantity, quality, and price of motor freight service depends on the intensity of competition between motor carriers (intramodal) and between motor carriers and other modes (intermodal). The small parcel market is dominated by the United Parcel Service which has an average size ship-ment of about 12 pounds. By limiting their shipments to a maximum weight (50 pounds) as well as maximum length and girth, they have been able to provide intensive competition for other small parcel shippers, such as parcel post, bus express, air freight, air freight forwarders, air parcel post, and other motor carriers. They are permitted, however, to pick up aggregated shipments weighing more than 100 pounds from one consign-or. In the less-truckload market (50 to 10,000 pound category), the regulated Class I and Class II general commodity motor carriers have preempted the market, transporting almost 90 percent of shipments in this weight range. Other competitors include parcel post, air parcel post, freight forwarders, air freight forwarders, rail less-carload and rail TOFC, air cargo express, and shipper nonprofit associations. Nearly every type of motor carrier competes for truckload traffic, and intermodal competition from railroads is strongest in this market.

The interaction of modal capabilities with the characteristics of transport demand determine the feasibility of competition by each mode. The limited capacity of airplanes and high line-haul cost of air transport does not allow air transportation to be a significant competitor for truckload freight. The ability of air transport to move freight speedily, however, does make it a competitive factor for moving high value, small shipments over long distances when speed and service are important considerations. The acquisition of air freight forwarder authority by some of the larger motor carriers is no doubt designed to mitigate this competitive factor.

In contrast, the high terminal costs and low line-haul costs of rail suggest that railroads possess inherent cost advantages over motor carriers in the movement of large shipments over long distances. At the same time, motor carriers provide superior service in areas such as transit time, reliability of pickup and delivery and loss and damage. Furthermore, shippers may incur higher inventory costs when they are forced to increase the size of their shipment to obtain lower rail rates.

During the past 20 years, there is ample evidence of changing management perspectives and control of the transportation and physical distribution function by shippers. This has resulted in a much greater sensitivity in mode selection on the part of shippers to rates and service performance. Shippers will pay some premium on similar shipments for the service advantages of truck transportation.[18]

Further insight into the degree of intermodal competition between truck and rail was developed in a study of Census of Transportation statistics.[19] Any block of traffic in which both of these modes had 10 percent or more of the tonnage was considered to be competitive, and any block of traffic in which either of them has less than 10 percent was considered to be noncompetitive. The study found that 26.57 percent of tonnage moved by rail and truck is competitive. Fig. 7-5 indicates that the 28.33 percent of tonnage that is rail dominated is freight that moves in large lots over long distances and the opposite situation exists for the 44.6 percent of tonnage that is truck dominated. An earlier study utilizing an identical methodology but different data came to similar conclusions but noted that competitive traffic would be much higher if shipment sizes were easily changed and not determined independently of the mode of transport.

An examination of data contained in the 1963 and 1972 Censuses of Transportation provides some insight into the total transportation market. The material in the two Censuses enables one to make a limited check of two points in time of the total market as well as the share of the market that is held by different modes of transportation. The Census data cover movements of manufactured and processed commodities that originate at manufacturing establishments as defined in the Census of Manufactures, based on the standard industrial classification.

| | UNDER 1,000 POUNDS | 1,000-9,999 POUNDS | 10,000-29,999 POUNDS | 30,000-59,999 POUNDS | 60,000-89,999 POUNDS | 90,000 POUNDS OR MORE |
|---|---|---|---|---|---|---|
| LESS THAN 100 MILES | | | | | | |
| 100-199 MILES | | | | | | |
| 200-299 MILES | | TRUCK DOMINATED | | | COMPETITIVE | |
| 300-499 MILES | | | | | | |
| 500-999 MILES | | | | | | RAIL DOMINATED |
| 1,000-1,499 MILES | | | | | | |
| 1,500 MILES OR MORE | | | | | | |

Fig. 7-5. Distribution of shipment size and distance modally dominated and intermodally competitive for all *manufactured products* (89 Product Classes or Types) for rail and truck shipment. Source: Roth, Ronald D., *An Approach to Measurement of Modal Advantage,* American Trucking Associations, January, 1977.

Twenty-four major shipper groups are examined in the two Censuses. The trends for the total transport market in the years 1963 and 1972 had been upward. At these two times our economy was expanding, and the significant fact is that the motor carrier relative share of the total market in most classes was increasing. The share of ton-miles by truck increased from 31.9 to 37.6 percent while the rail share decreased from 62.3 to 57.0 percent. One explanation for this trend was developed in a study that found there is increasing regional self-sufficiency which could result in a diminishing need for intercity movement of goods in various stages of manufacturing. This may result in shortened hauls for many high-valued manufacturing products in contrast to the general trend for longer average haul for all commodities due to more distant concentrated origins of bulk raw materials.[20] In addition, the increasing value of the freight, higher costs of holding inventory, and recognition of customer service favor the service advantages of truck over rail.

The railroad industry has taken action to increase competition in some areas and decrease competition in other areas. Railroads have virtually eliminated their less-carload services requiring freight terminal handling. This is reflected in the steady decline of rail participation in small shipment traffic. Railroads can compete indirectly for small shipment traffic by offering carload (CL) on trailer-on-flatcar (TOFC) rates that are low enough to compensate for the service disadvantages of shipping in larger quantities. The ability of rails to compete for medium-value manufactures traffic through the development of TOFC services is being thoroughly investigated. A study conducted for the Department of Transportation measured the potential diversion of truck freight to rail if optimal TOFC operations were instituted.[21] Focusing on one specific market lane, the study found about 85 percent of the merchandise freight traffic might be handled in intermodal service, but less than half of that amount actually had the potential for diversion; even less could be actually transported under the operational, economic, and service constraints.

Shippers of perishables have found railroad refrigerated service deteriorating in recent years, some of it deliberately, and have turned increasingly to motor carriers. The number of nonmechanical refrigeration cars, the so-called "ice" cars—in service by the railroads has been reduced for over the past 10 years. Even so, there were still 20,000 of these cars in 1973. In that year, the railroads stopped providing icing service for use in these cars. In addition, during that year they added no mechanically refrigerated cars to their fleets. Furthermore, the railroads started in 1970 removing from service railroad-owned or -leased mechanically refrigerated trailers that were used in trailer-on-flatcar service. By 1973, over 5,000 of these cars had been removed from perishable service. The effect of this action was to force the shippers of perishable agricultural commodities to use truck service, which resulted in a shortage of motor carrier equipment for perishable commodities. The railroads also announced that their TOFC service for meat movements would be phased out by the end of 1975 because of unprofitability.

It appears there are varying degrees of intramodal competition at different levels of service that are based on carrier economics and the size of markets. The degree of competition in truckloads appears to be reasonably strong. There are few economies of scale to cause monopolization of the market by a few carriers. Entry and exit are easy because of the low cost and mobility of the truckload carrier's principal asset—trucks. The general commodity carriers have truckload service as a part of their regular operations and, in some instances, have organized a specialized division to handle truckloads of a particular commodity or commodity class. Specialized carriers, too, handle truckloads of a commodity or commodity class and also provide a significant element of competition for this truckload traffic. In addition, railroads transport many manufactured commodities both in carload lots and truckloads in TOFC service, and this service is competitive with both general commodity and specialized motor carriers.

Another formidable competitor is the manufacturer or processor who, through provision of his own private carriage, transports his products to customers. The shippers of truckloads and/or carloads have skilled and knowledgeable managers of traffic, physical distribution, or logistics department who control large volumes of freight. They are able thereby to stimulate competition for the traffic.

Within the legal weight limits that can be transported on the highway, the principal competitor of regulated motor carriers is private carriage. Many motor carriers seem oblivious to the possible conversion to private carriage by traffic and physical distribution departments of corporate firms due to inadequacies of regulated carrier service and rates.

In analyzing the status of for-hire motor carriers, differentiation should be made between the regulated and nonregulated (exempt) carriers. There are two and one-half times more exempt carriers than there are regulated carriers operating interstate. These carriers are not subject to economic regulation. There is no restriction on entry into exempt hauling, and each may establish any price for its service that it desires. Even in exempt interstate transportation, however, carriers sometimes agree to charge a specific rate between certain origin and destination points. Some exempt carriers publish a tariff, although not required to do so, and charge shippers the same rates for transporting the same quantities.

There are some exempt carriers which have secured operating authority for handling return loads of certain specific commodities and have filed their rates for this traffic with the Interstate Commerce Commission. In some cases, this rate may be 25 percent less than the carrier which hauls only nonexempt commodities. The lower rate offered by the exempt carrier is often just a "paper" rate, however; it is not used because the provision of facilities for solicitation and other expenses, such as terminal expenses, is not justified, particularly for those exempt carriers which can lease their units for the return haul to regulated for-hire carriers. This supplies a certain amount of revenue and is much simpler. There have been instances during an equipment shortage in which exempt carriers charged 25 percent more than regulated carrier rates.

Greater tendencies toward concentration exist in the less-truckload and parcel segments of motor freight where economies of scale are more significant and the extensive use of terminal facilities makes entry and exit more difficult.

There are approximately 5,000 motor common carriers of general commodities and the top four firms account for 15 percent of total general freight revenues, and the top eight firms account for 22 percent of the total.

There are a few firms that are dominant in the long-haul (transcontinental) less-truckload markets and regionally. The number of competitors in specific point-to-point market lanes depends on the amount of traffic available between two points and feeder traffic from other points. Major population and industrial areas are assured of a large number of carriers because of the large volume of traffic and their strategic location as bridges between other population centers. The number of carriers authorized to serve selected market lanes is shown in Table 7-1. Despite the large number of authorized competitors, the actual level of competition may be low.

A recent study analyzed the market share of less-truckload traffic held by the top carriers in large traffic markets.[22] It found that the top four firms account on the average for more than three-fifths of the business. Another study examined service to small communities in the nine-state Rocky Mountain region.[23] The study found about one-fourth of the towns were served by no more than one carrier, and more than half were served by no more than two. In most cases, more carriers were authorized to serve the towns than actually provided service.

Substantial controversy exists as to the causes of the observed market concentration. Some observers argue that economic regulation has prevented new entry and rate competition that would dilute the dominance of the top firms in each market. Others believe that economies of scale and market lane density are the reasons. Market studies conducted by a major carrier indicate that the number of carriers authorized to serve many major traffic lanes exceed the daily less-truckload expressed as trailerload equivalents. If the freight were split evenly among all authorized carriers, substantially less than one trailerload could be accumulated for daily service. The situation is more evident with regard to service to and from small communities where traffic volume is much lower.

### Conglomerates

A growing factor that can affect the level of competition is the ownership of motor carriers by conglomerates. During the 1960's, the conglomerate movement in industry had its effect in takeovers of motor carriers, primarily by nontransportation companies but also by transportation companies. From 1960-65, 25 motor carriers were acquired by nontransportation companies, and in 1966-69, 100 such acquisitions occurred.[24]

Some of the reasons for conglomerate ownership of motor carriers include the following: financial opportunity; the conglomerate surge; possiblity of economies of scale through horizontal integration; vertical integration when the motor carrier operation fits into the nontransportation operations; preferential service from subsidiary motor carriers; diversification efforts of motor carriers which establish holding companies in order to enter nontransportation businesses.[25]

TABLE 7-1

Selected Market Lanes and Number of Authorized Carriers

| Traffic Lane | No. Authorized Carriers |
|---|---|
| New York, N.Y. and Baltimore, Md.[1] | 71 |
| New York, N.Y. and Washington, D.C.[1] | 58 |
| New York, N.Y. and Roanoke, Va.[1] | 10 |
| New York, N.Y. and Richmond, Va.[1] | 26 |
| New York, N.Y. and Lynchburg, Va.[1] | 9 |
| New York, N.Y. and Norfolk, Va.[1] | 14 |
| Toledo, Ohio and Chicago, Ill.[1] | 49 |
| Atlanta, Ga. and Cincinnati, Ohio[1] | 24 |
| Baltimore, Md. and Cumberland, Md.[1] | 18 |
| Pittsburg, Pa. and Cumberland, Md.[1] | 13 |
| Buffalo, N.Y. and Cleveland, Ohio[1] | 41 |
| Chicago, Ill. and Milwaukee, Wis.[1] | 52 |
| Chicago, Ill. and Kansas City, Mo.[2] | 44 |
| Chicago, Ill. and Omaha, Neb.[2] | 33 |
| Chicago, Ill. and Minneapolis/St. Paul, Minn.[2] | 40 |
| Kansas City, Mo. and St. Louis, Mo.[2] | 47 |
| Minneapolis/St. Paul, Minn. and Los Angeles, Ca.[3] | 8 |
| Minneapolis/St. Paul, Minn. and Portland, Ore.[3] | 5 |
| Chicago, Ill. and San Francisco, Cal.[2] | 15 |
| Chicago, Ill. and Portland, Ore.[3] | 10 |

Sources: [1]David R. Kamerschen and Cris W. Paul, II, "The Value of Operating Rights in Regulated Trucking: Paradigm Lost," *Proceedings—Nineteenth Annual Transportation Research Forum* (Oxford, Ind.: Richard B. Cross, 1978), pp. 383-86; [2]Tabulated from cover *National Highway and Airway Carriers and Routes*, Fall 1977; and [3]Michael L. Lawrence, "Some Observations on Motor Carrier Regulation," paper presented to the Transportation Research Board, Washington, D.C., January 8, 1978.

Conglomerate ownership of motor carriers at present exceeds 11 percent of the Class I revenue totals. Some of the largest motor carriers are involved. International Utilities owns Ryder, a large regional southeast-based carrier, and P.I.E., a large transcontinental carrier. Pepsico, Inc., owns LeeWay Motor Freight and North American Van Lines. The Del Monte Corporation owns six motor carriers; Texas Gas Transmission owns four motor carriers, and Fuqua Industries, Inc., seven motor carriers. Recently American Natural Resources acquired Associated Truck Line, Graves Truck Lines and Garrett Freightlines. Conglomerate ownership became a matter of increasing concern to the Commission after the bankruptcy of the Penn Central Railroad which was a part of a holding company. It has policy implications involving possible preference and discrimination, anti-competitive aspects as a result of increased concentration of motor carriers, and possible financial manipulations that may leave the affected motor carriers in weakened financial conditions.

## Pooling

In an effort to continue service in some sparsely settled areas, a few motor common carriers of general commodities have entered into pooling agreements with Commission approval. The pooling arrangement, which has been approved by the Commission for use among household goods carriers for a long time, was recently approved for use among general commodity carriers and is in operation in a few areas. Under one such agreement entered into by Consolidated Freightways and a number of other carriers, a single carrier provides pickup and delivery of all traffic at specified points within a given area in which all of the carriers in the pooling agreement are authorized to serve.[26]

In substituting motor-for-motor service in one area in Montana involving 44 communities with a total population of 5,000 for example, daily service is provided under the pooling arrangement.

According to one study of motor carrier pooling arrangements, less than 100 interstate motor carriers are engaged in Commission-approved pooling agreements, but it seems clear that pooling among certificated carriers will increase.[27]

### Energy Implications

Energy use in the United States increased 118 percent from 1950 to 1976 and currently is divided as follows: industrial use, 36 percent; household and commercial use, 32 percent; and transportation, 32 percent. Consumption of petroleum increased at an even faster rate, 159 percent in the same time period. It is estimated that about 52 percent of our petroleum fuels are used to produce transportation. Less than 7 percent is used by commercial trucks.[28]

The 1980's will see an energy crisis reflected in rising energy prices and energy shortages in all sectors of the economy. In the trucking sector, diesel fuel prices, excluding taxes, rose over 40 percent in the first half of 1979. Fuel expenses account for about 5 percent of total motor carrier expenses but motor carriers operate on very low gross margins. Regulated carriers can save 8 to 10 cents per gallon by purchasing fuel at wholesale. The fuel costs for the independent owner-operators are higher—as much as 15 percent of revenue—since they purchase fuel at truck stops at retail price. Rapid fuel cost increases have endangered the financial viability of many carriers and vehicle operators that cannot raise their revenues to match such rapid cost increases. Absolute and spot fuel shortages have disrupted many motor carrier operations, particularly those dependent on retail sources.

Short-term public response to the situation includes fuel allocation, expedited rate increases, and temporary relaxation of certain entry controls. A partial solution supported by motor carrier interests is to increase size and weight limitations on vehicles. It is estimated that over 230 million gallons of fuel could be saved annually if (1) all states would allow the federally-approved maximum gross weight of 80,000 pounds; and (2) all states would permit the operation of 60-foot tractor, semitrailers or 65-foot twin trailer combinations.[29]

Motor carriers are rapidly adopting add-on fuel saving devices that reduce air drag, reduce engine power parasitic loss and improve engine/drive train efficiency.[30] Operational alternatives include the greater involvement in pooling agreements and other cooperative arrangements.

It has been suggested that freight be shifted from truck to rail or barge because the national average ton-miles per gallon or ton-miles per BTU are higher for nonhighway modes. A careful refinement of different facets of fuel efficiency by mode of transport is necessary, however, before drawing conclusions. The examination of energy intensiveness as expressed in BTU's per ton-mile does not reflect the fact that the services performed by each of the modes are not comparable.[31] Trucks provide pickup and delivery whereas rail and water do not. Water transport does not possess the flexibility in terms of availability of routes, as do railroads and motor carriers. And none of the modes possess the versatility of transport that motor carriers do. Water carriers are basically transporters of bulk commodities; pipelines are highly specialized and transport but a limited number of liquid commodities; and rail transportation is predominantly a transporter of bulk commodities, such as coal, grain, ore, lumber, wood products, pulp and paper.

Another factor that should be noted is that the circuity factor is much greater between origin and destination points for some modes of transport than for others. From Kansas City, Missouri, to Houston, Texas, for example, the inland water distance is 1,642 miles compared with 841 miles by rail. This is a circuity of 95 percent and is illustrative of the danger of relying solely on energy intensiveness based on ton-miles, grounded as it is on a mile-for-mile and not a point-to-point comparison. If one wants to determine a more realistic measure of energy intensiveness of each mode of transport, it would be more reliable to choose common origin and destination points for identical commodities with comparable services provided.

One cannot draw the conclusion that railroads are more efficient under all circumstances by comparing the aggregate fuel performance of railroads and motor carriers. There is evidence that for short hauls and light loads that characterize the traffic on many lines proposed for abandonment, motor carriers are more fuel efficient than railroads.[32]

An unpublished report, "Transportation Energy Conservation Options," which was produced at the Transportation Systems Center, Department of

Transportation, dealt with both freight and passenger energy use in conservation. With regard to freight service it pointed out that increasing the operating efficiency of trucks could save six percent of our energy within 15 years at a cost of an additional three billion dollars. Permitting larger truckloads could save another three percent of fuel within 10 years but this would be at a "negative" cost. These combined trucking efficiencies could save a total of 9½ percent within 15 years at a total investment cost of about three billion dollars.

On the other hand, the report indicates that a shift of freight from trucks to railroads would save less than two percent of energy but would require an investment of $15 billion and 15 years.

TOFC is the case where such direct comparisons are possible. Results of one study indicate that when all fuel is accounted for, TOFC and through truck service are about equal in fuel efficiency with differences dependent on characteristics of the corridor and the commodities involved.[33] Another study estimated that twin trailer service was 32 percent more fuel efficient than TOFC and 5.6 percent more efficient than rail boxcars.[34] After an operational test of comparable truck and TOFC service, the Department of Energy in 1980 concluded there was no single standard of comparison that was acceptable to all concerned and applicable on a general basis for measuring fuel efficiencies.

Longer term public policies include the development of alternative fuels that will not only hold down energy costs but also decrease U.S. dependence on foreign petroleum sources which is currently over 50 percent. Alternative fuels include alcohols, hydrogen, synthetic fuels from biomass, synthetic fuels from coal, and synthetic fuels from shale. The alcohol, coal and shale alternatives are especially desirable because the United States has abundant supplies of each. Some energy specialists believe that a reasonably mature synfuel industry can be established by 1990 with the proper financing incentives. Gasohol, a 90/10 blend of gasoline and alcohol, is already marketed at over 1,000 service stations. An important factor affecting the value of alternative fuels to the trucking industry is feasibility and cost of converting present engine and tractor systems to use new fuels.[35]

## Measurement of motor carrier costs [36]

The accurate determination of the cost of providing specific services is necessary to determine appropriate prices for controlling costs, and for setting future budget estimates. The former is especially significant for regulated carriers who must justify their rate charges before regulatory bodies as well as the market place.

There are three levels of motor carriers' costs which, under varying circumstances, are of help in analyzing and testing the compensatory nature of a rate. All three levels are necessary to provide the complete cost picture, and all three are necessary on occasion to explain motor carrier rates. (*a*) The first and lowest cost level is that of those one-way out-of-pocket or variable expenses which are separable from the joint expenses incurred in the round-trip movement of the equipment. (*b*) The second level of cost is that of the out-of-pocket or variable expenses applicable to the operation as a whole. This level embraces those joint expenses such as the round-trip movement of the equipment which, although of a joint nature for an individual segment of the motor carriers' operations, are nevertheless variable with traffic volume when the motor carriers' operations are viewed as a whole. (*c*) The third level of cost consists of the so-called fully distributed costs which are the out-of-pocket or variable costs plus an apportionment of the constant expenses.

The economic significance and application of each of these three levels of cost are stated briefly as follows:

(*a*) The out-of-pocket or variable costs which are separable from the joint expenses incurred in the round-trip movement of the equipment serve as a minimum below which the so-called return-movement rates cannot fall without incurring an out-of-pocket loss. Justification for rates that approach this low level of cost may exist where the value of the service (the conditions of demand) varies widely by directions of movement, the low rates being necessary to obtain a more efficient utilization of the equipment in the direction of the empty return. Under such circumstances, rates may be economically justified at a level slightly above the separable expenses assignable to the one-direction movement—that is, the added cost for pickup and delivery, platform handling, billing, and collection, and some small amount for additional fuel and vehicle wear and tear occasioned by the added weight of the load. Such rates, however, are based on the ability of the remaining traffic handled on the round trip to cover all the joint costs for the trip not recovered from the low-rated traffic. Otherwise, the carrier would incur an out-of-pocket loss for the round-trip movement taken as a whole. The principle at issue is that the revenues secured from the performance of any part of the operations, such as the round-trip movement of a truck, should normally equal the out-of-pocket expense incurred in performing such a segment of the service.

The Commission recognizes that transportation conditions may justify one-way costing and authorized its use in several cases. In one case, motor carriers showed that they had lost a substantial volume of business to rails and that a "heavy and chronic imbalance of traffic" existed in the going direction of the proposed rate. In another case, the Commission allowed rates based on one-way costing because the traffic would otherwise not move or move in private carriage.

(*b*) The second and broader concept of the out-of-pocket long run or variable costs, that which is applicable to the operation as a whole, is the one more commonly used. Such out-of-pocket costs provide a minimum below which rates having widespread or general application cannot fall without resulting in an out-of-pocket loss. Since such costs reflect the relative amount of transportation service received by the shipment, they provide a measure in cents per 100 pounds of the differences in the rates for shipments of varying sizes, lengths of haul, density, and so forth, which can be justified by differences in the cost of performing the service. Any remaining differences in the rates for the various kinds of traffic must be based on considerations other than cost.

(c) The fully distributed costs, based on the out-of-pocket or variable costs plus an apportionment of the constant expenses, provide comparisons of the relative costs of transportation for different regions or territories, separate agencies of transportation, or single carriers, based on total expenses. They also show the extent of the constant costs which are present in the operation and which must be recovered out of the revenues received over and above the out-of-pocket expenses. The comparative showing of the fully distributed costs in addition to the out-of-pocket costs assists in the determination of the limits within which recognition can be given to the value-of-service or demand factor. The fully distributed costs also provide a standard or measure that is helpful in testing the compensatory character of rates and in evaluating the extent to which noncost considerations (value of service or declarations of public policy) have entered into the making of the rates.

The long run variable costs are currently computed as "90 percent variable," i.e., 90 percent of the carrier's operating expenses and cost of capital (debt and equity) are considered as being directly variable with output—with the remaining 10 percent being, relatively speaking, constant.

The range within which motor carriers can reduce rates below fully allocated costs to meet competition is much narrower than that of railroads. The fact that motor carriers have not always made rates on a cost basis because they are competing with railroads has perhaps caused them to lose sight of the fact that their real competition may be private carriage. The ease with which private carriage may be instituted through the leasing of equipment can mean substantial loss of traffic, particularly truckload traffic, if for-hire service is not priced on a cost basis.

The significance of "cost of service" as opposed to "value of service" in the making of rates may be stated as follows: Cost-of-service considerations go principally to the distribution of the out-of-pocket or long-run variable costs. Value-of-service or demand considerations go to the apportionment of the constant and joint costs. The distribution of the out-of-pocket costs is based on the relative use the traffic in question makes of the carrier's plant and facilities. The apportionment of the constant and joint costs is fundamentally based on an appraisal of the effect the rates themselves would have upon the movement of the traffic and the carrier's revenues. Of far-reaching significance in this latter connection has been the recognition and application of the principle that by reducing the rates on traffic having expansible or elastic traffic volume, the contribution to the constant costs or revenue needs can be increased, within limits, beyond that which can be obtained by limiting rate differences strictly to cost-of-service considerations.

### Efficiency and performance criteria

Operating and financial measures are used by carrier management, investors, and regulatory bodies to assess the efficiency and performance of both individual carriers and larger carrier groups. Only a few of many available measures are discussed here.

Average load per vehicle mile and vehicle miles per vehicle are broad indexes of the utilization of equipment capacity. One must be careful in utilizing these indexes when the performance of other carriers is used as a benchmark. For example, the average loads for household goods carriers, general freight carriers, and agricultural products carriers are 4.11 tons, 13.29 tons, and 16.40 tons respectively.[37] These figures reflect the density of the freight normally moved by each carrier group rather than inefficiency. Similarly, one would expect lower vehicle utilization from short-haul carriers than from long-haul carriers.

One can ascertain evidence of productivity through an examination of trends in the indexes of the following: dollar input per employee and per capital unit; transportation output per employee and per capital unit; dollar input per unit of transportation output; revenue per dollar of output; and total payroll to revenues. A refinement of the last measure is to include purchased transportation as part of total payroll, making it more useful to specialized carriers who rely heavily on purchased transportation. Capital productivity is measured by various turnover ratios. Gross revenues to net carrier operating property measures how much revenue is produced by each dollar of operating equipment. Gross revenues to equity and after-tax income to equity are other measures.

The motor carriers make use of their average operating ratio as a measure of their revenue needs and financial condition. The operating ratio is the proportion which operating expense bears to operating income. Operating expenses divided by operating revenues and multiplied by 100 give the percentage of the operating revenues which are required to pay the operating expenses, this being the operating ratio. The operating ratio considers only total cost in investment and labor inputs and does not consider how efficiently these inputs are used. It does not differentiate between the carrier whose costs are high due to inefficiency and one whose operating ratio is high because of other circumstances despite the carrier's maximum efficient use of capital resources.

An operating ratio in excess of 100 would indicate that the expense of the operation exceeded the revenues derived from it. It is desirable to keep the operating ratio as low as possible.

The operating ratio is one of the single most important indexes of profitability from the financial analyst's point of view. Management's success in achieving higher revenue yields per unit is just as important as producing at the lowest cost per unit. Operating ratios developed for different freight services indicate areas of cross subsidy such as between shipments of different weight, distance, or location. Thus, the operating ratio can guide rate restructuring.

### Rate of return

A fair-rate-of-return concept is generally used in the regulated industries in determining the need for rate increases. In the utility industry, though, a rate increase is based upon the rate of return on the investment. When the rate of return on the investment of a utility company falls below a desired level, the company seeks a rate increase in order to obtain a fair rate of return. In industries of this kind, the investment is large, however, in relation to total costs, and the risk is more closely related to the amount of the investment. In the motor carrier industry, on the other hand, the amount of investment is relatively small in relation to total costs.

Motor carriers do not have to provide their own highways (but do contribute substantial taxes toward them) and the bulk of their fixed assets are tractors and trailers whose life-span is short. The working capital needs for motor carrier service are not comparable to those of a manufacturer. However, the Commission has indicated that a motor carrier should have working capital equal to its operating expenses for one month. Motor carriers are in general agreement that stability and service-ability are impaired whenever the individual operating ratio rises above 95 percent. From the remaining 5 percent, interest payments and income taxes not included in operating expenses must be paid and net income secured. The danger point for a group of carriers providing service in a given territory is usually reached when the group average rises significantly above 90 percent.

These characteristics led the Commission and motor carriers to accept originally the operating ratio and not the rate of return as a valid method of determining the need for rate increases for the industry.

Motor carriers, in seeking rate adjustment approvals from the Interstate Commerce Commission and state utility commissions, use their operating ratios as the criteria for proving the need for a general increase in rates. For example, Division 2 of the Interstate Commerce Commission, treating one proposal for increased rates which contemplated a 10 percent increase in less-than-truckload rates and a four percent increase in truckload rates, ruled that such increases would produce an average operating ratio of about 93 percent, which it believed to be reasonable.[38] Another decision mentioned and used the 93 percent ratio.[39] Again, in another decision, the granting of a general 10 percent rate increase was found to be just and reasonable, for it would result in an operating ratio of about 93 percent.[40]

The need for additional revenue based on the operating ratio alone may have more validity for some types of motor carriers than for others, but it is used for all carriers. For example, a specialized carrier, such as a household goods carrier, which pays 70 percent of the gross revenue for the lease of a vehicle and 20 percent to a booking agent to solicit traffic has 10 percent of the revenue left to cover all of the administrative and other costs. These two expenses will result in the operating ratio seldom, if ever, being below 90 percent. If the revenue on a shipment was $100 and the transportation was purchased for 70 percent of the revenue, with an additional 20 percent commission paid for the solicitation, the expenses would amount to 90. The operating ratio would be 90 percent. Assume that the revenue is increased on this shipment to $200 and that the transportation was purchased for 70 percent of the revenue while a 20 percent commission was paid for the solicitation of the shipment. The increased revenue would then be $200, the expenses $180, and the operating ratio still 90 percent.

The Commission prescribes a uniform system of accounts and reports, and the data are used by the Commission in special studies and cost studies, as well as in granting rate increases. A widespread practice has developed among motor carriers which may be destroying the authenticity of these records. Many motor carriers have established affiliated companies that furnish equipment and services to the carrier. Some of these companies are wholly-owned subsidiaries of the carriers, whereas many more are owned by stockholders, officers of the carrier, or close relatives of the principal owner. The equipment and services furnished by affiliates include motor vehicles, terminals, gasoline and oil, tires, pickup and delivery service, maintenance of equipment, and managerial services. These controlled affiliates can make unreasonably high charges.

The regulatory problem created by this situation is that the expenses contained in carrier's reports may be distorted because profits are siphoned off to affiliates. This practice can nullify the uniformity of reported financial data. Illustrative of this problem is the example of the carrier that paid $620,000 to 15 affiliates. The carrier had a net income of $7,500 whereas the combined net income of the affiliated companies was $157,000. In one major rate territory affiliates account for 40 percent of the assets of the carrier's operating property and for the U.S. it is estimated to be 25 percent.

Reports do not have to be filed with the Commission on affiliate companies. Motor carrier holding companies, however, are required to file reports of financial transactions. There are about 30 of these companies. This order applies to persons who are not motor carriers but who have effective control over one or more motor carriers through ownership of securities issued.

TABLE 7-2

Operating Ratios, Returns on Net Investment in
Transportation Property Plus Working Capital, and
Returns on Equity: Class I Intercity Motor
Carriers of Property—1960-1977

| Year | No. of Carriers | Revenues (in Billions) | Operating Ratio | Return on Net Investment | Return on Equity |
|------|------|------|------|------|------|
| 1960 | 935 | 4.4 | 97.51 | 11.53 | 4.93 |
| 1961 | 972 | 4.6 | 96.11 | 17.83 | 10.20 |
| 1962 | 1004 | 5.1 | 95.87 | 19.22 | 12.36 |
| 1963 | 1004 | 5.4 | 95.90 | 18.53 | 12.06 |
| 1964 | 1025 | 5.8 | 95.46 | 20.22 | 13.63 |
| 1965 | 1114 | 6.6 | 94.80 | 22.56 | 15.72 |
| 1966 | 1159 | 7.3 | 95.04 | 20.90 | 14.48 |
| 1967 | 1198 | 7.5 | 96.36 | 15.07 | 9.23 |
| 1968 | 1252 | 8.8 | 95.16 | 21.18 | 12.87 |
| 1969 | 1296 | 9.8 | 95.96 | 17.44 | 8.84 |
| 1970 | 1376 | 11.1 | 96.64 | 9.00 | 6.69 |
| 1971 | 1355 | 13.0 | 94.05 | 17.17 | 15.85 |
| 1972 | 1571 | 15.2 | 94.18 | 17.45 | 17.17 |
| 1973 | 1576 | 16.5 | 94.75 | 16.82 | 15.62 |
| 1974 | 755 | 16.7 | 95.25 | 21.35 | 13.35 |
| 1975 | 770 | 16.1 | 95.59 | 18.59 | 9.30 |
| 1976 | 852 | 18.4 | 93.88 | 25.76 | 23.80 |
| 1977 | 813 | 22.2 | 94.81 | 23.67 | 16.15 |

Sources: 1960-1969: ICC 84th Annual Report to Congress, 1970, App. G., Tables 18, 19, 20; 1970-1973, ICC 88th Annual Report to Congress; 1974-1976, ICC 91st Annual Report to Congress, Table 10; 1977, ICC 92nd Annual Report to Congress.

The Commission began to reconsider the use of rate-of-return criteria when in its proceeding, *Ex Parte MC-82 1978,* it required motor carriers to submit evidence of the "sum of money" which they require, over and above operating expenses, to attract debt and equity capital, to provide financial stability, and the capacity to render service.[41]

A recent decision by the Commission seems to have reversed the historical dependence on the operating ratio.[42] This decision stated that the rate of return on stockholder's equity (net income after interest and taxes) is the most important financial ratio because it is the return measure which the equity investor, the source of capital, will use in determining whether the motor carrier industry is an attractive place to invest capital. Three other ratios will also be considered: return on investment; the debt/equity ratio; and the current ratio. The operating ratio is no longer considered a reliable indicator of revenue need in general rate increase proceedings.

The Commission, in the same decision (currently under litigation), also ordered that motor carriers of general commodities should be permitted the opportunity to achieve a return no greater than the average return earned by all manufacturing industries—approximately 14 percent. An important factor underlying the validity of the 14 percent criterion is whether the general commodity motor carriers face fewer or more risks than industry generally. Higher risk industries must pay higher rates of return, other factors being equal.

Table 7-2 shows the operating ratios for Class I motor carriers of property as well as the return on net investment and return on equity. The relationship of changes in the operating ratio as reflected in return on net investment or return on equity are clearly shown in the table. The return for Class I carriers has been a satisfactory return and exceeds that of businesses in a number of sectors in our economy.

### QUESTIONS AND PROBLEMS

1. What facts are there to support the statement that "motor carriers are essentially small business firms?" Compare the gross revenues of the largest motor carriers over the past decade with the largest carriers in other fields. How does the growth rate compare?

2. Are there scale economies in motor transportation? How do you account for the controversy in the field?

3. Define operating ratio. What is its use in motor carrier rate cases? Is the fair-rate-of-return concept used in the utility industry also used in the motor carrier field? Discuss.

4. The motor carrier industry feels that the operating ratio is the only fair and equitable standard by which to assay its financial needs. Do you agree? Why or why not?

5. Explain out-of-pocket costs. What are variable costs? What are marginal costs?

6. What are constant costs? Joint costs? List and explain differences between constant and joint costs.

7. Give some examples of joint costs in the motor carrier industry. Of what significance are joint costs?

8. "The utility of transportation service to the shipper comes ... from its ability to satisfy his needs or wants." Explain.

9. What is meant by the statement that "motor transportation of general commodities is essentially a transactions business?" What are the economic implications?

10. What criteria should be used in determining the adequacy of competition in the LTL market? The TL market?

11. Assuming the necessity for energy conservation for the next decade, what might be its impact on the trucking industry?

12. Prepare a paper on conglomerates and holding companies in the motor carrier field which encompasses the economic motivation and impact of such ownership upon competition.

### FOOTNOTES TO CHAPTER 7

[1]Garland Chow, *The Economics of the Motor Freight Industries* (Bloomington, Ind.: School of Business, Indiana University, 1978), pp. 107-118.

[2]Revenue statistics from *Commercial Car Journal* (June, 1979).

[3]Combined revenue of United Parcel Service of America's two major operating companies.

[4]Computed from statistics from *1977 Motor Carrier Statistics* (Washington, D.C.: American Trucking Associations, Inc., 1978).

[5]*Ibid.*

[6]American Trucking Associations, *Research Review* (June 15, 1979), p. 2.

[7]The empirical evidence on economies of scale is mixed. Some of the studies that have concluded there are no economies of scale include: Robert A. Nelson, "The Economic Structure of the Highway Carrier Industry in New England," *Motor Freight Transport for New England* (1956), p. 34; Merrill J. Roberts, "Some Aspects of Motor Carrier Costs: Firm Size, Efficiency, and Financial Health," *Land Economics,* Vol. 32 (1956), p. 228; Richard Klem, "The Cost Structure of the Regulated Trucking Industry," *Proceedings of a Workshop on Motor Carrier Economic Regulation* (Washington, D.C.: National Academy of Sciences, 1978), pp. 57-98; and Ann F. Friedlaender, "Hedonic Costs and Economies of Scale in the Regulated Trucking Industry," *Proceedings of a Workshop on Motor Carrier Economic Regulation, ibid.,* pp. 141-162.

Studies that have concluded that significant economies of scale exist include: Paul W. Emery, "An Empirical Approach to the Motor Carrier Scale Economies Controvesy," *Land Economics,* Vol. 41 (1965), p. 285; Stanley L. Warner, "Cost Models, Measurement Errors, and Economies of Scale in Trucking," in *The Cost of Trucking Econometric Analysis,* M.L. Burstein, et al. (Dubuque, Iowa: Wm. C. Brown Co., 1965), pp. 1-46; Michael L. Lawrence, "Economies of Scale in the General Freight Motor Common Carrier Industry: Additional Evidence," *Proceedings—Seventeenth Annual Meeting of the Transportation Research Forum* (Oxford, Ind.: Richard B. Cross Co., 1976), pp. 169-176; and Garland Chow, "The Cost of Trucking Revisited," *Proceedings of a Workshop on Motor Carrier Economic Regulation* (Washington, D.C.: National Academy of Sciences, 1978), pp. 57-98. For a comprehensive review and critique of the empirical literature on this issue see Chow, pp. 58-65, and Garland Chow, "The Status of Economies of Scale in Regulated Trucking," *Proceedings—Nineteenth Annual Meeting of the Transportation Research Forum* (Oxford, Ind.: Richard B. Cross, Inc., 1978), pp. 365-73.

[8]Middle Atlantic Conference, *Middle Atlantic Conference Continuing Traffic Study,* Report No. 22 (September 1978).

[9]Interstate Commerce Commission, Bureau of Economics, *Transport Economics,* Vol. 5, No. 1 (1978).

[10]Transportation Association of America, *Transportation Facts and Trends* (July 1978), p. 14.

[11]Computed from statistics from *1977 Motor Carrier Statistics, op. cit.*

[12]Special tabulation of motor carrier annual reports, 1973. See Chow, *The Economics of the Motor Freight Industries, op. cit.,* p. 120.

[13]Interstate Commerce Commission, Bureau of Accounts, *Cost of Transporting Freight by Class I and Class II Motor Common Carriers of General Commodities—Central Region, 1971,* Statement No. 2C9-71 (Washington, D.C., 1973), Table 13.

[14]Hoy Stevens, "Line Haul Trucking Costs Upgraded, 1964," *Highway Research Record* (1966), p. 19.

[15]Senate Committee on Public Works, *Transportation and the New Energy Policies,* 93rd Cong. 2nd sess. (Washington, D.C. 1974), p. 20.

[16]$W = 500 (LN/N-1 + 12N + 36)$, where W = overall gross weight of any group of two or more axles, L = distance in feet between the extreme of any group of two or more consecutive axles, N = number of axles in the group under consideration.

[17]American Trucking Associations, Inc., *The Case for Twin Trailers* (mimeo) (December 1978), p.3.

[18]Alexander L. Morton, *Competition in the Intercity Freight Market* (Office of Systems Analysis and Information, Department of Transportation, February, 1971), pp. 134-37.

[19]Ronald D. Roth, "An Approach to Measurement of Modal Advantage," *Transportation Research Record* (1977).

[20]Alexander Morton, "Freight Demand" (Dissertation, Harvard University, Cambridge, Mass., 1973. See also *Improving Railroad Productivity* (A report to the National Commission on Productivity, Washington, D.C., November, 1973).

[21]Reebie Associates, *An Improved Truck/Rail Operation: Evaluation of a Selected Corridor,* report prepared for Federal Highway Administration, Department of Transportation (1976).

[22]Background Information on Trucking Industry Concentration Data, press release from the office of Senator Edward M. Kennedy, June 24, 1979, cited in Carole Shifrin, "A Few Firms Said Ruling Truck Routes," *Washington Post,* June 26, 1979, p. D-7.

[23]Paul T. McElhiney, *Motor Common Carier Freight Rate Study for Nine Western States,* final report prepared for Federation of Rocky Mountain States, Inc., in cooperation with Department of Transportation (May 1975).

[24]Interstate Commerce Commission, Bureau of Economics, *Conglomerate Merger Activity Involving Motor Carriers* (October 1970).

[25]*Ibid.*

[26]*Consolidated Freightways Corp., et al., Pooling,* 109 MCC 596 (1971).

[27]Barbara Blom Anthony, *Motor Carrier Pooling Agreements,* staff study, Transportation Systems Center, Department of Transportation (December 1976).

[28]American Trucking Associations, Inc., *Truck Energy Data* (October 1977), p. 7.

[29]*Ibid.*

[30]See *Report of St. Louis Truck Fuel Economy Demonstration,* Regular Common Carrier Conference (mimeo).

[31]Alexander French, "Energy and Freight Movements," *Transportation Journal* (Fall 1976), pp. 39-40.

[32]Herbert Weinblatt, Donald E. Matzzie, and John Harman, "Effects of Railroad Abandonment on the Modal Distribution of Traffic and Related Costs," *Transportation Journal* (Summer 1978), pp. 86-96.

[33]French, *op. cit.,* p. 39.

[34]Reebie Associates, *op. cit.*

[35]Ryder Program in Transportation, University of Miami, *Alternative Fuels and Intercity Trucking,* report prepared for the U.S. Department of Energy, June 1978, p. 302.

[36]Largely adapted from Interstate Commerce Commission, Bureau of Accounts, Cost Finding, and Valuation, *Explanation of the Development of Motor Carrier Costs with Statement as to Their Meaning and Significance* (Washington, D.C., 1959), and Statement of A. Daniel O'Neal, Chairman, Interstate Commerce Commission, made before the Antitrust and Monopoly Subcommittee of the Senate Judiciary Committee, April 26, 1978.

[37]American Trucking Associations, Inc., *1978 Financial Analysis of the Motor Carrier Industry* (Washington, D.C., 1978).

[38]*Increased Common Carrier Truck Rates in the East,* 42 MCC 633 (1943).

[39]*Increased Common Carrier Truck Rates in New England,* 43 MCC 13 (1943).

[40]*New England, 1946 Increased Rates,* 47 MCC 509 (1947).

[41]*Ex Parte MC-82, New Procedures in Motor Carrier Revenue Proceedings,* 339 ICC 324 (1978).

[42]*I & S M-29772,* decided November 27, 1978.

# chapter 8

# Financing motor carrier operations

In the early development of motor carriers, they were confronted with innumerable problems of financing. Their primary concern was with equipment financing. Once a carrier was able to pay for one truck, it was usually used as collateral for a loan to purchase a second truck, and so on as the business grew. As carriers expanded, they found the need for more efficient terminals. This, too, was primarily a financing problem. Moreover, many of the early operators found it difficult to secure financing on what they considered to be reasonable terms, so that financing aspects were a major problem from the beginning.

Financing continues to be a matter of vital interest to motor carrier management. It has been estimated that the capital needs of the trucking industry for replacement and expansion of equipment alone from 1976 to 1999 will exceed $130 billion, based on constant 1975 dollars.[1] What efficiencies can be secured by a planned program of equipment replacement and terminal improvements? In committing additional capital, where would its use most improve customer service? Should the company issue securities to the public? These and many other questions face management as motor carriers expand their operations.

## Factors influencing the granting of loans

The financial structure of motor carriers is different from that of other businesses which carry large inventories. Working capital customarily comes first in any analysis of credit worthiness by a financing institution. However, the need for working capital for motor carriers is small. The ratio of quick assets to liabilities is not as favorable in the financial structure of a motor carrier because the motor carrier does not carry large inventories; it has no need to do so, since it sells service and since its inventories are in the form of equipment that is used in the rendition of service.

Usually considered next in any analysis of credit worthiness is the relationship of capital and debt. Here the impressive proportions evidenced in other industries are not necessary. The average motor carrier's normal debt ratio is more than 1:1, or a total debt approximately equal to or slightly more than capital. A larger debt proportion can be carried by a highly profitable motor carrier operation, and frequently is when abnormal replacements are required to rehabilitate truck fleets. There is no set limit to a debt ratio, but a company should have an overall equity in equipment greater than the collateral margin if its entire debt were secured.

The extent to which motor carriers have relied upon their retained earnings as a source of capital funds is not known precisely, but it is a very important source. A study of 381 common carriers of general freight found that one third of the capital funds of these carriers came from retained earnings. [2]

One of the principal factors considered by lending institutions is the caliber of management. If company management has been stable and has shown consistently capable administration of company operations, this is favorably. viewed by lenders. The depth of management is also important. The carrier's future well-being should not rest entirely upon one individual, but there should be a division of responsibilities among a number of executives to insure continuity of operations. Capable management should begin at the terminal level and proceed upward to the top executive.

Tonnage growth is another of the determinants in the consideration of carrier earnings expansion. This factor is dependent in large measure on general economic growth and follows quite closely the GNP although increasing at a slightly greater rate than the advancement of GNP. The expansion of larger carriers is at a higher rate than the smaller carriers as they capture a greater share of an expanding market.

Other factors considered are: (1) consistent record of earnings after all charges; (2) reasonably steady flow of income; (3) balanced replacement program so that repairs and replacements do not constitute a burden on future operations; (4) sufficient cash together with other liquid assets, including receivables, to meet payroll and other monthly expenses; and (5) long-term debt spread over a sufficient period of time so that income after ordinary expenses and taxes is sufficient to meet amortization requirements.

In the past, carrier operating rights were a factor of significant importance. Most lending institutions considered them as being 10 to 20 percent of the revenue generated by management. However, the liberality of ICC grants of authority, particularly since 1970, and the possibility of freedom of entry as proposed in recent deregulation legislation have lessened their importance. The prospect of new carriers and the expansion of private carriage would lessen the earning capacity of many carriers, thus lessening their attractiveness as a credit risk. Operating certificates will probably be used as backup security to other liens.

A paramount factor considered by a lending institution is the ability of a carrier to repay a loan. Opinions of a carrier are inadequate. Lenders are interested in a thoroughly prepared financial statement. The institution wants to know the borrower's present financial condition. The current balance sheet and a current income statement will provide these facts. If a large loan is sought, additional information will be needed, such as the age of accounts receivable and payable, depreciation policies, prepaid expenses and accrued expenses, and any contingent liabilities or commitments that would have a bearing on the carrier's financial position. A history of the carrier's operations will give some indication of the company's stability of earnings. This also provides a basis of comparison with the current position of the company. The balance sheets and profit and loss statements for a number of years, preferably five to ten, would be helpful in providing a history of a company's operations.

A loan presentation should also include the principal routes, competition on the routes, the largest customers and the percentage of revenue coming from them, and a description of management. In a few cases, motor carriers have been able to obtain unsecured loans due to their strong position in the field.

### Working capital

Working capital is the amount needed day to day to operate a business and to pay the normal everyday expenses. This is often referred to as "permanent working capital." "Temporary working capital" is that needed for seasonal or unusual purposes, such as motor vehicle licenses, accelerated payment of federal income taxes, or the purchase or renewal of large annual insurance policies, or an unusual expense due to a strike or fire.

The lack of adequate working capital has been cited as second only to poor management as a cause of business failure. Many investment firms are hesitant to make loans on reasonable terms to motor carriers because they feel that there is not adequate working capital. Motor carriers justify their lower working capital on the basis that they operate virtually on a cash basis as accounts receivable turn over approximately every 20 days. The billings and collections have to be made in accordance with Commission regulations. Another factor cited by motor carriers to justify low working capital is that there is no inventory to tie up working capital as in other industries. Since working capital is important to the lending institutions, however, the motor carrier should do everything possible to improve its working capital balance.

Motor carriers have found that they can improve their working capital position without seeking outside loans by increasing their revenue billing efficiency, improving accounts receivable collections, and by temporary curtailment of purchases. The conversion of accounts receivable by outright sale through clearinghouses, discussed in a later chapter, is a method of providing immediate working capital. Accounts receivable can also be assigned as security for a short-term loan to increase working capital. The pledging of accounts can be arranged so that it provides for a continuing loan. The carrier and the bank execute a loan agreement providing that all newly created accounts receivable are automatically covered, so that the collateral for the loan is replaced. Under such arrangements, the amount of the loan may remain fixed or may fluctuate upward or downward in direct ratio to the amount of collateral in accounts receivable.

## Equipment Replacement Schedule

At what time in the life of a unit of equipment should it be replaced? This is an important management decision and requires the compilation of data based on experience. Factors such as equipment cost, maintenance cost, depreciation, cost per mile, specific cost in each time period, and others must be considered.

The cost per mile for the various mileage brackets of 100,000 miles, 200,000 miles, 300,000 miles, etc. can be determined using the purchase price, the resale price at the various stages of life of the unit, the depreciation, and the maintenance cost. Depreciation costs are highest in the first year of life of a tractor and reduce thereafter for the remaining life. Unit utilization will be higher, however, during the first year of life, and maintenance or repair costs will be less and increase gradually in the following years. Some companies have found that utilization of a unit is stable through the 300,000 mile bracket and then drops considerably when the unit is in the 400,000 mile level. When the unit has been operated about 600,000 miles, its availability for use may be reduced by as much as 50 percent. If the unit has not been replaced, two units will have to be used to obtain the same amount of road use that was obtained from one unit with 300,000 miles. One carrier has stated that its experience shows that equipment should be replaced at the 400,000 mile level which is usually when the unit is 42 months old.

## Revolving credit

Many companies establish a line of credit with a bank as a specified maximum which can be borrowed for certain purposes. This is sometimes used to augment working capital or to purchase equipment and is generally made available over periods ranging up to 18 months. A larger company may have an agreement with a group of banks that provide revolving credit up to as large an amount as $35 million.

## EQUIPMENT FINANCING

The financing of motor carrier equipment has presented two major problems: (a) lack of sources of credit, and (b) unfavorable credit terms in the purchase of equipment. Many financial institutions were wary of loaning funds to the embryonic trucking industry, and certainly this conservative attitude was somewhat justified in view of the record of many early truck operators. The lack of responsibility toward their financial obligations on the part of some motor carriers in the early days of the industry has been a factor in the reluctance of banking institutions to grant applications for motor carrier equipment financing. Furthermore, prior to 1935, there was not the stabilizing influence in the motor carrier industry that was introduced with the passage of the Motor Carrier Act at that time and the subsequent placing of the for-hire interstate motor carriers under the jurisdiction of the Interstate Commerce Commission. Even today, banks generally are not anxious to make this type of loan except under terms that many motor carriers feel are too stringent.

### Legal instruments

Equipment notes can be made upon the security of chattel mortgages, conditional sales agreements, or leases, usually with the option to purchase at the expiration of the lease. Lease agreements for purchase of equipment are not uncommon in motor carrier financing. The form of legal instrument to be used for any financing must be based on consideration of state laws and other circumstances. Because the conditional sales contract gives the lender a title claim instead of a mortgage, it is the most favored instrument in the majority of states for loans on new equipment. It cannot be used for refinancing, and in some states it is not sufficient for collateral purposes because foreclosure requires the cancellation of the debt.

Under a conditional sales contract, the buyer makes specific payments and acquires ownership rights in the vehicle. When the payments specified in the contract are completed, the title is vested in the purchaser. In effect, under the conditional sales contract, the purchaser acquires a contingent interest but does not become the full owner until all of the required payments are made.

When the security is a chattel mortgage, the ownership of the vehicle is held by the borrower subject to the mortgage lien. Under a purchase money chattel mortgage, title is held by the borrower but is pledged immediately to the lender until completion of all required payments. A promissory note may or may not serve as evidence of the debt covered by a chattel mortgage. If there is such a note, its payment is secured by pledge of the equipment which is described in the chattel mortgage. The borrower, of course, has possession of the equipment, but his free ownership is limited by the provisions of the mortgage which continues in effect until all of the payments or other requirements in the mortgage have been satisfied.

Congress enacted a bill, effective January 1, 1959, that provides that the recording of a vehicle lien in any one state should be recognized as valid by any other state. This law is applicable to common and contract motor carriers subject to the Interstate Commerce Act in their purchase of trucks and trailers. It eliminated the necessity for recording vehicle liens in several states in order to give lending institutions security in their financing of vehicle purchases.

A bailment lease is another type of lien instrument which may be used. Even though it is written in the form of a lease, this instrument provides for the title to be passed to the lessee or borrower upon completion of the scheduled payments.

### Vendor credit

As a result of inadequate truck equipment financing, some of the truck manufacturers undertook the financing of motor carrier equipment. This type of credit is called "vendor credit" and is extended or arranged only for the purchase of specific equipment from the manufacturer. It was instituted in 1946 as an aid in selling their products. Equipment manufacturers organized their own financial companies, which were in turn financed by banks and other financial interests. This was often the only form of credit that some customers could secure. This type of credit is not selective and is based primarily on the collateral value of the equipment purchased by the motor carrier. The terms for this purchase are predicated not on the qualifications of the particular motor carrier purchaser but rather on the value and life of equipment in the hands of *any* motor carrier used under average conditions under average management. Terms of payment are worked out on a statistical average and result in comparatively standard down payments and length of payments. The average length of a contract is 40 months. Interest rates on this type of financing are relatively high.

The equipment of trucking companies represents a large portion of their assets. Inasmuch as equipment is easily sold, truck and trailer manufacturers extend loans with no hesitation. Secured loans rather than unsecured loans are the most widely used type of borrowing in the trucking industry. Manufacturers usually finance purchases of equipment through an affiliate or an agency of the equipment manufacturer. Equipment is purchased on either a chattel mortgage or conditional sales agreement. Fruehauf Trailer Company, for example, sells trailers to customers and receives a time-payment contract. These contracts are sold to the Fruehauf Finance Company. The latter company borrows money at commercial banking rates and charges competitive retail finance rates, retaining as collateral the trailer equipment until the obligation is paid. In a recent year, this company had almost $800 million in loans.

### Selective credit

Contrasted to vendor credit is selective credit in equipment financing. This is credit advanced by a lending institution to an individual motor carrier based on its individual credit worthiness. This is the type of credit which has presented difficulties both to those supplying credit and those applying for it. The need for understanding of the trucking business by lending institutions and the need for understanding of the banking business by truckers is evident. The promotion of understanding of problems and policies present in each operation will go far to ease credit restrictions.

Care should be exercised that the debt matures in amounts that can be handled by the motor carrier without difficulty. Too often, carriers are forced by financing institutions to concentrate too large a portion of their debt maturities within too short a period of time. As a result, revenue operations cannot provide funds for orderly payment. A piece of equipment with a six-year service life, earning ten percent on its average depreciated value, will not pay for itself for more than four years. Financed on a 25 percent down payment, this period can be shortened to a little more than three years. A selective credit analysis for an individual motor carrier should consider, in determining the length of maturities, the life of equipment, management, coverage, and other credit factors. Credit periods of three to six years should be justified for heavy equipment.

In making loans to motor carriers, the lending institutions must give careful attention to collateral. This is true primarily because loans are repaid out of revenue, not by the liquidation of assets, as in other businesses which have reasonably high accounts receivable and inventory. As has been pointed out also, motor carriers usually have little or no working capital, and their debt ratios are high. Careful attention is given, then, to the life of the equipment in determining maturities.

Payments on a monthly basis need not be the same for the life of the loan. If the original credit is based on a variety of equipment—light, medium, and heavy—payments in the early months may be heavier than those of the later months. In that manner, dependence is not placed on light equipment to serve as collateral beyond the middle period of its service life, though such equipment continues to serve as collateral. Also to be considered in such a scheduling of maturities is the fact that lower payments are made in the later stages of the loan, when maintenance costs are higher and collateral value of the equipment lower.

Terms of credit for the financing of used equipment must of necessity be more stringent. With equipment serving as collateral, the service life of the equipment will have to be determined. Substantial down payments and short-term maturities would appear to be desirable in financing of this kind.

When it is necessary to refinance equipment loans, the matter of maturities is important. Loans which are refinanced are usually paid on a monthly basis, but, like the original equipment loans, such payments do not have to be uniform for the period of the loan but may be larger during the early months than in the later period. A carrier which has heavy current debts may need refinancing, but most lending institutions are very careful in considering such loans to determine fully the nature and service life of the security which is to be used.

### Depreciation as a source of financing

Depreciation is a reasonable allowance for the wear and tear on property used in a business. The factor of obsolescence is included. No cash outlay is involved for any given year's depreciation, but unless the records of the business provide for depreciation each year during the estimated life of a piece of equipment, the day will come when the equipment will have to be replaced, and there may not be sufficient funds for its purchase. With high inflation rates, depreciation of current purchases will not provide sufficient funds for future purchases. There are several basic methods of computing depreciation: straight line; sum of the years' digits; and declining balance. The Internal Revenue Service permits other logically consistent methods that comply with generally accepted practices.

The simplest and the most commonly used method is the straight line. This method assumes that the wear and tear is uniform during the useful life of the equipment. Therefore, the cost of the item, less its estimated salvage value, is depreciated in equal amounts over the estimated useful life.

The sum-of-the-years'-digits method is predicated on the assumption that depreciation is higher in the early years and lower in the later years of the life of the property. Under this method, different fractions are

used each year against the original cost, less salvage value. Assuming a
five-year life, the sum of the years' digits would be 15, that is, the
accumulated total of one, two, three, four, and five. The accumu-
lation—15—is the denominator of a fraction. The numerator represents
the remaining useful life of the item each year. Thus, the first year 5/15
of the cost, less salvage value, would be depreciated. The second year
4/15; the third 3/15; the fourth 2/15; and the fifth 1/15.

The declining-balance method is also based on the assumption that
depreciation is higher in the earlier years. Under the declining-balance
method, the depreciation base is lowered each year by the amount of
the depreciation deduction, and a steady rate is applied to the balances
which result. The income tax provisions provide that the declining-
balance rate may be as high as 200 percent of the straight-line rate. The
manner in which these three methods are applied is illustrated as
follows:

| | Straight Line | | Sum of Digits | | 200% Declining Balance | |
|---|---|---|---|---|---|---|
| Year | Annually | Accumu-lated | Annually | Accumu-lated | Annually | Accumu-lated |
| 1 . . . . . . | 2,500 | 2,500 | 4,000 | 4,000 | 5,000 | 5,000 |
| 2 . . . . . . | 2,500 | 5,000 | 3,000 | 7,000 | 2,500 | 7,500 |
| 3 . . . . . . | 2,500 | 7,500 | 2,000 | 9,000 | 1,250 | 8,750 |
| 4 . . . . . . | 2,500 | 10,000 | 1,000 | 10,000 | 625 | 9,375 |

It is assumed in this illustration that equipment costs $10,000 and
has a negligible salvage value, with a useful life of four years. It will be
noted that under the straight line and sum of the years' digits, the
accumulated depreciation is $10,000 at the end of the fourth year,
whereas under the 200 percent declining-balance method, the accumulated amount is $9,375. One way of handling the balance of $625 is to
switch from the declining-balance method to the straight-line method
after the end of the third year, which is permissible under the federal
income tax law.

The use of the 200 percent declining-balance method makes it possible to postpone some of the income tax payments and increase capital
gains or decrease capital losses if obsolescence forces the carrier to sell
equipment before the end of its useful life. Such fast depreciation
methods are of value to the trucking industry because of the high
annual value of money, the high rate of return on invested capital, and
the obsolescence of equipment.

Economic Life Evaluation, or ECOLIF, demonstrates to management the alternative replacement policies of equipment in terms of cash flow. Obviously, other factors will be considered in the decision-making process but management must be aware of the economic consequences of various alternatives. The complete computer program with the necessary input data can provide a very quick response regarding the desirable service life of a vehicle. Much of the input data must be based on historical data for a number of vehicles, on the replacement value of vehicles at the time, and on the present cash flow value of money.

A factor of considerable importance in planning equipment financing is the relationship between depreciation charged off as expense on the carrier's books as compared with the annual rate of principal and interest payments to the lending institution. If depreciation expense is greater than the payments to financial institutions, cash is generated from operations, and a smaller cash reserve can be maintained.

## Leasing of equipment

As a means of securing equipment for operations, other than purchasing, motor carriers sometimes use one of the following leasing arrangements: (1) enter into a lease-purchase contract with equipment manufacturers; (2) lease equipment from wholly-owned subsidiaries or affiliated companies; (3) lease equipment from owner-operators; or (4) lease vehicles from commercial leasing or rental companies.

Lease-purchase contracts closely resemble conditional sales contracts in that they specify that title to the equipment will eventually pass to the so-called "lessee." This type of contract is not a commercial lease, since the purpose for which the lease is written is a "convenience" in extending credit under terms more favorable than might otherwise be available. Under a typical arrangement, the purchaser—or lessee—signs a contract obligating him to make monthly payments based on a percentage of the cost of equipment. No down payment may be required or as much as 20 percent may be required, depending upon the circumstances. In addition to the monthly payments, the vendor may collect his service and interest charges with the monthly rental or as a flat fee paid upon termination of the contract. Some truck and trailer manufacturers also engage in commercial leasing of equipment they produce, which is called "finance leasing." The title to the equipment does not pass to the original lessee and runs for a period, such as 60 months. The lessee pays a specified amount per month.

Motor carriers sometimes establish subsidiary companies from which the parent motor carrier leases its equipment. A carrier may have a subsidiary that owns its motive power, another company which owns the trailers, and yet another that maintains the equipment. The tax advantages of such arrangements are apparent for those carriers whose combined operations would place them in the upper tax brackets.

Vendor credit may be extended to for-hire motor carriers through individuals who purchase equipment and operate it under a lease contract for motor carriers. The carrier ordinarily leases the equipment on a long-term contract and employs the owner as operator. The carrier may or may not underwrite the credit of its owner-operator.

There are a number of what are termed "full-service" leasing plans under which commercial leasing companies provide carriers with equipment. Commercial leasing companies will supply the equipment desired and agree to service and maintain it for the duration of the leasing contract. The lessor company also pays all insurance and taxes on the equipment. The monthly rental on equipment held under full-service leasing is ordinarily a flat monthly fee established at the time the contract is made.

Another type of commercial leasing arrangement is called "all-expense" leasing. In addition to the services provided under full-service leasing, the lessor company also provides all fuel and oil. This type of contract usually requires that the lease run for a year or longer, and some often run for the life of the vehicle.

Commercial leasing companies also supply vehicles on a short-term rental basis. Under such arrangements, equipment must be selected from whatever is available at the time. Rental charges are a flat amount per day or per week, plus a mileage charge. This charge includes all vehicle costs, including fuel and oil.

Leased equipment is available in virtually every city of any size in the United States. There are national associations which issue franchises or licenses to local operators, as well as independent local companies. There are a large number of firms engaged in truck leasing and rental. Long term truck leasing has grown rapidly, and a number of companies specializing in this field have become very large. Among these are Ryder System, Truck Division of Hertz, Saunders Leasing System, Ruan Leasing Co., and Leaseway Transportation.

There are arguments for and against leasing of vehicles, and management should determine the facts about each method before committing itself. Probably the advantage most often cited for leasing is that it conserves or releases working capital that would otherwise be frozen in fixed assets. It should be pointed out in this connection that for leasing to be practicable, the lessee carrier must be in a position to reinvest or use the capital thus released in a more profitable or more important phase of its business. The value of the freed capital to the company should be at least sufficient to offset the overall cost of leasing, which includes a return to the leasing company on capital it has invested as well as a charge for the leasing service. Whether the equipment is owned or leased, the economic cost is borne by the party who uses the equipment.

## TERMINAL FINANCING

As terminal facilities have been outgrown by motor carriers and there has been greater recognition of the importance of efficient terminal operation to a motor carrier's success, more new terminals are being constructed. Terminals are financed largely by conventional mortgages or by sale and lease-back arrangements. Mortgage lenders generally look more to earnings and to working capital of trucking companies than to property values and the possibility of multiple use of terminals. Even where they are satisfied with the credit status of a carrier, lending institutions usually loan about one-half of the cost of terminals rather than the usual two-thirds, because of their feeling that the terminals are single-purpose buildings and can only be used by other trucking companies. Motor carriers have long felt that two-thirds should be loaned on terminals and that any well-built truck terminal could be converted to other use without loss to the mortgagee.

In financing a new terminal the carrier, before making any commitments on the purchase of land or construction, should discuss with a lending source or sources conditions about the financing of the proposed terminal. This initial action will save much time and effort and is likely to result in securing a loan on a basis which is satisfactory to both parties.

Truck terminal mortgages ordinarily do not exceed a 20-year term. There is considerable difference as to the rate of interest carriers have to pay on mortgage loans. Larger carriers have been able to get mortgage loans in the past at from two to three percentage points lower than smaller carriers.

The conventional source of capital for terminal financing is a lending institution such as a bank or an insurance company. Loans from individuals who wish to make investments are also available at times. Carriers usually negotiate directly with the organizations from which they desire to borrow money, although they may secure the services of the private placement staff of an investment banking firm or use mortgage loan brokers. If the services of the latter are used, a fee is charged which will run from one to two percent, depending on the size of the loan, the larger loans having a lower rate.

Publicly financed motor carriers may find the use of first-mortgage bonds feasible. Their use may permit the carrier to spread the retirement of its real estate obligations over a relatively long period.

Another method of terminal financing is the use of industrial revenue bonds. A carrier may apply to a community to utilize the tax exempt borrowing status of the community to build a terminal in that community. The carrier must convince the local authorities that the issuance of the industrial revenue bond would be in the community's benefit. The rates are far below conventional mortgage financing.

### Sale and lease back

It has become quite common for a motor carrier to sell a piece of property it owns and lease it back for a term of years. The sale and lease-back of terminals has been growing, and this has also been used for motor carrier equipment as well. The primary sources of capital for this type of financing are life insurance companies and pension funds. One of the advantages of the sale and lease-back is that rent is fully deductible for tax purposes. If the motor carrier owned the property, the deductions would be only depreciation and interest, and no depreciation could be taken on the land. Another advantage is that the motor carrier does not have to put up the difference between what can be borrowed in a mortgage and the amount the building costs—at least one-third of the cost and probably more. The carrier has the entire amount of money which would have been tied up in a building available for use in operations and then pays on an installment basis through rent. Real estate and related liability are also removed from the balance sheet.

A disadvantage of this type of arrangement is that the carrier does not own the building when he is through leasing. Further, in a long-term lease the rental will reflect the cost of property plus an interest rate on the investment which is generally about one-half or one percent above the interest rate the lessee carrier would pay if it were borrowing the money.

## PUBLIC FINANCING

As motor carriers have grown, there has been an increase in the number of companies that have turned to public equity financing. The first trucking company to issue its securities to the public did so in 1939. Currently, there are 48 carriers that have issued stock to the public, and the number is continuing to increase. The stock of 13 carriers is listed on the New York Stock Exchange, nine on the American Stock Exchange, and the others are traded over-the-counter. A number of the companies have issued more than one offering, one of them having issued seven to date. Of the offerings made since 1939, most of them were made since 1955. In recent years, the price-earnings ratio has been 12 for the typical motor carrier.

Most bankers feel that a motor carrier must have operating revenues of $15 million annually and $1.5 million of net profit after taxes before it is ready for equity financing. Currently, there are over 200 common carriers with operating revenues in excess of this figure, so many additional carriers are of a size to justify a public market for their stock. The advantages to the carriers of public financing are:

1. Provides new capital for future growth.

2. Reduces some of the debts created by growth.

3. Helps in acquisitions of other companies. A company having stock with an established market price gives an opportunity to offer another company a tax-free merger with stock that can be turned into cash. In the event that a cash purchase is desired, the cash may be raised by sale of additional stock.

4. Has a tendency to improve the credit rating because of the endorsement of investment bankers and the investing public. The price of the stock establishes a value for the company which is generally well above book value.

5. Provides a sound basis for executives and key employees to acquire a stock interest in the company.

6. Makes possible a stock option plan of marketable stock to provide greater incentive to executives and key employees.

Another advantage is that in a closely held corporation, the death of the owner can jeopardize a continuation of service because it may be necessary to liquidate the business. On the other hand, if stock has been sold to the public, it is more likely that the corporation will continue. There is the added advantage that the sale of any stock that the estate might need for the payment of estate taxes can be accomplished when a public stock is outstanding.

Another reason for equity financing is the tax advantage to the owner or major stockholders through the sale of the stock in that it can be treated as a capital gain. All of the stock need not be sold in any one year but can be sold at intervals when there will be an advantage taxwise; or part of the stock may be sold to allow diversification of investments.

When a carrier is offering stock to the public, a prospectus is prepared containing selected data about the company, such as capitalization, financial statements, legal opinions, and summary of earnings. A description of securities is also included. The basic data are provided by the motor carrier, and the prospectus is prepared by the carrier's attorney and the underwriter.

The cost of a public underwriting is from 9 to 12 percent of the offering price on initial offerings. Generally an additional 1 to 1½ percent is added, due to other costs, such as printing, attorneys, and other miscellaneous expenses. The cost of later offerings is usually lower than that of the first offering.

Interstate Commerce Commission approval must be secured for the issuance of securities when the par value of the securities to be issued, together with the par value of the securities then outstanding, exceeds $1 million. Prior to 1957, a carrier could avoid being subjected to this approval by fixing an arbitrary par value for its capital stock which had no reasonable relation to actual value, such as 25 cents a share. In 1957, however, an amendement was passed which prevented the use of arbitrary stock par value as a means of avoiding Commission jurisdiction.

### QUESTIONS AND PROBLEMS

1. How can motor carriers improve their working capital? Is inadequacy of motor carrier working capital really a problem for firms wanting to borrow?

2. As a loan officer of a large bank, how would you rank the factors that would influence your recommendations on granting a loan to a motor carrier?

3. What are some of the methods used in computing depreciation? Name some of the factors which would influence your choice of one of the methods. How important is cash flow in the motor carrier industry?

4. Enumerate the advantages and disadvantages of financing terminals by the use of sale and lease-back arrangements.

5. Critically analyze the statement that "leasing releases working capital that would otherwise be frozen in fixed assets."

6. Do you feel that publicly issued securities of motor carriers will ease the financing problems of these carriers? Why or why not?

7. What are the advantages of public financing?

8. How would you define a growth stock? Could any of the motor carrier stocks be so classified?

### FOOTNOTES TO CHAPTER 8

[1]Department of Transportation, *National Transportation Trends and Choices* (Washington, D.C.: U.S. Government Printing Office, 1977), p. 22.

[2]Interstate Commerce Commission, Bureau of Transport Economics and Statistics, *Survey of Class I Motor Carriers of Property, 1939-1954* (Washington, D.C., May, 1956), p.21.

# chapter 9

# Management and operations

## MANAGEMENT

The development of the motor carrier industry from its early struggle for recognition as a reliable form of transport to its present mature and stable position has provided a challenge to management. Many problems of management in this fast-growing industry were solved at the time they developed by a management possessing greater operational knowledge than executive ability. Some represented good judgment at the time they were made but would not stand up under critical analysis today.

The management techniques that were used when a company was small are inadequate in the light of the size and scope of many trucking operations. One of the major carriers, for example, employs more than 14,000, operates 228 terminals, owns 20,000 pieces of motor carrier equipment, is authorized to serve 17,000 points, and handles 30,000 shipments per day.

The management approach in the trucking industry is largely a reflection of the company president. The size of operation, geographic service area, whether a family company, a closed corporation, or publicly held, individual personality of the executive, and other factors have their impact on company management. In actuality, motor carrier management is as diverse as the motor carrier field itself.

The key ingredient in motor carrier management, as in other businesses, is the quality of management. Gross revenue has to be converted to net revenue through good management or a firm fails. There have been a number of general commodity carriers with virtually identical operating rights, that used comparable equipment, and operated under the same rate structure; yet some firms failed (Yale Express) or just prior to failure were acquired by another carrier, and others have been very profitable. Associated Transport in 1973 was the 11th largest carrier, based on gross revenues, and yet it sustained substantial losses that year. Earlier in 1972, 46 percent of its stock had been purchased by Eastern Freight Ways. But in 1974 Eastern wrote off its $8.9 million investment as a loss and by 1977, both Eastern and Associated had ceased operations. Another firm, Adley Corporation, a large New England based, north-south carrier, was taken over by Yellow Freight System.

Motor carriers need to utilize the best management principles and strategies in order to be successful in a very competitive field.

### Management approaches

There are three streams of management thought. One is referred to as *management science*, in which heavy reliance is placed on the quantification of many aspects in order to provide a more precise decision-making process. Another school of thought is the *behavioral approach* which draws upon psychology, sociology, anthropology, and the social sciences in personal and interpersonal relations among individuals. Between these two groups, one finds what is termed the *classical approach* to management which relies primarily upon the basic functions of management but draws, where appropriate, on other areas.

### Management functions

What are the management functions to be performed in order to have a successful trucking operation? *Planning* and *policy formulation* are critical factors. Planning requires the look ahead, and policy formulation is the framework within which planning can be realized. What is the market area for the future and the level of service to be achieved? The establishment of policies will serve as guides that govern some portion of the activities of the trucking company. Executives should be included to the maximum extent in the plans and policies that apply to most other employees. Another function of management is *direction*. In the trucking business, the degree of success in getting things accomplished through people depends largely upon management's ability to provide leadership. The fourth function of management is *staffing*. In a service industry such as trucking where effective management must occur through other people's actions, the selection and staffing of individuals with management potential is mandatory for success. The fifth function of management is *control*. This is the means by which the trucking company attains the objectives that have been set in the plans of the company. Control systems can be established which detect a fall-off in performance, or standards can be established to provide management with information as to whether or not goals are being met. If not, corrective action can be taken to improve the situation. The budget is probably the most common control device.

### Management by objective

In recent years, a management planning method, termed *management by objective,* has been introduced that may offer opportunities for improvement in management planning in some companies. Management by objective incorporates work planning, participative management, and performance appraisal. It begins with a company president and a planning group who establish objectives for the entire organization. With these company objectives in hand, each top level manager works with his management subordinates to establish the contributions to achievement that can be accomplished in his division. Each of these subordinates, in turn, specifies the objectives to his next lower level and requests them to indicate in what specific manner each can work toward meeting the objectives. This process can be continued to the level of terminal manager.

The work planning is an important phase as is the participation of all personnel at all levels of management. But beyond this phase is the measurement of performance of task objectives necessary to accomplish the goals. In the behavioral sense, the action plan for performance of tasks should be established jointly with each subordinate, from the top level of management to the lowest. The action plan should include the steps necessary to achieve an objective. The latter should not be too difficult for subordinates to attain nor should they be so easy that performance does not improve over what it had been. Specific time periods should be set for periodic review of performance, and a final review should be conducted at the end of a year. If performance appraisal of individual contributions to the goal reveals individual inadequacies in performing certain tasks, a self-improvement program can be established that will help the individual overcome any deficiencies in knowledge or ability.[1] Thus, management by objective can work as a management development program.

A program such as this can be effective in integrating the task objectives of the organization with the personal goals of individuals. Some companies have found it effective, whereas others feel that it is too time consuming.[2] It takes time for management to learn how to establish goals and how to review performance. But it does have the advantage of requiring specificity in plans and goals for the entire organization and individual contributions to the accomplishment of those goals.

### Motivation of employees

Because the trucking industry is a service industry in which many employees, either in person or by telephone, are in constant contact with the shipping public, the importance of optimal employee performance cannot be overemphasized. All employees must understand and support the efforts to provide the best possible service at a reasonable cost in order that profits are adequate to sustain the company's economic health. Every opportunity must be taken to inform employees of the important role each of them has in the financial success of the company. Sharing information with them will assist them also in understanding the company's strategies and goals.

Larger companies try to fill the information gap through employee meetings, company information memoranda, and company publications. One large motor carrier issues an employees' annual report, similar to the annual report to stockholders. The tie between job security and the margin of profit, and the significance of the employee at every level are stressed throughout this report. A graphic is included each year (Fig. 9-1) that shows where the revenue dollar goes and the amount that is expended for payroll expenses in comparison with other expenditures.

Management has often sought to develop incentive programs for supervisory as well as other employees. One such program ties salary bonuses for supervisory personnel to a reduction in operating ratio, the lower the operating ratio the higher the bonus.

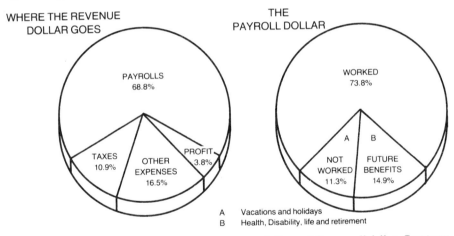

Fig. 9-1. Percentage expenditures from the revenue dollar and the payroll dollar. Courtesy: Garret Freightlines, Inc.

### Computers in decision-making

The extent of greater utilization and reliance upon computers as a management tool is found in a recent survey of Class I motor carriers.[3] In 1967, about 10 percent of the carriers had their own computers and, by 1979, the number had rapidly expanded so that more than 75 percent had computers; and others are planning to expand their present computer operations. In addition, many other carriers purchase computerized services from data processing service organizations. There are computer capabilities from small to very large.

There are a number of management-oriented uses of computers that can yield valuable data for decision-making. These include profitability by terminal, profitability by traffic lane, profitability by shipment and equipment control. An additional area for effective utilization of the computer is that of freight billing and its related activities, such as delivering, transfer of freight, unloading, etc. Other areas include central dispatching for the line-haul function, preventive maintenance scheduling, trailer control, tractor control, and line-haul driver control. Information on claims can also pinpoint problem areas where improvement can be effected.

A computer-based information system can be programmed to provide significant data in each of these areas. One can measure vehicle maintenance costs, for example, to any degree of detail desired. A maintenance information system can be a valuable aid in managing the vehicle fleet for these data provide comparative figures on many specific factors. Effective utilization of data from such areas should result in increased productivity through more efficient billing and records and utilization of equipment.

When a trucking company with a computer at headquarters makes the decision to broaden its computer operations by establishing computer terminals at its freight terminals that are tied to the central computer, it is establishing what is referred to as an "on-line system." The computer terminals, or devices as they are also called, are teletype or typewriter-like devices which might be GE Terminette 2740's or TV-like devices. Telephone lines or Western Union are used to connect the remote terminal sites to the computer. The entire system includes the computer, the disc, the tapes, the lines, and the terminal devices.

Several terminal devices may share a single phone line (which is a "multi-drop" operation) in which event the use of the line is usually controlled by a computer program. The computer sequentially invites, or "polls," each of such terminal devices to send data to the computer. A terminal line may also be dedicated to full-time use and not shared with voice activity such as dispatching. They are dedicated only to the data processing function. In addition, "dial-up" lines are regular voice-type lines that are attached to the terminal devices only during data transmission. Such a device may be set up to call the computer, or the dial-up device may be set up to receive calls from the computer with automatic answering.

The machine instructions or programs that control the computer or the lines are referred to as the "software." The trucking company usually prepares the programs for billing, transfers, delivery messages, and similar matters while the supervisory programs are usually provided by the computer, or hardware, vendor or purchased from a contractor.

The establishment of an on-line system requires extensive planning as it is an expensive system in its initial development and one that may require substantial financial outlays as the system is in use. A company may find that it needs additional terminals, possibly a second computer. Additional personnel may be required in the area of computer programmers, systems coordinators, computer operators, etc., especially if the system operations are expanded. Further, the education of the personnel to operate the system can be a great deal more expensive than was anticipated, particularly that of field personnel. An additional factor that must be considered is the "debugging" of programs and the inevitable down time, when the system, or part of it, is inoperative.

Smaller computers, termed minicomputers, are being increasingly used in the trucking industry. They are made up of a central processing unit with data storage capability, a keyboard device and data entry, a printer to record the result produced, and a magnetic disc unit for secondary data storage. Not only are these less expensive computers but also they do not require a programmer or a systems analyst in-house, since they function with the basic programs provided either by the hardward company or by an outside software company.

Although there has been significant progress in motor carrier use of computers, the possible link up with shipper computers has been an elusive goal. The shipper/carrier data exchange would make it possible for shipping information to move as fast as freight and would undoubtedly cut documentation costs. Moreover, the paperwork involved with freight bills that are processed through industry-sponsored freight bill collecting systems, as well as through some banks which perform the collection function, could be computer interfaced with shippers and carriers, which would reduce costs.

The electronic devices exist, the skills exist, and in many instances data have been accumulated. However, the standardization of codes is lacking. For several years, an organization has worked with carriers, shippers, government, and computer builders to determine the feasibility of standard codes, message format and systems interfaces. Much progress has been made toward standardization.[4]

### Value of organization

In every motor carrier organization, certain functions have to be performed. The assignment of functions to specific departments may vary from company to company, but that is of little significance as long as the functions are properly handled by the departments in charge. In a fast-growing organization, it does happen, however, that departments have been allowed to grow so large as to result in improper performance of component functions. Efficient management may find it wise to reexamine the functions of each department to ascertain if there should be a reallocation of duties.

In addition, top management may find that the organization has expanded to the point where a different type of organizational setup should be employed. In a dynamic industry, the organizational setup must be one in which immediate decisions can be reached and necessary changes effected expeditiously. The financial resources of most motor carriers are not sufficient that they can afford to delay action when some particular phase of their activity is losing money.

Of the types of business organization, such as line, staff, and functional, the most common type in the motor carrier field is line organization. For the small motor carrier, this type of organization fits its needs in a satisfactory manner. If a motor carrier organization outgrows this type of management, however, top management should not be reluctant to delegate authority and responsibility when efficiency demands such a move. A smooth-working organization and one that builds future management personnel does not place too much reliance upon one individual or several individuals. This is particularly significant in larger motor carrier organizations, for the greater the size and span of an organization, the greater the need for proper delegation of authority and responsibility.

### Line organization

The line organization (Fig. 9-2) is widely used in business management and is typified by a setup similar to that of a military organization, where there is one person who commands and who alone is responsible for the results. This is characteristic of business enterprises which can be traced to a small beginning, such as the motor carrier. The owner of a small motor carrier organization may find that management of his business is a relatively simple matter, for he has complete authority and responsibility, both operational and managerial. In many instances, however, in the motor carrier field, the small business has grown, and in the increased burdens upon the owner require that he delegate some authority and responsibility. Even here, the line organization of management continues, for all of the personnel are subordinate to the owner, who will disseminate downward his decisions and expect compliance therewith. With continuing expansion of his business, he may be forced to delegate further authority because there are not enough hours in the day for him to continue to handle all problems, large and small.

A line organization, then, represents highly centralized management. It is understandable that the founder of such an organization, which has grown and prospered, may find it difficult to relinquish the managerial control which he has maintained since the inception of his organization. On the other hand, what many owners do not realize is that they may retain control of their organizations by the proper delegation of authority and, by so doing, relieve themselves of burdensome details. Figure 9-3 shows the organization of a Class I carrier.

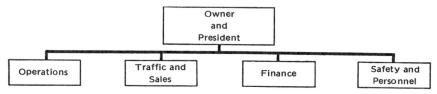

Fig. 9-2. A typical line organization.

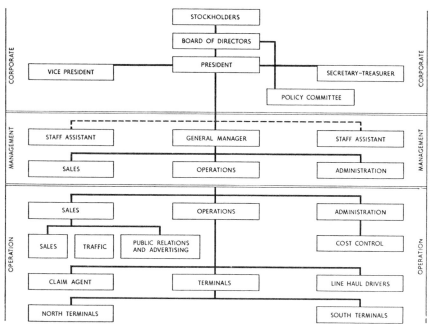

Fig. 9-3. Organization of a Class I carrier.

### Line and staff organization

This may give rise to the establishment of staff departments that are added to the basic line organization. When separate staff departments are created, they are manned by specialists who study and make recommendations on problems assigned to them and which they develop. Plans and methods for assisting other departments are formulated by them. Where separate staff departments are created, the head of each department has line control only over the people in his department. It has been pointed out in differentiating between line and staff executives that staff officers are assigned to an authority of ideas, whereas line officers are charged with the authority to command. In general, the staff or the group of managerial experts support the line executive in an informational and advisory capacity. The information or ideas of the staff flow up to a superior; and this executive, possessing authority, may transmit this information or ideas into orders down through the organization.

Large companies often reach a stage in their development where the line-and-staff organization needs to be modified in order to fulfill the management requirements of their companies. This is usually accomplished by the creation of committees which are not a form of management organization in themselves but are fitted into the organization at different levels. A number of standing committees are set up, usually one for each level of authority. A committee of top management, generally called an executive committee, may be established in order to keep the executives informed of the happenings in all departments of the company. Ordinarily, a committee does not have authority to make decisions. There is a discussion of the problem, and the committee makes a recommendation to the executive who is responsible for making the decision.

### Functional organization

Some motor carriers have found that the staff organization continues to place too much responsibility upon the top executive as their organizations continue to expand and hence have worked out a functional type of organization. The staff members are given broader responsibility concerning the particular functions of the business they represent. Whereas they formerly functioned in an advisory capacity, they now have authority to command within their own departments. These functional executives and those in lower managerial echelons will have channels established so that there is a free flow and interchange of work of a technical nature between them.

### Organization chart showing functions performed

Some companies publish an organization chart which shows the line of authority and the persons in charge. Back-up personnel may also be listed. A functional chart is also prepared which shows for each of the departments the basic functions which are performed by each department. Such a functional chart for a Class I motor carrier grossing less than $5 million a year is shown in Fig. 9-4. A number of these functions are discussed in more detail in chapters which follow. The number of departments in a company may be greater or less than shown in the chart. Some of the functions performed by the executive department may be delegated to other or new departments.

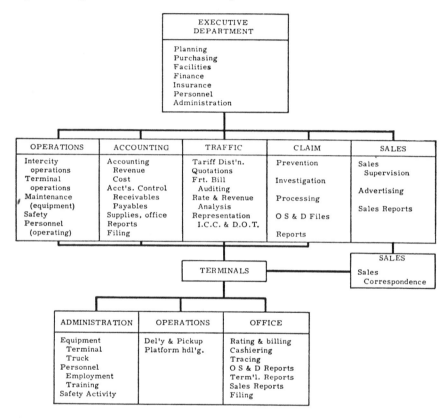

Fig. 9-4. Functions performed by departments.

There have been too many cases of motor carrier executives emphasizing those phases of management in which they have had practical experience; that is, the individual who started as a one-truck operator and has built the company into a 50-truck operation tends to concentrate his management efforts in operations. If the executive's background has been principally in selling, there is a tendency to emphasize that phase of management. There is a need for a balanced approach to management of the business enterprise and a perspective of the entire organization.

### Training programs

A number of motor carriers have become very large organizations, and many of the founders of these companies are approaching the age when they must retire from active management. There is a definite need in the motor carrier industry for the training of qualified personnel to assume future executive responsibilities. The people chosen for further training may be already employed in the carrier's organization, or additional personnel of potential executive capacities may be hired from outside the company. The majority of the top-management and junior executives in the motor carrier industry, thus far, have come from within the industry. Whatever the source of this group of potential future administrators, it is imperative that top management establish a program of training, formal or informal in nature, so that the benefits of well-trained personnel may be enjoyed in current operations and an adequate foundation built for the future.

Training may be divided into preservice, that is, training and instruction prior to the time that the individual becomes a regular employee in the job for which he is being trained, and in-service training for those who are already performing the particular functions for which they are receiving training. The length of the training period is dependent upon the job for which they are being trained and upon the caliber of trainees. Some of them exceed one year in length. On the other hand, one company gives rate clerks only six weeks of training in the general office before they are assigned to an operating job at a terminal.

A number of carriers have established a management training program in which the trainee is rotated through the departments of the company to get a better understanding of the company's organization and management. He must make progress reports and is given tests periodically. The management training program of one Class I motor carrier covers a 42-week period, during which the trainee spends from two to eight weeks on each of the following areas; dock supervision, pickup and delivery dispatch, line-haul, tracing, OS/D, terminal procedures, rating and billing, accounts receivable and collection, maintenance, sales and marketing, office management, and personnel administration. Fifteen of the 42 weeks are in dock supervision which is interspersed at intervals throughout the program.

A reservoir of potential management personnel which exists today and which is being tapped to advantage by motor carriers is that being trained by universities, which provide well-balanced business curricula, including comprehensive transportation offerings. When personnel derived from such a source is oriented to the particular procedures of an individual motor carrier, the advantages should soon be manifested.

## OPERATIONS

The efficient management of motor carrier operations is a necessity. The success of a company depends upon the provision of service that will satisfy shippers and result, at the same time, in sufficient profit to maintain financial well-being. In all companies, large or small, operations performs this very important role. In very small carrier organizations, operations tends to be *the* company but as the size of companies increases, operations becomes one of the departments.

Operational responsibilities encompass both internal or company problems and certain external constraints. The external constraints can and do have an impact upon the internal operational aspects of the motor carrier. Such internal aspects as safety, communication, maintenance, leasing, equipment utilization, interchange, and accounting will be covered as well as the external constraints that affect operations.

### External constraints

Motor carriers have been subject to varying degrees of federal regulation since 1935 and to state regulation prior to and since that time. Regulation enacted specifically for carriers, economic and safety regulation, is discussed in a later chapter. But there has been legislation in recent years that applies to motor carriers as a part of the total industrial complex which greatly broadens the spectrum of institutional constraints for carrier management.

One such legislative act, the Occupational Safety and Health Act, was passed in 1970. It is designed to reduce the number of job safety and health hazards through development, implementation, and enforcement of mandatory occupational safety and health standards applicable to any business affecting interstate commerce. The Secretary of Labor is charged with setting the standards, and currently over 400 traveling compliance officers are in the field. The Act also created a Presidentially-appointed Occupational Safety and Health Review Commission, to settle disputes arising from enforcement of the Act.

OSHA has no jurisdiction over the over-the-road equipment. However, many of OSHA regulations become effective once a truck is being loaded or unloaded.[5] Standards are also set for the operation of material handling equipment, walking and working surfaces, and storage areas. Noise standards and those for handling of certain chemical and other toxic substances are being developed. Inspections cover a wide spectrum of trucking activities from control of noxious gases and fumes to adequacy of dock boards and bridge plates.

Enactment of legislation designed to enhance the quality of our environment has included the National Environmental Policy Act (1969), the Clear Air Act (1970), and the Noise Control Act (1972). Under the Environmental Policy Act, a Council on Environmental Quality was established which has as its purpose the evaluation of required impact evaluations. In the first three years of the law's existence, about 1,440 impact statements regarding highways were submitted by the Department of Transportation to meet the requirements of EPA. Motor carrier management is also affected by the emission and noise standards established under the other Acts so that the interfaces with EPA will be continuing. The required governmental ecological changes provide new challenges for management in areas such as scope of operations, equipment selection, level of service, method of operations, and costs, to name but a few.

In view of these new externalities that have a direct impact on future policy and operation—OSHA standards, environmental requirements, and affirmative action as required under the Equal Employment Opportunity Act, it is apparent that motor carrier management will have to adjust to many additional regulations beyond those contained in the Interstate Commerce Act, and the safety regulations of the Department of Transportation.

### Safety programs

The promotion of safety pays in any motor carrier organization. This may take the form of a well-defined safety program carried out in conjunction with an insurance company but more often as a separate safety program. The usual emphasis in such a program is upon drivers, both over-the-road and pickup and delivery, and it is a most important phase of operations. The stepped-up regulatory activities of the Department of Transportation are causing new emphasis to be placed on these programs. The periodic road checks which they make at strategic highway points throughout the nation to determine the condition of vehicles and compliance with motor carrier safety regulations have shown that substantial improvement can be made in safety programs. Since the institution of road checks by the Department of Transportation, a number of states have conducted similar road checks to insure compliance with state regulations.

The responsibility for the safety program is placed directly under the safety director or the safety supervisor, who is responsible to the general manager for the satisfactory functioning of the program. A comprehensive program should include selection of driver personnel, driver training, awards or incentive plans, general safety information, inspections, and road supervision of drivers.

The success of this kind of program is dependent in large part upon the cooperative attitude of management. Inasmuch as management originates the program, it is necessary that policies be formulated and goals and standards established that can be used to measure progress. It is to the best interests of management to foster a well coordinated safety program. A good program can result in direct money savings and in improved company and industry public relations.

### Selection of driver personnel

Careful selection of driver personnel is of utmost importance. Avoidable accidents can be practically eliminated through the use of good judgment and the skill of a truck driver. The general requirements for the selection of driver personnel vary widely, but most companies establish certain requirements such as the following: the driver must be 26 years of age; he must have two years of experience on similar equipment and two years' employment with one employer; and he must successfully pass the Department of Transportation's physical examination, as well as driver aptitude and knowledge tests.

Visual speed and accuracy tests which measure an applicant's speed and accuracy in perception are used by some carriers. Since about 95 percent of the cues in traffic come through the eyes, the driver should be able to get a clear picture quickly and make an intelligent decision.

A carefully planned road test in traffic with a trained observer riding with the applicant over a route known to the observer is valuable in developing comparative records of the ability of different applicants. There are also driving tests that have been developed to demonstrate an applicant's ability to handle a vehicle in close quarters.

### Driver training

Driver training is given to the newly hired driver while he is making what are called "student trips." These student trips are familiarization training trips which are made in order to acquaint the new driver with the route. He is accompanied on these runs by a regular driver, who observes the new driver's driving techniques. Any apparent weaknesses are pointed out and ways of correcting them suggested. The new driver is indoctrinated in the driving rules and regulations of the Department of Transportation, as well as in the individual carrier's rules and regulations.[6] Recruiting, screening, and initial start-up costs can average $1,500 per driver. Therefore, reduction of turnover is rather important.

In addition to a specific program for the new drivers, a continuing driver-training program should be conducted for all driver personnel.

### Awards or incentive plans

Many different driver award plans have been instituted. One plan consists of merchandise awards which are earned through points given for each month's safe driving. The granting of this type of prize has the advantage of support and encouragement of the driver's family. The goal of merchandise coveted by his family makes a vigilant driver, thus cutting down on those accidents which are caused by carelessness.

In addition to the merchandise award plans, there are share-the-savings plans and cash bonus plans. There are two general types of the share-the-savings plans. One of these is the plan in which the savings on fleet insurance plans are shared with the drivers. Under such an arrangement, the company ordinarily assigns a percentage of any savings on lower premiums to be divided among the drivers, and the remaining savings to be retained by the company. A base operating period, such as the preceding year, must be established in order that premium savings can be determined. The other type of share-the-savings plan is that in which the savings on fleet operating costs are shared with the drivers. The carrier will establish the average operating cost per mile for a power unit. A specific power unit is assigned to each driver, who is then responsible for that particular unit. Each driver is given a percentage of all savings that he can produce through operating his vehicle at less than the average cost.

Under the cash bonus plan, the carrier gives a specified amount to each driver for each month he operates without an accident. Since the plan provides for a relatively small amount of money for each accident-free month, the driver may not receive anything of a substantial nature that will be a reminder that his safe driving was a direct benefit to him if he is paid at the conclusion of each month without an accident. When the monthly bonus is operated on a cumulative basis and is not paid until a 6-month or 12-month period has elapsed, the amount involved is more likely to be large enough that it will be a greater incentive.

## Inspections

Adequate equipment inspection prior to the operation of each vehicle is an important part of a safety program. This specific responsibility should be assigned so that all potential defects which might jeopardize safe operation of a motor vehicle may be detected. This inspection should include the checking of tires, lug nuts, air-brake hoses and connections, reflector windshield wipers, and so on.

The next step in inspection is to have each driver's log properly checked as to accuracy and completeness. The Department of Transpor-

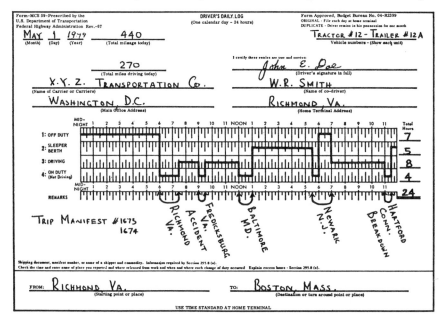

Fig. 9-5. Specimen log.

tation prescribes the driver's daily log and requires that these logs be properly maintained. Figure 9-5 is a specimen log, which covers a driver's activities on the first day of a trip in which he left Richmond, Virginia, with a shipment of miscellaneous freight to be delivered in Newark, New Jersey, and Boston, Massachusetts.

The driver reported for duty with his co-driver at the carrier's Richmond terminal at 6 a.m., at which time he was given papers for the shipments and instructions for making the trip. The vehicle combination was being loaded at the time he reported for duty, and the driver attended the vehicle until the loading was completed. He then made a pretrip inspection of the vehicle, made entries upon his driver's log to

7:30 a.m. as "on duty not driving" and started driving at that time. At 9 a.m., in Fredericksburg, Virginia, he was involved in an accident with an automobile, which was damaged to the extent of $250. He remained at the accident scene for one-half hour while the police conducted their investigation. He obtained information relating to the accident and performed an inspection of the vehicle. He then made entries upon his log to 9:30 a.m., showing this stop as "on duty not driving" and started driving at that time. At 12 noon, he stopped near Baltimore at a truck stop for gas and a meal. He then made entries upon his log to 1 p.m., showing this stop as "on duty not driving." He then entered the sleeper berth, while his co-driver assumed the driving duties.

At 5:30 p.m., he arrived at the carrier's Newark, New Jersey, terminal and reported to the dispatcher. He gave to the dispatcher his statement concerning the accident and other information needed to complete a report to the Federal Highway Administration. He was told by the dispatcher that helpers would not have the Newark-bound freight unloaded until 7 p.m. He then walked to a nearby diner, leaving the vehicle at the terminal, ate a meal, and returned at the specified time. He then made entries upon his log to 7 p.m., showing 5:30 p.m. to 6 p.m. as "on duty not driving" and showing 6 p.m. to 7 p.m. as "off duty" due to the fact that the vehicle and its cargo were under the care and custody of the carrier's dispatcher during this time, and then started driving.

At 11 p.m., the vehicle broke down near Hartford, Connecticut. He placed warning devices upon the highway while the co-driver telephoned the carrier's Hartford shop to ask that a shop man be sent to repair the vehicle. He made entries upon his log to 11:30 p.m. showing this stop as "on duty not driving" and entered the sleeper berth for the balance of the calendar day.

The name of the co-driver for this trip is shown directly below the driver's signature. Additionally, the total miles traveled during the day and the actual miles spent driving are shown on the appropriate lines near the top of the form.

The total hours for each line show seven hours off duty; five hours in sleeper berth; eight hours driving and four hours on duty (not driving) for the day covered by the log. The sum of these hours shown under "Total Hours" equals 24 hours.

Under "Remarks," a check on time markers and entries will show that the driver reported for work at Richmond at 6 a.m. and was on duty (not driving) until he started to drive at 7:30 a.m. The time spent driving is shown on line 3 and the time spent in the sleeper berth on line 2. All stops are shown on line 4. In the lower left-hand corner, the driver shows the transportation performed by entering the shipping document numbers.

As the destination of the driver on this trip is Boston, he enters the original starting point and the final destination on the appropriate line near the bottom of the form, thus: "From: Richmond, Va.; To: Boston, Mass." The original starting point and final destination are to be shown on the log for each day throughout the trip. If a driver departs from and returns to the same place on any day, the "destination or turnaround point" shall be the farthest point reached before the driver begins his return trip.

The DOT has permitted, on an experimental basis, the use of machine-handled punched cards for driver's daily logs. The use of this new form facilitates the handling and filing of the reports, as well as the taking of information from the reports to be used by various departments of the carrier.

If the motor carrier employs the use of a recorder, such as the Tachograph, the Servis Recorder, or the Speedograph, the charts from this equipment are inspected at this time. To be effective, the charts must be examined daily to check their agreement with the driver's logs, to check whether any driver is exceeding a company or other speed limit, and to see whether or not the device is being tampered with.

The Commission, when it had jurisdiction over safety regulation, denied a petition of a motor carrier in which the carrier sought to substitute the record produced by a mechanical recorder for the driver's daily log. The Commission held that the recorder record was essentially a vehicle performance record, whereas the daily log was a personally executed record of the driver's working time.

The "hours of service" rules prescribed by the Department of Transportation permit 10 hours driving time after 8 hours straight off-duty time. However, the driver may not drive again until he has been off duty for another 8-hour period. A driver may be on duty 60 hours in any continuous 7-day period if the company operates 6 days a week or may be on duty 70 hours in any continuous 8-day period if the company operates 7 days a week.

### Road supervision of drivers

Inasmuch as the operation of a truck fleet is conducted over wide areas, it is more difficult to supervise line-haul drivers. The supervision of drivers cannot be considered as the sole method of securing the greatest efficiency from the drivers. An important aspect of operations of this type is to have proper selection and adequate training of drivers in order to create self-supervision in drivers.

There are a number of methods which have been used in supervising drivers—road patrols, check stations, and mechanical operations recorders. There is no general agreement as to which is the most effective, since each of them has advantages and disadvantages.

The different types of road patrols will be discussed. The first of these is the *carrier's road patrol.* The road supervisor by direct observation can check the drivers' handling of the equipment as well as checking the equipment. Such a road supervisor will have other duties, such as those of driver training and conducting safety meetings. He also investigates serious or unusual accidents and maintains contacts with law enforcement agencies in the territory in which he operates. He maintains a continuous route survey to report on any unusual conditions on the routes used by his company's equipment. He is also to render assistance to any highway user who is in trouble.

The road supervisors may be furnished with properly marked cars or cars which are unmarked. The advantages of conspicuous marking of the road patrol vehicle far overshadow the disadvantages of marking.

The road supervisor's observation must be of sufficient length to give an accurate report of the operation and condition of the unit. On the open road, from three to five miles of observation is generally adequate. In urban areas, shorter observations are sufficient. Every effort must be made that the observations are accurate and factual. Although the supervisor has the authority to stop his company's vehicles on the highways, the accident hazard which may be created through such action limits this to a minimum number of cases.

In order for a road patrol to be an effective method of supervision, it is necessary that there be a prompt processing of the road reports and an adequate follow-up with the driver. Both favorable and unfavorable reports should be made. Where there are serious violations, there should be an interview with the driver in order that all aspects of the report can be covered. There have been some instances in the past of road supervisors serving as policemen, which has created a strong antipathy among drivers toward the use of road patrols generally. There should be good relations between the drivers and the road supervisor. An understanding of the road supervisor's job and the benefits to all parties concerned will do much to establish greater confidence.

The cost of a full-time company-operated road patrol has tended to restrict its use to the larger companies, inasmuch as its cost runs from $ 25,000 to $ 40,000 per year.

Another type of road patrol is that conducted by insurance companies which insure motor carriers. Most of the insurance companies have some type of road patrol supervision, although its extent varies among the companies. Reports are furnished to the motor carrier. They provide the insurance company with a degree of control over its risks as well as furnishing motor carriers with a road patrol report from an organization outside their own.

Road patrol service may also be secured from companies specializing in this service or from cooperatives established by local trucking associations.

Many trucks have a citizen's band radio which is licensed by the Federal Communications Commission. Their extensive use involves many things, including safety.

### Mechanical operations recorders

The use of mechanical operations recorders provides a means of road supervision of drivers and can be used in conjunction with maintenance management. In order to give somewhat better control over operations between terminals, motor carriers have made use of recorder devices, such as the Tachograph. This is a mechanism that can be installed in the cab of a truck and connected with the mechanical part of the truck. It will record on a circular chart inside the device information that shows when the engine started, how long the engine idled, when the vehicle was in motion, how fast it traveled, when the vehicle stopped, the duration of stops, and the distance traveled between stops. The chart is inserted only by authorized persons prior to truck departure and is marked as to unit, date, destination, driver, and any other pertinent information. The Tachograph clock is set to the correct time and wound. The chart is placed in back of the clock, and a small knife cuts the edge of the chart at the proper time setting. The mechanism is closed and locked. Upon completion of the trip, only a designated person with the proper key can unlock the unit and remove the chart. Clock movements are available which cover 36 hours, 72 hours, or even a full week's operation on one chart. A recorder which records speed of engine in revolutions per minute is desirable where speed of engine rather than speed of vehicle is the determining economy factor.

### Accident review board

An accident review board may be established by a carrier in order to screen accidents and establish responsibility for the purpose of maintaining safety records of drivers and their eligibility for safe-driving awards. A review board is usually composed of three to seven members, with driver representatives, management representatives, and an insurance representative. The driver representatives are generally required to have at least one full year of accident-free driving with the carrier. Quite often, one representative is required to be an over-the-road driver and the other a local driver.

In some companies, the board meets at regular intervals to determine those accidents which are chargeable and to recommend preventive measures. In other instances, the board serves as an appellate group to determine only what accidents are chargeable. When the board serves in the latter capacity, the safety director has initially determined the chargeability of accidents, and drivers may appeal to the board.

The primary purpose of conducting accident investigation is to prevent similar accidents in the future. A preliminary investigation and report is required from the most immediately available person who is qualified to make such a report. The complete facts concerning the circumstances, causes, responsibility, number and extent of injuries, number of fatalities, and amount and extent of property damage are secured in order to suggest the preventive measures and administrative or disciplinary action. Examination of records and witnesses, careful measurements, and mechanical condition of the vehicle are some of the specific matters that are thoroughly investigated.

### Communications

The many types of communication services available may be divided into two broad categories—written and vocal. Both types are used by carriers, and it is just a question of how much of each type should be used.

The types of written communication are mail, telegraph, and teletype. Teletypewriter service is available on a per-use basis and is called a teletypewriter exchange service (TWX). The equipment is installed for the carrier and is connected to a TWX switchboard in a telephone company's central office. Calls are connected with other teletypewriters installed at various points in the carrier's system. A nominal installation and monthly charge are made, plus billing for actual message use. The message charge is based on the first three minutes in a manner similar to long-distance telephone charges. It is possible to arrange a conference service among three or more subscribers, and unattended service (that is, without an operator) is also available. This service may be used for transmitting data processing information as well as form transmission, such as waybills. TWX service combines speed and two-way communication with a minimum of cost and is effective where a few connections a day meet the requirements between terminals.

There is also private-line teletypewriter (TT). TT service provides direct continuous contact between specified locations at a fixed monthly charge. This service is flexible and can be provided at 60, 75, or 100 words per minute with single operation, that is, transmission in both directions but only in one direction at a time; or duplex, that is, simultaneous transmission in both directions. Charges are based on the daily word capacity.

Since TWX and private-line service are compatible, it is often feasible to employ private-line service at the main terminal points only, and TWX service to the less important terminals. The great advantage of the types of written communication is that a record is made of the information transmitted. There are also systems which reproduce messages electronically—one receives a handwritten message while it is being written. Another, called "facsimile reproduction"—reproduces photographically written, drawn, or printed material.

The other basic category of communication is that of the voice services. The users of these services usually consider the direct oral contact between the connected parties to be the principal advantage of this service, although speed of service is also of particular importance. Long-distance telephone and private-line telephone service are the principal types. The latter is similar to private-line teletypewriter service. Some carriers have instituted a private microwave system that can be used for voice channel, teletype communication, and data transmission.

The use of radio frequencies is discussed in the chapter on terminal operations.

### Utilization of over-the-road equipment

In order to secure the best utilization of equipment, a carrier should ascertain the maximum average load weight which its fleet can produce. This can be done by finding out what each type of semitrailer will carry. These figures are then multiplied by the number of units and the number of runs per week. This will give the fleet semitrailer capacity. The average load weight which the carrier actually loads should be computed in order to compare actual operations with the optimum. The volume moving between two terminals is divided by the number of runs made between the terminals each week. When a terminal falls too far below the potential average load, steps should be taken to see that employees take advantage of as much of the potential capacity as possible. It is necessary to have some spare trailers because of customer demands, as well as certain inefficiencies in manpower. A company often operates on a ratio of 1½ semitrailers to every truck-tractor.

Experience shows that utilization of equipment cannot be increased by adding more equipment than is needed. Actually, by adding too much equipment, utilization may drop. Employees tend to let up, the average load weight may fall, and the pressure may not be on customers to release equipment. Another important factor in utilization of equipment is to accomplish balanced loading so that equipment is utilized in both directions. The sales force must be called upon to secure the best possible balance in directional movement of freight.

The matter of deadhead miles is of concern to motor carrier management. The importance of minimizing or eliminating deadhead miles is reflected in the cost per mile for motor carriers. It has been estimated by the Commission that for motor carriers of general commodities, deadhead miles amount to about 12 percent on the interstate system. This compares with 45 percent of empty freight car miles for railroads.

### Sleeper cab and relay

In addition to "peddle runs" in over-the-road operations, there are also sleeper cab and relay operations. The relay operation is commonly called the "slide seat," since one driver drives to a relay point, a distance of 300 or more miles, and then a new driver slides in the seat and drives to .he next point. The current trend is toward the use of the relay system and phasing out the sleeper cab operations for long-haul general commodity carriers. However, sleeper cab operations are widely used by specialized commodity carriers, private carriers, and exempt carriers operating in long-haul movements, including husband-wife teams.

In trying to determine the better method to be used, a careful analysis must be made of a specific operation. An important factor is the volume of road schedules. Another factor that must be considered is the out-of-pocket expenses. In a sleeper cab operation, the driver rate per mile doubles. This cost, though, is partially offset by a reduction in fixed expenses.

Under the relay system, the running times tend to become constant, which improves the dependability of service. A company also has a better opportunity to make regular checks with drivers. Drivers like it because they are able to be home at regular intervals, which can reduce driver turnover.

The ability to adjust relay runs to various terrain conditions often makes it possible to purchase power equipment adequate for one segment of the relay, and a lighter type for another portion of the run, with resulting reduction in equipment cost. Since fixed points are established under the relay system, costs can be reduced on fuel, oil, and parts through concentration of purchasing power in quantity at these points.

### Interchange and interlining

Instead of transferring cargos from the trailer of one motor carrier to that of another, motor carriers have found it much more efficient to interchange equipment. This makes it possible for one carrier to haul a load part of the way and, at a designated transfer point, to turn the equipment over to a connecting carrier, which will complete the haul. The physical exchange of equipment, which is generally confined to trailers, is effected between authorized carriers for the furtherance of through movement of freight over routes each is certificated to serve. In interchange, each carrier has authority to operate in the portion of the haul it performs. The trailer interchange is arranged on several different bases by means of individual agreements between carriers. Sometimes completely loaded trailers are interchanged; or, in other cases, a loaded trailer is offered by one of the two carriers in exchange for an empty trailer to be used by the first carrier while the second carrier is completing the through movement. Interchange between modes of transportation is growing and has been facilitated by the use of containers.

Although there is an increasing amount of trailer interchange, this practice is not as prevalent among motor carriers as it is among rail carriers. In rail transportation, 75 percent of rail tonnage moves interline, whereas motor carriers of general commodities interline only 25 to 35 percent of their tonnage. There have been a number of difficulties in the interchange of equipment, which include: (a) nonuniformity of fifth-wheel coupling device; (b) nonuniformity of braking devices; (c) differences in light connections; (d) state restrictions on vehicle weight, length, and width; (e) reluctance of some motor carriers to allow their equipment to be removed from their control; (f) reluctance of some motor carriers to allow equipment bearing their firm name to be operated in a foreign territory; (g) inability to make suitable agreements covering necessary repairs to a unit while it is in the possession of a foreign carrier; and (h) lack of uniform basis of compensation.

In an effort to improve trailer interchange practices and accomplish a degree of uniformity, action was taken regarding a uniform charge for the use of equipment. The Commission approved the National Equipment Interchange Agreement filed on behalf of over 300 motor common carriers, which provides the machinery for the establishment of a uniform charge for interchange for those carriers that wish to use it. The approval was granted under Section 5 (a) of the act and provides that carriers can be relieved from the operation of the antitrust laws with respect to agreements among themselves for joint action on rates and related matters when such agreements have Commission approval. The approval was subject to the conditions that it applied only to motor common carriers which are members to the agreement and that the Commission could prescribe additional conditions in the future.[7]

At present, there are 425 participating carriers in the agreement. A committee of 48 carrier representatives with geographic representation makes recommendations with respect to the rate of compensation for the use of equipment and rules and regulations concerning use. Currently, a uniform per diem, based on graduate size of equipment, is used (over 40 foot trailer, $15; 32 to 40 foot, $12, etc.).

In order to eliminate empty back hauls and to save fuel, the Regular Common Carrier Conference instituted a computerized interchange substituted service program (CISS). A similar program was instituted by the Irregular Route Common Carrier Conference and the Equipment Interchange Association called Computer Assisted Load Matching (CALM). Both programs are a means of matching excess loads of freight with available equipment and drivers on the same routes.

The Interstate Commerce Commission has prescribed rules governing the interchange of equipment. When power equipment is being interchanged for any through movement of traffic, there must be a contract which specifies the particular equipment to be interchanged, the points of interchange, the use to be made of the equipment, and the consideration paid. The carriers' operating authority must authorize the transportation of the commodities and the service to and from the points where the interchange occurs.

Interchanged equipment must be inspected by a qualified and authorized inspector in the manner prescribed in order to comply with the Department of Transportation's safety regulations. Such equipment must also carry a copy of the interchange contract. When using power units of the originating carrier, traffic transported in interchange service must move on a through bill of lading issued by the originating carrier, and the rates charged, and the revenues collected, must be accounted for in the same manner as if there had been no interchange of equipment. Charges for the use of equipment must be kept separate and distinct from divisions of the joint rate. The rules further provide that when power units are interchanged, they must be identified in accordance with requirements of the Commission's identification rules.

Leased equipment operating in interchange service can be subleased for return to the originating carrier, as well as used in interchange between more than two carriers. A lessee of equipment on a through movement involving more than two carriers shall be considered the owner of the equipment for the purpose of leasing it for movement to destination or return to the originating carrier.

A Uniform Intermodal Interchange Agreement has also been developed governing conditions for the use, as well as maintenance and repair, of interchanged containers, trailers, and other equipment. Currently, no railroads, 32 steamship lines and 1,400 motor cariers participate in the agreement.

*Interlining* is usually understood to mean the physical transfer of a shipment from one carrier to another rather than the transfer of equipment as in interchange. A carrier generally does not interline traffic with another carrier where the opportunity exists for the latter carrier to "back solicit" such traffic through knowledge gained from shipping documents. For example, an eastern carrier terminating in Chicago will try to make interline arrangements with a western carrier that does not serve east of Chicago. If the western carrier serves points east of Chicago that are competitive with the eastern carrier, it would doubtless contact the shipper, from information gained from the freight bill, to move the shipments without interlining.

In *Ex Parte MC-77, Sub 1, 1977*, the Commission permitted trucking companies to limit to three the number of carriers that are participating in an interline movement on a single through rate. A carrier is permitted to name the carriers with which it will not interline.

### Leasing

During the 1930's, leasing of vehicles from individuals who owned and often operated the vehicles became widespread among motor carriers. Some carriers employed these owner-operators, also referred to as "gypsies" or wildcatters," for a period of time under a contractual arrangement. This type of leasing has since become known as "term leasing." Most of the leasing, though, was for a particular trip—in many instances, for a one-way haul—and the arrangements were often oral. Leasing arrangements which are for a period of time of less than 30 days are now called "trip leasing." Ordinarily, owner-operators are independent contractors. Some, however, are covered in labor agreements, in which case they are employees, and minimum rates are specified for leased equipment, as well as other provisions.

The practice of augmenting carrier equipment by means of trip leasing became so widespread and resulted in so many malpractices that the Commission instituted an investigation, *Ex Parte No. MC-43, Lease and Interchange of Vehicles by Motor Carriers,* in 1948. Extensive hearings were held, and subsequently regulations were issued to become effective in 1951. Motor carriers were opposed to the regulations and carried the matter to the Supreme Court, which affirmed the right of the Commission to issue such regulations.[8] After this decision, several bills were introduced in Congress designed to divest the Commission of the power to regulate the duration of any lease or the method of compensating (a percentage of the gross revenue) for such a lease—two of the most controversial of the leasing rules. None of these bills became law, but the Commission postponed the effective date of these two provisions. In 1953 it reopened hearings on the two rules. These provisions of the leasing rules never became effective, and in 1956 Congress enacted legislation prohibiting the Commission from controlling the duration and the amount of compensation for leases of agricultural carriers. Finally, in 1957, the Commission issued new motor carrier leasing rules that superseded previous regulations. These rules remained in effect until the Commission issued new rules in 1979. The Commission's action was taken in order to insure full disclosure to the owner-operator of all aspects of the lease agreement with the regulated carrier. The Commission referred to these rules as promoting a "truth in leasing concept" that would insure that carriers and owner-operators were fully aware of the obligations and responsibilities of each.

The current rules provide:[9]

1. A written contract must be made by the parties which must state all items that may be charged back to the lessor, the responsibility of each party with respect to insurance costs, and the terms of any equipment purchase plan or rental contract that gives the carrier the right to make deductions from the lessor's compensation.

2. Equipment must be in the exclusive possession and control of the lessee.

3. Compensation is to be specific, and must be stated on the face of the lease; and the owner-operator must be furnished a copy.

4. Duration of the lease must be specific.

5. Copies of the lease are to be carried in the vehicle.

6. During the lease, the equipment must be identified as that of the ICC regulated carrier.

7. A receipt must be given by the carrier to the owner when possession is taken of the vehicle; and a receipt given the owner when possession of the equipment ends.

8. Payment to the lessor shall be specified in the lease and must be made within 15 days after submission of the necessary delivery documents and other paperwork and the documents required shall be clearly specified.

9. A copy of the rated freight bill shall be given the lessor when payment is based on a percentage of the gross revenue of a shipment.

10. Lessor cannot be required to purchase or rent any products, equipment, or services from the carrier as a condition of the lease arrangement.

11. If any escrow funds are required, the lease shall so specify.

12. Driver must be in compliance with safety regulations.

13. Certain records covering the leasing operations must be maintained.

There are a number of general exceptions to the leasing rules, however, as follows (exceptions do not apply relative to inspection and identification of equipment):

1. Trip leasing between authorized carriers in the direction of a point which the owner of the equipment (lessor) is authorized to serve is permitted. The point must be a place authorized in the operating authority, not just a terminal.

2. Leasing rules do not apply to equipment used in transportation performed within commercial zones.

3. The rules do not apply to vehicles leased without drivers from a rental company.

4. The rules do not apply to equipment other than power units, provided that such trailers or semitrailers are not drawn by a power unit leased from the owner of such trailers.

5. The rules do not apply to equipment used wholly or in part in the substituted motor-for-rail transportation of railroad freight moving between points that are railroad stations on railroad billings.

In addition to the preceding general exceptions, there are exceptions to *specific* rules as follows:

1. The 30-day requirement does not apply to leasing of equipment used in exempt agricultural transportation or perishable commodities. This use by a motor carrier of a motor vehicle is to be in the general direction of the general area where the motor vehicle is based; or if the motor vehicle has completed an exempt movement, the motor vehicle can be used in a loaded movement in any direction and/or in the general direction in which the motor vehicle is based.

2. The 30-day requirement does not apply to leasing between authorized automobile transporters or leasing between authorized tank-truck carriers. It also does not apply to dump equipment used in bulk transportation of salt and calcium chloride from November 1 to April 30.

3. Where household goods carriers have intermittent operations under a long-term lease, the rule requiring exclusive possession and responsibility applies only during the period the equipment is operated by or for the authorized carrier.

In order for a regulated common carrier to rent equipment with drivers to an interstate private carrier or shipper, such service must be specified in the operating authority of the carrier. (An exception is granted when the vehicles so rented are used in three exempt transport categories—vehicles used exclusively for distribution of newspapers, transportation incidental to transportation by aircraft, and commercial zone transportation.) The rules also prohibit authorized common carriers from renting equipment without drivers to private carriers or shippers. (This prohibition does not apply to authorized carriers transporting property wholly for and on the billings of railroads.)

Contract carriers, however, may rent equipment without drivers to private carriers or shippers provided the contract carrier first secures the approval of the rental contract from the Commission.

The existence of the exceptions, both general and specific, to the rules makes it clear that the interests championing these have been able to continue to be more flexible in certain sectors of trucking. For example, the exception to the rule which permits leasing of exempt vehicles to regulated carriers when the return trip is in the general direction of the exempt vehicle's base can be applied in the following manner. An exempt carrier from Orlando, Florida, to New York can lease his equipment on the return trip to an authorized carrier going to Chicago, thence to Nashville, Atlanta, and finally to Orlando, i.e., the vehicle is going in the general direction of the exempt trucker's base.

One of the basic sources of leased equipment is from owner-operators. Some lease their equipment to a regulated carrier on a term basis, possibly a year; and thus operate in a manner similar to company employees. Others may be engaged basically in transporting exempt commodities and will trip lease on the return trip to any regulated carrier in order to get gasoline money back to their home base of operations.

It is also a rather common practice for a regulated general commodities carrier which has a specialized division, such as steel or perishables, to make extensive use of lease arrangements.

Exempt carriers of agricultural commodities are permitted to trip lease to a for-hire carrier back to their home base; but the leasing arrangements must specify origin, destination, and time of beginning and ending of last movement which brings equipment under the agricultural exemption.

### Maintenance management

The magnitude of investment in equipment, particularly the tractor, has resulted in special efforts being made to secure its maximum utilization. Annual mileages of 150,000 to 200,000 miles are not unusual with many major carriers.

The effective management of maintenance of equipment is important in controlling maintenance costs and in minimizing the breakdown of equipment while it is being operated. Carrier management attempts to get maximum utilization from equipment and has no more units of equipment than necessary to conduct operations. For these reasons, it is mandatory that equipment be maintained in the best possible condition. Road failures and vehicles out of service are costly elements that must be avoided as much as possible.

There is a tendency in maintenance work to maintain inadequate records, yet such records can be effectively used for a variety of purposes. One of these is to compare the performance of one manufacturer's parts with those of another. Another use is to compare maintenance costs of a carrier's fleet with outside fleets.

For a long time, many motor carriers replaced parts when they had been in service for a certain number of hours or a certain number of miles. In recent years, increased use has been made of instrumentation as a management tool to improve maintenance. Instrumentation is the use of instruments by trained technicians to determine what maintenance needs to be done before any work is performed. The functioning of different parts of the engine can be tested to ascertain what repairs are necessary, if any, without dismantling the engine. Weaknesses can be detected, and the necessary maintenance performed to correct them. Instrumentation greatly facilitates regular service inspection procedure. The investment in this type of equipment depends upon the size of the fleet and ranges from $500 to $4,000.

A survey of Class I and Class II common carriers of general freight showed that equipment maintenance consumes 11.9 percent of their gross revenues.[10]

### Documentation

The Interstate Commerce Act does not prescribe a uniform bill of lading for motor carriers, although it does require that receipts for goods must be given by the carrier. Therefore, there is not a particular form of the bill of lading which is used by all carriers. Many of them use the bills of lading, both the straight and the order forms, which are reproduced in the current issue of the National Motor Freight Classification.

A uniform straight bill of lading serves as a shipper's receipt for the goods and a contract between the shipper and the carrier for the transportation of the shipment. The straight bill of lading is nonnegotiable. In other words, it cannot be reassigned or used for the purpose of transacting business between the shipper and the consignee, as is the case with the uniform order bill of lading. The majority of shipments move under the straight bill of lading. Under this bill of lading, the delivery may be made upon the proper identification and without the presentation of the bill of lading. The terms and conditions are contained on the back of the bill of lading.

Motor carriers and shippers may use the short-form bill of lading which does not have all of the terms and conditions printed on the back, although all the terms and conditions apply. Shippers often have their own bills of lading printed and are the principal users of the short form. There is little difference between the two forms, but the short form is not used on c.o.d. shipments.

The uniform order bill of lading constitutes a receipt for goods and a contract between the points and, in addition, constitutes title to the goods. Under its terms, it provides for delivery to the party who possesses the original copy of the bill of lading properly endorsed, that is, signed by the shipper and the origin carrier, upon receipt of the shipment. The endorsement constitutes the signature of the shipper and the signature of the party presenting the bill of lading to the carrier at destination. If the party who presents the order bill of lading is different from the party to be notified, as has been shown on the bill of lading, this would indicate that the order bill of lading has been transferred. Each of the transfers must be recorded by endorsement on the back of the bill of lading. Thus, the order bill of lading is a negotiable instrument, and the title to goods may be passed from one party to another by endorsement.

The order bill of lading is usually handled by having the shipper endorse it and forward it together with an invoice and sight draft covering the merchandise to his local bank. The local bank will then forward it to a bank at destination. The party named on the bill as the party to be notified will be notified by the bank at destination, and that bank will make collection from the customer for the amount of the invoice or sight draft and will receipt and surrender the original bill of lading. The customer will then surrender the order bill of lading to the delivering carrier and will receive his goods. The order bill of lading may be endorsed "in blank," that is, it could be negotiated by anyone; and it may be endorsed: "To the order of . . . ," which constitutes limited endorsement since it cannot be further negotiated. Motor carriers often refer to the uniform order bill of lading as a shipper's order, order notify, or sight draft bill of lading.

There is a minimum of three copies of the bill lading: the original, the memorandum copy which is usually retained by the shipper, and the shipping order copy which is retained by the origin carrier. The carrier's freight bills are issued from the information which is shown on this copy. Many carriers, however, have more copies made of the bill of lading. When there are but three copies of the order bill of lading, the original must be forwarded by the shipper to destination and turned over to the destination carrier before delivery of the goods, the shipper retaining the memorandum copy and the shipping order copy being retained by the origin carrier.

A carrier's liability for loss and damage is set forth in subchapter I of the Interstate Commerce Act and the Bill of Lading Terms and Conditions. Shippers sometimes make notations on bills of lading, such as "Protect from Weather." The terms and conditions of the bill of lading cannot be changed by such notations unless the carrier's tariffs offer protective service.

In addition to the commercial bills of lading, many motor carriers must be familiar with the government bill of lading. The government bill of lading is issued by the federal government for use in the movement of its property. This bill of lading is nonnegotiable, and the original copy of the bill of lading signed by the shipper and the origin carrier upon receipt of the goods must be forwarded by the shipper to the consignee for execution and surrender to the carrier upon delivery of the shipment. The carrier which seeks to collect the freight charges must have the original bill of lading to present to the proper governmental agency to receive payment.

When freight has been picked up and checked into a terminal, a waybill which is used as a routing document in internal operations by the carrier may be made from the shipping order or bill of lading. From the bill of lading a freight bill is prepared showing the total charges that the shipper or receiver is to pay for the shipment. Some carriers are combining the bill of lading and freight bill into a single document, in an effort to cut billing cots, which amount to $40 million annually.

The carrier assigns to the freight bill a number, which is termed a "pro number." This term is derived from the word *progressive,* and it indicates that the freight bills are numbered consecutively. Reference to the pro number is made in correspondence, loss and damage claims, tracing, and the like. If a carrier lists on a load sheet all of the freight bills covering freight loaded on the same truck or trailer, this is termed "scripting."

A manifest may be used by the operations department for control purposes. On a manifest is recorded each movement of line-haul equipment and its load which is dispatched between cities. Such manifests may be issued regardless of whether the equipment is empty or loaded. Each terminal will have manifests which are numbered with a prefix to identify the terminal. The information shown on the truck manifest includes the name of the consignee, destination, shipper, weight, number of pieces, and pro number, as well as information about the equipment and route. If freight is added at intermediate points, supplemental manifests may be issued. Many carriers have eliminated manifesting as being a costly and needless procedure. The information on the manifest can be secured from other documents.

The line-haul unit must be sealed in order to provide protection for the contents of the truck or trailer. The Congress enacted a law which covers the unlawful breaking of seals or locks on motor vehicles or unlawful entry of motor vehicles transporting property in interstate commerce.

On the terminal-to-terminal loads, the seal, which is a small piece of metal containing a number, is placed on the latch which secures the doors of the body of the vehicle. The seal should be applied by an authorized terminal employee, and properly recorded on the manifest. If there is a discrepancy, it should be reported.

### Accounting

For the purposes of prescribing a uniform system of accounts, carriers have been grouped by the Interstate Commerce Commission into three classes, as previously explained in an earlier chapter. Since January 1, 1979, Class I motor carriers are those with annual gross revenues of $5 million or more; Class II motor carriers are those with annual gross revenues of $1 million or over but less than $5 million; and Class III motor carriers are those with annual gross revenues of less than $1 million. Class I and Class II motor carriers are required to keep their accounts under a uniform system and to file quarterly and annual reports in a form prescribed by the Interstate Commerce Commission. Class III carriers subject to Interstate Commerce Commission regulations have not had to keep their accounts under the system prescribed by the Commission. Beginning in 1948, however, a simple annual report form of eight pages has been required from Class III carriers, in order that the Commission may obtain information about these carriers. These reports consist primarily of the reporting of revenues, expenses, vehicle-miles operated, tons transported, equipment operated, and some limited information as to the number of employees. The annual report required of Class I and Class II carriers, on the other hand, is over 70 page reports. A sufficient number of schedules are contained in the reports to give a comprehensive picture of Class I and Class II motor-carrier operations.

Because of the wide use made of financial data which are shown in motor carrier quarterly and annual reports in connection with the fixing of rates, the handling of general revenue proceedings, the handling of applications for the purchase, merger, and consolidation of operating authorities, and the issuance of securities which require Commission approval, it is important that there be close supervision by the Commission of motor carrier accounting practices. Many dispositions of applications for rate increases have been based principally on the data contained in the quarterly and annual reports of the motor carrier applicant. The reports are also of value in determining credit standings and the general financial condition of the industry. One of the largest credit rating firms maintains a small staff at the Commission to examine the reports. Extensive use is made of the reports by carriers which compare their own operating statistics with those of other carriers. Industry "norms," or averages of the figures, are compiled, and a carrier may compare the cost elements of its operations with those of the industry average.

Authorized Commission personnel, such as special agents, examiners, or accountants, have the right to inspect a carrier's records, including all accounts, records, correspondence, and similar material. This is true even though the records do not relate to transportation. This right of inspection by the Commission has been upheld by the Supreme Court.

The accounting system which motor carriers use may be either a centralized or a decentralized plan. Whether a centralized or decentralized accounting system should be used is influenced by factors such as the number of terminals and their geographical location and the size of the company. In smaller companies where there is but one accountant, the accounting system is generally centralized. However, many of the largest Class I carriers also use the centralized system.

The advantages of the decentralized plan are prompt collections, quicker availability of collected funds, records at hand for dealing with shippers, more prompt remittance of c.o.d.'s, better relations with creditors, and use of prevailing wage scales. In the decentralized plan, the cashier at the terminal collects accounts receivable.

The advantages of the centralized system are greater uniformity in the classification of transactions; specialization of accounting personnel; greater possibilities for job analysis, evaluation, and production; strict control of costs, closer supervision of accrued items; more current financial statements; and less necessary verification of branch records.

Larger carriers often adopt machine accounting when this is feasible. Manual methods, however, still predominate throughout the motor carrier industry.

### Interline accounts

A large number of shipments move over two or more main lines. Some carriers have felt that they should restrict their participation in so-called joint hauls to not more than two connecting carriers because of the difficulty in collecting. This is due in part to the financial risk if they agree to joint hauls with numerous carriers with which they have little contact.

Where motor carriers have joint rates and one carrier owes another carrier, the collection of the division which is owed is a matter for the carriers to settle or the courts. However, where the Commission by order has prescribed divisions as between carriers or has required retroactive adjustment of divisions, the carriers may base their court actions upon such orders.[11]

In the settlement of interline accounts, a motor carrier deals with two aspects, the so-called collectibles and the payables. The collectibles are amounts that the motor carrier secures from connecting carriers and include two categories: (a) shipments that are transferred to a connecting carrier with freight charges collect, which includes that division of revenue from origin to point of transfer; and (b) shipments that are transferred to a motor carrier from a connecting carrier with freight charges prepaid, which includes that division of revenues from point of transfer to destination.

The payables are charges that are due connecting carriers, as follows: (a) shipments that are transferred to a connecting carrier with freight charges prepaid, which means that division of revenue from interchange point to destination; and (b) shipments transferred by connecting carrier to a motor carrier with freight charges collect, which includes the division of revenue from origin to point of transfer at which the motor carrier received the shipment.

### Cooperative bill collection system

The collection of freight bills by motor common carriers from hundreds of different shippers can prove most burdensome. Depending on the volume of business, carriers must try to collect from 50 to 3,000 bills a day. Commission regulations permit motor carriers to extend credit to shippers for 7 days with credit extension to 30 days subject to a 1 percent, $10.00, service charge.

To facilitate the collection of freight bills and the settlement of interline debits between carriers, an organization called Transport Clearings has been formed. It is a nonprofit corporation owned and operated by and for its carrier members and is presently located in St. Paul, Seattle, Portland, San Francisco, Denver, Charlotte, N.C., and Los Angeles. Each one of the organizations is separately incorporated and locally run, such as Transport Clearings of Los Angeles and Transport Clearings of the Bay Area (San Francisco). Each one of these cooperative clearinghouses, representing carrier members in this area, buys outright all freight bills submitted by a carrier member which otherwise would be sent directly by the carrier to the shipper. The carrier member, in other words, is paid immediately for all freight bills submitted. Each submitting carrier guarantees that each bill is legal and bona fide in all respects.

Transport Clearings in turn re-sorts the freight bills by debtor (shipper) and submits all bills to the debtors in combined form. This enables the debtors to pay Transport Clearings with one check and one mailing covering bills to all carrier members of Transport Clearings which would otherwise have to be paid to each individual carrier. If a bill cannot be collected, Transport Clearings sustains all the loss; but it will control the carriers' choice of credit customers by advising them that it will accept bills against all shippers except those on a "cash list." This cash list is sent to all carrier members and names the firms which Transport Clearings has learned from experience are unsound credit risks.

A second type of operations conducted is that of interline settlements. Bills submitted against other carrier members are settled or cleared by the cooperative clearinghouse located in the city where the transfer from the line of one carrier to the line of the other carrier takes place. The bills so submitted are charged to and collected from the other carriers by deduction from their settlement check each day. Transport Clearings follows the same system as do banks in their clearinghouse operations, with the exception that banks pay their individual balances, whereas Transport Clearings collects by deduction from the money owing to the submitting carriers on all bills submitted.

This nonprofit organization is supported by fees collected from the carrier members. The excess of income over expenses is refunded to the carrier members on a prorate basis. The capital needed to start such an organization is put up by carriers plus borrowed funds. Although this organization is of recent origin, it is interesting to note that the Transport Clearings groups collect about $2.75 billion in freight bills a year.

There are many advantages to a carrier in this type of collection operation, one of the biggest of which is that the carrier's cash is not tied up in accounts receivable. One carrier is reported to have had $230,000 due in freight bills while it owed $170,000 to creditors. It had but $15,000 cash on hand. Upon joining Transport Clearings, the carrier immediately received the $230,000 due it from outstanding freight bills, less the cooperative's fee for collection; it then paid off the money it owed and had over $70,000 cash on hand.

Another advantage is that all carriers enjoy equal credit relationships with customers. Therefore, the customer cannot play one carrier against the other by stating that one carrier allows him 30 days' credit, whereas another will allow him only 20 days. The fraud potentials in a carrier's offices can be minimized through the use of this system, since one check will handle 95 percent of the collections. Furthermore, there is a reduction of disbursement requirements, since interline payables are paid by deductions from receipts. The reduction in clerical costs and inbound mail is another advantage.

Shippers, too, like this system of collection, not only because it simplifies their payment of bills to area carriers which are members but also because they are spared the unpleasantness that sometimes arises through misunderstandings over the collection of bills.

Transport clearinghouses and other collection agencies that are employed by carriers to collect their freight charges are not under the jurisdiction of the Commission, but as agents of the carriers they would be liable with the carriers to the penalties prescribed for violations of the act, such as the giving of rebates or unlawful extension of credit.

### Bank clearings and electronic funds transfer

In addition to the industry-sponsored freight bill collecting system of motor carriers, a number of banks have instituted operations which serve as clearinghouses for profit. The first of the clearinghouses for motor carriers was organized in 1949 by a Chicago bank. At the present time, about 42 such clearinghouses are operated by banks in major cities and they collect about $3 billion annually. Initially, all the banks which instituted the settlement systems confined them to interline accounts.

The bank which originally instituted this operation has over 200 motor carrier participants. A $1,000 balance for each carrier is required, although it has been stated that it is necessary to call daily for reimbursement for overdrafts in some accounts. Daily statements are furnished to carriers. Eighty percent of the transactions are paid without any difficulty.

A new, paperless way to settle freight charges is currently being developed. This is a method that brings together a combination of data communications and data processing with electronic funds transfer. This eliminates the need to mail freight bills and payment checks between the carriers who join such a system and their customers. A carrier's computer sends shipments data to the electronic funds transfer company and the carrier's customers' computers send matching shipment data to the system. The funds transfer company performs a computer printout of input items and makes transfer of funds from the payor to the payee account.

## QUESTIONS AND PROBLEMS

1. In what specific ways can the computer aid management in decision making? Would your answer be different for a Class III carrier in contrast to a Class I carrier? In what ways?

2. What is management by objective? How does it work?

3. What are the external constraints which face operations management? How would you suggest this area be dealt with most effectively?

4. Are the basic functions of management any different in a motor carrier organization than those found in other types of business organizations?

5. It is sometimes stated that an organization chart is tailored to accommodate the people in the company. How would you suggest overcoming this?

6. In what way could you ascertain weaknesses in a carrier organization structure?

7. What suggestions do you have for staffing the departments of a Class I carrier that is growing at an annual rate of 20 percent?

8. "The preparation of and the responsibility for a sound budget rests

with the respective department heads and not with the budget officer." Comment.

9. What is bootstrap management? Is there any evidence that it exists in motor transportation now?

10. What is the role of training in developing effective motor carrier management?

11. Trace the changes which occur in the organization structure from a 1-truck operation to a 300-truck, 20-terminal operation.

12. What should be included in a comprehensive safety program?

13. Describe an awards or incentive safety plan. What suggestions could you make to improve such a plan?

14. What are some of the difficulties that have arisen where interchange of equipment between motor carriers has taken place?

15. List the advantages and disadvantages of equipment interchange between motor carriers.

16. What types of road supervision of drivers are used? In your opinion which would be best for a Class I carrier with a 200-truck operation?

## FOOTNOTES TO CHAPTER 9

[1] Steven J. Carroll, Jr., "Research in Management by Objectives," *Journal for Humanistic Management*, September, 1973.

[2] *Ibid.*

[3] Management Systems Committee, American Trucking Associations, Inc.

[4] Transportation Data Coordinating Committee (founded by the National Industrial Traffic League and the Transportation Association of America).

[5] Joseph A. Reidinger, "OSHA—Its Effect on Transport and Logistics," American Society of Traffic and Transportation Proceedings, Annual Meeting, 1974, p. 119.

[6] Truck driver-training courses are sponsored by some state trucking associations, by the Regular Common Carrier Conference of ATA, and offered through the extension division of a few colleges. North Carolina State University has had such a course since 1949.

[7] *National Equipment Interchange-Agreement*, October 16, 1958. Developed by the Regular Common Carrier Conference of American Trucking Associations, Inc.

[8] *American Trucking Associations, Inc. v. United States*, 344 U.S. 298 (1953).

[9] *Lease and Interchange of Vehicles by Motor Carriers*, 64 MCC 361 (1957); see supplemental reports; also 51 MCC 461 (1951), 52 MCC 675 (1953); Ex Parte MC-43 (1974), and Ex Parte MC-43 (Sub 7) (1979).

[10] ATA Foundation, Inc., *Costs and Characteristics of Maintaining Motor Freight Equipment* (Washington, D.C., 1962), p. 7.

[11] Administrative Rule No. 14, August 26, 1936.

# chapter 10

# Labor relations

It is a curious fact that although Class I operators may be negotiating several labor contracts and engaging in the settlement of grievances throughout the year, there are few carriers that employ a full-time labor relations executive. Labor costs constitute approximately one-half of operating expenses, yet motor carrier management sometimes postpones preparation for collective bargaining until the present contract is expiring. Unions, on the other hand, have specialists whose full time is spent preparing for contract negotiations. In order to maintain an even keel in collective bargaining, motor carrier management must devote more attention to the labor relations problem.[1]

Motor carriers are particularly vulnerable to strikes or interruptions of any type in their service. Motor transportation is an intensely competitive field. A motor carrier faces competition from other motor carriers, from other modes of transportation, and from private carriage, and carriers lack the cash reserves to carry them through any long period of business interruption. Inasmuch as they are engaged in rendering service, they are unable to live off their inventory as production industries can. When they are not able to transport freight, it is just business lost. These factors have undoubtedly had an effect on their collective bargaining with unions.

### Classification of motor carrier employees

Employees of Class I motor carriers are classified by the Interstate Commerce Commission as equipment, maintenance, and garage; transportation which includes drivers and helpers; terminal; sales, tariff, and advertising; insurance and safety; and administrative and general. The average compensation for line-haul drivers is higher than that of supervisory personnel in terminals, transportation, and equipment maintenance and garage. In 1974, the average was $19,000. Officers, owners, and partners have average annual compensation of more than $40,000.

Many carriers will have individual classifications of employees which will differ from this classification. Furthermore, the classification of employees covered by union contracts varies also from contract to contract and from area to area. For example, one union contract may refer to a freight handler as a "lumper"; another contract may refer to such a worker as a "stacker"; and still another may refer to him as a "platform worker." This lack of uniform terminology can lead to misunderstandings, but it is so prevalent that it is doubtful whether uniformity can be achieved. There is even some carry-over of terminology from horse-and-wagon days, such as the term "hostler," which formerly referred to the man who took care of the horses at the stable and is now used by some carriers to refer to the man who takes care of the trucks at the garage.

| | |
|---|---|
| Officers & Supervisors | 16.4¢ |
| Drivers & Helpers | 53.5 |
| Owner-Operator Drivers | 2.4 |
| Vehicle Repair & Service | 5.6 |
| Clerical & Administrative | 8.6 |
| Cargo Handlers & Other labor | 13.5 |

Fig. 10-1. Distribution of the 1977 motor carrier wage dollar among the major employee classifications. Source: American Trucking Associations, Inc., *Trends* (Washington, D.C., 1977-78), p. 17.

The distribution of the Class I motor carrier's wage dollar by type of employee is shown in Fig. 10-1. The largest share of the wage dollar goes to drivers and helpers, that is, those engaged in the transportation of the over-the-road as well as pickup and delivery units. Cargo handlers rank next in the amount received as their share of the wage dollar. The amount received by these two groups of employees constitutes two-thirds of the entire wage dollar.

The importance of wages to gross revenue varies, depending upon the type of service rendered. The wages paid to the employees of common carriers of general freight exceeded those paid by other types of Class I carriers, amounting to over half of gross revenue.

### Federal labor legislation

The National Labor Relations Act enacted in 1935, which encouraged employees to organize unions and outlawed specific employer unfair labor practices, applied to motor carriers as well as to other businesses engaged in interstate commerce, excluding railroads and airlines. The National Labor Relations Board was created to administer the provisions of the act.[2]

The Labor-Management Relations Act (known as the Taft-Hartley Act) enacted in 1947 listed unfair labor practices of unions. Among other provisions, a "cooling-off" period is required when strikes threaten national health and safety. The Federal Mediation and Conciliation Service was created by this act and attempts to bring the parties to an agreement during the cooling-off period. If the parties cannot agree and the work stoppage might result in a national emergency, the President of the United States can secure an injunction to stop the strike.

In 1959, the Labor-Management Reporting and Disclosure Act (Landrum-Griffin) was passed. This act requires, among other things, financial reports from labor organizations, union officials, and labor relations consultants; provides a "bill of rights" for union members so that all have equal rights to nominate candidates, vote, and attend membership meetings; stipulates standards for elections and office holding; and requires that national and international unions must elect officers at least once every five years and locals at least once every three years.

Pension plans for employees must now be administered under the Employee Retirement Income Security Act of 1974 (ERISA). The Teamster pension funds involve substantial amounts of money. Three of the area conference pension funds have combined assets of $1.8 billion.

Under Equal Employment Opportunity legislation, motor carriers, as well as other business firms, have had to establish affirmative action programs indicating they are not discriminating in minority hiring and advancement opportunities. In 1974, the Department of Justice filed a class action-civil rights suit against 349 major trucking companies, as well as the Teamsters Union and the International Association of Machinists. Seven major truck lines signed a partial consent decree at that time in which they denied any violation of the law but agreed to try and meet hiring goals set by the decree to employ more minority workers.

As discussed in the Management and Operations Chapter, the Occupational Safety and Health Act was enacted in 1970 for the purpose of reducing the number of job safety and health hazards.

### Teamsters Union

The Teamsters Union comprises the largest international union with a current membership of more than 2.2 million, about 30 percent of whom are truck drivers. The membership of this union is composed of many other groups including vending-machine repairmen, automobile salesmen, service station employees, department store office workers, frozen-food plant employees, wholesale opitical workers, potato chip company employees, farm employees in some areas, and many others.

The Teamsters were one of three unions expelled from the AFL—CIO in December, 1957, for failing to eliminate corrupt practices. Although the AFL—CIO granted new charters to compete with two of the expelled unions, no new charter was issued to compete with the Teamsters. In 1968 the Teamsters and the United Auto Workers, another expelled union, formed the Alliance for Labor Action.

The international union is headed by elected officials including a general president, a general secretary-treasurer, 13 vice presidents, and three trustees. The latter have only the duty of auditing the union books twice each year. The convention which meets every five years elects the international officers and acts as an appeals group regarding disputed decisions by officers and lower units of the organization. Constitutional amendments, where necessary, are enacted by this body. The general president has a great deal of power as he can interpret the constitutional laws of the union and can settle all disputes submitted to him by lower bodies. He appoints union organizers; decides whether or not members who are on strike or who have been locked out are entitled to benefits; and approves the bylaws of the component elements of the Teamsters Union. Among other important powers, he has the authority to appoint trustees of local unions and Joint Councils who have power to select and remove officers and to conduct the affairs of the local or Joint Council under their control. The decisions of the president may be appealed to the general executive board which controls the legislative and judicial powers of the union between conventions. This body consists of the president, secretary-treasurer, and the 13 vice presidents.

Local unions, of which there are 744, are organized along craft lines, such as a local union of milk drivers, bread truck drivers, and so on. If there is an insufficient number of members of one craft, they can form a union of mixed crafts, or a mixed local. In those cities in which there are three or more local unions, a Joint Council is formed. About 50 of these are now in existence. They adjust jurisdictional disputes among local unions, rule on such matters as strike proposals or anticipated lockouts, and evaluate wage proposals to be submitted to employers.

The union is also divided into five area conferences—Eastern, Central, Western, Southern, and Canadian. The Western States Conference of Teamsters covers 11 western states; the Southern Conference of Teamsters, 12 southern states; the Central States Conference of Teamsters, 12 central states; the Eastern States Conference of Teamsters embraces the eastern states; and the Canadian Conference embraces Canada. Each conference is headed by a chairman appointed by the president from among the vice presidents or international organizers and by an executive board or policy committee appointed from among local leaders within the conference area. Each conference is divided into trade divisions and state divisions. The trade divisions are based upon the type of work performed by members in that area, such as bakery, beverage, building and construction, and chauffeurs.

The dues of the locals are not less than $8 per month, and the initiation fee is fixed by each local union. The amount of this fee depends on the type of job but is about $25 for many workers. The local union remits a per-capita tax of $3.15 per month to the international union. This provides revenues of over $75 million. Additional revenue comes from initiation fees and sale of supplies to the locals. In addition, income from investments amounts to more than $3.7 million. Seven of the local unions have a membership of over 10,000. The largest local, Local 705 in Chicago, has 19,500 members. If funds in the international union fall below $5 million, each member can be assessed $1. In the case of strikes, action may be taken by a vote of two-thirds of the local union; but, prior to taking this action, the local must notify the Joint Council of the union. For example, there are 25 locals in New York City which are joined together in a Joint Council. This is the largest Joint Council, with a membership of 153,000. The international president then must be notified and will be in charge of the strike in the event such action is taken. The strike benefits which the international union gives to the local are $25 per week per member.

Labor agreements over the years have evolved from local to area (Central States Agreement) and, in 1964, to a single uniform national contract called the National Master Freight Agreement, one for over-the road and one for local cartage. There were various supplemental agreements to this contract. The master agreements are negotiated every three years by the Teamsters Union and industry representatives.

A local union may negotiate a number of different contracts. This is because some companies will negotiate with the labor organization individually if they are not members of a trade association. The trade association (local or state) negotiates directly with the local union for contracts for all of its member carriers.

In Chicago, there are two unions, one a Teamsters local union and the other an independent union of drivers which have negotiated separately in the past. In 1970 when it appeared that a final settlement of the National Master Freight Agreement was concluded, these two unions went on strike, demanded and got a contract which was 55 cents higher than the national contract provided. The national contract was then renegotiated and a better settlement received.

The Teamsters have entered into mutual aid and assistance pacts and jurisdictional agreements with a number of other unions. These pacts provide methods of resolving questions of jurisdiction and methods of aiding each other should this be necessary.

Owner-operators are not usually members of the Teamsters and their status is that of an independent contractor, not as an employee of a trucking firm. The National Labor Relations Board has consistently applied the common law "right-to-control" test in determining whether an independent trucker is an employee or an independent contractor. If the right to control the manner and means to attain a given end is reserved, the relation is one of employer-employee, but if control is reserved only over the desired result then an independent contractor relationship exists.

A Class I regular route general commodity carrier recently embargoed all less-truckload traffic weighing less than 5,000 pounds and closed over 100 terminal facilities. It laid off or dismissed over 4,700 employees, many of them drivers, and hired owner-operators for their trucking operations. The Teamsters asked the Commission to investigate and possibly suspend or revoke the carrier's operating rights.

Those private carriers that have been organized by the Teamsters have individual contracts and are not a part of the National Master Freight Agreement.

### Other unions

The International Association of Machinists and Aerospace Workers, AFL–CIO, embraces a number of mechanics in its membership. In terms of numbers of organized motor carrier employees, this union ranks second to the Teamsters.

The Office Employees International Union, AFL–CIO, has organized some office employees in the motor carrier field. The Teamsters are also organizing office employees.

There are several other unions in the motor carrier field that have organized some employees. These include the Transport Workers Union of America and District 50 of the United Mine-Workers, and others.

**Independent truckers' organizations**

Owner-operators, of which there are an estimated 200,000 to 250,000, are considered to be independent entrepreneurs. Many are not affiliated in any way with the Teamsters Union although some interesting affiliates have been developing over the years. One such group is the Fraternal Association of Steel Haulers which broke from the Teamsters in 1967 and formed 13 chapters in the Pittsburgh, Youngstown, and Cleveland area. It is estimated the membership of this organization accounts for 65 to 95 percent of the steel hauling business. They have sought higher freight rates in order that the amount they receive as a percentage of the gross would be larger, and they were successful in establishing a limit of three hours on the time a company takes to load the independent's truck before paying overtime.

The potential strength of an affiliation of independent truckers lies in the fact that they haul such a large percentage of the perishables and livestock and, in addition, own their own equipment. When they engage in a work stoppage, their driving services are withdrawn as in any driver work stoppage but beyond that their vehicles are withdrawn also.

Other organizations, such as Midwest Truckers, Association of Independent Owner-Operators, Minnesota Independent Owner-Operators, Kentucky-Indiana Independent Owner-Operators and Drivers Organization, National Agricultural Transportation League, Unionized Truckers of America, and others have functioned over a period of time in different parts of the nation and dealing with the particular commodity they transport.

The fuel crisis in the winter of 1973-74 brought the organizations, albeit with factional infighting, together and demonstrated to them their strength in collective action. It was in January the independent truckers blockaded some highways and called for a work stoppage which was effective and lasted for several days. The government sought to work with representatives of the different independents which had created a temporary federation. An important result of the negotiations was recognition by the federal government that the independent truckers are a separate industry group distinct from the Teamsters Union. The agreement in February provided both temporary and permanent rate relief, raised the allocations of truck fuel, and pledged federal attention to a number of nonenergy-related regulatory matters, such as licensing and sizes and weights.

The National Independent Truckers Unity Committee set up a permanent organization in June, 1974, which consisted of 22 groups in the independent owner-operator field. The Committee adopted proposals on size and weight legislation, speed limits, and federal uniform licensing regulations. This type of organization injects a completely new force into management-labor relations that is going to be felt increasingly in the future.

Again in 1979 during the run-up of fuel prices and the accompanying fuel shortage, the independent truckers took a work stoppage action. They were striking for lower fuel prices, higher speed limits, removal of restrictive size and weight limits, and for a pass through on fuel increases. The federal government urged the states to modify their size and weight limits, which a number did, made more fuel available to them, and permitted the pass through of fuel price increases.

## Employers' groups

Employers have banded together for a number of reasons. Some have thought their strength, when combined, would be greater because a strike against one would be a strike against all of them. Further, by combining their forces, they could develop better cost data concerning the effect of union proposals and be prepared to present counterproposals to unions, thus improving their bargaining position. There is an advantage, too, in having a group administer an agreement. It enables employers to have a uniform interpretation of a contract rather than having provisions carried out differently by various locals. Some employers, also, have felt that the demands on their time would be lessened through group bargaining and the use of specialists. For smaller companies, employer groups present a better opportunity to stress the effect of a proposed contract upon their operations.

Employers' groups, in general, started as state organizations and then formed area confederations to bargain with unions on area contracts. Thus, there emerged a number of regional organizations. This type of organization existed for a number of years; and then as the union drive for a national contract developed, the employers banded together in 1964 in an organization called Trucking Employers, Inc., which in the 1973 negotiations represented trucking companies employing an estimated 400,000.

Dissatisfaction among a number of carriers with TEI led to the formation in 1978 of a group called Carrier Management, Inc. The two groups subsequently reconciled their differences and formed a new group, Trucking Management, Inc. (TMI), which then conducted the three-year labor contract with the Teamsters in 1979. Basically, TMI represents the regulated general commodity carriers.

The Teamsters had ordered a selective strike of 73 member carriers of TMI, and TMI responded by ordering their 500 members to lock out the Teamsters. The difficulties of normal negotiations were compounded by the voluntary wage-price guidelines of 7 percent of the Council on Wage and Price Stability and the fact that inflation was running above the guidelines. The federal government threatened to push for deregulation of the industry if the settlement did not fall within the 7 percent guidelines.

The lockout, which lasted for 10 days, had its greatest effect on the auto industry. Although the three-year contract that was signed at the end of this time exceeded the guidelines, the Administration chose to interpret the settlement as being within the guidelines.

A clause in the contract permitting contract negotiations to be reopened in the event of war was broadened at the union's request to provide for re-negotiation in the event of deregulation, imposition of mandatory wage and price controls, or the adoption of a National Health Insurance law.

Negotiations for specialized commodity carriers are not handled by this group. These are completely separate but follow the pattern of the national agreement. There are 32 supplements to a general contract that cover specialized carriers.

## Settlement of grievances

All contracts provide methods for the settlement of grievances. The following procedure is taken from a contract and is typical:

1. Any employee who has a complaint must first take the matter up with his employer. If not settled, then
2. The employee shall take the matter up with the business agent of his local union.
3. The business agent will take the complaint up with the employer. If not settled, then
4. The complaint is referred to the Joint Committee of the Employers and the Employees Council, which meets once each month. Any grievance so submitted which this group is unable to settle is referred to arbitration on the following basis:

    Two members will be selected by the employers' group, two by the employees, and these four so selected shall select an arbitrator for arbitrating the dispute. The decision of the arbitrator shall be final and binding on both parties. Pending a decision by this Board of Arbitration, there shall be no work stoppage, either by strike or lockout.

**Points covered in contracts**

The national agreement in 1979 was an umbrella contract covering 40 regional supplemental agreements. Each contains wages, hours, and working conditions.

Seniority rights prevail in union contracts. For example, if it becomes necessary to reduce the working force, the last man hired shall be laid off first. Seniority also is the primary basis on which various runs are allocated. The method being used may be that of posting the available run, with the man applying who has the most seniority getting

|  | Effective 4-1-79 | Effective 4-1-80 | Effective 4-1-81 |
|---|---|---|---|
|  | Per Mile | Per Mile | Per Mile |
| Single Axle Units | 24.425¢ | 25.175¢ | 25.925¢ |
| Tandem Axle Units (4 Axles) | 24.675 | 25.425 | 26.175 |
| Tandem Axle Units (5 Axles) | 24.8 | 25.55 | 26.3 |
| Tandem Axle Units Carrying a Cargo of 40,000 lbs. or more and Jeeps | 24.925 | 25.675 | 26.425 |
| Double Bottom Units or a Combination of Vehicles or Units | 25.825 | 26.575 | 27.325 |

the run if he is considered capable of handling it. Rates of pay are "spelled out" in the contracts, specifying the rate to be paid per hour or per mile and differentiating between over-the-road and local rates for drivers. Differentiation is made also in the rate of pay scale between driver personnel and nondriver personnel, as well as on the basis of equipment operated.

For example, rates of pay for over-the-road drivers contained in a contract for a particular area are on an hourly basis or on a mileage basis, whichever is the greater. Mileage rates are primarily used. The rates of pay for the various types of equipment are as shown above.

There are different methods of pay for local drivers, most of whom are on an hourly basis. The driver in local pickup and delivery receives $10.53 per hour. Average overtime is more than five hours per week for most drivers in local service. So-called "driver-salesmen," like the beverage, milk, or bread truck driver now frequently also handling detergents, lotion, and shampoo, are often referred to as the elite among drivers since they receive a stated amount on a specified sales minimum and a percentage on all sales above the minimum. The result is that they are paid considerably more than a local cartage driver.

Methods of payment for drivers are adapted to the particular type of run. Trip rates are found in some contracts and apply between specified points. Peddle runs within a 75-mile radius of the city are ordinarily paid on an hourly basis, and there is a minimum guarantee of eight hours for each run. The pay for a turnaround run is on an hourly basis and depends on the length of the run. All hours worked beyond 60 per week are considered overtime.

All regular employees are guaranteed $425 per week except the youngest employee in each classification. Other contracts may contain provisions such as the driver shall not deliver more than 50 feet from the truck, no agency shall follow a truck or investigate the driver, a driver shall not help another driver, and other restrictions.

Negotiations have been successful in eliminating restrictive provisions in some labor agreements. One contract provided that mileage pay was to be paid drivers for the miles scheduled between two given points even though the route had been shortened by highway improvements. Such a provision meant that drivers were being paid for "watered" miles they were not actually driving. Management and labor modified this through bargaining by adopting a formula whereby the excess-mileage payment was reduced by one-sixth per year over the life of the contract. Management agreed to the principle that the agreed-upon wage increases would offset the drivers' excess-miles pay loss.

When the speed limit was reduced to 55 miles an hour during the fuel shortage in 1973-74, the Teamsters felt this would reduce the earnings of their intercity drivers who were operating on a mileage rate. The union renegotiated the National Master Freight Agreement so that any employee who believes he has suffered a reduction in pay because of the lower speed limits should file with a local union representative (who will take the grievance up with the employer) to bring his earnings back to the pre-speed limit level.

With the development of trailer-on-flatcar and containerization, the union has negotiated contracts which it felt would minimize the effect of the shift to these operations on its membership. In 1959 a contract was made between a large motor carrier and the union under which the carrier could transport its trailers on flatcars between Chicago and points west when its volume of business exceeded that which could normally be handled by its regular complement of drivers. A settlement calling for reimbursement to drivers for earnings lost when the carrier started its piggyback was formulated.

An example of the provisions for layover pay taken from a contract is that layover pay shall commence following the 14th hour after the end of the run. If the driver is held over thereafter, he shall be guaranteed two hours' pay even if he is held over just 15 minutes. If he is held over more than two hours, he shall receive layover pay for each hour held over not to exceed eight hours' pay in the first 22-hour period, plus comfortable and sanitary lodging. On Sundays and holidays, only meals and comfortable lodgings will be allowed. There are additional stipulations for layovers beyond the first 22 hours.

Some contracts contain a provision that prohibits an intercity driver, coming into a city in which a union of local drivers has jurisdiction, from making any deliveries except to his company's terminal. Labor organizations may feel that this restriction is a sound practice; but, from the standpoint of flexibility of service, the public may be the loser.

There are many other articles covered in an employer-employee contract, such as vacations, meals, rest periods, deadheading, breakdowns or impassable highways, defective equipment, pay period, pickup and delivery limitations, minimum guarantees, mileage and hourly rates, and many others. The number of holidays is always stated in a contract. In one area, it was agreed that Washington's Birthday would constitute a holiday. After signing the contract, carriers found that shippers' stores did not close on this day as it was not a holiday in that state for most business firms. Employees who worked on that day had to be paid overtime. In another contract, the members of a local sought an extra holiday beyond the six national holidays. Truck operators proposed that each driver be given his birthday as the extra holiday, since the establishment of a standard holiday on one date would have resulted in overtime for those who worked on that day.

"Hot cargo" clauses are widely found in contracts.[3] These provide that members of the union will not handle cargo involved in labor disputes of which they are not a party. Although this action by unions was prohibited in the Labor-Management Reporting and Disclosure Act of 1959, contracts negotiated in 1961 contained a "hazardous conditions" clause which the union felt protected the individual driver against penalty by his employer for refusal to cross a picket line or handle goods of a company engaged in a labor dispute, since the act does not prohibit or penalize a worker for individual action.

The Commission ruled in a complaint instituted by a motor common carrier against a number of its connecting motor carriers that they had failed to carry out their duties as common carriers under the act by refusing to accept shipments tendered to them by the complainant because of obligations under labor contracts to which the defendants were parties. The Commission did not determine the legality of the so-called "hot cargo" clauses in such labor contracts, but found that the connecting carriers' refusal to accept the tendered interstate shipments was unlawful and that they, as common carriers, could not bargain away their statutory obligations to the public by means of contracts with third parties.[4]

Significant gains have been made by organized labor in health, welfare, and pension benefits for their members. These are often referred to as "fringe" benefits, and yet there have been negotiations in which employers have agreed to pay far more in fringe benefits than the wage increase provided in the contract. These plans cover the following: pensions, accident and sickness benefits, surgical benefits, life insurance, hospitalization, and medical benefits. The health and welfare provisions cover the employee's family as well. When these benefits are combined with workmen's compensation and social security, fringe benefits amount to over 35 percent of the payroll.

Most health and welfare and pension funds are jointly administered by trustees of employers and employees. In a recent contract, the employer's contribution was $75 per week for each member covered by the contract. These contributions will increase to $83 per week the second year of the contract and to $91 the third year.

The central Teamsters have a $700 monthly pension benefit after 20 years of service. Vesting exists in some pension plans. It gives terminating employees the right to a certain percentage of their earned benefits depending on their age and/or length of service. Thus, they do not lose what has been contributed toward their pension plan providing they stay with a company a specified minimum time, such as 10 years.

### Questionable practices

A practice has developed in unloading at some food chain warehouses that has added to the problems of cost and delivery of goods to these warehouses or distribution centers. At times, drivers have been coerced into employing casual laborers, often referred to as "swampers," "lumpers," or "gypsies." These people unload the trailer and the driver is not allowed to assist. Of course, such work is at a cash fee, and the fee varies widely. Some carriers have proposed that tariffs be published that relieve them of the responsibility for unloading.

## Nonunion employees

More attention should be given by management to an upward revision of the pay scale for nonunion employees. As was pointed out earlier, the average wages for intercity drivers are higher than for most supervisory personnel. In some instances, drivers are making more than middle management. Management which allows inequities of this type to occur is neglecting its obligation to nonunion employees and will have increasing personnel problems unless adjustments are made.

A study of salaried employees that covered 68 job classifications in the trucking industry, based on a sample of Class I motor carriers of general freight, provided insight into the level of compensation for these employees. The base salary and bonus, if any, are supplied in the study. It enables a carrier to compare company salaries with those that are contained in the sample.[5] For example, 50 percent of the terminal managers in the sample received bonuses, whereas 62 percent of the vice presidents of traffic received a bonus; but just 22 percent of fleet maintenance directors received one.

The compensation for terminal managers is related to the volume in terms of tonnage handled through the terminal as well as by the number of terminal employees.[6]

For nonunion employees, there should be a wage review conducted annually. This is done by department, division, or section heads, or a review board may be created which will conduct the interview with each nonunion employee. The employee's work should be reviewed and evaluated. Constructive criticisms and suggestions should be made. Where good work has been performed, the employee should be commended for it. As a result of this wage review, the employee should be informed of any action taken to adjust his salary. In the event that no salary adjustment is made, he should be told the reasons for the lack of action.

The health and welfare benefits for salaried employees are also important in terms of total compensation. A survey to ascertain the level of such benefits for nonunion carrier employees indicated that some form of sickness and accident coverage was provided by all of the responding carriers; hospital and medical coverage was provided by all, including dependent coverage to age 19 for children. Most of the responding firms provided noncontributory life insurance coverage, the amount based generally on the employee's salary level. Accidental death coverage was also provided by all but two of the responding carriers. These fringe benefits have become of substantial importance to employees, and the plans must be periodically reviewed to insure their effectiveness and adequacy.

A voluntary wage and price standard established in 1978 by the President's Council on Wage and Price Stability to combat inflation was set at 7 percent although there were provisions for exceptions. Federal monitoring of the wage aspects focused on management and nonunion employee groups as union employees were covered by collective bargaining contract charges.

### QUESTIONS AND PROBLEMS

1. With whom has the Teamsters entered into mutual aid and assistance pacts? How could you find out how effective the pacts have been?

2. What has been the Teamsters' attitude on employee productivity? How does it compare with that of other labor organizations in the transportation field?

3. What are "free riders?" What practical solution can you suggest to eliminate them?

4. What are "hot cargo" clauses? Trace their legality and indicate their effectiveness.

5. Trace the growth of fringe benefits indicating the present importance of these benefits in total motor carrier labor cost.

6. What constructive suggestions do you have to improve management's bargaining ability?

7. What are the advantages and disadvantages of nation-wide bargaining in the motor carrier field for employees? Employers? The public?

8. If a union embracing all transportation workers existed, do you feel their members would benefit more than in the existing situation? Why or why not?

9. As a union negotiator, indicate the importance of "real" wages vs. actual wages. Have you suggestions for reconciling these wages at the bargaining table?

10. Do you feel that the independent truckers will become a part of the Teamsters within five years? Why or why not?

# FOOTNOTES TO CHAPTER 10

[1] The ATA Industrial Relations Department holds an annual forum on some aspect of industrial relations. The papers and discussions of these meetings are published and are an excellent source of labor-management developments in this field.

[2] The National Labor Relations Board has asserted jurisdiction over all interstate freight transportation (excepting railroads and airlines) and that transportation which serves as essential links for interstate transportation if they derive at least $50,000 gross revenue from such operations.

[3] The Interstate Commerce Commission has granted certificates to nonunion motor carriers to operate in an area sufficient to provide service denied them by other unionized motor carriers who refused to interline shipments with them under the "hot cargo" clause (MC-116067, *Nebraska Short Line Carriers, Inc., Common Carrier Application*, June 1, 1959).

[4] *Galveston Truck Lines Corp.* v. *Ada Motor Lines*, 73 MCC 617 (1958).

[5] Industrial Relations Department, American Trucking Associations, Inc., *ATA Trucking Salaried Employees Compensation Study*, 1973.

[6] *Ibid.*

# chapter 11

# Terminal operations

Adequate terminal facilities have been and continue to be a problem of motor carriers generally. If all shipments made by shippers were of truckload lots, the matter of terminal facilities would not be so great, since an over-the-road truck would be dispatched to the shipper's place of business and loaded at that point for over-the-road shipment. Shipments of over 19,000 pounds rarely need platform handling. However, intercity common carriers of general commodities find that the bulk of their traffic is composed of small shipments of less-than-truckload quantities which must be consolidated with other small shipments going to the same destination or along the same route. Central terminals are established by over-the-road operators where these small shipments can be delivered by local trucks and then transferred to the over-the-road vehicle.

The necessity for recognized locations where small lots of freight could be received and handled led motor carriers to lease or purchase whatever room was available. In the early days of the motor carrier industry, they frequently used vacant lots or small garages. As the extent of their operations increased, they obtained the use of warehouses or other buildings suitable for this purpose. Even today, it can be said that as a rule truck terminals are remodeled structures originally constructed for some other purpose, although there is a trend now toward construction of new terminals built to meet the motor carrier's own needs and specifications. There is little doubt that this trend will continue.

Although development of terminal facilities has been somewhat slow in comparison with other phases of the development of the motor carrier industry, substantial progress has been noted in more recent years. Just as the motor truck has been developed along specialized lines to meet differing transportation requirements, truck terminals now are being built to meet the special handling requirements of the motor carrier or carriers for which they are designed. The terminal expense per ton of intercity freight for the Class I common carriers of general freight has risen from $2.03 per ton in 1950 to $8.53 in 1973.

and to $13.37 in 1979. However, there are wide variations among the regions. The upward trend in terminal expenses is a matter of concern to motor carrier operators.

The center of truck operations is the terminal. For many motor carriers, the terminals constitute their general offices, and all activities are concentrated there. For larger motor carriers, the terminals represent branch offices and have accounting, collecting, dispatching, sales, and all other phases of branch operation. Basically, the terminal serves as a consolidation and distribution point for LTL traffic. Large carriers may have as many as 300 terminals.

As metropolitan areas have grown and economic activity in the suburban areas has increased, some of the larger carriers have established several terminals, that are often termed satellite terminals, instead of a single terminal to serve an area. Management of motor carriers does not agree on the optimum size or number of terminals to serve these areas. Some feel a single terminal is the best solution. Others feel that a number of satellite terminals serving smaller areas is more manageable and hence have opted for this approach. However, the larger carriers have often also established breakbulk terminals, geographically located at a focal point, for feeding terminal traffic into the motor carrier system. This is an effort to secure economies in equipment utilization and labor. For example, a transcontinental carrier rather than dispatching a partially filled trailer from the east coast to a Chicago destination establishes a breakbulk terminal point, such as Harrisburg, Pennsylvania, into which all the less-truckload lot Chicago-bound traffic originating in terminals in New Jersey, Delaware, and Maryland can be funneled. The incoming loads are stripped and then reloaded to maximum capacity for Chicago and other destinations. The breakbulk terminal does nothing but strip and reload for particular destinations. One transcontinental carrier with 393 terminals has 24 breakbulk terminals.

### Terminal location in the urban area

The location of a terminal within an urban area must be selected with a number of factors in mind. These include the present and future needs of the terminal; cost of land acquisition; zoning restrictions; service to customers; accessibility to main highways; availability of power, water, and sewage; traffic congestion; and transportation for employees.

In some cities, there is a tendency for new terminals to be constructed adjacent to a main highway away from the city's business district, such as a beltway. In other cities, they are located within the industrial district but are grouped within a relatively small area. At the present time, there is no uniform pattern of terminal location.

From the studies that have been made to date, the distance from the heart of the city does not appear to matter, except in Chicago and New York; while the terminal may be a greater distance from some customers, it will be closer to others. In choosing a location in cities like New York and Chicago, the costs of different sites can be ascertained by laying a grid of coordinates over the city to measure the pickup and delivery routes from the present and proposed locations. "Stem time" is the amount of time from the terminal to the point of first pickup or delivery and from the point of last pickup or delivery to the terminal. This is unproductive time, and the location of the terminal in relation to customers has an important influence on the amount of stem time that a carrier has in its urban operation. The over-the-road costs, if the road units come all the way into the city, also have to be computed on the basis of the proposed locations. The areas from which business is received must also be carefully ascertained in order to evaluate terminal location properly.

Where the scheduled pickup and delivery trucks cannot handle a shipment or shipments, separate trucks are dispatched on what are called "shag runs" to handle it.

### Types of terminals based on ownership

The predominant type of terminal in use is the carrier-owned individual terminal. There are, however, other types of terminal operations based on ownership. Among these are the following: (a) the renting of space by a motor carrier to other motor carriers; (b) a cooperative association of motor carriers, with each paying a share of operating expenses; (c) a privately owned terminal company which operates on the basis of leases with carrier tenants; and (d) a terminal operated on a fee basis for each arrival and departure of an over-the-road unit, with a handling charge based on tonnage handled.

The foregoing types of terminal operations are self-explanatory. With one exception, they are slightly different phases of the same operation—joint use of terminals by motor carriers. Some of these terminal operations are referred to as "union truck terminals." The joint use of terminals by motor carriers is looked upon in metropolitan areas as a partial solution to the terminal problem. In a current motor carrier directory, there are listed 60 common and joint terminals, including union truck terminals. These vary in size from a terminal that serves only four carriers to a terminal that serves 56 carriers, including local carriers.

### Types of terminal design

A motor carrier does not have terminals at all points which it serves, but it does have terminals in the larger metropolitan areas. The desire of motor carriers to retain their identity and shipper relationships has, in general, caused them to establish their own terminals rather than make arrangements for joint use of terminals. In the construction of new terminals, a much used design has been that of the so-called island-type enclosed dock. The offices and dock form a T shape, with the offices forming the cross of the T. This type of terminal and dock operation is characterized by a cross-dock operation—that is, on one side of the dock, the over-the-road units are loaded and unloaded; on the other side of the dock are the pickup and delivery units. Incoming freight from over-the-road units is moved across the dock to the pickup and delivery units. Conversely, the outgoing freight is unloaded from the pickup and delivery trucks and moved across the dock to the over-the-road units.

Although the T design is the most popular, other designs include the I- and L-shaped structures in which the terminal headquarters are placed at one end of the dock. Most of the buildings are single-story rather than multistory buildings. The island-type design with cross-dock movement of freight has developed in part because of the need for different height loading platforms for the over-the-road equipment and the pickup and delivery trucks.

Another design is that of a modified X. The headquarters are located in the center, and the docks are diagonally situated in the fingers that extend outward from the center.

The distance from pavement to the floor level of the over-the-road semitrailer averages 51 inches but varies within a six-inch range, depending upon model, tire size, and load. Because of the spring deflection, a trailer when loaded may be three inches lower than when empty. Some of the newer semitrailers are equipped with air suspension springs that provide a constant loading height, since air can be added or taken from the air springs in order to maintain correct height. Despite this development, however, terminal docks must be designed to accommodate leaf-spring suspensions, since the majority of units are so equipped. The floor height of van-type city delivery trucks runs from six to eight inches lower than the typical over-the-road semitrailers. For this reason, it has not been possible to establish a height which works equally well for a pickup and delivery truck and an over-the-road unit.

When dock and trailer-bed levels are not equal, the dock level is usually designed to be lower than the trailer bed, since this will permit opening and closing trailer doors while in a loading position.

In the construction of terminals as well as in their operation, the dock height is important because savings in freight-handling costs and reduction of damage claims can be secured when the dock is suited to vehicle height or the vehicle body-bed height is suited to the dock.

A number of different types of ramps are in common use. One is the ramp from the vehicle body to the shipping platform, which is usually made of sheet metal alloy and is manually placed. Leveling may be accomplished, also, by mechanical means. One of these mechanical methods is the adjustment of the truck or semitrailer to a line with the platform by means of a lifting platform in front of the dock. Another mechanical method, which is more widely used, is the adjustment of the platform to a line with the truck or semitrailer bed through a power-operated ramp built into the platform. Experience has shown

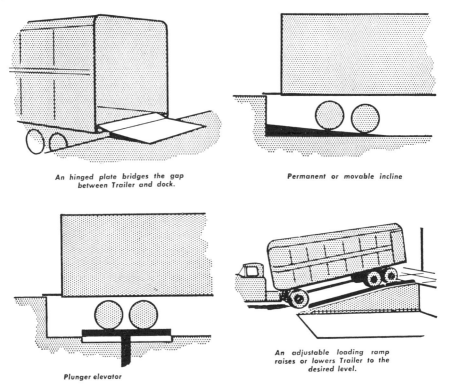

An hinged plate bridges the gap between Trailer and dock.

Permanent or movable incline

Plunger elevator

An adjustable loading ramp raises or lowers Trailer to the desired level.

Fig. 11-1. A number of permanent or movable inclines for dock use.

that the volume which can be handled through the use of three mechanically operated ramp-equipped berths is equal to the volume handled through the use of five ramp-equipped platform berths, manually operated. A permanent or movable incline can be placed at the dock to raise the semitrailer level. Figure 11-1 illustrates the use of these various methods.

Whether the ramp is manual or mechanical, the slope should not exceed ten percent in order to facilitate loading and unloading.

Many dock offices are located at the center of the dock which serves as a consolidating point for the collection and distribution of bills of lading, freight bills, and other paper work required for dock operation. The location of dock offices at this point, which is often referred to as a "doghouse," has not been entirely satisfactory. In some of the newer terminals, the dock office is centered on one side of the dock, with a portion of it elevated from one to two feet above the dock floor. This part of the office is constructed of sliding glass windows which afford a complete view of the dock platform. The dock foreman, city dispatcher, and the line haul dispatcher are located at this point, with loudspeakers and an intercommunication system for their use. The rating and billing department and OS&D personnel can be located adjacent to them.

Some carriers have separate facilities for inbound and outbound operations called split-dock construction. The carriers with facilities of this kind are those having a very large portion of their freight in less-truckload lots. The inbound terminal is a wider dock with truck bays extending along only one side and having a considerable amount of storage space. The outbound terminal is a cross-dock operation in which local trucks are emptied and freight loaded across the dock into over-the-road trailers. Between the two terminals is a yard space where trailers are "spotted" and local trucks are parked. The users of this system feel that it eliminates much confusion.

Generally, the length of a terminal dock is based on the number of units which must be spotted simultaneously at the dock.[1] To secure this figure, the morning, or inbound delivery phase, and the afternoon, or outbound phase, must be analyzed. The morning phase is found by combining the number of road units to be stripped or unloaded at one time and the number of city units to be loaded at one time. The formula is reversed for the afternoon phase, combining the number of city units to be stripped at one time with the number of road units to be loaded at one time. Four factors will give the basic information. These are: When shall stripping (or loading) begin? When shall stripping (loading) be finished? How many loads will there be to strip (or load)? How long will it take to strip (or load) a unit?

If, for the morning phase, it is found that ten spots are needed for simultaneous stripping of road units and 13 spots for city unit loading, a total of 23 berths are needed. Assuming that the afternoon phase demands ten spots for stripping city units and 20 for loading road units, a total of 30 spots are required.

By comparing the morning figure (23) with the afternoon figure

(30), the afternoon or outbound phase must govern the dock length. Therefore, the dock must be built to accommodate at least 30 units. Since most units are parked in pairs, with double doors, the dock will be designed to accommodate 32 units, 16 on each side. Allowing 12 feet for each unit, the dock length becomes a minimum of 192 feet.

The maximum width prescribed by most states for trucks or semi-trailers is eight feet. As a result, terminals are usually constructed with doors, stalls, or other positions at least 12 feet in width. Narrower position widths can be used when necessary but this increases the possibility of damage to the equipment, as well as the loss of time getting in and out of the more restricted positions. Another factor to be considered is that as the position width increases, the amount of yard space required for maneuvering decreases.

**Yard space**

The use of the island-type dock permits a flow of vehicles around the dock, and it is generally felt that this flow should be counterclockwise around the dock. This permits backing of units from the left side, which is preferred. It is necessary that there be adequate clearance between the dock and the wall or fence enclosing the yard in order to permit the shifting and backing of vehicles. Yard width should be at least twice the overall length of the vehicle or combination that is going to be backed into the dock platform. The ideal yard width for truck-tractor-semitrailer combinations is 100 feet, whereas a van-type city delivery truck requires approximately half this width. This ideal yard width makes for expeditious movement of truck units into and out of truck berths, although many truck terminals have from 25 to 35 feet less space than this ideal figure of 100 feet.

**Freight terminal handling methods**

The methods by which freight is handled at the terminal may be divided into two categories—manual and mechanized. The manual method, as far as equipment cost is concerned, is very inexpensive.

In the majority of the terminals, dock operations are *manual* and involve the use of equipment such as two-wheel hand trucks. A four-wheel platform truck which provides a level platform on which to stack shipments is being widely used. This basic type of industrial truck has the advantage of keeping the freight on a flat truck and not placing it on the floor. Its use also cuts down the number of operations involved in loading and unloading. However, some heavy commodities, such as filled barrels or drums, are not as easily loaded on the four-wheel hand truck as they are on the two-wheel hand truck.

Both of these hand trucks are usually rolled into the truck or trailer body for loading and unloading. Generally, only one shipment is placed on a four-wheel hand truck, although this is not as closely followed in manual operations as is true when four-wheel carts are used in mechanized operations. Widespread use is also made of portable section roller conveyors. Packages can be placed on the conveyor and then moved by giving a push, or if the conveyor is tilted sufficiently, it will operate on a gravity basis. These are also used in unloading at a shipper's dock.

When an island-type dock exceeds ten truck berths in length, it is considered to be sufficiently large for the economies of operating *mechanized material-handling equipment,* such as forklift trucks and draglines. Where there is mechanized dock operation, it is desirable for the dock to be somewhat wider than where manual equipment is used. Whereas 50 feet in width is satisfactory for manual dock equipment, the width of the dock for mechanical equipment usage should be approximately 65 feet, and the free aisle should be correspondingly wider than for manual equipment.

During World War II, forklift trucks and pallets began to appear in motor carrier terminals. Since that time, forklift systems have been used in the larger terminals of many motor carriers. The original forklift trucks in use were of the stand-up type and were gasoline propelled. There has been greater interest and use of the electric forklifts in recent years, although the initial cost, with spare batteries and chargers, is about twice that of a gasoline-engine forklift truck. There are many factors which should be considered, such as noise, operating cost, and salvage value. Since the forklift truck on the motor carrier dock is subjected to frequent stops, starts, and short runs, maintenance is also an important factor. Many other industries use the sit-down-type forklift truck, but since the driver in a motor carrier terminal may get on and off the forklift on almost every load, the stand-up type is still favored in motor carrier terminals.

Forklift trucks may operate directly into the body of the truck or semitrailer, or they may stop at the edge of the dock. Whether it operates into the truck or semitrailer body in both the city trucks and the line haul semitrailers is largely based on the strength of the floors of the vehicles. To add a heavy floor to carry the load of a forklift truck will add from 500 to 700 pounds to the tare weight of the vehicle, which reduces its payload.

When forklifts are not permitted in the bodies of vehicles, a pallet roller is placed inside. A pallet roller is a steel frame with wide rollers on which a pallet can be placed for rolling backward or forward in a straight line in the vehicle body. Thus, shipments can be rolled on or off the pallet roller in loading or unloading, and a forklift truck does not enter the body of the vehicle.

Usually only one shipment is placed on a pallet. A 40- by 48-inch pallet may handle as much as 3,000 pounds. However, if the shipments are very small with two shipments to the same destination terminal, some companies will carry two shipments on one pallet. The reason for handling a single shipment on a pallet is to avoid mixing shipments, which is an important factor in checking freight. Inasmuch as pallets usually are not loaded to maximum capacity under the single-shipment rule, it is common practice to tier partially loaded pallets if it is necessary to haul shipments on the dock for a time during the movement across the platform. They can also be tiered by using pallet racks in the terminal, thus permitting the temporary storage of goods in tiers without damage to the goods.

Some shippers have palletized and unitized their shipments and handled them with forklift trucks. Motor carriers with forklift trucks are therefore in a position to facilitate the terminal handling of such shipments.

Some of the points which will influence whether or not the terminal handling system should be a forklift truck and pallet operation are: (a) terminal volume, which should be less than 300,000 pounds per day; (b) distance of average one-way forklift travel, which should be less than 150 feet; and (c) volume which is distributed over the working day in such a way that only two forklift trucks are required normally, and not over three at peak volume.

The productivity of freight handlers in a well-managed truck terminal using such mechanized equipment runs more than 2,000 pounds per man-hour.

The *dragline* is a type of mechanized equipment. It is a conveyor with a powered chain or cable which runs overhead or in the floor and pulls carts from one area on the dock to another. The greatest advantage obtained from a dragline is when it is used for transfer of freight directly from the pickup to the outbound line-haul unit.

In the overhead-type dragline, the chain or cable is attached to rollers which ride in the open sides of a steel channel hung from a supporting structure. The cart has a mast or chain for engaging fixtures attached to the cable.

In the floor-type dragline, the chain is in a trench about 12 inches wide by 12 inches deep. The trench is covered except for a slot a little more than one inch wide through which a pin from the cart drops to engage the line. Generally the drag chain is located in the middle section of the dock in a long loop which extends from one end of the dock platform to the other, with turnarounds at the extreme ends of the loop so that the chain goes continuously in one track past the various doors opening on the vehicle-loading berths (Fig. 11-2).

Fig. 11-2. This terminal uses the floor-type conveyor system or carrousel. The four-wheel trucks are attached to the drag chain and are moved to proper locations for loading and unloading. Courtesy: American Trucking Association.

Most dragline conveyors have been put on docks which are more than 60 feet in width and over 450 feet in length. However, there have been draglines installed on old motor freight docks which are neither that long nor that wide. In St. Louis, for example, there is a dragline on a dock which is only 115 feet in length. Some of the older terminals have installed overhead draglines, whereas the trend in the newer terminals is toward the floor type. The latter has several advantages over the overhead type, although it is more costly to install.

A number of factors that are considered necessary to justify the installation of a dragline are: (a) a dock volume exceeding 300,000 pounds per day; (b) an average one-way travel of handling equipment of more than 150 feet; (c) the need for more than two forklift trucks to handle normal volume or more than three during peak periods; (d) a wide variation in volume of freight flow from hour to hour; (e) freight handlers and supervisors who are not too experienced; (f) little hauling of peddle freight; and (g) a large percentage of freight which is fragile or easily damaged.

Under the dragline system, only one shipment is placed on the four-wheel cart, or two small shipments if they are for the same destination terminal. When the four-wheel cart is loaded with a shipment, it is pushed out of the vehicle body manually and connected to the dragline. It is given a code number and stays on the dragline until it is removed by the loader at the loading berth or storage spot to which the truck has been coded.

An innovation in terminals is one in which there are two independent but integrated draglines for moving freight within the terminal. An outer dragline conveys shipments from the receiving dock to the control center through which all freight passes. The inner, or shunt line, carries a switch cart directly to any of the doors in the terminal for loading or unloading, upon instructions from the control center.

Motor carriers should certainly investigate the possibilities of material-handling equipment because under the right combination of circumstances, substantial economies can be effected through its use.[2] The type of material-handling equipment to be used at motor freight terminals should be chosen only after a careful analysis. Although there are a number of guides, of which some have been given, there are many factors in individual terminal operations which must be considered. For example, a motor carrier whose volume and operations appear to lend themselves to a forklift-pallet-type terminal operation has found that the nature of the LTL freight which it handles precludes the use of forklift trucks.

### Methods of freight checking

There are a variety of checking procedures that are used with different freight-handling systems in truck terminals. This is an important aspect of the control of freight, but there is wide disagreement as to the effectiveness of the different checking systems or the extent to which freight should be checked. On the carrier's docks, there are four different places at which freight may be checked. These are: (a) when the shipment comes off the city pickup truck and is put onto the dock; (b) when the shipment is moved on the dock to the outgoing line-haul vehicle; (c) at the destination city when the freight is checked as it comes off the line-haul vehicle; and (d) when the freight is being loaded onto the city delivery truck at destination.

In the past much of the checking at carriers' terminals was accomplished by assigning one checker to each one or two incoming vehicles. Usually he was given a stand-up desk with pigeonholes or clips for holding papers, which would be located on the dock near the vehicles to be checked by him. The bills of lading would be secured by him from the city pickup driver or the freight bills from the line-haul vehicle which was to be unloaded. The checker would then check the items as they were unloaded and would indicate to the dock workers where to transfer or place the freight. On unmechanized docks, this manual checking of freight is still quite general.

There are a number of variations of manual checking systems. In some instances, when the contents are being unloaded by a stripper (person unloading), he will call out to the checker the items which the checker checks against the bill of lading or the freight bill. In other instances, the stripper may also be the checker. Where the freight handling has been mechanized by the use of forklift trucks and pallets, a manual checking system is frequently used, although the tendency is to establish a centralized checking system when forklift mechanization is used.

One of the most widely used types of centralized checking systems is one which is handled by means of two-way telephone communication equipment. Under this arrangement, the checker is usually located near the center of the freight-handling area and is often housed in a glass-enclosed booth which is elevated so that the checker has a clear view of all dock activities. The booth is usually arranged so that the checker has desk space on three sides with adequate room to spread the bills covering several trucks. The checker has a multistation two-way telephone device in the booth, the central unit of which is connected to two-way transmitter speakers hung in each truck or trailer. The stripper can carry a portable microphone station throughout his work area equipped with a call in switch or button so that he can signal the checker at any time.

With the dragline conveyor, a somewhat different system from centralized checking is used. A pneumatic tube device carries bills from the dock foreman's office to loading berths. The city delivery truck is located at the receiving side of the platform. The checker, who is located on the dock, has a chart of the loading berths of the trailers assigned to specific destinations. An empty four-wheel truck is pushed to the end of the city delivery truck, and the driver, dock unloader, or stripper will sort and place on the dragline cart one shipment. The checker compares the number of pieces in the shipment as well as the destination shipping tag on the shipment with the bill of lading which has been given him by the driver. If all of these things check, he will mark on the dragline cart placard board the berth number at which the shipment is to be removed from the dragline. On the bill of lading, the identification of the truck and driver which made the delivery are noted after which the bill of lading is rolled into a tight roll and placed in a holder at the side of the dragline cart placard board. That cart is then hooked onto the dragline and travels to the dock space indicated. When it is not possible to place an entire single shipment on a dragline cart, the checker loads the first dragline cart and marks on the placard "1 of 4, MTF" (more to follow). Additional carts needed are similarly marked with the last cart bearing the notation "4 of 4, complete." The bill of lading is then placed in the holder with the final cart. If the shipment on the dragline cart can be loaded directly into the line haul vehicle, it is pulled to the outside of the dragline chain and loaded.

Shipments on carts that the loader is not ready for may be left connected to the dragline so that the cart goes around several times until the loader is ready to load it into the trailer; or it may be removed from the dragline and put in the center area within the dragline carrousel until wanted.

### Receiving shipments

A number of different matters must be covered in some way in order to indicate the conditions under which certain commodities may be accepted because of the destination points or for other reasons. One of these is the matter of points served. Most companies publish a routing guide which will indicate the points served. However, where the shipment has a destination not contained in the routing guide, the operations department will determine whether or not it can be accepted. When the shipments are given to the motor carrier for transportation, they should be accompanied by bills of lading or connecting carrier's freight bills. Most shippers will make out their own bill of lading, but if they have not, the motor carrier representative accepting the shipment will issue a bill of lading.

Shipments of unusual size or weight may require special equipment.

The classification and/or tariff rules of motor carriers will indicate the dimensions of a shipment which are acceptable. Frequently shippers will have a quantity to be shipped which constitutes a full load and will want it to be moved immediately. Such shipments usually are accepted when the equipment is available for its immediate movement.

Certain points served by motor carriers are designated as prepay points. Such points are usually those at which there are no terminals of the motor carrier. Therefore, shipments are not accepted to that point unless they are prepaid. The charges are generally collected from the shipper at the time the shipment is picked up. However, if the shipment is of such a nature that the proper description or weight cannot be ascertained, it will be brought to the terminal for weighing, rating, and billing, and held until the shipper pays the charges. Additional requirements of shipments destined to prepay points are that the carrier will not collect on c.o.d. shipments; the shipment will not be shipped on an order bill of lading; the shipment will not require refrigeration or protection from cold; and the bill of lading must show where the shipment is to be unloaded.

When perishable items are accepted, such as frozen meat or citrus juices, the shipper should indicate on the bill of lading the temperature at which the shipment must be maintained. This information is then copied on the freight bills. Fresh meat and poultry accepted for interstate movement must conform to existing government regulations and must be accompanied by a government meat inspector's certificate unless the shipment is marked with the government meat inspector's stamp. Some states have quarantine restrictions on nursery stock and fruit and vegetables, and they cannot be accepted unless accompanied by a transportation permit from the horticultural inspector.

In-bond shipments also are treated somewhat differently from the ordinary shipment. Ordinarily, in-bond shipments originate at a point of entry into the United States. They are shipments on which U.S. customs duty has not been paid. They are usually tendered to the motor carrier by a customs broker and released by a U.S. customs inspector who furnishes the carrier with a form which it must sign called "Transportation Entry and Manifest of Goods Subject to Customs Inspection and Permit." The carrier's copy of this document is attached to the freight bill or truck manifest and must accompany the shipment. The originating carrier signs in the usual manner a bill of lading or a document serving this purpose. If a full truckload of in-bond shipments is tendered, they can be loaded in one piece of equipment and sealed. Otherwise the shipments have to be individually labeled or tagged.

## Weighing and marking

The carrier need not weigh all freight that is received at the terminal, but spot checks should be made frequently to determine whether the weights on the bills of lading are correct. If the weight is incorrect, the shipper should be notified of the change in weight. Most companies have a form which is filled out termed a "correct weight advice." If there is an increase in the revenue as a result of the discrepancy in the weight, companies often will pay an employee an amount for discovering the discrepancy, such as ten cents for each 100 pounds up to the first 500 pounds of difference and five cents for each additional 100 pounds.

Before shipments are accepted from a shipper or a connecting carrier, all pieces of each LTL shipment should be tagged or marked showing the consignee's name and destination. It is the shipper's responsibility to mark and tag each piece of freight, but if he fails to do this the carrier's representative receiving the freight must mark or tag it.

## Stowing freight

Most carriers find that it is impossible to specify other than general rules for loading, since each commodity has some characteristic that should be considered when it is loaded. Two of the obvious rules are to see that light freight is stowed where it will not be crushed by heavy freight; and precautionary marks indicating how the freight should be loaded should be observed. For particular commodities, rules must be formulated to insure that the freight is properly stowed. Unpackaged items, such as pipe, cans, freight in bundles, batteries, and motors, present special problems. Rugs and other freight, which when packed or wrapped are long, bulky, and hard to load, also cause difficulty in loading. Baled or burlapped goods must not be stowed in contact with barrels of oil, greases, or other liquid-carrying containers and must be protected from chafing by wooden boxes and crates. Sacked goods, such as beans and flour, should be loaded in dry, clean places on the floor, using paper on the floor to keep the sacks clean. They should be loaded away from any items which have projections likely to injure the sacks.

If there are "drop" shipments to be made, that freight must be placed to facilitate its unloading. If a semitrailer has been loaded and there is visible space left, the load must be tapered off gradually in order to avoid tipping and smashing of the contents. If the over-the-road unit goes all the way through to another terminal, it will be sealed at the origin terminal.

### Dispatching

The operation of the dock in larger motor carrier organizations is the responsibility of a terminal manager. In smaller motor carrier organizations, however, the dispatcher is in charge of the dock activities. The dispatcher is a key man in the successful functioning of dock operations. Most dispatchers were at one time truck drivers themselves, so they have an understanding of the problems of operation. It is their responsibility to dispatch the freight properly, so that the units are kept rolling. They make certain that the over-the-road units are properly prepared and swept out before reloading for over-the-road operation. They insure that the freight is checked against the freight bill, piece by piece, before it is loaded. Some dispatchers have separate checkers and loaders, and the checkers' duties are only those of checking the freight against the freight bills. Freight checking is a very important factor because there may be 75 to 100 or more shipments in a single load coming out of a terminal.

Incoming freight must be carefully checked, sorted, and routed for proper distribution. It is the responsibility of the dispatcher to see that there is prompt sorting and routing, and that the activities of the pick-up and delivery units are correlated to bringing in shipments for loading and to delivering shipments to local consignees.

Some carriers use centralized dispatching under which a headquarters operations department authorizes each over-the-road trip. It assigns personnel and equipment to each trip and specifies departure times, routes of travel, intermediate pickups and drops, as well as connecting service at junction points and destination terminals. Central dispatching is responsible for the scheduled arrival of every load once the load is ready for the road. It is also responsible for having necessary action taken when breakdowns or accidents occur during road trips. Some carriers use computers in these dispatching operations.

Carriers using centralized dispatching feel that it provides flexibility in moving equipment into the areas where it is most needed. It is also felt that close coordination can be maintained with the carrier sales department in the following of important and rush loads and in providing the service that the sales department has promised.

Most companies operate under decentralized dispatching of over-the-road operations. The terminal manager is given the authority to dispatch the over-the-road equipment in order to meet commitments to shippers. Because of this responsibility, the company feels that the terminal manager will use ingenuity in loading and planning the dispatching of equipment into and out of his terminal. It is customary under decentralized dispatching to have coordination between the terminals and headquarters by means of teletype or telephone as required, in some instances daily.

Since most motor carriers do not have definite, scheduled hours of departure for over-the-road units, the dispatcher must have knowledge of the shipments that are being brought in by pickup and delivery trucks as well as the shipments that are already at the terminal, so that he will know about when to close out a unit and have a driver available. It is not always possible to secure a full load, so that a dispatcher has the responsibility of deciding when a unit should be dispatched. In motor carrier operations, a shipment cannot be held at the dock beyond a reasonable time or the inherent advantage of short transit time in motor carrier shipment is negated.

Dispatches are made so that deliveries will occur on certain time schedules, such as first morning, second morning, third morning, this being the manner in which the salesman has sold the service. Therefore, the dispatcher has to dispatch the units in order to meet the service requirements.

The dispatcher sends out the various pickup and delivery units each day to the points that fall into particular zones within the city which he has established. Drivers of these units then call in after picking up the shipments and receive additional instructions as to where the next pickup should be made in a particular zone or a neighboring zone. It depends upon the amount of freight handled by a motor carrier whether there are separate trucks dispatched to pick up shipments from those dispatched to deliver shipments.

In dispatching loaded less-truckload freight on city delivery equipment, the most widely used method is that of *route loading* or loading in proper sequence, that is, first on, last off. In this system, the city is divided into areas the number of which will depend on the volume of freight to be delivered. These areas are numbered or lettered, and a space is provided on the dock to correspond to each area. Upon the arrival of the inbound line-haul units, the bills are coded by the area to which they are bound.

The advantages of route loading are: (*a*) it is easier on the driver; (*b*) loading in sequence is less time consuming which, at present wage scales, is an important factor; (*c*) there is a saving in fuel cost and wear on the equipment because travel distance, time, and traffic are kept at a minimum; and (*d*) the reduction in the number of times the freight is handled in the delivery vehicle reduces claims.

There are disadvantages of this system, however. It takes longer to load in proper sequence, since most of the freight has to be floored and reloaded, which requires more space. More time is taken in the unloading-loading process, and individual shipments may not be delivered as early. The rehandling of the freight, since it is floored and then reloaded, can result in more claims in the terminal, although this is dependent in part upon the freight-handling system which is used.

The second method is called *loading by zone*. Under this arrangement, a city is divided into zones. The freight bills which accompany each over-the-road unit to the city are coded by zone according to the street locations of the consignees. The bills are handled by the stripper or checker, who sends these inbound shipments to the waiting delivery unit for the proper zone. Since a delivery unit is available for each zone, it is not necessary to floor any of the freight for any zone unless it cannot be loaded immediately without damage to itself or other freight.

Some of the advantages of the zone loading are: (*a*) a greater freight volume can be handled over less floor space in the terminal; (*b*) the total time which is required for unloading line-haul vehicles and loading city delivery vehicles is substantially reduced; (*c*) the incoming LTL shipments do not have to be routed, floored, and rehandled in sequence but the freight goes directly to the vehicle which is being loaded for the zone to which it is destined; and (*d*) delivery vehicles can be out delivering earlier which enables line-haul units to be scheduled for later arrivals and still be quickly handled.

On the other hand, it takes longer to make deliveries under the zone system because it is necessary for the driver to dig through the shipments and sort as he delivers, along with the rehandling and backtracking. There is, also, potential damage to freight due to its numerous handlings in the delivery vehicle.

A combination of sequence and zone is sometimes used. The first two thirds of the delivery truck is loaded without regard to sequence as it is under the zone system. Two or three stops on the rear of the truck are then arranged in sequence under route loading. As soon as the driver gets his first three stops off, he has room to segregate his freight and arrange his stops. Under this system, paper work can be minimized and congestion on the dock relieved.

The dispatcher will also dispatch "peddle trips," which are operated primarily for the purpose of pickup or delivery of freight at the shipper's or consignee's platform at intermediate station points outside a city, town, or commercial zone. Peddle trips usually operate within a radius of from 50 to 75 miles of the terminal and are generally loop runs originated and terminated at one terminal. The principal purpose of peddle runs is to gather and distribute freight en route at the platforms of consignors and consignees, rather than to move it from one terminal to another terminal.

There are some motor carriers which operate certain scheduled hours of departure for over-the-road runs. Others may have only one scheduled departure at a specific time, which is referred to as a "hot-shot" run. A number of carriers which have made use of the "hot-shot run have found that too many shippers desire all their freight to go on that particular run. Hence, many carriers which had instituted this service have discontinued the operation.

A report on the over-the-road schedules which are dispatched is maintained by the dispatcher. Such a report lists the driver, the loading time, departure time, the equipment, the destination, and other relevant information. This information can be placed on a form which consolidates the schedules dispatched from each terminal. This is usually done by teletype, so that it is possible that the headquarters of the company will have complete information about the status of the equipment and freight dispatched.

The terminals of larger carriers are operated seven days a week and provide for 24-hour service. However, these carriers are frequently spoken of as being on an eight-day week. This arises from the fact that the maximum number of hours prescribed by the Department of Transportation for drivers is 60 hours in 168 consecutive hours, or 70 hours on duty in 192 consecutive hours. Many carriers operate under the latter arrangement, which is referred to as an eight-day workweek.

## Pickup and delivery operations

A part of the need for better terminal operation is the problem of improving *pickup and delivery production*. The type of trucks used in pickup and delivery service may be a factor in improving operations. Some motor carriers have used the small city-type semitrailers, that is, 20-foot trailers, in pickup and delivery and peddle-run operations, although heavy reliance is still placed upon trucks. Some companies use two 26-foot trailers in tandem in over-the-road operations and then separate the two units for pickup and delivery in the city. There are also 40-foot tandem-axle trailers, built so they can be split into two 20-foot units, that can then be used for local pickup and delivery work. On some downtown streets of certain cities, semitrailers exceeding a specified length are prohibited for pickup and delivery use. When the vehicles must park at the curb to load and unload across the sidewalk, the truck is preferred equipment. Also, when the shipping or receiving platform can be reached only by backing down the length of a long alley, it is often easier to do this with a truck than a semitrailer. On the other hand, the 26-foot semitrailer is just as easily maneuvered as a straight truck with a 14-foot body. Further, it is possible to get the rear of the semitrailer square against a shipping platform in a loading area which is just slightly wider than the trailer is long.

If two semitrailers are used for each truck-tractor, one semitrailer can be loaded while the other is on the street making deliveries. The same operation exists for pickups, since a loaded semitrailer may be brought back to the terminal for unloading, an empty semitrailer picked up, and the driver start out to make more pickups.

Whether trucks or trailers are best suited for pickup and delivery and peddle operations depends upon individual situations. The important factor is that an analysis should be made to see the type or types which are best suited. At the present time, there is a trend toward placing more city-type semitrailers in the pickup and delivery fleets than has been done in the past.

Where management uses computers, better cost information is available which can be used to pinpoint areas where improvement is possible. One of the areas is that of the impact of congestion on pickup and delivery costs. In New York City, it is estimated that operating costs of motor carriers are 112 percent more than the costs in adjacent areas, with 70 percent of this due to congestion in pickup and delivery.[3] It was found that trucks in these operations work an average of four hours per day standing still in traffic, and the average vehicle speed is four miles per hour.[4]

In some cities, a number of noncompeting carriers have formed a consolidated pickup and delivery service because of higher labor costs and greater traffic congestion on the streets and at shippers' docks. A survey conducted in eight large cities concluded that pickup and delivery drivers spend an average of 9 percent of their time driving to and from their route; 28 percent driving on their route; 20 percent in contact and paper work; 20 percent in actual handling of freight; 15 percent on miscellaneous and personal; and 9 percent in delay time. The elimination of only one item—delay time—was found to increase pickup and delivery productivity by 20 percent. In addition, travel time consisting of 37 percent had the greatest cost-saving potential.

In order to accomplish greater efficiency under the consolidated pickup and delivery plan, the drivers act as agents for the carrier for which the freight is picked up or delivered, and the carrier assumes full responsibility for any loss or damage claims. Joint meetings are held between dispatchers and terminal managers of the carriers, and accounts are exchanged voluntarily by carriers without any charge. The plan appears to work best in congested midtown areas where either problems in alleys or at shippers' docks create substantial delay, or in fringe areas where excess travel time as related to limited tonnage is a factor. Shipments that are consolidated for delivery must be taken to the delivering carrier's terminal by the origin carrier. It has also been found that the terminal locations of the participating carriers should be intermediate or convenient to the location of the driver's home terminal.

There is a distinct cost-saving potential in the consolidated pickup and delivery plan under certain conditions if it is carefully planned and administered. Shippers and receivers benefit also from this consolidation since the number of pickups and deliveries is reduced and dock congestion is lessened.

### Two-way mobile radio

Mobile radio was first introduced in the trucking industry in 1949. Seven frequencies were obtained for truck operations in the Federal Communications Commission's Highway Truck Radio Service. These frequencies were shared with every type of truck operation, including heavy haulers, merchant delivery services, home delivery operations of fuel oil companies, and others. This service was predicated upon the need for the trucking industry to communicate with over-the-road vehicles while en route. Since that time, additional frequencies have been authorized, and use of this type of communications has increased.

Two-way radio can substantially improve productivity. There is a saving in driver time, since the driver does not need to call into the dispatch office at set intervals, such as every 30 minutes. In addition, nonproductive calls by pickup drivers on regularly assigned routes can be eliminated by the use of radio. The dispatcher keeps a record on each driver as he makes each stop, and the amount picked up is recorded at that time. The record is examined with the sales department at the end of a 30-day period, and the stops eliminated where no tonnage has been handled. The experience of carriers using two-way radio indicates that four radio-equipped trucks are equal to five not so equipped. A 20 percent increase in productivity is typical. One company that was using 25 street trucks making pickup and delivery reduced their fleet after the installation of two-way radios to 20 trucks. After the elimination of more than 100 nonproductive calls, the fleet was further reduced to 17 trucks in which more tonnage was handled than had been the case with the original 25.

Two-way radio can also reduce overtime. Its proper use actually enables a carrier to eliminate regular routes and establish assigned areas in which drivers can be moved around. It is also possible to take care of last-minute requests for late afternoon pickups without overtime, whereas under the old system it was often necessary to send a truck back out.

## Terminal controls for management

The terminal manager in many companies is in the same position as an individual conducting his own business. Where this is the case, a condensed picture of the operating results of a terminal for a specified accounting period, such as four weeks, furnishes the terminal manager with a profit and loss summary. This is not a substitute for cost reports but is a method of determining the area of the company operations in which profits are being made or losses incurred. It provides a breakdown of costs and enables him to analyze the various aspects of the operation. The data furnished the terminal manager should include revenue breakdown between outbound and inbound and according to size of shipments. Expense items should be shown, and when one expense item shows an unreasonable increase, it should be cause for special examination.

Other companies do not use the terminal profit and loss statement but establish cost accountability. In controlling terminal costs under these arrangements, such standards of performance as labor costs per ton of freight handled, load average, percent of empty miles, pounds per man hour, bills per man hour, and others are used. With the assignment of cost accountability, an effort is made to instill companywide profit incentive.

In the past, sufficient measures have not been undertaken to determine the profitability and efficiency of individual terminals. Terminal operation is a significant item in carrier's expenses. Since motor carrier operations are often conducted over a broad geographical area, it is important in terminal operation that cost control techniques be used. Such controls, which involve various types of reports, are in and of themselves costly and are impractical unless some action is taken after a review is made of them. These cost controls are of equal importance to the management of the organization at headquarters and the terminal manager of each of the terminals. To company management such reports make possible the efficient management of the organization, while the data which is secured is particularly useful to terminal managers in evaluating the productivity of the terminal. The manner in which cost controls may be applied is to divide the controls into such groupings as platform control, office control, pickup and delivery control, and any additional groupings that are desired for control purposes. Terminal cost controls should develop adequate data on which management can make intelligent decisions.

Platform costs can be compiled in a weekly report showing pounds per man-hour and labor costs per 100 pounds. A monthly report on platform costs would include both of these items plus the overall costs per 100 pounds. Pickup and delivery costs can be developed in a weekly report and a monthly report, with the costs broken down as was the case for platform costs. The terminal office costs can be developed in a weekly report showing labor costs per bill (shipment) and a monthly report which shows the same information plus the over-all cost per bill (shipment).

During the past several years, terminal costs have risen at a more rapid rate than intercity costs. In an effort to control such costs, additional management techniques are being used. The creation of the terminal as a profit center, simulation, and computer controls are some of the methods.

Some carriers have felt that an incentive method can be used to cut terminal costs. One Class I carrier has successfully correlated technical design with human appeal to secure efficiently operated terminals. An incentive plan has been established by this carrier in which terminal profits are adjusted to book profits. Twenty percent of the net profits of a terminal is shared with terminal employees in the following manner: 25 percent to the terminal manager and his assistants; 25 percent to the sales force; and 50 percent to clerical, platform, and pickup and delivery drivers.

Another type of incentive program is based on work standards. Standards of performance are established by time studies or by past experience. An incentive that will reward employees for meeting and exceeding the standards is set—usually in the form of a bonus on a graduated scale. For example, the standard represents 100 percent; if 105 percent of the standard is accomplished, five percent of the earnings may be paid; and a larger amount if 110 percent of the standard is performed, and so on.

Another Class I motor carrier has six freight handling experts called "terminal engineers" who travel among the company's terminals to examine dock procedures, loading practices, and freight-handling tech-niques. They check out loads and city drivers on the correct operation of freight equipment and indoctrinate new employees with the proper method of delivering and picking up shippers' freight. These experts make reports and recommendations to the terminal managers.

### Joint terminals

Motor carriers have shown a reluctance to participate in the union terminal or joint operation. There have been instances where motor carriers have made use of such terminal facilities only until their business has developed to the point where establishment of their own ter-minals has been possible. Rentals are usually on a per-door basis.

City traffic experts favor consolidation of terminals, particularly for less-than-truckload mixed merchandise, because they feel that it relieves traffic congestion. Many motor carriers, on the other hand, although not favoring joint terminal operations, have eased traffic problems by building their new terminals on sites removed from congested areas. As a result, their less-than-truckload shipments of mixed merchandise will be moved throughout the cities in pickup and delivery trucks instead of in over-the-road units.

A study of a consolidated pickup and delivery operation for Colum-bus, Ohio, used a simulation model to replicate the operations of a consolidated terminal. The terminal would handle all deliveries up to 5,000 pounds. It concluded that substantial benefits could be accom-plished through such an operation, both in terms of cost reduction and also in societal benefits through reduction in vehicular traffic in the central business district.[5]

A transportation facilitation center which would serve as a centra-lized consolidation and breakbulk terminal on shipments of less than 1,000 pounds has been suggested.[6] Instead of each carrier providing service, a fleet of special trucks from the facilitation center would handle the small shipments. The center would be owned by a third party (private, public, or combination ownership) which could not compete with the client carriers. It would be intermodal in nature and would handle both domestic and international freight. Extensive use of containerization would be utilized. The plan would call for the estab-lishment of a nationwide network of such centers. The study concluded such a plan was economically feasible.

Some of the advantages of joint use of terminals by noncompeting carriers are the savings on freight interlined to other carriers also using the terminal, reduction in inner-city congestion, and fuel savings. The savings on such freight are estimated to be as much as $4 per ton, since the handling cycle is eliminated as well as delivery costs to the second carrier.

It appears that the participation of motor carriers in union or joint terminal operations is not going to increase materially unless at some future time there should be pressure from metropolitan areas for their increased use to relieve congestion in city streets. The experience to date would indicate that the most successful type of joint terminal operation is that in which the carrier tenants perform complementary rather than competitive service.

Publicly financed, modern union motortruck terminals built in the 1950's in New York City and Newark have not been successful. In 1973, United Parcel Service signed a 25-year lease for a substantial part of the New York Motor Truck Terminal. The Newark terminal was advertised for sale in 1979.

## QUESTIONS AND PROBLEMS

1. What factors have caused motor carriers to give increased attention to terminal facilities?

2. Describe the island-type terminal. Compile a list of other terminal building types which, in your judgment, would be suitable for motor-carrier use.

3. Differentiate between cross-dock and side-by-side transfer of freight at a terminal.

4. Assume that you had an island-type dock, 20 truck berths in length, on which you were using manual equipment. How would you go about determining the feasibility of mechanizing the dock? Would you use the overhead conveyor, forklift truck, or other mechanized equipment? Explain why.

5. Of what importance is yard space in the operation of a terminal? What are some ideal yard widths?

6. Describe the work of the dispatcher.

7. What is a "peddle run"? Explain the terms "eight-day workweek" and "hot-shot run."

8. List the types of motor carrier terminals, based on ownership.

9. "Motor carriers have shown a reluctance to participate in the union terminal or joint operation." Discuss. How extensive is the common or joint terminal at the present time?

10. Do you feel that pressure from metropolitan areas may force joint terminal operations in some cities? Why?

11. What are the advantages and disadvantages of the different methods of freight checking?

12. Explain route loading and loading by zone. List the advantages of each system.

13. Why are terminal cost controls so important? What is the trend in terminal costs compared with line-haul costs?

14. Should terminals be organized and operated as profit centers? Defend your position.

15. Explain how you would analyze the economic feasibility of a transportation facilitation center.

## FOOTNOTES TO CHAPTER 11

[1] See The Operations Council, American Trucking Associations, Inc., *Shipper—Motor Carrier Dock Planning Manual,* Washington, D.C., 1973.

[2] The Operations Council of the American Trucking Associations, Inc., is active in furnishing the industry with information concerning material-handling activities and has published *Methods of Freight Handling.* There are several trade publications which deal with material handling that are helpful. The meetings of the American Material Handling Society and the Society of Packaging and Material Handling Engineers, two professional societies, provide much information on material handling.

[3] *Some Factors Tending to Increase Truck Cost in the Tri-State Region and Its Central Cities* (New York: Tri-State Transportation Commission, January, 1971), p. 3.

[4] *Goods Movement in the New York Region—A Study Proposal* (New York: City of New York Department of City Planning, April, 1970), p. 1.

[5] Dennis R. McDermott, "An Alternative Framework for Urban Goods Consolidation," *Transportation Journal,* Vol. 15, No. 1, Fall, 1975, p. 5.

[6] Department of Transportation, *A Study of the Transportation Facilitation Center Concept,* Washington, D.C., September, 1974.

# chapter 12

# Claims

The freight claims procedure used by motor carriers differs among the various carriers, and numerous systems are employed. The essential characteristics of any freight claims procedure should be that it be as simple in its operation as possible, in order to expedite as rapid processing of the claims as is consistent with good business policy. All motor carriers subject to the Interstate Commerce Act are required to investigate carefully all claims before settlement is made.[1] Since a claim is a demand made by a claimant, either shipper or consignee, for restitution for financial loss which was suffered because of the loss of or damage to freight or by application of erroneous rates, weight, or assessment of charges, it is necessary for the claimant to furnish a motor carrier with definite proof of financial loss. An adequately staffed claims department is essential to satisfactory customer relations.

Claims can be divided into two general types: (a) cargo claims, and (b) claims due to overcharge. Cargo claims are those claims which are filed for freight that the carrier has failed to deliver to the consignee because of the destruction, disappearance, or conversion of freight, or because of its being damaged by the carrier so as to render its value less to the consignee. Overcharge claims are those which are caused by erroneous application of rates, weights, and assessment of freight charges.

## CARGO CLAIMS

An average motor carrier in recent years has considered itself fortunate to earn a profit of five cents on each dollar in revenue. The average claim is for about $80, and in order to pay it, a motor carrier realizing five cents profit on each dollar must transport $1,600 of revenue freight without profit. To pay a claim of $100, the carrier would have to transport $2,000 of revenue freight to come out even, whereas a $1,000 claim would drain away the profit on $20,000 of revenue freight. The claim bill for Class I, motor common carriers of general commodities in a recent year exceeded $190 million. These facts emphasize the importance of close attention to causes and prevention of claims.

Cargo claims are of two varieties: (*a*) those which are attributable to known loss or known damage, and (*b*) those which are attributable to unknown loss or damage.

### Known loss or damage

The first type of cargo claims is that of freight received with loss or damage. visible and with exception at the time of delivery. Claims of

STANDARD FORM FOR PRESENTATION OF LOSS AND DAMAGE CLAIM
(Read Instruction on Back Before Filling in This Form)

To: _____
(Name of Carrier)     (Date)
(Street Address)     (Claimant's Number)
(City, State)     (Carrier's Number)

This claim for $_____ is made against your company for ☐ Damage ☐ Loss in connection with the following described shipment:

(Shipper's Name)     (Consignee's Name)
(Point Shipped From)     (Final Destination)
(Name of Carrier Issuing Bill of Lading)     (Name of Delivering Carrier)
(Date of Bill of Lading)     (Date of Delivery)
(Routing of Shipment)     (Delivering Carrier's Freight Bill No.)

If shipment reconsigned en route, state particulars: _____

If shipment moved from warehousing or distribution point, indicate name of initial shipper and point of origin, and, if known, name of prior carrier or carriers and prior billing reference: _____

DETAILED STATEMENT SHOWING HOW AMOUNT CLAIMED IS DETERMINED
(Number and description of articles, nature and extent of loss or damage, invoice price of articles, amount of claim, etc. ALL DISCOUNT and ALLOWANCES MUST BE SHOWN.)

Total Amount Claimed

The following documents are submitted in support of this claim:
☐ Original Bill of Lading
☐ Original paid freight bill or other carrier document bearing notation of loss or damage if not shown on freight bill.     ☐ Original invoice or certified copy
☐ Carrier's Inspection Report Form (Concealed loss or damage).     ☐ Shippers concealed loss or damage form.
☐ Consignee concealed loss or damage form.     ☐ Other particulars obtainable in proof of loss or damage claimed:

(Note: The absence of any document called for in connection with this claim must be explained. When impossible for claimant to produce original bill of lading, or paid freight bill, a bond of indemnity must be given to protect carrier against duplicate claim supported by original documents.)
Remarks: _____

The foregoing statement of facts is hereby certified as correct.

(Claimant's Name)
(Address)

Fig. 12-1. Standard form for presentation of loss and damage claim.

this nature usually will be submitted by the claimant on the standard form for presentation of loss or damage claims. Figure 12-1 is an example of this form. These claims should be supported by (a) the original bill of lading; (b) the original destination freight bill (or bond of indemnity); (c) the original invoice or certified or photostatic copy; and (d) any other particulars which are obtainable to aid in proof of the loss or damage claimed.

### Concealed loss or damage

The second type of cargo loss or damage, that of concealed or unknown loss or damage, is that freight which is received with no loss or damage visible at the time of delivery and therfore is received without exception. A claim of this kind should be supported by (a) the original bill of lading (or bond of indemnity); (b) the original destination freight bill (or bond of indemnity); (c) the original invoice or certified or photostatic copy; (d) any other evidence which may be obtainable to prove loss or damage claimed; and (e) inspection report by a carrier representative. If inspection is not made by a carrier representative, the claimant will be required to complete a standard form for the handling of concealed loss and concealed damage claims. Either a shipper's form or consignee's form is used, depending upon whether the claimant is a shipper or consignee.

Although carrier liability is well established, the ultimate recourse regarding it has not been made by the Interstate Commerce Commission but rather by the courts. However, the Commission has broadened its concern about this matter as a result of carrier effort in 1969 to effectuate new guidelines on concealed damage. This resulted in *Ex Parte 263, Rules, Regulations, and Practices of Regulated Carriers with Respect to the Processing of Loss and Damage Claims,* 1972. The Commission, in that proceeding, stipulated certain principles and practices for the investigation and voluntary disposition of loss and damage claims and the processing of salvage. Basically, the rules stipulate that shippers must file claims in writing within a time period specified by the carriers; that carriers must acknowledge receipt of each loss and damage claim within 30 days; that carriers must investigate claims promptly; that carriers must dispose of complaints within 120 days of their receipt; and carriers must maintain records of salvage they obtain from damaged shipments. Further, the carriers must account for all money recovered in the sale of such salvage.

## Damaged freight

The nature of the goods shipped, the container used, and the method of packing are all important in safe transportation of goods. Even though the shipper might be at fault, the burden of proof of negligence is upon the carrier after the carrier has signed the bill of lading. This is the case because it is assumed that if the shipment was not properly prepared, the carrier should have rejected it; or if it was quite susceptible to damage, the carrier should have accorded it special handling.

Damaged freight is in a different class from lost freight because, in the latter case, the payment of a claim may be averted if the shipment is found and forwarded to the consignee. Damaged freight, however, represents a permanent injury and one in which the shipper has suffered a monetary loss and expects the motor carrier to compensate him.

Loss and damage freight claim handling procedures vary widely among motor carriers. A suggested loss and damage freight claim handling procedure includes the following points:

1. Make inspections within 48 hours.
2. Acknowledge claim same day received.
3. Give claimant your claim number.
4. Investigate claim immediately; be sure of the facts.
5. Pay claim or deny liability promptly.
6. Keep claim files "active"—trace for replies to unanswered correspondence.

## Over and short freight

Over freight is freight with or without marks (including articles in excess of quantity on billing) which is found in possession of a carrier at any point without a regular revenue or astray waybill. There can never be an "over" piece of freight without a "short."

Astray freight is understood to be freight which has become separated from the regular revenue freight bill and is covered by an astray freight bill. Freight may be "over" with marks as to shipper or consignee or without marks. In the latter case, it is usually referred to as "dead over." In both of these cases, their freight has become separated from the waybill.

Upon discovery of over freight, an over report is prepared immediately. A copy of the report is sent to the transfer and/or the origin or billing point for investigation and determination of the reason for the freight checking out over at the unloading point. The origin or transfer terminal which receives this report should check the various reasons for freight going astray. If the origin terminal cannot account for the overage from its records, the shipper should be asked to help in the matter. The terminal which has the over freight should also request the consignee and shipper for proof of ownership when the origin terminal cannot provide the revenue billing within a reasonable time.

In the case of short freight, the carrier has a bill but no freight or less than the number of pieces called for by the billing. Short freight is a real problem, for the carrier has signed the shipper's bill of lading for the freight and the terminal which holds the bill does not know what has happened to it. Because of mismarkings or misdescription by the shipper, the carrier may share the responsibility for short freight. The common causes of such shortages are the failure of carrier's employees to count and pick up the freight signed for, errors made in billing, inadequate packing, loading onto the wrong unit, and theft, to name but a few.

Over freight which is discovered at an origin terminal should be forwarded to the destination terminal on an astray freight waybill after the original waybill reference has been secured. However, where over freight is found at an intermediate terminal, it is usually forwarded to the destination terminal immediately on an astray freight waybill and will include the original waybill reference if possible. If over freight is found at destination terminal, it should be held until the revenue waybill reference has been established. A free astray waybill is issued covering freight which checks over from a truck and cannot be applied on revenue billing. The free astray waybill should show the name and address of shipper, weight, description of freight, and at what point and from what vehicle it checks out over.

Every effort should be made to deliver over freight. After it has been carried on the over report of carriers for 90 to 120 days, however, some carriers then consider the over freight to be salvage freight. Under such arrangements, the headquarters freight claim department may authorize the shipment of the salvage freight to the appropriate department for disposal. When the operations department has exhausted all efforts to dispose of refused or unclaimed freight, it will be shipped to the headquarters claims office for appropriate disposition. Shipments of salvage material to the headquarters are usually handled on a deadhead bill of lading or waybill. If carrier returns salvage to a shipper, it will usually move on a revenue billing, unless the freight claim department authorizes a different procedure.

## OVERCHARGE CLAIMS

The second general type of claim is that of overcharge. Claims of this nature are made because of the application of erroneous rates, weights, and assessment of freight charges. An overcharge claim is usually submitted on a standard form for the presentation of overcharge claims. An overcharge claim is supported by the following documents: (a) original bill of lading, if not previously surrendered to carrier when shipment was prepaid or when claim is based on misrouting or valuation (or bond of indemnity); (b) original paid freight bill (or bond of indemnity); (c) original invoice or certified copy, when the claim is based on weight; (d) when the claim is based on weight, a weight certificate or a certified statement; and (e) other evidence which can be obtained in proof of the overcharge claimed. Increasing use is being made of computers in handling overcharge claims.

Although the law makes no exception when overcharges are discovered in such small amounts that they would be absorbed in bookkeeping and handling costs, and for which claims have not been filed, it seems questionable that the law would contemplate refunds under this condition. When a claim is filed, however, it is the carrier's duty to give it consideration and to pay or decline it on its merits regardless of the amount involved.

The Commission in *Ex Parte 342, Procedures Governing the Processing, Investigation, and Disposition of Overcharge, Duplicate Payment, or Overcollection Claims,* adopted regulations for the handling of overcharge, duplicate payment, or overcollection claims. It ruled that carriers have to pay, decline to pay, or settle each written claim within 60 days after receiving the claim. If agreed to by the parties, the time period can be extended. Claims for overcharges and duplicate payments must be accompanied by the original freight bill or copy.

When a carrier participated in a freight movement but did not collect the charges and then discovered that an overcharge had been made, it must immediately notify the collecting carrier which must refund the amount of overpayment within 30 days after discovering the overpayment.

Public Law 89—170 amended the Interstate Commerce Act to permit reparations suits against motor carriers or freight forwarders in cases where the applicable rates exceeded a maximum reasonable level to be filed in court. The Commission is to be called upon to aid the court by making administrative determinations relating to the amount of reparations.

Shippers must sue in court to obtain reparations. The carriers are not permitted to make reparations even where they are willing to do so. It has been suggested that Section 11705 should be amended to provide concurrent jurisdiction between the courts and the Commission, which would provide a simple and less expensive method of collecting motor carrier reparations.[2]

### Tracing

Tracing and OS&D's are closely associated, inasmuch as a tracer often means that the freight has gone astray and is covered by an OS&D report. When a request to trace a shipment is received, particularly one that has been in transit for some time, the OS&D files should be checked on overs and shorts. The trace file should be consolidated with the OS&D file if it is found that the freight is over or short in the hands of the carrier.

Frequently there are requests for information on freight movements which have not been delivered. Although tracers are annoying, carriers are not in a position to judge the importance of a customer's request. It is, therefore, important that each tracer be given prompt and courteous handling. It is desirable to have a tracer form in order that a record may be kept of the action taken. A tracer may be the forerunner of possible trouble in the movement of a shipper's goods, so that a record should be maintained that will be helpful if an overage or shortage of freight should occur.

A tickler file is used to maintain a check on traced shipments. When shippers use tracing for the purpose of expediting, the carrier soon finds that this type of tracer may become quite burdensome, diverting attention from those cases which merit greater consideration. As in other claims work, computers are being used increasingly in tracing.

## INVESTIGATION AND DISPOSITION OF CLAIMS

A number of principles and practices for the investigation and disposition of freight claims have been forumulated to secure uniformity among carriers and uniform treatment of claimants in the disposition of claims of like nature.[3] They are also planned to secure better relationships in claim matters among carriers as well as between carriers and their customers. These principles include the time limit for filing claims, the documents required in support of claims, description of claims for deterioration, description of claims for damage by delay, procedure to be followed when two or more claims are presented on the same shipment, and the measure of damages.

Although all of these principles are significant, the one which covers the measure of damages is of particular importance. This reads as follows:

Except in claims involving declared or agreed value, the responsibility of the carrier for loss, damage or injury which is caused to property by the carrier is the full actual loss, damage or injury to such property as suffered by claimant. The maximum liability of the carrier in any event is the destination value in the quantity shipped.

For the purpose of arriving at the correct measure of liability where destination value of the property is a factor (in the absence of a declared or agreed value), any recognized market quotations at destination, or point adjacent thereto, quoting commodity values in the quantity shipped, may be accepted. In the absence of such market quotations or other established market values in the quantity shipped, the bona fide invoice price, plus proportionate freight charges if paid and not included in invoice price, and duty if paid and not refundable, shall represent the reasonable destination value. Brokerage, overhead expenses, percentage above invoice, or other similar items added to the invoice price, will not be paid.

The practice of adjusting claims on non-perishable commodities on the basis of the difference between retail value in good condition and the marked-down value resulting from damage, shipment being sold without repair, is considered to be in the nature of an appraisal of damage and, accordingly, to be a proper practice and in conformity with other expressions regarding measure of damage in connection with property sold in a damaged condition.

In the event of refusal by consignee or owner of shipment not entirely worthless nor so materially damaged as to destroy its value, shipment shall be handled as provided by the bill of lading contract or applicable laws in a manner that will best conserve the interests of all concerned. On claims filed in connection with such refused shipments, carrier liability will be acknowledged only for such damage as appropriate investigation may develop is reasonably chargeable to carriers.[4]

The proper measure of damages is a controversial subject. It involves the determination of what yardstick should be used, after liability has been established, the retail or wholesale price, the market value at destination, or the replacement cost. Ordinarily the law does not contemplate the making of a profit out of a carrier's misfortune in losing or damaging goods. On the other hand, it cannot be definitely stated that a claimant should never include any profit in his claim. There are instances in which the profit has been earned.

The tendency in recent court decisions is to restrict the claimant to his actual loss, as determined from evidence placed before the court, depending upon the terms of sale, the business methods of the claimant, and the circumstances under which the shipment was made.

In 1976, an independent organization for the arbitration of freight loss and damage claims between motor carriers and shippers was established. The Transportation Arbitration Board consists of 10 shippers and 10 carrier arbiters. Each case is decided by a two-person team, one shipper and one carrier arbiter. The unanimous decisions of the teams are binding and enforceable by law. Numerous claims have been submitted to it for arbitration.

## Inspections after delivery

After a carrier has delivered a shipment to a consignee, the latter may notify the carrier of a shortage or damage which was not noticed at the time of delivery. Therefore, a notation regarding the shortage or damage was not placed on the freight bill. Such discrepancies often are not discovered for several days after delivery. Upon notification of the discrepancy the carrier should have an inspection made within 48 hours after receipt of the notice, having requested the consignee to discontinue unpacking until the inspector arrives. The carrier requires the consignee to submit the original container, wrapping, packing, and contents as delivered as evidence.

It is advisable for each terminal to maintain a record of requests which are received for inspections. This record should include the date and time of request; nature of request; name and address of the firm or person making the request; and the freight bill number or other reference on the shipment to be inspected. Each record should contain the time, date, and name of the inspector who is notified to make each inspection.

All of this information may be recorded on the reverse side of the delivery receipt copy of the freight bill. Before the inspection is made, the delivery receipt copy of the freight bill for the shipment should be examined to determine whether any exceptions were made at the time of delivery. If exceptions were made that are associated with loss or damage for which an inspection is being made, it is customary for a notation to this effect to be made on the inspection report.

Before the inspection is made, the inspector should secure the consignee's copy of the carrier's freight bill. It sometimes happens that exceptions are placed on the consignee's copy of the freight bill, although the carrier's delivery receipt does not contain the exceptions. If there are no authorized exceptions on the carrier's delivery receipt or the consignee's copy of the freight bill, the inspection report should state "concealed damage" or "concealed loss." In examining the shipment, it is necessary to determine whether the containers and packing are sufficient. Most inspection reports require that if packing is inadequate a statement to this effect should be contained in the report. However, the inspector should show the consignee how damage could have been prevented if better or additional packing were employed. In this manner, the consignee can call the attention of the shipper to the inadequacy of packing so that future shipments can be properly packed.

The invoice should be checked against the freight bill or the bill of lading to determine if they agree. The invoice should also be checked carefully to determine the cost of the shipment. The freight bill, packages, and packing slip should be examined to ascertain where the shipment was packed. The inspection may indicate that the goods have had prior transportation, or that they may have been previously offered for sale.

An inspection report is filled out on which all questions must be answered. The original copy is left with the consignee who will attach it to the claim if it is filed; the duplicate is forwarded to the headquarters claims department after examination by the terminal or branch manager and any notations as to disposition of salvage are made. The third copy is kept by the terminal and attached to the delivery receipt copy of the freight bill.

### Salvage

As a result of loss or damage to goods, there is the problem of disposing of commodities at their salvage value. If the carrier is responsible for the damage and the damaged goods have no salvage value, the inspector is instructed to dispose of them so that they cannot be used as evidence upon which to file a claim on another shipment. The salvage, in such a case, would be dumped or destroyed immediately. If the carrier is responsible for the damage and the goods have some salvage value, an effort is made to get the consignee to retain them in order that he can get the best possible salvage value from them. Many consignees will not retain damaged goods, in which case the inspector may pick them up and return them to the terminal. Here, a salvage record form is made out, and the matter is handled in accordance with company procedure for such goods. If the inspector cannot take the salvaged goods back to the terminal, they should be labeled with carrier's stickers in order to be identifiable. If possible, they should be sealed.

Where there is doubt as to the carrier's responsibility for the damage, goods are usually not picked up regardless of whether or not they have any salvage value. The inspection report, in this case, should indicate the reasons for not picking up the damaged goods.

A special salvage record form is used for the pickup of the goods. It is important to maintain a continuing record of this type of goods because 30 percent of the carrier's claim payments may be offset by salvage sales.

### Loss and damage claim register

The maintenance of a loss and damage claim register is recommended. Thus, when a claim is received it can be entered in the carrier's claim register or logbook, as it is sometimes termed, and a complete record made of the claim. In this manner, each claim is given a number and is logged. This expedites the prompt handling of claims which is essential both in maintaining customer goodwill and also in providing for orderly operation of a business. File cards are used in conjunction with this system.

## REFUSED OR UNCLAIMED FREIGHT

When a carrier has refused freight on hand, the notice of such refusal should be sent at once. If the freight is perishable, the shipper should be notified by wire. Unclaimed freight should not be held longer than 15 days before giving notice that the shipment cannot be delivered. In forwarding the refused or unclaimed form notice to the shipper and consignee, it is important that the shipper's name and street address be spelled correctly. Questions frequently arise as to whether the shipper received notice when the name is spelled incorrectly or is incomplete.

After the first notice, a follow-up should be made within a reasonable time. In rebilling a refused or unclaimed shipment, the proper storage charges are assessed. The requested disposition of refused or unclaimed freight should come from the shipper, and the consignee's requests for disposition are not acceptable.

## RECOOPERING

The recoopering of packages received in damaged condition immediately upon discovery eliminates the probability of theft by extraction from packages and minimizes possible damages which might be incurred if the shipment was allowed to go forward without reconditioning the package. It sometimes happens that several slats in a crate will become broken in shipment or a carton will break open because of pressures upon it, and this damage to the crate or carton may not have resulted in damage to the contents. At the time freight is transferred from over-the-road units to a terminal, these breaks will often be discovered and the freight set aside so that the packaging can be repaired immediately before notifying the consignee that the freight is on hand.

Section 3 of the Bill of Lading Terms and Conditions provides that "except where such service is required as a result of carrier's negligence all property shall be subject to necessary cooperage, packing, and re-packing at owner's cost." A motor carrier could perform a recoopering service when the container failure is due to defective or inadequate packing and add such expense to the freight bill, to be collected upon delivery. However, few motor carriers add this charge to the freight bill.

## CLAIM PREVENTION

The National Freight Claim Council has formulated recommendations that cover a wide variety of claim prevention activities. They include the maintenance of adequate statistics; causes of claims; OS&D procedures; educational programs; employee selection and training; and managerial recommendations on many other aspects of an effective program.[5]

There are many guides for determining the efficiency of a freight claim department. One of the most frequently used is that of the percentage of claims received and settled within a specified period of time. If the carrier settles within 30 days 70 percent of the claims received, its rating is considered to be excellent. If over 50 percent is settled, the carrier's rating is considered to be good. Less than 50 percent is considered to be poor, while lower than 40 percent is considered to be inexcusable. In 1945 only 48 percent of the claims were settled within 30 days. Currently, 64 percent are settled within that period of time.

The freight claim ratio is expressed as a percentage of revenue. It includes cargo insurance plus cargo loss and damage claims. It is the ratio of net claim payments to gross revenue. There are many factors which affect the claim ratio, such as amount of LTL traffic handled, volume of traffic, amount of interchange, types of commodities handled, number of terminal handlings, freight handling by employees, condition of equipment used, as well as others.

Because of the foregoing factors, it is difficult to compare one carrier's ratio to another's. The average ratio for Class I carriers is above one percent, but it is believed that most carriers can reduce their ratios to one percent or less. Some motor carriers with effective claim prevention programs have reduced their ratio to 0.50 percent and lower. One Class I carrier has 0.16 ratio.

The freight claim ratios shown in Fig. 12-2 are for Class I intercity motor common carriers of general freight. In recent years, there has been an improvement in the freight claim ratio as a percent of revenue, but the dollar amount is staggering. For one large carrier, it is more than $5 million a year, and for all Class I motor carriers over $190 million. Although there has been improvement, much remains to be accomplished.

It is essential that motor carriers strive for as nearly perfect a shipping record as possible, not only because of the savings that accrue to the carriers from such a record but because of the benefits to the shippers as well. After all, the speediest and most equitable settlement of a claim is at best a poor substitute for prompt delivery of freight in first-class condition. There is an attitude altogether too prevalent among motor carrier employees that a certain amount of loss and damage is inevitable in the handling of freight. When the loss and damage ratio for a carrier increases, a campaign is usually undertaken to cut down on these claims, but this is a temporary expedient. What is needed is not a sporadic program but a continuous one, in order to minimize loss and damage to freight through the cooperation of everyone concerned.

Studies in recent years have shown that about half the payments for

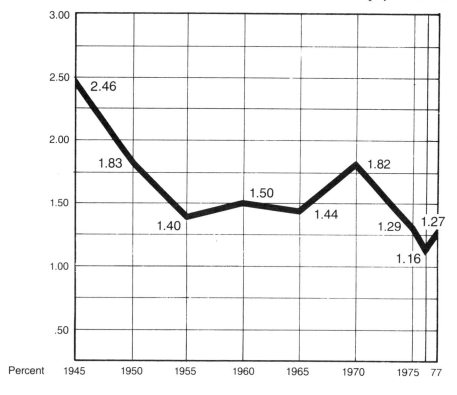

Fig. 12-2. Freight claim ratios of Class I intercity common carriers of general freight. Source: American Trucking Associations, Inc., *Trends*, 1977-78, p. 17.

loss claims by Class I motor carriers of general commodities were crime related. The Department of Transportation has estimated that about 85 percent of cargo theft occurs from within the system. It has published a pamphlet entitled "Cargo Security Handbook for Shippers and Receivers" outlining the importance of improved documentation procedures in controlling loss. It is estimated by the Department of Transportation that $1 billion is lost annually by the transportation industry to crime.

Various kinds of electronic security equipment is being utilized by carriers. Surveillance equipment used by some carriers includes sensors at perimeter points that report on intrusions, and closed circuit television monitored by a guard. Recording cameras trained on entry points and alarm systems are used by others. Access control systems requiring a special pass or an electronic card-key to a controlled area is another approach used to cut losses of freight. A total systems approach by management is needed to control loss claims effectively.

The President, by Executive Order in 1975, defined the roles of the Department of Transportation, the Attorney General's Office, and the Secretary of Treasury in fighting cargo theft. Among other things, DOT is to collect, analyze, and publish reports on the extent of cargo theft losses, coordinate federal activities to prevent cargo theft, and to report annually on the effectiveness of the federal antitheft program.

The top ten commodity groups susceptible to loss and damage ranked in descending order for Class I general commodity carriers were: clothing; fabricated metal products; TV's, radio sets and recorders; electrical machinery equipment; furniture; auto, bus and truck parts; household appliances; machinery; paper and paper products; and canned food. Yellow Freight's seven-months' experience in transporting hand calculators was $2,700 in revenue and claims for loss from theft of $52,000.

Since 1971, motor common and contract carriers of property with average gross revenue of $1 million or more have been required to file quarterly reports with the Commission on freight loss and damage claims. In classifying claims according to the cause of loss, the Commission uses the following categories: shortage; theft and pilferage; hijacking (stealing with use of force or threat of use of force); concealed damage; visible damage; wreck and catastrophe; delay; heat, cold, water; and other. The largest causes of loss and damage claims are shortages and visible damage, each of which amounts to about 40 percent of claims.

Petty pilferage can be minimized by using a Mercury Quartz light in conjunction with a dust-like powder that is sprinkled on the contents of a carton. If someone removes anything from the carton, the dust that is invisible to the naked eye clings to his hands and clothes. Cartons can be secretly sprinkled with the powder, and the terminal crew can be placed under the light when they go off duty. As a preventive measure, the men can be told about the light and shown how it works. If they are then told that cartons will be powdered and the light used, pilferage can be reduced considerably. If it increases at any time, the light can be used again.

A large part of the causes of claims paid are matters over which carriers could exercise a greater degree of control. For example, in bad weather the suction which is created at the rear of a semitrailer as it moves on the highway causes rain and snow to get through even the smallest cracks around the doors and damage the cargo. This often leads to extensive water damage. A most effective means of preventing this is the use of cloth tape which seals all the cracks around trailer doors.

There are many independent testing laboratories and container manufacturer laboratories in which tests are constantly being conducted to develop additional information on containers and improve transit of goods. Carriers, for a nominal fee, can have tests conducted on containers. In some instances, such tests are conducted on containers when the shipper has packed his shipment in accordance with standard shipping practices, but the carrier's experience has shown the packing to be inadequate. The shipper is usually more willing to accept the report of an independent testing laboratory than the carrier's opinion in this matter.

### Use of impact machines

A few motor carriers have made use of an impact recorder which records on a graph the jolts and shocks to which containers are subject. The use of this device has been helpful in giving the claims department more positive information on where the containers sustain the most shock. Several different makes of these machines are small enough to be put in a shoebox.

This machine can be used in claim prevention by placing it in a box and dropping it varying distances, such as six, 12, or 18 inches. Since the device is exposed, the employees who handle the freight can see the immediate results. Some of the facts that have been developed through the use of the impact recorder by carriers are that the rear section of a semitrailer sustains many more shocks; that there is a definite shock resulting from hooking the tractor and semitrailer; except for accidents, the shocks that are transmitted by line-haul vehicles in transit are not as great as those sustained in the handling of cargo to and from trailers; and spring suspensions on tractors and semitrailers are important in absorption of road shocks.

A lightly loaded vehicle moving at ten miles an hour when crossing a railroad grade crossing is estimated to transmit a shock to the lading which is as great as that encountered in shifting boxcars at 15 miles per hour.

### Truck alarms

Since there are numerous cargos of high-value freight, such as textiles, clothing, furs, tobacco, and drugs, which are vulnerable to theft and hijacking, particularly in metropolitan areas, alarm systems have been devised to counteract this danger. There are organizations which install a police-type siren alarm which can be heard for miles and will sound for hours if any unauthorized person attempts to enter, operate, move, or tamper with the protectively wired truck or trailer. These systems of protection have been perfected to the point where a trailer can be protected by the installation of a system that will cause a siren to blow if the trailer is moved in any way by anyone except the authorized operator. This means that the system must not be too sensitive, or it would be set off by street vibration; at the same time, it must be sensitive enough to respond immediately if the trailer is towed away.

This service is not sold to the motor carrier but is leased to it at a set amount for each unit per year. The manufacturer then maintains the equipment. The rental charge for the first year is higher because of the installation charge.

The alarm system has proved to be one of the most effective ways of minimizing pilferage yet devised. Its success is reflected in the lower insurance premiums a carrier secures by having his equipment thus protected, or the carrier may be able to obtain a higher policy limit in the insurance it is carrying as a result of the use of an alarm system.

### National classification rules

A number of National Motor Freight Classification rules, if followed, would constitute a means of claim prevention. Rule 680, for example, provides in part the "... kinds or specifications of the containers, packages or other manner in which the articles shall be packed or protected for shipment. ..." Section 2 of the same rule provides that "... carriers may for good reasons refuse to accept freight the transportation of which, in their judgment, would not be reasonably safe and practicable." The latter provision constitutes a carrier's tariff authority for refusing shipments which because of the nature of their packing would result in claims.

Concealed damage, which is a vexing claim problem, could undoubtedly be reduced through greater use by the carrier of one of the classification rules. Rule 360, Section 3, provides that "... when carrier's agent believes it necessary that the contents of packages be inspected, he will make or cause such inspection to be made or require other sufficient evidence to determine actual character of the property." A check could be made prior to the acceptance of the merchandise under the provisions of this rule, particularly of those shipments which involve frequent claims.

Rule 689 governing experimental or test shipments makes it possible for manufacturers to test packages which could not be accepted under the existing packaging requirements made in the governing classification. Test permits are issued by the National Classification Board, usually for a period of three months. Most requests for permits come from shippers who are required to supply the bill-of-lading number, date of shipment, name of carrier, and other information. Shippers requesting test permits have to send the package that they want to test-ship to the Classification Board. An example of a test permit is that of baby food in glass jars packed in cartons without inside protection or separators, other than lubricant applied to the jars. If the test shipment involves a package that is controversial, the Classification Board requires a monthly report.

Rule 780 provides for the nonacceptance of certain specified articles and articles of extraordinary value. The term "extraordinary value" has not been defined by the Commission or the courts. Some carriers have held that the term means a value beyond the normal liability of the carrier. Other carriers have felt that the term is comparative, i.e., an article with an ordinary value of $2 per pound when valued at $5 per pound would be considered to be of extraordinary value. There are articles under Rule 780 which a carrier should not accept but does.

The reason that there is a lack of adherence to any of these classification rules which could reduce claims is the factor of competition between carriers.

## WEIGHING AND INSPECTION BUREAUS

The Motor Carrier Weighing and Inspection Bureaus, of which there are 14, formed a nonprofit national organization in 1954 called the "National Association of Motor Carrier Weighing and Inspection Bureaus." The objectives of this association are: (1) to collect and disseminate information which will be helpful to the Bureaus and the industry generally; (2) to promote cooperation between motor carriers and the shipping public; (3) to publicize the necessity for the work which these Bureaus perform; (4) to encourage educational programs concerning the functions of these Bureaus by the membership and the National Classification Committee; and (5) to encourage the participation of representatives from the National Classification Board and the National Classification Committee at each national meeting of the Motor Carrier Weighing and Inspection Bureaus. These bureaus are usually a part of a rate bureau.

Included in an average W&I Bureau's scope of activities are such matters as: determining proper descriptions to be used on bills of lading; checking weights shown by shippers on bills of lading; determining causes of damage; inspecting damaged shipments; recommending improved packing and shipping methods; proposing changes in descriptions for packing in classification and tariffs; checking freight on carrier platform for proper description; testing carrier scales; recommending improved methods of freight handling, loading, and stowing for claim prevention; and assisting in disposing of over, short, and damaged freight. A representative bureau inspected 1,378 shipments during one year. If found that 48 percent did not comply in some respect with classification or other tariff requirements; and 43 percent were inaccurately or incorrectly described, thus affecting the charge assessed.

## QUESTIONS AND PROBLEMS

1. What are the types of cargo claims? What documents must support cargo claims? Why?

2. List the causes of cargo loss and damage claims.

3. What procedure may be followed in delivering damaged freight? What is refused freight?

4. After examining the loss and damage claim ratio for motor carriers, formulate a short- and a long-range program which you feel will reduce that ratio, and explain in detail how you would accomplish it.

5. What tangible benefit could you expect as a motor carrier operator through the use of an alarm system?

6. What are some of the typical carrier procedures for making delivery of over freight without benefit of the revenue waybill?

7. What is the National Freight Claim Council? Should membership be compulsory?

8. How would you determine the efficiency with which claims are handled by the freight claim department?

9. What are some of the methods of claim prevention which have been successful?

10. In what way do some of the National Motor Freight Classification rules provide a means of claim prevention?

11. How do the activities of motor carrier weighing and inspection bureaus assist in claims work?

## FOOTNOTES TO CHAPTER 12

[1] Section 222 (c).

[2] Peter Lynagh, "Motor Carrier Reparations, A Settled Issue?" *Transportation Journal*, Winter, 1973, Vol. 13, No. 2, p. 27.

[3] The National Freight Claim Council of ATA has formulated a number of freight claim rules, as well as establishing principles and practices covering loss, damage, and overcharge claims. Motor carrier members of the Council are pledged to handle claims promptly and efficiently. It has also established an arbitration and appeal procedure for use when carriers disagree on apportionment of claim for shipment over lines of two or more carriers.

[4] National Freight Claim Council, ATA, *Freight Claim Rule Book* (Washington, D.C., 1977).

[5] National Freight Claim Council, ATA, *Freight Claim Rule Book* 1977.

# chapter 13

# Insurance

Insurance plays a vital role in motor carrier operations. Some of the types of insurance which are used by motor carriers are comparable to those applicable to other business firms, such as insurance on terminals, office equipment, and the like. There has been, however, the development of different types of insurance especially adapted to motor carrier operations, together with elaborate programs designed to provide comprehensive coverage of all phases of carrier operations.

Various states established minimum insurance requirements before there were any federal requirements as one of the conditions for granting authority to operate intrastate, inasmuch as some of the motor carriers had not shown adequate financial responsibility. Even since the passage of the federal requirements, most state laws still provide for minimum insurance requirements for intrastate operation, although, in many instances, the Commission requirements are higher than those in some states on public liability and property damage.

Subchapter II of the Interstate Commerce Act requires that the Interstate Commerce Commission shall prescribe reasonable rules and regulations applicable to brokers and carriers in order to afford protection to travelers and shippers who utilize motor carrier transportation. As a result of this provision of the act, the Interstate Commerce Commission conducted an investigation and established rules and regulations (*Ex parte No. MC-5*) in 1936, and later added further provisions specifying insurance and surety bond requirements, as well as the requirements for a self-insurer.

Thus, before a certificate or permit may be issued to any person, evidence of security for the protection of the public in the form of insurance, surety bonds, or qualifications as a self-insurer must be on file with the Commission as follows:

1. Cargo liability: Not less than $5,000 on any one motor vehicle for common carriers of property; not less than $10,000 for loss or damage at any one time and place. However, certain low-value commodities, such as coal, lumber, and commercial fertilizer, do not require cargo liability security. Contract carriers of property are not required to file evidence of cargo liability security.

2. Bodily injury: Not less than $100,000 for injury or death of one person. For all injuries or deaths in any one accident not less than $300,000.

3. Damage to the property of others (excluding cargo): Each accident $50,000.

These minimum requirements are low, in the opinion of most carriers which secure coverage of these items in amounts up to $1,000,000. Transportation risks of the trucking industry are often considered to be "target" risks and are more susceptible to large jury verdicts. Those carriers that have seasonal operations with clearly defined dates of commencement and termination during a season are only required to comply with the insurance regulations for the periods in which the operations are authorized.

Private carriers and exempt for-hire carriers are not required to comply with Commission insurance requirements. The Commission has also exempted from the provisions of *Ex parte MC–5* those common or contract motor carriers which have leased their entire operating rights to others.

In arranging for insurance, carriers request their insurance agents to provide them with the desired amounts of insurance and not less than the minimum insurance specified by the Commission. Carriers must arrange to have evidence of such insurance filed with the Commission by the insurance company in the prescribed form. Most insurance companies are familiar with the Commission's requirements with respect to the procedure to be followed. There are currently about 300 insurance companies listed in Commission files. However, it is the carrier's responsibility to see that the necessary filing is made with the Commission. The insurance must be written by an insurance company or companies legally authorized to transact business in every state in or through which a carrier operates. A carrier may be prosecuted or its certificate or permit may be revoked if the security for the protection of the public is not kept in effect at all times.

Where owner-operators are used by motor carriers, it is the owner-operator's responsibility to secure the necessary insurance coverage. However, some motor carriers using these independent contractors have assisted them in securing insurance on a more favorable basis than would be available to them as individuals.

Insurance coverage, as filed with the Commission, can be canceled only upon 30 days' notice in writing by a party properly authorized to cancel the insurance.

Surety bonds are filed with the Interstate Commerce Commission and are of two types. There are a few large transportation companies for which the parent corporation acts as a surety. Therefore, if there are claims against the subsidiaries which they are unable to pay, the surety bond furnished by the parent corporation is used to settle claims. However, most of the surety bonds which are filed with the Commission are filed by surety companies, and such a company must be one contained on a list approved by the U.S. Treasury Department under the laws of the United States and the applicable rules and regulations governing bonding companies.[1]

---

Public liability and property damage   . . . 35.0%
Cargo Loss & damage  . . . . . . . . . . . . . 56.5%
Fire, theft & collision . . . . . . . . . . . . . . . . 5.3%
Other insurance expenses  . . . . . . . . . . . 3.2%
**Total** . . . . . . . . . . . . . . . . . . . . . . . . . . **100.0%**

---

Fig. 13-1. The distribution of the motor carrier insurance dollar. Source: American Trucking Associations, Inc., *Trends*, 1977-78, p. 17.

The risk manager is responsible for determining potential loss to company personnel and assets. He formulates the method best designed to protect personnel and assets from loss. In order to accomplish this, the manager must focus on the company's exposure to accidental loss. This requires identification analysis and treatment of the exposure. The manager deals primarily with pure risk which is only subject to loss, not with speculative risk such as the opening of a new market area in which there can be a gain.

After risks have been identified and analyzed, the sequence for treating exposure may be first to transfer risk such as using contracting in the leasing of property or using equipment rental so the owner must cover the risk. A second step is that of loss prevention and loss reduction, for which many useful techniques are available. A third step is the retention of risk, which may be undertaken because it is felt it would result in lower costs. Examples of retention by trucking companies are workmen's compensation and property damage to buildings and contents. The fourth step would be to transfer the risk by insurance. There are many types of coverage, and the risk manager for a trucking company must understand all of them.

Out of every dollar of motor carrier gross revenue, about 2.2 cents is spent in insurance premiums, claims, and other expenditures relative to insurance. The distribution of the motor carrier insurance dollar, based on the experience of Class I common carriers of general freight is 35.0 cents for public liability and property damage; 56.5 cents for cargo loss and damage; 5.3 cents for fire, theft, and collision; and 3.2 cents for other insurance expenses as shown in Fig. 13-1.

## Types of insurance companies

Several different types of insurance are available from insurance companies, which are organized as *stock companies, mutual companies,* and *reciprocal companies.* Some companies specialize in but one type of insurance, such as public liability and property damage, whereas others may handle a more complete line, such as cargo liability and Workman's Compensation. Another source of insurance is self-insurance, which is discussed later.

The stock company in most instances is a corporation that functions with the advantages of a corporation insofar as the buyer is concerned. It limits the carrier's liability to the actual premium charged for the coverage at the time the carrier originally purchased it. It holds no contingencies for any additional expense, nor is the carrier liable in any way in case of any deficit or in case the stock company becomes defunct.

Another type is the mutual insurance company. The policyholders who have mutual insurance own the company. There are assessable and nonassessable types of mutual companies. The policyholders are given a dividend providing the company makes money. A form of the mutual insurance company is the cooperative exchange owned by the members. Insurance is written on a cost basis, plus a small contribution to surplus to insure growth. Such exchanges are composed of companies which specialize in writing certain lines of insurance and which have banded together to offer policyholders a full coverage of all lines, as well as to spread the risk among the different companies.

The reciprocal company is one in which the individual policyholders sign a Power of Attorney, giving the "attorney in fact" power to manage their insurance dollars and authority to levy assessments to pay claims against policyholders.

Recently a new form of insurance company has been formed that is termed a captive insurance company. This is a separate insurance company created by a parent corporation, and the subsidiary company has been formed primarily to insure its parent corporation and other affiliates.

Most insurance is available from insurance companies which are engaged in that business, but some insurance companies have been formed by motor carriers. Probably the best known of these is the Truck Insurance Exchange founded in 1935 (now called the Transport Indemnity Company) in Los Angeles by the same group that had, earlier, organized the Farmers Insurance Exchange. At that time there were very few casualty companies in the United States which were interested in covering the hazards of the rapidly growing motor carrier industry. This limited insurance market was particularly acute in the 11 western states. As a result, a group of prominent western truck operators approached the Farmers Insurance Exchange organization with the request that they organize a company along the same lines as Farmers, which was done. Additional insurance companies have been added from time to time so that many types of insurance are available from this group, and it has grown rapidly.[2] In 1969 Transport Group, Inc., a holding company was formed which owns Transport Indemnity Company and Transport Insurance Company of Dallas. The assets of these companies exceed $150 million, and they insure over 700 motor carriers.

The Commission requires that each insurance company must possess minimum financial resources. The minimum will be determined on the basis of the values of assets and liabilities as shown in its financial statements filed with and approved by the insurance department of the home state of such company, except in instances where, in the judgment of the Commission, additional evidence with respect to such values is considered necessary.

Motor carriers usually secure insurance from agents of insurance companies or from an insurance broker. The latter acts as an insurance buyer for the motor carrier and seeks to secure the best coverage for the carrier consistent with cost. Some state laws define the insurance broker as an insurance buyer. Larger motor carriers tend to deal through a broker or directly with an insurance company.

Some carriers feel that it is desirable to consolidate all coverage with one insurance company if possible, since good experience on one coverage will compensate for a loss on another because the insurance company will look at the overall picture. Further, adjustment expense, which ordinarily claims about ten percent of the premium dollar, may also be reduced by adopting such a plan because many highway accidents involve more than one coverage. It is not infrequent to involve four separate coverages in one loss; that is, Workman's Compensation, when the driver is injured; collision or fire, when equipment is destroyed; cargo, where the load is lost; and bodily injury and property damage liability, when third parties are injured or damaged.

### Procedure of insuring companies

A number of companies specialize in writing insurance for fleet coverage and provide a comprehensive service. Usually, before such companies will write any insurance, they will have their safety engineers investigate the motor carrier requesting insurance coverage. Safety engineers conducting such investigations check a number of items that have effect upon the safety record of a motor carrier:

(*a*) A check is made of the condition of the carrier's equipment, its age, and other relevant information which would have any influence upon accidents. (*b*) A thorough investigation is made of the so-called "inside" personnel—that is, the office employees, the dispatcher, and other nondriver personnel—to ascertain attitudes that may have influence on safety records. (*c*) The territory the carrier is authorized to serve and the routes it is permitted to use are examined because substantial differences are found in operating conditions, both in terms of traffic and terrain, which affect safety. (*d*) The commodities the carrier is authorized to haul are also examined, since some commodities by their nature are subject to a higher percentage of loss and damage than others; the relative proportions of vulnerable commodities carried is taken into consideration in the establishment of an insurance program. (*e*) An investigation is made of the records of the owner-operators of equipment for the company, as well as the records of company drivers, to secure the complete picture as to the qualifications of the drivers. In addition, safety engineers will investigate any other factor which they feel is pertinent to the formulation of reports to the insurance company and the recommendations they will make on the feasibility of insuring the risks of the particular carrier.

An insurance company will continue to make available to its policyholders safety engineer services, including road patrol reports and recommendations on driver selection as well as advice on many other safety matters.

### Bodily injury and property damage insurance

The property damage policy covers loss and expenses arising from claims upon the carrier for damages due to damage to or destruction of property belonging to others by an accident because of ownership or use of the vehicle described in the policy. Liability insurance covers loss arising from claims upon the assured carrier for damages due to bodily injuries or accidental death because of ownership or use of the motor vehicle described in the policy, with minor exceptions.

For intercity operations, bodily injury and property damage insurance is rated on the basis of broad zones, countrywide, there being four zones in all. Zone 1 carries the highest rates and applies to the largest cities. The rates are graded downward, so that those for Zone 4 are the lowest. The applicable rule in the *Automobile Casualty Manual* is so constituted that whenever an intercity trucking risk is rated, Zone 4 is always utilized in developing the premium by averaging the highest-rated zone and the lowest-rated zone into or through which operations are conducted.

Bodily injury and property damage insurance may be purchased on a straight-rate or guaranteed-cost basis. It may also be purchased on a deductible basis, with some companies recommending use of a $100-$500 deductible on property damage only and no deductible on bodily injury because personal injury claims are more difficult to settle.

Contracts for bodily injury and property damage are often written on what is termed a "retrospective contract." Retrospective rating is a form of rating whereby the premium is finally determined after the contract has expired, by totaling the incurred losses and applying the conversion or cost factors for adjustment of claims, taxes, and a factor for service.

This contract is written by agreeing to a given deposit premium, termed a *standard or basic premium,* estimated in keeping with the past year's experience. The motor carrier and the insurance company agree, for example, to a two percent rate on gross income ($2 per $100 gross) for deposit. The insurance company will further agree to accept a fixed percentage of that deposit for service—a general average being approximately 20 percent, or the cost of services being predetermined at $0.40. The balance, of $1.60, is reserved for losses which are paid from this reserve. A preagreed adjustment expense, generally ranging from 12 percent to 20 percent of the losses, is added to the losses for adjustment services.

This type of contract may be purchased with a minimum premium; generally, the lower the minimum, the higher the maximum. The maximum premium guarantees that the costs will not exceed that certain figure. These contracts are written for limits of $10,000, or a prearranged figure in that range. A separate excess policy is provided for which the motor carrier pays a standard fixed rate.

The primary contract or the retrospective portion of the contract is basically a service contract. The insurance company agrees to take care of the losses and to service the risk. At the end of the accounting year the premium charged equals the losses plus the service charge. In effect, the costs are geared directly to the insured losses. The primary consideration in the selection of such a contract is the ability of the motor carrier to comply with the possible penalty charges between the standard paid in deposit and the maximum premium provided under the policy.

Restrospective contracts are a desirable form of rating for the following types of risks:

1. Risks which are better than the average in their classification but which are not large enough to be entirely self-rated and thus which

do not get full credit for their good experience under the experience plan.

2. Risks which may have operated over a period of years under an experience-rating credit and which due to a change of ownership must revert to manual rates.

3. Risks which have been self-insured or which are contemplating self-insurance. Retrospective rating permits them to secure the benefits of self-insurance to a large degree but still maintain the advantages of being covered by an insurance carrier.

4. Risks which are relatively large and which want their insurance premium for compensation and liability lines handled as a single expense, and which feel that the available experience, rating plan does not give them sufficient recognition of their good experience, particularly on the general liability and automobile liability lines.

The retrospective method has been recommended particularly for risks which have instituted more effective loss-prevention programs and wish to secure immediate benefit from reduced losses which are expected to result from such a program. It is not considered feasible if the insurance premium is less than $25,000 per year, although there is a trend toward three-year plans in order to level off the insurance costs from year to year and to make retrospective contracts available to risks which would be too small on an annual basis to lend themselves to retrospective rating.

When a trucking company vehicle causes an accident, the injured person may sue and collect compensatory damages from the company, i.e., the retroaction of the injured person to a position he was in prior to the accident. Where the facts warrant it, a jury may award additional punitive damages for punishment because of special facts or conditions disclosing deliberate violation of law or gross carelessness or negligence. Although not all state courts have awarded punitive damages, federal courts have done so if the facts justified it.

Excess liability contracts are being increasingly used as catastrophe protection. This type of insurance provides coverages above a specified amount up to a specified limit. The use of this insurance is on the rise because single occurence losses can be very great.

### Cargo insurance

Interstate common carriers carry cargo insurance to compensate shippers or consignees for loss of or damage to property belonging to shippers or consignees. Cargo insurance is inland marine insurance, inasmuch as it is a carry-over of ocean marine insurance to inland transportation. There are two types of cargo insurance contracts. The "named peril" policy provides insurance against named perils of fire, collision or upset, wind or cyclone, floods, and others. This type of insurance covers the causes that result in the majority of claims but leaves the possibility of a claim for some cause not listed as a named peril. Even with the perils named the motor carrier should know just what protection it has. For example, the phrase "collision of the vehicle" is different from "collision of the load."

The other type of cargo coverage is termed an "all risk" policy. This provides much broader coverage in that the insurance company guarantees to pay any cargo claim for which the motor carrier is liable for any cause whatsoever except war risk or nuclear energy. This form should be written on a deductible basis.

Cargo insurance may be bought on a straight-rate basis or on a retrospective-rating plan, but is usually bought on a straight-rate basis with a deductible in amounts up to the ability of the truck operator to meet claim payments. A $500-deductible provision is quite common, although deductible provisions may be as much as $2,000. However, the premiums on such policies are not as low as might be expected, since the Interstate Commerce Commission requires that the insurance company have the potential responsibility for all loss, including the deductible amount, in the event the motor carrier fails to pay.

The amount of cargo insurance carried varies widely depending on the commodities transported. For most carriers limits of $500,000 should be considered the minimum.

Recently there have been single shipments moved which were to be used in missile and nuclear development valued at as much as $3 million. For excess coverage, insurance companies may form pools in which they participate in the underwriting in order to spread the risk.

The Commission has exempted in its insurance regulations a number of low-value commodities from the requirement that carriers maintain insurance or other security. Such items as ashes, cinders, coal, corn cobs, garbage, scrap iron, and others are included.[3] This exemption in no way relieves the carrier from liability to shippers for loss or damage that may result from the transportion of such commodities.

### Workman's compensation

Workman's Compensation coverage is required in all states. It is written to comply with the compensation statutes of the state where the motor carrier operates. In most states these rates are established by a rating bureau and are subject to modification based on the past three to five years' experience. Coverage may be purchased at bureau published rates without modification or may be purchased in a policy subject to retrospective rating, whereby the published rate is paid and the final premium is not determined until after the policy has expired and the losses have been determined. The premium is then adjusted to the amount of losses incurred for the year. This insurance may also be written subject to a participating dividend plan under which the insurance company pays a dividend based on its claim experience. Some insurance companies pay the same percentage dividend to all insured companies, while others vary the dividend according to the losses of the individual insured.

### Personal lines group insurance

Employee benefits have been expanded to include insurance on life, accidental death, weekly indemnity disability, accident and health, comprehensive major medical, long-term disability income, dental, vision, and hearing care. These are provided by the employer and are covered under group insurance plans.

### Additional coverages

*Fire, theft, and collision* insurance is usually referred to as physical damage insurance and is used to cover equipment. The coverage should be adequate to enable the carrier to replace lost equipment. It should also be adequate to cover the concentration of vehicles.

Bodily injury and property damage claims arise from operation of motor vehicles. However, a *comprehensive general liability* policy is needed which will cover all legal liability for claims brought as a result of personal injury or property damage arising out of other causes. Comprehensive general liability covers all contingencies, known and unknown, whereas under a plain liability policy only the known hazards are covered.

*Fire insurance policies* may be secured in standard form to cover terminals and other real estate. An appraisal of all properties should be made for this coverage. Fire insurance is frequently sold with a coinsurance clause which is an agreement on the part of the motor carrier to carry insurance up to a percentage of the valuation of property insured. The failure to do so makes the motor carrier a coinsurer.

*Burglary and theft insurance* may be secured. Whether or not a theft of company-owned property or cash in its possession is likely to occur in sufficient amount to cause any impairment of working capital is a factor to be considered. The "3-D" policy is a combination policy insuring the results of dishonesty, disappearance, and destruction. It insures against employee dishonesty inside and outside the premises and forgery losses, as well as destruction of property and other listed coverages.

*Fidelity bonds* may also be taken out. The cargo policy should be examined to determine whether or not infidelity of employees is excluded. If it is, and valuable merchandise is transported, it is important that drivers be included in the fidelity bond.

Another type of insurance is what is referred to in the insurance field as *"bobtail" insurance.* Since there are many truck-tractors owned by individual drivers, or owner-operators, provisions are made for coverage under the carrier policy when the unit is operated in commercial service for the carrier. The "bobtail" insurance provides coverage for the truck-tractor after it leaves the carrier's docks and for all nonrevenue driving until it returns to the docks. This covers such driving as going to the owner-operator's home and any other driving which is not for revenue.

*Bailee liability* is a form of property damage liability in which an insurance company agrees to pay, on behalf of an insured, losses legally chargeable to him occurring to equipment he is renting under leases from others. A broader coverage is straight material damage on leased equipment. Under this form of coverage, there is no necessity that there be any legal liability for the loss on the part of the operator. All that is required is that there be a written lease of the equipment and that it be damaged while it is in the operator's custody or control.

*Fiduciary insurance* is liability protection for an individual, or individuals, who is in an administrative or advisory capacity on employee pension plans. Under the Employee Retirement Income Security Act of 1974 (ERISA), pension fund trustees and other fiduciaries can be held personally liable for actions in the handling of these funds. Various types of fiduciary liability protection are available from insurance companies, and some form of bonding of welfare and pension fund administrators, trustees, and other fiduciaries is required under the act.

It has also become common for motor carriers to secure liability insurance for directors and officers to protect them against financial loss resulting from claims alleging executive malpractice.

**Cost of insurance**

The payment of insurance may be one of several different types. The *gross-receipts plan* has been widely used by many insurance companies. In the early days of trucking insurance, the carrier might have had to pay the premium on a policy for an entire year, although equipment might be idle for a considerable period of time, unless the carrier wanted to cancel the insurance. Under the gross-receipts basis, the insurance premium is based on gross receipts, so that if a trucker's equipment is idle for ten weeks, there is no insurance premium payable for that period of time. However, there is a minimum premium on policies written on a gross-receipt basis. This is usually 20 percent of the estimated annual policy premium. The premiums paid by carriers for their insurance vary considerably. As a result of the investigations of safety engineers, there is an established "fence" rate, which is predicated upon their findings. After the first year's operation of the assured, it may be that the safety record will be above or below the predictions of the safety engineers; the insurance rate will then be changed accordingly. On the gross-receipts basis, a common rate is four percent, although some carriers pay as low as one percent and others pay above six percent.

Another basis is the *specified-car basis* in which an individual premium is charged for each truck or semitrailer which is insured. The *retrospective-rating plan* explained earlier constitutes a third basis.

In order to control insurance costs, a motor carrier should secure a statement two or three times a year from its insurance company itemizing each of the losses in the major insurance categories. On the basis of this information it is possible to determine before the insurance year has expired whether or not losses are increasing or decreasing from the amount on which the policy rate is predicated. An increase would mean that the operations department should be alerted to change the trend.

Some insurance companies furnish their policyholders with special registers in which to record essential information on each accident or loss or damage claim. These registers will provide the carrier with additional information beyond that secured from an insurance company loss statement and can be effectively used in insurance cost control.

The Interstate Commerce Act, under Section 215, permits a motor carrier to qualify as a self-insurer. In order to qualify, however, the motor carrier must establish to the satisfaction of the Commission its ability to pay final judgment recovered against it for bodily injuries to or death of any person resulting from the negligent operation, maintenance, or use of motor vehicles in transportation service subject to Subchapter II of the act; and for loss of or damage to property of others, which includes cargo, coming into the possession of the motor carrier. It must be able, in the judgment of the Commission, to do this without affecting the stability or permanence of its business as a motor carrier in interstate or foreign commerce. The Interstate Commerce Commission for a number of years required that motor carriers which wanted to self-insure must be qualified to self-insure completely. Since 1950, however, the Commission has permitted motor carriers to self-insure partially and be covered by insurance from insurance companies for the remainder. Currently, about 35 carriers are partially or completely self-insured. The primary reason why motor carriers turn to self-insurance is that they expect it to be less costly.

If, in the opinion of the Commission, the carrier has demonstrated sound management and has the financial resources to cover its liability obligations, it may be permitted to operate as a self-insurer. The Commission decides each request upon the merits of the case.

Those motor carriers, except those owned by railroads, which have been authorized to self-insure are required by the Commission to file a claims report every six months and a quarterly financial report.

Generally, unless a motor carrier has a premium expenditure of at least $150,000 a year, it is not feasible to self-insure. If a carrier's losses are $100,000 a year, normally the premium would be approximately $150,000, since $100,000 must be used to pay the pure losses, and an additional $50,000 to compensate the insurance company for the cost of administration and reinsurance, plus a profit. It is the experience of the insurance industry that the relationship between premium and losses is $3 of premium for every $2 of losses.

In this illustration, approximately $50,000 above losses would be available under a self-insurance program to provide reinsurance and a claims and safety service. Considering an average public liability and property damage insurance rate of $2 per $100 revenue and an average insurance rate of $2 per $100 revenue for full coverage cargo insurance, it has been concluded that a motor carrier would require an annual minimum revenue between $4,000,000 and $5,000,000 to provide an adequate premium spread to maintain self-insurance.

Self-insurance is generally considered as applicable to fleets that are in a position to handle their losses up to at least the first $10,000. Before selecting such a plan, however, consideration should be given to the ability to service and supervise losses; the availability of proper supervisory service to direct that work; and the application of handling losses as it applies to the furtherance of the safety program. Self-insurance may be used in connection with adequate excess insurance, carrying from the amount of losses the motor carrier can handle, on up to the limits necessary to protect properly the financial security of the company.

The fact that the premiums on insurance will vary depending upon the safety record of a motor carrier in itself provides justification for safety programs and any other measures which would insure a better carrier record, since this improved record would be reflected in carrier savings.

### QUESTIONS AND PROBLEMS

1. Point out the significance of adequate insurance coverage in motor carrier operations.

2. List the items that insurance safety engineers will check in investigating a motor carrier which is seeking fleet coverage.

3. How is public liability and property damage insurance rated?

4. Why has the Interstate Commerce Commission required minimum insurance requirements for motor carriers?

5. Explain the deductible provisions found in cargo insurance.

6. What are the advantages of a premium based on gross receipts?

7. "The Interstate Commerce Commission has for a number of years required that motor carriers which wanted to self-insure must be qualified to self-insure completely." Why?

8. What conditions have been imposed on a common carrier of general commodities which has been approved by the Interstate Commerce Commission to self-insure partially?

9. Ascertain and report on the trends at the present time in self-insurance, both complete and partial.

10. What is a retrospective contract? Is it used with all types of insurance?

11. Define named peril; bill of lading policy; mutual companies; and specified-car basis.

12. What are punitive damages? How can a trucking company prepare itself for such contingencies?

## FOOTNOTES TO CHAPTER 13

[1] This list entitled "Companies Holding Certificates of Authority from the Secretary of the Treasury under the Act of Congress Approved July 30, 1947 (6 USC Sections 6–13) as Acceptable Sureties on Federal Bonds (a)."

[2] Additional insurance companies have been formed by motor carriers. One large Class I carrier organized an insurance company as a wholly-owned subsidiary to cover its own operation, as well as to insure other motor carriers.

[3] 22 MCC 350 (1940).

# chapter 14

# Motor Freight Classification

When the Motor Carrier Act was passed in 1935, which established federal regulation of interstate motor carriers, one of its provisions required motor carriers to establish, observe, and enforce just and reasonable rates, charges, and classifications, and just and reasonable regulations and practices relating thereto. The classification serves to prevent unjust discrimination among persons, places, and descriptions of traffic.

### Development of motor classification

In November, 1935, a committee of 100 motor carrier tariff men and transportation experts was appointed to formulate a motor carrier classification. The original issue of the National Motor Freight Classification was filed with the Interstate Commerce Commission in March, 1936, and consisted of two volumes, one containing LTL ratings and the other volume ratings. Upon reissuance, the LTL and volume ratings were combined into one volume, which procedure has been followed since that time.

The freight classification is an index or a list of thousands of articles which shows how those commodities are grouped or classified for the purpose of applying rates or charges. It does not fix the rates in dollars and cents to be charged for transporting the articles. It merely states in which class or rating each commodity belongs. The rates or charges in dollars and cents for transporting the commodities are established by each motor carrier and published in tariffs. The freight classification arranges into groups articles with similar transportation characteristics; and to each group is affixed a number or letter, which is called the "rating." Thus, a hundred articles may be grouped, based on their transportation characteristics, into but five groups.

Because of this grouping, rates can be applied to these five groups, whereas in the absence of such classification, there would have to be separate rates on each of the articles. The classification then provides a means of establishing a relationship between articles which are grouped. Each number which is assigned to each class bears a definite percentage relationship to the other numbers. The Class 100 rating is equal to

100 percent; Class 85 is equal to 85 percent of Class 100; and so on down to Class 35. Above Class 100 are multiples, such as Class 125, which is 125 percent of Class 100, and so on up to Class 500 or five times Class 100. Currently, there are 23 ratings. These range from Class 500 to Class 35, and are Classes 500, 400, 350, 300, 250, 200, 175, 150, 125, 110, 100, 92½, 85, 77½, 70, 65, 60, 55, 50, 45, 40, 37½, and 35. Class 500 applies to ping pong balls and a few other items. The average density of the Class 500 items is one-half pound per cubic foot. After the rating is found, reference must be made to a tariff, which will give the class rate for the article.

There are many articles which are specifically described in the classification, and through the use of "NOI," which means "not more specifically described," the description is broadened so that virtually everything is classified. New articles are manufactured and introduced to the public continually. These commodities are not always properly indexed and listed in the classification, inasmuch as there has been no actual handling of these commodities before that time. The classification contains a rule-making provision for the classification of commodities not specifically indexed called the "rule of analogy." A specific description and rating in the classification for the new item is made by the classification committee in the event it is determined that the current descriptions do not apply.

## National Motor Freight Classification

The National Motor Freight Classification, in general, followed the older rail classification, partly because of the fact that when the Motor Carrier Act was passed—requiring, among other things, that tariffs be filed with the Interstate Commerce Commission—the task of formulating completely new classifications was so formidable that motor carriers simply followed the rail classification. As a result, originally almost all of the entries in the National Motor Freight Classification had descriptions that were the same as those in the railroad classification. Even at the present time it is estimated that over 60 percent is identical, due to the competition between rail and motor carriers.

The contents of the National Motor Freight Classification are as follows:

1. List of commissions with which the classification is filed.
2. Table of contents.
3. Participating carriers.
4. Index to articles.

5. Index to generic headings.
6. Index to rules.
7. Rules.
8. Prescribed forms for bills of lading.
9. Classification of articles.
10. Specifications for numbered packages.
11. Principles for investigation of freight claims.
12. Explanation of abbreviations and reference marks.

Figure 14-1 is a sample page from the National Motor Freight Classification. A brief summary of the sample page follows: The item number on the left side serves to identify the article. The page number on which the article is described is not listed in the index to articles, but the item is numbered so that it is necessary to use the item number in looking up the article. Item 172200 is Rustic Work Articles, NOI; which means that it is not more specifically described in the classification. If the shipment is other than flat or knocked down flat, the rating for less truckload is 200 and truckload 100. If it is flat or knocked down (KD), the rating is substantially less—for less truckload 85 and truckload 55. The right-hand column shows MW, which means minimum weight and is the division between what constitutes a truckload and less truckload. In the case of our first Item 172200, it is 10, which under Rule 997 of the classification shows the minimum for a truckload to be 10,000 pounds. In Subs 1 and 2, the minimum for the truckload, using Rule 997, would be 24,000 pounds. In other words, the classification ratings for Subs 1 and 2 are substantially less.

The bulk of the classification in terms of pages consists of a list of participating carriers, index to articles, classification of articles, and packaging. The articles which are classified are listed alphabetically under the noun. If this is not sufficiently descriptive, adjectives are used as well. When any part of the description of an article is indented from the left margin in a position subordinate to the text preceding it, the description must be read within its context especially under the preceding heading. For example, Item 172240, Safes or Safe or Vault Parts, Fire or Burglar Proof, controls Items 172260 through 172340.

There are approximately 200 generic headings contained in the classification similar to the one just cited, some of which have but two or three entries, but the majority are quite lengthy, an example of which is the heading "Machinery and Machines or Parts Named" which covers about 25 pages.

The classification also contains different types of motor carrier bills of lading. Since the classification has the widest distribution of any motor carrier tariff, it is felt that this accomplishes greater uniformity in the bill of lading used by motor carriers, since the exact form of the bill of lading for motor carriers has never been prescribed by the Interstate Commerce Commission.

As indicated earlier, the National Motor Freight Classification originally contained practically identical entries to the railroad's classification. Motor carriers soon found that certain of the items contained in the rail classification, particularly those which were light and bulky, could not be moved on a compensatory basis at the existing rating in the classification. Many of the light and bulky articles were docketed for a change in their classification, so that there are fewer identical entries between the rail and motor classifications than was originally the case.

With the establishment of the railroad's Uniform Freight Classification No. 1 (as a result of the Interstate Commerce Commission's action in *Dockets 28300* and *28310* covering rail classification and class rates, which rail classification became effective May 30, 1952), the National Motor Freight Classification No. A—1 was published and became effective on July 10, 1952. Although the Commission issued an order in *Docket MC—C—150* placing motor carriers on notice to effect uniformity of the National Motor Freight Classification, it did not issue a final order in this *Docket*. The National Motor Freight Classification No. A—1 (later changed to NMF 100 series with 100F currently effective) was published to be more competitive with its rail counterpart, the new Uniform Freight Classification with the exception of certain light and bulky articles. There are a little more than 14,000 truckload ratings. About two thirds of truckload ratings in NMF 100F are Class 55 and below. The total number of LTL ratings is a little over 11,000. Because of the nature of the service rendered, as well as packing containers and other matters, three fourths of the LTL ratings are Class 70 and above. NMF 100F contains over 11,000 items, of which over 1,700 are notes or Special Packages, and 10,000 are commodity descriptions.

A classification is applicable only when tariffs make specific reference to it. Since National Motor Freight Classification 100F is competitive with the railroads' Uniform Freight Classification, the motor carriers adopt the motor classification that will insure continuing competition. Generally, NMF 100F is used in most of the major motor rate territories. Currently, there are 4,822 motor carriers participating in the

| Item | ARTICLES | LTL | TL | MW |
|---|---|---|---|---|
| | **RUBBER MATERIALS GROUP:** subject to item 171600 | | | |
| 171860 | **Rubber,** scrap, hard rubber, pulverized, in bags | 50 | 35 | 36.2 |
| 171880 | **Rubber,** scrap, NOI, see Note, item 171884; in packages; also TL, loose | 50 | 35 | 30.2 |
| 171882 | NOTE—Tires, LTL, need not be in packages. | | | |
| 171884 | NOTE—Applies only on: Scraps, pieces or trimmings of rubber impregnated cloth; reclaimers' tailings or residue; old worn-out rubber boots, shoes, belting, clothing, rolls or rollers, hose mats, matting or packing; tires, with or without steel rims, see Note, item 171882; or similar worn-out articles; having value only for reclamation of raw materials. Such articles must be described on bills of lading and shipping order at time of shipment as "Scrap Rubber" | | | |
| 171980 | **Shavings or Turnings,** hard rubber, in packages | 85 | 55 | 30.2 |
| 171990 | **Sheet, Slab or Block,** sponge rubber, in boxes or crates, or in bales or rolls wrapped in burlap or waterproofed paper | 77½ | 45 | 30.2 |
| 172010 | **Straps, Strapping or Webbing,** upholstering, rubber or rubber and cord fabric with or without metal end clips, in boxes | 77½ | 45 | 30.2 |
| 172160 | **Rubber Preservative,** NOI, in barrels, boxes or Packages 823, 1112 or 1118 | 70 | 37½ | 36.2 |
| 172180 | **Rum,** denatured. See item 60000 for classes dependent upon agreed or released value: | | | |
| Sub 1 | In containers in barrels or boxes | 85 | 37½ | 30.2 |
| Sub 2 | In bulk in barrels | 70 | 37½ | 30.2 |
| 172200 | **Rustic Work Articles,** NOI, wood, with or without bark removed: | | | |
| Sub 1 | Other than KD flat | 200 | 100 | 10.2 |
| Sub 2 | KD flat | 85 | 55 | 24.2 |
| 172220 | **Saddles,** turkey body protective, canvas, in boxes | 85 | 55 | 24.2 |
| 172240 | **SAFES OR SAFE OR VAULT PARTS, FIRE OR BURGLAR PROOF:** | | | |
| 1/2260 | **Safes,** with hollow walls or with solid walls less than 1 inch thick, wrapped, see Note, item 172282, or in boxes or crates | 85 | 55 | 24.2 |
| 172280 | **Safes,** with solid walls 1 inch or more in thickness, in boxes or crates or wrapped, see Note, item 172282 | 70 | 45 | 30.2 |
| 172282 | NOTE—Safes must be wrapped with solid fibreboard or double-faced corrugated fibreboard, securely fastened with steel bands, or with burlap. | | | |
| 172300 | **Safe or Vault Doors or Vault Fronts,** wrapped in burlap, or in boxes or crates | 70 | 45 | 30.2 |
| 172320 | **Safe Deposit Boxes or Cases,** in boxes or crates, or loose, finished surfaces protected by crating | 70 | 45 | 30.2 |
| 172340 | **Vault Linings,** steel | 65 | 37½ | 36.2 |

| Item | Article | | | AQ |
|---|---|---|---|---|
| 172360 | Salesmen's Samples, other than boots, shoes, hats, caps, china or porcelainware, NOI, or earthenware or stoneware, NOI, in salesmen's sample trunks, locked, or in trunks in crates, or in salesmen's hand sample cases in boxes or crates: | 125 | 125 | |
| Sub 1 | When contents consist of articles which in boxes are classed class 110 or lower, the same as if in wooden boxes. | | | |
| Sub 2 | When contents consist of articles which in boxes are classed higher than class 110, class the same as if in wooden boxes. | 50 | 35 | 30.2 |
| 172370 | Sand, foundry core or foundry shell, containing not over 5 percent phenolic resin, in five-ply paper bags or in drums | 125 | 70 | 24.2 |
| 172400 | Sash, glazed or not glazed, or Sash and Frames combined, or Windows, airplane, boat, motor bus or railway car, in boxes or crates | 100 | 55 | 30.2 |
| 172420 | Sash Parts or Window Frame Parts, airplane, motor boat, motor bus or railway car, in boxes or crates | 70 | 45 | 24.2 |
| 172440 | Sausage or Food Product Casings, cellulose or plastic film, in boxes or in Package 121 | 85 | 50 | 24.2 |
| 172450 | Sausage or Food Product Casings, collagen, in boxes | 100 | 37½ | 30.2 |
| 172460 | Sausage Casings, dried, NOI, in barrels or boxes | 65 | 37½ | 30.2 |
| 172480 | Sausage Casings, frozen, pickled or salted, in barrels, boxes, kits, pails or tubs, or in metal cans in crates | 70 | 40 | 30.2 |
| 172490 | Saw Blade Stock, bandsaw, coiled ends not welded, in boxes | 85 | 55 | 30.2 |
| 172520 | Saw Blades, Saw Teeth or Saw Chain, viz.: | | | |
| Sub 1 | Blades, bandsaw, ends welded together, in boxes | 77½ | 50 | 30.2 |
| Sub 2 | Blades, circular saw or saw NOI, in boxes or crates, or wrapped in fibreboard, or on boards | 77½ | 50 | 20.2 |
| Sub 3 | Saw Chain, (chain with cutting teeth), or Saw Teeth, in boxes | 200 | 70 | 36.2 |
| 172524 | Scenery, theatrical, see Note, item 172526, or Theatrical Properties other than costumes or live animals, in packages | | | |
| 172526 | NOTE—Applies on borders, curtains, drops, flats or set pieces. | | | |
| 172530 | Screenings, flaxseed, in bags or barrels | 65 | 37½ | 36.2 |
| 172540 | Screens, textile printing, surfaces protected with fibreboard, in packages | 400 | 300 | 10.2 |
| 172560 | Screens, textile printing, surfaces protected with not less than ¼ inch wooden boards, spaces between boards not over ¼ inch, in packages | 250 | 150 | 18.2 |
| 172570 | Scrubbers, NOI, fume or gas, condensing, cyclonic or venturi type, plastic, with or without fittings or attachments, in boxes or crates | 200 | 125 | 10.2 |
| 172580 | Sculpture or Statuary, NOI, cement, concrete or iron, in barrels, boxes or crates | 125 | 85 | 12.2 |
| 172600 | Sculpture or Statuary, NOI, metal, NOI, plaster, stone or terra cotta, in barrels or boxes | 150 | 85 | 12.2 |
| 172640 | Seals, NOI, other than packing devices, forms or shapes, see Note, item 172642, in barrels or boxes | 70 | 55 | 36.2 |
| 172642 | NOTE—Applies on seals which are designed to prevent or to indicate tampering with or theft from containers or equipment on which they were designated to be used. | | | |

Fig. 14-1. Specimen page from National Motor Freight Classification 100F. Courtesy: National Classification Board.

classification. Generally speaking, these are general commodity common carriers.

### Classification rules

The National Motor Freight Classification contains 72 rules. Rules are added or dropped from time to time. Some of these rules are almost identical to the railroad classification rules covering the same subjects, whereas others are considerably different from the rail rules.

Classification rules and regulations have great significance, and the principles contained therein must be learned by the user of the classification. A knowledge of these rules enables the user to look up the ratings for individual commodities without referring each time to all of the 72 rules. Certain rules are often referred to in other tariffs as having application on shipments subject to that tariff. Thus, in many instances, classification rules and regulations may apply even on articles which are not subject to the classification and class rates.

A careful reading of the rules shows that the phrase "unless otherwise provided" appears in many rules. This indicates that there may be, and in many instances there are, exceptions to these rules. It is possible for so many exceptions to be made to a rule that it has very little effect.

The rules cover many matters, including acceptance of goods, marking shipments, definitions of shipments, loading or unloading heavy or bulky articles, and articles subject to the bill-of-lading conditions. There are 25 rules which describe general packaging requirements and specifications for them. In addition there are about 825 separate numbered packages which provide minimum packaging requirements for a wide range of commodities.

A number of classification rules are discussed in other chapters. The operation of Rule 997 is described here in order to illustrate the manner in which a rule is used.

The minimum weights relative to cubic capacity for a truck or trailer are provided in Rule 997. In the motor classification, commodities under the column titled MW, as shown in Figure 14-1, are subject to a minimum weight of 1000 times the figure in the column. The minimum weights apply per vehicle of not less than 30 feet in length.

### New England area classification

Another motor classification is used by motor carriers in addition to the National Motor Freight Classification. In the New England area, there is

the Coordinated Motor Freight Classification. The ratings in this classification, which are used in conjunction with class rates, have been established to produce about the same revenue per truckload on all commodities
transported. There are no truckload or minimum weights shown. Density
or weight per cubic foot of the commodity is the primary determinant of the
classification, with value a secondary factor. For example, the ratings and
the shipping weights per cubic foot are as follows:

| Rating | Shipping Weight per Cubic Foot (Pounds) |
|---|---|
| Class 1 . . . . . . . . . . . . . | 3—5 |
| Class 2 . . . . . . . . . . . . . | 5—10 |
| Class 3 . . . . . . . . . . . . | 10—15 |
| Class 4 . . . . . . . . . . . . | 15—20 |
| Class 5 . . . . . . . . . . . | 20 and over |

Coordinated Motor Freight Classification No. NEB 100C contains nine
classes:

Class
1
2
3
4
5
1½t1—150 percent of Class 1
2t1—200 percent of Class 1
2½t1—250 percent of Class 1
3t1—300 percent of Class 1

In this classification, there are four multiples of Class 1 that are
applicable on those articles having a density of less than three pounds
per cubic foot. These are: 1½ times 1; 2 times 1; 2½ times 1; and 3
times 1. There is no definite line drawn between these, but when
density is this low, the Classification Committee decides each item on
its own merits. Although density is the primary factor in the
construction of this classification, those articles which have unfavorable
transportation characteristics, such as a tendency to impregnate other
commodities with which they are loaded, or the degree of fragility is
such that other commodities cannot be loaded on them, or a
susceptibility to theft which would require extra precaution to avoid
loss, may be rated higher than the element of shipping density alone
would warrant. Figure 14-2 shows the ratings and description of articles

in a manner somewhat different from that used in the National Motor Freight Classification. In comparison with the National Motor Freight Classification, the New England Classification contains fewer variations in ratings which are dependent upon the way in which a particular commodity is packed for shipment.

| ITEM & S NOS. | RAT- INGS | ARTICLES |
|---|---|---|
| | | ABRASIVES: |
| 10 | 5 | Abrasive Cloth or Paper, including Emery or Sand Paper, in packages |
| 20 | 2 | Abrasive Material, consisting of synthetic fibre mesh and silicon carbide, in boxes |
| 30 | | Alundum, Corundum, Emery or other Natural or Synthetic Abrasive Material consisting chiefly of aluminum oxide or silicon carbide; |
| 40 | 5 | Crude or Lump, in packages |
| 50 | 5 | Flour or Grain, in packages |
| 60 | 5 | Refuse, including broken wheels, wheel stubs or wheel grindings, in packages |
| 70 | 5 | Wheels, other than pulp grinding |
| 80 | 5 | Wheels, pulp grinding, in packages |
| | | |
| | | ACIDS (See Rules 20 and 40): |
| 90 | 5 | Abietic, in barrels |
| 100 | | Acetic, glacial or liquid; |
| S1 | 3 | In carboys |
| S2 | 4 | In glass in barrels or boxes |
| S3 | 5 | In bulk in barrels |
| S4 | 3 | In tank trucks (See Rule 160) |
| 110 | | NOIBN, Dry: |
| S1 | 4 | In glass in barrels or boxes |
| S2 | 4 | In cans or cartons in barrels or boxes |
| S3 | 5 | In bulk in bags, barrels or boxes |
| 120 | | NOIBN, Liquid: |
| S1 | 2 | In glass bottles, each packed in rattan or willow baskets or hampers |
| S2 | 5 | In carboys not exceeding seven (7) gallons (See Note) |
| S3 | 3 | In carboys exceeding seven (7) gallons, completely boxed or necks projecting |
| S4 | 4 | In glass in barrels or boxes |
| S5 | 5 | In bulk in barrels |
| | | NOTE – Carboys completely encased; necks must not project. |
| 130 | 5 | Arsenic, fused, in barrels or boxes, or in bars wrapped in paraffined paper in wooden boxes only |
| 140 | | Arsenic, other than fused: |
| S1 | 3 | In carboys |
| S2 | 5 | In barrels |
| S3 | ? | In tank trucks (See Rule 160) |
| 150 | 5 | Azelaic, from animal or vegetable fats, in bags, barrels, or boxes |
| 160 | | Boric (Boracic): |
| S1 | 4 | In glass in barrels or boxes |
| S2 | 5 | In cans or cartons in barrels or boxes, or in bulk in bags, barrels, boxes or steel pails |

Fig. 14-2. Ratings and description of articles in Coordinated Motor Freight Classification No. NEB 100C. Courtesy: Coordinated Freight Classification.

After the passage of the Motor Carrier Act in 1935, New England area motor carriers used the National Motor Freight Classification for a time. However, they soon developed the Coordinated and Official Classifications; and the Official was absorbed by the Coordinated on January 1, 1955. The development of their own classifications was partly the result of a cost study and also because there was not the degree of rail competition faced by motor carriers in this area as compared with motor carriers located in other areas in the United States. Therefore, it was felt that there could be a departure from the classification procedure which had largely dictated the formulation of the National Motor Freight Classification, namely competition. The Commission authorized the New England area carriers to use these two classifications. The Coordinated Classification is used largely in conjunction with interstate class rates in New England, but outside of New England, and generally between points in New England and points in other rate territories, the class rates of motor common carriers are based on the ratings found in the National Motor Freight Classification.

The current Coordinated Motor Freight Classification contains rules numbered 10, 20, 30, etc., through 360.

## Rail classifications

In addition to the motor-carrier classifications, there are a number of motor-carrier participants in the railroads' Uniform Freight Classification. Some state regulatory commissions have required motor carriers to use the rail classification for intrastate shipments.

## Factors influencing classification of articles

The characteristics of the commodities which must receive consideration in fixing classification ratings are generally as follows:[1]

1. Shipping weight per cubic foot.
2. Liability to damage.
3. Liability to damage other commodities with which it is transported.
4. Perishability.
5. Liability to spontaneous combustion or explosion.
6. Susceptibility to theft.
7. Value per pound in comparison with other articles.
8. Ease or difficulty in loading or unloading.
9. Stowability.
10. Excessive weight.
11. Excessive length.
12. Care or attention necessary in loading and transporting.
13. Trade conditions.
14. Value of service.

15. Competition with other commodities transported.
16. Quantity offered as a single consignment.

The order in which the foregoing classification elements have been listed is not necessarily the order of their importance. It is necessary to weigh the importance of each factor from a classification standpoint, and this importance varies with each commodity or group of commodities with similar transportation characteristics.

Of course, some elements are given greater weight for particular commodities than is true of others. Often in classifying articles it must be determined if the correct description is applied. For example, the National Classification Board was asked to classify a product being placed on the market which was a dog shampoo. Is it a shampoo, an insecticide, a soap, or a toilet preparation? In this case, it was classified as a liquid soap.

Another item, throwing discs (commonly called frisbees), were reclassified to a higher classification based on density as the dominant characteristic of frisbees. They had been classified in the "Games and Toys" group and were reclassified as "Athletic Goods." The density of frisbees is between 5 and 6 pounds per cubic foot.

In a proceeding involving a number of light and bulky commodities, the Commission prescribed a table of ratings related to density which was to be used as a guide where density was considered to be the predominant element involved.[2] The Commission indicated that all commodities could not be rated solely on the basis of density and that its scale of ratings should not be construed as an inflexible guide in assigning reasonable classification ratings to all light and bulky articles. However, it ruled that in fixing ratings on articles moving by motor carrier the density of the articles must be accorded more consideration than has heretofore been the case and that other characteristics must also be given appropriate consideration.

Figure 14-3 illustrates the application of certain classification factors to two commodities and shows the truckload and less-truckload ratings for the items.

With greater emphasis on the simplification of documentation and paper work, coupled with analysis and data processing in transportation, use is being made of the Standard Transportation Commodity Classification. This is similar to the Standard Industrial Code. It may be that future classifications and tariffs will utilize the STCC.

In *Ex Parte No. MC-98, Sub 2, Released Rates in Conjunction With a Small Shipments Tariff,* the Commission in 1978 instituted a proceeding to determine how the classification could be made more effective or possibly dropped. In the hearings, general support for the classification was expressed but there were criticisms from shippers on what they viewed as inequitable applications of density as a factor in classification as well as the need to update actual value ratings to reflect current values.

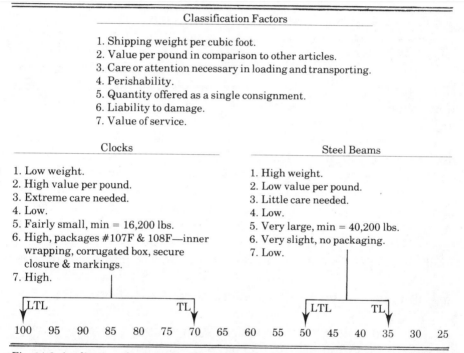

Classification Factors

1. Shipping weight per cubic foot.
2. Value per pound in comparison to other articles.
3. Care or attention necessary in loading and transporting.
4. Perishability.
5. Quantity offered as a single consignment.
6. Liability to damage.
7. Value of service.

| Clocks | Steel Beams |
|---|---|
| 1. Low weight. | 1. High weight. |
| 2. High value per pound. | 2. Low value per pound. |
| 3. Extreme care needed. | 3. Little care needed. |
| 4. Low. | 4. Low. |
| 5. Fairly small, min = 16,200 lbs. | 5. Very large, min = 40,200 lbs. |
| 6. High, packages #107F & 108F—inner wrapping, corrugated box, secure closure & markings. | 6. Very slight, no packaging. |
| 7. High. | 7. Low. |

Fig. 14-3. Application of certain classification factors to two commodities, showing the truckload and less-truckload ratings for the items.

## National Classification Board

The task of classifying commodities and other matters relating to the contents of the classification are performed for motor carriers by the National Classification Board. This Board is composed of not less than three and not more than seven full-time members, one of whom serves as chairman. It considers proposals for changes in descriptions of articles, minimum weights, packing requirements, ratings, and rules or regulations in the National Motor Freight Classification. Figure 14-4 is an application form for a change in classification. The Board holds public hearings, recommends the disposition of proposals, and instructs the publishing agent of the National Motor Freight Classification regarding resulting changes in the classification. In a recent year, which is typical, the Board issued six regularly scheduled dockets as well as "special" dockets as the need arose. The number of subjects on these dockets ranged from 41 to 116. Fifty percent of the proposals were filed by shippers, ten percent by carriers, and 40 percent by the Board.

Hearings on proposed changes that appear on the dockets are held in the Board's offices in Washington, D.C., by appointment. Hearings on each docket range from two to four days and include appearances and/or written statements from interested parties. After public hearings, a majority vote of those designated members governs the action of the Board. If the Board reports on proposal as adopted, and there are no objections within 30 days after date of notice of disposition, the Board instructs the publishing agent to publish it. The Board may deviate from the terms of a proposal but may not unduly broaden the issues defined in the published docket.

The Board may reopen or reconsider any docket subject upon which a disposition notice has been issued within six months following the date of the initial notice, providing reconsideration shall not be granted after the effective date of publication in the classification. When the Board reaches its final conclusions, a revised disposition notice subject to all of the procedural rules applicable to initial disposition shall be issued. The Board cannot reopen any docket subject which was previously appealed and acted upon by the National Classification Committee.

The appeals procedure provides that if the Board receives written objections with stated reasons within 30 days after its date of notice of disposition of a proposal from 15 participating carriers in the classification or from eight members of the National Classification Committee, the decision of the Board is automatically appealed to the Committee through its secretary. If the Board reports a proposal as having failed of adoption, the proponent may appeal the decision of the Committee within 30 days after date of notice of disposition by the Board by written notification to the secretary of the National Classification Committee, setting forth the basis for the appeal. The Board may permit additional time for filing appeals by proponents, but not more than 30 days.

The hearings which are held on appeals are made before the National Classification Committee. A majority of the Committee present decides whether an appealed proposal shall be approved, dismissed, or resub-

## National Classification Board
### of the Motor Carrier Industry

| 1616 P STREET, N.W. | WASHINGTON, D. C. 20036 | 202-797-5308 |
|---|---|---|

### PROPOSAL FOR CHANGE IN THE NATIONAL MOTOR FREIGHT CLASSIFICATION

DATE: _____

**ONE COPY** OF PROPOSAL AND SUPPORTING EXHIBITS OR STATEMENTS **MUST** BE SIGNED AND SUBMITTED BY THE PROPONENT. ALL QUESTIONS MUST BE ANSWERED AS COMPLETELY AS POSSIBLE. WHEN ACTUAL DATA IS NOT AVAILABLE BECAUSE PRODUCT IS NEW, PLEASE ESTIMATE. FAILURE TO COMPLETE THE PROPOSAL FORM MAY RESULT IN DELAY, AS THE PROPOSAL WILL NOT BE PROCESSED FOR DOCKETING UNTIL PERTINENT INFORMATION IN THIS FORM HAS BEEN FURNISHED. ALL INFORMATION WILL BE TREATED IN A CONFIDENTIAL MANNER, UNLESS OTHERWISE AUTHORIZED UNDER 2 (a) and (b).

**PLEASE TYPE OR PRINT CLEARLY**

1) PROPONENT'S COMPANY NAME _____

   STREET ADDRESS _____

   CITY _____ STATE _____ ZIP _____

   INDIVIDUALS' NAME _____ TITLE _____

   SIGNATURE _____ TELEPHONE NO. _____

2) PROPONENT IS REQUIRED TO ANSWER THE FOLLOWING QUESTIONS:

   (a) May your name be quoted as the proponent of the proposal? Yes _____ No _____

   (b) May the information contained in this proposal be released to the following interested parties? Carriers _____ Shippers _____ Others _____

   (c) What supporting data is attached? Photos _____ Blueprints _____ Catalogs _____ Samples _____ Advertising _____ Labels _____
       Empty Retail Sales Containers _____

3) Description of Article(s): _____

   _____

4) Trade nomenclature or registered trade name: _____

   _____

5) Sales invoice nomenclature: _____

   _____

6) PRESENT CLASSIFICATION: (Show specific NMFC item number and description under which commodity is now being classified)

| ITEM NO. | DESCRIPTION | CLASSES | | MINIMUM WT. FACTOR |
|---|---|---|---|---|
| | | LTL | TL | |
| | | | | |
| | | | | |
| | | | | |
| | | | | |
| | | | | |
| | | | | |

Fig. 14-4. Application form for change in classification.

PROPOSED CLASSIFICATION: (Show description, classes and minimum wt. factor exactly as you propose them to be established in the Classification. IF a packaging proposal amend item accordingly)

| ITEM NO. | DESCRIPTION | CLASSES | | MINIMUM WT. FACTOR |
|---|---|---|---|---|
| | | LTL | TL | |
| | | | | |

7) SHIPPING CHARACTERISTICS AND VALUE:

| TYPE OF PACKAGE USED (1) | MODEL OR STYLE NO. | NO. OF ARTICLES PER PACKAGE | OUTSIDE DIMENSIONS OF SHIPPING PACKAGE (2) | | | WEIGHT AS PACKED FOR SHIPMENT (POUNDS) | | WHOLESALE (CLAIM) VALUE PER PACKAGE |
|---|---|---|---|---|---|---|---|---|
| | | | Length | Width | Height | Per Package | Per Cu. Ft.(3) | |
| | | | | | | | | |
| | | | | | | | | |
| | | | | | | | | |
| | | | | | | | | |
| | | | | | | | | |
| | | | | | | | | |

(1) Wooden or Fibreboard Box; Crate; Drum (and capacity in gallons); Wrapped or Non-wrapped Bundle; or Roll (paper, plastic or cloth wrapped); Paper, Plastic or Cloth Bag; or Other Type of Package.

(2) If package is curved or irregular shape use extreme outside measurements.

(3) To ascertain the "weight per cubic foot" multiply the three dimensions of the article as packed for shipment and where the result is in cubic inches, divide by 1728 to reduce to cubic feet, then divide the weight by the number of cubic feet thus ascertained. To obtain the cubic feet of space occupied by a drum, pail, etc., square the greatest diameter and multiply by the height.

8) COMMODITY CHARACTERISTICS:

   (a) What are materials from which commodity is made, by percentage of volume and weight? _____

_____

   (b) Is commodity subject to U.S. Department of Transportation Regulations Governing Explosives and Other Dangerous Articles? Yes _____ No _____

   If yes, What commodity description and label are required? _____

_____

   (c) Is commodity Liquid _____, Paste _____, Dry _____, when shipped?

   (d) Does commodity require Heat _____ Refrigeration _____ Temperature Control _____ while being transported?

   (e) If commodity is wooden, is it "in the rough" _____, "in the white" _____, or "finished" _____?

     "IN THE ROUGH" REFERS TO WOODEN ARTICLES THAT ARE NOT FURTHER MANUFACTURED THAN SAWED, HEWN, PLANED OR BENT.

     "IN THE WHITE" REFERS TO WOODEN ARTICLES THAT ARE FURTHER MANUFACTURED THAN "IN THE ROUGH", BUT INCLUDING NOT MORE THAN ONE COAT OF PRIMER.

     "FINISHED" REFERS TO WOODEN ARTICLES AFTER THEY HAVE PASSED THE STATE OF "IN THE WHITE".

Fig. 14-4. *Continued.*

(f) If commodity is not wooden and is considered to be unfinished, what processes have been performed and what processes remain to be performed before consumption or use? _____

_____

_____

_____

## 9) FORM OF SHIPMENT:

(a) Is commodity SU_____ , SU in sections _____ ,
"SU" (Set Up) refers to articles in their assembled condition, or disassembled, folded or telescoped but not meeting the conditions described in paragraphs (b) through (f) below. Where an article does meet the conditions described in paragraphs (b) through (f), but such provisions are not published in item descriptions, the SU classes will apply.
"SU in sections" or "In SU sections" refers to articles taken apart in sections.

(b) Is commodity "KD" _____ , KD flat _____ ?
"KD" (Knocked Down) refers to an article taken apart, folded or telescoped in such a manner as to reduce its bulk at least 33 1/3 percent from its normal shipping cubage when set up or assembled.
"KD flat" refers to an article taken apart, folded or telescoped in such a manner as to reduce its bulk at least 66 2/3 percent from its normal shipping cubage when set up or assembled.

(c) Is commodity folded _____ , folded flat _____ ?
"Folded" refers to an article folded in such a manner as to reduce its bulk at least 33 1/3 percent from its normal shipping cubage when not folded.
"Folded flat" refers to an article folded in such a manner as to reduce its bulk at least 66 2/3 percent from its normal shipping cubage when not folded.

(d) Is commodity nested _____ , nested solid _____ ?
"Nested" refers to three or more different sizes of an article placed each smaller within the next larger or three or more of the same article placed one within the other so that each upper article will not project above the next lower article by more than one-third of its height.
"Nested solid" refers to three or more of the same article placed one within the other or upon the other so that the outer side surfaces of the one above will be in contact with the inner side surfaces of the one below and so that each upper article will not project above the next lower article more than ¼ inch.

(e) Is commodity compressed_____ , if so, by machine_____ , by hand_____ ?

(f) Is commodity disassembled _____ , partially_____ , completely_____ ?

(g) Is commodity wheeled, if so is it shipped with wheels on _____ , off_____ ?

## 10) CHARACTERISTICS OF SIZE AND METHODS OF SHIPMENT:

(a) What are predominant areas of movement? Nationwide _____ , East_____ , South _____ , Midwest_____ , Southwest_____ , Farwest_____ .

(b) What are predominant methods and sizes of shipments?
(1) Less than truckload lots _____% , average size of shipment _____ lbs.
(2) Straight truckload lots _____% , average size of shipment _____ lbs.
(3) Mixed truckload lots _____% , average size of shipment _____ lbs.

(c) What are the usual terms of shipment?
(1) Freight prepaid by shipper _____ .
(2) Freight collect_____ .
(3) Collect on delivery (C.O.D.) _____ .
(4) Freight prepaid by shipper and added to customer invoice _____ .

(d) What is annual tonnage of this commodity by motor common carrier? _____

(e) What percentage of movement is by motor common carrier? _____ %

(f) What percentage of movement is subject to class rates? _____ %

## 11) CLAIMS EXPERIENCE (Motor Common Carrier Shipments):

(a) Claims filed by: Shipper _____ , Consignee _____
(b) Number of claims (one year period) _____ , What period? _____ through _____
(c) Dollar amount of claims _____ Amount Paid _____

(d) Total number of shipments made (one year period) _____
(e) Total amount of freight paid (one year period) _____

Fig. 14-4. *Continued.*

12) What are major competitive commodities? _____

13) (A) Names and addresses of Manufacturers or Shippers (when proponent is carrier)

(B) Name and address of Competitors (when proponent is manufacturer)

14) Names of originating carriers (when proponent is shipper or manufacturer)

15) STATE FULL REASON(S) FOR PROPOSAL CHANGE OR ADDITION. (If, as justification, proponent refers to ratings of other articles in the Classification, complete information as to weight, value, loadibility and other pertinent factors of such comparable items, should be given. Use separate sheet if additional space is needed.

Fig. 14-4. *Concluded.*

mitted to the Board. Those appealed proposals which are approved by the Committee are published by the publishing agent. All interested parties are given notice by mail of hearings by the Board or of appeal hearings before the National Classification Committee. The same notice is given to the public by publication in a trade publication, *Transport Topics,* not less than 14 days preceding such hearing. The procedure for changes in the National Motor Freight Classification provides the right of independent action so that any participating carrier may publish, cause to be published, or concur in any tariff or tariffs containing exceptions to the classification and any or all provisions thereof.

When a carrier gives written notice to the National Classification Committee of independent action on any proposed change in the classification at any time within 30 days after date of notice of disposition has been issued, the publishing agent withholds publication of the proposed change for a period of 30 days from the notice of the independent action so that any such party may have independent publication made.

The National Classification Board is often requested to provide interpretations of matters contained in the classification. These interpretations, which number about 2,000 each year, are opinions not rulings. They are distributed to weighing and inspection bureaus and are available on request from the Board. Typical of this type was a request from a plastic hula hoop manufacturer for an opinion on the proper classification description of the hoop which was a rigid plastic tubing fastened together by means of a wooden peg. It was the opinion of the Board that it should be shipped under Item 45105—"Games or Toys, NOI, plastic flat."

## National Classification Committee

The National Classification Committee is composed of 100 elected representatives of common carriers with at least one member from each state and the District of Columbia. The primary duty of the Committee is to investigate, consider, and make recommendations with respect to matters affecting the classification of commodities; and finally to decide, fix, and prescribe the contents, provisions, and ratings of the National Motor Freight Classification. It considers policy matters affecting the publication of the National Motor Freight Classification and appoints members to the National Classification Board.

The administrative and detail work is handled by subcommittees, such as Light and Bulky Articles Committee and the Shipper Contract Committee, the membership of which varies from seven to 25 members. To qualify for membership on the National Classification Committee, the individual must be an officer, owner, or full-time employee of a motor carrier which is a party to the National Motor Freight Classification Agreement. Each participating carrier may nominate one qualified person who may be placed on the ballot to represent the state in which the nominating carrier is domiciled. A number of motor carrier tariff bureau officials are members of subcommittees but have no vote.

The schedule of fees for motor carriers that participate in the National Motor Freight Classification varies, depending upon whether the carriers are intrastate or interstate, and whether they are Class I or other than Class I carriers. The fees for Class I carriers are based upon the gross revenue.

## National Motor Freight Traffic Association

The National Motor Freight Traffic Association, Inc., consists of motor common carriers of property and investigates, analyzes, and disseminates information on classifications and tariffs. It serves as agent for the participating carriers in compiling, distributing, issuing, and publishing the classification. In addition, it analyzes and disseminates information on the classification, and rates, charges, rules, and regulations governing the transportation of property by motor vehicle. It conducts research and issues statistics, studies, reports, and information on carrier costs, and makes appearances before the Interstate Commerce Commission.

There are a number of standing committees, such as Commerce, Bill of Lading, Weighing and Inspection, and Form and Construction of

Tariffs, which handle many detailed matters. In addition, special committees are appointed to handle particular matters. There is also a Transportation Committee on Practices and Procedures composed of five members each from the National Motor Freight Traffic Association and the two common carrier conferences of the American Trucking Associations, which seeks to find ways and means to cut costs of handling small shipments.

The National Classification Committee is an autonomous committee of the National Motor Freight Traffic Association. This committee's duties are to investigate, consider, and make recommendations concerning the National Motor Freight Classification.

## QUESTIONS AND PROBLEMS

1. Carefully explain the development of the National Motor Freight Classification.

2. What is the purpose of classification? Is classification of greater or lesser importance today as compared to 20 years ago?

3. Describe the composition of the National Motor Freight Classification. Choose an item from NMFC and compare it with the same item as classified in the railroad's Uniform Freight Classification.

4. What is the purpose of the classification rules? Are they used only in conjunction with class rates?

5. How would you explain the basic differences between the National Motor Freight Classification and the Coordinated Motor Freight Classification?

6. What are the factors which influence the classification of articles? Is there any one factor that appears to be of more importance than others?

7. What is the composition of the National Classification Board? What is the procedure followed by it?

8. How are the members of the National Classification Committee chosen? What is its relationship to the National Classification Board?

9. If a carrier proposal fails of adoption before the National Classification Board, what steps may then be taken by the carrier?

10. Compare the factors used in classification of freight with those used in making rates. Point out the similarities and/or differences. What conclusions can you draw from your analysis?

### FOOTNOTES TO CHAPTER 14

[1] *Motor Carrier Rates in New England,* 47 MCC 660, 661 (1948).

[2] *Incandescent Electric Lamps or Bulbs,* 44 MCC 501 (1945); and 47 MCC 601 (1947).

# chapter 15

# Rates

Historically, motor carrier rates have been said to be on a level with the rates of the railroads. When the motor carriers filed their original tariffs in 1936 with the Interstate Commerce Commission, their rates were predicated largely upon those charged by rail carriers. It has been pointed out, however, that there are many rates, both interstate and intrastate, which are commonly believed to be based on rail rates but prove upon research to be rates historically fixed by a particular motor carrier for a particular shipper and thereafter followed first by other motor carriers and then by the railroads.

Prior to the passage of the Motor Carrier Act in 1935, it was customary for motor carriers which handled substantial amounts of interstate traffic to publish and distribute to shippers "rate books" or "rate guides" which quoted rates. Some of these rates applied to movements in which two carriers participated. These rate guides resembled railroad tariffs in form, and the rates in these guides were incorporated in the tariffs that were required to be filed with the Interstate Commerce Commission with the passage of the Motor Carrier Act in 1935.

In rate making, there are a number of theories that are useful in an explanation of particular rates. A practical explanation of the method by which rates are made is the rule of the "Four C's"—Custom, Competition, Comparison, and Compromise. Although regulation has modified the rule of the "Four C's," it has not fundamentally changed this pattern.

### Relationship of size of shipments to rates

Motor carriers make a distinction between truckload and less-than-truckload shipments. In order to secure a truckload rate, which is lower than that applied to less-than-truckload shipments, a shipment of minimum weight as established by the carriers must be tendered or the minimum paid. The truckload minimum will be that weight which can be transported in a single vehicle. However, it need not fill the truck to its visible capacity. Any shipment less than this minimum is called a "less-than-truckload lot." In addition to truckload and less-than-truckload categories, motor carriers have established a "volume minimum." This can be described as a minimum weight which is in excess of what can be loaded in a single truck. When a shipper tenders the volume minimum weight of a commodity, the volume rate applies even though it may exceed the carrying capacity of the largest vehicle available and must be carried in two or more vehicles.

Rates on graduated quantities have been established in some areas on quantities of 5,000, 10,000, and 20,000 pounds. If a shipper can tender shipments of 10,000 instead of 5,000 pounds, he can secure a lower rate; and, if he can tender shipments of 20,000 pounds, he can secure a lower rate than that applicable to the 10,000-pound shipment.

Shipments fall into three general classes; (a) shipments loaded at the shipper's door in the over-the-road unit which occupy the entire vehicle and are unloaded at consignee's door from the over-the-road unit; (b) shipments picked up at the shipper's door in the over-the-road unit and carried with other freight for all or a substantial part of the journey, without being handled over the platform of original terminal; and (c) shipments picked up at the shipper's door, delivered to consignee in pickup equipment, and handled over platform at both origin and desti-nation. Truckload shipments or shipments weighing more than 10,000 pounds usually fall in the first category; those weighing between 5,000 and 10,000 pounds, in the second category; and less-than-volume ship-ments (less than 5,000 pounds), in the third category. The less-than-volume shipment differs from the less-than-truckload shipment in that it requires relatively more pickup and delivery service and more plat-form handling, the cost of which has increased at a much faster rate than over-the-road costs.

There has been a great deal of dissatisfaction among carriers and shippers with the manner in which rates on small shipments are com-puted. Numerous suggestions have been made on ways to improve this situation, most of which would eliminate the use of a classification and much of the paper work in the handling of the shipments. Prepayment of freight charges with stamps, graduated charges based on weight with-in a given area, and the establishment of a single agency to handle all small shipments are some of the plans that have been suggested. The fact that some of the elements of terminal costs are independent of the weight of the shipment has made small-shipment pricing difficult.

There is no general definition of what constitutes a small shipment but, for statistical purposes, the Commission includes those shipments weighing less than 10,000 pounds. The volume of such shipments is staggering. Weights under 50 pounds are usually termed small parcels. Motor carriers often refer to small shipments as those in the 500 pound to 750 pound range. However, motor carrier rate bureaus use 1,000 pounds as the weight break. Based on the continuing traffic studies of the motor carriers, they handle about 86 percent of all intercity shipments weighing under 10,000 pounds and derive about $8 billion from such shipments.[1]

### Broken stowage

It is recognized in motor carrier operations that it is impossible, in general, to load shipments to the full width, length, and height of a vehicle. This is termed "broken stowage," because of the existence of spaces unavoidably left unfilled. These unfilled spaces occur on account of irregularities in the sizes of packages in mixing common loads of crates, bundles, boxes, bales, rolls, pipes, barrels, drums, and the like. In addition to the unfilled spaces between packages, the empty spaces at the sides, the ends, and the top of the cargo constitute broken stowage. Thus, waste space may exist even where the packages are uniform in their dimensions. An over-the-road unit with a van body 7 feet x 7 feet x 30 feet has a loss of eight percent of the total cubic space of that body if there is empty space of three inches below the roof, three inches along one side, and three inches between the back of the load and the rear doors. Upon analysis, a number of less-than-truckload loaded vehicles filed with general cargo were found to have a space of six inches to one foot at the top of the load. In a van body with a height of seven feet, a space of 1 foot at the top of the load is equal to a loss in total space of 14 percent. Ordinarily, the horizontal space between packages will amount to from two to five inches out of the total body width of seven feet. If an allowance is made for an average loss of six inches at the top of the truck and a loss of two inches of load space across the width of the truck and a loss of four inches between the front end of the body and the rear doors, the total waste space would be slightly over ten percent. Terminal managers have estimated that broken stowage for the average over-the-road vehicle runs from five to 15 percent of the space capacity. This element of waste space must be considered in the formulation of rates.

### Density

Because the cubical content for the maximum weight-carrying capacity of an over-the-road unit is limited, density is an important factor. A study made by one of the committees of the Transportation Research Board as to economics of size and weight contained an analy-

sis of the densities of many commodities moving in intercity truck transportation. They ranged from five pounds per cubic foot to 254 pounds per
cubic foot with commodities having densities of 50 pounds or more accounting for 52 percent of total truck tonnage.[2] The average density of packaged general freight is about 12½ pounds per cubic foot. As shown in

## TRAILER SPACE and CARGO LOADINGS

73,000-Pound Gross Loading in 40-Foot and 45-Foot Semitrailers with
2,286 and 2,571 Cubic Foot Capacities

(Tare weight: tractor 14,000 pounds, trailer 11,000 pounds)

| | | |
|---|---|---|
| 21 LBS./CU.FT. 19 LBS./CU.FT. | | 24 LBS./CU.FT. CIGARETTES |
| 40 FT. 0% Empty 45 FT. 0% Empty | | 13% Empty 22% Empty |
| 30 LBS./CU.FT. VENEER & PLYWOOD | | 35 LBS./CU.FT. ORANGES & GRAPEFRUIT |
| 40 FT. 30% Empty 45 FT. 38% Empty | | 40% Empty 47% Empty |
| 40 LBS./CU.FT. SOAP | | 45 LBS./CU.FT. CANNED & FROZEN FOODS |
| 40 FT. 48 % Empty 45 FT. 53% Empty | | 53% Empty 59% Empty |
| 50 LBS./CU.FT. PAINT | | |
| 40 FT. 58% Empty 45 FT. 63% Empty | | |

Fig. 15-1. The relation of density to cargo loadings.

Fig. 15-1, the 40-foot semitrailer would be loaded to its capacity with a
commodity which possessed a density of 21 pounds per cubic foot, and
the 45-foot semitrailer 19 pounds per cubic foot. This ideal seldom
prevails inasmuch as an item as light as cigarettes has a density of 24
pounds per cubic foot which loaded to the 73,000 pound gross load
would leave the 40-foot semitrailer 13 percent empty and a 45-foot

semitrailer 22 percent empty. Commodities such as paint, soap, and canned and frozen foods may leave the trailer 50 percent or more empty.

Although there is variation among carriers, an increasing volume of freight in recent years has consisted of lighter shipments. Many manu-factured items are made of lighter weight material, such as plastic pipe or fiberglas pipe instead of metal or concrete pipe. Fiberglas pipe may weigh just five percent of concrete pipe but occupy the same space. In early 1974, a sample survey of 48 carriers made by the National Classi-fication Committee showed that only 26 percent of 111,000 dispatches were released with the maximum legal weight whereas 44 percent were released with the maximum space occupied without reaching maximum weight, i.e., they "cubed" out. The other 28 percent were released to meet service needs. A transcontinental carrier operating in 44 states currently has 74 percent of its miles operated by its twin trailers be-cause they provide more space than a semitrailer.

Freight rates are usually quoted on a weight basis; but the amount of weight that can be carried in a truck, except as limited by state laws and the weight-carrying capacity of the vehicle, depends upon the density of the commodity or commodities. The lighter and bulkier articles will, in general, be charged at a higher rate to compensate for the lack of weight, even though they fully load the vehicle's cubic space.

### Class rates

A class rate is one that is governed by a rating in a classification. In establishing a class rate, there will be factors similar to those enumer-ated as receiving consideration in fixing classification ratings which will have influence. Class rates have a broader application than other rates in that they apply to and from all points which have motor carrier service. There is widespread use of mileage scales, which results in the rate increasing as the distance increases but not in exact proportion to in-creases in distance. To simplify rate construction, class rates are usually made on a group basis; that is, the principal city in each group is known as the base point, and the rates are published between the base points. However, in some instances, towns in a group are over 70 miles from the base points, so that there may be a lack of uniformity in rates on a distance scale except between the base points.

The rate scale used by motor carriers is generally either one which is being used by railroads or one with the necessary modifications. In 1952 the railroads had a class rate scale prescribed by the Commission in *Dockets 28300* and *28310* to be applicable throughout the United States east of the Rocky Mountains.[3] This scale has become known as the *28300* scale and has been adopted in a number of rate territories. Deviation from the *28300* class rate scale usually occurs where the competitive situation requires or permits it.

The structure of motor carrier class rates has changed from the original single class scales. Separate scales were established for less-truckload and truckload traffic, and later these scales were segmented by weight of shipment. Thus, in one rate territory, there are scales for less truckload under 1,000 pounds; 1,000-1,999 pounds; 2,000-4,999 pounds; and 5,000 pounds and over. Truckload scales were established for loads of less than 30,000 pounds, and for 30,000 pounds and over. Separate scales were also developed for minimum-charge shipments. There is a minimum charge for a single shipment, and a minimum charge for multishipments. This refinement has provided a class rate structure more reflective of motor carrier operations.

Some class rate tariffs incorporate what is termed a "class rate stop" or a "minimum-rate stop." This means that, although goods may be rated at a lower class in a classification, the class rate applicable will be the same as on a higher class. In other words, the article may be rated Class 40 in a classification; but, because it cannot be carried profitably at a Class 40 rate, the carriers establish a rate stop at Class 45 in the rate tariff. Anything rated below a Class 45 rating carries a Class 45 rate. The need for the class-rate stop is attributed to the fact that the motor carriers largely adopted the railroad classification but soon discovered that the rail class rates on lower-rated, long-haul traffic were not compensatory to the motor carrier, especially where there was a joint-line movement. The establishment of the class-rate stop was the solution to this problem and is widely found in the tariffs of the motor carriers.

The effect of the minimum-rate stop is to provide a bottom rate on class traffic and to raise the classification rating on all traffic which would move at lower rates in the absence of the rate stop up to a rating equivalent to the rate stop. There are numerous individual minimum-rate stops on less-truckload, single-line movements. Ordinarily joint-line hauls are subject to higher individual stops than single-line hauls. The Commission has felt that the use of class rate stops "not only results in undue disadvantage to freight rated in the lower classes but in effect to a certain extent constitutes avoidance of the duty imposed by law upon all motor common carriers to afford reasonable transportation service at reasonable rates in all classes of traffic."[4] The Commission has reemphasized the desirability of eliminating class-rate stops but has continued to permit their use. One agency tariff was found to contain individual stops for about 517 carriers, with each carrier maintaining a variety of stops for different movements. For one large carrier, there were 90 statements of minimum-rate restrictions containing about 330 separate minimum rates.

## Commodity rates

The second general type of rate is that of commodity rates, which generally are published to provide for the movement of traffic believed to require a rate lower than a class rate. The commodity rate is usually a point-to-point rate applicable to a specific commodity between certain points and thus has a limited application. This type of rate based primarily on volume and regularity of shipments is widely used by motor carriers. It is possible for a commodity rate to be higher than a class rate, but the reverse is usually the case. Carriers usually provide an alternating application rule in their tariffs so that if commodity rates are higher the shipper may apply the class rate.

## Exception ratings

The publishing of exceptions to the classification in a separate tariff removes articles from the classification and establishes rules or rates that modify the normal class rates. These are, in general, below the class rates. The exceptions, in effect, might be looked upon as amendments to the classification and are established for a variety of reasons: to meet competition, to accomplish a more restrictive application of particular rates, and to move a considerable volume of traffic of a particular type. These exceptions contain rules and regulations governing the application of rates and practices which are not covered in the classification. Exception ratings and rules in a rate tariff, unless otherwise indicated, take precedence over the classification. The exception ratings are used in conjunction with class rates.

No exact figure is known as to the percentages of traffic which move under class rates, commodity rates, or exception ratings for the United States as a whole. Some indication of the revenue derived from each type of rate in one of the important rate territories in 1979 is that approximately 26 percent moved on commodity rates, 65 percent on class rates, and 7.4 percent under minimum charge. In another large geographical area, the class-rated traffic was 46 percent, commodity traffic 48 percent, and four percent minimum charge.

## OTHER RATES AND RATE FORMULATION

Many other types of rates are published, some of which are discussed in this chapter. There may be arbitraries to an off-line point, to a particular area, or to piers, which are charges in addition to the basic rate. In addition, differentials may be added to the basic rates. The basic transportation service is that rendered between origin and destination. There are many accessorial or additional services that carriers may offer for which there are extra charges. These services and the charges applicable to them are contained in the tariffs and are usually in the form of rules. Examples of these are pickup and delivery service in addition to normal pickup and delivery, such as inside delivery; protection service for perishable freight; segregation of truckload shipments of foodstuffs; and exclusive use of the vehicle.[5] In the absence of tariff provisions covering the exclusive use of the vehicle, a shipper who tenders a truckload quantity would not be entitled to the exclusive use of the vehicle.

Shippers have complained that additional charges were made by carriers for which no additional service was performed. In response the Commission, in *Ex Parte 254, Additional Charges of Motor Carriers and Forwarders, 1978*, instituted rulemaking procedure to eliminate these surcharges. The focal point was on arbitraries.

Some carriers provide an express service which is a premium service utilized mainly when conditions at point of delivery make its use by the shipper economically feasible despite relatively higher transportation costs. Because express service is marked by an undertaking to provide transportation service superior to that normally required and furnished for ordinary freight, relatively higher charges are established for it.

In 1974, P.I.E., a transcontinental motor carrier, proposed that in return for a modest surcharge, shippers would receive a written guarantee that if shipments were not delivered on schedule for reasons within control of the carrier, P.I.E. would refund all transportation charges, including the surcharge. After investigation, the Commission rejected it on the basis that it violated the Interstate Commerce Act.

Recently a motor carrier was permitted to give discount coupons of 10 percent on less-truckload shipments of 500 pounds or more of class-rated shipments transported during December, 1979, between points in Texas and 22 states. the coupons were redeemable during the following January and February on the same type of shipments.

Although the shipper has the option provided by contract carriers of low cost motor transportation in contrast to the regular common carrier service, the wide range of choices from high quality, high price items to low cost, low price items that is available in other goods and services has not developed in motor transportation. The tendency of the general commodity carrier has been to provide a high level quality and performance service and not provide lower level service at rates of 10, 20, or 30 percent less.

## Tariffs

Rates and rules are published in tariffs, which in effect are price lists of carriers, in accordance with general tariff circular requirements prescribed by the Commission. There are many different kinds of tariffs, such as class, class and commodity, general commodity, specific commodity, grouping (points around a principal city may be grouped), accessorial charge or allowance, scope of operations (area served by carriers), mileage, rules, terminal service rules, and tariff indexes. Tariffs may be divided into two broad types—governing and specific. Illustrative of the governing tariffs are rules tariffs and routing tariffs; illustrative of the specific are class, commodity, and exceptions tariffs. Local

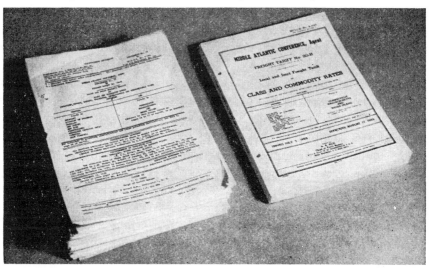

Fig. 15-2. Supplements (left) to a class and commodity tariff (right) issued in a period of one year. The volume of the supplements is about four times that of the original tariff.

tariffs contain rates which apply between points served by one carrier. Joint tariffs contain rates which apply for two or more carriers; and there are other types of tariffs based on the types of rates which are contained. There are many changes which are made in the rates so that supplements are issued to the tariff. Figure 15-2 shows a tariff and the supplements issued to it in one year's time.

Computers are being used to aid in the compilation of tariffs. Electronic data processing equipment provides copy to be used in printing and reduces the time needed to check copy. Its use also increases the accuracy of the data. To be of maximum utilization, the use of point and commodity codes should be more widely instituted and the problem of rate retrieval resolved.

In a policy statement, the Commission in 1979 began efforts to encourage the standardization, simplification, and modernization of tariffs, particularly through the application of modern data technology.

Two levels of rates may be published in a tariff. For example, one level may include all increases that have been made, and the other may not include certain increases but may be published to apply only via certain carriers which wish to protect the lower level. In one tariff, the lower level is published in Section 2½ of the tariff, and the higher level is published in Sections 1 and 2. Section 2½ applies only via carriers and to the extent shown in Item 1321 of the tariff. For this reason these carriers are known as "1321 Carriers." Generally the 1321 carriers are the ones which protect both classification and exception rates in the tariff. Carriers other than the 1321 carriers are those which protect only the exception rates and apply the rates in another tariff on classification-rated traffic.

Intrastate rates are subject to the state regulation in most instances. These rates are often below interstate rates.

A federal court ruled in 1979 that intrastate rate making by rate bureaus is not immune from anti-trust law even though states have regulatory commissions and procedures. This has raised doubt as to the legality of intrastate rate making by rate bureaus which publish intrastate tariffs.

### Average or incentive rates

In a number of cases, railroads have published dual rail commodity rates which are often referred to as "incentive" or "discount" rates. Under this plan, two rates are published. For example, one is a base rate which is applicable on the first 40,000 pounds in the shipment, and the other is a rate which is 20 percent lower than the base rate and applies on portions of the shipment which weigh more than 40,000 pounds if the excess amount is loaded into the same car as the initial 40,000 pounds.

Motor carriers, in order to be competitive on such traffic, have established commodity rates which are referred to as "average rates" or "incentive rates." These rates are made by computing the rate in cents per 100 pounds which would be applicable under the dual rate system of rail rates based on the average weight of a commodity when it is moved by rail. If the average weight of a commodity moved by rail was 50,000 pounds, 40,000 pounds would be moved at the base rate by motor carriers and 10,000 pounds at 80 percent of the base rate. Motor carriers compute what the rail rate is for the 50,000 pounds, that is, they secure the average rate and make this the rate that they charge. Shipments which exceed the vehicle capacity under average rates are placed in a second vehicle with less-truckload shipments or divided into two or three parts if loaded in a vehicle with less-truckload shipments.

### Distribution service rates

Some line-haul carriers in connection with their intercity rates have published distribution tariffs which provide that truckload or volume shipments may be consigned for distribution by the line-haul carriers. There are both individual carrier tariffs and agency tariffs which contain these rates. These tariffs are generally applicable on freight of all kinds, with certain commodities excepted. These shipments, in effect, are pooled shipments which require numerous separate deliveries at destination.

Local cartage companies also perform distribution at destination for railroads which render pool-car service. Often truck shipments are distributed at destination by local cartage companies.

The distribution rates which are established by the line-haul carrier provide for a small additional charge to be added to the line-haul rate. The carrier will then render multiple split delivery service to a number of consignees. A prior haul by the carrier offering the distribution service is not required in all tariffs. Some require the consignor to furnish a bill of lading for each part of a pooled shipment to be distributed, whereas others require a bill of lading and distribution sheet covering the truckload or volume shipment from origin to destination point. A pooled shipment may require as many as 30 deliveries or as few as five.

Distribution rates are generally below those of local cartage carriers which also perform pooled shipment service. These carriers have sought to have the Commission prescribe minimum reasonable rates for distribution rates, but the Commission has declined to do so. It has held that there is nothing in the act which specifically prohibits a line-haul carrier from performing a distribution service at a point which it is authorized to serve.[6]

In general, distribution rates have been maintained at about the same level for a number of years, although there have been substantial increases in a number of other rates. Usually, long-haul carriers adjust local rates according to the over-the-road distance so that the longer the haul the lower the distribution rate.

### Split deliveries and stop-offs in transit

Split delivery means that there can be several deliveries at one destination. Stopping in transit to unload partially means that the service must be performed at a point or points between origin and destination. A charge is made for each of the stop-offs and, in one of the rate territories, this is currently $27.50 for each stop. In one case, the Commission approved tariff rules limiting the number of stops.[7] In a more recent case, on the other hand, the Commission imposed no limitation on the number of such truck stops.[8] The typical number of stops under such tariff provisions are three.

Stopping-in-transit to complete loading or to unload partially does not constitute transit service within the usually accepted meaning of that term as applied to motor carriers, according to the Commission. This is an extra transportation service for which the motor carrier is entitled to receive reasonable compensation.

### All freight—freight-all kinds

Section 10766 (b) provides that if line-haul transportation between concentration points and break-bulkpoints in truckload lots for a total distance of 450 miles or more is performed under contracts, such contracts should not permit payment by freight forwarders to motor common carriers of compensation lower than would be received under rates or charges established under subchapter II of the act. This amendment to the act became effective in 1951. Later, a number of motor carriers filed tariffs containing all-commodity rates or all-freight rates (merchandise in mixed truckloads) which were to replace former joint rates and divisions with freight forwarders.

The all-commodity or all-freight rates are patterned to some degree upon the railroads' all-commodity rates. The all-commodity rates of motor carriers do not apply on all commodities because the tariffs contain some classifications of property in which certain commodities are excepted and certain restrictions apply. For example, one tariff provides that the rates apply on a mixed shipment which consists of ten or more commodities, no one commodity to exceed 50 percent of the weight of the lading or of the minimum weight, whichever is greater. Some of the articles which are excepted include commodities in bulk, explosives, livestock, and perishable freight, as well as others.

One motor carrier which hauls only for freight forwarders maintains its charges in its tariffs in dollars by truck for various stated maximum weights ranging from 20,000 to 24,000 pounds and rates in cents per 100 pounds for "overage," i.e., weight in excess of the maximum which produces charges relatively lower than its truckload charges. Some motor carriers maintain all-commodity rates which are available to any shipper who can meet the conditions contained in the tariff, although the primary users of such rates are freight forwarders.

### Assembly and distribution rates

Section 10725 (b) authorizes motor common carriers to establish for freight forwarders and others who employ or utilize the instrumentalities or services of such common carriers under like conditions less-truckload assembling and distribution rates which differ from their normal less-truckload rates between the same points. These rates apply only *to assembling points and from distribution points*. They cannot cover terminal-to-terminal movements. Individual shippers and shippers' cooperative associations have utilized assembly and distribution rates under conditions similar to those prevailing for freight forwarders. The assembly and distribution rates are usually lower than rates on nonforwarder traffic.

The reasons for assembly rates which were 85 percent of class rates were cited in one case as being the elimination of solicitation expense, a reduction in the cost of rating, billing, and adjusting claims, and a saving in delivery expense.[9]

In another case, assembly and distribution rates which were approximately 70 percent of the ordinary rates were found to be reasonable.[10]

### Intermediate point rates

Numerous tariffs have intermediate-point rules that are generally used to make applicable rates from or to points named in a tariff as well as from or to unnamed intermediate points. Such rules serve to reduce the size of tariffs and provide rates at new origins and destinations. A typical rule provides that when an origin is not supplied in a tariff with a commodity rate, and is between the destination and a point from which a commodity rate is published to the destination, the rate to be applied for that specified is the next most distant point from the origin.

### Section 10721 rates

Section 10721 of the Interstate Commerce Act permits reduced or free rates to the government. The primary user of these rates is the federal government. A substantial volume of Department of Defense and General Services Administration traffic and a large volume of household goods is moved for the Department of Defense under such rates. The

Section 10721 quotations must be filed with the Commission and be open for public inspection.

### Allowances

Carriers sometimes permit the shipper an allowance when the shipper performs a part of the transportation service, such as picking up his shipment at the terminal rather than having the carrier deliver it to him. Allowances are not made to a shipper or consignee for performing a service unless it is one which the carrier is obligated to perform under its tariffs as an essential part of a transportation service.[11]

Clerical services, such as billing and collection of charges, performed by a shipper cannot be classified as "allowances." Allowances must also be reasonable in relation to the facilities furnished and service performed. Allowances of 10 cents, 12 cents, 20 cents, and 50 cents per 100 pounds have been found to be reasonable in different instances. The allowance is usually greater on high-rated traffic than on low-rated traffic. An allowance has been permitted a shipper who aggregates multiple shipments of class-rated traffic into a single shipment weighing 12,000 pounds or more. Allowances may also be made when shipper-owned equipment is furnished, and this occurs more frequently with specialized equipment.

Parties who perform pickup and delivery service for rail and motor carriers and freight forwarders may be permitted to receive more than the shipper's allowance in the tariff only under a written contract. The terms of this contract must provide that such a person shall be required to furnish the service as an agent or as an independent contractor of the carrier or freight forwarder and shall be required by such contract to issue, or to accept, in the name of the carrier or freight forwarder, receipts for the goods picked up or delivered by him in such service.[12]

Payments which are in excess of the tariff allowance and not under such contractual arrangements are held to be the giving of an undue and unusual preference and advantage and constitute rebating.[13]

These contracts do not have to be filed with the Commission but are retained by the carrier. They do not have to cover general pickup and delivery service, but rather an allowance contract could be made with a number of local cartage companies or an allowance contract with a warehouseman to pick up and deliver only shipments moving to and from that warehouse.

### Minimum charges

In some urban areas, such as New York and Chicago, a minimum charge based on less than 100 pounds is maintained on restricted types of traffic, but generally the minimum charge is stated to be the applicable Class 100 rate for 100 pounds subject to a minimum of $3 or more depending upon the rate territory. There are higher minimum charges which are provided for specified services.

When minimum charges are stated as the applicable Class 100 rate for 100 pounds, it is necessary to find a rate scale number of the Class 100 rate in the tariff to which the minimum charge is tied. This number is then converted into the minimum charge or that amount which may be charged on a higher basis according to the class tariffs. It is then necessary to check back against the minimum charge to determine which is higher. To compensate for this, a surcharge of $1.50 is added to the freight charges computed at the applicable weight and rate on all shipments of less than 5,000 pounds in one rate territory. In this rate territory, it was stated that more than 70 percent of shipments in excess of 5,000 pounds moved in line-haul from shipper's door to consignee's door, with nearly 20 percent handled by trailer spotting. Thus, a minimum use of terminal facilities or equipment was involved. In contrast to this, just 12 percent of the shipments under 5,000 pounds was picked up and delivered in line-haul semitrailers and only 1½ percent by trailer spotting. Further, it was stated that it cost four times more for pickup and delivery of less-truckload traffic than for a ton of volume or truckload freight.[14] In this particular case, decided in 1955, the Commission ordered cancellation of the surcharge and authorized a minimum charge of $3; and increased rates for two weight groups to make up for revenue produced by the surcharge. Later, minimum charges of $5 were permitted.

However, when motor carriers imposed a surcharge to compensate them for the expense of a weight-distance tax enacted by the state of New York, the Commission found that the surcharge established for this purpose was not just and reasonable. The Commission stated that this tax, like other operating taxes, should be treated as a normal operating expense and be reflected in the rates rather than in surcharges.[15] In a later case a modest surcharge of 50 cents per shipment was approved in one rate territory.[16]

The experience of carriers has been that the minimum-charge rate structure for the smaller shipments is a method to price a service which consists of weight, distance, terminal, and clerical functions, whereas the rate scale is based on only weight and weight-distance. It is possible that shipper members of the American Retail Federation who have many small shipments are paying a minimum charge on one out of every four shipments received.

**Net weights**

Although most rates are based on the gross weight of the shipment, i.e., the package and its contents, the Commission has approved motor carrier truckload rates based on one weight of the contents of a package and on the inclusion of the rate of empty containers in the rate for the loaded movement. It also has approved the supplying of containers by the carrier, as well as the interchange of containers for others with consignor and consignee provided there is no discrimination and that the charges collected are reasonable for the entire service performed.

An increasing number of shippers and receivers utilize material-handling equipment involving the use of pallets. Motor carriers are permitting such shippers who load and unload the palletized shipments to move them on a net weight basis. A rate reduction is granted for the return of the pallets, with the tariff rules specifying the quantity on which the rate reduction applies, such as 1,000 pounds of pallets. These rates have been established in part because motor carrier equipment is not tied up as long in loading and unloading.

**Actual-value and released-value ratings**

Although the Interstate Commerce Act[17] provides that motor carriers are to be responsible for the full value of merchandise transported by them where freight is lost or damaged, it also provides for a limitation of that liability in specific instances where approved by the Commission. Applications to provide such limited liability have been made to the Interstate Commerce Commission to cover certain commodities and have been approved by the Commission. The effect of these approvals by the Commission has been to provide at least two ratings on certain commodities. These are actual-value ratings and released-value ratings. The rating to be applied in some of these commodities where limitations of liability have been approved by the Commission, whether it is to be an actual-value rating or a released-value rating, will depend upon the shipper's designation of the rating in the bill of lading.

The actual-value ratings have been published on commodities where the range of value has been so wide that it is difficult to establish one rating based on an average value. When this rating is used in a bill of lading or on shipping orders, the shipper must designate the use of the rating and certify the actual value of the commodity. An example of a commodity so rated in the National Motor Freight Classification is shown in Table 15-1.

A shipper can specify an arbitrary valuation on certain commodities which may or may not be the actual value of the commodity to be

## TABLE 15-1

### Examples of Actual-Value Ratings of Commodities in the National Motor Freight Classification

| Item | ARTICLES | CLASSES | | MW |
|------|----------|---------|------|------|
| | | LTL | TL | |
| 57670 | **DRAWING INSTRUMENTS, OPTICAL GOODS OR SCIENTIFIC INSTRUMENTS:** | | | |
| 57760 | **Binoculars, Field Glasses, Monoculars, Opera Glasses or Magnifying Reading Glasses** other than eye glasses or spectacles, toy or other than toy, with or without carrying cases or tripods or stands, in barrels or boxes, see Note, item 57762: | | | |
| Sub 1 | Actual value not exceeding $1.00 each.......................................... | 100 | 70 | 20.2 |
| Sub 2 | Actual value exceeding $1.00 each but not exceeding $50.00 each........................... | 125 | 85 | 12.2 |
| Sub 3 | Actual value exceeding $50.00 each.............................................. | 300 | 150 | 10.2 |
| 57762 | **Note**—Shipper must certify on shipping order and bill of lading the actual value of the property as follows: | | | |
| | *Actual value of the* ................... *(insert name of commodity) is hereby stated by the shipper to be 'not in excess of* ...... *dollars each' or 'in excess of* ...... *dollars each', as the case may be.* | | | |

## TABLE 15-2

### Examples of Released-Value Ratings of Commodities in the National Motor Freight Classification

| Item | Articles | Classes | | MW |
|------|----------|---------|------|------|
| | | LTL | TL | |
| 110800 | Leather Scrap, NOI, value declared in writing by the shipper, or agreed upon in writing as the released value of the property, in accordance with the following; see Notes, Items 110802 and 110804: | | | |
| Sub 1 | If not exceeding 3½ cents per lb., in packages..... | 60 | 35 | 30.2 |
| Sub 2 | If exceeding 3½ cents per lb., in packages........ | 70 | 37½ | 30.2 |
| 110802 | *Note.* The value declared in writing by the shipper, or agreed upon in writing as the released value of the property, as the case may be, must be entered on the shipping order and bill of lading, as follows: "The agreed or declared value of the property is hereby specifically stated by the shipper to be not exceeding.............cents per pounds." If consignor declines to declare value or agree to released value in writing, the shipment will not be accepted. (Ratings herein based on released value have been authorized by the ICC in Released Rates Orders MC No. 1 of January 16, 1936, and FF No. 2 of January 19, 1943, subject to complaint.) | | | |
| 110804 | *Note.* Ratings apply only on old worn-out leather articles, other than belting, boots, or shoes, or on scraps of old (used) leather, or on tanners' tearoffs or rough roundings, or on leather refuse from the manufacture of leather or leather goods, and do not apply on bellies, heads, shanks, or shoulders, nor on leather cut or stamped into forms, shapes, or strips. | | | |

shipped. However, the amount that the shipper specifies in the bill of lading will determine the rating that will apply on the shipment, as well as the estimate of the carrier's liability in the event of loss or damage by the carrier, and is termed the released value of the commodity. Examples of released-value ratings to be found in the National Motor Freight Classification are shown in Table 15-2.

The ICC criteria for determining a released value rating are as follows:

1. There must be a wide range of value such that the amount of any claim which may arise would be difficult to estimate;

2. Susceptibility to loss or damage must be comparatively high;

3. There must be a relatively high ratio of claims to freight charges;

4. There must be a high ratio of the number of claims to the number of shipments;

5. There must be difficulty by the carrier in obtaining adequate insurance coverage;

6. The cost of insurance must be unreasonably high;

7. There must be competitive necessity.

In 1979, the Commission permitted released rates on shipments weighing 500 pounds or less when the rates are published in a small shipments tariff. The carrier may provide excess value charges if it believes the charges would improve its competitive position.

Where a commodity is subject either to an actual or to a released valuation, the value of the commodity should be expressed in the rating in essentially the same manner as indicated in the classification. If the classification provides a rating based on a value in cents per 100 pounds, the value of the commodity on the bill of lading should be expressed in that manner. If a carrier representative prepares a bill of lading covering such a shipment, the value of the commodity—that is, the value in cents per pound, per 100 pounds, and so forth—must be secured from the shipper. The shipper should be informed that there is more than one rating in effect, depending on the actual or released value of the commodity. In all cases where commodities are accepted at actual-value or released-value ratings, the bill of lading must be signed by the shipper. As discussed in an earlier chapter, practically all household goods are moved at released value ratings.

Small parcel carriers also use released value ratings and typically limit their liability to $100 per package. However, they will insure parcels valued in excess of this amount at a rate of 25 cents per $100 value.

The increased value of commodities due to inflation and technological advances has resulted in greatly increasing liability for motor common carriers. The use of released rates in which the liability of the carrier is limited to a specified amount per pound or per article has been one method of meeting this problem. Another method that some motor carriers advocate is to accept only prepaid shipments, i.e., no c.o.d. or "order notify" shipments. The latter shipments are more expensive to handle.

### Transit privileges

The development of the transit privilege (other than stopping in transit to load or unload partially) has been limited, although an increasing number of carriers have authorized such privileges by tariff provisions since the end of World War II. The motor carrier tariff files of the Commission contain roughly 20 motor carrier agency tariffs which authorize transit. There are relatively few individual line tariffs covering transit privileges which have been issued.

The storage-in-transit privilege has been the privilege which has been more widely granted by motor carriers than any other. This has been granted on frozen citrus juice concentrates and juices; storage of frozen eggs; storage and repacking, and/or rehandling of dairy products; freezing and storage of foodstuffs; and storage of unfinished fabric.

Other transit privileges that have been granted include fabrication of iron and steel articles; reconditioning of iron and steel pipe; dipping-in-transit on shipments of tire fabric; liquid chemicals for rehandling, further treatment, and storage, which permits mixing of chemicals; and processing in transit of paper and paper products, which permits cutting and trimming of the paper.

Generally, the commodity is billed into the transit point and charges paid thereon on the basis of the local rate applicable from initial point of origin to the transit point. When the product is reshipped from the transit point to final destination, it is rebilled from the transit point on the basis of the difference between the rate paid to the transit point and the applicable through rate on the transited commodity from initial point of origin to final destination.

### C.o.d. charges

Frequently, a carrier is called upon by a shipper to collect charges for the commodities at the time they are delivered to the consignee. This is commonly referred to as collection on delivery, or c.o.d. service. The carrier collects a c.o.d. charge for this service. The Interstate Commerce Commission has prescribed rules and regulations governing the handling of c.o.d. shipments and collections which require that the carrier must publish, post, and file tariffs that contain the rates and rules governing such service. Briefly, they are required to remit each c.o.d. collection within ten days after delivery of the c.o.d. shipment to the consignee, and they must keep certain records concerning such shipments. C.o.d. charges are listed in the rules of the National Motor Freight Classification. Transportation, consolidation, insurance and storage charges, paid or to be paid by the consignor and which he seeks to recover from the consignee, may be included in the sum shown in the bill of lading as the amount to be collected from the consignee, provided the carrier's tariffs do not forbid such inclusion.

The Commission has permitted rules requiring prepayment of freight charges where there is a need for such a rule. For example, such rules have been permitted requiring prepayment on shipments destined for large cities, such as New York. However, the Commission in *Ex Parte 272, Investigation Into Limitations of Carrier Service on C.O.D. and Freight Collect Shipments*, requires c.o.d. and freight collect as a part of motor carrier service except in special circumstances.

### Detention

Although carriers had published detention rules in their tariffs, many had not attempted to collect them and, when they did, not all shippers would pay them. In *Ex Parte MC-88, Detention of Motor Vehicles— Nationwide, 1978*, the Commission issued uniform detention rules that carriers are required to publish in their tariffs and to enforce. These rules do not apply to some specialized carriers, such as household goods, bulk carriers, and heavy haulers. The rules are assessed on a time basis with different rules applying on vehicles with power units and those without power units. The free-time period is based on the actual weight in pounds and varies for power units from 120 minutes for less than 10,000 pounds and graduated upward to 420 minutes for 44,000 pounds or more. When the delay per vehicle beyond free time is one hour or less, the charge is $18.00 and for each additional 30 minutes, the charge is $9.00. If 90 percent of the shipment is on pallets, free time is one half the time normally applicable for the weight, not to exceed 120 minutes.

Vehicles without power units are allowed 24 hours of free time for loading or unloading. After the expiration of free time, the charge is $25.00 for the first and second 24-hour periods; for the third and fourth, $35.00; and for the fifth and thereafter, $50.00.

The carrier is required by the Commission to keep a record of the times for each vehicle and collect any amounts due from the shipper.

**Diversion and reconsignment**

Diversion or reconsignment is an accessorial service. Rules governing diversion or reconsignment of truckload shipments can be found in tariffs that have the rates, but there is wide variation in the wording and charges under the rule. An example of such a provision is shown as follows:

(*a*) When upon instructions of shipper or consignee a shipment is diverted or reconsigned at destination or at some point intermediate to original destination, such diversion or reconsignment will be effected at a charge of $5.85, and the tariff rate from origin to final destination via the reconsignment point will be applied. In the absence of a joint through rate via the route of actual movement (through the reconsignment point), the lowest combination of intermediate rates will apply.

(*b*) When a shipment is reconsigned en route and its continued movement involves a backhaul to the original shipping point, or in the direction of the original shipping point over the route of original movement, charges will be assessed at tariff rates to and from the point of reconsignment.

*Note A:* Carriers do not obligate themselves to divert or reconsign shipment at points short of original destination, but when requested, a reasonable effort to do so will be made.

There are many additional services for which charges are made, but the ones discussed are representative.

**Routing**

There is contained in some tariffs routing that is applicable for the movement of certain commodities. In addition, highway routing guides are issued by an individual carrier, showing the routing to points it serves; and some routing guides have been published for two or more carriers engaged in joint hauls. The publication of a highway routing guide so that a shipment could be routed from point-to-point throughout the United States, however, would be a very difficult task. Many highway carriers have terminal facilities at only a few of their points, which limits them to one-way or inbound service only to the many points where they do not have terminal facilities. Therefore, point-to-point routing is not available with highway transportation except between points having terminal facilities. Terminal facilities are maintained by one or more motor carriers at all the principal points at which freight originates, to which it is delivered, and at which it is interchanged. Many motor carriers maintain terminal facilities at gateway points, through which goods move to terminal junction points for local distribution. Point-to-point routing is possible to the major commercial points, as well as to most intermediate points, through the use of some routing guides which are now available. [18]

Although subchapter I of the Interstate Commerce Act gives the shipper the right to route his freight via rail, there is no provision similar to this in subchapter II governing motor carriers. At the time that the Motor Carrier Act was passed in 1935, there were very few through routes involving two or more motor carriers. Furthermore, motor carriers were primarily concerned with the operation of their own routes and did not seek interchange traffic because of the difficulties involved in divisions between carriers.

During the early years of federal regulation, there were a number of cases in which the Commission reiterated that subchapter II did not empower the shipper to specify routing. However, a careful reading of more recent cases reveals that the shipper's position in routing is receiving greater recognition. The Commission held that although subchapter II of the act does not specifically grant to shippers the right to designate the routes by which their property should be transported by motor common carriers, such carriers are charged with the duty under Section 11101 to establish, observe, and enforce just and reasonable regulations and practice relating thereto. Misrouting is an unreasonable practice according to the Commission.[19] Furthermore, the Commission has jurisdiction to determine whether a shipment has been misrouted.[20]

### Importance of costs in rate making

Although a good start has been made in the development and use of cost data in rate making, the regulated for-hire trucking industry has yet to build a motor carrier price structure starting with the foundation. Rate scales reflecting the distinctive characteristics, the economies, the inherent advantages, as well as cost disadvantages, have not been devised. The basic rail scales still constitute the foundation of the price structure of motor carriers.

Mistakenly, many motor carriers feel that the railroads are their primary competition; if they provide better service at much the same rates, they will be able to compete successfully for the traffic. Private carriage, however, is the real competition for-hire carriers must meet. To do so, for-hire carrier rates should give more consideration to marginal or incremental costs.

Variable, or out-of-pocket, expenses in cost studies are directly assignable to commodities, whereas constant expenses, being related to the operation as a whole, are apportioned to commodities on a statistical basis. It has been suggested that a basic cost rate scale should be developed by determining out-of-pocket costs for all operations, including over-the-road costs for different mileages. With this rate scale as a basis to apply on all truckload shipments, another rate scale could be prepared which would be made up of constant costs, overhead, and profit. The latter scale could be used as the basis of classification principles because motor carriers could take true percentages of this scale to superimpose upon the out-of-pocket scale to arrive at rates for different classes. Every class would be a combination of true cost for handling shipments of that particular size plus a percentage reflecting the proper classification principles, variable costs for that type of traffic, and a reasonable profit based upon the ability to pay.

The same procedure could be followed in building a less-truckload rate structure. A rate scale of this kind would provide an easy method of making rate adjustments since the scale would be composed of four sections—the terminal and over-the-road costs from the basic scale, and terminal and over-the-road costs from the classification, including overhead and profit.

### Rate increases

The procedure followed in rail rate proceedings and in motor rate proceedings is different because the railroads have been under maximum rate orders for many years and must petition the Commission to permit an increase and simultaneously waive the effectiveness of the maximum order or orders. Motor carriers, on the other hand, do not have maximum rate orders issued by the Commission to prevent an increase, with the result that motor carrier rate bureaus, as a matter of practice, have filed tariffs containing the desired increase in each case without petitioning for a hearing on a proposed temporary increase.

The request for increases may be by a percentage, such as five percent, which would increase all rates by that amount. This is termed a "horizontal" increase. In other instances, the requests are for selective increases that are applicable on a commodity or commodity group. These are sometimes termed "vertical" increases. General rate increases are typically of an X-Y-Z nature; i.e., three percent on shipments of less than 500 pounds, two percent between 500 and 1,000 pounds, and 1.5 percent on the remainder of the traffic. If the carrier's labor costs increase by six percent, and labor constitutes 65 percent of the carrier's costs, one might assume that all rates could be increased by about four percent and reflect such costs. This does not occur, however, because on shipments weighing more than 1,000 pounds, the competitive pressures from private carriers, TOFC, and specialized truckload lot motor carriers result in increases being proposed on an graduated scale.

Under *Ex Parte MC-82, New Procedures in Motor Revenue Proceedings,* if the increase in carrier revenue is in excess of $1 million, the justification required by the Commission of the need for the general increase is much more comprehensive, and 45 days' notice is required rather than 30 days.

The rules that were applicable in 1971 to the ten major tariff publishing bureaus stated that those carriers participating in continuous traffic studies accounted for about 90 percent of the revenues earned by Instruction 27 carriers in the nation. (Instruction 27 carriers are those selected by the Commission to submit certain traffic data to it each year). Bureaus had to include those Instruction 27 carriers that earn $1 million or more in annual operating revenues from the issue traffic (issue traffic consists of those shipments on which the freight rates or charges would be affected by a rate proposal).

During the 1970's, motor carriers initiated the restructuring of their rates by major bureaus in which they sought to increase the rates on smaller shipments so they more nearly reflected costs and, at the same time, reduced rates on certain larger shipment categories on which rates had been too far above costs. This action was interrupted by the Commission which began extensive hearings on this subject in *Ex Parte No. MC-98, New Procedures in Motor Carrier Restructuring Proceedings, 1976.*

Motor carrier rate increases are not filed or established on a national scale but are largely initiated by the many freight rate conferences or bureaus on behalf of their carrier members. When increases have been granted, they have been applicable only to the particular territory which requested the increase. The regional nature of rate increases is due to differences in costs and other factors within the various rate territories. Rates may be suspended by the Commission. The author's study covering a five-year period showed that two-thirds of the suspensions in that period were for two months or less. The principal reason given for all suspensions during that period was rate reduction, which accounted for 65 percent of the suspensions.

As a part of the government's move to end a transportation stoppage by independent owner-operators, the Commission by a special permission order issued February 7, 1974, allowed motor carriers to apply for a six percent fuel surcharge on 24-hours' notice without the necessitating of submitting supporting data. The order required the pass-through of increases authorized under the permission to the persons actually incurring the fuel increase prices. Subsequent shipper protests resulted in the Commission cancelling this surcharge but allowing motor carriers in *Ex Parte MC-92,* July 1974, to file rate increases of up to nine percent. Of this nine percent, three percent would represent the surcharge and would be incorporated into their general rate structure. This, too, became very controversial.

Again in 1979 during the fuel shortage and the run up in fuel prices, the independent owner-operators struck for relief. The Commission reactivated the quick rate relief procedures allowing rate increases to go into effect with 10 days notice, and granted an immediate six percent surcharge increase to owner-operator traffic or truckload traffic, and 2.7 percent on less truckload and that provided by other than owner-operators. Future increases were to be indexed to the base fuel prices of January 1, 1979, and weekly notices were to be issued by the Commission. By February, 1980, the TL surcharge increase was 11.5 percent and the LTL was reduced to 2.0 percent.

**Joint-rate divisions**

When a shipment is transported by two or more carriers, it is often done on the basis of a joint through rate. The division of the revenue for the shipment depends upon the agreement between the carriers. One of the following methods—the first four of which are "arbitrary prorate" methods—may be used:

1. A flat percentage rate of through gross revenue.
2. A flat rate per 100 pounds which is applicable regardless of any class, commodity, or exception rating.
3. A flat rate per 100 pounds dependent upon the class, commodity, or exception rating used to determine the through rate.
4. A flat percentage rate of net revenue.
5. A mileage prorate. The mileage factors used are generally the short-line mileage between junction points, with reliance upon Rand McNally map distances. The mileage factors are added, and this total is then divided into each mileage factor, having first reduced each mileage factor to percentage by multiplying by 100. The figure secured from so dividing represents the percentage due each carrier.
6. Rate prorate. Determine percentages as in No. 5. However, the factor used is the normal first class rate between junction points.
7. A mileage-rate prorate. This combines No. 5 and No. 6, and the procedure is as follows: The percentages should be determined both by mileage, as in No. 5, and by rate, as in No. 6. Then add the percentage to each line by mileage to the percentage to each line by rate, and divide by the number of lines considered in the computation.

Many carriers use the rate prorate method of dividing revenues.

One of the primary problems involving joint-rated traffic is that of division of revenues.[21] Few cases involving division of revenues come before the Commission, as the carriers usually reach an agreement without seeking a ruling. In a case of major proportions involving division of motor joint rates, the Commission upheld the existing division that had been attacked by some short-haul truckers which felt they were not receiving an adequate share on joint hauls.[22] Some revenue division agreements are not revised to reflect the rate increases, and this often gives rise to friction between the carriers.

### Rate conferences and rate bureaus

After the passage of the Motor Carrier Act in 1935, which required interstate motor carriers to file and publish their rates, rate bureaus and rate-making conferences were developed in the motor carrier field. These bureaus were patterned after those that had been established in the rail field, and today there are more than 65 motor carrier rate and tariff bureaus. These bureaus provide the rate-making machinery through which a rate change or proposal is formulated. They also compile tariffs for carriers in accordance with tariff circular requirements of the Interstate Commerce Commission. These requirements specify the size of the tariff, the size of type, and other matters. Of the tariffs that are filed by motor carriers, the Commission examines them on a random sampling basis.[23]

Motor rate bureaus are usually operated by groups of carriers, but there are some bureaus in the motor carrier field which are operated by individuals. Some of these motor carrier rate and tariff bureaus limit their membership to common carriers, whereas others permit both common and contract carriers to participate. Other rate bureaus include any type of motor carrier, large or small. Furthermore, some rate bureaus have created rate-making machinery for a specific type of commodity or haulers, such as household goods. Most of the motor carrier rate bureaus are incorporated as nonprofit organizations and serve their members in the following manner:

1. Aid in preparing, filing, and amending tariffs, schedules of rates, and services.
2. Provide a means for concerted action in handling problems arising under regulatory laws within the areas of business operations of the membership.
3. Disseminate pertinent information to the membership and other interested parties.
4. Serve as a means for interchange of views on technological developments in the motor carrier industry.
5. Cooperate with other motor carrier agencies and appropriate government agencies.

Each motor carrier rate bureau has a Standing Rate Committee composed generally of full-time employees and an Appeal Committee (often called General Committee) composed of representatives of the carriers. Figure 15-3 is an organization chart of a typical motor carrier rate bureau.

The rate bureaus are supported by dues, assessments, or other revenue contributions, such as the publication and sale of tariffs. There is considerable variation among the bureaus in their means of support, some of them charging dues that are sufficient to cover a major portion of their expenses and depending upon the sale of the published tariffs to augment their revenues. There is generally an admission fee, ranging from $20 to $50, and dues paid on the basis of percentage of gross receipts; and, as is to be expected, the bylaws of such bureaus provide a definition as to what constitutes gross receipts. This results in a range of charges from $13 to $325 per month in one rate bureau, whereas another bureau has a range of from $15 to $60 per month. In addition to being a practical method of formulating rates and publishing tariffs, the rate bureau procedure is inexpensive for carrier members.

### Intraterritorial motor carrier rate bureaus

Motor carriers in an area or region usually have a bureau to insure a simple and economical method of considering such traffic matters as freight rates and rules and regulations to govern the traffic to be moved. These bureaus act as clearinghouses for the traffic problems which concern the carrier members, as well as the carriers and the shipping public, and the carriers and the Interstate Commerce Commission. Intraterritorial rate bureaus handle and publish rates applicable to points within a defined territory. However, some intraterritorial bureaus also publish rates to points outside the defined territory; in other words, interterritorial as well as intraterritorial rates. The map shown in Fig. 15-4 indicates the primary intraterritorial rate bureaus and the areas covered by each.

When tariff changes are proposed, the proposals are made through the rate bureaus. A proposal is made by a shipper or carrier on a form provided by the rate bureau. Figure 15-5 gives the procedural steps that are followed in regular rate proposals.

In addition to the regular procedure, the motor carrier rate bureaus also provide for emergency procedure. Emergency proposals can be initiated by the bureau, carriers, or the federal government when specific conditions, such as competition, national defense, or tariff errors, are present (Fig. 15-5).

### Interterritorial motor carrier rate bureaus

To facilitate the adjustment of rates between areas, a number of interterritorial motor carrier rate bureaus have been established. Figure 15-6 is a map which shows the intraterritorial areas to which interterritorial rates are published by interterritorial rate bureaus.

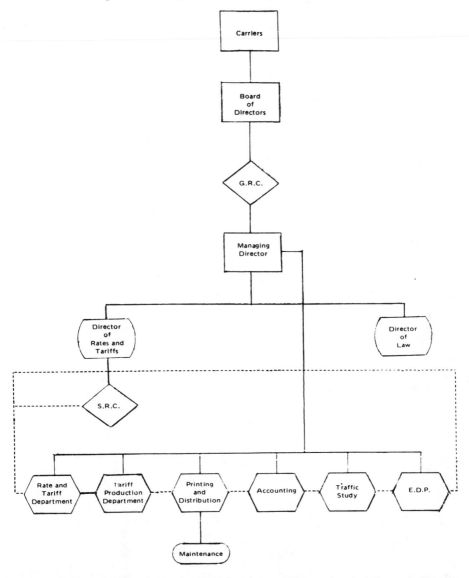

Fig. 15-3. Organization chart of a typical motor carrier rate bureau. Source: Central and Southern Motor Carrier Tariff Association.

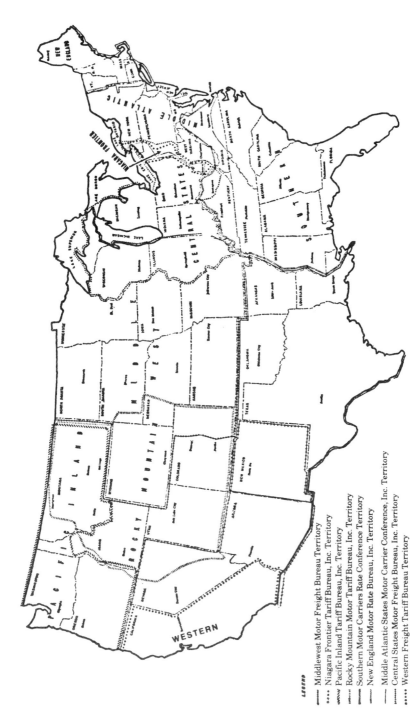

Fig. 15-4. Approximate boundaries of major intraterritorial motor freight territories.

LEGEND

Middlewest Motor Freight Bureau Territory
Niagara Frontier Tariff Bureau, Inc. Territory
Pacific Inland Tariff Bureau, Inc. Territory
Rocky Mountain Motor Tariff Bureau, Inc. Territory
Southern Motor Carriers Rate Conference Territory
New England Motor Rate Bureau, Inc. Territory
Middle Atlantic States Motor Carrier Conference, Inc. Territory
Central States Motor Freight Bureau, Inc. Territory
Western Freight Tariff Bureau Territory

In general, the procedure in presenting interterritorial rate proposals follows the pattern of that described for intraterritorial rate proposals, with the exception that independent action can be taken immediately after a proposal is denied and no appeal is necessary. In both interstate intraterritorial and interterritorial rate proposals which have been favorably acted upon by the committees after public hearings at which carriers, shippers, and the public have had the opportunity to participate, the proposed rate is filed with the Interstate Commerce Commission for action. In the event of independent action by a carrier, as previously described, the rate proposal involved, if applicable to interstate traffic, must be filed with the Interstate Commerce Commission for its action.

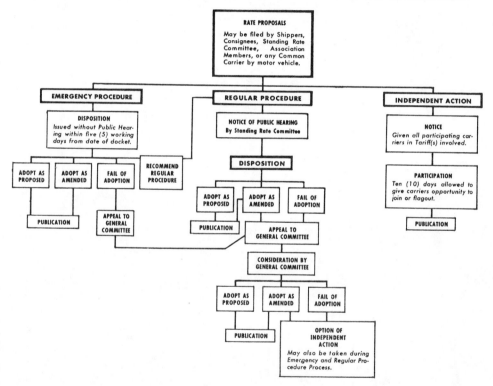

Fig. 15-5. Procedural steps followed in rate proposals—regular, emergency, and independent action. Source: Eastern-Central Motor Carriers Association.

### Conference method of rate making

The method whereby a carrier or shipper originates a rate proposal and submits it to a rate bureau, as previously described, is referred to as the conference method of rate making and was in general use for many years in railroad rate making prior to the development of the motor

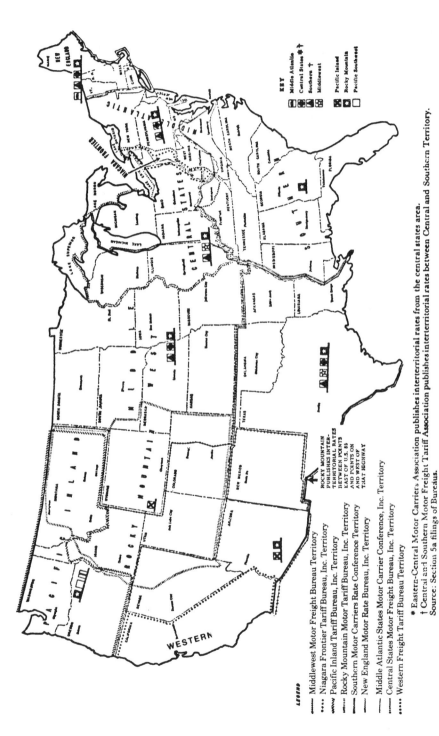

Fig. 15-6. Intraterritorial areas to which interterritorial rates are published by interterritorial rate bureaus.

carrier industry. Some doubt as to the legality of the conference method of rate making was raised by the Department of Justice as a result of investigations questioning whether the operation of a rate bureau is contrary to the antitrust laws. The Department of Justice accordingly brought a criminal suit (which was tried in 1944 and resulted in acquittal) against a number of motor carriers. The questions raised by this suit and a similar suit instituted by the Department against railroad rate bureaus resulted in the introduction of legislation in the Congress to legalize the conference method of rate making. Extensive hearings were held concerning various proposals which would permit rate agreements among carriers. It is significant that there was overwhelming support by shippers' organizations of the bill which was finally passed, and became Section 10706 (b) of the act, which is known as the Reed-Bulwinkle Act. The effect of the investigations and subsequent congressional hearings has been beneficial to the industry as a whole, for minor abuses were pointed out and corrected.

The amendment exempted from the antitrust laws regulated carriers whose agreements of rates and charges have been approved by the Interstate Commerce Commission. An order issued by the Interstate Commerce Commission on July 6, 1948, stated in detail the rules, regulations, and procedures required for the filing of applications for approval of agreements with other motor carriers covering the establishment of rates. In 1959 the Commission issued rules governing the maintenance and preservation of accounts and other records and required annual reports from these bureaus. The major rate bureaus filed for permission to act jointly on interrelated rate matters.

The right of independent action is used by the carriers in an estimated 20 percent of proposed rate changes; and in instances where such prerogative is exercised and the rate in question approved by the Interstate Commerce Commission, succeeding tariffs or supplements thereof often show adoption by other carriers of the rate in question. Shippers and carriers generally are in agreement that the conference method of rate making represents the most practical and orderly procedure for the formulation of rates.

The Commission undertook an investigation in 1973 and elicited comments on 28 areas of inquiry concerning the current practices of groups of carriers engaged in collective rate making under Section 10706 (b).[24] The Commission's report issued in 1975 constituted general approval of rate bureaus.

In 1978, under pressure from the Department of Justice and the Senate Judiciary Committee's Subcommittee on Anti-trust and Monopoly, the Commission in *Ex Parte No. 297, Sub. 3, Motor Carrier Rate Bureaus*

*Under Section 5a of the Interstate Commerce Act* again undertook an investigation of the 65 rate bureaus and issued recommended rules in 1979 on which there was protracted litigation. The following rules were proposed:

... bureaus would not be permitted to vote or agree on single line rates (an estimated 70 percent of the movements of general commodity carriers are single line);

... voting or agreement on interline rate proposals would be limited only to those carriers that could practicably participate in the movement;

... discussion of single and joint line rates by carriers not eligible to vote on such proposals must be limited to whether the proposal would result in discrimination;

... bureaus would be prohibited from protesting any rate or classification established by any carrier of the same mode under its right of independent action;

... bureau members would be able to vote and agree on general increase or decrease proposals or on broad tariff changes.

The Commission questioned whether anti-trust immunity would be necessary if carriers were to continue to use a common tariff for publication of their single line rates.

If major changes such as these are made, the operations of the rate bureaus will be radically altered. However, there will be opposition from some shippers as well as carriers. Whether all, or any, of the proposed rules become effective, consideration should be given to the reduction in the number of major rate bureaus, of which there are presently ten. Some duplicative effort is involved in the work of these bureaus. Both from the standpoint of operations and economics, some reduction appears feasible. At the present time, iron or steel commodity rates within the Central States Motor Territory are published by at least four bureaus—Central States Motor Freight Bureau, Motor Carriers Tariff Bureau, Steel Carriers Tariff Association, and the Interstate Tariff Bureau.

The conference method of rate making allows for more rate flexibility than is generally recognized. For example, one of the major regional rate bureaus in a recent year acted upon approximately 3,000 rate proposals of which 31 percent were reductions in less-truckload lot rates and 56 percent were reductions in truckload rates. Moreover, during the same period, there were 1,200 independent actions of which 83 percent were rate reductions.

## ICC POLICY ON RATES—COMMON

Prior to the development of intercity motor carriers, the rate structure of railroads reflected the influence of the value-of-service consideration in existing rail rates. Generally, rates were relatively high on desirable traffic, as well as on shorter hauls, since such traffic could pay the higher price. With the railroads being virtually the only means of transportation for such traffic, the higher rates did not cause the loss of much volume of this traffic. The revenue derived from these rates enabled railroads to establish low rates on traffic when this was virtually mandatory if there was to be movement of goods.

The rail rate structure was very vulnerable to the competition engendered by the growth of motor carriers because the relatively high rail rates made it possible for motor carriers with a faster, as well as a more complete, service to render such service at the same or lower rates.

The railroads have somewhat belatedly recognized that the nature of their rate structure has lent itself to the development of competitive motor carrier services. Rail carriers have reduced rates to hold or to regain traffic in a number of instances. Frequently the superiority of motor carrier service has restrained shippers from returning their traffic to railroads.

### Reasonableness of rates and rate competition

The Commission has held that rates lower than those of other carriers in the same general territory are not necessarily unreasonable. It has been stated that the rates of the other carriers would have to be found just and reasonable before the rates of the first carrier could be condemned.[25]

Although subchapter II of the act contains no long-and-short-haul clause as is found in the Fourth Section of Part I, the Commission has ruled that when the charge for a short haul exceeds that for the long haul such rates are *prima facie* unreasonable.[26]

Some of the tests applied to rates which have been established to meet competition are: (a) they must be reasonably compensatory so they will not cast a burden upon other traffic; (b) they must not be lower than is necessary to meet competition; and (c) they must not result in a violation of any section of the act.

For a number of years prior to 1958, railroads had maintained that the Commission in its rate decisions forced them to maintain rates at levels that would protect competing modes of transportation. Furthermore, it was stated that the Commission was allocating shares of traffic to the various modes through its rate rulings. The Transportation Act of 1958 amended the rule of ratemaking in Section 15a of the Act by adding the following paragraph:

In a proceeding involving competition between carriers of different modes of transportation subject to this Act, the Commission, in determining whether a rate is lower than a reasonable minimum rate, shall consider the facts and circumstances attending the movement of the traffic by the carrier or carriers to which the rate is applicable. Rates of a carrier shall not be held up to a particular level to protect the traffic of any other mode of transportation, giving due consideration to the objectives of the national transportation policy declared in this Act.

This has become a very controversial provision, as railroads feel that it is intended to bring about a substantial change in rate making, whereas motor and water carriers feel that little or no change is intended. The decisions in some early cases have permitted the railroads to lower rates on certain traffic, some of which is competitive with motor carriers and some of which is not.[27]

Among the selective rate adjustments the railroads have been permitted to establish is a "guaranteed" or "contract rate." The shipper agrees to ship a certain percentage, such as 90 percent, of the annual tonnage of a particular commodity in return for which the rate is lower than the normal rate, perhaps 17 percent lower. Railroads have also been permitted to establish annual volume rates. These are rates in which the rate to the shipper is based on a specified annual minimum quantity. If more than this quantity is shipped, the rate declines on a graduated basis.

The competitive aspects of motor and rail transportation will result in an increasing number of cases testing the exact meaning of the amendment, and unquestionably some of these will reach the courts. A recent case involving intermodal competition in which reliance upon a particular type of cost was at issue is that involving the shipment of ingot molds. In this case, the railroads sought to reduce their rates for handling ingot molds' traffic below their fully distributed costs of handling traffic and that of the competing barge-trucks service, although it would still be above the railroads' out-of-pocket costs. The Commission ruled against the proposed rate reduction, but the railroads appealed the decision to a district court, which set aside the Commission's order. The district court held that the Commission had failed to state a rational basis to support its conclusion that fully distributed costs of the two competing modes must be compared to determine which mode has an inherent cost advantage. Upon appeal to the Supreme Court, the district court decision was reversed. The Supreme Court felt there was no reason why the Commission should not have wide latitude to decide not only where but how it will solve the problem of what costs to apply.

The Commission authorized the use of one-way costing in a recent ruling.[28] The traffic would be lost to private carriage unless rates were reduced by using one-way costing.

The competition which motor carriers face is not only that from other modes of transportation but from other motor carriers as well. This has frequently led to the establishment of motor carrier rates which are noncompensatory. These rate wars have resulted in the Commission's prescribing minimum rates in a number of rate territories in order to stop the practice. The first of these was decided in 1937. Since that time minimum rates have been prescribed in a number of other territories. [29]

The Transportation Act of 1958 brought a number of carriers of certain agricultural commodities under regulation that had formerly been exempt from regulation. The transportation of such items as frozen fruits and vegetables, tea, coffee beans, and others is now regulated. The Commission instituted a general investigation into the rates, charges, and practices of carriers transporting such commodities and found that, in general, the rates were compensatory. In the case of coffee beans, however, minimum rates were prescribed. [30]

The large number of motor carriers, the nature of their operations, and the ease with which volume shippers can engage in private motor carriage have been factors which have tended to keep motor carrier rates in the lower zone of reasonableness. In those instances where minimum rates have been prescribed by the Commission, such rates often became, in practice, maximum rates because they are the rates which are charged. There have been some instances in which rate proposals have been made by the rate bureaus to increase rates, which action would not be followed by a number of carriers belonging to the respective bureaus. This has made it necessary for the Commission to prescribe a higher minimum. The establishment of minimum rates may be the only method for securing stability of rates in competitive areas.

The majority of the protests received by the Commission in motor carrier rate dockets that are against reduced rates come from motor carriers which are opposed to reduced rates proposed by individual carriers.

### Volume minimum

The conditions under which shipments are moved in motor transportation are not favorable to volume minimum rates which exceed the capacity of a vehicle. The Commission has not found that it is less expensive to move two or three truckloads from a factory in one day than to move one load. There are numerous motor classification ratings which apply on minimum amounts of 50,000 pounds or more, although in some territories there are no such ratings. In the case of commodity rates, there are few which provide for minima above the capacity of the vehicles.

Some years ago the Commission announced that in the case being considered and in the future it would follow a policy of considering to be unreasonable those volume rates of motor carriers subject to minimum weights which are greater than they are able to transport on one unit of equipment unless there was a showing that operating economies would result from maintenance of such greater minimum weight. The Supreme Court, in reversing this, held that other factors than operating costs must be considered, such as the need to meet competition of rail carriers.

Volume minimum weights have been used by motor carriers in order to be competitive with railroads. The Commission has approved a commodity rate subject to a minimum of 100,000 pounds but the size and weight limitations of the states prevent this quantity from being moved in a single vehicle, so the motor carriers may transport it in two vehicles. The Commission examines the reasonableness of the revenue per truck-mile or per ton-mile when the minimum is above the vehicle capacity.

### Through routes and joint rates

Motor common carriers of property may but are not required to enter into through-route and joint-rate arrangements with other such carriers or with common carriers in other fields of transportation. There are many arrangements between common carriers of motor vehicles; but, except in special cases, motor carriers of property and railroads have not been parties to these voluntary arrangements.

The Commission in 1974 ruled that its regulations require motor freight tariffs to conform strictly to operating authority.[31] The major objective of the Commission was to open the way for participation by motor carriers in joint rates and through routes. Some exceptions tariffs had included restrictions against shipments that required a two- or three-line-haul or more than a specific number of lines. The Supreme Court held in 1973 that the Commission may compel motor carriers to continue joint rate agreements they have filed with it.

### ICC POLICY ON RATES—CONTRACT

As a result of an amendment to the Interstate Commerce Act in 1957, motor contract carriers are required to file with the Commission their actual rates and charges, whereas formerly they were required to file only their minimum rates. There is an exception to the effect that a contract carrier which has served a single shipper for more than one year need file only its minimum rates unless the Commission decides otherwise. It is probable that this exemption arises from the fact that a contract carrier serving a single shipper is in effect a substitute for private carriage and thus is not competitive with common carriers.

Contract carriers are not required to maintain the same rates, rules, and regulations for the same services for all shippers served. The new definition provides that no contract carrier shall demand, charge, or collect compensation for such transportation different from the charges filed with the Commission. No reduction can be made in any such charge except after 30 days' notice. This does not apply to increases in charges. Under the 30-day requirement, it is possible that the rates will be protested and perhaps suspended for investigation. Heretofore, the rate might be changed without prior notice or publication. Furthermore, when only a minimum rate was required and not actual rates, a carrier that had contracts to perform identical services for more than one shipper could charge different rates, and the schedule filed with the Commission would show only the lowest charge—the minimum—made for such service. The Congress felt that this placed common carriers at a disadvantage, since it was not possible to determine whether the minimum rate filed was charged all shippers for the same service. It was also possible to charge those contract carrier rates which were above the minimum without prior notice or publication.

Armored-car operators holding motor contract carrier authority to transport bullion, currency, coins, etc., are not required to file schedules of actual rates and charges. It was held that the amount of service rendered each customer and the conditions, time, and place under which the service is rendered vary to such an extent that it would be difficult to describe the service sufficiently to permit the publication of fixed rates in a public rate schedule. They are required, however, to file copies of their minimum rate schedules with the Commission.

The contract carrier's schedule must show the extent of the service which is included in the rate which is filed. The Commission has held that when additional services are provided, such as split pickups, the charges for such services should be shown.[32] When a contract carrier's schedule provides mileage rates or charges, a definite means of determining the mileages must be specified. There are a number of motor carrier agency mileage guides which are used for this purpose. In other instances, the services are performed on an hourly rate basis.

A contract carrier may begin service immediately upon the signing of a new contract if the schedule on file covers the movement as to commodities, rates, rules, and similar matters, the only required change being the addition of the shipper's name. The contract has to be filed within 20 days, and, at the same time, the shipper's name must be added to the schedule by issuing a supplement or a reissue.

Schedules of rates and charges and any amendments to them are required to be open for public inspection, so that they may be examined by competitors, shippers, or others. On the other hand, the Commission may not make public contracts which are filed with it except as a part of a formal proceeding when it considers such disclosure to be in the public interest or to disclose discrepancies with the carrier's schedule of rates.[33]

The Commission has also held that contracts with no definite formula for the rates and under which periodic adjustments are made to assure that neither party will have undue profits or losses are not acceptable.[34]

## QUESTIONS AND PROBLEMS

1. Should motor carriers of general commodities establish four levels of rates based on service provided—premium, superior, standard, and delayed? Why or why not?

2. Define the following: class-rate stop; commodity rate; exception ratings; actual-value ratings; released-value ratings; volume minimum; and detention.

3. Of what importance is broken stowage in rate making? What is the significance of density in motor carrier operations?

4. Explain the nature and extent of motor carrier rate increases in recent years.

5. "There has been a very substantial increase in the development and use of cost data in rate making by the Interstate Commerce Commission and the motor carriers, placing service primarily on a cost basis." Are they using the "right" costs?

6. Explain how motor carrier rate bureaus serve their members. How are they supported?

7. Describe how a rate proposal is docketed.

8. Enumerate the reasons why the conference method of rate making is the only practical way to formulate rates. Do you agree?

9. What is the essence of the Reed-Bulwinkle Act as applied to motor carriers?

10. How does a class rate scale work? Have motor carriers adopted the *28300* scale used by railroads?

11. What are distribution rates? Average rates?

12. Do you anticipate a greater development of motor carrier transit privileges? What are some of the problems involved in granting transit privileges?

13. Should the shipper have the right to route motor shipments? Do shippers have any recourse if motor carriers do not follow the routing?

14. What are some of the tests applied to rates which have been established to meet competition?

15. Does the determination of the reasonableness of rates for common carriers differ from that for contract carriers?

16. What are instruction 27 carriers? What is issue traffic?

### FOOTNOTES TO CHAPTER 15

[1]Transportation Association of America, *Transportation Facts and Trends* (1979), p. 11.

[2]Malcolm F. Kent, "The Freight's the Weight," *Highway Research Board Proceedings*, Vol. 37 (Washington, D.C., January, 1958).

[3]*Class Rate Investigation, 1939*, ICC 5 (1952).

[4]*Minimum Class Rate Restrictions, Central & Eastern States*, 44 MCC 367 (1945).

[5]Exclusive use of the vehicle is designed to accord truckload service to less-truckload shipments. The Commission was held that exclusive use of vehicle charges cannot be applied when the entire shipment cannot be loaded in one vehicle.

[6]*Local Cartage National Conference* v. *Middlewest Motor Freight Bureau, Inc.*, 62 MCC 239 (1953).

[7]*Stopping in Transit, Central Territory*, 52 MCC 59 (1950).

[8]*Multiple Deliveries—N.Y., N.J., and New England*, 69 MCC 77 (1956); and 309 ICC 437 (1960).

[9]*Definitions of Freight Consolidators*, 43 MCC 527 (1944).

[10]*Distribution Rates, Newark, N.J., to N.J. and N.Y. Points*, 46 MCC 745 (1947).

[11]*Mid-Western Motor Ft. Tariff Bureau, Inc.* v. *Eichhootz*, 4 MCC 755 (1938).

[12]*Allowances for Pick-Up-and-Delivery at Kansas City*, 272 ICC 331 (1948).

[13]*Ibid.*

[14]Brief of Central States Motor Freight Bureau filed in *I and S M—4462 Surcharge on Small Shipments Within Central States*, 1953.

[15]*Surcharges—New York State*, 62 MCC 117 (1953).

[16]MC—C—2022, *The Atchison Chamber of Commerce et al.* v. *A & B. Transfer et al.*, June, 1958.

[17]Section 20 (11).

[18]*National Highway and Airway Carriers and Routes* (Chicago: National Highway Carriers Directory, Inc.; published semiannually). See American Trucking Associations, Inc., *Motor Carrier Directory*.

[19]*Metzner Stove Repair Co.* v. *Ranft*, 47 MCC 151 (1947).

[20]*Hausman Steel Co.* v. *Seaboard Freight Lines, Inc.*, 32 MCC 31 (1942).

[21]Gerald E. Hawkes, "Motor Carrier Divisions of Revenue on Joint Rated Traffic," *Transportation Journal*, Vol. 8, No. 2 (Winter 1968), p. 19.

[22]*Advance Transportation Co. et al. v. Edward E. Allard*, 350 ICC 751 (1959).

[23]*Ex Parte No. 367, Tariff Integrity Board*, 1979.

[24]*Ex Parte No. 297—Rate Bureau Investigation*, June, 1973; findings issued June 3, 1975 (349 ICC 811).

[25]*Fifth Class Rates between Boston and Providence*, 2 MCC 530 (1937).

[26]*Hausman Steel Co. v. Seaboard Freight Lines, Inc.*, 32 MCC 31, 39 (1942).

[27]*Coal from Kentucky, etc., to Virginia*, 308 ICC 90 (1959); *Gasoline & Fuel Oil from Friendship, N.C.*, 305 ICC 673 (1959); *Sugar to Ohio River Crossings*, 308 ICC 167 (1959); *Lumber from California & Oregon*, 308 ICC 345 (1959); *Paint in Official Territory*, 308 ICC 439 (1959); *Tobacco—N.C. to Central Territory*, 309 ICC 347 (1960); *Carpets and Rugs—Amsterdam, N.Y. to Chicago—Contract Rates*, 309 ICC 124 (1960).

[28]*Aluminum Extrusions from Miami to Chicago*, 325 ICC 188 (1977).

[29]*Middle Atlantic States Motor Carrier Rates*, 4 MCC 68 (1937); *Central Territory Motor Carrier Rates*, 8 MCC 233 (1938); *New England Motor Carrier Rates*, 8 MCC 287 (1938); *Trunk Line Territory Motor Carrier Rates*, 24 MCC 501 (1940); *Midwestern Motor Carrier Rates*, 27 MCC 297 (1941); *Iron and Steel Articles—Eastern Common Carriers*, 68 MCC 717 (1957) and 305 ICC 369 (1959).

[30]*Rates on Formerly Exempt Commodities*, 329 ICC 61 (1966).

[31]*Ex Parte MC-77, Restrictions on Service by Motor Common Carriers (Compliance Reports and Interpretations)*, 1974.

[32]*Dairy and Packing House Products—Iowa, Nebr.—Chicago*, 51 MCC 77 (1949).

[33]*Glass Milk Bottles, Elmira, N.Y., to Md., Pa., and W. Va.*, 29 MCC 191 (1941).

[34]*United Parcel Service of Pa., Inc., Filing of Contracts*, 43 MCC 689 (1944).

# chapter 16

# Selling, advertising, and public relations

## SELLING

The primary duty of the sales department is to sell the services provided by the operating department of the company. In order to accomplish this, a salesman must have a thorough knowledge of the operations of the company. He must know the services which are performed day after day, as well as services which can be rendered by each department of the company when it appears desirable or necessary. The advantages and limitations of his company's interline arrangements should also be a part of a salesman's general knowledge. The salesman must be familiar, then, with the entire operations of the company and the boundaries within which service can be promised and fulfilled. He must understand and be in accord with the policies of the company he represents. The salesman must also have a natural liking for people.

The men who sell transportation service are often called "traffic soliciters." The term that will be used in this text, however, will be that of *transportation salesmen,* because in the present-day competitive transportation era, sales methods, techniques, and effort must be employed to meet the challenge of continuing competitive relationships.

The transportation salesman must maintain contact with the established customers of the company at reasonable intervals dependent upon (a) the value of the account to the company; (b) leads sent in by other transportation salesmen on prospective business; (c) the ability to secure leads for forwarding to other company transportation salesmen; (d) the special service required by the customer; (e) the attention necessary for maintaining goodwill; and (f) the common courtesy owed a customer who is using the service of the company.

All prospective customers should be contacted by the transportation salesman to familiarize them with the services of the company and how these services will benefit the prospective user. This requires a knowledge of market research and physical distribution. The transportation salesman will also handle complaints and try to solve any problems on a fair and equitable basis. In all matters, he must work closely with the operating department, the terminal manager, and other departments in order to meet the service requirements of the customer.

The selling of motor freight transportation represents the selling of a service, which is not a simple matter. The salesman who demonstrates the superiority of a fountain pen has tangible evidence which makes the selling job easier. This is not the case in selling a service. In this type of selling, the salesman has no product to show which can sell itself at the time of the call on the prospect. Rather, it is necessary that the salesman convince the shipper that he should buy a service, the advantages of which he cannot know exactly until he has purchased and used it.

Further, it is difficult to produce a service uniformly as can be accomplished with a product. The buyer of transportation service is interested not only in the extent of service offered by a carrier but also in the consistency of the service, because consistency, like uniformity of product, permits more orderly planning. It enables the traffic or physical distribution manager to coordinate activities of his department with those of other departments of his company on a firm basis.

The growth of motor carrier companies and the increase in personnel necessitates control of the sales functions through sales management. Responsibility for all the sales activities are centralized under a sales manager whose control of these functions governs the degree of effectiveness of the sales department. If the motor carrier is a large firm, there may be regional sales managers as well.

The sales manager's functions include the following: (1) the sales operation, which embraces such matters as selection, training, and supervising of salesmen; (2) sales control, which includes allocation of accounts (national and local), quotas, and budgets; (3) market research, which involves analysis of markets and research on potential tonnage; (4) sales promotion, which is primarily the use of advertising as a sales aid; and (5) the establishment of a sales policy consistent with overall company policy.

Prospects for motor freight transportation can be classified into four groups: (a) those shippers who are already using motor service and therefore are aware of its advantages and know that it meets their transportation requirements; (b) those shippers who make inquiries concerning motor transportation services and charges and who think such transportation service may meet their needs; (c) those shippers who are using a competitive agency of transportation and do not know the advantages of motor transportation; and (d) those shippers who will not try motor carrier service because they feel that a competitive transportation agency meets their transportation needs. The latter group presents the greatest selling problem.

One of the common methods used to locate these prospects is for the transportation salesman to become a member of, and attend the meetings of, numerous business groups, luncheon clubs, traffic clubs, and other organizations where the opportunity to meet businessmen and traffic men exists. The purpose of membership in these organizations, aside from the personal benefits accruing from such participation, is to open a channel through which the motor transportation salesman can make contacts. It has been truly said that much valuable business is obtained through social contacts. After making these contacts, it is possible for the salesman to ascertain whether or not an individual constitutes a logical prospect for a future call. Having met the prospect at one of these informal meetings, it is generally easier for the salesman to secure the interview and establish a friendly basis for the job of selling.

### Shipping motives

In this type of selling, the transportation salesman is required to know thoroughly the transportation needs of the shipper—those things a shipper looks for in a transportation service. Some motor transportation salesmen believe that a knowledge of their prospects, their needs, and their problems is of more value even than a knowledge of selling techniques. There are often times when a transportation salesman can make suggestions that will improve packing methods or aid in solving problems in the shipping department.

There are a number of different reasons why shippers choose a particular transportation agency: (a) habit, (b) economy, (c) convenience, (d) dependability, (e) protection against loss, (f) speed, (g) extra or special service, (h) friendliness or courtesy, (i) liability or responsibility, (j) reputation, (k) trade requirements, (l) policy, (m) friendship, and (n) market competition. These motives, or combinations of them, will influence the choice of a transportation agency by a shipper. It is essential that a transportation salesman, in dealing with a prospect, recognize the motivation that can be effectively used for that particular prospect. Many times a prospect volunteers what it is that he looks for in a transportation service. It should be noted that these motives are largely rational; that is, a traffic manager who is buying transportation service is going to buy on a rational basis, not on an emotional-appeal basis.

### Importance of planning

A transportation salesman has to budget his time carefully in order that he can see a sufficient number of prospective shippers. Some shippers have established limited hours during the day or set days of the week in which they will meet with motor carrier salesmen. A simple method of accomplishing this is for each salesman to keep a card index of all his prospects. On each of these cards, he should place pertinent information which will assist him in selling motor carrier transportation service. Some salesmen may feel that this will include personal information about the prospect, such as his hobbies, as well as business information about the volume of traffic handled, destinations shipped to, and other data of that nature. By recording on a card for each prospect the date of his call and the length of time spent in the call, the transportation salesman has a basis for analyzing whether or not the results he is obtaining are commensurate with the time he spends with each potential customer. In maintaining a card index file on his prospects, it would seem wise for a salesman to arrange a tickler system so as to insure frequent or regular calls on his prospects to show his sincere interest in securing the business.

Furthermore, a salesman should secure from other departments relevant information to be entered in the card index file on the correct cards, showing the tonnage and revenue he secured from each shipper; and the status of any damage claims may profitably be recorded on the cards. This enables the salesman to talk intelligently with those shippers he has been serving. Every call should be planned and thought given to the purpose to be accomplished. It may be to gain new or additional business or to satisfy a complaint.

### Traffic evaluation

It is true that in too many cases emphasis has been placed upon tonnage rather than upon the revenue aspects of the traffic. Tonnage of certain types will render a small amount of revenue because of the depressed rates. Unless a salesman watches this carefully, he may find it much easier to sell the tonnage on which his company secures low revenue. One large motor carrier evaluates traffic by the following criteria:

1. *Tonnage.* There must be a proper balance of various classes. Little credit can be given a salesman for securing a lot of tonnage if his average less-than-truckload rating is Class 50. It is necessary that there be a proper balance of traffic of various classes.

2. *Weight density.* The matter of weight density is very important to all agencies of transportation, but more so to truck transportation than

to rail because of less cubical capacity. Therefore, in the solicitation of traffic, it is important that a transportation salesman know the loadability of the freight being handled or solicited.

3. *Risk and damage susceptibility.* In an analysis of the value of traffic, consideration must be given to the question of risk of damage, theft, or pilferage. The fact that an article may be rated Class 100 does not mean that this particular traffic is desirable. The matter of risk is not limited to damage to the article itself; consideration must be given also to articles which may cause damage, such as acids or carbon black.

4. *Unit value.* Thought must also be given to the question of whether the article is of unusual value, which, of course, adds to the risk. Such traffic, too, may require extra care in handling, thus increasing costs. Claims on this class of traffic add unduly to insurance expense or cargo losses.

5. *Size of shipment and its relationship to cost.* The size, shape and weight of an article affect the cost of handling and should be considered in analyzing the value of traffic. The quantity shipped should be taken into account; whether the shipments are many and small, or whether they are single shipments of large quantities, must also be considered.

### Knowledge of company services

A well-trained transportation salesman must know his company and the service it offers, and he must apply that knowledge to the needs of individual shippers. He should be able to quote rates and should be conversant with the operating authority, both as to routes and commodities. Typically, salesmen are selling a service for which they can rarely quote the price. It is not only important to know the rate structure of his own company but also it is almost of equal importance for the transportation salesman to know what his competitors' price structures are. He should know what service his company is prepared to offer or desires to offer in conjunction with connecting-line carriers. If questions arise concerning matters about which the salesman is unfamiliar, he should always check with his company before giving any information. Although erroneous information may lead to securing traffic one time, it precludes securing future tonnage from that shipper.

### Off-line representation

When the headquarters of an industrial organization is responsible for the routing of traffic, and the motor carrier does not serve the headquarters point but does serve a part of the territory in which the industry ships, the motor carrier will often establish an off-line representative to solicit this traffic. These are often termed national accounts. It is common to establish a national account representative in several cities throughout the United States. One type of off-line selling is that in which the salesman devotes his full time to off-line calls and interline contacts. Another, and less costly, type of off-line salesman is the man who represents several noncompeting carriers. The multiple-carrier salesman often finds that the "lead" he receives from one office may not be useful for one carrier which he represents but may be of value to another carrier. Multiple representation is found particularly in the handling of government and national accounts.

### Selection and training of salesmen

Salesmen must be carefully selected in order to insure an effective sales program. The job requirements are very important as a factor in the selection. A company should first determine what it wants in the prospective salesman. Such matters as the level of experience, the age level, the salary level, and the level of responsibility will be decided before hiring is undertaken. Both formal and informal means may be used to secure applicants from which a selection is made. Applicants should be carefully investigated, interviewed, and screened. Basically, most companies desire to select salesmen who want to work and will produce, and who can be trusted.

### Sales management

It is a common practice in the motor carrier field to hire a salesman with a "following"; that is, a motor carrier will hire a transportation salesman who has made a successful record in the employment of another motor carrier, in order that this new salesman will bring with him the accounts that he has serviced with his former employer. This type of "raiding" is expensive; and it is questionable, over a period of time, whether it is wise procedure. It may turn out that the transportation salesman is unable to maintain a large share of his former accounts. What is needed is adequate sales training in transportation selling. The attribute of the old-time salesman in the transportation field was largely that of a being a "good fellow." Today, it is necessary that a transportation salesmen be a trained individual who is thoroughly grounded in the rudiments of salesmanship in order to serve his company and his clients.

Motor transportation salesmen are usually paid on a straight salary basis, a set amount per week, semimonthly, or monthly. There are two other types of compensation that may be used in paying salesmen—commission and bonus or incentive. It is estimated that about 20 percent of carrier salesmen receive a share of the company's profits under some type of an incentive program.

Some companies establish quotas on both inbound and outbound traffic and then match the results with the quotas. The quotas may change from month to month, not only in terms of desired increases in business, but also in terms of type of traffic in order to achieve a balance of traffic.

It is generally easier to sell single-line service than interline service, yet many carriers must establish interline arrangements in order to provide service to customers because of a lack of operating authority.

The sales training program should cover many areas of carrier policies and practices and be required of new salesmen, established salesmen, and sales supervisors.

The basic steps in selling need to be emphasized. These are: (a) the preapproach, in which background data are secured about the prospect; (b) the approach or interview; (c) the demonstration in which the presentation is made of a company's superiority; (d) overcoming objections; (e) securing the order; and (f) following up the sale. The provision of supplementary material on the techniques of selling will also add to the value of such training.

As a means of improving sales training, a sales manual should be prepared to serve as a guide or an outline in the training program. The information contained in this manual should cover such topics as company policies and procedures, selling techniques, description of salesman's duties, and information about the company's service. It will also be a valuable reference source for salesmen in day-to-day selling.

Salesmen should recognize the value of the numerous forms they are required to fill out and keep current. They relate to their job responsibilities. Illustrative of these are new business leads, rate proposals, routing requests, shipper's record, interline record, monthly sales report, key account lists, and records to help balance traffic.

## ADVERTISING

One of the most effective tools of the modern businessman is advertising. The motor carrier industry could well afford to devote more attention to this aid to selling, for advertising in the motor carrier field is largely of the hit-or-miss variety. Motor transportation service must be merchandised, and advertising can help to accomplish this task efficiently and at reasonable cost. Many motor carriers believe that a salesman alone should take care of supplying the traffic volume, not realizing that this is an expensive way to do business. Since the salesman is the most expensive item in the selling budget, an advertising program which will increase the productivity of his personal contacts with shippers will result in lower overall unit selling costs. Advertising is proxy salesmanship which acquaints a shipper with the motor carrier before a salesman's visit. An advertising program correlated to a salesman's activities makes the selling job easier and effects savings in time for the salesman. Savings in time are savings in money for the motor carrier when translated into a greater number of calls made each day by a salesman.

A number of advertising media are available; and each possesses merit, depending upon the desired objectives of the advertising program. Local newspapers, national advertising, magazines, trade papers, direct mail, radio, and television are some of the most widely used forms of advertising today. Many motor carriers make use of advertising in local trucking directories and national traffic directories, which are in the hands of most shippers or traffic men. Certain types of motor carriers, such as household goods carriers, may keep their name before the public by employing numerous media, including radio advertising, whereas carriers of general commodities tend to aim their advertising to reach a special group. One of the most favored methods of advertising used by motor carriers is that of direct-mail advertising. The effectiveness of this medium of advertising could be increased by making it more personal than the ordinary pamphlets, folders, and blotters, although these types of advertising are better than no advertising at all.

The value of advertising is twofold. From it should be secured (a) the direct results, measured in traffic, that are obtained; and (b) indirect results in aid to salesmen in making known the name of the company and its service, thereby simplifying the task of selling. It has been pointed out that a salesman of motor transportation service must know where his potential shippers are. An advertising program, likewise, to be effective in increased volume of traffic, must know where potential shippers are and must transmit to those potential shippers through the best possible medium or media the facts about the motor carrier which are of importance to the shippers. An effective advertising program for a motor carrier, and one which works with a motor carrier's salesmen, analyzes the shippers' desires and needs and stresses the manner in which the particular motor carrier can fulfill those needs.

Perhaps one of the reasons why advertising is not used more extensively by motor carriers is that too much is expected in the way of tangible results. Motor carrier operators are very practical men and look for a precise measure of benefit from any expenditure of time and money. The benefits of advertising, however, do not always take a tangible form. Particularly is this true of the advertising of a service such as motor transportation, for much of the result of an advertising program will be indirect. Advertising serves the motor carrier as an inexpensive contact, as well as being a method of creating interest in and preference for a carrier's service. Thus, advertising takes the intermediate steps necessary to the production of an order.

## PUBLIC RELATIONS

A part of the selling program of any motor carrier must be that of public relations. Public opinion is of vital importance to the motor carrier industry. Definite responsibility must be assigned for the formulation of an adequate public relations program. This task frequently falls to the sales department, since the members of this department have many contacts with persons outside the motor carrier industry. This is, by no means, a project that should be confined to the sales field, however, but is one that must permeate a carrier's entire organization at every level. All too often, the development of an internal public relations program of proper indoctrination for all employees is neglected. It is certainly true that motor carrier drivers, operating as they do on public highways, are under close scrutiny of the traveling public to a degree much greater than is true of any other intercity property carrier. The result is that the actions of a truck driver on the highway are a decisive factor in the formulation of public opinion concerning the motor carrier he represents, as well as of the industry as a whole.

A good public relations program emphasizes the importance of every individual in a motor carrier's organization. It starts with the answering of a telephone in the motor carrier's place of business. It is the result of impressions its salesmen make in their contacts with the public, the conduct of its drivers on the road, and the impressions formed by people who call at the carrier's place of business. A good public relations program is a composite picture of all the elements of a motor carrier's organization. Everyone in a motor carrier's organization should realize that his part in creating good public relations for the company is vital.

An aspect of public relations often neglected by motor carriers is participation in community affairs. A company, like an individual, should be an active and participating citizen in service and fraternal organizations, in such business organizations as the chamber of commerce, in youth work, and in community health and welfare projects and drives. The impression a community has of a company is due in part to the performance of civic responsibility by company personnel.

Funds for public relations and advertising are often inadequate. Carriers will agree in labor contracts to pay as large an amount in one area as $30.50 per week for each employee into health and welfare funds, but when funds for public relations and advertising are considered, they will not provide sufficient money for a thorough program. If only 25 cents a week for each employee were set aside by the carriers in the area in which this labor contract was negotiated for public relations and advertising, it would amount to $50,000 a week.

The motor carrier national and state trade associations bear the brunt of the public relations program which is carried on in the industry. The three major aims of the national trade association are: (1) to establish the indispensability of trucks; (2) to emphasize that truck drivers are safe and courteous in jointly sharing the highways; and (3) to establish the facts about truck taxes and alleged highway damage.

If a motor carrier makes use of the factual information supplied by an industry association and makes certain that the information is transmitted directly to all employees, it has made a start on good public relations. Public relations workshops conducted by the American Trucking Associations in recent years have been developing a great deal of helpful material.

In 1953 the ATA Foundation, Inc., was created for the purpose of enabling suppliers of the trucking industry to offer special assistance in the public relations problems of the industry through education, research, and publicity. The Foundation is a public relations arm of ATA, but it does not conflict with the basic ATA public relations program, since the Foundation is open only to the nonoperating side of the industry. Each contributor, to the extent of its financial contribution, has the option of specifying that its own advertising agency specify and place advertising or other projects undertaken on behalf of the trucking industry and underwritten by its contribution. All advertisements, direct mail, publicity, or other public relations projects of the Foundation, which are financed by the Foundation, are signed "American Trucking Industry—ATA Foundation." Various media, such as newspapers, magazines, radio, and television, are used. There are now about 51 contributing members of the Foundation. It is administered by a Board of Trustees consisting of a minimum of 11 members and is helpful in assisting in the public relations activities of the trucking industry.

The publication and distribution of a company paper offers an excellent and informal means of conveying those ideas which a motor carrier wishes to emphasize. Such a paper need not be lengthy. It may be in mimeographed form and consist of several pages of "news" about employees, citing examples of good employee public relations and facts about the company and the industry which can be helpful to employees in meeting the public.

### QUESTIONS AND PROBLEMS

1. Do you agree that the term "transportation salesmen" is the best one to be used in describing those who sell motor transportation service? Why or why not?

2. What makes the selling of a service difficult?

3. Of what significance is the application of shipping motives in selling motor transportation? What are rational motives?

4. "It is true that in too many cases emphasis has been placed upon tonnage rather than upon the revenue aspects of the traffic." Why is an understanding of this statement important? On what basis or bases would you evaluate traffic?

5. What is sales diplomacy? How would you go about learning who controls the traffic in a firm? Why?

6. Draw up a list of "do's and don'ts" for motor transportation salesmen.

7. Assume you have been hired by a regular-route motor common carrier of general commodities to draw up a sales program for a ten truck fleet, operating interstate, which has just started business. Describe your program.

8. How are transportation salesmen compensated? Formulate a sound compensation incentive system for the transportation salesmen of a motor carrier employing ten transportation salesmen.

9. Explain the reasons why motor carriers do not utilize advertising to a greater extent as a selling aid. What is your opinion on greater use of advertising?

10. "Public opinion is of vital importance to the motor carrier industry." Explain. How would you organize a public relations program for a specific motor carrier?

11. Is the motor carrier industry faced with a continuing public relations job? Why? What part do the motor carrier trade associations have in public relations work?

12. As a motor carrier salesman, would you rather work "national accounts" or "local" accounts? Why?

# chapter 17

# Regulation and transport policy

State regulation preceded federal regulation in the field of motor transportation. By 1928 property carrying by motor vehicle was regulated in 33 states and the District of Columbia, and passenger carrying by motor vehicle was regulated in 43 states and the District of Columbia.[1] However, there was great variation among the states in the regulatory statutes which were enacted, and many have been modified or augmented. The states undertook regulation for a variety of reasons, which were reflected in the statutes enacted. Some tended to emphasize safety regulation. Others undertook the regulation of the for-hire property and passenger carriers, and still other regulation was undertaken in order to safeguard the highways through the establishment of weight and size limitations. There is evidence that some of the states had statutes enacted in behalf of special interest groups which sought to restrict the development of motor carriers. Other states, however, had more liberal attitudes, as reflected in the statutes that were enacted to regulate the commercial carriers. Early state regulation of commercial motor transport in many instances was successful because of the manner in which the statutes were administered.

The states ran into considerable difficulty in attempting to regulate the property-carrying common and contract carriers. In three states, cases before the U.S. Supreme Court held that state statutes which attempted to regulate motor vehicle contract carriers were unconstitutional.[2] Until 1925 it had been believed that, in the absence of federal regulation, the state had power, if it desired, to control interstate traffic within the boundaries of the state. The U.S. Supreme Court in two cases stated that regardless of the absence of federal regulation the state did not have the right to restrain interstate operations.[3] Another important case which had effect upon the developing pattern of regulation was that of *Stephenson* v. *Binford.*[4] The decision in this case upheld a Texas statute which provided for separate and somewhat different treatment of the contract carriers and common carriers. As was followed later by the federal government in its regulation pattern, Texas statutes required contract carriers to secure permits and required common carriers to secure certificates of public convenience and necessity.

The state regulatory agencies which were given the job of regulating the commercial motor carriers varied in different states; such agencies were variously called the Public Service Commission, the Public Utilities Commission, the Commerce Commission, the Railroad Commission, and the like. These state agencies were already exercising regulatory control over intrastate operations of certain other modes of transportation. Today, the administrative control by state regulatory bodies over intrastate operation is extensive, covering safety as well as economic regulation. All states have these regulatory bodies to regulate property carriers, with the exception of New Jersey. In a few states, private carriers and local cartage companies are regulated. In addition there are presently 23 state Departments of Transportation, some of which have certain regulatory responsibilities.

The granting of certificates of public convenience and necessity to common carriers or permits to contract carriers enables the state to exercise control over the number of for-hire carriers operating intrastate. The general procedure is to regulate the rates of the common carriers, which must be just and reasonable, and to require the filing of tariffs with the regulatory body. The rates must be made public and must be adhered to. Somewhat similar requirements are imposed upon contract carriers. Certain records must be maintained and reports made periodically to these state commissions. Rules to be followed in the establishment of accounting systems must be observed by the commercial motor carriers. Some of the state regulatory bodies have been empowered to administer the special taxes which are levied upon commercial carriers in their states, such as ton-mile, mileage, and gross receipts taxes. Insurance requirements or the bond requirements for the different classes of carriers are generally stipulated by the state agency. In the safety field, the hours of service are generally regulated for the common and contract carriers but not for the private carriers. Relevant data concerning the regulation of commercial motor carriers by the various state agencies can be found in the *State Motor Carrier Guide,* published by Commerce Clearing House, Inc. After the passage of the Motor Carrier Act in 1935, a number of states patterned their state requirements, either through modification of existing statutes or the enactment of new statutes, upon the new federal requirements so that there was a greater degree of uniformity among the states than had hitherto been the case.

However, there is still variation in intrastate regulation because of the numerous problems that exist.[5] For example, in California, regulatory records show that 92 percent of all revenue for hauling freight and express is received by motor carriers. In regulating motor carriers, this state has two laws: one a public utilities code governing regulation of common-carrier trucks operating under certificates of public convenience and necessity; and the Highway Carriers Act of 1935 which governs operations of other for-hire trucks under a permit system. A permit is very easy to secure and originally required only the payment of a nominal fee. Until 1951 the fee was $3; then $50 until 1955; and $100 since that time. The result was that by 1978 there were about 640 certificated motor carriers to which certificates and permits had been granted, whereas there were 13,000 permitted carriers.

The records of the California Public Utilities Commission indicate that there is a great turnover among the permitted carriers, with 20 percent of the revoked permits having been issued less than a year and 23 percent between one and two years. One-third of the revocations are due to failure to carry required insurance, and 24 percent are due to failure to pay their fees.

### Development of federal regulation

A Supreme Court decision in 1925 declared that a permit could not be refused an interstate operator.[6] Serious question then arose as to whether the states could control the operation of interstate commercial motor carriers, and the state regulatory bodies became active in the sponsorship of federal regulation. A bill was introduced in Congress in 1925, and in every session thereafter, until the passage of the Motor Carrier Act in 1935. For a period of almost ten years, then, prior to the passage of the Motor Carrier Act, there had been pressure upon Congress for the enactment of federal motor carrier legislation. The state regulatory agencies were joined in seeking legislation by competitive transport agencies, the Interstate Commerce Commission, certain commercial interests, organized labor, and some of the larger motor carriers. The report of the Federal Coordinator of Transportation, recommending the regulation of both common and contract motor carriers, was made in 1934. The recommendations in this report served as the basis for the Motor Carrier Act of 1935.

The Motor Carrier Act of 1935, later incorporated as Part II of the Interstate Commerce Act in 1940, provided for the safety (since 1967 under the Department of Transportation) and economic regulation of interstate motor carriers engaged in the transportation of persons or property in interstate or foreign commerce, which includes those motor carriers engaged in the handling of interstate shipments but operating wholly within the confines of a state.

The congressional policy, as set forth in the act, was to preserve the inherent advantages of motor transportation, foster sound conditions in the motor carrier industry, promote an adequate motor carrier service at reasonable rates, encourage coordination among the different agencies of transport, and facilitate cooperation between federal and state regulatory authorities. The administration of this act was placed in the hands of the Interstate Commerce Commission. There was some feeling in the motor carrier industry that the Interstate Commerce Commission might be unable to regulate motor transportation in a manner that would benefit the industry because of the Commission's long experience in regulating competitive transport agencies.

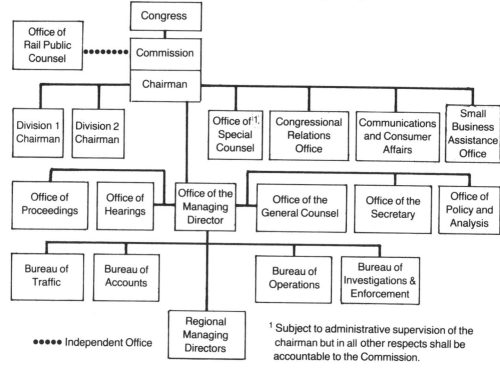

Fig. 17-1. Organization of Interstate Commerce Commission.

## Interstate Commerce Commission

The membership of the Commission is divided into the following divisions: Division 1—operating rights; and Division 2—rates and finance. The total complement of the Commission is 11. The chairman, who is selected by the President to serve in that capacity, does not serve in any division, but the other Commissioners are assigned to the divisions. The Commission has three committees—legislative, rules, and policy and planning. There are five offices that report directly to the chairman.

The staff of the Commission is divided into four bureaus (Fig. 17-1): Accounts, Investigations and Enforcement, Operations, and Traffic; and six offices: Managing Director, Proceedings, General Counsel, Secretary,

Office of Hearings, and Policy and Analysis. Division 1 deals primarily with issuance of certificates, permits, and licenses for motor carriers and brokers; and Division 2 handles freight rate cases and cases involving acquisitions and mergers.

Administrative law judges conduct hearings and submit reports and recommendations to the Commission on motor carrier matters. An approximation as to the percentage of AL judges' recommended reports which are followed by the Interstate Commerce Commission in rate cases is about 50 percent where the reports are uncontested. In instances where exceptions are filed to the AL judges' reports and there are additional hearings, the AL judges' reports in rate cases are followed about 85 percent of the time. In cases that involve operating authority, the Interstate Commerce Commission follows the reports about 60 percent of the time when they are uncontested. When exceptions are filed to these reports in operating authority cases and additional hearings are held, the reports are followed in about 80 percent of the cases.

Since there are many thousands of motor carriers, a tremendous volume of work is involved in the regulation of this segment of transportation. One phase of this regulation, the granting of operating authority, is a huge task in itself. For example, a motor carrier that received its original grant of operating authority in 1935 may have applied from time to time for extensions of the authority to cover new points or additional commodities. These subsequent grants, or subnumbers as they are termed, exceed 400 or more for some carriers. It costs the Commission about $400 to handle each of these applications, and it undoubtedly costs each of the carriers far more to present the application.

Applications for temporary authority for service by common or contract motor carriers by motor vehicle are handled by an employee Temporary Authorities and Transfer Board, except those involving broad questions of policy as well as certain other exceptions. It also deals with applications under one section of the act relating to transfer of certificates or permits that have not involved the taking of testimony at a public hearing.

Other special boards that were created include the Operating Rights and Finance Boards and five Review Boards that handle specific matters, such as insurance and leasing.

To aid in the administration of the Motor Carrier Act, now subchapter II of the Interstate Commerce Act, certain types of cases involving not more than three states can be referred to joint boards by the Commission. The Commission may also at its discretion refer cases of a kind not specified which may involve more than three states to joint boards for action. The membership of these joint boards consists of one member from each state within which the motor carrier operations are conducted or proposed. Their decisions are binding, although appeal may be made to the Commission. The members of the joint boards are usually members of state regulatory commissions or individuals nominated by the governors of the respective states. These joint boards are an unusual administrative device; but, inasmuch as the members have knowledge of the state regulatory patterns, some measure of benefit can be expected.

On the other hand, there is a feeling that members are inclined to give undue weight to the testimony of those living in the home state of the members. Of all motor carrier cases, one-third to one-half are initially issued to joint boards. In many instances, an AL judge of the Commission will conduct joint board hearings. In some instances, only one member of a joint board is present and constitutes a one-man quorum. The reports of joint boards are accepted unless an exception is made to a report.

### Administrative rulings, rule making and general policy statements

One method of establishing Commission policy, used to a great extent in earlier phases of regulation and to a lesser degree at the present, is the issuance of Administrative Rulings. These rulings are numbered and dated and carry a reference to the section of the Interstate Commerce Act involved. Each of the rulings carries a heading indicating that it is an administrative ruling of a bureau or section and has been made in response to questions raised by the public. A ruling is considered by the bureau and/or section to be the correct interpretation of the Act and/or regulations and is made in the absence of an authoritative decision by the Commission.

In the motor carrier field, 127 rulings have been issued of which 93 were issued prior to May, 1943. Some are now obsolete or superseded but others are followed.

During the past several years, the Commission has increased its reliance on rule making as a policy device. In its 1971 annual report, it stated that it was placing greater emphasis on rule making as an effective tool to help solve problems and to adapt regulation to rapid changes in transportation.[7] More recently, it has made use of general policy statements.

A review of these rule making proceedings indicates that some are instituted as a result of past difficulties encountered by the Commission or in anticipation of problems created by changes in circumstances, such as those affecting carrier operations or operating authority. The Commission may institute a proceeding or a petition may be filed by an interested party requesting the initiation of a proceeding. Filing of a petition seeking initation of a rule making proceeding does not automatically bring such results. The Commission must first determine if it will grant the petition. If petition fails to present adequate evidence or reason for a proceeding, the petition will be denied. If the Commission does grant the petition, it then initiates the proceeding by publishing a notice of proposed rule making in the *Federal Register,* as it does for all rule making proceedings.

It is usual for the Commission to issue an order specifying the problem or problems and, at times, possible solutions or alternatives. The order invites interested parties to file representations. Based on these representations, the Commission either issues a tentative report inviting further representations on matters on which it feels the record is inadequate, or issues a final report setting forth its decision.

The rule making proceedings fall into two categories—those affecting a broad area of transportation, and those applying to a type of carrier, rail, motor, water or freight forwarder (as well as broker). Illustrative of recent rule making applying to the broad area of transport are *Ex Parte No. 55, Implementation of National Environmental Policy, Ex Parte No. 278, Investigation of Discrimination Practices of Carriers,* and *Ex Parte No. 251, Joint Rates and Practices of Surface and Air Carriers.* Those applying to a single mode of transportation may be instituted to apply to all carriers in that mode or only a particular type of carrier. *Ex Parte No. 37, Commercial Zones and Terminal Areas* is applicable to different types of motor carriers in contrast to *Ex Parte No. MC–19, Practices of Motor Common Carriers of Household Goods* which applies to household goods carriers.

While *Ex Parte* findings have been challenged in the courts, the court action is generally instituted because of a disagreement over findings not over the Commission's rule making power. The latter has been upheld in the courts.[8]

The rule making and general policy statement procedure provides a tool which the Commission can use effectively in adapting to changes in transportation. It enables the Commission to investigate an issue thoroughly and institute general policy guidelines rather than utilizing a case-by-case method.

### Extent of regulation by the Commission

There were 18,050 motor carriers authorized under the Interstate Commerce Act to engage in transportation in interstate or foreign commerce for compensation on January 1, 1980. Of this number, 16,874 were carriers of property, the remainder being carriers of passengers.

Another segment of interstate motor carrier transportation of property is performed by an estimated 42,033 carriers which transport "exempt" commodities exclusively, primarily agricultural commodities and fish. There were also an estimated 103,344 private carriers which were used to transport property bought or sold by them incidental to their manufacturing or mercantile business.

Approximately 40 percent of the Commission's work deals with motor carriers, and the large number of carriers makes the task of regulation a formidable one. A great many carriers comply with the rules and regulations of the Commission but, with such a large number, it is understandable that there are violations. Motor carriers are subject to criminal prosecution in the federal courts for failure to comply with the provisions of the act and with the rules and regulations of the Commission. Violations include engaging in transportation for compensation without first having obtained Commission authority, rendering transportation service beyond the limitations of the authority issued, failure to file tariffs or schedules, collecting charges different from those filed, not complying with the insurance requirements, not keeping records, falsification of reports or records, or violation of any requirement of the Commission.[9]

To insure greater compliance, the Commission has authorized one of its bureaus to participate in proceedings in which carriers seek new operating authority, or to extend existing authority, or seek to purchase or merge with other carriers, for the purpose of examining the applicant's fitness to operate. The Department of Transportation also furnishes safety information about a carrier's fitness for use in operating authority application, transfer, and revocation proceedings. If there is evidence of failure to comply with safety regulations or with other rules and regulation, this would be a factor in consideration of the application.

The volume of unlawful, or "grey area," operations as it is often termed is unknown. A sufficient number of violations have been detected, however, to lead to more effective enforcement of both state and federal regulatory laws in an attempt to apprehend and prosecute violators. Efforts to reduce the incidence of these violations include cooperative agreements between the Commission and state commissions for investigation of operations suspected of being unlawful, the establishment of uniform standards of state registration of interstate operating authorities, state-federal training schools for enforcement officers of the regulatory agencies, and joint road checks by the Commission and state commissions.

The Commission has also asked shippers to assist in eliminating violations of the act. Such shipper practices as seeking transportation at less than the lawful charges, securing services of the carrier not provided for in its tariff, and extension of credit beyond the period established by the Commission are examples of areas in which shipper cooperation is requested.

### Economic regulation

There are two broad fields of regulation—economic and safety. Economic regulation is the regulation of business practices. The so-called "regulated for-hire" motor carriers are subject to both economic and safety regulation, whereas certain other carriers are subject only to safety regulation. Economic regulation is under the jurisdiction of the Interstate Commerce Commission, while safety regulation is under the Department of Transportation. Private carriers of property and some classes of carriers (exempt) which transport property for compensation are subject only to the provisions of the act and the regulations pertaining to safety which cover qualifications and maximum hours of service of employees, standards of equipment, and safety of operation.

If a motor carrier's application for operating authority is granted, the prospective carrier must comply with the Commission's tariff and insurance requirements before a certificate or permit will be issued. Further, no operations may be lawfully conducted until a certificate or permit is actually issued by the Commission.

Common carriers are issued certificates of public convenience and necessity, and contract carriers are issued permits. These permits and certificates constitute the operating authority of those carriers which meet the requirements of the act as interpreted by the Interstate Commerce Commission. A certificate is granted to a common carrier only if required by public convenience and necessity. The contract carrier's permit can be issued if it is consistent with the public interest and the National Transportation Policy. These operating authorities serve to control the availability of motor transportation service.

Under the provisions of the act as it has been amended, there are a number of "grandfather" clauses. Under the original provisions of the act, those carriers that had bona fide operations (and operated continuously except in circumstances beyond their control) as of June 1 and July 1, 1935 (for common and contract carriers respectively), were permitted to secure their operating authority without proof of public convenience, public necessity, or public interest. Similarly, those carriers operating wholly within the United States but engaged in interstate commerce between points in the states and points in territories and possessions were granted "grandfather" rights at the time they were subjected to regulation under an amendment to the act in 1950.

The Transportation Act of 1958 accorded "grandfather" rights to those motor common and contract carriers that were transporting commodities formerly exempt from economic regulation, such as frozen fruits, berries, vegetables, cocoa and coffee beans, tea, and certain other items if they were transporting them on or before May 1, 1958, and operated continuously thereafter.

The Alaska Statehood Act did not provide "grandfather" rights authorizing the issuance of operating authority to those performing services subject to the Commission's jurisdiction when Alaska became a state. The Congress provided for these rights for motor carriers in Alaska and Hawaii in a bill passed in 1960.[10] Those operating on August 26, 1958, in Alaska and June 27, 1959, in Hawaii may continue operations under the "grandfather" provisions pending determination of their applications.

The Commission in *Ex Parte MC–59, Motor Carrier Operation in the State of Hawaii,* December 9, 1960, exempted Hawaiian motor carriers from federal regulation except those that are affiliated with other carriers operating outside Hawaii. Such affiliated carriers must obtain operating rights.

The regulation of business practices (economic regulation) for common carriers includes the following: (a) certificate requirements, as outlined above; (b) requirements of reports and prescription of a uniform system of accounts for Class I and Class II carriers; (c) publication of rates and observance of rates, which must be reasonable and nondiscriminatory; (d) prescription by the Interstate Commerce Commission of maximum and minimum rates can be exercised; (e) requirement of 30-day notice for changes in rates; (f) suspension of proposed rates for a period not to exceed seven months; (g) requirement of insurance or surety bonds, including public liability and property damage and cargo loss and damage; (h) requirement of approval of the Interstate Commerce Commission for security issuances of over $1 million; (i) requirement of Commission approval of consolidations and mergers, as well as other forms of control (not applicable if annual gross revenues are less than $300,000); (j) reasonable requirements as to the rendering of continuous and adequate service; and (k) receipts or bills of lading must be issued for freight accepted for transportation.

The regulation of business practices of contract carriers, in addition to those regulations already listed for common carriers which affect accounts and reports, consolidations and acquisitions of control, and security issuances, includes the following: (a) prescription of actual charges; and (b) requirement of surety bonds or insurance, not including loss or damage.

In deciding whether transportation is interstate or intrastate, the Commission has held that if the facts disclose a persistent and continuing intention of the shipper that the shipment will move in interstate commerce, it will be held to be interstate transportation even though not under a joint rate with another carrier or under any common control, management, or arrangement for continuous shipment to or from points outside the state. When there is a break in the continuity of movement, such as storing or commingling goods in a warehouse, with the ultimate destination unknown, the subsequent truck movement within the state is in intrastate commerce.[11]

## Department of Transportation and transport policy

There were many studies over a long period of time dealing with transportation problems, and numerous recommendations were made. Among the recommendations was that of the creation of a Department of Transportation. After extended hearings, legislation was enacted in 1966, and the Department of Transportation was officially established April 1, 1967. It consolidated about 30 existing transportation agencies employing about 100,000 with a budget of about $6 million at that time. It is now the fourth largest federal agency with a budget of $15.8 billion and 123,000 employees. It is responsible for leadership in the development, direction, and coordination of transportation policies, functions, and operations of the federal government. Safety functions of the transportation regulatory bodies were transferred to the Department, but not the economic regulatory functions.

As established, the Department is the focal point within the executive branch for federal activities relating to transportation policy, research, safety, and administration. Congress was unwilling to bring the Maritime Administration into the new Department, due in large measure to the opposition of maritime interests to a new maritime policy and program advocated by the then Secretary of Transportation designate.

The original objectives of the Department set forth in 1968 were economic efficiency, environmental quality, safety and support of other national interests, including national defense, economic growth, social development and advancement of scientific research. Following more than two years of study, a fifth objective was added in 1971, namely to facilitate the process of local determination by decentralizing decision making and fostering citizen participation.

The policy process has been defined as: (1) establishment of national goals of primary importance in which there is agreement on priorities and levels of efforts for areas such as defense, public and private sector roles, regional growth, urban development, etc.; (2) agreement on policies to advance these goals; and (3) development and implementation of programs to carry out the policies.[12]

This report delineated ten principles that should be used to guide in the development of National Transportation Policy. These are: (1) to insure the provision of a national transportation system that reasonably meets the nation's needs; (2) to provide this system insofar as possible through the competitive forces of the private sector; (3) where federal expenditures are necessary to finance transportation investments or operations, to recover these expenditures from users and other beneficiaries in relation to the benefits received; (4) to reexamine economic regulation thoroughly in order to determine what parts are necessary to protect, at a minimum, the public interest; (5) to pursue transportation issues involving conservation of scarce resources, the provision of safe transportation, the protection of environment and the availability of satisfactory transportation for the poor, handicapped, and elderly; (6) to provide some federal support to relieve the severe transportation problems present in our large urban areas and the relationship of these problems to other urban issues; (7) to reexamine rural public transportation policy in the numerous isolated rural areas; (8) to remove unneeded restraints on intermodal cooperation and encourage joint use of terminals and other facilities by all transportation modes; (9) to direct a limited number of research programs with high potential payoff to the nation as a whole that have little likelihood of being undertaken without adequate federal support; and (10) to advance the overall knowledge of the nation's transportation system, its capabilities, and its problems. There have been subsequent statements of National Transportation Policy by DOT.

In the formulation of a National Transportation Policy, as directed by Congress in the act creating the Department, the Department must secure approval of the policy by Congress before such a policy is operative.

Four assistant secretaries and a general counsel were established in the Office of the Secretary. Basically, they are advisors to the Secretary. Their responsibilities are with functional areas which cut across the entire Department, and they do not have line authority. The Assistant Secretary for Policy and International Affairs is the principal staff advisor to the Secretary for development, analysis, and review of policy, plans, and programs for domestic and international transportation. The Assistant Secretary for Environment, Safety, and Consumer Affairs has responsibility for insuring that the Department's programs will protect the nation's environment, enhance the safety and security of passengers and cargo, handle the requirement for transportation of hazardous materials, and facilitate the movement of cargo and passengers. The Assistant Secretary for Governmental Affairs maintains liaison with Congress and other federal, state, and local governments regarding Departmental programs. The Assistant Secretary for Administration handles personnel and training and general administrative operations. The General Counsel advises the Secretary on all legal matters affecting the Department. The Assistant Secretary for Budget and Programs is responsible for the budget and planning.

The eight major operating divisions of the Department are Aviation, Highway, Railroad, National Highway Traffic Safety, Urban Mass Transportation, and Research and Special Programs Administrations, the Coast Guard, and the St. Lawrence Seaway Development Corporation, which carry out the day-to-day execution of the operating programs. The Research and Special Programs Administration is responsible for research and development programs to advance transportation capability as to safety, economy, and effectiveness. The Transportation Systems Center, which performs research and development, is also a part of its responsibility. The Federal Aviation Administration is responsible for registration of aircraft, issuance of air safety regulations, certification of pilots, operation of air navigation facilities, development of supersonic transport aircraft, and administration of federal grants-in-aid for public airports. The Federal Highway Administration is in charge of the Federal-Aid Highway Program and the national traffic and highway safety programs. The National Highway Traffic Safety Administration has responsibility for safety of the highways, including vehicles, drivers, passengers, and pedestrians. It establishes standards for newly manufactured vehicles and their components. In addition, it issues state program standards to assist states in implementing their safety programs for drivers and vehicles. The Federal Railroad Administration is responsible for railroad and oil pipeline safety, operation of the Alaska Railroad and the Administration of the High-Speed Ground Transportation Program. The Urban Mass Transportation Administration is responsible for the federal-aid programs, including loans, grants and operating subsidies, to improve urban mass transportation systems and facilities. It also conducts research and development projects and mass transportation demonstration programs. The Coast Guard handles marine aids to navigation, administers a merchant marine safety program, provides search and rescue operations, and enforces federal laws on the high seas or waters subject to the jurisdiction of the United States. The St. Lawrence Seaway Development Corporation is responsible for the operation and administration of the U.S. locks portion of the Seaway and works with its Canadian counterpart on many aspects of development, operations, and financing in facilitating use of the St. Lawrence Seaway.

A very important part of the Department involves safety. A semiautonomous National Transportation Safety Board was created, charged with investigating and determining the cause of aircraft, railway, highway, and pipeline accidents and with formulating recommendations for promoting transportation safety. The five members serve five-year terms. Under the Transportation Safety Act of 1974, the Board became an independent agency.

The Department initially emphasized safety aspects and the formulation of future action programs and policies. More recently, it has markedly increased research funds and activities in transportation and has sponsored a number of legislative proposals, some of which were enacted. The latter include an Airport and Airway Development Act for five-year improvements in each area, funded by the concept of a trust fund financed by user charges. Programs in mass transportation systems with federal funds for both capital grants and operating subsidies have been passed. The creation of a National Railroad Passenger Corporation, Amtrak, to operate most of our nation's rail passenger service is another of its accomplishments, as well as elimination of the interest payments of the St. Lawrence Seaway debt.

As the focal point in the government for articulation of transportation programs, the Department has been successful although it has not been as successful in instituting some policy changes. Several attempts at regulatory modernization legislation have not been successful but they have injected a greater degree of new ideas and approaches. Many people do not realize that two groups within the Office of the President—the Council of Economic Advisers, and the Office of Management and Budget—have a larger role in shaping policy as well as program changes than has the Department. This often leads to substantive modifications of Department proposals. There are also other organizational groups within the Office of the President that function from time to time in this area that may further modify proposals.

The National Transportation Policy Study Commisssion in 1979 identified the extensive patchwork of federal involvement in transportation policies and programs. In the intercity market, there were 338 policies, 346 programs, 52 federal agencies, and 17 congressional committees. In the urban transport market, there were 162 policies, 357 programs, 46 federal agencies and 13 congressional committees. The rural transport market also had 243 policies, 404 programs, 51 federal agencies, and 17 congressional committees, and in the international transport market 193 policies, 290 programs, 47 federal agencies, and 19 congressional committees.

## Brokers

The operating authority of a broker is a license which is issued by the Interstate Commerce Commission, and 70 licenses for property brokers have currently been issued. The Commission prescribed rules and regulations, which became effective in 1952, governing the practices of brokers of transportation of property. The rules require that each broker must keep and retain for a period of three years an exact record of each transaction in which he participates. He is required to keep open for public inspection at each place of business which he maintains a schedule stating the maximum charge for each brokerage service which he holds out to perform, and he cannot collect any more than that amount. Schedules stating the minimum charge for nonbrokerage service to shippers, consignors, and consignees and the maximum charge for such service for carriers must be kept open for public inspection. The Commission did not establish what the minimum or maximum charge should be.

The rules prescribe that a broker's license may be transferred if approved by the Commission. There is also no prohibition against a person holding a license as a broker and a certificate or permit as a carrier, and there are some instances when such a dual status has been authorized. The license may be restricted in order to exclude from its scope transportation which the person is authorized to perform as a carrier. However, in other instances, such as in the case of household goods brokers also authorized as carriers, such restrictions may or may not be included.

A broker's license will indicate the point or points at which he may conduct his business and from which he may arrange transportation to other points or areas. A number of household goods brokers' licenses authorize service ". . . to all points in the United States."

A licensed broker may lawfully arrange for exempt transportation unless the license restricts this. Exempt transportation may be arranged for by brokers who do not hold authority. Thus the brokerage rules and regulations do not apply to brokers of transportation who arrange for hauling exempt commodities under Section 10526 (b). The regulations do apply to brokers of transportation performed under Section 10924 (a).

In contrast to the small number of regulated freight brokers, there are over 1,000 brokers of unregulated transportation, especially agricultural commodities. Some of the brokers have annual gross revenues of $10 million and handle from 4,000 to 100,000 truckloads per year. They play a major role in the establishment of rates in exempt transportation and, under partial or complete deregulation, the exempt truck broker's role would likely be increased.[13]

### Reexamining regulation

Regulation of an industry may be instituted for a variety of reasons. It may occur because a large sector of the public feels the market mechanism produces inequitable or unfair results. In other instances, an industry may feel it is unable to operate within a free market and ask for government regulation. Other reasons are cited in statutory provisions creating various regulatory agencies. In time, regulatory body rulings and court interpretations provide refinement.

As new modes of transportation have developed, competition has increased among the different modes. In addition, the ease with which private carriage can be substituted for for-hire carriage, even by relatively small shippers, has resulted in very effective competition prevailing. As an outgrowth of these factors, as well as alleged inefficiencies caused by regulation, consideration is being given to the relaxation of regulation.[14] Suggestions range from complete abandonment of economic regulation to continuance of regulation with no change.

When economic regulation is instituted, as in the trucking industry, there are a number of goals of regulation which when achieved are often subsequently overlooked. After economic regulation has been operative for a period of time, questions may be raised about the costs of regulation, especially by economists who then quantify the costs. Periodically, statements of general economists have appeared that economic deregulation would result in savings of as much as $1 billion to $10 billion. Unfortunately, the magnitude of these figures is such that they make good headlines, but such proposals are silent as to what would take regulation's place.

It is suggested in the case of economic regulation of motor transportation that an examination of benefits, as well as costs, might provide a better framework for decisions on future action. The benefits could also be quantified if that were the basis for decisions. Among the benefits of regulation often cited are service availability to small as well as large communities, rate stability, absence of unjust discrimination by carriers among shippers, commodities, and locations, greater employment stability, and reliability and continuity of service. An economic analysis of "The Costs and Benefits of Surface Transportation" by the Bureau of Economics of the Commission concluded that the benefits of economic regulation amounted to $4.8 billion and the costs were $1.7 billion.

If deregulation occurs, the larger general commodity carriers, undoubtedly, would drop 30 percent of the points they now serve, which would be the smaller points, and there would be a greater measure of concentration in what is presently the regulated sector than is now the case. This is not to suggest that no changes should be made but rather that various facets of regulation should be modified, in the author's judgment, which would result in greater economic efficiency, at the same time retaining regulation.

The Department of Transportation in 1971 submitted to Congress the Transportation Systems Act and the Regulatory Modernization Act. This proposed legislation would have, among other things, liberalized entry into motor transportation, would have limited the power of the Commission to suspend rates, would have stipulated that Section 5a could be applied only to joint rates and through routes, would have permitted rates to be lowered or raised without regulatory interference when they fell within a zone of reasonableness, and rate charges that were protested could not be changed more than 20 percent the first and second years.

Certain parts of this legislation became very controversial, and it did not pass. The same year, rail, truck and barge carriers formulated a less controversial legislative program but it also failed to pass. The Transportation Improvement Act was introduced in 1974 by the Department of Transportation and consisted primarily of assistance to railroads. However, Congress introduced the Surface Transportation Act, which incorporated some aspects of the Transportation Improvement Act but it too died in Congress.

In 1974, when the rate of inflation in the economy was running at a rate of about 12 percent, the new President had a number of "economic summit meetings" which were aimed at bringing together proposals to control the rate of inflation. Among the proposals were the removal of all route and commodity descriptions for motor carriers, automatic Commission approval of railroad and truck rates within a zone of reasonableness, elimination of barriers to entry into the trucking industry, and repeal of the antitrust exemptions for rate bureaus. The proposals represented essentially wholesale deregulation that would apply to transportation in particular, but also to other governmental regulatory aspects. In June, 1975, the President met with 24 Congressional leaders and in July met with the members of the ten regulatory bodies to try to formulate regulatory reforms.

The Justice Department has played a leading role in the deregulation effort and, in early 1975, proposed to the White House that the trucking industry be completely deregulated in three years. It had drafted legislation to accomplish the deregulation.

The Department of Transportation, at that time, prepared a draft bill which was more moderate. Its proposed legislation prohibited rate bureaus from discussing single-line movements, extended the incidental-to-aircraft exemption to 100 miles, permitted intercorporate hauling by private carriers, exempted from economic regulation for five years transportation to new plants, permitted trip leasing of private carrier equipment to regulated carriers, provided easier entry by requiring the Commission to consider efficiency gains to a carrier applicant and also provided for more competition by withdrawing the authority of the Commission to protect existing carriers if the new carrier proposed a rate above fully allocated costs, prohibited rate suspensions for common and contract carriers within a certain percentage of the prior rate if above variable cost and placed a time limit on suspension, provided that rates above variable cost could not be found to be unjust or unreasonably low, established a $100 million fund to construct or improve roads or bridges where rail line abandonment occurred, and provided for the use of highway funds for improvements to or operations of a rail freight line to prevent abandonment of the line.

The National Transportation Policy Study Commission was established by Congress in 1976 and made its report in 1979. The committee consisted of six members of the House of Representatives, six members of the Senate, and seven public members.

Its report indicated that the transportation system could not be preserved at the present spending level and might not be able to meet the nation's future needs in the year 2000 in an expanding economy. The report contained more than 80 recommendations for action covering all modes and the infrastructure, 33 of which were considered major recommendations. The following are the principal ones affecting motor transportation:

. . . The three regulatory bodies, the Interstate Commerce Commission, the Federal Maritime Commission, and the Civil Aeronautics Board, should be abolished and a single transportation commission should be created;

. . . The Department of Transportation should be restructured so that it would become the primary agency in all non-regulatory federal actions involving transportation;

. . . Congress should consider consolidating committee transportation jurisdiction rather than having it spread over 30 committees as is currently the case;

. . . Carriers should be allowed to raise or lower rates within a zone of reasonableness defined by Congress, and the anti-trust laws should apply to these firms;

. . . Only carriers that can actually provide service to particular customers should be permitted to participate with other carriers in rate bureau activities to establish a collectively-arrived-at rate;

. . . Carriers should be permitted easier access to and from servicing particular markets;

. . . Federal and state regulations should be applied equally to all carriers;

. . . The federal government should increase its efforts to promulgate equitable and cost effective standards;

. . . Federal policy should encourage private ownership and operation of transportation by relying on the market place;

. . . The federal government should study the benefits of a uniform federal standard on the Interstate Highway System but states should maintain their authority to establish weight and length standards for trucks;

. . . Federal laws and regulations impeding ownership of more than one mode of transportation should be eliminated;

. . . Transportation firms should be allowed to merge subject to antitrust law enforcement;

. . . Modal trust funds for highways, airports, and inland waterways should be retained;

. . . Users of transportation facilities should be assessed charges that reflect the costs occasioned by their use except where non-transportation social and economic objectives are served;

. . . The federal government should foster energy conservation efforts and encourage the development of alternative fuels and energy saving technologies, such as improved equipment design;

. . . Federal involvement in regulation should be minimized;

. . . Effective economic analysis should be required of all existing and proposed major federal policies, programs, and regulations.

The activity involving regulatory modifications was intensified by several factors. The appointment by the President of the chairman of the Interstate Commerce Commission, a recent development, resulted in making this body more reflective of the political changes the Administration desired. Another factor in creating the climate for deregulation was the substantial social legislation passed in the 1970's that affected businesses. These programs involved the environment, occupational and safety hazards, and equal opportunity, all of which produced broad government regulation and expense and red tape for business. The cumulative effect of this social regulation was to focus attention on regulation in general and its impact on both small and large businesses. As a result, proponents of economic regulatory change found more receptivity to deregulation of the trucking industry.

The President's Council on Wage and Price Stability established in 1978 voluntary guidelines on wages and prices. When the National Master Freight Agreement was being negotiated between the Teamsters and regulated motor carriers in 1979, the chairman of the Committee publicly stated that if the negotiated agreement was not within the guidelines, the Administration would press for deregulation of the trucking industry. Both the regulated carriers and the Teamsters were opposed to deregulation. According to the Administration the outcome of the negotiation was in conformance with the wage-price guidelines. However, in spite of this, the President supported proposed legislation introduced by the Senate Committee entitled "Trucking Competition and Safety Act of 1979," which proposed substantial deregulation of the trucking industry. The following are the principal provisions of this legislation:

. . . Outlaw rate bureaus by removing their existing antitrust immunity;

. . . Remove restrictions on commodities which may be transported and eliminate backhaul prohibitions;

. . . Ease entry restrictions but require applicants for new authorities to prove that they are fit, willing and able to meet financial, insurance and safety requirements;

. . . Give carriers freedom to raise or lower rates within a zone of reasonableness without I.C.C. suspension. This would be phased in over a period of two years;

. . . Stiffen penalties for safety violations.

Prior to this time, the regulated trucking industry had consistently resisted efforts at change but had indicated that at the appropriate time they would submit a bill of their own. This they did shortly after the Committee's bill had been introduced. Their recommendations dealt with the areas of entry control, rate regulation, and collective ratemaking and were meant to strengthen the regulatory process. The principal recommendations were:

. . . Legislation should emphasize the adequacy of existing service in grants of authority, the degree of competition, and the energy impact of grants of authority. Only legitimate protests to application for authority should be considered. Upon application and appropriate showing, the Commission should be required to reasonably broaden commodities listed in certificates;

. . . A 7 percent no-suspend zone should be included on an experimental period of 5 years, with suspension only if it were prejudicial or discriminatory;

. . . In collective ratemaking, carriers would be prohibited from voting or participating in traffic in which they could not or did not carry. Individual rate bureaus would be prevented from protesting independent actions of member carriers. Collective ratemaking would be extended to intrastate rates, and specialized carriers could not be denied collect ratemaking process.

An I.C.C. task force in 1977 made 39 recommendations regarding motor carrier entry regulation, some of which were adopted and have been covered in earlier chapters. In 1979, another I.C.C. task force recommended substantial deregulation of certain motor carrier industry segments, such as heavy haulers, temperature controlled service, lumber and building material, metal, bulk material carriers, and household goods carriers. Also included were deregulation aspects for limited market segments, such as armored truck, vehicle transporters, boat haulers, wrecker service, courier services, and film carriers.

The Task Force plan proposes to ease entry restrictions and rate control in market segments *where* an initial determination has been made by the I.C.C. that increased competition will lead to more efficiency, better service, and lower rates. In the sectors where this determination is made (Master Certification) carriers wishing to compete in such market segments need only make a declaration specifying the markets that they commit themselves to serve. Individual tariffs would be required, and a zone of reasonableness rate structure would be employed.

A rulemaking procedure was instituted by the I.C.C. in 1979 in *Ex Parte No. 230 (Sub No. 5), Improvement of TOFC/COFC Regulation*, to consider the following proposals: (1) exempt from regulation rail transportation of TOFC/COFC shipments, either in whole or in part; (2) provide expedited and simplified procedures for licensing new TOFC/COFC service by motor carriers, including those affiliated with railroads; (3) establish a zone of reasonableness within which carrier TOFC/COFC rates could be raised or lowered; (4) modify existing regulations which prohibit motor common carriers from exchanging TOFC/COFC shipments with railroads at other than authorized service points; and, (5) clarify the circumstances under which motor contract carriers can subtitute rail service for all-motor service. The proceeding is limited to rail-motor TOFC or COFC shipments and does not embrace those shipments having a prior or subsequent movement by water.

Also in 1979, the Commission established a rulemaking procedure in *Ex Parte No. MC-127, Special Procedures Governing Return Hauls Applications for Motor Carrier Authority Complementary to Movements of Exempt Agricultural Commodities* to consider permitting motor carriers that haul exempt agricultural commodities to obtain summary grants of authority to haul regulated commodities on the return portion of their movement.

The support for deregulation in some form continued to grow and, as a result of Congressional hearings, the Senate and the House in 1980 introduced separate bills on trucking deregulation, S. 2245, "The Motor Carrier

Reform Act of 1980" in the Senate, and H.R. 6418, "The Motor Carrier Act of 1980" introduced in the House. The major differences and similarities of the two bills are as follows:

*Entry*: S. 2245—The I.C.C. would grant certificates unless it finds that the service provided would be inconsistent with public convenience and necessity, considering the National Transportation Policy, evidence of public need, and existing service.

H.R. 6418—the I.C.C. would grant certificates if applicants are fit, willing, and able, and if it finds that service provided is consistent with public convenience and necessity, considering the National Transportation Policy, public support or other demonstration of public need, and quality and quantity of service.

*Fitness Only Test*: S. 2245—a finding of fitness alone is sufficient for applications to provide transportation: to points not now served by a regulated carrier; as a substitute for abandoned rail service; government traffic; and packages of less than 100 pounds if transported in a vehicle in which no one package exceeds 100 pounds.

H.R. 6418—a finding of fitness alone is sufficient for applications to provide transportation to points not now served by a regulated carrier; as a substitute for abandoned rail service; government traffic; and shipments weighing 100 pounds or less if transported in a vehicle in which no one shipment exceeds 100 pounds.

*Master Certification*: S. 2245—master certification would be prohibited except in the above four instances where the fitness test applies.

H.R. 6418—master certification would not be prohibited.

*Protest Standards*: S. 2245—no carrier could protest an application unless it has the authority to handle the traffic for which authority is applied and has performed service within the scope of application during the previous 12 months; or unless it has filed a prior application for substantially the same authority; or unless the I.C.C. grants leave to intervene upon showing of legitimate interests.

H.R. 6418—generally the same as provided in S. 2245.

*Certificate Restrictions:* S. 2245—within 180 days, the I.C.C. must eliminate all gateway restrictions and circuitous route limitations. It must adopt expedited procedures to allow processing of individual carrier applications to remove other certificate restrictions.

H.R. 6418—within 180 days, the I.C.C. must adopt expedited procedures to allow processing of individual carrier applications to remove all gateway restrictions and circuitous route restrictions and all other certificate restrictions.

*Rate Bureaus*: S. 2245—after January 1, 1981, only carriers with authority to participate in the transportation to which the rate proposal applies may vote on such rate proposal. Effective July 1, 1983, discussion or voting on single-line rates would be prohibited.

H.R. 6418—after January 1, 1981, only carriers with authority to participate in the transportation to which the rate proposal applies may vote on such rate proposal.

*Zone of Reasonableness:* S. 2245—a no-suspend and no-investigation zone of ± 10 percent per year would be established, but no collective ratemaking would be permitted in the zone. The I.C.C. could suspend or investigate rates in the zone for discriminatory, predatory, or destructive competitive practices.

H.R. 6418—similar to S. 2245. (See p. 548, 1980 truck bill provisions.)

Both the Senate and the House separated the household goods movers from the rest of the trucking industry in formulating trucking regulatory reform in 1980. The principal provisions of the proposed household goods bill were the establishment of two standard rate levels—one for line haul rates and one for accessorial charges. Under this bill, carriers would be permitted individually (not collectively) to adjust their rates up or down from the I.C.C. established standard rate level, 10 percent for line haul and 20 percent for accessorial services without Commission interference. The Commission would be required to review and change the standard rate semiannually on the basis of operating costs and would retain authority over discriminatory pricing practices. The Commission could not impose a mandatory binding estimate rule on movers. In regard to entry of new applicants, they would have to prove that there is a necessity for their services. Antitrust immunity would apply only to joint consideration and discussion of the formula and procedures relating to changes in the standard rate level. (See p. 548, 1980 household goods bill provisions.)

Entry control was instituted in the motor carrier field, in part, to provide a balance of capacity with the potential market. At the time it was established, there was a problem of overcapacity, but conditions have changed substantially in recent years. There are artificial restrictions in operating rights that make for inefficiencies. Too many of the rights are specialized as to commodities, routes, direction of movement, territory, and others. Consideration should also be given to eliminating the circuitry for regular route carriers by permitting the carrier authorized to serve two points to follow the most direct route between them.

Greater use could be made by the Commission of limited-term operating authorities that might run from three to five years. The performance record developed during that period by the carrier could be used as the basis for determination as to whether permanent authority should be issued.

Another improvement in the efficiency of regulated carrier operation would be to permit exempt commodities to be transported by regulated carriers in the same vehicle with regulated freight without the exempt commodities losing their exemption.

Exempt carriers would also have more flexibility if those operating not more than three tractor-trailer units were permitted to transport regulated commodities on the return haul of an exempt commodity movement. This would be designed for the independent owner-operator.

Another method would be to provide regulated authority to motor carriers whose primary business is transporting exempt commodities. Such general commodity irregular route authority would be available when at least 50 percent of total transportation tonnage was of exempt commodities.

A greater measure of flexibility in carrier pricing could be accomplished if competitive rates could be established without the normal 30-day notice. If this were permitted without any notice whatsoever, regulated carriers would be able to institute rates immediately which, in their judgment, were necessary in order to meet competition.

Another proposal that would introduce more flexibility to meet competitive conditions would be to stipulate that rates could not be suspended until they had been in effect for 60 days. As it now stands, a carrier can have its proposed rate suspended for a period of seven months. The rigidities caused by this may preclude its adoption of a rate structure to meet competitive conditions. Certainly, it would be reasonable to permit rates to become effective for a period, such as 60 or 90 days, and if the dire consequences forecast as a result of the rate change came to pass, then the regulatory body could suspend the rate. Under existing conditions, there are altogether too many instances of rate suspension occasioned by competitive carrier protests.

Another area in which improvements might be made in the rate structure is that of elimination of cross subsidy in rates, which exists in many rate structures, i.e., rate revenues on some shipments are used to recover the costs on other shipments, the rates for which do not cover all costs. This would necessitate a restructuring of rates. The evidence is that very small shipments are subsidized by larger shipments, and that short-haul mileage traffic is subsidized by long-haul traffic. One of the possible solutions to this problem is the development of standard costs so that rates can be properly based. These costs, developed through industrial engineering techniques, could be used to provide an approach to rates that would reflect efficiency criteria.

The elimination of the National Transportation Policy statement in the Act might also allow for a better basis of competitive rate making. It is a broad statement that contains no adequate guidelines for the Commission's use, whereas the Act itself is based on substantive law. This might clarify the standard to be used by the Commission.

The primary competitor of regulated motor carriers is now private carriage. Once a firm converts to private carriage the possibility of recapturing that traffic is remote since service factors are often improved. In addition, private carriers can and usually do take the most direct route whereas grants of authority of regular route carriers often contain circuity which, unless it is modified, prevents effective competition with private carriage if the latter has a semblance of balance in its haul.

The objective of regulation should be resource commitment adequate to insure that no serious distortion in allocation exists over time within the structure of private and public requirements. This is difficult to accomplish. But transportation regulatory statutes and their administration should be revised to give effect to the following principles: facilitate technological advancement; make costs the primary tests of rates; encourage market-oriented decisions; encourage individual initiative; and improve the quality and safety of transportation services.

During the past three years, numerous actions by the I.C.C. have resulted in a liberalization of economic regulation. In spite of opposition from the trucking trade association and the Teamsters' Union, there is growing pressure on Congress for further deregulation, the extent of which, at time of writing, is problematical.

It is unfortunate that trial periods have not been devised to test certain deregulation proposals. Their effects could then have been determined before the finality of legislative deregulation. As it is, uncertainties and conjectures have caused apprehension among many carriers and many shippers as well. Concern has been expressed, for example, by some shippers as to possible recourse if the Interstate Commerce Act statutory provisions regarding rates are eliminated. The courts would have to be substituted for the I.C.C. on such matters as reasonableness of rates, discriminatory rates, preferential treatment, or prejudicial practices. For some shippers, this would represent no hardship, but for others it would. There are other areas, too, in which the outcome of deregulation will have indeterminate results.

### Exemptions to the Motor Carrier Act

The current estimate is that 56 percent of the intercity ton-miles by truck is not subject to economic regulation. This is accounted for by private and exempt carriers. On the face of it, exempt carriage appears to offer the perfect example of marketplace decisions relating to the amount, quality, and rates for the services without abuses of power for shippers and carriers. It has the appearance of possessing complete rate flexibility. However, it has more rate stability than appears on the face of things. The author's research in the exempt sector indicates the existence of a market information system that functions through truck brokers in which growers, exempt carriers, and consignees have advance knowledge of the rate to be paid. This information system is manifested in some sectors through the publication of rates for truckloads from origins to destinations in a manner very similar to that which occurs in the regulated sector. The result is a measure of stability in the rate structures.

There are a number of exemptions to subchapter II of the Interstate Commerce Act, at the present time. Some of these exemptions are discussed in other chapters. These exempted groups are subject to the safety regulations which the Department of Transportation prescribes, such as the qualifications and maximum hours of service of employees, standards of equipment, and safety rules. Specifically excluded are school buses; motor vehicles owned or operated by hotels; trolley buses; motor vehicles incidental to air transportation; motor vehicles under the authority of the Secretary of the Interior which are used in transporting persons in national parks and monument areas; motor vehicles controlled and operated by farmers to transport agricultural products from the farms and transport supplies to the farms; motor vehicles controlled and operated by cooperative associations or federations of cooperative associations as defined in the Agricultural Marketing Act of 1929; motor vehicles used principally in carrying livestock, fish, or agricultural commodities, not including manufactured products thereof; motor vehicles used exclusively in the transportation of newspapers; vehicles operated exclusively on rails; and motor vehicles used by railroads or express companies, freight forwarders, or persons as incidental to rail transportation pickup and delivery service, since this is already subject to regulation by the Interstate Commerce Commission under subchapter I of the Interstate Commerce Act.

The second group of exemptions are those that are termed conditional in that the Commission may continue these exclusions from the act to the extent that it finds necessary to carry out the National Transportation Policy of the act. The conditional exemptions included the transportation of persons or property wholly within a municipality; between contiguous municipalities, or within a zone adjacent to and a part of a municipality or municipalities; and casual, occasional, or reciprocal transportation for compensation by any person not engaged in transportation by motor vehicle as a regular occupation or business.

The reason why a number of these exemptions were given was to ease the problem of regulation, inasmuch as certain exempted carriers were essentially local in their operations. Careful examination of these exemptions frequently gives rise to the charge that certain of them cover special-interest groups, and therefore it is questionable whether or not such an exempt status should be permitted to continue for such groups. It would appear that it would be extremely difficult to change the status of these exempt carriers after permitting them such a long period of freedom from regulation.

The language in the exemptions which are contained in Section 10526 is not uniform regarding the use of vehicles. Some of the exemptions are more stringent than others regarding this matter. The hotel and newspaper exemptions require that the vehicles be "used exclusively" in the exempt transportation. The school children exemption contains the restriction "employed solely," whereas the national parks exemption uses "operated . . . principally." The commercial zone, casual or occasional, and aircraft exemptions refer to transportation and make no mention of the use of vehicles.

The agricultural commodity, livestock, and fish exemption applies only if the vehicles "are not used in carrying any other property, or passengers, for compensation." The farmer, cooperative association, and taxicab provisions exempt certain motor vehicles but do not contain language which might be interpreted to restrict their use at other times. The problems involving agricultural cooperatives' transportation of nonfarm related traffic for nonmembers (on backhauls) has led to considerable Commission and court activity. The courts ruled that the "incidental and necessary test" must be used. Where cooperatives transport nonfarm related traffic for nonmembers, which is incidental and necessary to the effective performance of its primary farm-related functions, such transportation is exempt.[15] In 1968 Congress enacted legislation (P.L. 90–433) limiting for-hire hauls of nonfarm traffic exempt from Commission regulation to 15 percent of a cooperative's total interstate tonnage in a fiscal year. Cooperatives must notify the Commission they are hauling such traffic and open their records for inspection.

In 1978, Congress directed the Administration to establish a Rural Transportation Advisory Task Force to assess the needs of agriculture, determine the adequacy of the current transportation network in meeting those needs, and make recommendations to Congress for a national agricultural transportation policy. The report issued in 1980 recommended, among other things, the following:

. . . feeds, feed ingredients, grain mill by-products used in feeding, fertilizer, agricultural limestone, and other soil conditioners be added to the list of commodities exempt from I.C.C. regulations under the agricultural-commodities exemption;

. . . legislation be enacted to remove the 15 percent restriction now applied under the agricultural cooperative exemption to the noncooperative, nonmember, regulated traffic of farmer cooperatives;

... the enactment of legislation that will give the Secretary of Agriculture the authority to develop standard contracts of haul for trucking fresh fruits and vegetables and to establish both waivable and non-waivable regulations to govern the use of these contracts;

... USDA continue to provide historical cost, rate, and other information that will be useful to truckers in deciding where to look for loads; and

... Congress consider legislation which would provide adequate incentives to the States to resolve the problem of varying State regulations.

The transportation of newspapers is an exemption which requires that the vehicles have to be used exclusively in the exempt transportation. The Commission has interpreted this to mean that the vehicle can only be used in the transportation of newspapers if it is to be exempted.[16]

The comic supplements or illustrated supplements are considered to be a part of the newspaper. Ordinary magazines, however, are not. Newspapers may be transported under this exemption in the same vehicle and at the same time as U.S. Mail moving under contract with the Post Office Department.[17]

The casual, occasional, or reciprocal exemption is a conditional exemption which is applicable to transportation which is casual, occasional, or reciprocal by any person not engaged in transportation by motor vehicle as a regular business. An example of this exemption is that of a farmer who might occasionally carry his products or his neighbor's products to a market area. This exemption might apply to persons who now and then carry property but do not do so regularly.

The incidental-to-transportation-by-aircraft exemption has been defined as that confined to the transportation in bona fide collection, delivery, or transfer service of shipments which have been received from or will be delivered to an air carrier as part of a continuous movement under a through air bill of lading covering, in addition to the line-haul movement by air, the collection, delivery, or transfer service performed by the motor carrier.[18] This exemption also applies to the indirect air carrier-air freight forwarder.

Prior to this decision, there had been earlier determinations by the Commission in which varying distances between cities and outlying airports were used in determining the exemption, with a rule-of-thumb limit of 25 miles. Intercity motor common carriers had urged the Commission to prescribe the commercial zone of a city as being the limit of the exemption. However, the Commission recognized that a reasonable terminal area for an air carrier at particular points may be different from that for a surface carrier. There have been a number of cases in which the Civil Aeronautics Board has extended terminal areas beyond the 25-mile radius but, in 1966, an application to extend the limits between Indianapolis and Terre Haute, Indiana, which are 65 miles apart, was accepted by the Board. Subsequently, the Commission using its criteria would not allow the extension as it was beyond the limit permitted under the incidental-to-air transportation. In 1979, the Commission issued new rules establishing the zone as extending 35 miles from the boundaries of the airport as well as from the corporate limits of any municipality any part of whose commercial zone falls within 35 miles of the airport. However, the Commission later issued another rule permitting the continuation of service beyond the 35-mile limit where such service had previously been performed.

Section 10526 (6) provides an exemption for motor vehicles used in carrying property consisting of ordinary livestock, fish (including shellfish), or agricultural (including horticultural) commodities (not including manufactured products thereof), if such motor vehicles are not used in carrying any other property or passengers for compensation.[19] This exemption is a very important one because it is estimated that there are 45 percent more carriers engaged in the hauling of exempt agricultural commodities than there are regulated carriers.[20]

The Commission in a number of proceedings in the years following the passage of the Motor Carrier Act determined what fell within the exempt agricultural commodity group. As a result of a series of court decisions which began in 1948 and continued through 1957, however, the list of commodities was greatly enlarged by court interpretation beyond those listed by the Commission as exempt. In 1956 the Supreme Court held that fresh and frozen dressed poultry were exempt agricultural commodities and stated that when the commodity retained a continuing substantial identity through the processing stage, it had not been "manufactured."[21] In another case, the Supreme Court affirmed a lower-court decision that frozen fruits and vegetables also came within the exemption.[22] In order to prevent further erosion of traffic into the exempt category, Congress in the Transportation Act of 1958 returned certain commodities to the regulated transportation category and froze the exempt status to a commodity list issued by the former Bureau of Motor Carriers in Administrative Ruling No. 107.

Under the present exemption, motor vehicles used in carrying property consisting of ordinary livestock, fish (including shellfish), or agricultural (including horticultural) commodities (not including manufactured products thereof), if such motor vehicles are not used in carrying any other property, or passengers, for compensation, are exempt. The commodities included in this exemption are those shown as "exempt" in the commodity list and do not include property shown therein as "not exempt."[23] The exemption does not include frozen fruits, berries, and vegetables; cocoa and coffee beans; tea; bananas; kelp; or wool imported from a foreign country, wool tops and noils, or wool waste. The exemption includes cooked or uncooked (including breaded) fish or shellfish when frozen or fresh (but not including fish or shellfish which have been treated for preserving, such as canned, smoked, pickled, spiced, corned, or kippered products). The Supreme Court, in 1972, reversed the Commission and broadened the agricultural exemption to include frozen fried chicken inasmuch as the law exempted cooked fish. Administrative Ruling No. 119 currently lists more than five single-spaced pages of exempt commodities.

The Transportation Act of 1958 accorded "grandfather" rights to those motor common and contract carriers that had been transporting on or before May 1, 1958, and continuously thereafter commodities formerly exempt from economic regulation in interstate or foreign commerce. The "grandfather" rights allowed the continuation of these operations until a properly filed application for operating authority had been acted upon. The act also provided certain "interim" rights to those carriers which, after May 1, 1958, and prior to August 12, 1958, instituted transportation as motor common or contract carriers in interstate commerce of commodities formerly considered exempt. The interim rights allowed the continuation of such operations until an application for operating authority, properly filed, had been acted upon. It was estimated by the Commission that there would be about 3,000 filings for "grandfather" rights for the transportation of formerly exempt commodities.

The motor carrier applicants for "grandfather" rights under the Transportation Act of 1958 to haul the formerly exempt commodities were permitted an opportunity to apply for authority to haul both groups of commodities, those still exempt and those now nonexempt, in the same vehicle at the same time without subjecting the exempt commodities to economic regulation.

Since February, 1951, the Commission has followed the decision of the courts in two cases, in which it was held that a vehicle may be used for transportation under the exemption in Section 10526(6), even though at other times it is used for intrastate or interstate transportation for compensation of commodities not mentioned in the exemption. [24]

Where a "train" of trailers is drawn by one motive unit or one or more trailers are drawn by a loaded vehicle, it is permissible for one or more units of the train, or combination of vehicles, to transport exempt commodities while the other units are transporting regulated commodities.

There are two provisions in the act which apply to motor carriers which operate physically intrastate but are transporting goods in interstate commerce. The first of these is Section 11501 (2), and the second is the certificate of exemption. In 1962, a new section, Section 10525 (a), established a procedure by which a state commission had the power to authorize a carrier operating solely within its state to engage in both intrastate and interstate operations within the limits of its intrastate authority.

The purpose of the other exemption, the certificate of exemption, which is contained in Section 10525 (b) , is to permit transportation in interstate or foreign commerce when it is of such character or volume as to be of little, if any, consequence in effectuating the National Transportation Policy by carriers engaged in intrastate operation solely within a single state in conformity with the laws thereof without imposing upon such carriers the burden of federal regulation. This exemption is a total exemption, applying also to safety and service requirements. There are approximately 30 such domestic exemptions. In addition, it is under this exemption that Hawaiian motor carriers are exempt from regulation. The phrase "solely within a single state" which is used in this exemption precludes the issuance of a certificate of exemption to one who conducts any operations outside the one state, even those exempt carriers hauling agricultural commodities under Section 10526 (6) .

### Safety regulation

The Motor Carrier Safety function was transferred from the Interstate Commerce Commission in early 1967 and established as the Bureau of Motor Carrier Safety in the Federal Highway Administration in the Department of Transportation. The Bureau is responsible for administering and enforcing the motor carrier safety regulations insofar as highway transportation is concerned. The Federal Highway Administration establishes requirements for the qualifications and maximum hours of service of employees, and safety of operation and equipment of motor carriers, the safety and comfort of migrant workers, while in transit, and reporting to the Interstate Commerce Commission on the fitness, with respect to safety, of motor carriers to receive operating authority.

The Bureau of Motor Carrier Safety has the statutory requirement to promulgate safety regulations for all interstate motor carriers. These relate to the truck, the driver, and the method of operation. Compliance, enforcement, and investigation responsibility includes, among other things, roadside checks and terminal checks. Currently, there are 60,000 motor vehicle inspections per year.

Since April, 1969, motor carrier accident reports filed with the Department of Transportation are open to the public.

About 34 state regulatory agencies have adopted all or parts of the Department of Transportation motor carrier safety regulations. Under Public Law 89-170, cooperative enforcement agreements can be entered into with state agencies to provide free exchange of information and to conduct joint investigations. Currently, there are 29 such agreements.

To administer enforcement of the motor carrier safety program, there are about 123 investigators throughout the United States or one for every 1,100 motor carriers. The Bureau does not have the power to assess any penalties, but evidence of violations is presented to a U.S. attorney, and it is filed in the courts. This amounts to about 400 cases per year.

The motor carrier has the obligation to maintain the vehicle in safe operating condition. Under the regulations, it is not to be operated unless it is inspected and found to be in safe condition.

Although the motor vehicle is most convenient, it is quite destructive, as reflected in our highway casualties. Currently, about 43,000 persons are killed annually on highways.

Two legislative acts were passed in 1966 in an effort to attack the problems involved. The National Traffic and Motor Vehicle Safety Act (P.L. 89-563) authorized the Secretary of Transportation to issue federal performance standards for new and used motor vehicles and their equipment. By 1969 over 30 standards had been issued applicable to manufacturers of new cars. Additional standards are being developed, some of which will be applicable to used cars. Safety rules on new trucks and buses applicable to strength of door locks, uphill performance and acceleration, stability and control of coupled vehicles, and truck braking performance were also issued in 1969. Certain regulations have also been proposed to apply to trucks and buses in use. The Highway Safety Act (P.L. 89-564) authorized the Secretary of Transportation to issue federal standards of highway safety programs to which the states must conform and provided grants-in-aid to assist in implementation of the standards. Thirteen standards were issued covering such programs as periodic motor vehicle inspection, motor vehicle registration, motorcycle safety, driver education, driver licensing, traffic codes and laws, traffic courts, alcohol in relation to highway safety, emergency medical services, traffic records, highway design construction and maintenance, and traffic control devices. One part of the act established federal matching grants to assist the states and their local communities in meeting the federal standards. It stipulated that the governor of each state was responsible for bringing his state into conformity with the federal standards. The Federal-Aid Highway Act of 1970 placed the jurisdiction for most of the standards under the National Highway Traffic Safety Administration. Currently, there are 18 federal safety standards. The Federal-Aid Highway Act of 1973 allowed the 18 safety standards to remain in effect but it prohibited the

Department of Transportation from setting any new standards without action by Congress.

The Transport Safety Act of 1974 consolidated into the Office of the Secretary of Transportation responsibilities over movements of hazardous materials. It included broad expanded powers of regulation and enforcement. Under the Act, the Department may require registration of all carriers (including private) and shippers handling such materials.

The Secretary of Transportation is authorized to conduct highway and motor vehicle safety research, testing, and development and training.

## QUESTIONS AND PROBLEMS

1. Trace the development of state regulation of motor carriers, and cite the pertinent court decisions pertaining thereto.

2. What tests would you apply in determining whether regulation is effective?

3. What factors prompted the passage of the Motor Carrier Act? Why are joint boards an unusual administrative device? Do you feel that their use is sound? Why or why not?

4. List and explain the exemptions listed in the Motor Carrier Act. Which exemptions, in your opinion, are justified at the present time? Explain your answer.

5. Outline what is included in the regulation of business practices for motor common carriers.

6. Carefully differentiate between a common and a contract motor carrier based on the statutory definition and Interstate Commerce Commission decisions. Why is this important to shippers? To the public?

7. Why has the Department of Transportation prescribed safety regulations for all interstate motor carriers?

8. It has been suggested at times that we should eliminate economic regulation of motor carriers by the Interstate Commerce Commission and allow competition to serve as the regulator of rates and services. What are some of the consequences that might be expected if this proposal were followed? Do you feel it would benefit the public?

9. What is the purpose of the employee boards?

10. Is there an overlapping of safety regulation between the states and the federal government?

11. Compare the regulations governing interstate motor common carriers and brokers and indicate what differences, if any, exist.

12. Outline the major proposals made by the Administration since 1970 to modify regulation. What suggestions would you make for regulatory change?

### FOOTNOTES TO CHAPTER 17

[1] *Motor Bus and Motor Truck Operation,* 140 ICC 741 (1928).

[2] *Michigan Public Utilities Commission* v. *Duke,* 266 U.S. 570 (1925); *Frost* v. *Railroad Commission of California,* 271 U.S. 583 (1926); *Smith* v. *Cahoon,* 283 U.S. 553 (1931).

[3] *Buck* v. *Kuykendall,* 267 U.S. 307 (1925); *Bush* v. *Maloy,* 267 U.S. 317 (1925).

[4] 287 U.S. 251 (1932).

[5] See particularly: Donald V. Harper, *Economic Regulation of the Motor Trucking Industry by the States* (Urbana, Ill.: University of Illinois Press, 1959).

[6] *Michigan Public Utilities Commission* v. *Duke,* 266 U.S. 570 (1925).

[7] Interstate Commerce Commission, 85th Annual Report to Congress, 1971, p. 7.

[8] *American Trucking Ass'n* v. *Atchison, T. & S.F.R.R.,* 387 U.S. 397, 416, 18 L. Ed. 2d 847, 87 S. Ct. 1608 (1967).

[9] The three largest transporters of mobile homes which received more than 85 percent of all revenues in that field pleaded no contest to three counts of antitrust violations in 1974. The indictment alleged that the companies attempted to fix and stabilize rates for hauling mobile homes, tried to limit the growth of competition by coercing other transporters of mobile homes into joining a rate conference, and protested virtually all applications for new operating rights by competing carriers.

[10] Public Law 86–615.

[11] *Determination of Jurisdiction Over Transportation of Petroleum and Petroleum Products by Motor Carriers Within a Single State,* 71 MCC 17 (1958).

[12] Secretary of Transportation, U.S. Department of Transportation, *A Progress Report on National Transportation Policy,* May, 1974, p. 2.

[13] Charles A. Taff, "A Study of Truck Brokers of Agricultural Commodities Exempt From Economic Regulation," *Transportation Journal* (Spring, 1979), Vol. 18, No. 3, p. 15.

[14] National Resources Planning Board, *Transportation and National Policy* (Washington, D.C.: U.S. Government Printing Office, 1942); Dudley F. Pegrum, "The Economic Basis of Public Policy for Motor Transport," *Land Economics,* Vol. 28 (1952), p. 224; Department of Commerce, *Issues Involved in a Unified and Coordinated Federal Program for Transportation* (Washington, D.C.: U.S. Government Printing Office, 1949); Presidential Advisory Committee on Transport Policy and Organization, *Revision of Federal Transportation Policy* (Washington, D.C.: U.S. Government Printing Office, 1955); Department of Commerce, *Federal Transportation Policy and Program* (Washington, D.C.: U.S. Government Printing Office, 1960); Senate Committee on Commerce, *National Transportation Policy* (87th Cong., 1st sess. [Washington, D.C.: U.S. Government Printing Office, 1961]); Presidential Message, *The Transportation System of Our Nation* (87th Cong., 2d sess. [Washington, D.C.: U.S. Government Printing Office, 1962]). Numerous annual reports of the President's Council of Economic Advisers.

[15] *Northwest Agricultural Coop. Assn.*, v. *Interstate Commerce Commission*, 350 F 2d 252 (1965) and certiorari denied 382 U.S. 1011 (1966).

[16] *Elliott Extension of Operations*, 6 MCC 578 (1938).

[17] *Blau Common Carrier Application*, 61 MCC 705 (1953).

[18] *Kenny Extension—Air Freight*, 61 MCC 576 (1953).

[19] For an account of the background of the agricultural commodities exemption see Charles A. Taff, *Operating Rights of Motor Carriers* (Dubuque, Iowa: Wm. C. Brown & Co., 1953).

[20] An analysis of state exemptions for transportation of agricultural commodities shows that six states have no special statutory provisions exempting for-hire transportation of agricultural commodities. Three states exempt such carriage only if it is the transporter's own goods, and one state exempts only grain moving from the producer to a place of storage or sale for a distance of not more than 50 miles. In 37 states, there is a wide variation in exemptions of for-hire transportation of agricultural commodities. A few are broader than the federal statute while some are limited to transportation from farm or other place of production, or specifically provide that title to the goods must be held by the producer. In other states, the exemption is restricted to transportation performed by farmers for themselves or by farmers for other farmers. See *State Motor Carrier Guide*, published by Commerce Clearing House, Inc., for additional data.

[21] *East Texas Motor Freight Lines, Inc., et al.* v. *Frozen Food Express et al.*, 351 U.S. 49 (1957).

[22] *Home Transfer and Storage Co.* v. *United States*, 141 Fed. Supp. 599 (1957).

[23] Issued March 19, 1958.

[24] *U.S.* v. *Dunn*, 166 Fed. 2d 116 (1948); *ICC* v. *Service Trucking Co., Inc.*, 186 Fed. 2d 400 (1951).

# chapter 18

# Commission policy—operating authority and mergers

## OPERATING AUTHORITY

As motor carriers have grown, they have often sought an extension of operating authority in order to fill in or round out their service pattern. Often they have purchased the operating rights of others. An examination made in early 1965 of the records of 1,200 Class I carriers showed that they have a total of about 40,000 grants or an average of about 33 grants per carrier. The average for 2,500 Class II carriers was over seven per carrier—a total of about 19,000 grants—and for the 10,000 Class III carriers, the average was about three grants per carrier. It is apparent that the Class I carriers have been more aggressive in extension of their operating authority. About 140,000 permanent grants of operating authority are currently outstanding. By 1978, the Commission was granting new permanent operating rights at the rate of nearly 8,000 a year.

The extent to which restrictions apply in operating authorities varies greatly. Some restrictions deal with equipment, others with operations, or service, or tacking, or interchange, or combinations of them. Typical equipment restrictions apply in grants to transport chemicals and petroleum, for example, in which tank trucks are designated. In many grants, the backhaul restriction is included which prohibits a return haul of the same commodity. Probably between 15 and 20 percent of common carrier certificates contain this prohibition.

Substantial refinements have occurred through the years in operating authority, as one might expect, due to a variety of factors. Restrictions were imposed on operating authorities by the Commission which subsequent technological developments have undermined. Carriers, in such circumstances, may feel they are well qualified now to transport certain commodities they were prohibited from transporting when their certificates were granted. For example, a specialized type of carrier today may feel as well qualified to transport general commodities as any general commodity carrier because of the availability of equipment and its operational knowhow. Additionally, as highway improvements have been made and size and weight restrictions of the states have been modified, commodities that could be shipped by individual carriers and distances that could be economically served have changed. Carriers that had been essentially localized may have found they could become inter-city carriers; an intrastate carrier might wish to become an interstate carrier; a regional carrier could become interregional.

Added to the technological changes that have occurred that could serve as the basis for eliminating some of the historic barriers between types of operations, there have been the equally important changes in our distribution patterns. These have occurred because of changes in marketing channels, broadening of production lines, the increase in movement by bulk, the minimization of inventory carrying costs and warehousing costs, the increase in refrigerated movement, and other developments. The method the Commission has used in handling oper-ating rights cases has been an additional factor. Where a case-by-case method is utilized, the Commission is often called upon to adjudicate narrow definitional aspects often opposed by other carriers. The op-ponents may feel that the proposal would result in broadening the authority in some manner. The Commission must find some rationale for its decision but too often consistency is lacking in the decisions as a result of a case-by-case approach.

For many years the Commission was more restrictive in the grants of authority for regular route carriers of general commodities than for irreg-ular route carriers. Irregular route carriers were able to get initial grants easily as well as subsequent grants, so-called "subs." In the past several years, the Commission has adopted a much more liberal approach in re-gard to grants of authority to regular route carriers and has approved a high percentage of all applications.

### Common and contract carriage

Although the Motor Carrier Act (later Part II of the Interstate Com-merce Act) defines a common and contract carrier, it has not always been easy to draw a line between the two types of carriers. The ul-timate test of common carriage has been the fact of holding out or not holding out to serve the general public. By 1953 the lack of a clear line of demarcation caused motor contract carriers to request the Commis-sion to institute an investigation relative to the need for legislative amendments to clarify the status of contract carriers. A subsequent decision of the Supreme Court in *United States* v. *Contract Steel Car-riers,*[1] which held that a contract carrier is free to search aggressively for new business within the limits of its permit and that indiscriminate solicitation and advertising did not constitute a holding out to serve the general public, resulted in virtual obliteration of the distinction be-tween common and contract carriage. Following this decision, the Con-gress in 1957 redefined contract carriage.

As a result, the Commission in the issuance of a permit considered a number of factors, among which are the following: (1) the number of shippers to be served by the applicant; (2) the nature of the service proposed; (3) the effect the new service would have upon the services of the protesting carriers; (4) the effect that denial of the permit would have upon the applicant and the shipper; and (5) the changing character of the shipper's requirements.

The new definition of contract carriage gave the Commission the power to institute proceedings on or before February 18, 1958, either on its own initiative, upon application of a permit holder, or upon the complaint of an interested party, to revoke contract carrier permits and issue in exchange common carrier certificates for those carriers whose operations were found to be common rather than contract carriage under the amended definition. Of the 2,620 contract carriers in existence in August, 1957, 1,801 were found by the Commission to be contract carriers under the amended definition. Of the remaining 819 carriers, 92 voluntarily requested revocation of their permits; 417 filed applications to convert to common carriage; 309 proceedings were instituted by the Commission on its own motion; and one complaint proceeding was instituted by another carrier. Some of the conversions were to specialized common carriage.

In a conversion application case involving the issuance of a certificate in lieu of an outstanding permit, questions were raised whether certificates should contain (1) restrictions against tacking of separate grants of authority; (2) restrictions against interchange with other common carriers; (3) restrictions designed to perpetuate the "Keystone" restrictions;[2] and (4) whether to grant common carrier authority in lieu of contract carrier authority where contract operations are dormant or the subject of only token operations. The Commission, in this case, applied the "substantial parity" test, which means that a parity should be established between future operations and prior bona fide operations.[3]

In the redefinition of contract carriers, the phrase "contracts with one person or a limited number of persons" raised the question: What constitutes a limited number; is it two, four, ten, 15, or perhaps more? In testimony the Commission did not answer the question by giving a specific number but stated that it would be based on the circumstances which the Commission found in each case.[4] Its rulings, though, limited the number of shippers to 6 to 8. Despite the limitation on number of shippers, the author's research shows that 70 percent of all Class I and II contract carriers received subsequent grants of authority in the years 1970-1975.

In 1979, under deregulation pressure the Commission rejected the "rule of 8" and put no ceiling on the number of contracts.[5] It indicated that it would consider a motor carrier to be a contract carrier if it met one of the following criteria:

. . . performed exclusively one type of specialized service, which because of the degree of specialization involved, is usable only by a particular type of shipper or industry; or

. . . served exclusively firms which are affiliated with one another; or

. . . assigned equipment to the exclusive use of each shipper served for periods of at least 30 days.

Contract carriers cannot interchange traffic with each other,[6] nor can they interchange traffic with common carriers.[7] However, contract carriers may receive shipments from a common carrier or deliver shipments to a common carrier for completion of the transportation haul if this is done in the name of the shipper. Thus the shipper employs the contract carrier as his agent to arrange for transportation beyond points to which the contract carrier is authorized to serve. The bill of lading issued by the common carrier should show the shipper as the consignor rather than his agent, the contract carrier, because the contract carrier cannot furnish service beyond its own line in its own name.

### Dual operations

The act prohibits dual operations, that is, the holding of a permit as a contract carrier and a certificate as a common carrier, unless specifically approved by the Commission. The Commission may permit dual operations if it is shown that there is a good cause. The principal objection to dual operations is that they can result in a particular shipper being given common carrier service at the contract carrier rate, thereby discriminating against other shippers. The tendency of the Commission has been to permit dual operations where the services are of such different nature as to be noncompetitive or where they are between different points or in different areas.

After following a restrictive policy for a long period of time, the Commission in 1978 indicated it would permit dual operations unless there was a specific showing that abuses would be likely to occur.[8] This ruling was upheld by a U.S. court of appeals in 1979.

### Competition

When there is sufficient traffic available to permit it, the Commission has held that competition should be encouraged. In cases involving property carriers, the question of monopoly has seldom arisen, although the Commission stated, in one case, that the existence of a monopoly, standing alone, is not sufficient to justify a new operation in the absence of a showing of some inadequacy in the existing service.[9] The Commission has stated that whether the competition comes from within the motor carrier field or from other modes of transportation will have a bearing on the granting or denial of authority by it. In numerous cases, the Commission has indicated that merely because a point had adequate rail service was not justification for denying motor carrier service, and that shippers were entitled to adequate service by both modes of transportation. The Supreme Court has ruled that the Commission must evaluate the inherent advantages of motor over rail, including rate advantages, when passing on motor applications.[10] The Court stated that a lower rate attributable to differences between two modes of transportation is an "inherent advantage" that cannot be ignored by the Commission in passing upon applications.

Later, the Commission held that a motor carrier was not entitled to a grant of authority merely because there was no other motor service available. The Commission stated that it was incumbent upon the applicant to establish by affirmative evidence that the shippers had a need for motor service because existing rail service had proved completely inadequate to meet their transportation requirements.[11]

Competition from private carriage is sometimes a factor in the grant or denial of operating authority. The Commission has said that a shipper's stated intent to engage in private carriage if the application was denied was not a good reason for approval.[12] In a later case, however, the expressed intent of a shipper to turn to private carriage was cited as a reason for granting an application.[13]

## Public convenience and necessity

The Commission may issue certificates to motor common carriers under Section 10922 (a) (2) if the service is required by the public convenience and necessity. The statute does not define the phrase "public convenience and necessity" and the courts have left it to the Commission. The meaning of the phrase is considered by the Commission to be more than the mere adequacy or availability of transportation agencies but less than an acute need.

The standards for determining public convenience and necessity are found through the answers to a number of questions:

1. Will the new operation or service serve a useful public purpose responsive to public demand or need?
2. Will the public purpose be served as well by existing lines or carriers?
3. Can the public purpose be served by an applicant with the proposed

new operation or service without endangering or impairing the operations of existing carriers contrary to the public interest?

4. Will the advantages to those of the public using the proposed service outweigh the disadvantages, real or potential, that may result to existing services?[14]

Public convenience and necessity has been judged to exist in operating economies and factors which will result in a greater degree of safety, expedition, and more efficient operations, as well as other factors.

A case which had been before the Commission and the Courts for ten years was ended in December, 1974, by the Supreme Court upholding the Commission as the arbiter of public convenience and necessity *(73–1055 Bowman Transportation, et al.* v. *Arkansas Best Freight System et al.).* The issue was the granting by the Commission of general commodity authority between points in the southeast and southwest to three carriers, the effect of which was to increase significantly motor carrier competition. A number of applicants in the case who sought but failed to win authority challenged the decision in the U.S. District Court. The latter set aside the Commission's order and directed the Commission to dismiss the proceeding. The effect of the Court's action was to block the issuance of the certificates. The Court refused to remand the case to the Commission.

The three carriers who were granted the authority by the Commission appealed the lower Court's ruling to the Supreme Court. The latter agreed that the Commission conclusion that consumer benefits outweighed any adverse impact upon the existing carriers reflects the kind of judgment entrusted to it, namely a power to weigh the competing interests and arrive at a balance that is deemed the "public convenience and necessity." The Court stated that the Commission approach was congenial to new entry and the resulting competition. By this decision, the Supreme Court should dispel any notion that the Commission's primary obligation is the protection of firms holding existing certificates. The Supreme Court further stated that where Congress has chosen government regulation as the primary device for protecting public interest, a policy of facilitating competitive market structure and performance is entitled to consideration.

In a later case, the Commission ruled in favor of a grant of operating authority and stated that protests to new motor carrier applications would be rejected unless *substantial harm* to the existing carrier was demonstrated.[15]

In another policy statement, *Ex Parte No. MC-116, Change of Policy Consideration of Rates in Operating Rights Application Proceedings (1979),* the Commission indicated that in the future it would consider the issue of rates as a factor in determining whether the proposed service would be required by the present or future public convenience and necessity.

### Fit, willing, and able

Under Section 10923 (a) (1) a certificate may be issued to a qualified applicant if, among other things, the applicant is found to be fit, willing, and able properly to perform the proposed service. Therefore, the question of the carrier's "fitness" is a very important matter.

The Commission has felt that past violation of the act is a factor to be considered in determining the fitness of a carrier but is not an absolute bar to the grant of operating authority. There have been numerous cases in which there were unauthorized operations which have been termed "inexcusable," although the applicant has been held to be fit. However, when operations have been deliberately conducted without authority over a long period of time with the full knowledge that they were unauthorized, the Commission has held the applicant to be unfit.

In determining the fitness of a carrier with regard to violations of safety regulations, the Commission has generally not denied applications of carriers of general commodities for this reason when the service was needed by the public. Carriers of dangerous commodities, such as munitions, are assumed to have a higher degree of responsibility, and the Commission has denied applications by finding the applicant unfit due to violations of safety regulations. With the transfer of safety regulations to the Department of Transportation, the Commission and DOT entered into an agreement to insure that safety compliance information regarding an applicant for operating authority be transmitted to the Commission, and to provide for DOT intervention in proceedings before the Commission for the purpose of presenting evidence regarding a motor carrier applicant's safety compliance record.

An applicant whose only submitted evidence of its financial fitness and ability consisted of generalized declarations by its representative to the effect that the applicant had always realized an operating profit and that the proposed operations could be conducted at a profit, was held not to be fit and able financially, since the evidence submitted was insufficient. Something more substantial in the way of specific financial data is required to meet the fundamental requirement of financial fitness and ability.[16]

A more precise position regarding an applicant's fitness, willingness, and ability to perform the proposed service was set forth by the Commission in 1952. At that time the Commission ruled that the applicant's past failures to comply with the act and Commission rules and regulations as well as the gravity of certain past offenses, despite penalties and admonitions, warranted the conclusion that the applicant failed to show that it was fit and willing properly to conduct the proposed operations.[17]

The Commission, in 1960, established procedures of looking further into an applicant's record of fitness in any case in which there is evidence to indicate a failure by the applicant to comply with the applicable provisions of the law and the Commission's rules and regulations.

### Operating authority based on duration

The Interstate Commerce Commission grants to qualified motor common and contract carriers two primary types of authority based on duration: *permanent operating authority* and *temporary operating authority*. Temporary certificates and temporary permits are not issued—merely temporary operating authority as referred to in the act. Most operating authorities are of a permanent nature. Temporary authority may be secured from the Commission under Section 10928 to provide service for such period of time as the Commission shall specify but not more than a total of 180 days. This authority may be granted without hearings or other proceedings, providing there is an *immediate* and *urgent* need for the service and there is no carrier service presently operating which is capable of meeting the need. There appear to be two categories of temporary authority. The first is an emergency temporary authority for 30 days or less, while the other is regular temporary authority for a longer period of time, up to 180 days.

When temporary authority is issued, the carrier is subject to all provisions of the act and rules and regulations of the Commission just as is true of the carrier which holds permanent operating authority.

Section 11349 (a) states that when the Commission has pending before it for determination a consolidation or merger of two or more carriers, it can grant temporary approval for the acquiring carrier to operate the entire property involved in the merger application for a period not to exceed 180 days. This insures continued operation of the motor carriers involved pending a Commission determination of the merger application. Beginning in 1954, the Commission attached a statement to orders granting temporary authority in motor finance cases which informs the parties that the temporary authority should create no presumption that final approval will be given the application. The Commission has authority to extend temporary operating rights beyond 180 days based on a ruling of the Supreme Court.

### Limited-term certificates and permits

There are also what are termed "limited-term" certificates and permits. These certificates and permits are issued to expire at a specified time. Such a limited-term certificate might be granted to a lessee who applied for an extension, the certificate being conditioned to expire with the termination of the lease. The construction of a dam that requires three years is another example in which limited-term rights might be granted to motor carriers. Thus, when the circumstances indicate that the public interest would be served by such action, this type of certificate or permit may be issued.

The entire Commission approved the issuance of limited-term certificates in 1955 for the transportation of dangerous explosives for a period not exceeding five years. It thus inaugurated a general policy to confine the grants of operating authority for the transportation of dangerous explosives, radioactive materials, and certain types of compressed gases by motor carriers to limited-term certificates and permits for periods not exceeding five years. Grants of operating authority have been made for one-year periods, also.[18] This action was prompted by the desire of the Commission to review the carrier's safety record if and when renewal of such operating authority was sought.

The limited term operating authority provides an opportunity for the Commission to issue a type of authority that is intermediate in nature between temporary authority and permanent authority. Although little used by the Commission, it appears that the use of limited term authority, combined with performance report requirements for such authorities, would provide greater flexibility in the issuance of authority. The recipients of such grants, recognizing that a review would be made prior to renewal, might be more responsive in serving public need than is sometimes the case with permanent operating authority. It also would allow the Commission to assess the public need for the authority and the degree to which a particular grant is filling that need at the time of renewal.

### Regular and irregular routes

The operating authorities granted to common and contract carriers which prescribe the highways to be followed are termed "regular-route" authorities. If highways are not specified in the operating authority, the carrier may operate over irregular routes. Operating authorities of irregular-route carriers are further divided into *radial* and *nonradial* operations. Generally the permits of contract carriers contain authority to operate over irregular routes, while common carriers may be either regular- or irregular-route carriers. About 31 percent of the common carrier and seven percent of contract carrier grants are regular route.

The Commission has not been able to prescribe a general rule by means of which the regular- or irregular-route nature of all operations can be determined, although it has listed eight practices to serve as criteria in the determination of the nature of an operation, whether regular or irregular. These practices are:

1. Predetermined plan. Regular route operation is repetitive and is according to a predetermined plan. This is in contrast to operations strictly on call, as demanded, and where demanded.
2. Character of traffic. A large number of shippers are served and aggregated lots of miscellaneous truckload shipments are carried.
3. Solicitation. Full time solicitors are employed at principal points to secure less-truckload and truckload shipments.
4. Terminals and call stations. Regular route carriers usually maintain terminals at principal points for the handling of less-truckload shipments.
5. Fixed routes. Regular route carriers habitually use certain routes.
6. Fixed termini. Regular route carriers always have fixed termini.
7. Periodicity of service. Regular route service is repetitive in nature so as to become fixed in pattern but it does not depend upon the interval between offerings.
8. Schedules or their equivalent. Regular route carriers observe fixed published schedules of departures and arrivals.[19]

The Commission has stressed that none of these criteria standing alone is conclusive except possibly that of definite published schedules.

In a 1967 case, the Commission pointed out the various types of restrictions that are and are not acceptable to it. The Commission indicated that in the filing of applications the applicant should be careful to show correctly the commodities to be transported, the points to be served, restrictions to be imposed, whether tacking or joinder of operations are proposed, and whether regular- or irregular-route service is proposed.[20]

Some consideration has been given by the Commission to the elimination of the distinction between regular- and irregular-route common carriers so that certificates issued to common carriers in the future would not be divided into these two groups, but this has not been accomplished. In 1964 the Commission issued special rules to govern the conversion of irregular route to regular route. There were 155 applications filed under the special conversion rules and 120 became regular-route common carriers.

There are several types of irregular-route operations: (a) a carrier of specific commodities or class of commodities which originates freight at one or a limited number of origin points and distributes the freight at all points in a defined destination territory; (b) a carrier of general commodities which receives such freight in truckload quantities and distributes to numerous consignees in a defined destination territory; (c) a carrier which transports a particular class of commodities between certain points and serves no intermediate points; and (d) a carrier which transports products of a limited-base area to all destination points in a broad destination territory and returns with general merchandise and supplies that are used in the limited-base area.[21]

Carriers specializing in the transportation of a single commodity or a commodity group, such as paper and paper products, building materials, frozen foods and meat, and steel, often have irregular route authority. This transportation is usually in truckloads. The grants to individual carriers may number several hundred, with transportation from a specific plant site to a number of states, sometimes the entire 48, authorized. These grants have proliferated at a rapid pace during the past decade. An analysis indicates that 1,530 Class I and Class II motor carriers have irregular route authority, and among this number are many regular route common carriers.

Irregular-route common carriers and contract carriers may cross states for which they have no interstate operating authority in order to join their authorized origin and destination points or areas. Such states are called "traversal" states.

The Commission adopted rules and regulations applying to the utilization of superhighways (including interstate highways) on a permanent basis for certificated regular-route motor carriers, later modified in 1975.[22] Also revised were its *deviation* rules. The Commission used a "corridor" service concept that was designed to preserve existing competitive relationships. The rule allows a regular-route motor carrier of property to operate over superhighways between the point of departure from and to the point of return to the carrier's authorized regular service route, as an incident to its certificated authority, provided that either: (1) the superhighway route between such points; (a) extends in the same general direction as the authorized service route, and (b) is wholly within 25 airline miles of the carrier's authorized service route; or (2) the distance over the superhighway route between the point of return to the carrier's authorized service route is not less than 80 percent of the distance between such points over the carrier's authorized service route. For those motor carriers authorized to serve all intermediate points (without regard to nominal exceptions) on their underlying authorized service routes, operations pursuant to (1) above also confers the implied right to serve intermediate points on and within one airline mile of the superhighways routes.

### Off-route points

A regular-route carrier may desire to serve a point that is off its regular route, which is referred to as an off-route point. The off-route point is usually considered to be one which can be served by making a short side trip with over-the-road equipment, which then returns as soon as possible to its regular route and schedule. There is no prescribed distance which constitutes an off-route point. Distances of five miles have been considered to be off-route points, as well as one of 25 miles but not one of 100 miles. In 1952 the Commission permitted deviation from regular routes in delivering or picking up U.S. Mail within ten airline miles of the authorized routes.

Regular-route scheduled service may be performed to and from such points. Carriers may also have terminals at such points and may interchange at these points. Service may be performed between two off-route points incident to the same route only when such service is performed in connection with, and as an integral part of, a good-faith operation of that route.

### Alternate routes

Carriers sometimes seek alternate routes, which may be granted if there is evidence that shows that the use of the alternate route will result in operating economy and efficiency, that a more expeditious or economical service will result, or a safer operation may be conducted. If the alternate route does not amount to a new or different service which would materially affect other carriers already supplying adequate service, the application for an alternate route may be granted. If it does amount to a new or different service, the carrier must prove public convenience and necessity.

The Commission has established three concurrent requirements which must be affirmatively met before authority can be granted for an alternate route solely on the basis of operating economy and convenience. These are: (1) applicant must presently operate between both termini under appropriate authority over a practical and feasible route; (2) applicant must be in competition with the present carriers operating between these termini by reason of handling a substantial amount of traffic; and (3) the competitive situation must remain unchanged if the authority is granted.[23]

### Follow the traffic

For a number of years, the Commission ruled that a carrier could be allowed to follow traffic of certain shippers to new origin points when the traffic was of such importance as to have a substantial effect on the carrier's revenues or ability to continue its overall operations.

The Commission has not been consistent in applying a follow-the-traffic principle. In one case, it was ruled that the fact that the traffic would be new traffic from the new point was controlling,[24] while the same fact was given as a reason for granting authority in a later case.[25]

The Commission has provided, however, that when a carrier's service is limited to a particular type of service, the carrier's commodity description may be broadened. For example, truckaway service was granted to a carrier to enable it to retain the traffic of a shipper who was discontinuing the use of driveaway.[26]

### "Tacking" rights

The right to join two or more certificated routes of one common carrier having a common service point is termed "tacking." The tacking which occurs at the common service point enables the carrier to serve all the points on the routes that are affected by the joinder at the common point. There can be tacking of regular and irregular routes but the more common practice has been the tacking of irregular routes. An irregular route carrier may purchase additional irregular route rights that have a common point between the two operating authorities. This is referred to as a "gateway point." The requirements are that service rendered between the two points must be via the gateway. One can visualize that two radial route authorities joined in such a manner could result in substantial circuity since service has to be rendered through the gateway.

In November, 1973, in an energy-related action,[27] the Commission, in a rule making proposal, recommended modification of the gateway restriction for irregular-route carriers. This permits carriers to serve points on their routes by operating over more direct routes providing this does not shorten the route by more than 20 percent. Specific application can be made, however, to shorten the route by more than 20 percent. More than 300,000 elimination requests resulted, and the rule change was also applied to regular route carriers.

Contract carriers have not been permitted to render a through service by tacking two or more permits. However, the Commission has allowed a contract carrier to arrange for interchange of traffic with a common carrier providing the contract carrier acts as an agent for the shipper in a capacity apart from that as a contract carrier in arranging the transportation beyond the point it is authorized to serve.[28] This practice is not extensive, however. In addition the Commission has felt that a single contract carrier cannot render through service between points specified in separate authorities held by it.[29]

### Commodity descriptions

One of the difficult regulatory problems has been the interpretation of commodity descriptions which are contained in certificates and permits. All certificates except a very small number, possibly 25, have some limitation upon the commodities which the carrier may transport. Since under the "grandfather" provisions of the act, the carriers themselves described the articles which they were moving at the time regulation was imposed, there was little uniformity in the wording of the descriptions used. There have been many individual determinations made by the Commission as to the interpretation of commodity descriptions. This approach has led to an atomizing of operating rights.

Railroads, because of availability of all types of equipment, hold themselves out to transport all types of freight. This is not the case with motor carriers, for which they have often been criticized. Prior to the Motor Carrier Act, the motor common carrier rendering interstate service had no legal duty to transport all of the traffic tendered to it. Therefore, its holding out fell into a well-defined channel. It transported only such commodities as would readily load into its equipment without damage to other lading or to equipment and which would not exceed the carrying capacity of its vehicle. Thus, motor common carriers of general commodities, not being equipped to handle commodities moving in bulk, dangerous articles, and others, simply did not solicit this business. With the passage of the Motor Carrier Act, motor common carriers were permitted to continue such operations as they had been conducting, with the result that the exceptions now, as then, reflect the self-imposed limitations of the carriers of general commodities.[30]

Based on the commodity descriptions in operating authorities, common carriers of property may be divided into two groups. The first is that of carriers of general commodities with the usual exceptions, which are dangerous explosives, commodities of unusual value, household goods as defined in *Practices of Motor Common Carriers of Household Goods*,[31] commodities in bulk, and those requiring special equipment. The second category is that of common carriers of property authorized to transport special commodities either by name or under generic headings.

Some commodity descriptions are based on the use to be made of the commodities. In order to fall within such a description, a given commodity must meet the "intended-use" test. Originally, this test required that the commodities at the time of transportation had to be in the form and condition ready for the particular use and be definitely earmarked and intended for such use. In later cases, this was modified by the use of the phrase "virtually no other use" and still later, by the phrase "predominant use."[32]

When an industry's new products have been developed, carriers have often requested broadened commodity descriptions in order to transport these commodities. In one of these cases, a common carrier serving the textile industry asked to have its "wool" authority broadened to include synthetics, which was authorized despite available service.[33] This "field-of-service" doctrine has also been applied in the transportation of cheese and meat products. On the other hand, the Commission has not applied this principle when many industries are served by the carrier. For example, a carrier was denied authority to haul liquid commodities of all kinds.[34]

At the time that most carriers secured their operating authority, traffic moved in disposable containers and dunnage which did not need to be returned. When shippers began using reusable containers, common and contract carriers were required to have specific operating rights to permit the backhauling of empty containers used in moving shipments. As a result of increasing use of reusable containers, the Commission in 1960 ruled that all certificates and permits authorized the return transportation of such items as empty boxes, crates, cases, barrels, drums, pallets, cans, and other containers and shipping devices from destination to origin by a carrier having proper authority for the outbound movement.[35]

In another ruling, the Commission eliminated a restriction that had become too difficult to administer. The truckload lot restriction was found in many early motor carrier certificates as it represented a method of operation by certain carriers that were handling only volume shipments. It became apparent, however, that the Commission when called upon to interpret the restriction over the years could not find a single definition covering all of the situations that arose in the administration of such a limitation. It hadapproved truckload tariff minimums of 10,000 pounds, 20,000 pounds, and 30,000 pounds. The problems involved in determining what constituted a truckload lot resulted in the undertaking of an *Ex Parte* proceeding by the Commission. The Commission subsequently ruled that the public convenience and necessity required the removal of truckload lot restrictions on all existing motor carrier certificates which had been issued by it up to that time.[36] This was a restriction which was imbedded for years and was vexing to the Commission because of the difficulty in its interpretation. It finally removed all such restrictions as a result of the *Ex Parte* proceeding.

### Revocation, suspension, and abandonment

Motor carrier operating rights can be revoked only in accordance with the procedure established in Section 10925 (b) of the act. This section provides that:

... certificates, permits, and licenses shall be effective from the date specified therein, and shall remain in effect until suspended or terminated as herein provided. Any such certificate, permit, or license may, upon application of the holder thereof, in the discretion of the Commission, be amended or revoked, in whole or in part, or may upon complaint, or on the Commission's own initiative, after notice and hearing, be suspended, changed, or revoked, in whole or in part, for willful failure to comply with any lawful order, or with any term, condition, or limitation of such certificate, permit, or license.

The Commission procedure in revoking operating authority is one in which the burden of proof is upon the complainant. Since the act specifies that the holder of operating authority is to be given not less than 30 days to comply with an order of the Commission, this period of time is adequate to comply with any Commission order. It usually happens, therefore, that even when proof is submitted, the Commission gives the carrier a specified time in which to comply with the order of the Commission, with the result that compliance follows in most cases.

The Commission also has authority under Section 10925 (b) to suspend operating authorities. There have been numerous proceedings involving the fitness of carriers in which the Commission has required compliance with Commission orders or suspension would follow. However, the number of suspensions has been relatively small. If the carrier wants to comply with the Commission's orders, it is given the opportunity to do so. The effect of suspension is a temporary interruption of operations which can be resumed upon compliance with the Commission's requirements. Suspension does not carry the finality that revocation does.

Revocation is a cessation of operations with the likelihood of resumption remote.

Often a carrier may stop operations on a particular segment of his operating authority, and such operating rights are termed "dormant." Dormant rights may be sold or service may at some later date be reinstituted. In a particular case because of carrier financial problems, all but 67 of 391 individual territorial authorities that a carrier held were dormant.

The Commission was not given the power under the act to compel a motor carrier operating in interstate or foreign commerce to continue in business if it desires to discontinue operations entirely. The relatively small investment required for operations was a factor which influenced Congress in permitting the motor carrier to cease operations any time that it wanted to do so. However, as long as the carrier holds a certificate authorizing it to conduct certain operations it is under the Commission's jurisdiction to the extent provided by the act and must comply with any lawful requirements which the Commission may establish with respect to continuous and adequate service if the carrier wants to continue its operations.[37] The Commission has stated that there must be active and sincere efforts to obtain traffic. When there had not been any traffic moved for a number of years and the evidence indicated that the holder of operating authority was engaged in activities not connected with transportation, however, it was held that there had been abandonment.[38] The Commission has permitted the abandonment of portions of an operation when they were not profitable and there was little public need for their continuance, even though the carrier's operations as a whole were in sound financial condition.[39]

### Railroad operation and control of motor carriers of property

Railroads, to a limited extent, engage in motor transportation directly as well as through noncontrolled motor carriers[40] and through their own subsidiaries. Operations of the two former types are auxiliary or supplemental to train service. Operations of the controlled motor carriers (those in which a railroad has a greater than 50 percent interest) by railroads may be of the auxiliary or supplemental type or, in some cases, are independent of rail business.

The Interstate Commerce Commission has felt that Section 11344 (c) of the Interstate Commerce Act requires that a railroad or its affiliate seeking authority to acquire control of a motor carrier shall be required to show that the proposed transaction will be consistent with the public interest and that it will enable such railroad to use service by motor vehicle to public advantage in its operations and will not unduly restrain competition. Under Section 10922 of the act, railroads may file applications for grants directly to them of authority to initiate new motor carrier operations. The Commission has, almost without exception, conditioned the grants of certificates under Section 10922 so as to restrict the authorized motor operations to service that is auxiliary to or supplemental to rail service.[41]

The conditions which are usually imposed on rail operations of motor carrier services are as follows:

1. The service by motor vehicle shall be limited to service which is auxiliary to or supplemental of rail service of the railroad involved. This condition requires that the traffic be that of the railroad moving under rail responsibility on rail billing and on rail rates. Unless limited by the third condition explained later, the first condition permits all-motor movements of rail traffic. However, it does not permit all-motor movements on motor billing and motor rates.

2. An applicant shall not serve or interchange traffic at any point not a station on the railroad. The terminal area of the railroad station is the area which is meant by the word "point" and not merely the station.

3. The shipments transported by the carrier shall be limited to those which it receives from or delivers to the railroad under a through bill of lading covering in addition to movement by applicant a prior or subsequent movement by rail. The through bill of lading which is referred to is a rail bill of lading. Often this condition has been revised by the establishment of a key-point system, in which case the condition is that no shipments can be transported by the railroad as a common carrier by motor vehicle between any of the following points or through, or to, or from more than one of said points (with the points being named). The establishment of a key-point condition was instituted in order that local shipment or ex-forwarder traffic or ex-pool-car traffic could be handled by motor carrier. In some instances, there has been a combination of the prior or subsequent rail haul and the key point system.[42] Key-point restrictions have been removed when it was shown that to do so would allow the substitution of a faster, more economical, and more efficient service without endangering the operations of independent motor carriers.

If "special circumstances" can be shown which would negate any possible disadvantage to the public resulting from the granting to a railroad affiliate of unrestricted authority to engage in motor carrier operations, the Commission has approved.[43]

Pacific Motor Trucking Company (Southern Pacific) is presently seeking unrestricted motor carrier operating authority from California to other southwestern states, and this has been in litigation for a number of years. The Commission is somewhat more liberal now if the rail motor carrier subsidiaries can show an improvement in the efficiency in carrying existing traffic. In some other instances, where shippers and/or receivers have felt that existing motor carriers have not provided adequate service, the Commission has appeared more willing to liberalize the operating authority of the railroad-owned motor carrier subsidiary.

4. All contractual arrangements between the motor carrier and the railroad shall be reported to the Commission and shall be subject to revision as necessary.

5. The Commission reserves the right to impose further specific conditions as it may find necessary in order to restrict the motor carrier service to that which is auxiliary to or supplemental of rail service.

The imposition of restrictions on railroad operation of motor carriers does not apply to those operations which are conducted by the railroads under "grandfather" rights.[44]

The primary purpose of the policy of imposing restrictions is to prevent the railroads from acquiring motor operations through affiliates and using them in such a manner as to unduly restrain competition of independently operated motor carriers. This policy, the Commission feels, was and is sound and should be relaxed only when the circumstances clearly establish (1) that the grant of authority has not resulted and probably will not result in the undue restraint of competition; and (2) that the public interest requires the proposed operation, which the authorized independent motor carriers have not furnished except when it suited their convenience.

In 1979, there were 16 U.S. railroads that owned one or more Class I and Class II motor freight carriers. However, eight of these railroads owned carriers of which each had combined operating revenues of more than $10 million. These are: Conrail, Rock Island, Missouri Pacific, Santa Fe, Rio Grande, Southern Pacific, St. Louis and Southwestern, and Burlington Northern. There are a small number of Class III motor carriers owned by railroads but they do not have to file separate annual reports with the Commission. The combined revenues of all separately reporting railroad—owned motor carriers account for less than three percent of the total revenues of all ICC regulated Class I and Class II general freight carriers. This percentage has remained unchanged for more than a decade. Other major railroads either have no motor carrier subsidiaries or very small localized service.

There appears to be considerable variation as to the manner in which railroad-motor carrier subsidiaries operate. One of the large trucking subsidiaries, the Pennsylvania Truck Lines (Conrail) operates essentially as the railroad's contractor for truckload TOFC/cartage substituted service and for TOFC terminal operations. On the other hand, another motor carrier subsidiary, Missouri Pacific Truck Lines, provides a system-wide LTL service that is completely dependent on using the parent railroad's TOFC service.

### Dual status, private-public

Private carriers have often requested authority to operate also as a for-hire carrier. This usually happens when a private carrier has a one-way haul and seeks to overcome this disadvantage by securing operating authority for the return haul. The Commission for many years ruled that a combination of public and private operations of this type was not desirable and denied many such applications.

There were a few cases involving small operations in which there was not much possibility of detrimental results, such as favoritism, discrimination, and unfair competitive practices, when the Commission approved public-private operations. Another exception to the principle of the *Geraci*[45] case was when authority was granted for public-private operations but conditions were imposed to prevent undesirable practices. The usual conditions were that (*a*) public operations should be conducted separately from the applicant's other activities; (*b*) separate accounting systems be maintained; and/or (*c*) there be no admixture of property in both the public and private carriage at the same time in the same vehicle. One or more of these conditions was usually imposed, and frequently all three were imposed.

In the *Veon* case, the Commission indicated that in the future the exceptions to the policy of the *Geraci* case would be rare and denied a grant of contract carrier authority to a private carrier.[46] In the interval between these two cases the Commission denied entry in 41 cases and granted it in 20 cases.

From 1964 to 1978, the Commission followed much the same policy granting some dual rights and denying others. In 1978, however, the Commission in *Toto Purchasing and Supply Co.*, 128 MCC 873 (1978) permitted dual operations. Subsequently, in *Ex Parte MC-118* the Commission upheld the action in the *Toto* case and stated that the need for energy-efficient operation and greater coordination between public and private transportation required a change in interpretation.

### MERGERS

There has been a gradual reduction in the number of carriers from 26,200 in 1939 to 16,874 presently. Some of the reduction is the result of mergers, and this type of action is on the increase. In 1946 there was one carrier that had transcontinental operating authority as the result of mergers and acquisition; there are now 14 whose transcontinental operations were the result of mergers and acquisition.

The antitrust laws, whose basic aim is the preservation of competition, closely complement the aims of our surface transportation policy, and the enforcement of Section 7 of the Clayton Act is entrusted to the Commission. Another link between antitrust policy and transportation policy is the goal in the National Transportation Policy of fostering "sound economic conditions . . . among the several carriers." This provision has relevance to the question of mergers or stock acquisition in transportation because of their potential for injuring other carriers through the diversion of traffic.

The subject of consolidations, mergers, and control is a particularly important one in view of the vast number of certificates and permits which have been issued and the growth aspects of the industry. As the assets of property carriers have grown, further expansion through acquisition of the operating rights of other carriers often appears desirable because it may be less difficult to purchase rights than to secure a new grant of authority from the Commission. Further, persons outside the motor carrier industry are seeking to acquire operating rights through purchase. The determination by the Commission of what constitutes control of a carrier is also of great significance.

The policies of the Commission in transfer, or "finance cases" as they are termed, are of interest not only to carriers but also to shippers and the public, since there are many aspects, such as service and competition, which are included. Motor carriers generally purchase rights from other carriers at a cost in excess of their carrying value. (See Fig. 18-1 for advertisements of rights wanted, rights for sale and solicitation of a proposed merger.) A sample of 43 finance proceedings before the Commission in 1970-72 revealed that in 37 of them the selling price of the operating rights exceeded the carrying value on the seller's books. In 1976, 19 trucking companies paid a total of $20.6 million for the operating rights of Associated Transport. If acquisitions are to be undertaken by a motor carrier, management should develop an overall acquisition program looking ahead as to where it wants to be ten years or more in the future. An overall plan can then be developed including the priorities for acquisition. It is Consolidated Freightways' acquisition experience that early growth with new authority is 1½ to two times the historical local annual growth rate of manufacturing within the market area.[47] The value of the intangible assets of a motor carrier, the operating rights, goodwill, etc., are usually valued on a par with the dollar value of the tangibles. The move toward consolidation is much further advanced in the passenger field than in the property field.

The majority of transfers involve certificates rather than permits. This undoubtedly is due largely to the fact that contract carriers cannot render a through service by "tacking" the rights which they acquire.[48] In the transfer of operating rights, there are two broad groups of transfers, those provided for under Section 11343 (d) (1) and those covered by Section 11343 (a).

Section 11343 (d) (1) of the act states that, except as provided in Section 11343 (a) any certificate or permit may be transferred pursuant to such

Fig. 18-1. Advertisements of operating rights for sale and operating rights wanted.

rules and regulations as the Commission may prescribe. This particular section deals with transactions between small motor carriers where together their annual gross interstate operating revenues are less than $300,000 (prior to 1965 the basis was 20 vehicles) and a noncarrier in which the transaction involves operating rights only. This section does not apply when the proposed transfer involves only the sale of equipment or the lease of equipment, while Section 11343 (d) (1) approval only is required when a person who is not connected with a carrier purchases or leases the rights of a motor carrier.

Section 11343 (a) of the act embraces all consolidations, acquisitions, and mergers of two or more carriers when operating revenues are more than $300,000. A person not connected with a carrier can acquire control of a corporate motor carrier through stock holdings. When there is no change in the record holder of the certificate or permit, this requires no Commission approval under either Section 11343 (a) or Section 11343 (d) (1). Similarly, a person not connected with a carrier or one in control of a carrier can acquire control of one or more corporate carriers through stock ownership which does not require Commission approval providing the $300,000 exemption is not exceeded and a railroad or other carrier, as defined in Section 10102 (17) of the act, is not a party. With these exceptions, motor carrier operating authority can change hands only if Commission approval is granted, since under Section 11343 (a) approval and authorization by the Commission is required while a transfer under Section 11343 (d) (1) is covered by one of the rules issued by the Commission. A proposed transfer under Section 11343 (a) is required to be consistent with the public interest. Further, there are additional requirements as well when a rail carrier or affiliate is an applicant in a case involving a motor carrier.

One study points out the paradox of various Commission decisions that sometimes preserve or increase monopoly power of larger carriers that have achieved their present position largely as a result of mergers and administrative decisions dealing with market concentration. Commission actions sometimes result in insulating these larger carriers from possible competition by denying merger approval to lesser-sized carriers on the grounds that "undue concentration" already exists. Thus, protection is sometimes afforded larger companies that do not need it, while stronger competition from the merger of smaller and medium-sized companies is not allowed to develop.[49]

This study discusses the uncertainties of merger decisions. It points out that by allowing the merger of smaller and medium-sized companies, as just discussed, greater competition may be created for the larger company that has a dominant position in a market and thus shippers and carriers might experience an equalization in bargaining power; or, on the other hand, it might create greater hazards for the smaller companies not in the merger proposal; or even intensify the merger pressure in the competitive market.[50] Further, the Commission's task is complicated by lack of sufficient data on carrier industry structure and its effect on economic performance of individual carriers.[51]

Another study by the same author which examined more than 950 merger cases in both Sections 11343 (a) and 11343 (d) (1) proceedings contains a vast amount of data and analysis. Among its recommendations is a suggestion that the Commission should institute an *Ex Parte* proceeding to investigate motor carrier unifications in relation to the National Transportation Policy, and the implication of concentration which is manifesting itself.[52] It also recommended that the Commission should devise a set of procedures by which effective post-evaluations of unifications could be accomplished to determine if the claimed economic benefits actually resulted from the merger.

The formulation of holding companies and conglomerates has had some impact on the merger rate. Another study, which dealt with Section 11343 (a) merger cases and was based on a random sample examination of 450 cases, concluded that the current trend of trucking mergers has accomplished favorable results but would recommend that very careful scrutiny be given to mergers that do not involve end-to-end unifications. This study feels that the Commission's role in mergers is an active one.[53]

### Reasons for mergers

One of the primary factors affecting consolidation is that of acquiring routes and access to markets rather than equipment or other physical assets. A motor carrier may desire to acquire a new route or area with additional traffic to enhance its competitive position or to eliminate interlining and interchange. The carrier can emphasize to shippers the benefits of single-line service. Competition with other modes of transportation and other motor carriers can be altered favorably through consolidations.

In addition to route acquisition, some motor carriers consolidate in order to provide diversification. A large western carrier in seeking to purchase certain motor carriers operating in the East felt that this move would tend to offset economic reversal in the West or vice versa. Another type of diversification is that of a general commodity carrier purchasing a carrier with specific commodity authority, such as a petroleum transporter.

The fact that investment capital may be secured on more favorable terms by the purchasing carrier is sometimes a motivating factor. This may occur when the acquisition improves the financial well-being and potential of the carrier. The purchasing status of a carrier may also be favorably changed, since the combined fleet and equipment requirements may improve the bargaining position of the carrier with its suppliers.

Internal operating improvements and economies may also be effected. Better scheduling and increased utilization of equipment may result from mergers. The acquisition of another carrier may increase the average length of haul; or conversely, a carrier may have a long average haul and want to add intermediate points to increase tonnage through principal terminals. The elimination of multiple freight handling and documentation may provide operating economies.

The Commission refers to cost savings that are economies of utilization, i.e., density. This occurs when the capacity of a given plant is more fully utilized. Another cost saving presumably would be economies of scale which would occur when a carrier utilizes its capacity more efficiently. There is considerable disagreement regarding the degree of scale economy that is possible in the motor carrier field.

Another aspect of mergers is that many motor carriers are first-generation companies, with the founders still active. Some of these individuals are reaching the age of retirement and, because of capital gains, find it advantageous to sell their operations. The death of the founder may be a motivating factor if the heirs do not wish to continue the operation.

### Types of mergers

Based on geographical aspects, there are several types of motor carrier consolidations. Overlapping consolidations often embrace parallel routes with service to some common points. The overlapping may be confined to larger points. Another common type is end to end. Typical end-to-end consolidation involves the uniting of connecting carriers, often involving carriers that have been interlining freight. This type of consolidation combines carriers whose routes are complementary. Tentacular consolidations sometimes are referred to as the right-angle type. The acquired lines extend outward like tentacles from the main route. Another is the area type. Operations may include a large number of regular routes or points but be concentrated in a relatively small area of two or three states.

### Section 11343 (a)

There are three primary means by which control of a carrier operation may be unified. These are: (1) leasing, which is applicable only for a limited period; (2) acquisition of stock control; and (3) actual ownership by merger, consolidation, or purchase.

Some of the ramifications of stock acquisition and competition are found in a recent case before the Commission.[54] Navajo Freight Lines, a transcontinental carrier, acquired 26 percent of the stock of Garrett Freightlines, a large western regional carrier with route authority as far east as St. Paul, Denver, and Albuquerque. Garrett opposed the acquisition, however, and the Commission instituted an investigation under

Section 11343 (b) of the Interstate Commerce Act to determine whether or not Navajo, without approval of the Commission, had unlawfully effectuated control or management of Garrett through stock ownership; and whether through its stock interest in Garrett it might have the effect of substantially lessening competition under the antitrust provisions of Section 7 of the Clayton Act. The Commission restrained Navajo from acquiring additional shares. As the litigation developed, Navajo filed an application with the Commission seeking authority to acquire control of Garrett.

The initial decision of the Administrative Law Judge found the acquisition of Navajo of the capital stock of Garrett to have been a violation of the Clayton Antitrust Act and ordered it to cease and desist from the violation and to divest itself of holdings in Garrett within one year. The ALJ also denied Navajo's motion seeking Commission acceptance of a voting trust between Navajo and the Valley National Bank of Arizona as settlement of the issues. The ALJ denied Navajo's motion to dismiss its application to acquire control of Garrett through ownership of capital stock and also denied Navajo's application to acquire control of Garrett through ownership of capital stock in MC—F—11198. The ALJ further ruled that control of Garrett in a common interest with Navajo not to have "been effectuated in violation of Section 5 (4) (now 11343 (b)) of the Interstate Commerce Act."

The ALJ concluded that movement of less-truckload general commodity traffic via regular-route motor common carriers of shipments weighing between 100 and 10,000 pounds constituted a specific and relevant product market (line of commerce) within the meaning of the Clayton Act. The next step under Section 7 was to delineate the geographic market in which the two companies do business and compete. The delineation of the first geographic market was the traffic lanes of four city pairs—Denver-Las Vegas, San Francisco Bay Area-Las Vegas, Los Angles-Denver, and San Francisco Bay Area-Denver. If the merger were permitted, the new carrier would have handled 56 percent, 17 percent, 20 percent, and 40 percent of the traffic along the respective routes; and the top four companies, including the Navajo-Garrett combination, would have been 93 percent, 94 percent, 74 percent, and 85 percent of these markets. This constituted a market combination among a few firms.

A second geographic area of competition involved transcontinental routes (Pacific and Rocky Mountain regions and points east of the Mississippi River). It was stated that with about 19 carriers (including Navajo and Garrett) in this market, the requirement of large investments to enter the market and the disappearance of any carrier would result in a higher concentration.

The third geographic area of competition was the gateways of Denver and of St. Paul where Garrett connected with carriers competitive with Navajo in varying degrees of traffic moving to or from points east thereof. The amalgamation of Garrett and Navajo would have had adverse effect on the eastern carriers which formerly interchanged traffic with Garrett. Since Navajo serves many of the same points as the eastern carriers, it would "back solicit" the shippers of eastern carriers.

The ALJ ruled that there had been a violation of Section 7 of the Clayton Antitrust Act and that the Act is prohibitive and imposes an obligation upon the Commission to act. He pointed out that Congress made it clear that no lessening of competition shall occur between carriers through stock acquisition, and that such acquisitions shall not be cloaked with immunity from the provisions of the antitrust laws except after Commission approval of an application initiated by a carrier under Section 11343 (a) of the Act, but prior to any consummation of the acquisition. Navajo filed exceptions to the decision in April, 1975.

The Commission in 1976 ruled that control of management of Garrett by Navajo was found not to have been effectuated under Section 11343 (a), but acquisition of capital stock of Garrett by Navajo, et al., was found to have violated Section 7 of the Clayton Antitrust Act. Navajo was required to cease and desist from such violation and divest itself of this capital stock. The Commission also denied the motion of Navajo to create a voting trust with Valley National Bank, denied Navajo's motion to dismiss the application to acquire control of Garrett, as well as the motion by Navajo to withdraw the application to acquire control of Garrett.

Subsequently, Garrett was sold to a noncarrier and Navajo was merged into Arkansas Best, a conglomerate with large motor carrier holdings.

Numerous factors are considered in determining consistency with the public interest. There are, however, certain factors which under Section 11343 (b) must be considered. These are: (1) the effect of the proposed transaction upon adequate transportation service to the public; (2) the total fixed charges which will result; and (3) interest of the employees affected.

The term "public interest" as used in this section has a direct relationship to adequacy of transportation service, to its essential conditions of economy and efficiency, and to appropriate provision and best use of transportation facilities. To meet the test of consistency with the public interest does not require consideration of specific matters but rather the broad considerations in the preceding sentence.[55]

It is absolutely necessary that there be a showing of consistency with the public interest. Serving the interest of the vendee only is not enough, it has been ruled.

The effect of the proposed transaction upon adequate transportation service to the public is one in which the competitive aspect is very significant. As interpreted by the Commission, the term "public interest" which is found in Section 11344 (b) includes the interest of competing carriers.[56]

One of the provisions that must be considered in a transfer case under Section 11344 (b) (4) is its effect on carrier employees. When the Commission felt in a particular case that future developments might affect employees, it reserved, for two years, jurisdiction to add conditions regarding employees.[57] In a subsequent case, the Commission reserved jurisdiction for three years to hear complaints of employees but refused to set up a formula with respect to employee seniority rights.[58] It has also held that when the transaction includes intrastate rights, the effect of approval on the intrastate employees has to be considered.[59]

A long-term employment agreement at high salaries which was proposed to be entered into between the buyer and some employees of the seller was found to be undesirable and not in the public interest.[60] It should not be inferred that employment agreements are not permissible. If they are true employment contracts and are not merely a means of increasing the consideration to vendors, such contracts have been held to be not subject to the Commission's jurisdiction under Section 11343 (a).[61]

The Commission reopened a case and modified the findings to provide severance pay for employees affected by the purchase. Any employee who lost his job because of the approved transaction was to receive, for a period of not more than three months, severance pay at the rate of his average monthly pay for the 12 months immediately preceding the month in which he was discharged. These payments, however, were to be reduced by the amount of total wages earned during the three-month period if he was otherwise employed, or by the amount of unemployment benefit payments. In the event of a disagreement arising as a result of this labor protective provision that could not be settled by the carrier and employee within 30 days, the matter was to be referred to an arbitration committee.[62]

One of the factors that is considered in transfer cases is the price which is to be paid for operating rights. Some of the elements which influence price are the value of the operation as a going concern, the number of years of development, the right to operate, and the extent to which the public is aware of the service rendered.

*Fitness* is one of the important elements involved in determining consistency with the public interest. The Commission has held that such matters as the number of safety violations, operating beyond authority, and the failure to keep records are elements considered in determining fitness. Actions such as these have been the basis for denial of purchase.[63] The practices in which an exempt freight forwarder engaged were also considered in determining the forwarder's fitness to acquire a motor carrier.[64] It should be noted that lack of experience in transportation is not in itself a sufficient reason to deny an application to acquire control.[65]

Frequently a lease of operating rights is sought with a view toward ultimate purchase of the rights. The Commission's attitude has been that these leases should be limited to short or trial periods no longer than necessary to secure an appraisal by the lessee of the operation.

The Commission has said that approval will not be given to a lease when there is not the intention to acquire the rights.[66] The proposed purchase of operating rights for the sole purpose of leasing them to another carrier is frowned upon by the Commission.[67]

Some of the other factors which have been considered in unification proceedings under Section 11344 (b) are a reduction in the cost of transportation,[68] the elimination of duplicate operations over a congested route,[69] and more efficient use of combined resources.[70]

A motor carrier may cease to operate and the service that it was formerly rendering may be absorbed through the expansion of facilities by other motor carriers. Unless the operating authority possessed by the carrier that has ceased to operate has been revoked, it may begin to operate again at some future time under its dormant rights. These dormant rights pose a problem, for "any substantial interruption of one carrier's service tends to result in expansion of other facilities to meet the continuing needs of shippers and thus to cause overcrowding if the suspended service is resumed."[71] Some motor carriers look for dormant rights to expand their operations. The present policy of the Commission in regard to dormant operating authority is that as long as a motor carrier actually holds itself in readiness to perform the service, the Commission will refrain from action to require operation or revocation unless there is reason to believe that the dormant operating authority is being held solely for purposes of profitable sale. There must, however, be readiness to perform the service, and insurance must be maintained and filed with the Commission.

### Section 11343 (d) (1)

The basis of Section 11343 (d) (1) is to make possible the transfer of rights under that section in the simplest manner possible with the least expense to the parties involved. The Commission adopted "Rules and Regulations Governing Transfers of Rights to Operate as a Motor Carrier in Interstate or Foreign Commerce" for transfers under Section 11343 (d) (1). These rules and regulations do not require a hearing, and the applications are handled informally.

Although the rules and regulations which apply on transfer cases under this section do not require hearings, there is a hearing, in some cases, if it is not known whether the case is a Section 11343 (a) or Section 11343 (d) (1) case at the time the application is made.

After applications have been acted upon, the Commission publishes in the *Federal Register* notices of orders granting applications under Section 11343 (d) (1). It defers the effective dates of the orders for 20 days to permit interested parties to file petitions for reconsideration. A copy of the application is sent by the Commission to the state regulatory authorities in those states in which are located the headquarters of applicants. It is assumed that the state regulatory bodies will have more knowledge of any matter that might disqualify either of the parties.

If there is denial of a Section 11343 (d) (1) application, there can be appeal to the courts. Some concern about securing judicial review has been expressed, since no transcript and findings exist on which the refusal has been based. However, since the Commission requires that there be an application, the appeal would be on the record of the application and its declination.

### QUESTIONS AND PROBLEMS

1. How can "public convenience and necessity" be proved? Does this differ from the phrase "consistent with the public interest?"

2. Explain the different types of operating authority.

3. What criteria are used by the Commission in determining whether the carrier is a regular- or irregular-route operator?

4. Define: off-route points; follow the traffic; and alternate routes.

5. What is the meaning of "fit, willing, and able?" Are there any standards used to measure it?

6. What is the procedure for suspending or revoking operating authority? Is it effective?

7. Has the problem of commodity descriptions contained in certificates and permits been solved?

8. Why is regulatory control over abandonment of routes by motor carriers different from that for railroads?

9. What problems may exist under dual operations? Public-private operations?

10. Under Section 5 (2) what factors must be considered in determining whether the transfer is consistent with the public interest?

11. What is Commission policy on the leasing of operating rights? Do you feel that leasing should be more restricted?

12. What problems are posed by dormant rights?

13. Under Section 5 may a person not affiliated with a motor carrier purchase a motor carrier without Commission approval?

14. How does a transfer under Section 212 (b) differ from one under Section 5?

15. Could an application under Section 212 (b) which was denied by the Commission be appealed later?

16. Prepare a research paper on the relationship of antitrust laws and the National Transportation Policy contained in the Interstate Commerce Act.

17. There has been some criticism of the Commission regarding the small number of grants of authority to new operators. Do you feel the criticism is justified? Why or why not? How does the Commission's record compare with that of the Civil Aeronautics Board?

## FOOTNOTES TO CHAPTER 18

[1] 350 U.S. 409 (1955).

[2] The ruling in *Keystone Transfer Co. Contract Carrier Application*, 19 MCC 475 (1939), restricted operations thereunder to those performed under contracts solely with persons who operate wholesale and retail food business houses or food processing plants.

[3] *T. T. Brooks Trucking Co. Application*, 81 MCC 561 (1959).

[4] Senate Committee on Interstate and Foreign Commerce, *Scope of Authority of I.C.C.* (Washington, D.C.: U.S. Government Printing Office, 1957), p. 205.

[5] *Ex Parte MC-119*, dated January 8, 1979.

[6] *Luper Transportation Co. (Kansas)—Purchase—McCarter*, 38 MCC 263 (1942).

[7] *Barton—Robinson Convoy Co. Ext.—Moffet, Oklahoma*, 19 MCC 626 (1939).

[8] *Ex Parte No. 55, Sub 27, Dual Operations of Motor Carriers* (1978).

[9] *York Interstate Trucking Inc. Ext.—Muriatic Acid*, 67 MCC 626 (1956).

[10] *Schaffer Transportation Company and American Trucking Associations, Inc.* v. *United States of America and Interstate Commerce Commission et al.*, 355 U.S. 83 (1957).

[11] *Union Pacific Motor Freight Co.—Key Point Restrictions*, 74 MCC 274 (1958).

[12] *A.J. Metler Ext.—Crude Sulphur*, 61 MCC 335 (1952).

[13] *George C. Winn & L. Winn Ext.—Calvert City, Ky.*, 66 MCC 340 (1956).

[14] *Pan-American Bus Lines Operations*, 1 MCC 190 (1936); and *All American Bus Lines, Inc., Common Carrier Application*, 18 MCC 755 (1939).

[15] *MC-72997, Sub 26, Liberty Trucking Co., Extension—General Commodities* (1979).

[16] *Producers Transport, Inc., Extension—Benzol,* 54 MCC 621 (1952).

[17] *Mathews Trucking Corp. Extension—Maine and New Hampshire, 1952,* 53 MCC 737 (1952).

[18] *Riss and Co., Inc., Extension—Explosives,* 64 MCC 299 (1955). The right of the Commission to limit the duration of a certificate has been upheld by the court in *Scott Truck Lines, Inc.* v. *United States et al.,* 163 F. Supp. 118 (1958).

[19] *Transportation Activities, Brady Transfer & Storage Co.,* 47 MCC 23 (1947).

[20] *Fox-Smythe Transp. Co., Ext.—Okla.,* 106 MCC 1 (1967).

[21] Senate Committee on Interstate and Foreign Commerce, *Study of Domestic Land and Water Transportation* (81st Cong., 2d sess. [Washington, D.C.: U.S. Government Printing Office, 1950]), p. 1503.

[22] *Motor Service on Interstate Highways,* 110 MCC 514 (1970); also *Ex Parte M-C65* (Sub No. 5) 1975.

[23] *Hayes Freight Lines, Inc., Extension—Alternate Routes in Michigan,* 54 MCC 643 (1952).

[24] *Girton Bros., Inc., Ext.—Louisville, Ky.* 69 MCC 299 (1956).

[25] *Kendrick Cartage Co., Ext.—Paducah, Ky.,* 72 MCC 35 (1957).

[26] *Blain Drive-away System, Inc., Extension—Truckaway,* 62 MCC 199 (1953).

[27] *Ex Parte 55, Gateway Elimination,* 119 MCC 530 (1973).

[28] *Holmes Contract Carrier Application,* 8 MCC 391 (1938); and Barton-Robinson Convoy Co. Extension, 19 MCC 629 (1939).

[29] *Longshore Extension—Salem—Youngstown, Ohio,* 43 MCC 759 (1944).

[30] *Descriptions in Motor Carrier Certificates,* 61 MCC 209 (1952).

[31] 17 ICC 467 (1939).

[32] *Mural Trucking Service, Interpretation of Certificate—Store Equipment,* 63 MCC 47 (1954).

[33] *Nelson and Sons Transp. Co. Ext.—Synthetics,* 62 MCC 271 (1953); this was upheld in *A.B.C.* v. *U.S.,* 155 F. Supp. 367, Sept. 13, 1956.

[34] *Quality Carriers, Inc., Ext.—Liquid Commodities,* 71 MCC 617 (1957).

[35] *Ex Parte MC-53, Interpretation of Operating Rights—Returned Containers,* June 1, 1960.

[36] *Removal of Truckload Lot Restrictions,* 106 MCC 455 (1968).

[37] *Towns of Bristol and Hill, N.H.* v. *Boston and M. Transp. Co.,* 20 MCC 581 (1939).

[38] *Rocket—Purchase, Ford,* 62 MCC 503 (1954).

[39] *Massachusetts N.E. Transp. Co.—Abandonment of Routes,* 51 MCC 573 (1950).

[40] A noncontrolled carrier is a motor carrier whose course of action the railroad did not have the ability to determine, other than through contractual arrangements for the performance of service for the railroad. Interstate Commerce Commission, Bureau of Transport Economics and Statistics, *Motor Operations by or for Class I Railroads, 1944,* Statement 4829 (Washington, D.C., September, 1948), p. 8.

[41] *Kansas City Southern Transport Co. Common Carrier Applications,* 10 MCC 221 (1938); *Kansas City Southern Co. Common Carrier Application,* 28 MCC 5 (1940).

[42] *Southern Pac. Transport Co. Common Carrier Application,* 51 MCC 695 (1950).

[43] *Great Northern Ry. Co., Ext.*, 114 MCC 321 (1971).

[44] *Pacific Motor Trucking Company*, 34 MCC 249 (1942).

[45] 71 MCC 369 (1938).

[46] 92 MCC 248 (1963).

[47] D.E. Moffitt, "Economic Evaluation of Carrier Authority," ATA National Accounting and Finance Council, 1973.

[48] Charles A. Taff, *Operating Rights of Motor Carriers* (Dubuque, Iowa: Wm. C. Brown & Co., 1953), p. 79.

[49] Jay A. Smith, Jr., "Concentration in the Common and Contract Motor Carrier Industry-A Regulatory Dilemma," *Transportation Journal*, Summer, 1973, Vol. 12, No. 4, p. 32.

[50] *Ibid.*, p. 43.

[51] *Ibid.*

[52] Jay A. Smith, Jr., *The Interstate Commerce Commission's Policy Regarding Mergers and Acquisitions of Regulated Interstate Motor Carriers: An Industrial Organization Analysis* (A doctoral dissertation, University of Maryland, 1972).

[53] James C. Johnson, *Trucking Mergers* (Lexington, Mass.: D.C. Heath & Company, 1973).

[54] No. MC–F–11094, *Navajo Freight Lines, Inc.–Investigation of Control–Garrett Freightlines, Inc.*, January 8, 1975. This also embraced No. MC–F–11198, *Navajo Freight Lines, Inc.–Control–Garrett Freightlines, Inc.*

[55] *Conklin Truck Lines, Inc.–Purchase–Bushroe*, 37 MCC 467 (1941); and *Associated Transport, Inc.–Control and Consolidation–Arrow Carrier Corp., et al.*, 38 MCC 137, 146 (1942).

[56] *Shein's–Purchase–Central New Jersey*, 59 MCC 534 (1953).

[57] *Schaefer et al.–Control; Transit, Inc.–Purchase–Tyson-Long Co., R. Howerter and W.R. Schaefer*, 50 MCC 433 (1948).

[58] *Safeway Trails, Inc.–Control and Merger*, 70 MCC 573 (1958).

[59] *Hudson Bus Lines, Inc.–Purchase–Boston and Maine Transp. Co.*, 58 MCC 73 (1951); and 58 MCC 133 (1951).

[60] *Transport Co.–Control–Arrow Carrier Corp.*, 36 MCC 61 (1940).

[61] *Rogers Cartage Co.–Control and Merger*, 55 MCC 145 (1948).

[62] *Baggett Transportation Co.–Purchase–Hunt Freight Lines, Inc.*, 75 MCC 147 (1958).

[63] *Powell–Purchase–Rampy*, 57 MCC 597 (1951).

[64] *Abco Moving & Storage Co., Inc.–Purchase–Dierking*, 47 MCC 557 (1947).

[65] *Weinstein–Control–Capital Transit Co. and Montgomery*, 56 MCC 127 (1949).

[66] *Wheaton Van Lines, Inc.–Lease–House*, 58 MCC 703 (1952).

[67] *Hancock Transp. Corp.–Purchase–Middlesex Transp. Co.*, 49 MCC 433 (1949).

[68] *Associated Transport, Inc.–Control and Consolidation–Arrow Carrier Corp. et al.*, 38 MCC 137, 146 (1942).

[69] *Eastern Michigan Motor Buses–Control–Great Lakes Motor Bus Co.*, 5 MCC 120 (1937).

[70] *Consolidated Motor Lines, Inc.–Purchase–Simpson Transportation Lines, Inc.*, 5 MCC 109 (1937).

[71] *Gregg Cartage and Storage Company v. United States*, 316 U.S. 74 (1941).

# chapter 19

# Operations of private carriers

Private carriage will be the primary competitor of for-hire motor carriers in the future, in the author's opinion, if it is not that at the present time. For that reason, some of the aspects of private carriage are discussed here to provide a knowledge of the development of this area of transport.

Certain of the same factors that coalesced to facilitate the development of for-hire truck transportation—improved highways, technological improvements in equipment, and modest capital outlays for equipment—provided similar opportunities to companies which wanted to perform their own transportation services. In the period of early development of truck transportation, some business firms that had been relying on for-hire carriers concluded that operating their own trucks offered service and cost advantages in many instances. As managerial interest in the use of the physical distribution concept grew, which embraced the components of inventory control, warehousing, transportation, material handling, packaging, and customer service, additional attention was focused upon the use of private carriage as a means of achieving better integration of these functional areas.

Initially local private operations in the distributive type of service were common. Identification was an important factor in early conversion to private carriage and remains one of the advantages. An oil company, such as Gulf, wanted to make deliveries to its service stations in a truck that had the Gulf markings on it. From such local service beginnings, many industrial firms turned to intercity private truck transportation.

There is no standard pattern in the institution of private carriage but the principal reason that appears in studies is that of service improvement. It is apparent that many managers have found certain advantages in the use of such operations over the services provided by for-hire carriers. One company that manufactures steel and steel products uses its private fleet primarily to deliver its products to contractors at jobsites on flatbed trailers. In some of its operations, it delivers joists as long as 140 feet so expandable trailers and escort vehicles must be used. Periodic movements are made between jobsites as well as from yards from which it also ships lumber, plywood, and building forms. Most of the jobs are delivered at specific times when a contractor has a crane and crew available to unload steel reinforcing bars, joists, and other products at the site. Although use had been made of common carriers with special commodities divisions to make deliveries, it was next to impossible to pinpoint delivery times. As a result, the company was faced with backcharges for crane and crew standing by awaiting delivery or, conversely, detention time on the part of the carriers because of either late or early arrival, which necessitated a delay in discharging until a crane and crew was available. Similarly, many private carrier operations transporting general commodities have been established for reasons of service.

Through provision of all or a part of their own transportation, shipper companies have a yardstick by which performance comparisons with for-hire carriers can be made. Such transportation may also serve as an effective competitive spur to improvements in the for-hire service of individual carriers.

### What constitutes private carriage?

As stated in Chapter 5, private carriers are shippers (manufacturers or merchants) who provide their own transportation service in whole or in part. Their primary business is other than transportation. The primary business test established in the *Woitishek* case is the controlling factor in the determination by the Commission of private carriage.[1] The principle enunciated is that the company's primary business must be other than transportation, and the transportation must be incidental to and in furtherance of the nontransportation business. This was upheld by the Supreme Court in 1951.

There has been a substantial amount of litigation before the Commission and the courts contending that the primary business test should not be the controlling principle but rather it should be whether or not the carriage was performed without compensation. This was rejected by the Supreme Court in 1951.[2] A later case permitted a transportation allowance equivalent to the lowest rail rate given to the company that operated the private carriage when the latter transported goods which its parent company had purchased from suppliers in its own trucks.[3]

The Federal Trade Commission in 1973 issued an advisory opinion that it was of the view that questions probably would not arise under the law the FTC administers if sellers using valid, uniform, delivered pricing systems offered to all customers on a nondiscriminatory basis the option of purchasing at a true f.o.b. shipping point price in lieu of a delivered price. Thus, such sellers could provide freight allowances for customer pickup. A transportation charge or allowance is legal whether or not an incidental profit is realized from the service.

Where goods are sold on a zone or uniform price basis with the cost of delivery included as an element of the product price, the vendor has been reluctant to provide a backhaul allowance because of possible discrimination charges by the Federal Trade Commission. If a backhaul allowance were applied, it would be the amount of the actual transportation cost deducted from the delivered price. Industries that have their own private fleets are desirous of providing such transportation themselves and securing the backhaul allowance.

An early ruling by the Commission, and upheld by the Supreme Court,[4] prohibits a corporation from performing transportation services for a subsidiary, parent, or other commonly-owned or -controlled company on a compensation basis. This is referred to as *intercorporate transportation*. The Commission refused to "pierce the corporate veil" and permit transportation services to be performed for compensation between commonly-controlled companies. However, the Commission allowed divisions of a multidivisional company to transport for each other for compensation even though the divisions may be engaged in unrelated businesses. As a result of conglomerate merger activity in nontransportation companies during the past 15 years, in many of which companies there are private carrier operations, the desire to transport between commonly-controlled companies has been manifested. The fuel shortages added impetus to this movement, and a petition was filed by the Private Carrier Conference in 1974 for a declaratory order by the Commission to formulate policy that would allow related or commonly-controlled corporations to haul for each other for compensation as private carriage.

In 1979, the Commission in *Ex Parte MC-122, Intercorporate Hauling* permitted intercorporate hauling where the parent company owns 80 percent of the affiliated companies. The 80 percent figure set as the subsidiary ownership minimum is the same as the Internal Revenue Service permits for consolidated financial reports. Shippers and carriers were to provide information over a 15-month period on the impact of this ruling, and the data would be used in determining whether the restrictions should be further relaxed.

Private carriers possess several advantages over for-hire carriers in serving their firms. They may take the most direct route between points served and may serve any point. Their advance knowledge of production schedules and plant and warehouse orders allows them to schedule their trucks in and out of company docks ahead of other trucks, and loads can be channelled or consolidated readily. A recent Commission study made on interstate highways found that the percentage of empty truck miles for private trucks was 27 percent, which was the highest percentage of any trucking operations, higher than regulated and exempt. If the private carrier is able to develop backhaul loads, it will be extremely difficult for a for-hire carrier to be competitive with it.

## Magnitude of private carriage

Private motor carriers constitute the largest group of motor carriers of property. They have grown in number from 77,000 in 1968 to a known 103,344 interstate private motor carriers of property in 1979.[5] Inasmuch as these carriers are not required to secure operating authority from the Commission, there is no single source that tabulates the actual number performing interstate and intrastate service. The number that are operating one or more trucks may be as many as five or ten times the recorded number.

The operations of some private fleets are equivalent to those of large regional Class I motor common carriers. One private carrier has 820 trailers and 268 truck-tractors in operation between plants. It transports finished products to the customer and carries inbound raw materials to its plants. Its private operations include 11 terminals and its average shipment size is 500 pounds. Such a carrier operates in much the same manner as a commercial carrier but since private carriers do not report their business operations to the Commission the picture of private trucking is a collage of information derived from a number of sources. Numerous surveys have been conducted in the last several years in attempts to provide a clearer perspective of the diversity and growth of this segment of transportation.

A survey was made of 370 nontransportation companies which were known to have sizable private trucking operations to ascertain information on the growth rate of private carriage, the motivation for conversion to private carriage, and whether or not a company with private carriage is as rigorous in evaluating its performance as it is the performance of common carriers it uses.[6] Based on a 45 percent return, some interesting results were obtained. There was a general expectation among the respondents that volume of traffic would increase but the proportionate share to common carriers might actually decline. The rate of conversion in recent years has been faster than in previous periods.

The decisive factors that led to the institution of private carriage in these companies were (1) to improve service, and (2) to cut transportation costs. In comparing performance or effectiveness of common and private carriage, the respondents indicated that the yardsticks used for common carriers were as follows: total cost per mile, 21 percent; transit time, 16 percent; other standards (customer service, utilization, operating ratio, claims service, dependability), 16 percent; and more than one of the foregoing standards, 41 percent. There were individual observations from shipper companies regarding the rigor with which an evaluation of performance of private carriage v. for-hire carriage is pursued, which indicated a rigorous evaluation. But the survey results contained no general conclusions on this matter.

Another survey that provides data about the companies that have undertaken some private carriage is one made by the Department of Transportation as a part of the *National Transportation Report of 1974.* It was instituted in order to secure a better understanding of the transportation problems faced by producers of manufactured products and, specifically, to secure shipper appraisal of the quality of service offered by different modes of transportation. Using a representative sample by region of the country and by metropolitan area size, 193 manufacturing plants which employed 100 or more individuals and were located in 14 metropolitan areas throughout the United States were surveyed. Over three-fourths of the plants shipped to a nationwide market.

About 82 percent of these companies stated that they used trucking more than any other mode, and 70 to 89 percent indicated there was an adequate number of competitors to maintain good service. Despite this fact, the survey found that about half of the shippers transported part of their output in their own trucks. Slightly more than 25 percent of the total volume of all shipments made by the respondents in the survey were delivered in private trucks. Further, there was an indication that an even greater share might move in that manner in the future.

Another survey found that approximately the same percentage of shippers, almost half of those responding, were engaged in private trucking. *Traffic World,* a weekly traffic and transportation trade journal, undertook a survey in 1973 through a mailed questionnaire to one of every three of its major shipper subscribers.[7] A total of 1,925 shipper subscribers were queried, a net return of 53.2 percent was complete and usable, and 47.2 percent of these shippers stated that they had private carrier operations. The average length of haul was found to be 350 miles, and the average fleet recorded about 3 million miles per year. The average shipper company had been in private trucking for about 18 years, although 24 percent had started private carriage operations within the past five years. Of the respondents, 62.6 percent expected their freight operations to increase the following year.[8]

There seems to be a consistent pattern among those companies with private carriage to expand their operations.

The preponderance of all trucks used in truck transportation are in private transportation. Even in the larger combination units of three or more axles, 53 percent are in private carriage.

**Managerial approaches to private trucking**

Strategies used by management in the utilization of its private carrier operation differs markedly among companies. Management's initial approach may have been to limit its use to a particular product or product line and in truckload lots only. Subsequently, the operation is often extended to other product lines. At other times, a company may have initially transported only its finished products and broadened its transportation to that of inbound raw materials for its plants and movements entirely between its plants. Some companies that have only less-truckload shipments consolidate the shipments in their private trucks and deliver them to break-bulk centers. Distribution from these centers is by for-hire, short-haul common carriers. Or the approach may be to confine private carriage to a particular geographical area or market segment and not expand its trucking operations as long as management feels it has satisfactory service and rates from for-hire carriers. However, as was stated earlier, about half of those companies that have private operations plan to expand those operations.

*Utilization.* The Department of Transportation had case studies made of ten interstate private truck operations from ten industry groupings which provide insight into the utilization of private fleet operations.[9] These companies were selected because it was felt the nature and scope of their private trucking would yield valuable data on the reasons for their undertaking, on cost elements, and on the utilization of private carriage in total corporate distribution. Some of these private carriers operate long-haul, some short-haul, some regional, some transcontinental, some only truckloads, others truckloads and less-truckloads combined. Some transported light and bulky products whereas others handled dense commodities. Some cargos were packaged, and others were bulk, dry, or liquid.

Unlike other studies in which service improvement is listed as the primary motivation for conversion, this study indicated that cost reduction was the primary factor. The range of savings was stated to be from five to 40 percent. The most profitable shipments for them to handle were in the 1,000 to 10,000 pound weight range.

The operating data in Table 19-1 reflect the diversity of their operations. As shown, the average length of haul is from 65 miles for a major producer and distributor of oil, gas, and other petroleum products to 1,000 miles for a company that is a large manufacturer of industrial machinery and supplies with 16 divisions. The preponderance of the latter company's shipments are less truckloads moving between plants or to warehouses. The average shipment size ranged from 3,000 pounds for a fabrics manufacturer to 44,000 pounds for a producer of indus-

# TABLE 19-1

## Private Carriage Operation
## Fleet Operating Data by Company

**1. What is the general nature of operations?**

| | A | B | C | D | E | F | G | H | I | J |
|---|---|---|---|---|---|---|---|---|---|---|
| a. Average length of haul (miles) | 240 | 150 | 65 | 120 | 1,000 | N | 330 | 750 | 805 | 875[a] |
| b. Average shipment size (thousands of pounds) | 37 | 3 | 43 | N | N | N | 44 | N | N | 34 |
| c. Average TL weight (thousands of pounds) | 37 | 25 | 43 | 29 | 33 | N | 44 | 33 | 16 | 34 |

**2. What is the cost experience?**

| | A | B | C | D | E | F | G | H | I | J |
|---|---|---|---|---|---|---|---|---|---|---|
| **a. Operating personnel** | | | | | | | | | | |
| Percent of total | 40 | 42 | 52 | 76.5 | 42 | 46 | 50 | 33 | 35.5 | 54.0 |
| Cost per mile (cents) | 32 | 30 | 31 | 122 | 26 | 39 | 23.5 | 20.5 | 17.8 | 39.5 |
| **b. Equipment** | | | | | | | | | | |
| Percent of total | 33 | 27 | 45 | 16 | 44 | 38.5 | 35.0 | 42.5 | 52.5 | 37.5 |
| Cost per mile (cents) | 26 | 19 | 27 | 25 | 27 | 34 | 17.0 | 27 | 26 | 27 |
| **c. Incidental operating expenses** | | | | | | | | | | |
| Percent of total | 4 | 3 | –– | 4 | 1 | 3 | 7.5 | 10 | 7.5 | 2.5 |
| Cost per mile (cents) | 3 | 2 | –– | 6 | 0.5 | 3 | 4 | 6.5 | 4 | 2 |
| **d. Facilities** | | | | | | | | | | |
| Percent of total | 6 | 3 | –– | –– | 2 | 2 | 1 | 1 | N | N |
| Cost per mile (cents) | 5 | 2 | –– | –– | 1.5 | 2 | 0.5 | 0.5 | N | N |
| **e. Insurance and claims** | | | | | | | | | | |
| Percent of total | 1 | 2 | –– | 0.5 | 1 | 3.5 | 0.5 | 2 | 2.5 | 2 |
| Cost per mile (cents) | 1 | 1 | –– | 1 | 1 | 3 | 0.3 | 1 | 1.5 | 1.5 |
| **f. Administration** | | | | | | | | | | |
| Percent of total | 16 | 23 | 3 | 3 | 10 | 7 | 6 | 11.5 | 2 | 4 |
| Cost per mile (cents) | 13 | 17 | 2 | 5 | 6 | 6.5 | 3 | 7.5 | 1 | 3 |
| **Total** | | | | | | | | | | |
| Annual cost (millions of dollars) | 2.2 | 17.7 | 2.5 | 4.9 | 2.1 | 2.0 | 2.4 | 0.9 | 1.1 | 0.7 |
| Cost per mile (cents) | 80 | 71 | 60 | 1.59 | 62 | 87.5 | 48.3 | 63 | 50.3 | 73 |
| Cost per hundred-weight (cents) | N | 84 | 7 | 64 | N | N | 35.8 | N | N | N |

**3. What are the measures of performance?**

| | A | B | C | D | E | F | G | H | I | J |
|---|---|---|---|---|---|---|---|---|---|---|
| Percent of empty miles | 21 | 12 | 50 | N | N | N | N | N | N | N |
| Pounds per load (thousands of pounds) | 37 | 25 | 43 | 29 | 33 | N | 44 | 33 | 16 | 34 |
| Miles per unit annual (thousands) | 90 | 100 | 100 | 32 | 180 | 52 | 126 | 105 | 83 | 75 |
| Percent of time not operating[b] | N | 45 | 20 | N | N | N | N | N | N | N |
| Waiting time | N | 0.98[c] | N | N | N | N | N | N | N | N |
| Operating speed mph | N | 42 | N | N | N | N | 40 | N | N | N |
| Transit time (percent on time) | N | 93 | N | N | N | N | N | N | N | N |
| Loss and damage claims experience | S | S | S | S | S | S | S | S | S | S |

N = Not reported.
S = Superior.

---

[a] Average for long-haul operation only.
[b] Based on 168-hour week.
[c] Hours per stop.

Source: Assistant Secretary for Policy and International Affairs, Department of Transportation, *Case Studies of Private Motor Carriage*, November, 1973, pp. 22-23.

trial and agricultural chemicals. Half of the companies, however, did not report shipment size.

Due to the diversity of operations, there is a wide variance in the cost per mile from $1.50 per mile for a full-line grocery chain located in the northeast which transports from distribution centers to its retail supermarkets to 48.3 cents for the private fleet transporting in bulk its industrial and agricultural chemicals. The two primary costs—operating personnel and equipment—also reflect differences in nature and scope of operation.

Many of the performance measures for the individual companies were not reported, as is indicated in the table. For one of them, however—loss and damage claims experience—all reported private carriage was superior.

A number of aspects of private carrier operations were studied, among which was the control systems used. It was found that the basic performance measure is the total cost per mile. The control systems were more advanced regarding vehicle operation and maintenance costs than in other costs. Only one company had measures of service performance.

The study found that nine of the ten companies had not taken a systematic approach to identifying corporate-wide movements by customer location, by supplier location, or interfacility to determine the specific application of private carriage in total corporate distribution. It concluded that the full potential of private trucking was only in its initial stages. The companies all expected to expand their private carrier operations and anticipated increasing the volume of less-truckload lots handled by their own fleets.

As a part of the study, a limited sample of representative common carriers was interviewed to ascertain the impact of private carriage on their operations. Although all of the common carriers acknowledged that traffic had been lost, they did not view private carriage as a threat to their existence. These common carriers felt that many industrial firms which instituted private carriage did not recognize the total costs of operation.

A follow-up study of private trucking for the Department of Transportation dealt with 14 private carriers.[10] They were selected from ten industrial groups and ranged in size from $200 million in annual sales to almost $3 billion. The companies were all manufacturers, and some part of their finished products were distributed with a private fleet. Their fleets were essentially general commodity-type, tractor-trailer combinations and ranged in numbers from 25 tractors to those of about 500 tractors. A wide range of utilization of these company fleets was reported from one percent of a company's transportation to 99 percent of total products moved.

Although there was a wide variation among the companies in the amount of empty backhaul miles, all of them were interested in improving the situation. The study focused on three areas where modifications of federal economic regulation by the Commission might offer private carriers opportunities for better equipment utilization—intercorporate hauling, cooperative transportation, and trip leasing.[11] It concluded that the elimination of restrictions on intercorporate hauling offered the major area of opportunity for economic benefits. Total fleet miles could be reduced by 28 percent in 27 parent-subsidiary instances. Of the miles saved, 61 percent were from private carrier operations and the remainder from for-hire truckers and railroads. Additional areas which would be beneficial to private carriers would be the development of cooperative transportation arrangements, and permitting trip leasing on a limited and controlled basis.

The study also surveyed eight regulated for-hire carriers to ascertain their views regarding the impact that modifications in these three areas might have on their operations. In general, they felt they would be adversely affected by the possible modifications.

Private carriage has not reached its present growth without challenges along the way from regulated carriers. Many of them have been adjudicated by the Commission or the courts. Moreover, periodic suggestions are made from different sources that all private carriers should be required to register with the Commission or that a common carrier should not have the same degree of common carrier obligation to serve a shipper when that shipper has a private carriage operation. Other proposals to add restrictions have also been made.

Two significant developments have recently occurred. In the *Toto* case, the Commission has permitted private carriers to apply for transportation of regulated commodities for back hauls which can be a means of minimizing empty miles. The other is the ruling which permits intercorporate hauling.

*Corporate Structure.* Private carriage operations are usually organized within the corporate structure with a relationship to traffic and/or physical distribution departments. In most of the large private carrier operations, private trucking is under this department. Figure 19-1 is the organization chart of a large industrial firm and shows the Vice President of Private Trucking on the same management level as the Vice President of Traffic. In this company, however, the Vice President of Traffic exercises control over the routing of shipments, and the result is that their private carrier operation must compete with motor common carriers for the traffic. This firm insists that from a management point of view the accomplishment of company objectives must be dominant in the management of transportation. Therefore, private carriage must stand on its own, with the full costs assigned against it. The Vice President of Private Trucking in this organization has a group of administrators dealing with managerial areas, as shown in Fig. 19-1, down through the terminal managers.

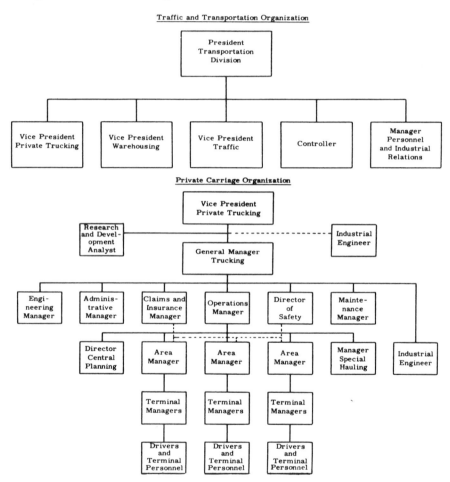

Fig. 19-1. Organization chart of a traffic department and the corporate relationship of the private trucking operation.

The organizational structure and reporting relationships may vary among private carriers. Some appear to be carefully formulated and integrated in the management heirarchy whereas others appear to be appendages.

TABLE 19-2

## PROS OF PRIVATE CARRIAGE

1. Makes it possible to penetrate and become competitive in areas previously out of reach due to inadequate or non-existent transportation service and/or uneconomical costs.
2. Allows proper continuity in flow of interplant materials. Therefore, material inventory and warehouse requirements are reduced.
3. *Quality* service with equal-or-better transit time, and *Special* service that is readily available for emergencies.
4. Reduction in loss and damage claims. Condition of goods better due to knowledgeable handling by own people.
5. General, lower overall cost of transportation and related services; also, further cost reductions realized through consolidations of goods to and from central points.
6. Packing requirements, particularly interplant, can be greatly reduced or eliminated.
7. Use of returnable containers can be most profitable.
8. Flexibility in handling restrictions—in loading and unloading, is available.
9. Flexibility (and competitive advantages) in meeting individual customer demands, especially where special or unique requirements exist.
10. Personal control of freight en route—also, capability of timing arrival or delivery of freight.
11. Can select equipment specifically suited to freight being hauled—latest technological improvements such as sealdtanks, special roller-bar trailers, etc., can be used.
12. In many cases trailers can serve as holding platform or warehouse.
13. Potential for development of new sales accounts because of improved service and customer relations.
14. Hedge against strikes and resultant loss of business because of inability to deliver goods to customer.
15. More security potential to prevent theft and hijacking.
16. Availability of advertising on trucks and, also, drivers have opportunity to further good customer relations for the Company.

## CONS OF PRIVATE CARRIAGE

1. Lack of backhaul movements can make cost prohibitive.
2. Necessity for highly-skilled, knowledgeable management and personnel.
3. Competitively-priced service now available through TOFC Piggyback program.
4. Challenges being presented by air carriers and their affiliates.
5. Substantial equipment investment.
6. Cost of Administrative overhead.
7. Costly, burdensome equipment maintenance.
8. Compliance with safety regulations also costly and burdensome.
9. Seasonal business fluctuations can seriously affect a private operation.
10. Private carriage sometimes injuries your reciprocity in dealing with common carriers.
11. Possibility of increased freight rates by common carriers because of loss of tonnage.

TABLE 19-2 (cont.)

12. If private carrier is unionized, unions take up a considerable amount of time.
13. Private carrier operations can be difficult to plan, to run a balanced operation.
14. Purchasing policy may be affected in that purchasing agents may be "locked in" with a supply due to vendor location and backhaul advantages.
15. Inclination of operations with large investment in Private Carriage to sustain and expand operations even in the face of changing conditions.
16. Full-cost responsibility on lost or damaged cargo and drivers' actions.
17. Advertising on trucks could be invitation to thieves and inform them of the availability of XYZ PRODUCTS carried in this truck.

Source: G.J. Agamemnon, Transportation Consultant, Burlington, N.C.

## Pro's and con's of private trucking

When a company is considering converting to private carriage in whole or in part, there are many factors that should be critically analyzed. A study by the Department of Transportation of ten interstate private truck operations concluded that private carriage was undertaken by a number of these companies without adequate analytical evaluation.[1,2] Such factors as existing and prospective for-hire carrier service and costs, and current and prospective service and cost of a private truck operation including return on investment should be included in an evaluation. In considering various aspects of private carriage, it is of value to look at both the pro's and con's of such operations. The compilation in Table 19-2 provides a basis for understanding some of the advantages and disadvantages of private carriage.

## Operations

The operations of private carriage, especially those of large private carriers, are similar to those of for-hire carriers which have been covered in earlier chapters. They must evaluate the selection and financing of equipment, location and numbers of terminals, frequency of scheduling, determination of routing, selection and supervision of drivers, compliance with state and federal regulations, and other matters. The forms that are used by large private carriers are as numerous as those of any commercial carrier. Control and data information are computerized in the larger operations and include terminal, employment, performance, and control records, and management control reports. Private carrier operations are service and cost centered but some operate as a profit center as well.

*Drivers.* Some private carriers follow the same procedure that for-hire carriers do in driver selection, but others do not have the personnel facilities for the necessary vision and physical tests that are required by safety regulations. As a natural evolvement of this need for qualified drivers, a type of company developed that supplies *contract drivers* under specific arrangements. The drivers have been recruited, screened, and tested by contract driver companies, sometimes called driver leasing companies. These companies supply the driver, usually on a long-term basis, to the private carrier but the driver remains on the payroll of the driver company. The private carrier, however, has exclusive and complete operational control over them, covering such points as routing, scheduling, loading, unloading, and DOT safety regulation compliance instructions, as if they were directly employed by the private carrier. The driver agency, having furnished the drivers on a long-term, dedicated-use basis to the private carrier, performs the administrative payroll function. When union drivers are used, the driver agency assists the private carrier with labor relations matters. One very large private carrier, which used only contract drivers, pointed out that the office for a contract driver agency was located in the private carrier's building. An estimated 20 percent of all private fleets now use such drivers.

There has been a considerable amount of litigation before the Commission regarding the lawfulness of use of contract drivers. A 1969 ruling by the Commission, (upheld by a federal district court and by the Supreme Court in 1973), stated that the use by private carriers of vehicles leased from one source and drivers contracted from a separate source, such as a contract driver company, was approved providing the private carrier had exclusive operational control over the driver and the vehicle and bears substantial financial burdens with respect to these two instrumentalities of transportation.[13]

*Use of Owner-Operators.* The provision of equipment for private carriage differs among companies. Some companies using specialized equipment are more likely to own their equipment. Others may lease their equipment from a leasing company or owner-operators, as do some for-hire carriers who lease either their entire fleet or a portion of it.

In one case that was adjudicated, the private carrier leased the vehicles for no more than 30 days and placed the owners on their payroll as drivers. This practice of securing the two instrumentalities of transportation, vehicles and drivers, from the same or related sources was challenged by several for-hire carrier trade associations. The decision by the Commission ruled that seasonal private carriage through the use of owner-operators was lawful.[14]

In the *Keller* case, the Commission found that joint operations in which leasing of vehicles, employment of drivers, and sharing of costs jointly by Keller Industries for the outbound transportation of its products and for 24 other companies for the inbound transportation of their products, under an arrangement solicited by Keller, was not lawful leasing and private operations but unauthorized for-hire carriage.[15] The

Commission found that each shipper had exclusive operational control over the vehicle and driver on its respective movement. It also ruled that each shipper had divested itself of the "normal burdens" involved in transportation. The latter situation developed, it was felt, since the arrangement enabled the shippers involved to avoid the risk and burden of an otherwise empty backhaul for the initiating outbound shipper's movement. The solicitation by Keller's agent was also referred to as a characteristic of for-hire transportation. The Commission's decision was upheld by the U.S. Court of Appeals.[16]

*Equipment Utilization Factors.* It is not uncommon for private carriers to have a ratio of three trailers to one truck-tractor and engage in what is called a "drop and run" operation. With tight scheduling, the trailers are dropped off for unloading while the truck-tractor picks up a loaded trailer at that point and moves it on to another destination where the process is repeated. By this means, truck-tractor utilization can be improved, which is an important factor in cost inasmuch as the truck-tractor constitutes the largest equipment cost component.

Some private carriers have made equipment replacement studies using analytical techniques on which to formulate a basis for policy decisions as to when truck-tractors should be replaced—varying from two to five years. Such studies may include both economic and sensitivity analysis. On the other hand, a number of supermarket private fleets rely on their experience to move equipment through a particular cycle. In one company, truck-tractors are used six years in over-the-road service (100,000 miles per year) and then switched to city runs for four years at which time they are replaced. In another type of operation, equipment is downgraded from long-haul to short-haul and eventually to yard or plant operations.

## QUESTIONS AND PROBLEMS

1. As the Vice President of the Physical Distribution and Transportation Department of a large manufacturer of consumer products distributed nationwide, you are called upon to study the feasibility of private trucking for your company. Outline the research that you feel necessary to respond to the request.

2. How do you account for the wide variations in the truck cost per mile that are found in various reports on private trucking?

3. Provide a brief account of the landmark cases in determining what constitutes private carriage.

4. Explain some of the strategies used by management in the operation and expansion of their private truck fleet.

5. "A shipper who converts to private carriage should no longer expect a regulated common carrier to fulfill its common carrier responsibility." Critically analyze this statement.

6. What are the regulatory issues in intercorporate hauling? Develop a rationale to oppose or support such private carriage.

7. What are the factors one might consider in determining whether a private carrier operation will use contract drivers?

8. The Marketing and Sales Departments of companies which have a private fleet have sometimes called upon the private truck operation to make emergency deliveries for them due to mixups in orders, communications, or other reasons. What problems do you see in these situations?

9. In intercity passenger transportation the private automobile is the dominant means of moving people. What will be the private truck percentage of the intercity freight market in 1990? Justify your answer.

### FOOTNOTES TO CHAPTER 19

[1] 42 MCC 193 (1943).

[2] *Brooks Transportation Company* v. *U.S.*, 93 F Supp. 340 U.S. 925 (1951).

[3] *Burlington Mills Corp.*, 53 MCC 327 (1951).

[4] *Schenley Distilleries Motor Division, Inc., Contract Carrier Application*, 44 MCC 1717 (1944), affirmed 326 U.S. 432 (1946).

[5] Federal Highway Administration, Bureau of Motor Carrier Safety.

[6] *Transportation and Distribution Management*, July-August, 1974, p. 52.

[7] *Traffic World*, February 11, 1974, p. 77.

[8] *Ibid.*

[9] Assistant Secretary for Policy and International Affairs, Department of Transportation, *Case Studies of Private Motor Carriage*, November, 1973.

[10] Department of Transportation, *Evaluation of Potential Changes to Federal Economic Regulations Governing Private Carriage*, October, 1974.

[11] *Ibid.*

[12] Assistant Secretary for Policy and International Affairs, Department of Transportation, *Case Studies of Private Motor Carriers*, November, 1973.

[13] *Personnel Service, Inc., Investigation of Operations and Practices*, 110 MCC 695 (1969); *National Motor Freight Traffic Association, Inc., et al.* v. *U.S. of A.*, Civil Action No. 339—71, U.S. District Court (D.C.); Supreme Court No. 72—632 (1973).

[14] *Ontario*, 112 MCC 211 (1970); Civil Action No. 480—71, U.S. District Court (D.C.), 1973.

[15] 103 MCC 520 (1966).

[16] *Keller Industries, Inc.* v. *United States*, 449 F 2d 163 (1971).

# chapter 20

# Intercity passenger operations

Linking thousands of communities today and forming an integral part of the passenger transportation system is the intercity motor bus operation. Paralleling to a great extent the improvements in our vast highway system, intercity bus operations have developed so rapidly that it is little short of phenomenal. The services rendered by these companies have become the accepted standard for thousands of passengers each year. The origin of intercity bus operation was humble. Most of today's operations had their origin in short-route sedan automobile service which in some cases was originally a sideline of a local livery man. Some began as operations of automobile dealers who were unable to find purchasers for their buses. Others were instituted by railroads in order to permit the abandonment of expensive rail service to rural points which produced low revenues. Still others represented efforts of electrical interurban railways to economize in their operations, as well as to provide a more flexible service.

Intercity buses provide the only means of for-hire intercity transportation to and from an estimated 14,000 communities in the United States. Bus transportation is available to 96 percent of the 3,377 important communities on the 42,500-mile interstate and defense highway system. As the size of the community decreases, the availability of rail and air passenger service drops rapidly, whereas bus service does not.

A total of 191 billion intercity passenger-miles were transported by for-hire carriers in 1978.[1] This represents 14 percent of total intercity passenger-miles, the other 86 percent being accounted for by automobiles. Since 1960 the percentage of the for-hire total carried by railroads has steadily declined to 0.7 percent, that transported by air carriers has steadily increased to 12.5 percent, and that transported by bus has decreased in the past several years to 1.6 percent. Of total intercity passenger-miles by for-hire carriers, 25.1 billion passenger-miles were by bus, 10.3 billion passenger-miles by rail, and 155.6 billion passenger-miles by air.

In terms of number of passengers, intercity bus operators transported more (330 million) than either railroads (275 million) or airlines (225 million). The average distance these passengers traveled by air was 719 miles, 126 miles by bus, and 37 by rail. The average distance traveled by air passengers has increased; for rail passengers it has substantially decreased; and for bus passengers it has increased.

There are 1,176 companies engaged in intercity bus service which operate interstate and are issued certificates or permits by the Interstate Commerce Commission. For the most part, intercity bus operations have developed separately from property-carrier operations. There are only seven carriers reporting to the Commission that transport both passengers and property. Of the approximately 478,339 buses of all types in use today, about 20,200 are engaged in intercity service, and an additional 78,960 are used in local transit, and by sightseeing and private organizations. There are about 379,178 school buses.

Like most other intercity for-hire passenger carriers, bus operators experience a wide seasonal variation in their operations. The first quarter of the year furnishes 19 percent of annual revenue, whereas the third quarter with its heavy vacation travel generates 30 percent of the revenue.

The intercity bus industry employs about 43,600 people including the personnel of bus operating companies, as well as those companies engaged primarily in providing bus station or garage services. Slightly more than one-half of these are drivers.

The growth of intercity bus common-carrier operation has been very rapid and appears to have reached a stable basis more quickly than the property-carrying aspect of highway transportation. This has been due, in some degree, to the fact that passenger operations are somewhat simpler than freight operations, since passengers assemble at a terminal and are discharged en route or ride on through to a terminal.

The members of the intercity bus industry are in general small business organizations, with a few outstanding exceptions. Most of the bus companies originated as individual or partnership enterprises. The stock in the individual companies today is owned by only a few people. The small business nature of the majority of the carriers was an important characteristic of the passenger-carrying industry. However, currently Class I motor carriers of passengers owned by nontransportation companies involved in conglomerate activities account for 69.5 percent of all revenue passengers carried and earn 88.9 percent of all revenue from passengers in regular-route intercity service.

The Interstate Commerce Commission classifies motor carriers of passengers into three groups for statistical purposes, in the same manner as that of property carriers. Class I passenger carriers are those with annual gross revenues of $3 million or more;[2] Class II, from $500,000 to $3 million; and Class III, under $500,000. There are 62 Class I carriers, and this group grosses approximately 80 percent of total revenues from all sources. Class II and Class III carriers, of which there are 1,114, account for only 20 percent of revenues. The revenues of Class I carriers (65 percent) are derived for the most part from regular-route operations, with the remainder from other services, such as charter and package.

There are a number of variations in types of operations. The first group provides scheduled service on regular routes. Some bus operations are long-haul trunk-line operations with almost no intrastate or short-distance traffic. Others are trunk-line carriers with extensive branch-line or local or intrastate operations and traffic. Still others are bridge carriers which enjoy volumes of long distance through traffic, as well as substantial local traffic and revenue. Another service is that of charter party and special party with routes and schedules arranged to suit individual passengers or groups of passengers. Another group provides local and suburban transportation, which may include service over regular routes or local sightseeing, charter, or airport limousine service.

### Equipment and load factor

Approximately 44 percent of the 20,200 buses in intercity operations are operated by Class I carriers. Most of the vehicles purchased by intercity bus operators are as replacements rather than additions to fleets. About three-fourths of the buses used by Class I carriers have seating capacities of 43. The buses that are engaged in local or suburban service have tended to have higher seating capacities. Many of these buses seat in excess of 49 passengers.

The intercity bus is heavier than the local or suburban-type bus and costs over $100,000. It provides more space and comfort for passengers, including reclining seats, special reading lights, washrooms, snack bars, and public address systems for music and announcements.

Class I carriers are relying heavily on diesel-powered buses. Currently, about 90 percent of the buses of these carriers use diesel fuel, which averages about six miles per gallon. A few buses are powered by liquefied petroleum gas, but these are confined to short-haul or suburban service. Most new buses have air suspension instead of metal springs.

Although the average seating capacity of intercity buses has increased over the years, this increase has not been nearly as extensive as the increase in the size of commercial air equipment. In buses, the average seating capacity has gone from 28 passengers in 1938 to an average of 43 passengers in 1979. The average seating capacity of airplanes, however, has increased from 21 to 137 passengers, and many planes have a capacity of more than 300 passengers. One of the reasons that buses have not had a greater increase in size is the restrictions imposed by states on length and width of buses. Another is the fact that the average passenger load on buses in regular-route intercity service in 1979 was 19.6 persons for Class I carriers and was estimated to be less than half of that figure in the Class II and Class III groups —8.1 persons. The average loads have decreased since the wartime peak, which was almost 25 persons per bus for Class I carriers, in spite of the fact that larger buses have been put into operation. Currently, the load factor (passenger-miles as a percent of seat-miles) is about 46 percent. The maximum practicable load factor based on World War II experience was 80 percent.

### Advantages of intercity bus transportation

Convenience is a very significant factor in the choice of a carrier, and therein lies part of the success intercity buses have experienced in securing a share of the passenger market. The routes of intercity buses are projected into the most convenient city areas. Depending upon operating rights, they may pick up or discharge passengers at almost any point on their route which the passenger desires. Intercity bus operators have provided service to thousands of intermediate communities between major cities; in addition, they have rendered service to sparsely populated areas which have been without for-hire transportation.

Closely associated with its accessibility to passengers is the advantage given to passenger convenience by the frequency of schedule. The relatively small size of the intercity bus as compared with a train makes it much more simple to adjust schedules to the needs of the traffic. In areas of light traffic, buses may operate two daily schedules in each direction each day, but in areas of heavy traffic density, there are often 18 or more schedules daily in each direction. The frequency of scheduling depends largely upon traffic patronage.

The element of speed influences the choice of carrier by a passenger. The improvements in the highway system and the reduction in the number of comfort stops since such facilities are now available in many buses have resulted in buses becoming more competitive with railroads in this respect. The advantage of speed has been lessened, however, as a result of the 55-mile an hour speed limit. Trailways has installed governors on its buses that limit speed to the legal limit.

Cost to the traveler also influences his choice of passenger agency to a degree. The intercity bus offers fares that average somewhat below those of the other commercial passenger carriers. The tendency has been for the fare per mile to decrease the longer the journey in intercity bus operation, with some shorter trips bearing a charge comparable to the rail coach fare. Intercity bus operations which are competitive between two points do not adhere to the same fare, and this practice is common in intercity bus operations. Solely on a transportation cost basis to the passenger, the advantage in intercity travel rests with the bus.

The average revenue per passenger-mile in a recent year for Class I motor carriers was 5.67 cents; for rail coach, excluding commutation, 6.69 cents; and air coach, 7.92 cents. On a price basis, intercity bus operations appear to be in a good position to hold their own in securing a good share of the commercial intercity passenger traffic.

### Service differentiation

With the development of intercity bus transportation, there has been experimentation with various standards and types of service. Sleeper buses, express service, free meals, and free pillows have been some of the innovations used to differentiate service, although the overwhelming portion of service has been and still is what might be termed standard.[3]

With a large portion of the interstate system open and an increased mileage of limited-access highways, intercity buses are more competitive in terms of total travel time with rail coach service. Rail service should be appreciably faster than bus yet a recent study comparing the average time savings of rail and bus for a sample of intercity trips in which the rail corridors served various sample cities found only two instances where time savings were significantly better by rail. On all other routes, the savings in travel time by rail was either slight or negative. It also concluded there was no apparent increase in time savings for the longer routes.[4]

There has been an expansion and improvement of through bus schedules involving both express and limited service in line with the trend toward longer trips by bus. It is possible to go from coast to coast without change of bus.

Some intercity bus operators have found that the establishment of a limited service has achieved success during the summer season only. One such company, in view of its experience, has no extra fare and provides limited service by stopping at only a few important terminals, so that the time en route is much less. Another firm providing limited services requires reservations to be made for the seats, provides a pillow for each passenger, and uses the newest equipment with a schedule that provides very few stops. Neither of these services is of the deluxe limited type, yet each represents a differentiation in service from that found in other forms of passenger transport.

In an effort to tap a new market, some bus companies have established a limited amount of what is termed "luxury" service. This service includes a hostess aboard, the serving of light refreshments, background music, washrooms, free reading material and pillows.

### Special services

The primary service of the typical intercity bus company is that of furnishing passenger transportation over regular routes. In addition, their special services are important and rapidly expanding. These include charter and special-party transportation, bus package express, and mail service.

Charter service involves the transportation of groups, such as athletic teams, bands, lodges, clubs, or other similar groups, which have been assembled by someone (other than the carrier) who collectively contracts for the exclusive use of certain equipment for the duration of a specific trip or tour to transport charter parties to any point. Special party service generally contemplates that such service will be rendered on weekends, holidays, or other special occasions within certain geographical areas to a number of passengers which the carrier itself has assembled into a travel group through its own sales activity. In addition to the increasing volume of tourist travel in chartered and special party service, there is extensive transportation of military units moving in groups and groups of selectees entering military service.

Buses have package and express compartments with capacities of 450 cubic feet. This provides adequate space for handling express shipments. Ordinary express shipments are tendered to the carrier and delivery is made by it only at terminals, agency stations, or bus stops. In some instances, arrangements are made by shippers or consignees with local trucking companies, taxicabs, or messengers to transport packages from the shipper's place of business to the bus terminal or from the terminal to the consignee's home or place of business. Shipments are made on a prepaid or collect basis.

A coordinated package service by air and bus has been established by a number of the airlines and the Greyhound operating companies. Shippers and receivers in some 6,000 communities without direct air service may use Greyhound bus service to ship items to the nearest airport city where packages are flown to any part of the country and then in turn delivered by Greyhound. Shipments using this service usually may not weigh more than 100 pounds.

Another special service is that of carrying U.S. mail. The Post Office Department in its effort to speed the transportation of mail has found that buses can be effectively used for many short-haul runs.

### Operating costs

As the capacity of the bus increases, the operating cost per seat-mile decreases, and operating expenses do not increase proportionately with bus size. The use of larger intercity bus equipment has taken place in part because experience has shown that increased bus size has brought about no material change in operating costs per vehicle and has definitely reduced the weight and operating expense per passenger carried. However, it has been found that areas of operation have great influence on operating expenses, and there may be a difference of as much as five cents per bus-mile due to area of operation. Vehicle age, on the other hand, has little effect on operating expense, being accountable for a range in operating expense of about one cent per bus-mile. Gross vehicle weight, it has been shown, has very significant effect, for vehicle weight results in differences of almost 20 cents per bus-mile. The latter factor has been a strong incentive for increased use of lightweight metals, as well as improved methods of bus construction.

As a result of rising wages, 35.2 percent of operating expenses were expended for labor costs in 1939 and increased to 59.8 percent in 1979. A rise of ten percent in wages today requires a fare boost of almost five cents on the dollar just to meet expenses, even if there are no increases in the cost of equipment, operating supplies, license fees, or any of the various other items required for bus operation.

Other expenses, although also greater, represent declining proportions of total expenses. Materials, supplies, and other nonlabor costs amounted to 40.2 percent.

Slightly more than 85 percent of all Class I bus operator drivers are paid for most or all of their work on a mileage basis. The remainder of the work is paid for by the hour, by the trip, or at a specified salary. The drivers are organized to a higher degree than any of the other segments of the bus labor force and are represented by the Amalgamated Transit Union, AFL-CIO.

One basic fixed expense is depreciation which is almost five percent of the total operating expenses of the Class I intercity bus operators. Generally, Class I bus operators depreciate their equipment on an eight-year basis, although the bus may not be retired at the end of that time. Some operators prefer the use of the vehicle-mile for computation of depreciation. Good business practice has been to retire a bus when the maintenance costs added to the annual amortization of the investment will be greater on the old bus than on a new one.

Since 1946 the expenses per bus-mile for Class I intercity carriers have risen from 28.8 cents to $1.22 in 1979. Half of this increase is accounted for by the increase in wage and salary costs. While costs have been constantly rising, carriers have been turning to other sources of revenue—charter and special party, and package express. These services often offset marginal revenues on regular route services.

The operating ratio for Class I carriers in 1979 (the percentage of operating revenues which are absorbed by operating expenses) was 96.2. The Commission has indicated that an operating ratio of 85 or less before income taxes would be appropriate.

A salient factor characterizing intercity bus operations is that the traffic volume varies so greatly from season to season, day to day, and hour to hour. It is customary for a carrier to maintain 25 percent or more of its fleet for the sole purpose of meeting the peak season demands. It is not unusual for the bus operator to have almost 100 percent more passengers during the summer months than during the winter season. A long-distance carrier may have to double its service on a weekend, as compared with a weekday. A carrier operating between a city and a surrounding rural area has a large outbound movement from the city before a weekend or holiday and a heavy inbound movement at the end of that period. Carriers may experience directional fluctuations as well, for the revenue per mile going in one direction may be double that going in the opposite direction. The industry establishes basic year-round schedules and augments these schedules with extra sections or establishes new schedules to meet the peak demands.

### Pricing and competition

The primary source of revenue for Class I carriers is from regular-route passenger services, although in recent years bus operators have been building up other revenue sources, particularly charter and express, because these are more profitable operations. Class I carriers derive 66 percent of their revenue from intercity schedules; and 15 percent from charter and special party service, which accounts for ten percent of the passengers. Approximately 16 percent of revenues comes from package express, and this has been growing substantially in the past decade. For Class I carriers, the revenue per passenger-mile has steadily increased from 4.41 cents in 1974 to 5.18 cents in 1979.

Historically, the most important factor influencing the bus fare structure has been competition. Although buses have competed for years with railroads, the passage by Congress of the Rail Passenger Service Act of 1970, which created the quasi-public corporation Amtrak, has injected a somewhat different competitive element into the field in the form of subsidy. Under provisions of the Act, Amtrak was provided initial federal subsidies but the sponsors of the legislation creating it indicated that after a two-year experimental period it would become self-sustaining. After several years of operation, however, it appears that the likelihood of it ever becoming self-sustaining is remote. Amtrak had its guaranteed loan authority increased from $500 million to $900 million. In its first three years, it had $489 million appropriated for its operation. In 1975, $1.1 billion subsidy was authorized for a two-year period. About one-third of the cost of Amtrak service is paid by its passengers, and the remainder by the general taxpayer. In 1978, the average cost of Amtrak service was 25.5 cents per passenger mile. This is a loss of 16.5 cents per passenger mile for each mile travelled by each passenger. Moreover, Amtrak is free to change its fares without state or federal approval which bus operators are not permitted to do. Amtrak cut its one-way fare between Boston and New York by 22 percent in 1971 in spite of more than $500,000 loss between these points. This route was still losing money in 1979. The basic Amtrak network was designed around terminal cities with populations over 1 million.

One segment of air transportation, the local service airlines, is also subsidized. Some of them are competitive with intercity bus transportation. The local service airline subsidy is presently about $69 million annually. A recent ruling by the Civil Aeronautics Board that a local service carrier could pass some of its subsidy through to a third level carrier—air taxi operator—adds an additional subsidized competitive element since these third level carriers have heretofore been unsubsidized.

In spite of the competitive aspects of other for-hire carriers, passenger travel by bus is somewhat less than air and rail fares on a national average.

The motor bus meets its greatest competitor in the private automobile inasmuch as the latter possesses the advantage of complete flexibility in time, direction, and place of movement. The advantage that the bus has in this competition is the lower cost to the passenger.

It is in the short-haul market, distances of up to 200 miles, that the bus possesses its greatest advantage and potential for future development. The long-haul market, which was a source of passengers in earlier years, has been lost to the airlines. Developing a hub of larger cities that serve as a center for short hauls of up to 200 miles appears to be promising.

Future intercity passenger mobility may be influenced by the availability of fuel which could substantially alter competitive relationships.

The energy efficiency of buses in comparison with private automobiles could result, under these circumstances, in a significant improvement in the competitive position of intercity buses.

The present fare structure is not the result of any analytical planning. It is the result of the operation of several compelling influences, such as the competition of the private automobile, rail competition, competition within the industry itself, and the ability of the traffic to bear the charges. The latter element is particularly important in the case of long-haul traffic.

Intercity bus fares are subject to the tapering principle, which means that the longer the journey the lower the cost per mile. A 10-mile trip may cost 6.5 cents a mile, whereas a 1,500-mile trip may cost only 3.5 cents per mile. The bus industry feels that the tapered principle of fares reflects their costs. It may be that the sharp drop in the fare for the very long journey is an attempt to attract passengers for the long journeys, as there is a great elasticity of demand for such service.

A large number of companies are providing a special fare at a flat amount which offers unlimited bus travel throughout the United States for a period of 30 or 60 days. While this type of fare ignores mileage, it can build load factor which has been low.

Prior to federal regulation, there were many instances of changes in fares almost from hour to hour. At one time, when the standard charge from St. Louis to Kansas City, Missouri, was $7, one carrier charged only 75 cents. Fares varied as quickly as agents could change "blackboard" prices in shop windows. Agents of some bus companies were sold a book of 25 tickets from Chicago to Los Angeles for $16 per ticket, and they would dispose of these tickets for any price above $16 that they desired. The passage of the Motor Carrier Act eliminated these fluctuating fares. There were, however, and still are many instances of two or more lines operating between competitive points and charging different fares. This gives rise to variations in the rate per mile which a carrier charges throughout its system.

As a result of an investigation of Class I intercity carriers of passengers which was instituted by the Interstate Commerce Commission in 1946, there was an endeavor on the part of the industry to bring about greater uniformity in bus fares. However, it was found that the intercity fares and charges of the carriers were, on the whole, lower than those in effect in 1934, prior to federal regulation, and did not require uniform fares. The Commission further ruled that fares and charges of the carriers, except for transportation in special, charter, and certain local mass transportation services, were not unreasonable or otherwise unlawful.[5]

In *Ex Parte No. 125, Fare Flexibility for the Bus Industry (1979)*, the Commission proposed a new rule under which it would allow bus companies to raise or lower fares within a fixed zone without prior Commission approval. Moreover, the companies could negotiate charter rates. This rule would not apply to rates through rate bureaus.

Additional revenue is derived from transporting newspapers and some mail for the U.S. Post Office; and a minute portion is secured from charges for baggage in excess of the minimum of 250 pounds per adult fare.

### The Greyhound Corporation

As stated earlier, there are many small intercity motor carriers of passengers. However, there are a number of very large organizations, the largest of which is the Greyhound Corporation. This organization was operating 100,000 route-miles and 5,500 buses in the United States and Canada in 1979. It accounts for over 60 percent of the total intercity bus traffic. Twenty percent of the Greyhound bus fleet is in charter service. Bus package express has grown rapidly and now accounts for more than 15 percent of the transportation revenues. There are 150 so-called "combo-buses," in which the rear portion of the passenger section is blocked off and fitted with special shelves and tie-down straps to handle some of this business. An expedited premium service is available, which is termed "next bus out," to key city pairs that assures that the package will be moved on the next available bus to that destination.

The Greyhound system had its beginnings prior to 1926, but it was in November of that year that a $10 million holding company was formed to take over some of the interstate bus lines operating in the Middle West. One company that joined the group that became the Greyhound system used a racing Greyhound dog as its trademark. Patrons of that company referred to it as "the Greyhound line." Although the firm name was entirely different, this was the name adopted by the entire system.

The Greyhound Corporation, a conglomerate, has been diversifying in recent years. It has 150 subsidiary companies in food, transportation, insurance, finance, aircraft service, leasing, and equipment manufacturing.

Greyhound operations, which are conducted through a limited number of geographically segregated divisions, permit coordination and an expansion of the distance over which buses operate. Large fleets of buses or "pools" are established. This enables the company to secure maximum utilization of buses and a more efficient maintenance program. Each bus is operated in service on the average of 90,000 miles a year. A national teletype network provides control and better service in the daily operation of schedules. The average life of a Greyhound bus is five to six years in mainline service, three to four years in secondary service, and then standby service. The new Americruiser, which seats 43, is shown in Fig. 20-1. On some of the suburban runs, a transit-type bus containing more seats is often used.

The Justice Department, a few years ago, alleged that Greyhound Corporation was restraining competition. The result of this allegation was a consent decree in 1957 (an agreement entered into without trial

Fig. 20-1. Greyhound Americruiser. Courtesy: The Greyhound Corporation.

and without admission by any party), containing a number of provisos regarding competitive practices. For a long period of time, Greyhound had purchased all of its buses from General Motors Corporation. As a result of the consent decree, Greyhound agreed to seek new sources of supply for buses.[6] This led to the establishment of its own equipment manufacturing, and it now fills all its own equipment needs through a subsidiary company and sells to others.

The percentage amount of revenue of the transportation subsidiaries of the Greyhound Corporation has been dropping sharply in recent years. In 1957, the transportation subsidiaries accounted for 93 percent of the revenues of the Greyhound Corporation. This had dropped in 1967 to 72 percent, and by 1979 amounted to only 18 percent.

The load factor for Greyhound Corporation as a national system is currently about 50 percent. Beginning in 1941, the load factor rose rapidly, reaching a high of almost 80 percent in 1944. After World War II, it declined sharply and then leveled off at around 50 percent. The load factor for Greyhound has been felt to be higher than the national average for the Class I motor carriers of passengers.

## Trailways

Trailways is the second largest intercity bus carrier in the United States with 22 percent of bus traffic. It was a part of TCO Industries, which is a holding company that, in turn, was a wholly-owned subsidiary of Holiday Inns of America, Inc. TCO Industries is the sole owner of 15 Class I bus carriers of which the principal carrier is Trailways, Inc., formerly Continental Trailways, Inc.

The Trailways Bus System was organized in 1935 with five member companies as a nonprofit association to coordinate schedules and services of independently owned operations into a nationwide bus system. This has grown to 46 member companies; however, through merger and acquisition, 30 of the companies were a part of Continental Trailways and 16 were outside the Continental system.

A number of additional independent bus companies are not members of this system and operate over a limited-route system.

In 1979, Holiday Inns sold Trailways to a Pittsburg conglomerate controlled by the Hillman family for $100 million.

## Terminals

Terminal facilities provided by bus operators for passengers have generally deteriorated during the past years. Improvement in supplying better accommodations through the construction of modern terminals is badly needed. Recognition of the importance of bus terminals to their operations was not lacking on the part of many early bus managements; rather, there was a reluctance to commit themselves financially during a formative stage when one of the keys to success was low operating cost. It was felt that the inadequacies of the so-called "terminals" and the inconveniences to the passengers were more than offset by the low fare.

The advantage of modern bus terminals is based in part on experience to date which shows that bus lines which offer terminal facilities to passengers have less fluctuation in their traffic because of seasonal and weather conditions. It is becoming increasingly evident that terminals can generate not only passenger-related revenue but nonpassenger-related revenue as well. There are several methods whereby a company can provide its own terminal. One is for the motor carrier itself to purchase and build the terminal property. Another is to lease the property and construct the building. Another method is to form a terminal company.

In New York, the Port Authority has constructed a bus terminal which is used by 29 intercity bus companies. This is a municipally owned and operated bus terminal.

When a terminal is constructed by an organization such as Greyhound and then other bus companies utilize that terminal, one method by which the latter contribute their share to the expenses of the terminal is by turning over an amount equal to 15 percent of their ticket sales at that terminal. If the total terminal expense is less, then the percentage that the tenant lines will pay under such an arrangement may be 13½ percent. Usually, noncompeting connecting carriers enter into an agreement with Greyhound for the use of the latter's terminals.

In hundreds of small communities, an intercity bus operator will arrange with a local merchant, such as a drugstore, filling station, beauty shop, or cafe, to act as agent on behalf of the bus company in selling tickets; the merchant's store, in effect, provides the terminal. Under such an arrangement, the agent typically receives a commission of ten percent on the one-way or round-trip tickets, five percent on commuter tickets, and five percent of any charter sales he makes.

In the larger communities, facilities are commonly provided by the bus companies, individually or collectively.

The motor bus industry either maintains a passenger station or a ticket agency in virtually every town of 1,000 or more. As a rule, it is not economical for a carrier to operate a passenger station in towns of less than 5,000 population. However, it is sales volume and not population which determines the feasibility of a carrier's station. No recent data are available on the percentage of revenue secured from carrier stations and commercial establishments acting as agents. Information gathered some years ago, however, shows that carrier stations originated 74 percent of the revenue, commercial establishments, 21 percent, and cash fares, 5 percent.

Tickets sold at commercial establishments are for about half the distance of those tickets sold at the carrier stations. Travel bureaus which sell bus tickets, as well as tickets for other transportation companies, sell essentially long-distance tickets. The bus lines do not concentrate only upon the major sources of traffic, although their major traffic volume originates at, or is destined to, the major metropolitan centers.

The development of rest stops and meal-stop facilities has presented one of the major problems of intercity motor bus operations. Meal stops originally were governed to some degree by the drivers. Whoever gave the drivers free meals received the business from them when they came through the town. In metropolitan centers, adequate rest-stop facilities are arranged; but in the smaller communities, it is customary to make an arrangement with the owner of a highway restaurant to take care of this phase of the bus industry's service. Larger bus operators have adopted a program of building and operating meal-stop and rest-stop facilities at key points, in addition to the provision of light refreshments on some buses.

### Federal regulation

In most states, legislation affecting intercity bus operators was initiated for safety purposes. Later, state statutes were enacted for the economic regulation of fares, tariff publications, and certificates of public convenience and necessity. By 1928, 43 states and the District of Columbia regulated the transportation of passengers by motor vehicle, with all states but Delaware having some regulatory control over transportation of passengers by 1932.[7]

Phases of the prefederal regulation period have been traced in an earlier chapter, on regulation of property carriers, and are equally applicable to passenger carriers. It is worth noting that intercity bus operators are said to have asked for federal regulation for several years prior to 1935. The Motor Carrier Act of 1935 became effective in 1935, and carriers subject to the act are regulated by the Interstate Commerce Commission. The regulation of interstate motor common carriers of passengers prescribed by this act is substantially the same as that prescribed for interstate motor common carriers of property.

Since 1935 a common carrier of passengers engaging in interstate commerce has been regulated as follows: (a) it must secure a certificate of public convenience and necessity to operate; (b) a uniform system of accounts is prescribed for Class I carriers; (c) rates and fares must be reasonable and nondiscriminatory, with publication of rates required; (d) the Interstate Commerce Commission can prescribe maximum and minimum rates and, in addition, possesses rate-suspension power; and (e) consolidations and mergers are subject to approval by the Commission. The foregoing is a partial but representative list of the Interstate Commerce Commission's regulatory powers over interstate motor carriers of passengers. Even though operating authority is granted, operations cannot be commenced until a certificate of insurance and a schedule of rates have been filed with the Commission. The Department of Transportation has regulatory safety control power, since maximum hours of service are set and qualifications of employees are prescribed, as well as other matters relating to safety.

The minimum age for drivers of for-hire equipment is set at 21 years of age. A physician's certificate of physical examination for each driver is required at least once every 36 months and must be kept on file. Drivers have to have at least eight hours of rest after each ten hours of driving and may not be on duty more than 60 hours during any period of 168 consecutive hours. The Department of Transportation prescribes other safety regulations concerning such matters as inspection and maintenance of vehicles and reporting of accidents.[8]

Most bus common carriers render a regular-route service between fixed termini, about 95 percent of the service being of this type. The regular-route bus operator that has been authorized to transport passengers between two or more points over a defined route and to serve all intermediate points on this route may serve, as off-route points, all municipalities and unincorporated areas situated wholly within one airline mile of the highway on its authorized service route; and military establishments, airports, schools, and similar establishments not located in a municipality that may be entered within one airline mile of the highway, provided that operation within any part of such an establishment more than one airline mile from such authorized highway is not over a public road.[9] Motor common carriers of passengers that are subject to the act are not required to secure permission from the Commission to make changes in their schedules. The Commission's *deviation* rules were modified in 1970 to permit deviation from authorized regular routes not located on a superhighway. Deviation of up to 15 percent from regular routes is authorized.

The permission for an intercity bus common carrier to carry express and newspapers must be secured by specific grant from the Interstate Commerce Commission, whereas mail may be carried without such specific authorization. When express is carried in the same vehicle with passengers, it must be limited to shipments of a weight, bulk, and volume that can be transported without disturbing the comfort and convenience of passengers or interfering with the safety, speed, and other essential qualities of the common carrier passenger service.[10] The same credit regulations that apply to the transportation of property by truck operators also apply to express shipments transported by passenger carriers. Baggage is a part of all passenger operations, and a common weight allowed on an adult ticket is 100 pounds. In 1974, the baggage liability limitation was raised to $250 by the Commission. It also required all travelers to label their baggage properly. Excess value declaration for baggage can be secured from the carrier.

The financial responsibility of common and contract carriers must be established to the satisfaction of the Interstate Commerce Commission through the filing of adequate insurance policies to cover liability or by acting as self-insurers. The Interstate Commerce Commission minimum requirement for motor passenger carriers for bodily injury and property damage is $100,000 limit for bodily injuries to or death of one person and $50,000 limit for loss or damage in any one accident to property of others. The limit for bodily injuries to or death of all persons injured or killed in any one accident ranges from $300,000 for passenger equipment with seating capacity for 12 or less passengers to $500,000 for equipment with seating capacity over 12 passengers.

The Interstate Commerce Act has no provisions relating to liability of connecting carriers for injuries sustained by passengers. Courts have held that the provisions of Section 11707 (a) (1) of the act relating to liability of originating and delivering carriers for loss or damage occurring on connecting lines do not include the transportation of passengers.[11] It has been held in the absence of statutory liability that the initial carrier's liability depends upon the terms of its contract with the passenger as evidenced by the ticket, and the provisions of its published tariffs.[12] Many passenger carriers have tariff provisions that state that they assume no liability for transportation over other lines except as to baggage.

Reasonable through rates are to be established with other common carriers by the bus common carriers. Section 10703 (a) (3) requires carriers to establish reasonable through routes. However, the rate may be a joint one or it may be a combination of locals if the carriers agree. Through routes and joint rates which have been established by an order of the Commission cannot be canceled without securing the permission of the Commission. If such routes and rates have been established voluntarily, they may be canceled on 30-days' notice or less if short-notice permission is secured, subject to suspension.[13]

Contract carriers of passengers are issued permits for interstate bus operation by the Commission. During World War II, some industrial plants, because of the stringent gasoline and tire rationing problems applicable to motor vehicles, used buses on a contract or private basis in order to insure an adequate labor force. However, this was an emergency expedient. In 1979 there were only 23 contract carriers. Passenger brokers are required to have licenses from the Commission, as is the case for property brokers.

The degree of maturity possessed by intercity bus operations by 1935 largely accounts for the relative freedom from problems which often accompanies the imposition of regulation. No difficulties were encountered in determining the legal status of operations, as there were practically no contract or private operations (other than school buses); and determination of the relationship of federal to state authority over bus operations presented no particular problem. Tariffs for passenger operations are relatively simple, and the industry was well prepared to file them with the Commission. Accounting and statistical requirements incident to federal regulation occasioned little trouble, largely because of the experience of the passenger carriers in reporting to the states. The securing of compliance with the regulation has called forth little in the way of educational work on the part of the Commission.

There has been a relatively greater degree of consolidation and mergers among Class I bus operations than there has been among regulated property-carrier operations. Intercity bus transportation possesses attributes which, in the absence of regulatory checks, tend toward monopolistic operations, and the industry presently might be characterized as an oligopoly. The Commission has fostered competition by authorizing additional long-haul motor carriers, such as Trailways, Inc., and by granting bridge-route extensions (which are roads that connect the routes of two geographically separated companies), particularly to member carriers of the Trailways system, in order to provide competition on through routes. Although the Greyhound Corporation has been authorized to acquire numerous carriers, which often has lessened competition, the Commission in many such cases has felt that the improved service to the public justified the grant. In following a policy of regulated competition, the question has been raised whether there is a need for two large nationwide bus systems or whether this would result in unwarranted duplication of service and facilities.

### Passenger-carrier exemptions to economic regulation

The Motor Carrier Act, now subchapter II of the Interstate Commerce Act, provides certain exemptions for passenger operation. School buses, taxicabs, motor vehicles owned or operated by hotels exclusively to transport hotel patrons between hotels and local common carrier stations, motor vehicles for exclusive use in the transportation of persons when incidental to transportation by aircraft, and transportation of persons in national parks or monuments by motor vehicles under the control of the Secretary of the Interior are carriers exempt from the Motor Carrier

Act. Motor vehicles controlled and operated by a cooperative association, as defined in the Agricultural Marketing Act, are also exempt.

Two conditional exemptions, that can be removed at the discretion of the Commission, are, first, the transportation of passengers wholly within a municipality or between contiguous municipalities or within a zone adjacent to and commercially a part of any such municipality, which means most local transportation in and around cities, and second, the casual, occasional, or reciprocal transportation of passengers by motor vehicle.

Commission rulings which serve as guides in the determination of the scope of the exemptions are briefly cited.

*Motor vehicles owned or operated by hotels* used exclusively to transport hotel patrons are exempt. At the time that the act was passed, it was common practice for hotels to furnish local transportation between the hotel and local common carrier stations. Free transportation was used as a means of securing business for hotels during the depression of the 1930's. Most of such transportation has been discontinued. The Commission pointed out in an early case that this exemption applied for local transportation only.[14]

*The transportation of persons in national parks or monuments* by motor vehicles under the control of the Secretary of the Interior is exempt under the act, but this exemption does not include sightseeing carriers.[15]

Where there were bus operations limited to passengers traveling between the railheads and Yellowstone Park, although much of the operation was outside the Park, it was held to be within the exemption.[16]

Although a similar holding was made as to Yosemite Park, a 173-mile operation from the Park to the Lake Tahoe resort area, which was not a railhead but an additional point of scenic interest, was held to be not within the exemption.[17] This exemption applies only to carriers moving passengers.

The *school bus exemption* applies to motor vehicles employed solely in transporting school children and teachers to and from school. "Solely" is interpreted by the Commission to mean "employed at the time solely," so that at other times it is possible for the vehicles to be used in nonexempt transportation without affecting the exemption. When there are official functions of the school sponsored and paid for by the school, such as athletic games or field trips, the exemption applies.

When a summer sightseeing tour is made in a bus owned and operated by a public school or bona fide parochial or private school, such operation if actually an occasional one is exempt under Section 10526 (1). However, if the bus is owned by a person operating during the school year under contract with the school, neither the casual or occasional nor the school children exemption applies.[18]

*Taxicab operations* which are exempted by Section 10526 (2) are essentially local operations conducted within a municipality and its environs. What constitutes the mileage limitation within which taxicabs must operate in order to be within the exemption has not been prescribed, but where the transportation is to points beyond 25 miles from a city, it is not usually considered to be local in nature. When transportation was performed in taxicabs and sightseeing limousines which sometimes carried two or more groups together, the vehicles having a capacity of not more than six passengers, this was held to be a bona fide taxicab service where it extended within the Washington, D.C., commercial zone to points as far distant as 18 miles. [19]

The service provided by taxicabs which were used to transport athletic teams in several states was held by the Commission to be a chartered party service and was not within the exemption. [20]

The *casual, occasional, or reciprocal exemption* does not apply when passenger travel is arranged by a travel bureau for compensation. [21] The ruling by the Commission that the transportation of passengers as a regular occupation or business did not fall within this exemption was upheld by the Supreme Court. [22]

The transportation by a worker of one or more of his fellow workers to and from work on a share-the-expense basis where the transportation is over routes and in vehicles which would be used if the worker traveled alone falls within this exemption.

In interpreting the exemption of *transportation incidental to transportation by aircraft,* the Commission has indicated that distance is not the controlling factor but rather the essential character of the traffic. Another consideration is whether the motor operations between a city and an airport are designed for the use of customers of the airlines which serve that city. [23]

When weather conditions caused passenger flights to be diverted to an alternate airport and a motor carrier moved the passengers in what would ordinarily be construed as line-haul transportation at the airline's expense, it was held to be within the exemption. This was true even though the distance was approximately 90 miles between Chicago and Milwaukee because such operations were sporadic, irregular, and emergency in nature, serving as a substitute for air operations and not as a complement thereto. [24]

The motor carriers in the exemption categories, although not subject to economic regulation, are subject to safety regulation by the Department of Transportation.

## Federal and state assistance to intercity bus systems

In 1977, the intercity bus lines proposed legislation that would fund an Amtrak-like federal program of operating subsidies, capital grants, tax breaks, and rate flexibility for intercity bus systems. The Surface Transportation Assistance Act of 1978 authorized two new programs to assist intercity bus carriers. A terminal development program provided grants to states and local public bodies with which to acquire, construct, or alter facilities for use in coordinating intercity bus service with other modes of transportation. The second program was that of operating assistance to intercity bus systems serving rural and non-urbanized areas.

Six states have instituted transportation systems programs for which intercity bus companies are eligible. One of the states, Michigan, has been very active in providing subsidy for the intercity bus industry operating within the state through a bus loan program, operating systems program, and intercity passenger terminal program.[25]

## Special or charter party service

Charter and special party service represents the rapidly expanding part of the intercity bus industry. It now accounts for almost half of intercity bus passengers. All regular-route operators, which applied for authority on or before January 1, 1967, have charter authority from points served by all their routes to all points in the United States and back. About 300 carriers have certificates for only charter or special service. The latter have specific authority permitting transportation of charter parties over irregular routes within designated territories. Those carriers that hold certificates authorizing some regular-route operations possess incidental authority in regard to charter operations, since the latter are incidental to their regular service. Charter operations contemplate the transportation of groups assembled by someone other than the carrier, who collectively contracts for the exclusive use of certain equipment for the duration of a particular trip or tour. Charter rates are at tariff rates per bus-mile, or time rates, which is higher.

Special service generally contemplates that such service will be rendered on weekends, holidays, or other special occasions within defined territorial limits to a number of passengers which the carrier itself has assembled into a travel group through its own sales activity. Each passenger has a ticket covering a particular trip or tour which has been arranged by the carrier.[26] Passengers are assessed the tariff fares per individual passenger, whether special tour movement rates or the standard fare for special party service.

Passenger brokers, of which there are currently 350 may use the services of carriers which hold charter authority, either specific authority or incidental authority. The Commission has ruled[27] and been upheld by the Supreme Court that brokers of passenger transportation by motor vehicle and travel bureaus may lawfully organize tour groups selling individual tickets (special transportation) and, in turn, purchase group (charter) transportation from the carriers provided that each tour patron at the time of purchasing his ticket and becoming a member of the tour group authorizes the tour organizer or broker to act as his agent in purchasing group transportation.[28]

The regulations which have been established to govern the transportation of special or charter parties, authorized under Section 10922 (3) have been prescribed by the Commission. They define special or charter parties, specify the origin and destination territory, specify a tariff provision regarding deadhead mileage and separate transportation rates and charges in connection with all-expense tours, limit the frequency of operation so that it will not amount to a regular service, prohibit the sale of individual tickets, and prohibit seasonal carriers from operating other than seasonal operations.[29] The Commission has stated that a tour must involve something more than expeditious point-to-point service; otherwise it is a regular-route carrier. It has granted authority to conduct special operations in the transportation of airline passengers, employees to and from work, cattle breeders to and from stockyards, automobile owners in their own vehicles, and sports fans to and from racetracks.

Tariff provisions for charter service ordinarily include separate charges for "live" miles and "deadhead" miles. The live miles are those involved in carrying the charter party. There is usually an hourly layover charge for the driver when the charter is stopped at a given point for more than a certain number of hours, such as three. The Commission, in 1960, required that motor common carriers of passengers which performed charter service had to issue an itemized bill covering the services performed. The type of information required in the expense bill is substantially the same as that required to be shown on motor carrier freight bills.[30]

One of the rules in reference to origin territory specifies that the charter service can be rendered ". . . at any point or points within the territory served by its regular route or routes." This has been rather liberally interpreted. For example, a point 23 miles from the carrier's nearest regular route was held to be within the territory served by its regular route.[31] Two rulemaking proceedings were instituted to explore the possibility of defining more precisely the respective areas of service of motor carriers providing special and charter service and passenger brokers.[32] In 1968 the examiners' reports recommended against the Commission's adoption of specific regulations on special operations and conditions in passenger brokers' licenses. In 1977, the Commission issued a ruling in *Ex Parte MC 96, Entry Control of Brokers,* which liberalized entry control but this ruling was voided by a federal court action in 1979. As a result, the Commission reinstituted *Ex Parte MC 96* to re-examine entry control for passenger and property brokers.

### State size and weight restrictions

The degree of enforcement of the state size and weight limits varies. Generally, whether intercity passenger motor buses operate intrastate or interstate, they are subject to these state restrictions. The statutes which establish these limits have been enacted, in general, for the same reasons as those enumerated in the restrictions on property carrying. These include the desire on the part of the states to promote safety, to protect highways, and to control competition among the different agencies of transportation. The influence of these state and local limitations has had considerable effect on the development of intercity passenger motor carriers in many phases of operation. In addition, sizes and weights of intercity buses are subject to regulation by incorporated cities and towns to a limited degree. The recommended code of the American Association of State Highway and Transportation Officials for height, length, width, and axle load of buses is as follows:

Height . . . . . . . . . . . . . . . . . . . . . . . . 13 feet 6 inches
Width . . . . . . . . . . . . . . . . . . . . . . . . 102 inches
Length, single bus (2 axles or 3 axles) . . . . . . . . 40 feet
Axle load . . . . . . . . . . . . . . . . . . . . . . 20,000 pounds

A six-inch wider bus would permit wider seats. Where state law permits, there are more than 100 such buses in intercity service. Most new buses used in transit service are of this width, and some of them are used in charter service on interstate highways. The wider bus and heavier axle loads would permit greater productivity opportunities for the intercity bus industry.

The diversity of regulations relating to economic and safety aspects of intercity bus operation from state to state has led to the creation in all states and the District of Columbia of state officials who negotiate with other state representatives to secure reciprocity agreements concerning such items as licenses, taxes, regulatory laws, and similar matters. As might be expected, the privilege of reciprocity has not been granted by all states in all aspects. If no reciprocity is granted, it is common practice for the nonresident owners to pay the same license fees as resident owners.

Since most interstate bus operations are also intrastate operations, complete and unrestricted reciprocity did not apply to them under generally existing laws. The result has been that vehicles operated by interstate carriers are now assessed considerably more than a full registration fee on each of their buses; in some cases as many as 12 are required. Some relief from this is secured in about half the states under proration laws. This law permits operators to pay registration fees in proportion to the percentage of the carrier's total operating mileage within the taxing state. In about one-third of the states, the motor fuel tax is paid only on the fuel consumed within the state. In other states, however, the fuel tax is on a sales basis, that is, the tax is paid on all fuel purchased irrespective of where it is used. This means that fuel purchased in a sales tax state and consumed in a use-tax state is subject to two levies.

The most common types of third-structure taxes are vehicle-mile, passenger-mile, seat-mile, and gross-revenue taxes. Two-thirds of the states levy third-structure highway-use taxes on buses. Some of these taxes are levied for highway purposes, like the third-structure taxes on property carriers, while others are for general revenue.

The three principal types of licensing and registration requirements in an 11-state area on the Atlantic seaboard are as follows: (a) the license or registration fee; (b) the registration of the vehicle with the regulatory commissions in each state; and (c) title fees and, in some states, sales or use taxes on buses. The problem of properly licensing and registering equipment in a multistate operation is a full-time job in larger companies.

### QUESTIONS AND PROBLEMS

1. Amtrak, the federally-subsidized rail passenger service, is not subject to Commission economic regulation. Why should interstate bus operators not be freed from economic regulation?

2. "The members of the intercity bus industry are in general small business organizations, with a few outstanding exceptions." Ex-

plain. What is the ownership distribution of Class I intercity motor carriers of passengers?

3. Enumerate the advantages of intercity bus transportation. Of what importance is schedule frequency to the public? To the carrier?

4. What are the types of motor passenger operations? How does the Interstate Commerce Commission classify motor passenger carriers?

5. List the reasons for or against coordination of passenger services by the various modes of transportation.

6. How important is passenger-related service revenue to the bus operator? How important are these services to the public? Comment.

7. If you wanted to start an interstate charter bus operation, to what regulatory aspects would you be subjected? What is the trend in the growth of charter service compared to regular route service?

8. What are the usual arrangements for the joint use of a bus terminal? Are union bus terminals desirable from the standpoint of the public?

9. "At one time, when the standard charge from St. Louis to Kansas City, Missouri, was $7, one carrier charged only 75 cents." Does the public actually benefit by such a condition? Justify your conclusion.

10. How does the determination of the legal status of the intercity bus operator as to private, contract, or common carrier compare with that of property carrying?

11. List the exemptions for passenger operation under Part II of the Interstate Commerce Act. At the present time, are all of these exemptions valid, in your opinion? Why or why not?

### FOOTNOTES TO CHAPTER 20

[1] A passenger-mile is a statistical unit used in measuring distance and passengers. One passenger transported ten miles is expressed as ten passenger-miles.

[2] Effective 1965, carriers reporting both intercity schedules and local and suburban schedules are classified as intercity carriers if the revenues received from intercity traffic equal or exceed 50 percent of the total revenues received from intercity and local or suburban traffic. Formerly, carriers whose average fare was 20 cents or less were classified as local carriers.

[3] There was the development of some second-class bus service in which rates were as much as 30 percent below the standard first-class bus rates; there were no terminal facilities, with the loading at a designated point on a street; and older equipment was used. However, the low cost to the traveler of the first-class or standard bus service has resulted in the elimination of the second-class service. See 51 MCC 87 (1939).

[4] Department of Transportation, Office of Transportation Planning Analysis, *An Analysis of Intercity Passenger Transportation in the United States* (Washington, D.C., August, 1974), p. 19.

[5] *Investigation of Bus Fares,* 52 MCC 332 (1950). Bus fares are published by the National Bus Traffic Association.

[6] It further agreed that it would not seek special privileges from its suppliers; and that it would not put unlawful pressure on its competitors. It agreed not to discriminate against a bus operator that uses a Greyhound terminal, nor can Greyhound, as a condition of terminal use, require the operator to refrain from competing with Greyhound.

[7] *Motor Bus and Motor Truck Operation,* 140 ICC 685 (1928).

[8] As a result of Public Law 939 (84th Cong., 2d sess.), DOT prescribes rules and regulations for carriers of migrant workers by motor vehicle. These requirements cover the comfort of passengers, the qualifications and maximum hours of service of operators, and safety of operation and equipment in interstate transportation for distances of more than 75 miles.

[9] *In the Matter of Administrative Ruling No. 102,* dated January 24, 1957, MC–C 2077.

[10] *Meisinger Stages,* 1 MCC 471 (1937).

[11] *Chicago, Rock Island, and Pacific Railway Co.* v. *Maucher,* 248 U.S. 359 (1919).

[12] *Louisville and Nashville Railroad Company* v. *Chatters,* 279 U.S. 320 (1929).

[13] Administrative Rule No. 8, August 19, 1936.

[14] *Shores and Brown Common Carrier Application,* 26 MCC 243 (1940).

[15] *Motor Carrier Operations, Wash., D.C., Mt. Vernon, Va.,* 51 MCC 197 (1949).

[16] *Yellowstone Park Lines, Inc., Common Carrier Application,* 7 MCC 195 (1938).

[17] *Yosemite Park & Curry Co. Common Carrier Application,* 49 MCC 522 (1949).

[18] Administrative Rule No. 80, May 23, 1939.

[19] *Motor Carrier Operations, Washington, D.C., Mt. Vernon, Va.,* 51 MCC 197 (1949).

[20] *Peters Common Carrier Application,* 23 MCC 611 (1940).

[21] *Exemption of Casual, Occasional or Reciprocal Transp.,* 33 MCC 69 (1942).

[22] *Norris Edward Bass* v. *United States et al.,* 358 U.S. 333 (1959).

[23] *Picknelly Extension of Operation–Bradley Field,* 47 MCC 401 (1947).

[24] *Graff Common Carrier Application,* 48 MCC 310 (1948).

[25] Interstate Commerce Commission, *The Intercity Bus Industry* (Washington, D.C., 1978), p. 101.

[26] *Fordham Bus Corp. Common Carrier Application,* 29 MCC 293 (1941).

[27] *Tauck Tours, Inc., Extension–New York, N.Y.,* 54 MCC 291 (1952).

[28] *National Bus Traffic, Inc.* v. *United States,* 352 U.S. 1020 (1957).

[29] *Regulations, Special or Chartered Party Service,* 29 MCC 25, 47 (1941); and *Regulations, Special or Chartered Party Service,* 48 MCC 521 (1948).

[30] *Ex Parte MC–56, Issuance of Expense Bills of Motor Common Carriers Performing Charter Operations,* dated December, 1959.

[31] *Indiana Motor Bus Co. Extension–Charter Parties,* 41 MCC 577 (1942).

[32] *Ex Parte No. MC–29* (Sub No.1), *Passenger Transportation in Special Operations,* and (Sub No. 2), *Operations of Brokers of Passenger Transportation.*

# chapter 21

# Urban mass transit

Urban transportation involves the movement of people, as distinguished from that of vehicles, and is mass transportation (generally defined as transportation by a public carrier during a year of passengers equal to the population of the city served). Transit operations include for-hire passenger transportation provided by local motor bus lines, electric street railways, elevated and subway lines, commuter railroads, and trolley bus lines. These types of mass transit operations have large capacity equipment and operate basically on a scheduled basis. They are discussed in a manner designed to describe the relative position presently held by each in urban transit operations, with an analysis of the factors present in today's passenger transit industry and an examination of future alternatives. Another type of urban passenger service is taxicabs. Unlike mass transit, they provide personalized transit using small capacity vehicles and operating on a demand schedule.

Early transit operations were carried on with horse-drawn streetcars; later, cable cars were developed in some cities. The growth of the American cities provided a sufficiently dense traffic to necessitate a faster mode of transportation than that of the horse-drawn streetcars, and the average speed of passenger service was increased by the use of electric traction. With the utilization of electric power, the transit industry took shape, and electric traction lines were developed in many cities. As the larger metropolitan areas continued to grow, the resulting congestion led to the introduction of subway and elevated railways in some areas. The next vehicle to appear on the transit scene was the motor bus, which was in use before World War I, although the expansion of this means of transport came after that war. The trolley bus was primarily developed in the late 1920's, there being only 41 such buses in service in 1928.

For many years, the only source of transportation to work and to shopping and recreation centers for the great majority of the urban population was the transit line. Many transit lines owned amusement parks and provided transportation directly to the parks on weekends. A 5-cent ride across the city in a streetcar and a day spent at an amusement park was a very popular diversion during this period, and transit lines enjoyed unusually profitable operations.

The investment of the surface, subway, and elevated railways has always been appreciable. The subway and elevated provide their own roadbed; and the surface street railways are required to provide their roadbed, which includes the property extending 18 inches on each side beyond the car tracks. This roadbed has to be maintained, and property taxes must be paid on it by the transit company. Transit companies operate under franchises, some covering periods as long as 50-75 years. In the larger cities, these franchises were often coveted in the earlier days; political aspects frequently entered into the granting of these operating rights, awarding, as they did, the exclusive right to operate within a city. A transit line still operates under a franchise from the city, although there are some instances where the state has assumed

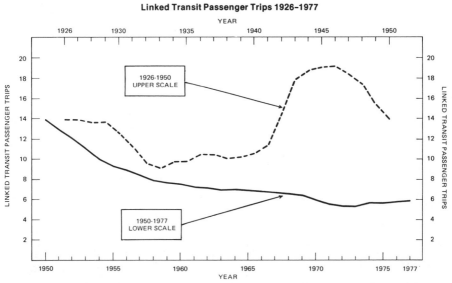

**Linked Transit Passenger Trips 1926–1977**

Fig. 21-1. Number of linked passengers carried by mass transit. (Linked passengers are all originating transit passengers and exclude all transfer and charter rides.) Source: American Public Transit Association, *Transit Fact Book* (Washington, D.C., 1977-78), p. 26.

regulatory jurisdiction over local services. In the beginning and for many years, most of the transit companies were subsidiaries of local utility companies which furnished electric service, but the Public Utility Holding Company Act of the 1930's contained divestiture procedures that enabled many of them to unload what by then had become generally unprofitable transit operations.[1]

At present, there are 1,034 companies transporting 5.7 billion passengers. Despite urban growth and population increases, the number of passengers carried has dramatically decreased by more than two billion since 1960 (Fig. 21-1). This has further aggravated the grave financial problems. The most important competitor of the urban transit lines has been and still is the private automobile. With the greater use of automobiles in the late 1920's, the favorable financial position of transit companies materially changed.

As shown in Fig. 21-2, 90.3 percent of all trips in standard metropolitan statistical areas in 1970 were made in private performance of transportation—in the automobile as driver or passenger, 86.6 percent; in motorcycles, 0.2 percent; and in trucks, 3.5 percent. The remaining 9.7 percent was in public transportation including rail rapid transit, buses, taxis, school buses, and other means.[2]

### Urban growth and transit plans

About 75 percent of all persons in the United States live in 267 metropolitan areas covering about six percent of our land area.[3] Although some rural areas in 1970-78 were regaining population, the percentage of population in metropolitan areas is projected to reach 80 percent or higher in the future. From 1970-78, there was a net migration from metropolitan areas in the Northeast and North Central regions whereas growth increased in the smaller cities and suburban areas in the Sun Belt.

The growth that is occurring in our urban population is not in the central city but in the suburban metropolitan areas. In the future, the outside central-city portion will probably double in population. We will then be primarily an urban noncentral-city population with the bulk of employment, residences, and urban travel in urban areas outside the central city. The central city appears to face a continuing decline in manufacturing and trade, but there will be expansion of service activities of government, business, and personal services.

As the metropolitan area has grown and income levels have risen, the move has been to areas where there is greater space, with the result that the great suburban development that has occurred has been of a lower density than the central-city pattern. Facilitating suburban home ownership has been the guarantee of lower interest rate loans by the Federal Housing Administration and the Veteran's Administration. In the urbanized areas, the average density (number of persons per square mile) has dropped and future estimates are for a continuing decline at a somewhat slower rate.

Historically, urban travel has been funneled to the central city, and many early transit operations were instrumental in the development of land areas adjacent to their routes. With the shift in population in metropolitan areas and the relocation of employment centers, urban travel patterns have changed with significant increases in intrasuburban and intersuburban travel, and from the central city outward. Census Bureau data show that since 1975 more people both live and work in rural areas or live and work in suburban areas than commute between suburbs and inner cities. Less than 15 percent of the working population fit the conventional pattern of suburbanites who commute into town to work. Only 6 percent of the working population used mass transit in that year.

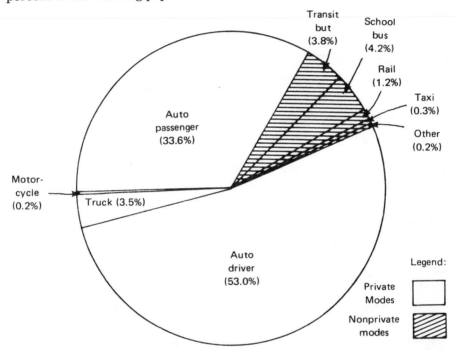

Fig. 21-2. Percentage of trips by modes, standard metropolitan statistical areas, in 1970. Source: Department of Transportation, *1974 National Transportation Report* (Washington, D.C., 1975), p. IV-1.

With the ever increasing number of automobiles in cities, traffic congestion has become a critical problem. Based on figures for 1975, 85 percent of all employed persons in the urbanized areas traveled to work in automobiles or trucks. Moreover, it is estimated that in every metropolitan area more than 86 percent of all trips are made by car. Parking facilities are inadequate, and large cities are faced with heavy expenditures to provide expressways for a continually increasing automobile traffic and a simultaneous decline in transit riders. Ordinarily, 30 to 40 percent of the space in our cities is devoted to transport facilities. In Los Angeles, two-thirds of the area in the downtown district is devoted to serving the automobile—28 percent for streets, freeways, and serviceways, and 38 percent for off-street parking facilities, loading areas, and other auto-servicing functions. City officials in many cities are having to decide the comparative desirability of

providing facilities such as expressways and parking areas or of rehabili-
tating and promoting greater public use of transit facilities.

The National Transportation Policy Study Commission forecast in 1979
that the federal government's contribution to capital investment in urban
mass transit for the period 1976-2000 would be $100.5 billion. This repre-
sents the 80 percent federal share in 1975 dollars and is a medium-growth
estimate. Forecast estimates predicted that rail fixed facilities would receive almost two-thirds of the expenditures.

The government's share of operating subsidy at the present time is 48
percent and is projected in this study to increase to 60 percent of the transit
operating subsidy by the year 2000. Presently two-thirds of the federal
share of operating subsidies goes to about 12 cities.

Urban areas have numerous alternatives for meeting their transportation objectives, such as highways, rail transit, rail commuter lines, and
others. Parking facilities must also be considered in support of highway
and transit options. Further consideration includes modernization and/or
expansion of present facilities, development of new facilities, or development of more capital intensive improvements.

## Trends in equipment and its use

Motor buses operated about 80 percent of the total revenue vehicle-
miles accounted for by all public transit vehicles in 1979. This is in
sharp contrast to the situation that existed in 1938, when motor buses
accounted for a little more than one-third of the total revenue vehicle-
miles. In that year, motor buses operated only slightly more revenue-
miles than the surface railways. A comparison of the motor bus reve-
nue-miles to those of subway and elevated shows a ratio of three to one
in 1979.

The transit equipment which is used in a particular city varies somewhat with the size of the city. All of the subway and elevated railway
cars are found in cities with populations of one million or more. There
are none in use in smaller cities. The preponderance of surface railway
cars are in cities of 250,000 or more, with only a small number in use in
any smaller cities. Motor buses, on the other hand, are found in cities of
all sizes. Bus transit is currently the only form of mass transit in nine-
tenths of the urban areas of over 50,000 population.

The seating capacity of the different types of transit equipment
varies, with the streetcar and commuter rail car having the greatest
seating capacity. The newer equipment in use on the subway and elevated lines has a seating capacity of from 44 to 56 persons. Streetcars
(light rail cars) have a seating capacity of from 49 to 61; trolley buses, from
40 to 48. Of the new buses delivered in recent years for urban transit use, the

seating capacity of 90 percent was 40 or more. Many of these buses seat 50 or more. In general, the restrictions on size and weight limitations which are applicable to intercity motor buses do not apply to urban transportation. The trend is toward motor buses with greater seating capacity. The improvement in riding comfort, and the addition of air conditioning in new buses have made bus riding more attractive.

There are a variety of reasons for the adoption of buses in transit operations, among which are the following: (a) flexibility in traffic; (b) individual power supply; (c) ability to pass each other; (d) through service to off-route locations; (e) ability to combine routes, with one vehicle rendering the service; (f) low initial cost; and (g) curb discharge.

Although the amount of new equipment used in subways is small in relation to the total, it is far more comfortable than the old. Since the life of a rail car is so long, one-third of all the equipment in use is over 25 years of age. The useful life of a subway rail car is about 35 years.

An increasing number of urban buses are diesel powered, particularly the larger units. About 25 transit systems use buses operated on liquefied petroleum gas, commonly called propane or butane gas. Buses with this kind of power emit no noxious odors and no visible smoke. Some cities that are striving to rid the air of exhaust fumes are requiring that owners of commercial vehicles take steps to eliminate exhaust fumes, either through the installation of certain devices or through the use of a fuel additive.

Air and noise pollution have affected the quality of urban life, and efforts are being made to minimize this factor. The Environmental Protection Agency, created by the Congress, through the standards which it issues on automobiles, trucks, and buses, may modify the degree of personal choice that the American public has enjoyed. Its efforts will doubtless move toward the greater use of public transit where it is available.

### Economic factors

The shifting population of urban areas has intensified the transit problems, for the low-density population in the metropolitan area results in fewer riders. In addition, the average trip length is increased, which necessitates more equipment and more drivers. Other operational factors also present problems. The overcrowding of subways and buses during rush-hour periods tends to drive people away from mass transit operations; and the traffic peaks themselves make operations more expensive. The big traffic loss of the last decade, which appears to have been arrested in 1973 and 1974, has been in the off-peak period and weekends. To meet the peak traffic demands, it is necessary to maintain equipment in excess of that which otherwise would be needed. These peak periods add to schedule difficulties, also. During the peak period, the schedule may call for a transit vehicle over a particular route every two or three minutes; whereas, during the off-peak period, a vehicle every ten or 12 minutes or less often may be adequate. This necessitates a certain amount of split shifts for drivers, who may work, for example, four hours in the morning, with three hours off, and four hours again in the afternoon. The splitting of shifts has always been a matter of contention between transit management and transit employees, with the latter contending that there should be extra compensation for the time between shifts. During World War II, the staggering of working hours at industrial plants and of store and office hours increased the carrying capacity of the existing transit vehicles by spreading the peak hours and so effecting greater utilization of existing equipment.

With surface transportation, the low average speed during the rush hours due to the frequency of stops and traffic congestion results in increased costs of operating equipment and the need for more equipment; and the frustrations of the longer transit time probably mean loss of riders as well.

Both the drivers and the maintenance workers of transit companies are organized and are primarily represented by the Amalgamated Transit Union, AFL–CIO. However, there are other unions. In Boston the Transportation authority bargains with 27 unions. Runs are allocated on a seniority basis, and the employees are paid on an hourly basis. Most labor agreements call for a minimum guarantee if an employee is asked to report for duty and no work materializes. These factors, combined with a high ratio of expenses to revenues, make the transit company very vulnerable to increases in wage levels and unable to absorb them to any appreciable extent. In 1978 the average number of employees in the transit industry was 162,510, and the payroll amounted to about 80 percent of operating expenses. Since 1970, employment has been stable or has increased. The average annual earnings per employee were $16,569.[4]

With operating subsidies being covered in part by federal funds under the federal transit aid legislation and labor costs constituting 80 percent of operating costs, the pressures of organized labor to secure higher transit labor settlements will be much stronger. Given the federal subsidy, one must raise the question as to whether hard bargaining between transit management and labor will occur. For example, a liberal change was negotiated for pension benefits with New York Metropolitan Transportation Authority, which based retirement benefits on the average pay of the final 12 months' service rather than an average of the five highest paid years. (Employees with 20 years' experience can retire at age 50). Following the change in the base, some employees were permitted by their supervisors to draw $15,700 in overtime in the final year compared to an average of $595 overtime in the three prior years. As a result, their retirement pension was $12,500 even though the final year base salary had been $9,364.[5]

A factor in transit operations increasingly being used is that of the express run, which has fewer stops and thereby appreciably cuts down on running time. It is estimated that the time for boarding and alighting is about 13 percent of scheduled running time, so the elimination of stops can speed up the run. The elimination of a number of stops reduces operational expense, since the many stops in urban operations cause a large amount of maintenance of equipment and make for a much higher consumption of gasoline and oil than is found in intercity passenger operations. In some of the new subway systems, the stations in the central core are so far apart that anticipated ridership has not developed, and may not.

One of the advantages in city operations is the flexibility of the bus. But this advantage is not used in serving transit riders to the extent that it should be. Transit routes are not modified to meet the changing needs of the central city unless there is a concerted effort by effective citizen groups to establish new routes that reflect riders' needs. It is the lower-income groups in the central city that are most dependent upon transit, and they often find that the trend to the relocation of industries in the suburban areas or across town results in trips that are excessively long. The distances involved are often not great, but because of routing rigidities, the trips require several transfers. Illustrative of this fact is the trip from south central Los Angeles to Santa Monica, an employment center, of 16 miles. The transit trip takes one hour and 50 minutes, requires three transfers, and costs 83 cents one way. This limits the riders' job opportunities and social and recreational opportunities and puts difficulties in the way of meeting their health needs. As widespread as automobile ownership is, there is almost one-third of the urban population which either is not served adequately or at all by automobiles.

Since the end of World War II, the factors of increased costs and increased competition from the private automobile have combined to narrow the margin between operating revenues and expenses for transit companies. The financial plight of the transit industry, which is caught in a squeeze between falling passenger traffic and increasing costs, is critical. The Urban Mass Transportation Administration (UMTA) has indicated that the fare box revenues typically cover about 45 percent of total transit operating expenses, local and state subsidies contribute another 35 percent, and federal assistance makes up the remaining 20 percent.

There are a number of fares which are used in transit operations: cash fares, tokens at slightly less than cash fares for a specific number, children's fares, school fares, senior citizen fares, zone fares, and weekly or monthly passes. The cash fare has long been favored by many companies, inasmuch as it is the simplest fare under which to operate. When a cash fare is used in combination with tokens or weekly or monthly passes, the tokens and passes may be somewhat lower. Where the savings on token fares are appreciable, token fares may constitute 95 percent of the total fares. The principle involved in the higher cash fare is that the cash fare is used by the occasional rider and therefore costs him somewhat more than for the rider who uses the transit system regularly, such as the purchaser of tokens or the pass. In the postwar period, there has been a trend toward more cash fares and the elimination of the pass.

Due to robberies, particularly of bus drivers, a growing number of systems in larger cities began in 1968 to require bus riders to present the exact fare. Thus, the driver does not carry any money nor does he sell tokens. If a rider does not have the exact change and has to deposit a larger amount in the fare box, he is given a slip, often called scrip, by the driver for the excess, to be cashed later by the rider at the bus company office.

Utilities, such as gas and electric companies, ordinarily establish a demand charge or standby charge against those who are responsible for the size of the plant, that is, the peak users. It is the peak users who make it necessary to have a larger plant and more equipment and manpower than would be necessary if use of the service was spread more evenly. In the transit industry, there are no demand charges. Actually, the fare structure in which tokens or weekly passes are used encourages peak-period riding and does not encourage the off-peak occasional rider. The rates charged, under these circumstances, may have little relationship to the cost of providing the service. Any effort to make peak riders pay a higher fare than off-peak riders, on the other hand, would meet with a great deal of rider resistance. These riders believe that because they are regular riders it is they who support the transit system. Therefore, they should receive preferential treatment, in their opinion. It is estimated that in our large urban areas 40 percent of total passenger traffic moves within a three-hour period, or, based on the available time per day, during 12½ percent of the day. Some companies have instituted lower slack-day, slack-hour fares to stimulate off-peak riding. This aspect of transit pricing will have to be more carefully examined by transit management in the future.

Several transit companies have established bus clubs in which suburban residents pay a monthly fee, such as $10, plus a per-ride charge. The buses stop in front of the club members' homes, and each person is assured a seat. Upon completion of loading, the bus operates express to the downtown area.

In 1950, 84 percent of the cash fares in cities of 25,000 or more were ten cents or less. Transit fares have steadily increased since that time, and by 1979 the average cash fare amounted to 37 cents. Base fares ranged from a low of 15 cents to a high of 75 cents. It is estimated that for every three percent increase in transit fares, there is a one percent loss in passengers. The effect of the fare increase is usually more severe on off-peak travel than on rush-hour travel. It also works more of a hardship on the lower-income rider of the central city. It is this group of riders which is most dependent on public transit. Since this population segment is developing more political muscle, fare increases are meeting more opposition, and a greater rigidity in fares is likely to result. This will inhibit transit operations for privately owned companies and undoubtedly will increase either subsidy of private companies or result in public ownership.

One of the problems faced by many of the transit companies has been the changing pattern in the average length of ride due to suburban growth. For example, one company had a ratio of short rides (½ mile or less) to long rides in the earlier days of one to six. Today, this company experiences one short ride for every 24 long rides, or a ratio of one to 24. This has given rise to increased use of a zone-fare system. The basic idea of a zone fare is to have an inner zone centered in the business district, which constitutes Zone 1; then concentric circles of radii of one mile, two miles, or three miles (whatever the predetermined zonal dimensions) will be established. In this manner, it is possible to set up a graduated fare structure by zones which more closely reflects the distance traveled. A zone-fare system must provide information on where the passenger boarded, his direction of travel, the time of boarding, and to what point he has paid. Furthermore, it must provide unalterable identification to the passenger to prevent overriding and must be fast and economical.

There are a few zone systems which depart from the central zone idea, and there are flat-fare systems which incorporate zoned service. The latter type of system is one in which certain routes from the center of the city out into the suburban areas are set up with express, limited, and local service, operating different distances for different fares, premium fares being charged for the express and limited service. Under the zone system, those individuals who from choice or accident live two or three miles or less from their place of employment will pay less for their daily commuting rides than those individuals who live five or seven or more miles from where they work. In other forms of transportation as well—taxi, private automobile, suburban bus line, or commuter service on a railroad—distance is the determinant. In most cases, the first zone is coextensive with the city limits.

Space is used more intensively in the densely populated urban areas by mass transit than automobiles. This makes it less costly of space requirements. Analytical forecasts of capacity of transit vehicle types are based on optimum assumptions of high utilization. In reality, the critical factor in optimum utilization is to attract passengers to the system. This involves a wide range of consumer preference factors including pricing, comfort, convenience, and others. One should not expect too much from mass transit immediately. In New York, with its heavy population density, mass transit moves as many as half of the people to work and back. Such cities as Philadelphia, Chicago, and Boston might possibly be expected to transport 25 to 30 percent but the limit during the next decade for all other communities would be 15 to 20 percent because it takes time to build a system and to attract riders.

The current mass transit is basically limited to fixed guideway systems, primarily rail, and to buses. At present, a fixed guideline rail system, such as the subway, costs more than $40 million a mile. The Secretary of Transportation in 1974 stated that ". . . in all but a very few situations, buses are cheaper, more quickly available, and can be more flexibly adapted to changing community patterns."[6]

Despite the difficulties in mass transit, about 7,200 taxicab fleets performing their personalized transit service in some 3,300 communities which regulate them are all privately owned. Their revenues exceed the total of all mass transit. Additionally, in 1978 they carried more passengers than the combined total of rail, trolley coach, and commuter rail and more than one-half as many as buses.

### Public ownership

A rapid erosion of private ownership of transit systems has been occurring. At the present time, 465 of the systems are publicly (city) owned. These companies account for 90 percent of total industry operating revenues, 89 percent of vehicle-miles operated, and 91 percent of revenue passengers carried. These publicly-owned systems own 84 percent of industry buses, all of the subway, elevated and trolley coach equipment, and 96 percent of surface railway equipment.

In some instances, the city has taken over the transit company under a leasing arrangement whereby private management continues to operate the system under a contract management arrangement. Since the system is owned by the city, taxes do not have to be paid on the operations, and the system becomes eligible for federal assistance. Currently, there are 72 transit systems that are using contract management.

Public operation of urban transit lines does not provide an easy solution to transit problems. It does mean that no profit has to be realized, and that the company can be subsidized through waiver of municipal taxes and through direct subsidy from general funds. This means the subsidy funds that are used come then from taxes on the general public. However, public service seems to be subject to just as much criticism from the passengers as private companies. In a few cases, outright subsidies have been granted to private companies to continue their operations, particularly where they were required by regulatory or public bodies to provide noncompensatory services, such as transportation of school children.

A principal result of conversion to public ownership in recent years has been the freezing of the fare, which means that deficits in operations must be recovered from other sources. A Transit Aid bill was enacted by Congress in 1974 that provided $11.8 billion for the ensuing six years, $3.9 billion of which was for operating subsidies for transit service of the six-year period. This bill, for the first time, provided federal subsidies to help cities pay the operating deficits of their transit systems which, in 1974, were more than $700 million. The operating subsidy was based on each metropolitan area's total population and its population density. The money could be used at local option either for capital grant outlays at a federal share of 80 percent, or for operating subsidies at 50 percent federal share. The remaining $7.9 billion was distributed over the six-year period for specific projects based on applications filed by cities, with the federal share 80 percent.

The Surface Transportation Act of 1978 authorized federal funding of $13.6 billion for a four-year period. This act is discussed in detail later in the chapter.

At the present time, it costs the city of New York $1.05 for every transit rider who deposits a 50-cent token in the fare box. The fare box yields about $723 million annually, and the deficit is made up by the payment from the city of New York of $302 million; by state contributions of $100 million; and by federal contributions of $115 million. Tolls from automobiles using the bridges and tunnels amounts to $69 million. Included in the total provided by the city of New York is $97 million for a 2,900-man police force that operates solely in the subway system. This system has lost 22 percent of its riders since 1969.

### Possible solutions to the transit problem

The provision of an adequate urban transportation system in our urban communities is considered to be essential. However, the increased use of private automobiles, including car-riding pools; the increase in the number of new and modern shopping centers built in residential suburbs, eliminating the need for so many trips downtown into the centers of cities; and the increased traffic congestion, which has materially slowed up streetcars and buses in most cities, causing a greater expenditure of fuel and labor time without any corresponding increase in services or passenger revenues, are some of the factors which have combined to jeopardize the future of the transit industry.

In order to have any long-range improvement in the transit problem, there must be coordinated planning by city officials, business organizations, transit officials, planning organizations, and the public. There are several areas in which the transit problem must be attacked. These include traffic control, transit operations, and urban land-use planning.

Traffic control covers such matters as parking regulations, one-way streets, synchronized traffic lights, the assignment of the curb lane to transit vehicles during rush hours, restrictions of turning movements, truck loading restrictions during rush hours, and enforcement of traffic control regulations. In a number of cities, the assignment of curb lanes to transit vehicles has speeded the move from 15 to 40 percent.

Transit operation improvements include modern equipment, more express runs, more frequent scheduling during peak periods, staggered working hours in order to spread rush period travel, better coordination between transit vehicles, and the park-and-ride service. This is the development of perimeter or fringe parking whereby drivers of vehicles park them in outlying areas and use an express transit service into the center of the city.

One proposal is that of having free transit service provided, either by the city or a private company, and subsidizing it through general taxation. Since there would be no fare collections, service would be faster and the cost to the city of this service would be less than to provide additional highways and parking facilities for private automobiles.[7] To provide free transit service, it was estimated in 1959 that it would cost about $2 billion per year and would provide the greatest relative benefit to those who are currently transit riders and the poverty groups who do not have access to an automobile and who find transit expensive. A recent study concluded that free transit would not attract substantial numbers of individuals who use automobiles to the use of transit. It was concluded that free transit might divert 13.8 percent of the trips to work from auto to public transit but few or no shopping trips by auto.[8] There are many riders who are not only able to pay present fares but could also pay higher transit fares. The general public should not be subsidizing this group of riders.

Rather than the free-transit approach, this study suggested that methods should be sought to subsidize directly low-income groups to insure adequate mobility. This could take the form of tax deductions or negative income tax.[9]

Free transit was tried in 1978-79 in Denver in a one-year experiment, financed by UMTA, in which all riders rode free except during rush hours. It cost UMTA $3.4 million and increased ridership during the off-peak hours by almost 50 percent. However, vandalism increased sharply, bus drivers objected to driving overcrowded buses, bus scheduling problems occurred, and regular paying riders often could not find a seat. This program was being evaluated by UMTA.

Public officials are encouraging greater utilization of transit facilities in order to relieve traffic congestion.[10]   A common problem they face is that of congested traffic in the downtown areas which is driving business to outlying shopping centers. According to surveys made in metropolitan areas, most city travel is by private passenger car in spite of the fact that the bus is nine times as efficient as the automobile in the use of street space to move persons. If the average automobile carriers 1.5 persons, it would take 33 automobiles to carry the 50 people who could easily ride in a transit vehicle.

Urban land-use planning must consider transportation as an integral part of such plans. Similarly, transportation should not be planned without consideration of land use. Certainly, the different land uses place varying traffic demands upon transportation facilities, and planning in urban land use must consider these effects. Transportation facilities that must be provided for present and future needs will have to be assayed in the light of the uses to which land will be put and the relative efficiency with which people can be moved. With the space limitations which cities are encountering, efficient land use becomes imperative. An example of good land use is in Chicago, where the median strip of several expressways is being utilized for rail rapid transit lines. This can be provided at a fraction of the normal cost of such facilities.

Subways provide a means by which transportation facilities are provided without taking land from other uses.[11] Six cities have these systems. Some of the larger metropolitan cities without subway systems are planning a subway system or have begun construction, due in part to federal aid and increasing problems of congestion.

In spite of modernizing efforts to make the transit system attractive to riders—and there have been instances of this—people may refuse to return to the transit system and continue to drive their automobiles. As traffic congestion continues to increase, it may be that drastic measures will be taken sometime in the future, such as banning private automobiles from downtown areas or imposing a toll upon certain of the main streets leading into downtown areas. The sharp increase in fuel prices in 1979 may do more than any other factor to increase transit ridership.

The imposition of a flat annual fee per vehicle on all vehicles registered in an urban area, such as $15, is another method suggested for encouraging transit riding.

It is estimated that between 30 and 35 million automobiles are used daily in commuting. Inasmuch as the automobile is so popular, how can we make it a more effective mass transit vehicle? The usage of the automobile represents about 120 million transit seats each day or more than 40 times the available seats on the nations' public transit systems. The current work-trip occupancy of automobiles averages 1.4 persons. A real car pooling effort could measurably increase the effectiveness of the automobile as a mass transit vehicle.

An emerging development is the use of vans owned by individuals or by corporations and used in vanpooling. Ten to 12 people can be transported in a van. Over 150 large corporations have purchased vans for vanpooling, with riders paying the operating expenses.

### Role of the federal government

The concern of the federal government in mass transit is apparent in the legislation that has been enacted in this area. The Federal-Aid Highway Act of 1944 first made provision for funds for use in the federal-aid system for cities and urban communities of over 5,000 population. The federal-aid allocation formula used was based on a ratio relating to urban population. However, the support of the federal government for urban mass transportation began with the passage of the Housing Act of 1961. It provided federal demonstration grants for experimentation; loans for new equipment; and specified that the Housing and Home Finance Agency (now Department of Housing and Urban Development) funds were to be used to formulate comprehensive transportation and land-use planning. The Federal-Aid Highway Act of 1960 stipulated that there had to be cooperation of state and local communities in the planning for highways in urban areas of more than 50,000 population as a requirement for project approval.

Other legislative enactments affecting mass transit and urban planning have broadened the federal role. The Urban Mass Transportation Act of 1964 provided coordinated assistance between the federal government and public and private transport companies to help develop mass transit; planning and establishment of regional transit systems; and assistance to states and localities in their support of transit finances and needs. Most of the demonstration grants have involved experiments in service, pricing, and technology. The earlier program of demonstration grants and loans was continued, but of more importance, this act authorized a new program of grants for capital equipment. These grants cannot exceed two-thirds of the net cost of a transportation project.

The eligibility for federal aid is based on the existence of an urban transportation plan, but where no such plan exists, emergency aid is available to the extent of one-half of the cost. Generally, grant funds for each state are limited to one-eighth of the national total. The 1964 act authorized $375 million for demonstration and capital grants through fiscal 1967. An amendment in 1966 continued the grant expenditures through fiscal 1969 at an annual rate of $150 million.

The National Capital Transportation Act of 1965 authorized $150 million in funds to plan, construct, and provide for the operation of an area-wide rail rapid transit system to serve the national capital transportation region. All but token appropriations were held up by Congress, however, until problems involving area freeway construction were resolved.

The High-Speed Ground Transportation Study of 1965 authorized the establishment of a program of research and development in high-speed intercity ground transportation and provided for a series of demonstration programs to evaluate public response to new equipment, higher speeds, variations in fares, improved comfort, and more frequent service. This was undertaken in the highly populated northeast corridor from Washington, D.C., to New York City, to Boston.

The legislation that has been enacted indicates that the federal government has committed itself to a program of subsidy in the urban mass transit field, which is in contrast to the whole thrust of its program in the intercity field of freight and passengers, where for many years it has been striving to eliminate any element of subsidy.

The creation of the federal Highway Trust Fund was designed to facilitate highway development, which it has accomplished. At the same time, federal highway policy has moved toward more comprehensive planning, has become more urban oriented, and has reflected social awareness in its programs. The urban transit field has many problems, but a critical one is that of adequate financing. For most transit companies, this factor dictates virtually every decision of company management.

The Urban Mass Transportation Administration of the Department of Transportation is responsible for the administration of the federal loan program and the financial assistance program of capital investment in urban transportation facilities and equipment.[12] The original administrator of UMTA indicated that the primary work of his then staff of 24 was to "give away money." Fifteen years later in 1979, it took more than 600 employees to handle UMTA's responsibilities.

The Department of Housing and Urban Development has federal responsibility for technical and financial assistance for comprehensive planning, including urban transportation. For research and demonstrations, the Department of Transportation has primary responsibility in the area of internal systems and program effects and requirements; and Housing and Urban Development has the primary responsibility in the area of external personal and community effects and requirements.

The 1970 Urban Mass Transportation Systems Act provided for extensive federal assistance to mass transportation. It indicated the intent of Congress to provide for a 12-year, $10 billion grant and research development program for rail and bus mass transportation with an authorized five-year spending level of $3.1 billion. The program, administered by Urban Mass Transportation Administration of the Department of Transportation was funded on a two-thirds federal and one-third local formula.

The Federal-Aid Highway Act of 1973 provided for Highway Trust Fund revenues to be used in a specified manner for urban mass transit. New contractual authority for federal grants for capital investment of $3 billion was also provided. The latter fund provided 80 percent and the states were required to provide 20 percent. Where there was a mass transit substitution for an urban highway system, the federal share of financing was 70 percent and state 30 percent. Since 1965 capital grants amounting to $10.2 billion have been made that have been used to help buy over 28,000 new transit buses, 2,431 new rail transit cars, 1,400 rail commuter cars, and the construction of about 200 miles of rapid transit rail track. Of the $5.7 billion in capital grants to mass transit, New York City received more than $1.4 billion, which is almost three times as much as any other major city received.

The National Mass Transportation Assistance Act of 1974 (the Transit Aid bill), described earlier in the chapter, provided significant new funding of $11.8 billion for a six-year period, to be used for either capital grants or operating subsidies. This was followed by the Rail Revitalization and Regulatory Reform Act of 1976, which contained as one of its provisions funding for subsidization of commuter rail operations.

Federal funding of $13.6 billion covering a four-year period was included in the Surface Transportation Assistance Act of 1978 under Title III, and was the legislation that covered urban mass transit. This act extended the basic features of the Urban Mass Transit Act of 1964 and provided more balance and program assistance between fixed rail and bus transit systems.

Four formula grant programs were funded for the four-year period for a total of $6.5 billion to be divided as follows: (1) *basic tier*, which applied to the operating and capital assistance program, $900 million annually; (2) *second tier*, which was for operating and capital assistance, $250 million per year, 85 percent of which was to be apportioned to 33 urban areas of over 750,000-in population and the remaining 15 percent to smaller urban areas; (3) *commuter rail/fixed guideway category*, two-thirds of the funds to be apportioned on a combined rail train-mile, route-mile formula and one-half to be apportioned on a fixed guideway route-mile basis; and (4) *bus assistance formula* program, which covered bus purchases, equipment, and construction of bus-related facilities. All of these programs were to be apportioned on the basis of urban population and population density.

A new formula grant program was also created for public transportation projects in rural and small urbanized areas. It provided operating and capital assistance funds for the establishment and maintenance of transit programs for areas of less than 50,000 population. Private operators of public transportation services were eligible for grants through purchase of service agreements from local public bodies. At the present time, there are over 400 transit authorities that receive federal grants.

The infusion of federal funds, together with some state and local funds in urban mass transportation, has stimulated, in a relatively short period of time, intensive research and development efforts where they had been almost nonexistent before. When combined with the demonstration grants, the result has been provision of funds to existing systems, and the development of new services. However, the initial infusion of several billions of federal funds was not effective in arresting ridership decline. The fuel shortage of 1973-74 appeared to have a more positive effect in stimulating more ridership. The ridership declined again after the crises were eased and did not increase until the fuel crises in 1979 with their steeply rising gas prices.

Following the rapidly escalating construction costs and fiscal problems that developed in 1973-74, the federal administration felt that the federal share of some of the capital projects,particularly for subways, would be so expensive that it started emphasizing the use of low cost capital public transportation alternatives, such as busways, increased use of buses, and possibly jitney service, and improved traffic control procedures to secure a better utilization of existing facilities.[13]

Some of the new transit systems that have been developed are what are termed *demand-responsive* systems that are referred to by various names, such as dial-a-bus, dial-a-ride, etc. These systems provide a personalized transportation service where customers are given door-to-door service. The customers call in their travel requests to a control center where trips with similar origins and destinations are grouped together. The vehicles do not have fixed routes and schedules but through grouping the individual travel requests, the costs per trip are considerably less than taxi fares. Another term applied to such demand responsive systems is *paratransit* but this also includes other arrangements, such as; (1) hire and drive service (daily and short term rental car) in which the vehicle is hired and driven by the traveler, and (2) prearranged ride sharing (car pool, subscription bus, and charter bus) in which a group of passengers makes a prior arrangement to travel together in a vehicle driven by one of them or by a driver hired for that purpose. Taxis and jitneys which are hailed or whose services are requested by telephone are sometimes considered part of paratransit.

Other demonstration grants have provided personal rapid transit in which small vehicles travel over exclusive rights-of-way and are automatically routed from origin to destination over a network guideway system; technologically advanced systems involving automatically controlled vehicles; continuously moving belts; and consideration of numerous other approaches. The inflationary impact of the early 1970's, however, dampened the move toward the newer, more expensive systems.

A $26 million UMTA contract to develop a design for an advanced prototype, 40-foot urban bus, resulted in a new vehicle called *Transbus* being introduced in 1975. After testing, UMTA requested bids from domestic and foreign manufacturers for production of the bus. No manufacturer submitted a bid to build the bus which was estimated to cost $230,000 each. A bus of industry's own advanced design would have cost less than half that much.

Old equipment concepts, such as double-deck and articulated buses and light rail vehicles (streetcars), are being reintroduced. To what extent and how rapidly systems are improved and technological advances materialize will depend upon such factors as the quality of transit management, the availability of funds, and the establishment of priorities about the needs of urban transit. In 1979, the President proposed that $16.5 billion be allocated to transportation as a part of the new energy program spending between 1980 and 1990 to improve mass transit systems and to bring about greater automobile efficiency. Ten billion dollars was specifically earmarked for mass transit.

In 1979, DOT issued new rules that would require all subways and buses to be fully accessible to handicapped passengers. This was to be phased in over a period of years at an estimated cost of $1.8 billion (DOT estimate) or $5.0 (industry estimate). The industry instituted a suit to prevent the new rules from being implemented.

### Private automobiles

The position of the transit industry today and the principal factor affecting its future is the private automobile, of which there are about 109 million. At least one car is owned by 85 percent of all households and two or more by 35 percent of all households. Twenty percent of all households own light trucks. As family income rises, the rate of car ownership increases.

Based on current trends, 90 percent of the eligible population could be licensed to drive by 1980.

It is understandable that the private automobile should be favored for recreational purposes, but surveys show that 75 percent of car trips are for the purpose of transportation to work or for business. About 30 percent of all trips are less than two miles in length, and 55 percent are less than five miles in length. Trips in the range of 20 to 50 miles and over comprise 6 percent of the trips but account for 22 percent of the travel.[14]

Studies made of individual use of autos for urban trips have concluded that individuals prefer to spend a great deal more to operate their autos than to use mass transit, something in the magnitude of four to six times as much.[15] The estimated costs of buying and operating an average standard-size automobile that has a ten-year life, during which it would be driven 100,000 miles, is 24.6 cents per mile (Fig. 21-3). This does not include any interest or financing charges. For the compact, the estimated costs per mile is 21.7 cents; for the subcompact the cost is 18.5 cents per mile, and for the 10-passenger van 36.2 cents. The figures assume a surburban-based operation.

| | ORIGINAL VEHICLE COST DEPRECIATED | MAINTENANCE, ACCESSORIES, PARTS & TIRES | GAS & OIL (EXCLUDING TAXES) | GARAGE, PARKING, & TOLLS | INSURANCE | STATE & FEDERAL TAXES | TOTAL COST |
|---|---|---|---|---|---|---|---|
| STANDARD SIZE | 6.3¢ | 5.5¢ | 5.5¢ | 3.2¢ | 2.5¢ | 1.6¢ | **24.6¢** |
| COMPACT SIZE | 5.2¢ | 4.8¢ | 4.9¢ | 3.2¢ | 2.3¢ | 1.3¢ | **21.7¢** |
| SUBCOMPACT SIZE | 3.8¢ | 4.1¢ | 4.1¢ | 3.2¢ | 2.2¢ | 1.1¢ | **18.5¢** |
| 10-PASSENGER VAN | 10.2¢ | 6.1¢ | 7.4¢ | 3.2¢ | 7.2¢ | 2.1¢ | **36.2¢** |

Fig. 21-3. Estimated costs of buying and operating various size automobiles in 1979. Source: Department of Transportation, Federal Highway Administration, January, 1980.

Another study on consumer preferences of transportation concluded that there was an overwhelming preference expressed for automobiles over the most likely form of mass transportation.[16] ·The advantages of convenience, comfort, and privacy provide to the automobile driver a high quality of transportation which mass transit has not been able to duplicate. It is questionable that mass transit can be made more competitive with the private automobile if all the funds have to come from the fare box.

The ownership and operation of an automobile is a major expense. For some car owners, it is their largest single expense, and for many, it is exceeded only by food and housing. To the majority, however, the computing of automobile costs includes only expenditures for gasoline and oil. The items of insurance and depreciation are seldom considered. The appearance of the compact cars made the public more conscious of the cost of operating automobiles. The weight of an automobile has an important bearing on its fuel usage. A 5,000 pound vehicle consumes 100 percent more gas than its 2,500 pound counterpart. An increase of 500 pounds from 3,000 to 3,500 can reduce mileage per gallon by 14 percent. This is one of the reasons that some individuals have advocated establishing a maximum weight on automobiles—for example, 2,500 pounds—in order to conserve fuel. With sharply rising fuel prices in 1979 as well as limited supplies of fuel, new automobile sales in the 1980's will likely be predominantly small cars.

The private automobile accounts for almost 80 percent of the energy used for passenger transportation, and about 55 percent of the energy used in passenger and freight transportation. As a major transportation user of fuel, there have been numerous proposals to discourage its use to conserve fuel, including an additional gasoline tax of ten cents, 20 cents, or even 50 cents a gallon, gasoline rationing, emergency-only Sunday driving, a special tax on higher horsepower automobiles, prohibitive parking fees, and prohibitive bridge tolls. These are penalty approaches whereas we should devise positive incentives. Car pooling is urgently recommended. If the average occupancy level of 1.4 persons commuting to work each day in 50 million private automobiles so used could be raised to 2.0 persons, it would remove 15.0 million automobiles from the daily commuter traffic and save 5 billion gallons of gasoline annually.

In December, 1974, the Congress enacted legislation making permanent the 55-mile an hour speed limit, which had been enacted as a temporary fuel conservation measure.

Despite the manifold advantages an automobile has for its owner, there are a number of critical problems which its extensive use creates and to which greater attention must be given—air pollution, safety, and congestion. If voluntary programs in urban areas are not successful in alleviating these problems, more stringent action may have to be taken. Taxing or pricing techniques may have to be employed, and more dramatic attacks launched to lessen driving errors and improve vehicle engineering and highway design.

## QUESTIONS AND PROBLEMS

1. Explain why one urban mode of transit—taxicabs—which is privately owned has been successful whereas mass transit has not.

2. What is mass transportation? What are the different kinds of equipment used in urban passenger transportation?

3. What are the ramifications of free transit?

4. What are the trends in transit equipment?

5. With federal subsidy now provided for mass transit operations, how would you insure that there be hard bargaining between transit management and labor?

6. Enumerate the reasons for the adoption of buses in transit operations.

7. What is the projected transit operating deficit in your community? What positive program could you suggest to make your transit system viable?

8. List and explain some of the economic factors in transit operations.

9. How do you account for the different types of fares which are used in transit operations?

10. What effect has the changing pattern in the average length of ride had upon transit company operations? Would you favor a zone fare? Why or why not?

11. Why is the private automobile the primary competitor of the urban transit systems?

12. In view of the financial plight of transit companies, what are some possible solutions which can be undertaken by cities? Transit companies?

### FOOTNOTES TO CHAPTER 21

[1] During the 1930-34 depression, National City Lines was formed by five brothers. They purchased numerous transit properties from electric utility companies and rehabilitated the properties with new buses. A 5-cent fare was generally charged. By 1939 National City Lines was operating in 37 cities. There were subse-

quent additions as well as substantial investment in some of the larger city transit systems, making a total of 21 wholly owned urban transit companies by 1968. Now a holding company with principal assets in trucking companies, manufacturing, distribution, and land development, its transit interests have been sold except for six operations, plus ten others it manages on a contractual basis.

[2] Department of Transportation, *1974 National Transportation Report*, Washington, D.C., 1975.

[3] A standard metropolitan area is considered by the federal government to be a city of 50,000 or more inhabitants, the county in which it is located, and such adjoining counties as are by various economic and social criteria oriented to the central city. An urban' area, on the other hand, is one of 2,500 or more population. The standard metropolitan area embraces 56 percent of our population, the central cities about 30 percent.

[4] American Public Transit Association, *Transit Fact Book* (New York, 1978-1979), p. 34.

[5] *Wall Street Journal*, August 19, 1974, p. 1.

[6] Presentation to Highway Users Federation Annual Meeting, Chicago, Illinois, October 30, 1974.

[7] For a logical development of this proposal, see L. Leslie Waters, "Free Transit: A Way Out of Traffic Jams," *Business Horizons*, Vol. 2, No. 1 (Spring, 1959), Indiana University, p. 104.

[8] Lewis M. Schneider, "The Fallacy of Free Transportation," *Harvard Business Review*, January—Feburary, 1969, p. 84.

[9] *Ibid.*, p. 85.

[10] In some cities, traffic congestion has become so critical that traffic experts have facetiously suggested: "Let cars drive north on odd days and south on even days."

[11] Little consideration is given today to construction of elevated rapid transit. There is considerable interest in the monorail, although many urban planners object to it from an aesthetic standpoint. A monorail system has been used in Germany, but so far none has been constructed in the United States except for demonstration models.

[12] For a critical analysis of UMTA, see George W. Hilton, *Federal Transit Subsidies* (Washington, D.C.: American Enterprise Institute, 1974).

[13] Assistant Secretary for Policy, Plans, and International Affairs, Department of Transportation, *Low Cost Urban Transportation Alternatives*, Vols. 1 and 2 (Washington, D.C.: Prepared by R.H. Pratt Associates, Inc., January, 1973).

[14] Federal Highway Administration, *Nationwide Personal Transportation Study*, Reports 1 and 7.

[15] Sidney S. von Loesecke, "Cost of Car Operations," *The Automobilist*, March, 1968, p. 13.

[16] F.T. Paine, A.N. Nash, S.J. Hille, and G.A. Brunner, "Consumer Conceived Attributes of Transportation" (College Park, Md.: Department of Business Administration, 1967), p. xiii. A study conducted for the Bureau of Public Roads.

# Selected bibliography

**Books**

Abouchar, Alan, *Transportation Economics and Public Policy: With Urban Extensions*. New York: John Wiley & Sons, 1977.

Aitchison, Clyde B., *Fair Reward and Just Compensation, Common Carrier Service*. Washington, D.C.: Association of Interstate Commerce Commission Practitioners, 1954.

Black, Ian, *Advanced Urban Transport*. Lexington, Mass.: Lexington Books, 1975.

Blanding, Warren E., and Hopper, W.S., *Common Carrier Advertising Handbook*. Washington, D.C.: Traffic Service Corporation, 1960.

Boot, Harry E., *Motor Carrier Leasing Regulations of the Interstate Commerce Commission*. 3d ed., Washington, D.C.: American Trucking Associations, Inc., 1969.

Brewer, Stanley, H., *The Utilization of Motor Common Carriers of General Freight in Distribution Patterns*. Seattle, Wash.: Bureau of Business Research, University of Washington, 1957.

Broehl, W.G., Jr., *Trucks, Trouble, and Triumph*. New York: Prentice-Hall, Inc., 1954.

Burstein, M.L.; Cabor, A.V.; Egan, J.W.; Hurter, A.P.; and Warner, S.L., *The Cost of Trucking: Econometric Analysis*. Dubuque, Iowa: Wm. C. Brown Co., Pubs., 1965.

Colquitt, Joseph C., *The Art and Development of Freight Classification*. Washington, D.C.: National Motor Freight Traffic Association, Inc., 1956.

Davis, Grant M., *The Department of Transportation*. Lexington, Mass.: Heath and Company, 1970.

———. *Increasing Motor Carrier Productivity: An Empirical Analysis*. New York: Praeger Publisher, 1977.

Davis, Grant M., ed., *Transportation Regulation: A Pragmatic Assessment*. Danville, Ill.: Interstate Printers & Publishers, 1976.

Domencich, T.A., and Kraft, G., *Free Transit*. Lexington, Mass.: D.C. Heath and Company, 1970.

Fair, M.L., *Economic Considerations in the Administration of the Interstate Commerce Act*. Centreville, Md.: Cornell Maritime Press, Inc., 1972.

Fair, M.L., and Guandolo, J., *Transportation Regulation.* 7th ed., Dubuque, Iowa: Wm. C. Brown Co., Pubs., 1972.

Fair, M.L., and Plowman, E.G., ed., *Coordinated Transportation.* Centreville, Md.: Cornell Maritime Press, Inc., 1969.

Fair, M.L., and Williams, Ernest W., Jr., *Economics of Transportation and Logistics.* Dallas, Tex.: Business Publishers, 1975.

Falcocchio, J.C., and Cantilli, E.J., *Transportation and the Disadvantaged.* Lexington, Mass.: D.C. Heath and Company, 1974.

Farris, Martin T., and McElhiney, P.T., ed., *Modern Transportation, Selected Readings.* 2d ed., Boston: Houghton Mifflin Co., 1973.

Filgas, James F., *Yellow in Motion.* 2d ed., Bloomington, Ind.: Bureau of Business Research, Indiana University, 1971.

Friedlaender, Ann F., *The Dilemma of Freight Transport Regulation.* Washington, D.C.: The Brookings Institution, 1969.

Fromm, Gary, ed., *Transport Investment and Economic Development.* Washington, D.C.: The Brookings Institution, 1965.

Guandolo, John, *Transportation Law.* Rev. ed., Dubuque, Iowa: Wm. C. Brown Co., Pubs., 1973.

Harper, Donald V., *Economic Regulation of the Motor Trucking Industry by the States.* Urbana, Ill.: University of Illinois Press, 1959.

———. *Transportation in America, Users, Carriers, Government.* Englewood Cliffs, N.J.: Prentice-Hall, Inc., 1978.

Harris, Curtis C., Jr., *Regional Economic Effects of Alternative Highway Systems.* Cambridge, Mass.: Ballinger Publishing Company, 1974.

Hazard, John L., *Transportation Management, Economics, Policy.* Centreville, Md.: Cornell Maritime Press, Inc., 1977.

Hille, Stanley J., and Poist, Richard F., ed., *Transportation: Principles and Perspectives.* Danville, Ill.: Interstate Printers and Publishers, 1974.

Hilton, George W., *The Transportation Act of 1958.* Bloomington, Ind.: Indiana University Press, 1969.

Hollander, Stanley C., ed., *Passenger Transportation.* East Lansing, Mich.: Bureau of Business and Economic Research, Michigan State University, 1968.

Hovell, Peter J., *The Management of Urban Public Transport.* Lexington, Mass.: Lexington Books, 1975.

Hudson, William J., and Constantin, James A., *Motor Transportation.* New York: Ronald Press Co., 1958.

Johnson, James C., *Trucking Mergers.* Lexington, Mass.: D.C. Heath and Company, 1973.

Kahn, Fritz R., *Principles of Motor Carrier Regulation.* Dubuque, Iowa: Wm. C. Brown Co., Pubs., 1958.

Kain, J.F., and Wohl, M., *The Urban Transportation Problem*. Cambridge, Mass.: Harvard University Press, 1965.

Kneafsey, J.T., *The Economics of The Transportation Firm*. Lexington, Mass.: D.C. Heath and Company, 1974.

————. *Transportation Economic Analysis*. Lexington, Mass.: Lexington Books, 1975.

Kolsen, H.M., *The Economics and Control of Road-Rail Competition*. Sidney, Australia: Sidney University Press, 1968.

Leiter, Robert D., *The Teamsters Union*. New York: Bookman Associates, 1957.

Lieb, Robert C., *Freight Transportation, A Study of Federal Intermodal Ownership Policy*. New York: Praeger Publishers, 1972.

————. *Transportation: The Domestic System*. Reston, Va.: Reston Publishers, 1978.

————. *Labor in the Transportation Industries*. New York: Praeger Publishers, 1974.

McFarland, R.A., and Moseley, A.L., *Human Factors in Highway Transport Safety*. Boston, Mass.: Harvard School of Public Health, 1954.

Miller, David R., ed., *Urban Transportation Policy: New Perspectives*. Lexington, Mass.: D.C. Heath and Company, 1972.

National Bureau of Economic Research, *Transportation Economics*. New York, N.Y.: Columbia University Press, 1965.

National Tank Truck Carriers, Inc., American Trucking Associations, Inc., *Tank Truck Transportation of Chemicals and Other Bulk Liquids*. Vol. I, Washington, D.C., 1956.

————. *Tank Truck Transportation of Chemicals. Vol. II, Washington, D.C., 1957*.

————. *Techniques of Tank Truck Transportation*. Washington, D.C., 1958.

Oi, Walter Y., and Hurter, Arthur P., Jr., *The Economics of Private Truck Transportation*. Dubuque, Iowa: Wm. C. Brown Co., Pubs., 1965.

Owen, Wilfred, *The Metropolitan Transportation Problem*. Rev. ed., Washington, D.C.: The Brookings Institution, 1966.

Powers, C.F., *A Practical Guide to Bills of Lading*. Dobbs Ferry, N.Y.: Oceana Publications, Inc., 1966.

Quandt, Richard E., ed., *The Demand for Travel: Theory and Measurement*. Lexington, Mass.: D.C. Heath and Company, 1970.

Rakowski, James P., *Transportation Economics: A Guide to Information Services*. Detroit, Mich.: Gales Research Co., 1976.

Scheppach, R.C., Jr., and Woehlcke, L.C., *Transportation Productivity*. Lexington, Mass.: D.C. Heath and Company, 1975.

Schneider, Lewis M., *Marketing Urban Mass Transit: A Comparative Study of Management Strategies*. Cambridge, Mass.: Harvard University Press, 1965.

Seburn, Thomas J., and Marsh, B.L., *Urban Transportation Administration*. New Haven, Conn.: Yale University Press, 1959.

Seng, R.A., and Gilmour, J.V., *Brink's, The Money Movers*. Chicago, Ill.: The Lakeside Press, 1959.

Sheldon, N.W., and Brandwein, R., *The Economic and Social Impact of Investments in Public Transit*. Lexington, Mass.: D.C. Heath and Company, 1973.

Sigmon, R.R., ed., *Miller's Law of Freight Loss and Damage Claims*. 3d ed., Dubuque, Iowa: Wm. C. Brown Co., Pubs., 1969.

Smerk, George M., *Urban Transportation: The Federal Role*. Bloomington, Ind.: Indiana University Press, 1965.

————. *Readings in Urban Transportation*. Bloomington, Ind.: Indiana University Press, 1968.

————. *Urban Mass Transportation, A Dozen Years of Federal Policy*. Bloomington, Ind.: Indiana University Press, 1974.

Steiner, Henry M., *Conflict in Urban Transportation: The People Against the Planners*. Lexington, Mass.: Lexington Books, 1978.

Taff, Charles A., *Operating Rights of Motor Cariers*. Dubuque, Iowa: Wm. C. Brown Co., Pubs., 1953.

Traunig, J.S., and Barrett, C., *Paying the Freight Bill*. Washington, D.C.: Traffic Service Corporation, 1971.

*TRINC Redbook* and *Bluebook (Motor carrier statistics)*, published annually with quarterly supplements by Trinc Transportation Consultants, Washington, D.C., 20024.

University of Denver College of Law, and Motor Carrier Lawyers Association, *Transportation Law Institute 1968, Operating Rights Applications*. Papers and Proceedings. Indianapolis, Ind.: Bobbs-Merrill Company, Inc., 1969.

————. *Transfer, Finance, and Security Cases (1969)*. Transportation Law Institute, 1970.

————. *Tariff Rules and Practice, 1970*. Transportation Law Institute, 1971.

Volotta, Alexander, *The Impact of Federal Entry Controls on Motor Carrier Operations*. University Park, Pa.: Center for Research of the College of Business Administration, Pennsylvania State University, 1967.

Waring, Dabney T., *The Story of the Middle Atlantic Conference and the Development of Its Rate Structure 1935-1956*. Washington, D.C.: Middle Atlantic Conference, 1957.

Way, William Jr., *Elements of Freight Traffic.* Washington, D.C.: Regular Common Carrier Conference, American Trucking Associations, Inc., 1956.

Weiner, P., and Deak, E.J., *Environmental Factors in Transportation Planning.* Lexington, Mass.: D.C. Heath and Company, 1972.

Williams, Ernest W., Jr., *The Regulation of Rail-Motor Rate Competition.* New York: Harper & Bros., 1958.

Wilson, G.W.; Bergman, B.R.; Hirsch, L.V.; Klein, M.S., *The Impact of Highway Investment on Development.* Washington, D.C.: Brookings Institution, 1966.

Wyckoff, D.D., *Organizational Formality and Performance in the Motor-Carrier Industry.* Lexington, Mass.: D.C. Heath and Company, 1974.

―――. *Truck Drivers in America.* Lexington, Mass.: D.C. Heath and Company, 1979.

Wyckoff, D.D., and Maister, D.H., *The Owner-Operator: Independent Trucker.* Lexington, Mass.: D.C. Heath and Company, 1975.

―――. *The Motor Carrier Industry.* Lexington, Mass.: Lexington Books, 1977.

## Monographs

Association of American Railroads, *Highway Motor Transportation.* Washington, D.C., 1945.

ATA, *Highways, Trucks, and New Industry.* Washington, D.C.: American Trucking Associations, Inc., 1963.

ATA; Batts, Lana R.; Roth, Ronald D., *Motor Carrier Regulatory Environments.* Washington, D.C.: ATA Foundation, 1978.

ATA; Glaskowsky, Nicholas A.; O'Neail, Brian F.; Hudson, Donald R., *Motor Carrier Regulation: A Review and Evaluation of Three Major Current Regulatory Issues Relating to the Interstate Common Carrier Trucking Industry.* Washington, D.C.: ATA Foundation, 1976.

ATA, Irregular Route Common Carrier Conference, *Motor Carrier Leasing and Interchange Under the Interstate Commerce Act,* by Robert J. Corber. Washington, D.C., 1977.

Black, Guy, *Long-Haul Truck Transportation of California Fresh Fruits and Vegetables.* California Agricultural Experiment Station, University of California, 1955.

Crandall, Burton B., *The Growth of the Intercity Bus Industry.* Syracuse, N.Y., 1954.

Curry, Neil J., *The American Motor Transport Industry.* Cambridge, Mass.: Bellman Publishing Co., 1956.

Davis, Dan R., *A Study of the Highway Distribution of Gasoline*. College Station, Tex.: Texas Transportation Institute, 1957.

Davis, Donald M., *Tariff Practice Book*. Akron, Ohio: Eastern Central Motor Carriers Association, Inc., 1970.

Davis, Frank W., Jr., *Intercity Bus Transport: The Tennessee Experience*. Knoxville, Tenn.: Center for Business and Economic Research, University of Tennessee, 1974.

Fitch, Lyle C., and Associates, *Urban Transportation and Public Policy*. San Francisco: Chandler Publishing Co., 1964.

Gillingham, J.B., *The Teamsters Union on the West Coast*. Berkeley, Calif.: Institute of Industrial Relations, University of California, 1956.

Haning, Charles R., *Private Trucking Costs and Records*. College Station, Tex.: Texas Transportation Institute, 1958.

Institute for Urban Transportation, *Mass Transit Management: A Handbook for Small Cities*. Bloomington, Ind.: Graduate School of Business, Indiana University, 1971.

Interstate Commerce Commission, Bureau of Economics, *Conglomerate Merger Activity Involving Motor Carriers*. Washington, D.C., 1970.

———. *A Preliminary Assessment of Empty Miles Traveled by Selected Regulated Motor Carriers*. McLean, Va.: Mitre Corp., 1976.

Kaiser Aluminum and Chemical Co., *Containerization, An Outlook to 1977*. Oakland, Calif., 1968.

McCarty, J.F., *State Regulation and Taxation of Highway Carriers*. Berkeley, Calif.: Bureau of Public Administration, University of California Press, 1953.

McWilliams, John C., *Motor Carrier Cost Techniques*. Washington, D.C.: National Motor Freight Traffic Association, Inc., 1956.

Miller, Mark S., *Motor Carrier Terminal Location in the Chicago Area*. Chicago Area Transportation Study. Chicago, Ill., 1974.

Moore, Thomas G., *Freight Transportation Regulation*. Washington, D.C.: American Enterprise Institute for Public Policy Research, 1972.

New England Governors' Committee on Public Transportation, *Motor Freight Transport for New England*. Boston, Mass., 1956.

———. *Intercity Bus Transportation in New England*. Boston, Mass., 1956.

———. *Local Public Transportation in New England*. Boston, Mass., 1956.

———. *New England Rail and Highway Freight Rates*. Boston, Mass., 1957.

———. *Public Transportation for New England*. Boston, Mass., 1957. (Contains a series of reports on transportation.)

Organization for Economic Co-operation and Development, *The Urban Movement of Goods*. Proceedings of Third Technology Assessment Review, 1970.

Owen, Wilfred, *The Accessible City*. Washington, D.C.: The Brookings Institution, 1972.

Rush, Herbert S., *Freight Rate Retrieval and Freight Bill Payment*. Washington, D.C.: Traffic Service Corporation, 1969.

Salzberg Memorial Lecture (Ninth) and Proceedings of the Syracuse Transportation Conference, *The Motor Trucking Industry—Its Future*. Syracuse, N.Y.: Syracuse University, 1957.

Smith, Wilbur, and Associates, *Future Highways and Urban Growth*. New Haven, Conn.: Automobile Manufacturers Association, 1961.

———. *Parking in the City Center*. New Haven, Conn.: Automobile Manufacturers Associated, 1965.

Transportation Committee on Practices and Procedures (National Traffic Committee, Regular Common Carrier Conference, Common Carrier Conference-Irregular Route), *Report of Survey: Recommendations for More Efficient Handling of Small Shipments*. Washington, D.C.: American Trucking Associations, Inc., 1954.

———. *Guide to Better Motor Carrier Operations*. Washington, D.C.: American Trucking Associations, Inc., 1954.

———. *Principles of Freight Terminal Operations*. Washington, D.C.: American Trucking Associations, Inc., 1954.

———. *Shipper-Motor Carrier Relations*. Washington, D.C.: American Trucking Associations, Inc., 1954.

Truck-Trailers Manufacturers Association, *Containerization*. Washington, D.C., 1967.

Vreeland, Barrie, *Private Trucking from A to Z*. 2d ed., New York: Shippers Conference of Greater New York, 1969.

Williams, Ernest W., Jr., ed., *The Future of American Transportation*. Englewood Cliffs, N.J.: Prentice—Hall, Inc., 1971.

**Government publications**

Defense Transport Administration, *Report on Revenue Vehicles Owned and Operated by Class I Carriers of Property*. Washington, D.C., 1952.

———. *Automobile Transportation in Defense or War*. Washington, D.C.: U.S. Government Printing Office, 1951.

Department of Agriculture, *Interstate Barriers to Truck Transportation*. Washington, D.C., 1950.

———. *The Transportation and Handling of Grain by Motor Truck in the Southwest*. Washington, D.C., 1952.

———. *Transportation of Frozen Citrus Concentrate by Railroad and Motor Truck from Florida to Northern Markets*. Washington, D.C.: U.S. Government Printing Office, 1951.

————. *Trucks Haul Increased Share of Fruit and Vegetable Traffic.* Washington, D.C., 1953.

————. *Length of Haul to Leading Markets by Motortruck, 1941 and 1950.* Washington, D.C., 1953.

————. *Motor Trucks Operated by Farmer Cooperatives.* Washington, D.C., 1978.

————. *Trucking: Lease or Buy?* Washington, D.C., 1977.

————. *Piggy Backing Fresh Vegetables.* Washington, D.C., 1979.

————. *Transportation Services to Meet the Growing Needs of Agriculture: Preliminary Report of the Rural Transportation Task Force.* Washington, D.C., 1979.

Department of Agriculture, Agricultural Marketing Service, *Protecting Perishable Foods During Transportation by Truck.* Washington, D.C.: U.S. Government Printing Office, 1956.

————. *Motortruck Transportation of Freshly Killed Beef.* Washington, D.C.: U.S. Government Printing Office, 1956.

————. *The Agricultural Exemption in Interstate Trucking.* Washington, D.C.: U.S. Government Printing Office, 1957.

————. *Highway Transportation Barriers in 20 States.* Washington, D.C.: U.S. Government Printing Office, 1957.

————. *Interstate Trucking of Fresh and Frozen Poultry Under Agricultural Exemption.* Washington, D.C.: U.S. Government Printing Office, 1958.

————. *Shifts in Rail and Truck Transportation of Fresh Fruits and Vegetables.* Washington, D.C.: U.S. Government Printing Office, 1958.

————. *The Agricultural Exemption in Interstate Trucking.* Developments in 1957-58, Washington, D.C.: U.S. Government Printing Office, 1959.

Department of Agriculture, Economic Research Service, *For-Hire Motor Carriers Hauling Exempt Agricultural Commodities.* Washington, D.C.: U.S. Government Printing Office, 1963.

————. *Comparision of For-Hire Motor Carriers Operating Under the Agricultural Exemption with Regulated Motor Carriers.* Washington, D.C.: U.S. Government Printing Office, 1966.

————. *Economic Performance of Motor Carriers Operating Under the Agricultural Exemption in Interstate Trucking.* Washington, D.C.: U.S. Government Printing Office, 1969.

————. *Over-The-Road Costs of Hauling Bulk Milk.* Washington, D.C., 1971.

Department of Agriculture, Farmer Cooperative Service, *Causes of Losses in Trucking Livestock.* Washington, D.C.: U.S. Government Printing Office, 1958.

————. *Piggyback Transportation for Pacific Northwest Cooperatives.* Washington, D.C.: U.S. Government Printing Office, 1960.

Department of Agriculture, Marketing Economics Division, *For-Hire Trucking of Exempt Farm Products*. Washington, D.C.: U.S. Government Printing Office, 1964.

Department of Agriculture, Science and Education Staff, *Transportation for Agriculture and Rural America*. Washington, D.C., 1973.

Department of Agriculture. The Agricultural Experiment Stations of many of the land grant universities have conducted research and published reports dealing with truck transportation by agricultural cooperatives and/or the truck transportation of exempt commodities.

Department of Commerce, *Charges for Private Use of Federally-Provided Transportation Services and Facilities*. Washington, D.C., 1953.

Department of Commerce, Bureau of the Census, *Pilot Survey of Commodity Movements by Truck*. March-May, 1953. Washington, D.C., December, 1954.

————. *Modern Transport Policy*. Washington, D.C., 1956.

————. *Federal Transportation Policy and Program*. Washington, D.C.: U.S. Government Printing Office, 1960.

————. *Rationale of Federal Transportation Policy*. Washington, D.C.: U.S. Government Printing Office, 1960.

Department of Energy, Division of Transportation Energy Conservation, *Alternative Fuels and Intercity Trucking*. Washington, D.C., 1978.

Department of Transportation, Federal Highway Administration, *Highway Statistics*. (Summary to 1965; annually since that time.) Washington, D.C.: U.S. Government Printing Office.

————. *Allocation of Highway Cost Responsibility and Tax Payments, 1969*. Washington, D.C., 1970.

————. *Parking Systems Analysis*. Washington, D.C.: U.S. Government Printing Office, 1972.

Department of Transportation, National Highway Safety Administration and Federal Highway Administration, *Safety of Wide Buses*. Washington, D.C., 1973.

Department of Transportation, Office of Systems Analysis and Information, *Economic Characteristics of the Urban Public Transportation Industry*. Washington, D.C., 1972.

————. *Transportation 1970-1980 Projections*. Rev., Washington, D.C., 1973.

Department of Transportation, Office of the Secretary, *A Survey of American Attitudes Toward Transportation*. Washington, D.C., 1978.

Department of Transportation. The published reports of many DOT research studies are available from Clearinghouse for Federal Scientific and Technical Information, Springfield, Va., 22151.

Research reports on highways and urban transportation are available through computer on-line access to summaries of current research projects and recent reports and articles through the Highway Research Information Service of the Transportation Research Board.

House Committee on Interstate and Foreign Commerce and House Committee on Public Works. There are a large number of publications issued as a result of hearings of these committees, among which are many pertaining to motor carriers and highways.

House Committee on Ways and Means, *Final Report of The Highway Cost Allocation Study.* 87th Cong., 1st sess. Washington, D.C.: U.S. Government Printing Office, 1961.

House Committee on Ways and Means, Subcommittee on Oversight, *Impact of Truck Overloads on the Highway Trust Fund: Hearings.* Washington, D.C., 1977-1978.

House Committee on Ways and Means, *Supplementary Report of The Highway Cost Allocation Study.* 89th Cong., 1st sess. Washington, D.C.: U.S. Government Printing Office, 1965.

―――. *1968 National Highway Needs Report.* 90th Cong., 2d sess. Washington, D.C.: U.S. Government Printing Office, 1968.

Interstate Commerce Commission, *Annual Reports* to the Congress. Washington, D.C.: U.S. Government Printing Office.

―――. *Motor Carrier Cases.* Vols. 1-121, Washington, D.C.: U.S. Government Printing Office.

Interstate Commerce Commission, Bureau of Economics, *Air-Truck Coordination and Competition.* Washington, D.C.: U.S. Government Printing Office, 1967.

―――. *The Role of Regulated Motor Carriers in the Handling of Small Shipments.* Washington, D.C.: U.S. Government Printing Office, 1967.

―――. *Transport Statistics in the United States.* Part 7 covers motor carriers. Washington, D.C.: U.S. Government Printing Office. Annual.

―――. *Transport Economics.* Washington, D.C. Issued monthly.

Message from the President of the United States, *The Transportation System of Our Nation.* 87th Cong., 2d sess. Washington, D.C.: U.S. Government Printing Office, 1962.

National Transportation Policy Study Commission, *Motor Carrier Task Force.* Washington, D.C., 1979.

―――. *National Transportation Policies.* Washington, D.C., 1979.

Office of Defense Transportation, *A Review of Highway Transport and Transit Industries during the War.* Washington, D.C., 1945.

―――. *Civilian War Transport.* 1941-1946, Washington, D.C.: U.S. Government Printing Office, 1948.

————. *Report of the Federal Manager of Motor Carrier Transportation Systems and Properties.* Washington, D.C., 1947.

————. *Supplemental Report of the Federal Manager of Motor Carrier Transportation Systems and Properties.* (Prepared by Bureau of Transport Economics of the Interstate Commerce Commission.) Washington, D.C., 1946.

Presidential Advisory Committee on Transport Policy and Organization, *Revision of Federal Transportation Policy.* Washington, D.C.: U.S. Government Printing Office, 1955.

Senate Committee on Small Business, *I.C.C. Administration of the Motor Carrier Act.* 84th Cong. 1st sess. Washington, D.C.: U.S. Government Printing Office, 1956.

————. *Competition, Regulation, and the Public Interest in the Motor Carrier Industry.* 84th Cong., 1st sess. Washington, D.C.: U.S. Government Printing Office, 1956.

————. *Trucking Mergers, Concentration, and Small Business: An Analysis of Interstate Commerce Commission Policy, 1950-56.* 85th Cong., 1st sess. Washington, D.C.: U.S. Government Printing Office, 1957.

————. *Trucking Mergers and Concentration.* 85th Cong. 1st sess. Washington, D.C.: U.S. Government Printing Office, 1957.

Senate Committee on Small Business, Bureau of Economics, *A Cost and Benefit Evaluation of Surface Transport Regulation.* Statement No. 76-1. Washington, D.C., 1976.

————. *I.C.C. Productivity Measurement Conference.* Washington, D.C., 1974.

————. *The Independent Trucker.* Washington, D.C., 1978.

————. *Truck Leasing: Staff Report on Motor Carrier Leasing Practices and the Owner-Operator.* Washington, D.C., 1977.

Senate Committee on Interstate and Foreign Commerce. There are a number of publications issued as a result of hearings of this committee, among which are some pertaining to motor carriers.

**Other reports**

American Bus Association, *Bus Facts.* (Annual) Washington, D.C.

American Public Transit Association, *Transit Fact Book.* (Annual) Washington, D.C.

American Trucking Associations, Inc., *Trends.* (Annual) Washington, D.C.

————. *Financial and Operating Statistics, Class I and II Motor Carriers of Property.* (Annual) Washington, D.C.

————. *Current Report Modern Transport Economics.* Reports are periodically issued. Washington, D.C.

Highway Research Board (now the Transportation Research Board) of the National Academy of Sciences. Washington, D.C. The Board publishes bulletins, research reports, and special reports on many highway subjects. An extensive bibliography of board publications is available from the Board without charge.

Highway Users Federation for Safety and Mobility. Many reports are issued by the Federation. Washington, D.C.

Motor Vehicle Manufacturers Association, *Motor Vehicle Facts and Figures.* (Annual) Detroit, Mich.

National Academy of Sciences, *Proceedings on Motor Carrier Economic Regulation.* Washington, D.C., 1977.

National Research Council, *Proceedings of Workshop.* Washington, D.C., 1977, 1978.

The October, 1958, issue of the *Vanderbilt Law Review* is devoted to a Symposium on Motor carriers and contains nine articles.

Traffic Service Corporation, *A Bibliography of Research Papers in Transportation, Traffic and Distribution Management.* Washington, D.C., 1968.

The Transportation Research Forum annually publishes papers presented at its annual meeting which may be purchased from The Richard B. Cross Co., Oxford, Ind.

Waters, W.G., II, compiler, *A Bibliography of Articles Related to Transportation in Major Economic Journals, 1960-1971.* Vancouver, B.C.: Centre for Transportation Studies, 1972.

### Periodicals

The rapid developments which take place in commercial motor transportation are reported in the many periodicals in the field, some of which are footnoted in the text. *Public Roads,* published bimonthly by the Federal Highway Administration of the Department of Transportation, is a valuable source of information. The reader is referred also to the following representative trade or professional publications for current articles dealing with various aspects of motor transportation.

*Commercial Car Journal.* Published monthly by Chilton Company, Inc., Philadelphia.

*Fleet Owner.* Published monthly by McGraw-Hill Publishing Co., New York.

*Heavy Duty Trucking.* Published monthly by Heavy Duty Trucking, Newport Beach, Calif.

*I.C.C. Practitioners' Journal.* Published monthly except July and August by Association of I.C.C. Practitioners, 2218 I.C.C. Bldg., Washington, D.C.

*Journal of Advanced Transportation.* Published three times a year by the Institute for Transportation, Durham, N.C.

*Logistics and Transportation Review.* Published quarterly by the Faculty of Commerce and Business Administration, University of British Columbia.

*Mass Transit.* Published monthly in Washington, D.C., 20004.

*Modern Bulk Transporter.* Published monthly by the Sutherland Publications, Inc., Washington, D.C.

*Overdrive.* Published monthly, Los Angeles, California.

*Owner Operator.* Published bimonthly by Chilton Company, Inc., Radnor, Pa., 19089.

*Passenger Transport.* Published weekly by American Public Transit Association, Washington, D.C.

*Southern Motor Cargo.* Published monthly by Motor Cargo, Inc., Memphis.

*Traffic Quarterly.* Published by Eno Foundation for Transportation, Westport, Connecticut, 06880.

*Traffic World.* Published weekly by Traffic Service Corporation, Washington, D.C.

*Transport Topics.* Published weekly by American Trucking Assoc., Inc., Washington, D.C.

*Transportation Journal.* Published quarterly by American Society of Traffic and Transportation, Inc., Box 33095, Louisville, Ky., 40232

*Trucking Business.* Published monthly by Motor Truck Publishing Company, Inc., Chicago.

# Major Provision of Motor Carrier & Household Goods Acts of 1980

Major provisions of the Motor Carrier Act of 1980 include: easy entry into industry; simplified commodity and territorial descriptions as well as removal of many restrictions, including gateways; greater rate flexibility with a zone of rate freedom of 10 percent above or below the rate in effect one year prior to the proposed increase permitted without ICC approval, and additional increases permitted in subsequent years; agricultural and shellfish exemptions broadened as well as incidental-to-air exemption; and exemptions to ICC jurisdiction over intercorporate hauling permitted if parent corporation owns 100 percent of subsidiary. Antitrust immunity will be removed after January 1 or July 1, 1984 for carriers to discuss collectively any rate proposal other than general rate increases, commodity classifications, and changes in tariff structures. As of January 1, 1981, carriers not participating in transportation to which rate proposal applies are not permitted to vote on such proposal. Other provisions cover lumping, brokers, finances, pooling, mixed loads, mergers, and insurance. The ICC has instituted rule making to implement the Act.

Major provisions of the Household Goods Transportation Act of 1980 include: improve consumer advice and assistance; permit estimate to be binding on a moving company; change weighing regulations; strengthen rules for reasonable on-time pickup and delivery; and reduce industry paperwork burdens. The provisions of the Motor Carrier Act of 1980 that cover general entry, rate bureaus, and general pricing flexibility also include the household goods carriers. The ICC has instituted rule making to implement the Household Goods Transportation Act of 1980.

# Index